CHRISTIAN RESPONSES TO ROMAN ART AND ARCHITECTURE

Laura Salah Nasrallah argues that early Christian literature addressed to Greeks and Romans is best understood when studied in tandem with the archaeological remains of Roman antiquity. She examines second-century Christianity by looking at the world in which Christians "lived and moved and had their being." Early Christians were not divorced from the materiality of the world, nor did they always remain distant from the Greek culture of the time or the rhetoric of Roman power. Nasrallah demonstrates how early Christians took up themes of justice, piety, and even the question of whether humans could be gods. They did so in the midst of sculptures that conveyed visually that humans could be gods, monumental architecture that made claims about the justice and piety of the Roman imperial family, and ideas of geography that placed Greek or Roman ethnicity at the center of the known world.

Laura Salah Nasrallah is Associate Professor of New Testament and Early Christianity at Harvard Divinity School. She is the author of *An Ecstasy of Folly: Prophecy and Authority in Early Christianity* and co-editor of *Prejudice and Christian Beginnings: Investigating Race, Gender, and Ethnicity in Early Christian Studies* and *From Roman to Early Christian Thessalonikē: Studies in Religion and Archaeology*.

CHRISTIAN RESPONSES TO ROMAN ART AND ARCHITECTURE

THE SECOND-CENTURY CHURCH AMID THE SPACES OF EMPIRE

LAURA SALAH NASRALLAH

Harvard University

CAMBRIDGE UNIVERSITY PRESS
Cambridge, New York, Melbourne, Madrid, Cape Town, Singapore,
São Paulo, Delhi, Dubai, Tokyo

Cambridge University Press
32 Avenue of the Americas, New York, NY 10013-2473, USA

www.cambridge.org
Information on this title: www.cambridge.org/9780521766524

First published 2010

Printed in the United States of America

A catalog record for this publication is available from the British Library.

Library of Congress Cataloging in Publication data

Nasrallah, Laura Salah, 1969–
Christian responses to Roman art and architecture : the second-century church amid the
spaces of empire / Laura Salah Nasrallah.
p. cm.
Includes bibliographical references and index.
ISBN 978-0-521-76652-4 (hardback)
1. Church history – Primitive and early church, ca. 30-600. 2. Art, Roman.
3. Architecture, Roman. I. Title.
BR163.N37 2010
261.5′70937 – dc22 2009025688

ISBN 978-0-521-76652-4 Hardback

FOR MARC

CONTENTS

PART II: INTO THE CITIES

PART III: HUMAN BODIES AND THE IMAGE(S) OF GOD(S)

LIST OF FIGURES

ACKNOWLEDGMENTS

MANY INSTITUTIONS AND INDIVIDUALS HAVE MADE THIS PROJECT POSSIBLE AND my pursuit of it a joy. I am grateful for American Association of University Women and Lilly Faculty Fellowships. My dean at Harvard Divinity School, William Graham, has generously supported my work. I have been grateful for invitations to test ideas at the Pappas Patristic Institute of Holy Cross/Hellenic College, Furman University, Williams College, and the "Women, Gender, and Religion Forum" at Harvard Divinity School, as well as in various conferences: "Revelation, Literature, and Community" (Princeton University), "Sanctified Violence in Ancient Mediterranean Religions" (University of Minnesota), and "Beyond Eden" (Istituto Svizzero Roma).

Harvard Theological Review and the *Journal of Biblical Literature* kindly allowed me to include revised versions of articles published in their journals, which have become Chapters 2 and 3, respectively. I am grateful to scholars who permitted use of plans and images under their control: Renate Bol, James Packer, and R. R. R. Smith. Neil Elliot and Joshua Messner of Fortress Press kindly provided images for several photographs and plans in Chapter 1. Dr. Martha Ronk and Omnidawn Press allowed use of lines from her poem, "In a Landscape of Having to Repeat." Andreas Geißler, Daria Lanzuolo, and Jonas Ryborg went out of their way to help me to find and receive images.

Many have helped me along the way with this book and deserve thanks; I hesitate to list them because I will undoubtedly forget some generosities. This book would not have come about without the help of Andrew Beck, James Dunn, Beatrice Rehl, and Jason Przbylski at Cambridge University Press. At Harvard, Felicia Share, as well as Daniel Hawkins and his staff, made it possible for me to get the book to press. I am grateful to my research assistants Arminta Fox, David Jorgensen, Jeffrey Keiser, Matt Ketchum, David Mihalyfy, Margot Stevenson, Robyn Walsh, and, most of all, Thomas Christopher Hoklotubbe, Michal Beth Dinkler, and Rebekah Junkermeier. Learning often happens more happily in community than alone, and I have enjoyed discussions with students in my 2005–2006 seminar on Apologetic Literature and my 2008 course Early Christianity in the Roman Empire.

Many colleagues, friends, and even strangers have sacrificed their time to read my work or to help me. All the errors that remain are mine. Anonymous readers for Cambridge University Press have contributed greatly to the project by their meticulous and encouraging comments. For reading or advice I am thankful to François Bovon, Joan Branham, Ann Braude, Cavan Concannon, Alexandra Cuffel, Michal Beth Dinkler, Carol Duncan, Yaron Eliav, David Frankfurter, Chris Frilingos, Caroline Johnson Hodge, Amy Hollywood, Karen King, Helmut Koester, Jon Levenson, AnneMarie Luijendijk, Amy Lyford, David Gordon Mitten, Kimberly Patton, Shelly Rambo, Fatima Sadiqi, Jonathan Schofer, Elisabeth Schüssler Fiorenza, and Larry Wills. I am honored by Natalie Boymel Kampen's and Herbert Kessler's generosity in reading portions of the manuscript.

My kind friends and great encouragers Melanie Johnson-DeBaufre and Michael Puett spent many patient hours listening and reading as I tried out various versions of the book. I am grateful. For long conversations and the willingness to read many versions of various chapters, I also thank Denise Kimber Buell, Shelly Matthews, and Andrew Jacobs. Their scholarly imprints are everywhere on this book, and all these friendships leaven my days and late working nights. I am grateful for a tremendous scholarly community – one that is incisive and kind.

My family's generosity, patience, kind sacrifice, and love have sustained me through this project and much more: Mother Pelagia, Salah and Nancy Nasrallah, and August Muench-Nasrallah make work possible and life joyful.

In the midst of this project, my small son asked me nearly every night at dinner: "Mama, how is your book?" He has offered to write for me and has kindly left on my desk many folded books of his own, scribbled pages, and heart-filled drawing on the backs of my drafts. His sweetness and preternatural maturity, and the laughter that his younger sister Beata brings to us, are sustaining joys. I work always conscious of the absence of my mother and brother. This book is dedicated to the memory of my sweet brother Marc, and to my son, his namesake.

ABBREVIATIONS

Abbreviations of ancient titles generally follow the third edition of the *Oxford Classical Dictionary*. They are also further detailed in the Index Locorum.

AA	*Archäologischer Anzeiger*
AJA	*American Journal of Archaeology*
ANF	*Ante-Nicene Fathers: The Writings of the Fathers Down to 325 A.D.*, edited by Alexander Roberts et al. Reprint. Hendrickson: Peabody, 1995
ANRW	Aufstieg und Niedergang der römischen Welt
Bib. Int.	*Biblical Interpretation*
CCSL	Corpus Christianorum Series Latina
CH	*Church History*
CR	*The Classical Review*
DAI	Deutsches Archäologisches Institut
DAIR	Deutsches Archäologisches Institut Rom
FAT	Forschungen zum Alten Testament
GCS	Die griechischen christlichen Schriftsteller
Hesp.	*Hesperia: Journal of the American School of Classical Studies at Athens*
HSCP	*Harvard Studies in Classical Philology*
HTR	*Harvard Theological Review*
HTS	Harvard Theological Studies
IG	*Inscriptiones Graecae*
JAAR	*Journal of the American Academy of Religion*
JBL	*Journal of Biblical Literature*
JECS	*Journal of Early Christian Studies*
JEH	*Journal of Ecclesiastical History*
JHS	*The Journal of Hellenistic Studies*
JRA	*Journal of Roman Archaeology*
JRS	*Journal of Roman Studies*
JTS	*Journal of Theological Studies*
Lampe	Lampe, *A Patristic Lexicon*
LCL	Loeb Classical Library

LIMC	*Lexicon iconographicum mythologiae classicae.* 8 vols. in 16. Zürich: Artemis, 1981–2009
LSJ	Liddell-Scott-Jones, *A Greek-English Lexicon*
OED	*Oxford English Dictionary*
Rend	*Rendiconti*
RömMitt	*Mitteilungen des Deutschen Archäologischen Instituts: Römische Abteilung*
RSV	Revised Standard Version
SBL	Society of Biblical Literature
SC	Sources chrétiennes
Stud. Theol.	*Studia Theologica*
SVF	Stoicorum Veterum Fragmenta
Theol. Jahr.	*Theologische Jahrbücher*
TLG	*Thesaurus Linguae Graecae*
WUNT	Wissenschaftliche Untersuchungen zum Neuen Testament
VC	*Vigiliae Christianiae*

INTRODUCTION

How perfectly ordinary someone says looking at the same thing or
I'd like to get to the bottom of that one.
from Martha Ronk, "In a Landscape of Having to Repeat"[1]

When second-century Christians penned their thoughts, they usually wrote from cities crowded with monumental buildings whose erection was funded by emperors and elites. These Christian apologists were concerned with themes of justice, power, culture, and ethnicity; they wrote about how the world around them blurred the lines between human and divine, and how it defined piety and proper religious behavior. In the streets, Christians and their neighbors were jostled amid a growing population of statues that depicted the wealthy and powerful as gods, or nearly so. Christians among others crowded into agoras and forums full of architecture that proclaimed the triumph of the Roman Empire, even as such spaces often retained or repeated architecture and images from classical Greece and the Hellenistic cities of Alexander and his successors. Christians among others questioned the truth and value of these representations.

In this book I bring together literary texts and archaeological remains to help us to understand how religious discourse emerges not in some abstract zone, but in lived experiences and practices in the spaces of the world. I read early Christian writings addressed to the Roman emperors and to the Greeks in relation to select buildings and images, especially statuary. This juxtaposition allows me to show how Christians, like their non-Christian neighbors,

[1] Martha Clare Ronk, *In a Landscape of Having to Repeat* (Richmond, CA: Omnidawn, 2004). My thanks to the author and to Omnidawn for allowing the use of this quotation.

responded to their material world as they negotiated their ethnic, religious, and cultural identities in the Roman Empire. Second-century Christians engaged in diverse struggles over representation. They accused others of using words and images incorrectly; they accused Roman imperial power of misrepresenting its own claims to justice, piety, and even divinity. While Christians were not systematically persecuted in the second century,[2] many Christians wrote about Roman intolerance and commented on the dangers and bravery of proclaiming Christian identity at this time. Christians thus negotiated their place amid the culture wars of the day. These culture wars involved theological debates and had real social, political, and economic effects.

Early Christians "lived and moved and had their being" in the spaces of the Roman Empire. The New Testament Acts of the Apostles puts this Greek philosophical phrase into the mouth of the apostle Paul as he stands on the Areopagus in Athens (Acts 17:16–34). In the early second century, Acts crafts a Paul who not only widely travels the spaces of the empire, but also crosses ethnicities and cultures.[3] His Jewish roots mingle with his fluent Greek cultural skills; his Roman citizenship shields his new Christian identity. Paul as hybrid – never singularly Jewish, Greek, or Roman – stands in Athens, the center of Greek culture, under the rule of Rome, preaching the one God of the Jews in what is arguably our first New Testament text to use the term "Christian." Overlooking the ancient agora where Socrates walked, looking down on altars, buildings, and statues, Paul offers a better religious or philosophical way, trying to turn people toward a God who does not dwell in structures made by human hands. This literary moment captures many of the themes of this book: Interactions with the built environment are not neutral, but for some would have provoked struggles over ethnicity and religious identity, ruminations on the deep power and marketability of foreign or ancient cultures in the context of empire, and debates over what is true religiosity.

Like early Christians, we are shaped by the spaces in which we "live and move and have our being." Our responses to the world – ethical, theological, political – are formed not only by our interaction with literature but also, and probably even more, by our interactions with the images and architecture which surround us, by our movements through cities and other spaces. These responses vary, of course, depending upon who we are. There are places where some of us, given the particularities of our bodies, can walk with confidence while others walk with fear, in danger. What is often missing from studies of early Christian literature is this attention to space, architecture, and art – an understanding of the broader material environment in which this

[2] See, e.g., Timothy D. Barnes, "Legislation against the Christians," *JRS* 58 (1968) 32–50.

[3] Throughout, my arguments about ethnicity and how ethnic and religious self-definition are inextricable are indebted to Denise Kimber Buell, *Why This New Race? Ethnic Reasoning in Early Christianity* (New York: Columbia University Press, 2005).

literature was written and the varieties of responses that Christians had to the spaces of empire.[4] Moreover, we do not adequately consider the range of meanings such spaces may have for various peoples with different privileges of status, race, and sex.

In this book I tell a story of Christians in the second century at three levels. Beginning with the broadest spaces of the empire, I focus in the first chapters on Christian contributions to a rhetoric about the shape and space of the world. Among others who were writing in Greek, and in the midst of Roman imperial rhetoric of mapping that was manifest in word and image, Christians said something about the geography of the world and Roman power over it. In the next chapters, I shift to the cityscape, turning to certain key cities of the empire and sites within them that elucidate early Christian debates about justice, power, religion, and culture. I turn in the final chapters to individual bodies and statues, body doubles – life-sized and oversized – that deliberately blur boundaries: Do they depict humans or gods?

CHRISTIAN APOLOGISTS AND THE SECOND-CENTURY BUILT ENVIRONMENT

Five Christian texts written in the second century in Greek are the focus of this book: the Acts of the Apostles, Justin's *Apologies*, Athenagoras's *Embassy*, Tatian's *To the Greeks*, and Clement of Alexandria's *Exhortation*. Among the most discussed and earliest Christian "apologies," these texts raise key issues of Christian identity in relation to Greek and Roman culture. Apologies have often been interpreted as marginal texts opposing Romans, Greeks, Jews, and other "heretical" Christians. Alternatively, they have been read as keys to the earliest Christian theological debates. In both instances, such texts are read as separate from the surrounding culture. Yet early Christian apologetic literature is not in any simple sense distinct from or in opposition to contemporaneous "pagan" culture, an insight that Werner Jaeger among others developed years ago, but which is too often forgotten.[5] I understand these early Christian apologists to be full participants in the cultural, ethnic, philosophical, religious, and political struggles of their time.

The second century was a time when there was an explosion of writing by the first Christian apologists, some of whom expressed concern about rising

[4] See, however, Robin Jensen, *Face to Face: Portraits of the Divine in Early Christianity* (Minneapolis: Fortress, 2005) chaps. 1–2; Yaron Z. Eliav, "Roman Statues, Rabbis, and Graeco-Roman Culture," in Yaron Z. Eliav and Anita Norich, eds., *Jewish Literatures and Cultures: Context and Intertext* (Providence, RI: Brown Judaic Studies, 2008) 99–115.

[5] Werner Jaeger, *Early Christianity and Greek Paideia* (Cambridge: Belknap, 1961); Charly Clerc, *Les théories relatives au cultes des images chez les auteurs grecs du IIme siècle après J.-C.* (Paris: Fontemoing, 1915), whose collection of sources I unfortunately discovered only after having searched through the ancient literature myself.

persecution. Scholars have a penchant for pithy definitions of the second century. Edward Gibbon described it as "the period in the history of the world during which the condition of the human race was most happy and prosperous," sustained by the so-called good emperors.[6] (They were, of course, not so good, and the empire not so happy, if you happened to be a Jew or a Christian, among others.) E. R. Dodds, in his 1963 Wiles lectures, instead characterized the second century as an "age of anxiety," interested as he was in "religious experience in the Jamesian sense": that is, religion as found in the heart of the individual person of the second century. He painted the inhabitants of the Roman Empire as concerned about barbarian incursions and sweaty with hopes and fears for the immortality of the individual soul.[7] While I am less inclined to make sweeping statements about a historical epoch, I argue in this book that we do not find in the second century so much an age of anxiety, as we find "a landscape of having to repeat," to borrow poet Martha Ronk's phrase.

The second century is famous for its great proliferation – a repetition – of imperially sponsored building projects, especially under Hadrian. It is also a time when many sculptures were produced, especially honorific statues of civic elites, many of which looked like the imperial family and/or re-presented forms from classical- and Hellenistic-period Greek sculpture.[8] Metropolitan centers under the Roman Empire, especially in the first through third centuries CE, were haunted with a ghostly, cool "other population."[9] Pliny, writing in the first century, complained about the three thousand bronze statues that aedile M. Scaurus erected on the *scaenae frons* ("scene building") of a theater (*Nat. hist.* 36.114). Cassius Dio reported that in early first-century Rome "it was possible for anyone who wanted freely to display themselves in public in a painting or bronze or stone" to do so.[10] He literally uses the Greek term for "mob" (ὄχλος) to talk about how many statues there were – a crowd that clustered in particularly prominent places within the city and hung off its architecture. Dio lived at the height of statuary proliferation in the late second and early third century. Perhaps feeling crowded, he celebrates the sobriety of the first century, when the emperor Claudius insisted that statues could be

6 Edward Gibbon, *History of the Decline and Fall of the Roman Empire* (2 vols.; Cincinnati: J. A. James, 1840) 1.39.

7 E. R. Dodds, *Pagan and Christian in an Age of Anxiety: Some Aspects of Religious Experience from Marcus Aurelius to Constantine* (Cambridge: Cambridge University Press, 1965); quotation is from p. 2. See Judith Perkins, *The Suffering Self: Pain and Narrative Self-Representation in the Early Christian Era* (New York: Routledge, 1995) for a different understanding of this second-century rhetoric.

8 See discussion and nuance in Paul Zanker, *The Mask of Socrates: The Image of the Intellectual in Antiquity* (trans. Alan Shapiro; Berkeley: University of California Press, 1995).

9 See esp. Peter Stewart, *Statues in Roman Society: Representation and Response* (Oxford: Oxford University Press, 2003) 1–8, 118, chap. 4: "The Other Population of Rome."

10 Cassius Dio 60.25.3; ET Ernest Cary and Herbert Baldwin Foster, *Dio Cassius Roman History* (9 vols.; LCL; Cambridge, MA: Harvard University Press, 1914–27) 7.431; see also Philostratus *Vit. soph.* 2.558, regarding Herodes Atticus and an excess of statues.

erected in Rome only by decree of the Senate or if someone built or repaired a public work.

The statuary mob of which Dio disapproved was not small or easy to miss, but was characterized by "high technical elaboration and finish," usually in polished marble, and by an "imposing scale . . . well over lifesize."[11] Across the empire, and especially in the Greek East, statues were displayed for many reasons, but they were often commissioned and erected to honor the recipient as a benefactor or prominent person in the city. Their final form, like portrait photography today, said subtly through clothing, stance, and hairstyle something about the person's ethnicity, education, wealth, status, religiosity, family connections, and power. Such statues not only acknowledged benefaction or power but also sought to bind the dedicatee, imperial, elite, or just wealthy, even more closely to a city, encouraging further benefaction. Although Dodd's characterization of the second century as an age of anxiety is not quite right – it is too driven by the issue of individual religious experience, a concern more of the twentieth century than the second – there is something anxiously performative about this time period. We find a massive repetition of statuary as if to reassure the city that the gods and true religion exist, and as if to reassure or to assert that the imperial family is in control. Statuary confirms to the elite that they are in power and suggests to the cities that benefit by them that these elites will continue to be here, offering their wealth for the benefit of the city.

This repetition occurs in a world that valued tradition and antiquity over innovation. A new religion would be labeled a *superstitio*, not something truly religious or pious. There was at this time no "anxiety of influence" in producing writings or images but rather a desire to echo prestigious ancient forms. This "landscape of having to repeat," however, should not be dismissed as derivative and thus debased. Scholars have begun to use terms like "emulation" or "repetition" to avoid the derogatory tone of "copying" or "imitation," which misrepresents why such artworks were reproduced.[12] Such

[11] R. R. R. Smith, "Cultural Choice and Political Identity in Honorific Portrait Statues in the Greek East in the Second Century A.D.," *JRS* 88 (1998) 63; he puts the usual size at 2.10–2.20 m.

[12] See Miranda Marvin, *The Language of the Muses: The Dialogue between Roman and Greek Sculpture* (Los Angeles: J. Paul Getty Museum, 2008); Elaine Gadza, "Roman Sculpture and the Ethos of Admiration: Reconsidering Repetition," *HSCP* 97 (1995) 121–56; Richard Gordon, "'The Real and the Imaginary': Production and Religion in the Graeco-Roman World," *Art History* 2 (1979) 5–34; see also Brunilde Sismondo Ridgway, *Roman Copies of Greek Sculpture: The Problem of the Originals* (Ann Arbor: University of Michigan Press, 1984); Miranda Marvin, "Copying in Roman Sculpture: The Replica Series," in Eve D'Ambra, ed., *Roman Art in Context: An Anthology* (Englewood Cliffs, NJ: Prentice-Hall, 1993) 161–88. See also Elaine Gadza, ed., *The Ancient Art of Emulation: Studies in Artistic Originality and Tradition from the Present to Classical Antiquity* (Ann Arbor: University of Michigan Press, 2002) and the work of Ellen Perry, *The Aesthetics of Emulation in the Visual Arts of Ancient Rome* (Cambridge: Cambridge University Press, 2005) and the excellent review essay that treats both: Christopher Hallett, "Emulation *versus* replication: redefining Roman copying," *JRA* 18 (2005) 419–35.

evaluative terms arose especially under the influence of eighteenth-century scholar Johann Winckelmann's hierarchical periodization of ancient art, in which the last stage was one of devolved imitation.[13] Roman-period sculptors are often characterized as hacks, copying Greek masterpieces mechanistically, missing the spirit of Greece that breathed life into the original statues and cloaked them in beauty. Such a critique consciously or unconsciously echoes Walter Benjamin's analysis of the loss of "authenticity" and the "aura" of an image in an age of mechanical reproduction.[14]

The Roman period was not a time of blind imitation or copying. These objects had their own context and "authenticity," to use Benjamin's term, even if there was repetition of literary and imagistic themes from classical and Hellenistic Greek culture. Yet because of this landscape of repetition, the second century was also a time of crises of *mimēsis* or representation, crises that had to do with ethnicity, *paideia* (the term for "culture" or "education" in Greek), and piety. How is identity adjudicated? How can one know if someone is Greek? Philosophical? Roman? Barbarian? Cultured? Who is really pious, and who denies the gods, and can the person who denies the gods do so precisely because s/he is pious? Who has the right to give a name, and based upon what criteria? Is a given image a god or a human? An elite or an emperor? How should one respond to the expansion and evolution of imperial cult, in which the imperial family was honored or even worshipped as gods or demi-gods, or at least as similar to the gods? This crisis over representation was visually evident through statuary and other images; for writers like Justin or Athenagoras, it was also manifest in a justice system more interested in names than deeds, and in emperors who claimed to be philosophical and pious but whose actions demonstrated something else entirely.

The second century is also the time when the term "Christian" first appears in our literary evidence – when some Christians come to name themselves as something distinct from Judaism – and when we have the first writings penned by Christians educated in elite Greek learning and culture, who are or want to be in conversation with their educated non-Christian peers. My argument that Christian writers argue about religion *alongside* "pagan" writers is not particularly controversial. Yet, in the study of Christian apologists, the traditional divisions of pagan-Jew-Christian have obscured possible alliances between those of high status who engaged in a culture war about the value of Greek *paideia* in the high Roman Empire. These divisions have obscured the possibility that Christian "apologists" do not define Christianity against

[13] Johann Joachim Winckelmann, *History of the Art of Antiquity* (trans. Harry Francis Mallgrave; Los Angeles: Getty Research Institute, 2006) 232–38.

[14] Walter Benjamin, "The Work of Art in an Age of Mechanical Reproduction," in Hannah Arendt, ed., *Illuminations: Essays and Reflections* (trans. Harry Zohn; New York: Schocken, 1969) 217–51.

paganism or Judaism as much as they define Christianity against certain *kinds* of other ethnic and religious practices, practices they usually attribute to the "many" or the crowd, on the one hand, and to the imperial family, on the other. One contribution of my book is to show these Christian voices within a controversy on the nature of true religion, as both the "tolerance" and the religious influences of Roman imperial cult blanketed the Mediterranean basin like strange snow. Christian "apologists" thus engage large, cross-cultic and cross-ethnic conversations about the nature of true religion and right ritual, defining themselves alongside educated "pagans" as part of a thin stratum of cultured elites who can see the folly of the low religious practices of the poor and the very, very rich.[15] Christians participate in the world, including its material aspects, in complex ways, sometimes assimilating, sometimes resisting, sometimes engaged in "colonial mimicry." They use available arguments and debates to carve out a space where Christians, too, are cultural and political critics in and of the Roman world.

BRINGING TOGETHER LITERATURE AND ARCHAEOLOGICAL REMAINS

All historical work is an imaginative enterprise, but many analyses are constricted by their over-reliance on literary sources. As I worked with the literature of second-century apologetic Christian texts, puzzling at the confluence I found in them of concerns about justice, piety, culture and ethnicity, and the blurring between human and divine, moments of clarity came when I pictured my teaching and research trips to the cities of the Greek East. In Olympia one can still see remains of the Fountain of Herodes Atticus and Regilla at the edge of the city's *altis* or sacred grove. This second-century family, famed for its wealth that rivaled the emperors and the oratorical and cultural skills of Herodes Atticus, imposed itself into the ancient cityscape. Nearby stood Pheidias's famous sculpture of Zeus, many altars to gods and statues of athletes, and other markers of classical-period Panhellenism – the glory days of Greece. Ancient visitors could stand at the fountain's cool waters, looking up at statues of the wealthy family of Regilla and Herodes, on one level, the imperial family on another, both levels punctuated by statues of Jupiter/Zeus. Surely this, like the Christian texts of focus in this book, is a form of "address" both to the emperors and to Greeks, one that directly treats the topics of piety and Greek culture under Rome.

Moving across the Aegean to Aphrodisias in modern-day Turkey, the visitor enters the narrow space of the Sebasteion, two long porticoes that end in a

[15] On the topic of religious tolerance in the Roman Empire, see Clifford Ando, *The Matter of the Gods: Religion and the Roman Empire* (Berkeley: University of California Press, 2008) 43–58 and chaps. 5–6 on the rite of *evocatio*.

temple dedicated to the goddess Aphrodite, to the "emperor gods," and to the city itself: an eastern city wedding itself in its myth, cult, and politics to Rome. Relief sculptures in fine marble on each of the porticoes depict personifications of the nations (*ethnē*) of the world as well as the emperors in heroic poses, conquering and pious, gathering this world to themselves. The architecture and art of this jewel of a building complex render violence divinely supported, maps the ethnicities of the world as belonging to Rome, and suggests that Roman power is pious and inevitable, blowing across the Mediterranean like a force of nature.

The study of art, architecture, and early Christianity should encompass not only catacomb paintings or the first churches, but also the earliest Christian responses to the built environments of the Roman Empire. A central argument of my book is that Christian apologists' *literary* texts can be best understood alongside *archaeological* remains from the spaces of the Roman world, and particularly the cityscapes of the second century. Disciplinary boundaries, however, have impoverished the study of early Christianity *and* the study of classics, ancient history, and art and archaeology: We have not been able to recognize how themes such as power, justice, piety, and culture are part of far-ranging ancient conversations that are manifest not only in literature but also in archaeological remains. We are like the blindfolded people in the fable who surround and touch the elephant, each characterizing the object of his or her interest according to limited knowledge. The elephant's side is a wall, the leg is a tree, the trunk is a snake, the tusk a spear, the ear a fan, the swinging tail a rope.

Because Christian texts are often sequestered from "classics," historians of early Christianity have too rarely recognized that "our" authors participate, for instance, in the so-called Second Sophistic, a cultural surge of interest in ancient Greek philosophy, rhetoric, images, and *paideia*, which extends roughly from the first to the third centuries CE. Moreover, specialists in literary texts have too rarely recognized that the themes of the so-called Second Sophistic and its resistors were not restricted to the power of oratory and words; such themes are also found in the built environment – "citations" of classical architecture and motifs, archaizing forms of worship supported by building renovations, representations of the diversity of *ethnē* (nations or ethnicities) and how they fit into the high valuation of Greek *paideia* and Roman power.[16] Not all cities of the Greek East "said" the same thing; not all literary texts of the so-called Second Sophistic were the same. Yet themes thread through this period, and Christians participate in the common debate.

[16] Susan Alcock, *Archaeologies of the Greek Past: Landscape, Monuments, and Memories* (Cambridge: Cambridge University Press, 2002) esp. chap. 2; Tonio Hölscher, *The Language of Images in Roman Art* (trans. A. Snodgrass and A. Künzl-Snodgrass; Cambridge: Cambridge University Press, 2004).

Similarly, Roman historians and art historians have not recognized the extent to which Christians conversing about images and representations were not engaged in knee-jerk rejections of iconography – an old scholarly prejudice – but thoughtful investigations of the powerful effects of iconography on those who moved about the empire. This book takes seriously what second-century Christians, among others, took seriously, even if they wrote satirically: that statues of theomorphic humans and anthropomorphic gods were significant theological statements. The theological stakes of such objects are expressed clearly in the North African writer Tertullian's insistence that Christian sculptors who "make" gods become priests to them, and their salvation becomes a fat, gilded sacrifice to the gods (*De idol.* 6). There is good reason in antiquity and today to take seriously the topic of the image of god(s), because it raises larger questions about what it means to be human, how the real or statuary human body stands in danger of becoming a commodity, who is considered worthy to be a god or in the image of god(s).

Of course, by reading Christian and non-Christian texts together, and by bringing together both literary and archaeological remains, my own reconstruction of the second century cannot entirely capture the elephant that we, blindfolded by the limits of our sources and methods, touch. All of our historical reconstructions are provisional and partial, all inevitably and happily the best attempts of our imaginative enterprise.

Yet to try to see more fully the second-century Roman world, we must attend not only to literature and material remains together, but also to how we conceptualize space itself. Michel de Certeau, David Harvey, and others have encouraged an analysis of space that would involve "walking in the city" in "wandering lines" rather than attempting to find a panoptic point from which to survey the scene. Such an analysis demands thinking beyond the elites who walked the metropolitan centers of the Roman Empire and taking seriously feminist and postcolonial criticisms, which ask questions about imperial power and its (ab)use of its subjects' bodies. Despite the elite male focus of many of our sources, this book tries to catch a glimpse of those who were less than elite: those, like Paul and even lower in status, who might stand in the center of Athens to offer some critique of culture, cult, and power; those, like the slaves and women we find at our texts' margins, who also might move through civic spaces busy with marble bodies of elites as gods. What would it mean to walk those cities and to travel between cities these roughly two thousand years later, and to resist being seduced by the pedagogical power of monumental architecture, a crowded statuary population, and their persuasive messages about ethnicity, *paideia*, and knowledge?[17]

[17] Michel de Certeau, *The Practice of Everyday Life* (trans. Steven Rendall; Berkeley: University of California Press, 1984); David Harvey, *Spaces of Hope* (Berkeley: University of California Press, 2000); Edward Soja, *Postmetropolis: Critical Studies of Cities and Regions* (Oxford: Blackwell,

Although many would argue that archaeological finds and material culture offer us hard evidence, rock-hard in fact, empirical and scientific and easier to trust than literary texts, I think otherwise. Architecture makes statements; statues speak, too. Feminist and postcolonial criticisms teach us to ask about the rhetoricity of literary evidence; we can extend this questioning to material remains.[18] What arts of persuasion do they employ and to what ends? How can we imaginatively reconstruct a viewer who sees and resists? A viewer who walks the city not with the knowledge of an elite but with that of a slave who does not own or control his or her own body, who is aware from his or her own experience of bodies of all sorts and their uses?

Asking these kinds of questions can help us to expose that interpretations of of statuary and monumental architecture in the Roman Empire were dynamic and contested. From this period emerged new views of the civic landscape and indeed new mappings of the *oikoumenē*, the "inhabited world." Vitruvius, who addresses his *De architectura* to Augustus, centers the map on Italy and the Roman people and concludes: "Thus the divine intelligence established the state of the Roman People as an outstanding and balanced region – so that it could take command over the earthly orb" (*De arch.* 6.1.11).[19] Yet geographical thinking about the first- and second-century Roman world is not stable; it shifts even within this one text. In the same passage, Vitruvius celebrates the man who is shipwrecked, the universal traveler: "An educated person is the only one who is never a stranger in a foreign land, nor at a loss for friends even when bereft of household and intimates. Rather, he is a citizen in every country (*sed in omni civitate esse civem*)" (6.preface.2).[20] Vitruvius oscillates between two poles. In one, the map of the world centers on Rome; in the other, the map of the world has no center but is traced by the universal traveler. This citizen of everywhere has in hand both *ars* ("skill") and a universal education – and in this period, such education was usually defined as antiquarian Greek *paideia*.[21]

2000); Dolores Hayden, *The Power of Place: Urban Landscapes as Public History* (Cambridge, MA: MIT Press, 1995); see esp. Henri Lefebvre, *The Production of Space* (trans. Donald Nicholson-Smith; Oxford: Blackwell, 1991).

18 See esp. Elisabeth Schüssler Fiorenza, *Rhetoric and Ethic: The Politics of Biblical Studies* (Minneapolis, MN: Fortress, 1999) and *The Power of the Word: Scripture and the Rhetoric of Empire* (Minneapolis, MN: Fortress, 2007).

19 ET Vitruvius, *Ten Books on Architecture* (trans. Ingrid D. Rowland; commentary and illustrations by Thomas Noble Howe; Cambridge: Cambridge University Press, 1999) 77.

20 ET Rowland, 75; the Latin is from Vitruvius Pollio, *De Architectura* (ed. F. Krohn; Leipzig: B. G. Teubner, 1912).

21 Vitruvius himself explains this emphasis on art and education in terms of ancient Athenian law (*De arch.* 6.preface.3–4). On the value of Greek education and on the *pepaideumenos theatēs*, or educated viewer, see Simon Goldhill, ed., *Being Greek under Rome: Cultural Identity, the Second Sophistic, and the Development of Empire* (Cambridge: Cambridge University Press, 2001); see also William Hutton, *Describing Greece: Landscape and Literature in the* Periegesis *of Pausanias* (Cambridge: Cambridge University Press, 2005) 32–41; Smith, "Cultural Choice and Political Identity," 56–93.

Much of this book studies the rhetoric of Vitruvian men. That is, it will address those men who by virtue of their sex and their *paideia* are like the lost and yet never lost traveler that Vitruvius describes. The term conjures Leonardo da Vinci's famous drawing of the perfectly balanced man, inscribed within a circle. Vitruvius comments about the ideal symmetry of the human body and the analogy of this body to architectural measure. He explains the origins of the symmetry of temples: "Nature has composed the human body so that in its proportions the separate individual elements answer to the total form.... Therefore, when they were handing down proportional sequences for every type of work, they did so especially for the sacred dwellings of the gods.... They gathered the principles of measure, which seem to be necessary in any sort of project, from the components of the human body" (3.1.4–5).[22] The human body is a site from which an understanding of space emerges;[23] architecture, Vitruvius claims, is derived from the very proportions of the human body. But buildings should also be calculated to please and to overwhelm the body: Vitruvius famously discusses *entasis*, the technique of adjusting a column with a slight bowing so that the "ascending glance of our eyes" can be humored in its pursuit of beauty (5.3.13).[24] His comments on the organization of steps indicates an even deeper understanding or manipulation of the human body in relation to the temple. "The steps in the front should be constructed so that they are always an odd number. In this way, if one begins to mount the temple steps with the right foot, it is again the right foot that will step into the temple proper" (5.4.4).[25] The very rhythm of the body's movements is calculated and controlled in relation to the temple, so that the walking human and the temple are both symmetrical and related in their rationalized steps one towards the other. The temple is based on the (perfect) body; and the body, comfortably mounting the stairs, perfectly confronts the place of the divine.

Vitruvius also suggests that architecture can be pedagogical, planned in order to teach the human his or her status in relation to divinities. He states: "Altars should face east, and should always be placed lower than the cult images that will be in the temple, *so that those who make supplication and sacrifices may look up at the deity; the heights of these differ and should be designed to fit the dignity of each particular god*. Their heights should be set out so that those for Jove and all the other celestial divinities are set as high as possible, whereas they are placed low for Vesta, Earth, and Sea...." (4.9.1).[26] Altars and gods should be placed at various heights in relation to the human body in order to create the proper

22 ET Rowland, 47.

23 He also gives a gendered etiology for columns (*De arch.* 4.6–7).

24 ET Rowland, 50; see also *De arch.* 5.4.4.

25 ET ibid., 51.

26 ET ibid., 62. Emphasis mine.

effects for awe and worship, and in order to remind the worshipper of the various levels and kinds of power of the gods.

Of course not everyone followed Vitruvius's advice, but his ideas about architecture being based on the human body, on the one hand, and the manipulation of the human body in relation to architecture, on the other, derive in part from practices of city planning and monumental architecture at that time. Vitruvius lays bare a broader phenomenon: Like literature, architecture (and we can extend the logic to the iconographic programs on buildings, to decorative elements, and to the statuary found on and around such buildings) can seek to persuade the human of something. Whether the person – Christian, "pagan," Jew, poor, rich, woman, man, child, slave, free – *is* persuaded is another matter entirely. Part of the project of this book is to map a range of responses, especially Christian, to the surrounding landscape.

My hope is that the work done in this book will stimulate the reader's imagination to question the prescriptive rhetoric of elite sources, to think spatially, and to look to archaeological materials as well as literary. Tearing literary texts from the material world in which they were produced leads to an impoverishment of our historical imaginations. No matter an apocalypse or a philosophical treatise, literary texts are produced on and respond to the dusty paths of the empire and the hard paving stones of the city. If we fail to include in our imaginative enterprise some sense of the bounds of the earth, the rhythms of the cityscape, and the power of images, we have cut ourselves off from a robust understanding of what scholars often study by means of literary texts: that is, persons in the Roman Empire, their bodily movement in and between cities, and their philosophical, theological, and political responses to their environment.

CHAPTER OVERVIEW

The majority of the chapters of this book juxtapose literary and archaeological materials, whether the latter be a forum, a temple, or sculptures. By bringing together images, statues, buildings, and archaeological sites with the writings of the early Christian apologists, I do not argue or imply that the authors had direct interactions with a given site or object. Nor, by juxtaposing the themes of a "pagan" orator with a Christian "apologist," do I indicate that there is necessarily a genealogical relationship between the two, that one read the other's work and copied from or responded to it. Rather, I bring these voices and spaces together so that we can overhear and glimpse the discursive world in which literature, images, and architecture were produced, and among which both Christians and non-Christians formulated their arguments.

Literature, architecture, and art alike offer rhetorical arguments. In the first chapter, I examine the rhetoric of literary apologies and the rhetoric of a monumental fountain in Olympia. Those who study early Christianity have often been stuck at the questions: "Whom did the apologists really address? What is an apology? Were the earliest Christians polluted by their interaction with surrounding Greek culture and the Roman world, or did they choose wisely to express their Christian essence in another idiom?" In more recent definitions, early Christian apologists function in scholarship to demonstrate Christian difference from Jews, pagans, and heretics – nearly everyone in the Roman world.

This chapter elucidates not only how Christians were different from others, but also how they were similar, by illuminating the focal texts of this book in relation to the so-called Second Sophistic. Christians are not the only ones to produce monumental addresses to the Roman emperors (as did Justin and Athenagoras) and the Greeks (as did Tatian and Clement), or to tell a story about themselves that would be attractive to those steeped in Greek *paideia* and comforted by Roman law and order. We find an analogous impulse in a second-century fountain in Olympia funded by the family of Herodes Atticus, one of the key figures of the Second Sophistic. By its placement and its iconography, the fountain constitutes a kind of pious "address" to the Roman emperors, in Greek idiom and in a quintessentially Greek city. An exploration of this site allows us to place contemporaneous Christian apologists into a broader context where performing Greek *paideia*, appealing to the Roman imperial family, and marking one's piety were common practices of the educated and elites.

Continuing with this expansive, border-crossing view, Chapter 2 presents how various kinds of "geographical thinking" peaked in the Roman Empire of the first and second centuries. This "geographical thinking" included novels about exotic lands, accounts by traveling merchants, fantastic tales of the cults of the world, and map-making and other representations of the world. Postcolonial theorists have observed that geography is a tool of colonizing power; thus the rise in geographical discourses at the height of the Roman Empire is no surprise. Two focal texts for this book – those of Justin, from Neapolis (modern-day Nablus) and Tatian, the "Assyrian" – engage in this conversation about geography and space as they find room for themselves and for Christianity within the ethnic and cultural map of the empire. I read them alongside the Syrian satirist Lucian. Each presents himself as an outsider who has nonetheless mastered Greek knowledge and culture. At the same time, each presents himself as a vulnerable body traveling the spaces of what people of the time called the *oikoumenē*, the "inhabited world," largely conquered by Rome.

We find such vulnerable bodies represented in relation to imperial space at the Sebasteion in Aphrodisias (in modern-day Turkey). This building complex provides a context for understanding Christian apologists' (and Lucian's) conversations about ethnicity, religion, and power in the spaces of the Roman

Empire. Commissioned by Aphrodisian elites to honor the Julio-Claudian imperial family, the Sebasteion contained images of various *ethnē* (nations) depicted as the exotic and beautiful other, immediately juxtaposed with images of the emperors conquering that feminized other.

In the third chapter, I treat the broad spaces of empire and then move to a particular city, Athens. "These things were not done in a corner," insists the apostle Paul about the ideas and origins of the Christian movement, according to Acts. This assertion, placed in Paul's mouth, leads us to wonder: In the midst of Roman power and claims to possess the inhabited world – claims manifest literarily and in the built environment – how did some early Christian communities imagine the space of the world? I suggest that the geographical imagination of Acts is best understood in the context of discourses of Greek cities under Rome. These include the writings of Aelius Aristides and especially archaeological and epigraphic evidence of the Panhellenion, a coalition of Greek cities led by Athens but partially supported by the Roman Empire. Indeed, it seems to have been the brainchild of the emperor Hadrian, who had his own agenda in promoting antiquarian religion and classically Greek culture. In the imagination of the second-century Acts, Paul asserts his Roman identity and his adeptness with Greek culture, and with his traveling body traces a kind of league of Christian cities under the Roman Empire. The logic is similar to that which produced the Panhellenion. Acts imagines a Christianity that fits easily within the Roman Empire, producing a Christian community that hybridizes with Greek culture and Roman imperial ideology.

In the fourth chapter, I juxtapose Justin's *Apologies* with the Forum of Trajan in the heart of the city of Rome. In the second century, the Forum was architecturally innovative; especially striking were its Column of Trajan, which rose over 40 meters (131 feet) to celebrate the emperor Trajan's piety and military might over "barbarians," its libraries with their cultured Greek and Latin texts, and its Basilica Ulpia, a law court for determining justice. Studding the architecture were over-life-sized carvings of conquered Dacians, beautiful yet humiliated before Rome. Trajan's complex was thick with messages of power, piety, culture, and justice.

In the face of such imperial claims, exemplified in the Forum of Trajan but also articulated elsewhere, Justin points to crises of *mimēsis* or representation in the Roman Empire. The emperors are not what they claim to be. Imperial justice is a sham; the emperors will stand before a greater and truly divine court. Imperial piety is a joke; without knowing it, the emperors have hung banners of their own divinized faces on crosses, the signs of Christianity. Yet Justin is no postcolonial hero. He formulates an argument that elides Christians with philosophical elites, over and against the imperial family and those of low status, who are all involved in the dirty business of making and honoring images.

In Chapter 5, I shift from cities to statuary, focusing especially on a portrait of the emperor Commodus as the ambivalent hero-god Herakles, with club, lion's skin over his head, and the apples of Hesperides in his hand, now in the Capitoline Museum in Rome. Commodus and other male elites of the empire wear the lion's skin of Herakles as part of their propaganda regarding their power and divinity, as did Alexander the Great and others before them. In the arena, some criminals were executed as they were forced to reenact myths, even the myth of Herakles, including his famous death in flames. An ambivalent sign indeed: Both emperor and imperially-sentenced criminal take on the form of Herakles. It is in this context of statues and literature that we can better understand the semiotic, philosophical, and theological concerns of the early Christian Athenagoras. His *Embassy* to the emperors Marcus Aurelius and Commodus offers a consistent philosophical argument about a crisis of representation that is going on in the empire: There is a slippage between signs – both linguistic (nouns) and visual (images) – and the things which they are supposed to represent.

While Chapters 4 and 5 treat writers who address their works to the Roman emperors, Chapters 6 and 7 study those who address "the Greeks." Chapter 6 outlines one ancient discourse about the origins of images, which states that images emerged from human desire, love, and longing, whether for the departed lover, the dead child, or the absent king. In this way, an image of a human – itself a potentially destructive or misleading simulacrum – came to be taken for an image of a god. Tracing this discourse from the first-century BCE *Wisdom of Solomon* through the second-century CE Maximus of Tyre, I delineate a debate over the theology and power of images, especially famed and quintessentially Greek images like Pheidias's Olympian Zeus.

Moving from stories of the origins of images to issues of connoisseurship and images, I analyze Tatian's rhetorical positioning in terms of ethnicity, namely, his embrace of a barbarian identity, and the way in which he characterizes Greek *paideia* as fragmented and morally bankrupt. He discusses Greek statuary (booty, really) that he viewed in Rome as monstrous and corrupting. Tatian's *To the Greeks* is not propelled by aniconism or fanatical bitterness, I argue, but by a satirical critique of Roman connoisseurship of Greek culture.

Perhaps no object was more subject to connoisseurship in the Roman period than Praxiteles' fourth-century sculpture, the Aphrodite of Knidos. Chapter 7 discusses how one early Christian writer, Clement, dealt with the proliferation of this image in literature and sculpture of the second century. Praxiteles' sculpture – Aphrodite, naked, shields her pudenda with one hand, and usually raises her other arm across her breasts; her face is often turned to one side – was explosively popular then. Rumors swirled around the Knidia in the second century. The original statue was said to have been modeled after Praxiteles' courtesan lover; a tale was also told of the statue's rape by an obsessed young man. The Knidia was replicated in various material forms at this time, including as funerary monuments. The portrait heads of Roman aging matrons perched on the young, rounded body of Aphrodite/Venus: These elite women are sculpted in the image of the goddess.

Both Tatian and Clement mention the Knidia negatively as part of a discussion about where such images lead a person: to wrongful lust and desire. Clement, Tatian, and non-Christian writers try to train their readers' eyes in response to the images filling the cityscapes of the Roman Empire. This is not mere prurience, but a cultural and political response to the proliferation of ancient Greek statue forms in the Roman period, including copies and interpretations of Praxiteles' Aphrodite of Knidos. According to Tatian and Clement, Greek objects, purchased by and valued by Romans, are full of monstrosities that produce illicit desire, including lust for the very possession of art. Christians among others resist this Roman obsession with plunder and booty or, to put it in other terms, connoisseurship and collecting.

Using the creation stories of Genesis, with its ideas of the human as image of God, on the one hand, and God as sculptor-creator, on the other, Clement argues that all humans are "living, breathing statues" in the image of God. The incarnation of the Logos – "reason," or "word," and also a title Christians applied to Christ – was intended so that all humans could "become gods," in Clement's words. This theology of *theōsis* is best understood in light of the spaces investigated throughout the book, where elites appear in statuary form as gods, and where Roman imperial power makes claims to its origins in divine providence and its role in perpetuating true religion. Clement's argument has a profoundly egalitarian potential: All, it seems, are worthy statues and gods, instead of only the elite and the imperial family, or those Greek objects valued by the same. Yet Clement insists that a peculiarly philosophical and controlled self is worthy to be the image of God, thus implying that becoming a god is mainly the purview of a male philosophical elite.

This limiting and cordoning off of the possibilities of god-becoming-human or humans-becoming-gods brings us back to the theoretical and ethical underpinnings of this book. It brings together material culture and literary texts not only because I believe that literature is elucidated by as full as possible an analysis of the broader culture in which it arose, but also because of my feminist commitments. The realm of matter, philosophically elided with the feminine in antiquity and even the present, is too often overlooked in preference for tracing a history of ideas through literary and philosophical writings. Part of the joy of this project has been to read not only literary materials but also to think about the material conditions in which buildings were erected and sculptures produced, to imagine the chisel's ring against marble and the echoing vibration in the ear and the bone. Part of the sorrow of the project – sorrow that makes me reflect on my own bodily privileges in the present – has emerged from the same focus: Thinking about the material conditions under which architecture and images are produced leads to a broader focus on materiality, including the body. A focus on artifacts and archaeology can lead us to reflect on the conditions of those bodies in the ancient world that were considered objects for use, servicing the building projects and the bodily wants of the elite.

To take again the words of Martha Ronk's poem, some might look at early Christian apologists and think "how perfectly ordinary," reading them as the balanced or vituperative responses of persecuted Christians in the midst of the Roman Empire, in the midst of a foreign culture. My response to these texts instead has been, "I'd like to get to the bottom of that one." My experience in researching and writing this book has been one of being continually surprised and a little confounded by the variety of Christian responses to the cultural currents of the second-century Roman Empire. This project represents my wonder at this period of history and my hopes to begin (because, given the vagaries of historical evidence and the limits of historiography, we can only just begin) to get to the bottom of it all.

PART ONE

FRAMING THE QUESTION, FRAMING THE WORLD

CHAPTER ONE

WHAT IS AN APOLOGY? CHRISTIAN APOLOGIES AND THE SO-CALLED SECOND SOPHISTIC

When I teach about early Christianity in the Roman Empire, I explain to my students that the early Christian apologists are not apologizing. The second-century Christian Justin writes:

> To the Emperor Titus Aelius Hadrianus Antoninus Eusebes [i.e., Pius] Augustus; and to his son Caesar, Verissimus the Philosopher; and to Lucius the Philosopher, the natural son of Caesar and the adopted son of Pius, a lover of *paideia*; and to the sacred Senate, with the whole People of the Romans, I, Justin, the son of Priscus and grandson of Bacchius, from the city of Flavia Neapolis in Syria Palestine, have made this address and petition on behalf of those of every race who are unjustly hated and abusively threatened, myself being one of them.[1]

Justin's slightly later contemporary Athenagoras pleads: "I need, as I begin to defend our doctrine (ἀναγκαῖον δέ μοι ἀρχομένῳ ἀπολογῖσθαι ὑπὲρ τοῦ λόγου δεηθῆναι ὑμῶν), to beg [you], greatest emperors, to listen equitably to us, and not to be prejudiced, carried off by the common and irrational rumor – to beg you to turn your love of learning and love of truth toward our speech" (*Leg.* 2.6).[2] But certainly Justin and Athenagoras are not sorry.

1 *1 Apol.* 1.1. The Greek edition is Miroslav Marcovich, *Iustini Marturis Apologiae Pro Christianis* (Berlin: De Gruyter, 1994). For a full discussion, including text-critical issues, see pp. 132–33.

2 The Greek edition is Athenagoras, *Legatio and De Resurrectione* (trans. William R. Schoedel; Oxford: Clarendon, 1972). Throughout the book, unless otherwise noted, translations are mine.

They are not backing down or making up. Rather, through their rhetoric they assert a situation in which they defend themselves, their religion, and their communities in the face of the oppressive powers and possible persecution of the Roman Empire.[3]

The Greek term *apologia*, famously used to describe Plato's account of Socrates' trial and death, means "defense," and many early Christians were familiar with this story and even argued that Socrates was a Christian before the fact of Jesus' appearance on earth, through the power of the Logos in the world.[4] Much of Christian literature, especially second-century literature labeled as "apologetic," offers evidence of resistance to the Roman Empire and its high valuation of Greek *paideia* ("culture" or "education"). It can be understood as literature of defense: *apologia*, not apology.

But the terms "apologists" and "apologetic literature" cover over a host of important questions about the *differences* between the various Christian voices in this debate, about the ways in which Christian arguments are *similar* to contemporaneous non-Christian arguments, and about the term "apology" itself. In the first part of this chapter I ask: What, exactly, is a Christian apologist, and how and why has the category of apologetics arisen? Is defense literature an ancient genre, a political stance, a label the writers themselves would have used? What work does this category do in the historiography of early Christianity? In unfolding answers to these questions, I pursue this book's double goal of reconstructing early Christian history more richly by embedding it within the material culture of its day, on the one hand, and telling a story of early Christians within the Roman Empire, on the other. We shall see that scholarly discussions divide like oil and water between those who admire the apologists' articulations of Christianity in light of Hellenistic philosophical traditions and those who disdain these as an offensive syncretism, a compromise of Christian revelation and a devolutionary merger with "pagan" philosophy.

3 On the definition of apologetics, see Annewies van den Hoek, "Apologetic and Protreptic Discourse in Clement of Alexandria," in A. Wlosok et al., eds., *La littérature apologétique avant Nicée. Entretiens sur l'antiquité classique* (Vandoeuvres-Genève: Fondation Hardt, 2005) 69–102; see also the responses to and discussion of the paper. Rebecca Lyman's "The Politics of Passing: Justin Martyr's Conversion as a Problem of 'Hellenization,'" (in Kenneth Mills and Anthony Grafton, eds., *Conversion in Late Antiquity and the Early Middle Ages: Seeing and Believing* [Rochester, NY: University of Rochester Press, 2003] 36–60) also points to the dangers of the category of apologetic, which might distract us from Justin's broader cultural context (esp. pp. 43–44). Those in antiquity, whether Christian or not, who debate education, myth, and cult often aim their critiques at non-elite cult practices and are part of a broader trend in "pagan monotheism." See the introduction to Polymnia Athanassiadi and Michael Frede, eds., *Pagan Monotheism in Late Antiquity* (Oxford: Clarendon, 1999) 1–20, esp. pp. 8–9.

4 See Loveday Alexander, "The Acts of the Apostles as an Apologetic Text," in Mark Edwards et al., eds., *Apologetics in the Roman Empire: Pagans, Jews, and Christians* (Oxford: Oxford University Press, 1999) 20–21.

The second part of the chapter re-situates early Christian apologetic literature by focusing on Olympia. This may seem to be an unusual move – certainly, no early Christian apologist claims to have written from that city. Nevertheless, Olympia, a Greek, even Panhellenic, city in the Roman period, is an exemplary site where I can begin to demonstrate the project of this book: reading so-called Christian apologies alongside others who represented themselves as addressing the Roman emperors and Greek culture, and within their rich cultural, material context, as participants in a fierce debate over ethnicity, power, culture, and religion. In Olympia, we find a monumental fountain dedicated by Regilla, wife of Herodes Atticus, a man famously educated, famously part of the so-called Second Sophistic, and himself an educator in the service of the imperial family. This fountain, I shall argue, constitutes a form of address to the Roman imperial family, articulated in Greek idiom. In the third part of the chapter and the conclusions, I show that this material address provides a new context for understanding early Christian texts that inscribe as their audiences the imperial family and "the Greeks."

I. WHAT DOES IT MEAN TO APOLOGIZE?

Scholars defining apologetic have long been intellectually snagged on the issue of audience, wondering whether Christian "apologies" really made it to their inscribed audiences, or whether other hearers – namely, Christians – were the main recipients of these writings. Tatian addresses "the Greeks" and Clement mentions the "Panhellenes"; Justin and Athenagoras appeal directly to the emperors; the canonical Acts of the Apostles is often understood as apologetic literature, a story that defended Christian origins and appealed to those in the Roman Empire with cosmopolitan and philhellenic sensibilities. We have been confused about how to read Christian identity within these writings: Scholars have often misunderstood how Christian writers fluidly engage the ethnic-religious nomenclature of Greek and Roman, sometimes positioning themselves against and sometimes within these categories.[5] We have been puzzled by the context that spurred such writings: Second-century Christians wrote at a time when there was no clear legislation against Christians, no clear judicial contexts in which to produce multiple *apologiai*.[6] We have been muddled about what these texts even are: There is not even a clear ancient generic definition of the *apologia* against which to measure our Christian sources.

[5] On the fixity and fluidity of ethnic/racial designations in early Christian rhetoric, see Denise Kimber Buell, *Why This New Race? Ethnic Reasoning in Early Christianity* (New York: Columbia University Press, 2005).

[6] Timothy D. Barnes, "Legislation against the Christians," *JRS* 58 (1968) 32–50.

It would be easier to understand so-called early Christian apologetic texts if we had a clearly defined ancient context of *apologia*, and thus could interpret them alongside other similar texts. Scholars have sought an ancient genre of *apologia*, or ancient practices of addressing the imperial family or broad populations ("the Greeks," "the nations," "the Jews"). But there is no ancient definition of *apologia* as a genre, as Loveday Alexander and Jean-Claude Fredouille have explored so well.[7] For Aristotle, apologetic and accusatory rhetoric are subcategories of forensic or judicial discourse (*Rhet.* 1.3). Pseudo-Demetrius's *Epistolary Types*, finalized perhaps in the third century CE but containing sources from as early as the second century BCE,[8] mentions the apologetic letter as a subcategory of epistolary forms. This brief reference, however, is not illuminating.[9] The texts collected under Menander Rhetor's name instruct on how to address the emperors; directions on how to compose the "royal speech," the "crown speech," and the "embassy" list structures and flourishes that sound like what we find in Justin's and Athenagoras's writings to the emperors. Menander suggests, "If you have to act as an ambassador (πρεσβεῦσαι) on behalf of a city in trouble, you should say what has been prescribed for the Crown Speech, but amplify at every point the topic of the emperor's love for humanity (τῆς φιλανθρωπίας τοῦ βασιλέως), saying that he is merciful and pities those who plead with him, and that God sent him down to earth because God knew that he was merciful and acted well towards people."[10] Some scholars of early Christian literature point to Menander to define early Christian apologies. Yet, even if Justin and Athenagoras clearly make recourse to terminology of *philanthrōpia* ("love for humanity") and justice, Menander dates to the late third or early fourth century CE, and thus may draw from second-century literature to prescribe literary forms. He may be an epitomizer, not a model.[11]

[7] Alexander, "The Acts of the Apostles," esp. 15, 24, 44; van den Hoek, "Apologetic and Protreptic Discourse in Clement of Alexandria," 69–73. Jean-Claude Fredouille notes that the term proper does not arise in the French language until the nineteenth century: "L'apologétique chrétienne antique: naissance d'un genre littéraire," *Revue des Études Augustiniennes* 38 (1992) 218–34 (see esp. 219); see also his "L'apologétique chrétienne antique: metamorphoses d'un genre polymorphe," *Revue des Études Augustiniennes* 41 (1995) 201–26. If we try to explore what apologetic might be by searching for *apologia* and its cognates in what is usually termed early Christian apologetic, we find very little. For example, Tatian's *To the Greeks* contains no such terms, and within his *Apologies*, Justin uses *apologia* or its cognates only four times, and once in the *Dialogue with Trypho*.

[8] Hans-Josef Klauck, *Ancient Letters and the New Testament: A Guide to Content and Exegesis* (Waco, TX: Baylor University Press, 2006) 195.

[9] Abraham J. Malherbe, *Ancient Epistolary Theorists* (Atlanta: Scholars, 1988) 41 (Pseudo-Demetrius 18). See also sections on apologetics in Stanley Stowers, *Letter Writing in Greco-Roman Antiquity* (Philadelphia: Westminster, 1986) 166–73.

[10] Menander Rhetor 423, in ET D. A. Russell and N. G. Wilson, eds. and trans., *Menander Rhetor* (Oxford: Clarendon, 1981) 180–81, with slight modifications.

[11] Ibid., "Introduction," xi.

If there is no ancient genre of apologetics to provide criteria for defining early Christian apologies, perhaps one can turn to early Christian writings that present together several apologists in order to understand how to interpret these texts. Eusebius, bishop of Caesarea at the time of Roman imperial persecution of Christians in the early fourth century, claims to have been in the service of Constantine. His early fourth-century *Ecclesiastical History* lists several writings that modern scholars consider apologetic. "Quadratos sent him [the emperor Hadrian] a speech, drawing up a defense on behalf of our religion (ἀπολογίαν συντάξας ὑπὲρ τῆς καθ' ἡμᾶς θεοσεβείας)"; Aristides "like Quadratus has left behind a defense concerning the faith, addressed to Hadrian" (τῷ Κοδράτῳ παραπλησίως ὑπὲρ τῆς πίστεως ἀπολογίαν ἐπιφωνήσας Ἀδριανῷ καταλέλοιπεν) (*Hist. eccl.* 4.3).[12] Here it seems, finally, that we have a catalog of apologies and the marking of some sort of genre of apologetics. Yet Eusebius's list of several texts that modern scholars consider to be *apologiai* does not delineate apologetics as a genre, but invents it as a category after the fact, via a chronological account of prominent early Christians who wrote to certain emperors or engaged in defensive debates.[13] It might seem that the Arethas codex of 912 CE (*Parisinus gr.* 451) is evidence of a fairly ancient concept of a corpus of early Christian apologies, because it collects several texts which scholars today assign the name apologetic. Yet the codex does *not* contain much of what scholars consider apologetic, such as Justin's works, Theophilus's *To Autolycus*, Hermias's *Irrisio*, and the *Epistle of Diognetus*.[14]

When, then, do we find the traditional apologists bound together? The French Benedictine Prudentius Maran produced the first printed collection of Greek apologetic writers in the mid-eighteenth century.[15] In 1742, he published an edition of Justin, Tatian, Athenagoras, Theophilus, and Hermias, arguably a strong subset of what most people consider to be the corpus of apologists. In 1734 Maran was briefly expelled from his monastery because

[12] The Greek edition is Eusebius, *Die Kirchengeschichte* (eds. E. Schwartz and Th. Mommsen; GCS; 3 vols.; Berlin: Akademie Verlag, 1999) 2.302, 304.

[13] van den Hoek, "Apologetic and Protreptic Discourse in Clement of Alexandria," 71; Fredouille discusses similar lists in Jerome, and Lactantius's treatment of Tertullian, Minucius Felix, and Cyprian ("L'apologétique chrétienne antique: naissance d'un genre littéraire").

[14] Regarding the Arethas codex, see van den Hoek, "Apologetic and Protreptic Discourse in Clement of Alexandria," 70. Johannes Quasten stated that this codex "was designed to be a *Corpus Apologetarum* from primitive times down to Eusebius," yet admitted that it did not include certain significant works (*Patrology* [3 vols.; Utrecht: Spectrum, 1964–66] 1.188). Nevertheless, the Arethas codex remains inextricably linked with apologetic literature of early Christianity; we find this in Maran's edition, incorporated a century later into Migne's *Patrologia Graeca*, in Otto's *Corpus apologetarum*, and in Harnack's *Die Überlieferung*. Harnack's work on the transmission of Greek apologetics is literally bound together with a book by Oscar von Gebhart about the Arethas codex.

[15] S.v. "Maran, Prudentius," in Samuel Macauley Jackson et al., eds., *The New Schaff-Herzog Encyclopedia of Religious Knowledge* (New York/London: Funk and Wagnalls Company, 1908–14).

of fears that he was agitating against the *Unigenitus* decree, which condemned Jansenist thought in France at the time. It is significant that Maran wrote in a tense context where definitions of Christian identity were debated. Some of what might be at stake in Maran's interest in apologetics is revealed in the titles of some of his other works: his three-volume *La Divinité de Jésus-Christ prouvée contre les hérétiques et les déistes* (*The Divinity of Jesus Christ Proven against the Heretics and the Deists*, 1751), *Les Grandeurs de Jésus-Christ avec la défense de sa divinité* (*The Glories of Jesus Christ with a Defense of His Divinity*, 1756), and *La Doctrine de l'écriture et des pères sur les guérisons miraculeuses* (*The Teaching of Scripture and of the Fathers about Miraculous Healings*, 1754). Through Maran we begin to see that apologetics is not a generic term from antiquity or an organic literary phenomenon arising from Christian persecution. Rather, as Maran's life hints, apologetic literature as a set of texts emerges in the taxonomic impulses of eighteenth-century European scholars who struggled in such contexts as the rise of Protestantism, the force of the Enlightenment, and the clash of religion and science.[16]

Yet, even if there is no ancient genre of apology or canonical list of early Christian apologies, we saw in the first lines of this chapter that both Justin and Athenagoras framed their writings as appeals to their rulers. Moreover, we do know something about dangerous embassies to rulers and emperors – and perhaps defenses presented before them – in the ancient world. According to Fergus Millar, the Roman emperors' days were bleary with ambassadorial requests from individuals and groups; there were "interminable embassies from cities, mainly Greek."[17] Where the emperor traveled, the machinery of bureaucracy did too, so that appeals from cities or even individuals could be quickly redressed or dismissed. This fact inspired writings that may or may not have made it to the emperor. We find examples of such literature in Philo of Alexandria's mid-first-century *Embassy to Gaius*, in Dio of Prusa's second-century *Kingship Orations*, or, slightly later, in Aelius Aristides' "Letter to the Emperors concerning Smyrna," which appeals to the mercies of Marcus Aurelius and Lucius Verus after the earthquake in Aristides' beloved home city.[18] In the late second and early third century especially, we find epigraphic evidence of *libelli* ("petitions") and *rescripta* ("imperial responses").[19] Even in the Roman Republican period, we read in Cicero a defense of the erection of

[16] S.v. "apologetic," "apology," *OED*; the first uses of such terms in English were in the seventeenth century.

[17] Fergus Millar, *The Emperor in the Roman World (31 BC–AD 337)* (Ithaca, NY: Cornell University Press, 1992) 3–11; 465–511; quotation on p. 6. For the phenomenon of envoys and appeals among those of lower status, such as the Pauline mission, see, e.g., Margaret Mitchell, "New Testament Envoys in the Context of Greco-Roman Diplomatic and Epistolary Conventions: The Case of Timothy and Titus," *JBL* 111 (1993) 641–42.

[18] *Or.* 19; see also *Or.* 21 ("The Smyrnean Oration").

[19] Tor Hauken, *Petition and Response: An Epigraphic Study of Petitions to Roman Emperors 181–249* (Bergen: Norwegian Institute at Athens, 1998).

a bronze statue of Servius Sulpicius, who died while on an embassy to Mark Antony on behalf of the Senate.[20] Thus Christians like Justin or Athenagoras claimed for themselves an ambassadorial role that was found not only in the literary and documentary records, but that was also expressed in the rhetoric of images – Cicero appeals to precedent, and statues of murdered ambassadors had been erected in the Roman Forum in 438, 230, and 162 BCE[21] – as a potentially dangerous act of self-sacrifice on behalf of a greater body. As Millar puts it, "Christian apologies of the second century . . . cannot be fully understood unless set against the background of those exhortatory or informative works so commonly addressed to emperors in this period. At the very least they owe their literary form to this custom; and we must be open to the possibility that some were actually sent, or even read, to emperors."[22]

The emperors may have received constant embassies and speeches, but we do not know if Christian apologies were sent to them or received by them, nor, if they were received, if they were taken seriously. Would the imperial family have followed Justin's minute arguments about how to read correctly the Jewish scriptures to see in them Christ's prefiguration? On a busy day, would Emperors Marcus Aurelius and Commodus have bothered to rifle through Athenagoras's long *Embassy*, much less have listened to him in person? And what does it mean for Tatian and Clement to address Greeks or Panhellenes in the second century? Tatian writes, "Do not maintain a totally hostile attitude toward barbarians, men of Greece, nor resent their teachings" (*Ad Graec.* 1.1); "Don't scorn our *paideia* nor busy yourself with a quarrel directed against us" (*Ad Graec.* 35.1).[23] How would one reach such a broad audience in the midst of a trend in the Roman world of acquiring Greek education and culture? The question of whether Christians in fact addressed the second-century imperial families is, given our data, impossible to answer, and we do not know what early readers of these texts thought about Tatian's or Clement's claims that these writings should make their way into the hands of the Greeks. Yet scholars continue to ask questions about the "real" audience of these writings, in part because of concerns about Christian authenticity. They worry: Would the apologists' theological or political assertions have any truth if we discovered that they did not *really* write to the imperial family or to "outsiders"?[24]

[20] Cicero *Philippic* 9; see Jeremy Tanner, *The Invention of Art History in Ancient Greece: Religion, Society and Artistic Rationalisation* (Cambridge: Cambridge University Press, 2006) 26.

[21] Tanner, *The Invention of Art History*, 26–29.

[22] Millar, *The Emperor in the Roman World*, 498; he makes this comment in the context of an example like Dio of Prusa's *Kingship Orations*, which claim to have been delivered before or sent to Trajan; see also p. 511 where Millar discusses the book of Acts.

[23] The Greek edition is Miroslav Marcovich, *Tatiani Oratio ad Graecos; Theophili Antiocheni ad Autolycum* (Berlin: De Gruyter, 1995).

[24] For such debates regarding Justin, see Niels Hyldahl, *Philosophie und Christentum. Eine Interpretation der Einleitung zum Dialog Justins* (Copenhagen: Munksgaard, 1966) 272–92; and Oskar Skarsaune, "The Conversion of Justin Martyr," *Stud. Theol.* 30 (1976) 56–59, who argue that Justin understands there to be a rift between Platonism and Christianity. See J. C. M.

We must take seriously the claims of early Christian apologetic literature to address the imperial family or the Greeks because such claims reveal much about their rhetoric – the intricacies of their arts of persuasion. Justin and Athenagoras rhetorically construct the imperial families as addressees; Tatian claims to address Greeks; Clement at one point invokes "Panhellenes" (*Prot.* II 34.1). Even if these addresses never occurred before emperors or all of the Greeks (how could they?!), the effect of inscribing such audiences is to place Christians on a larger ethnic–cultural map where their voices participate in Greek and Roman conventions and identities, and should be heard by Greeks or Romans. These texts claim that Christians can and should address the emperors, that Christians stand upon a stage large enough to address an entire race or language group, and that the imperial family and the Greeks should sit down and take notice. Yet although these Christian writers address the Greeks or the Roman imperial family and Romans more generally, this does not mean that we should understand Christians as something other than Greek or Roman. Their initial addresses and vocatives deliberately obscure how these Christians position themselves as Greeks or as subjects of Roman rule, as participants in Greek *paideia* and Roman piety and justice.

II. ADDRESSING THE ROMAN EMPERORS, BEING GREEK

The early Christian apologetic texts that are at the center of this book – the Acts of the Apostles, Justin's *Apologies*, Tatian's *To the Greeks*, Athenagoras's *Embassy*, and Clement's *Protreptikos* – can and should be read together, although they do not constitute an ancient genre or a contained corpus from the ancient world. All five texts weave back to certain themes: All five respond to the blurring of the human and divine in statuary, other images, and in religious practice; to the debate about what constitutes true religion or piety; to the question of what constitutes true justice under the empire; and to the negotiation of identity in a world where Greek ethnicity and forms of culture are special commodities in the global market of the Roman Empire.

So-called early Christian apologies are best understood in light of a broad set of contemporaneous literature and artifacts of the Greco-Roman world. This is not a radical thesis; Werner Jaeger developed the idea in his 1960 lectures, published a year later as *Early Christianity and Greek Paideia.*[25] Nevertheless,

van Winden, *An Early Christian Philosopher: Justin Martyr's Dialogue with Trypho Chapters One to Nine. Introduction, Text and Commentary* (Leiden: E. J. Brill, 1971) 24 for a review of the history of scholarship on Justin's philosopher's cloak, and what it might indicate about the continuity or discontinuity of his relationship with philosophy. For a sophisticated reading of the categories of Christianity and Hellenism as they relate to Justin, see Lyman, "The Politics of Passing," esp. 36–40, 44–45.

25 Werner Jaeger, *Early Christianity and Greek Paideia* (Cambridge: Belknap, 1961) 24–26. It has long been recognized that so-called apologists for early Christianity had much in common with their intellectual counterparts in other cults. See, e.g., Harry Austryn Wolfson, *The Philosophy of the Church Fathers* (3rd ed.; Cambridge, MA: Harvard University Press, 1970);

it bears repeating, because second-century Christian apologists have often been read as a contained corpus of Christian writings over and against others, or plumbed for early glimmers of christology or trinitarian thought, rather than understood within their wider literary world, much less amid the art and architecture that surrounded them. Moreover, these Christian writings are often read as dead serious as, indeed, parts of them often are. Yet if we glance more broadly at the literary world in which these Christian texts are written, we find ourselves in the cultural wars of the second century, where both Roman power and the value of Greek education and *paideia* under the Roman Empire were widely and satirically debated. Perhaps parts of Christian apologetic writings are much funnier than we had thought.

Defining the So-Called Second Sophistic

The apologetic writings at the center of my book should be understood in terms of this satirical and political literature, the cultural criticism of their day. That is, these Christian writings should be read in light of the so-called Second Sophistic. Scholars have borrowed this term from the third-century CE writer Philostratus, who coined it as he discussed important persons of the immediately prior centuries who had been interested in rhetoric like the ancient Greek sophists before them. Philostratus's phrase thus artificially crystallizes a range of trends that predate his writing. So too, modern scholars use the term "Second Sophistic" as a convenient shorthand for a range of phenomena that look similar, after the fact. Like the term postmodernism, the term Second Sophistic has no clear definition; like postmodern writers, writers of the Second Sophistic took part in a culture war with common themes variously treated by warring sides.

Even if, however, there was no community defining itself as the Second Sophistic in the first and second centuries CE (or even thereafter), the term is still useful if we understand it to refer to a broad context in which Greek identity was valued on the Roman imperial market.[26] The second century was a peak in the production and exhibition of an elite, antiquarian Greek identity[27] that was variously an act of resistance towards the Roman Empire and an item of social capital to be acquired by provincial and Roman elites

Harold W. Attridge, "The Philosophical Critique of Religion under the Early Empire," *ANRW* II.1 (1978) 45–78; Robert Grant, *Greek Apologists of the Second Century* (Philadelphia: Westminster, 1988) esp. 9.

26 Simon Swain, *Hellenism and Empire: Language, Classicism, and Power in the Greek World AD 50–250* (Oxford: Clarendon, 1996) 1–7, esp. 2. See also Rebecca Lyman, "Hellenism and Heresy: 2002 NAPS Presidential Address," *JECS* 11.2 (2003) 209–22, esp. 212–16; Tim Whitmarsh, *Greek Literature and the Roman Empire: The Politics of Imitation* (Oxford: Oxford University Press, 2001) esp. chap. 2; Glenn Bowersock, *Greek Sophists in the Roman Empire* (Oxford: Clarendon, 1969).

27 On the construction of Greek identity in antiquity, see Jonathan Hall, *Hellenicity: Between Ethnicity and Culture* (Chicago: University of Chicago Press, 2002) esp. 225–26.

alike.[28] Among those who participated in and resisted this cultural trend, "Greek" marked not only a region, ethnicity, or language, but also a set of practices that included antiquarian impulses; an emphasis on Plato, Homer, and other "classical" writers; the use of the Attic dialect of Greek; and the manipulations of genres associated with classical Greece, such as the dialogue. In the center of this trend were often struggles over definition. Those who were categorized as sophists eschewed the term, preferring to think of their work as philosophical.

Contemporaneous Christian writings seriously engaged the *paideia* of the world in which Christians took part and by which they were formed. But they also – and it is difficult to hear humor in cultures not our own – offered jokes and satire in order to stake out their place, among others, in the midst of the cultural pretentions and theological diversity of the variegated Roman world. Thus we should not think of the Second Sophistic as a club that Christian apologists joined or resisted, but rather as a larger set of rhetorical practices that produced debate over culture or *paideia* ("education"), piety, and ethnic identity under Rome in which writers such as Luke, Justin, Tatian, Athenagoras, and Clement participated, alongside non-Christian writers like Dio of Prusa and Lucian of Samosata.[29] Christian apologists participated in a broader culture of persuasion and defense.

Traveling to Olympia: Material Manifestations of Greek Paideia *and Imperial Address*

Scholars have correctly critiqued the term "Greco-Roman" for its careless lack of nuance with regard to chronology, culture, and power; like the term "Judeo-Christian," it flattens difference and unequal power into a pat compound adjective. Yet many of our second-century texts, as well as a city like Olympia in the second century, embodied the term well.[30] In Olympia on the Greek Peloponnesos we find an example of another second-century "address" and even an *apologia* or defense that evokes the Roman imperial family and the Greeks. Olympia is important because it is a city that materializes some of the key issues with which Christian apologists dealt: the power and prestige of Greek identity even in the Roman period, a power and prestige that caused

[28] See Maud Gleason's neat formulation: "*Paideia*, for both Greek and Roman gentlemen, was a form of symbolic capital" (*Making Men: Sophists and Self-Presentation in Ancient Rome* [Princeton, NJ: Princeton University Press, 1995] xxi).

[29] Timothy Horner, *Listening to Trypho: Justin Martyr's* Dialogue *Reconsidered* (Leuven: Peeters, 2001) esp. 72–83; Mark S. Burrows, "Christianity in the Roman Forum: Tertullian and the Apologetic Use of History," *VC* 42.3 (1998) 212–13.

[30] On seeing the debates and ideologies of the Second Sophistic in archaeology, see, e.g., Susan Alcock, "Old Greece within the Empire," 36–98 in her *Archaeologies of the Greek Past: Landscape, Monuments, and Memories* (Cambridge: Cambridge University Press, 2002); see pp. 88–89 on the term Greco-Roman.

various groups to fabricate Greek heritage; the use and glorification of ancient Greek history; the imbrication of culture, power, and religion; the significance of sculpture, namely, Pheidias's representation of Zeus; and the blurring between human and divine.

"Indeed, one sees many and varied things in Greece, and also one hears things worthy of amazement! But, above all, the mystic rites in Eleusis and the competition that is in Olympia has claim to the care of god," wrote Pausanias in his second-century travel narrative (*Descr.* 5.10.1).[31] Olympia was a city of fame and of long memory; ancient Greeks asserted that the games there began in 776 BCE and this date became their starting point for recorded history. At an early stage, the important monuments of the city fanned outwards from the tomb of Pelops, the legendary king of Olympia, and an archaic or archaizing ash altar of Zeus (Fig. 1). On either side of these were temples: To the north, at the base of the Hill of Kronos, was the early Archaic temple of Hera; on the south, built onto an artificial platform, was the larger temple of Zeus (ca. 470–357 BCE), at one time the largest temple on the Peloponnesos.[32] In the 430s, Pheidias made the famous chryselephantine sculpture of Zeus enthroned within the temple.[33] Along the base of the Hill of Kronos were located treasuries, lined up at a sacred center in a practice similar to that of the Panhellenic center and games-festival site of Delphi. Just south of these treasuries was the Metroon, a sanctuary for the Mother of the Gods, built in the fifth century BCE. Olympia had the prestigious role of hosting Panhellenic festivals, including games and religious ceremonies, every four years, a practice that occurred nearly continuously from the early eighth century BCE until the fourth century CE.

Even before the Roman imperial period, of course, Olympia had been a quintessential site of Panhellenic identity and a site for benefactors of various ethnicities to advertise victory or to offer a donation that would place them in the heartland of Greek identity. For example, in celebration of his victory over the Greeks at Chaironeia, the Macedonian king Philip II built a small *tholos* or round structure in which were placed statues of his family in the northwest corner of the Altis, near the sanctuary of Hera. According to Pausanias, the statues were ivory and gold (5.20.10); thus, they echoed the materials of Pheidias's famous statue of Zeus. The statues associated the Macedonian royal family with Zeus and with the lavish and culturally valued artistic tradition already

[31] The Greek edition is *Pausaniae Graeciae Descriptio* (ed. Maria-Helena Rocha-Pereira; 3 vols.; Leipzig: Teubner, 1903).

[32] Charles Gates, *Ancient Cities: The Archaeology of Urban Life in the Ancient Near East and Egypt, Greece and Rome* (New York: Routledge, 2003) 234–36.

[33] Ibid., 236. The workshop of Pheidias has been found in Olympia; see also Pausanias *Descr.* 5.15.1 regarding the workshop; 5.11.1–4 regarding the statue and throne. The statue was taken to Constantinople and destroyed in 476 CE in a fire. For Dio of Prusa's discussion of the statue and his "trial" of Pheidias, see pp. 230–33.

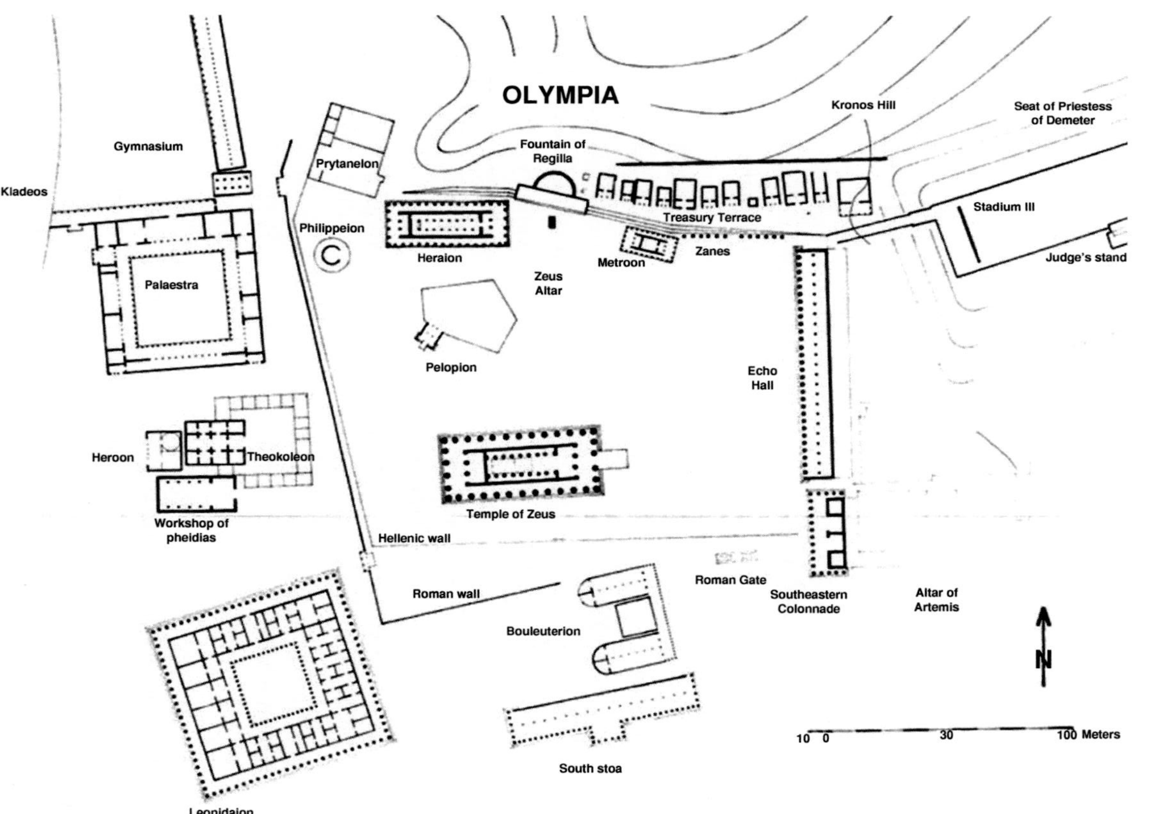

1. Olympia: Plan of city center, Roman period. Courtesy of Fortress Press and Helmut Koester (*Cities of Paul: Images and Interpretations from the Harvard New Testament Archaeology Project*).

located in Olympia. They also – even in their base materials – demonstrated an imperial family blurring the line between human and divine.[34]

In the Roman imperial period, ancient Panhellenic centers for games and festivals (Olympia, Delphia, Isthmia, Nemea) continued to flourish, renewed by new benefactions, and aggrandized through hosting imperial cult.[35] Of these, Olympia flourished the most consistently; after the turmoil of the Republican period, the Olympics "were rescued and restored by benefactions of (among others) Agrippa and Herod the Great, and Tiberius and Nero themselves competed in the games."[36] Through Pausanias we can see Olympia in the Roman period as a "memory theater"; it is an ancient site filled over the centuries with rich and contradictory statements about victory, power, and who should be remembered for what. On the temple of Zeus alone, according to Pausanias, were two important monuments to victory (or humiliation). Under a gilded *Nike* at the pediment was a golden shield with a Medusa in relief, booty dedicated by the Spartans to celebrate their triumph over the Argives, the Athenians, and the Ionians (5.10.4). On the frieze, Pausanias notes that there were "gilded shields twenty-one in number, a votive offering made by Mummius, general of the Romans, when he conquered the Achaeans in war, seized Corinth, and made the Dorians depart" (5.10.5). From the Spartan war to the pre-imperial, 146 BCE Roman conquest of Corinth by Mummius, the temple of Zeus was a billboard to announce triumph, to construct and preserve memory, and to place one's *ethnos* – whether Spartan or Roman, in

34 Not only did the statues of the Macedonian royal family stand in Olympia; Philip himself even competed in the Olympic games. At Olympia the Hellenizing Macedonian royal family materially made the argument that Macedonia belonged at the heart of Greece, and it asserted the right of Macedonian culture to stand alongside and to combine with ancient Greek history and religion.

35 Susan Alcock, *Graecia Capta: The Landscapes of Roman Greece* (Cambridge: Cambridge University Press, 1993) 189. For basic information on the *periodos* or circuit of these four games/sites, see Gates, *Ancient Cities*, 239. On Alexander-mania in the Roman period, see Diana Spencer, *The Roman Alexander: Reading a Cultural Myth* (Exeter: University of Exeter, 2002); Carmen Arnold-Biucchi, *Alexander's Coins and Alexander's Image* (Cambridge, MA: Harvard University Art Museums, 2006) 39–42. Pliny *Nat. hist.* 35.36.94 discusses how Augustus took paintings from the court of Alexander the Great, and then Claudius cut out Alexander's face from two works and substituted Augustus's.

36 Alcock, *Graecia Capta*, 190. Sulla plundered the sacred site in 86 BCE and had the games that were scheduled for 80 BCE moved to Rome for his triumph. See "Olympia: General Materials: Drachma of Elis: Eagle and Serpent" in Helmut Koester, ed., *Cities of Paul: Images and Interpretations from the Harvard New Testament Archaeology Project* (CD-ROM; Minneapolis: Fortress, 2005). Agrippa (son-in-law of Augustus) and Herod may have been the benefactors who completed the so-called Echo Stoa, begun by Alexander and eventually perhaps dedicated to the emperor Augustus (Ulrich Sinn, *Olympia: Cult, Sport, and Ancient Festival* [trans. Thomas Thornton; Princeton, NJ: Marcus Wiener Publishers, 2000] 105). If this is true, the Echo Stoa becomes an example of Hellenized Jewish benefaction to a structure begun by the most famous Macedonian Hellenophile, Alexander, and then connected in turn with the first Roman emperor, Augustus. It is a physical demonstration of how persons spanning various ethnic and cultic affiliations wished to associate themselves with a foundational site of ancient Greek identity.

these cases – at a Panhellenic center. Within the temple, presiding over these claims, sat Pheidias's chryselephantine Zeus, so large that were he to stand up, he could be seen over the temple's roof-line. This Zeus was still much discussed in the second century.[37]

Pausanias's account of Olympia leaves the impression that it was impossible to move through the Altis, the sacred grove around the Temple of Zeus, without squeezing one's body past the largely male statuary bodies of emperors (Hadrian included), gods (Zeus especially), athletes (both honest and dishonest), and "somebody" (6.3.1).[38] Pausanias tries at a taxonomy, distinguishing statues associated with victory awards (οἱ δὲ ἀνδριάντες τῶν νικώντων ἐν τοῦ ἄθλου) from votive offerings to the gods (τὰ ἀναθήματα) (5.21.1). But the sheer number of subjects depicted and inscriptions that Pausanias includes make it difficult to imagine how one would visually distinguish their statuses. The imperial, the divine, and the heroic visually blurred in statuary, on the one hand, and crowded the real bodies of tourists and worshippers, on the other.[39]

Within the Altis stood the fifth-century BCE Metroon, or sanctuary to the mother of the gods. By the Roman period, however, there was no *agalma* ("image") of her within it, but instead *andriantes* ("statues") of Roman emperors (5.20.9). Found at the south foundation of the Metroon's stylobate was a torso in Pentelic marble of what must have been the central cult statue of the temple. The torso, along with other fragments, must have come from a statue that measured 4.5 m high, including the base, and likely depicted Augustus in heroic nudity with a scepter in the left hand and the right forearm outstretched.[40] An inscription on the architrave of the Metroon allows us to surmise that despite Pausanias's attempt to distinguish cult image from mere statuary in his terminology, this statue may have indeed been that of Augustus as Zeus or Jupiter: "The Elians [dedicated this temple] of the Son of God, Caesar Augustus, Savior of the Greeks and of the whole world."[41] The Roman Augustus here becomes savior of one key ethnicity represented and remembered in Olympia – the Greeks – and also the savior of the entire

[37] See especially discussion of Dio's *Or.* 23 ("To the Olympians") in Chapter 6; on Zeus's size, see Strabo *Geog.* 8.3.30 and discussion in Gordon, "The Real and the Imaginary," 13–14.

[38] Altars too littered the area, including one to the "worker goddess" (Ἐργάνη), to whom those of Pheidias's descendents who cleaned the statue of Zeus sacrificed (Pausanias *Descr.* 5.14.5).

[39] On such blurring in Pausanias, see Gordon, "The Real and the Imaginary," 7–8.

[40] Koester, *Cities of Paul*, "Olympia: Metroon and Fountain of Regilla: Statue: Torso of Augustus"; Konrad Hitzl, *Die Kaiserzeitliche Statuenausstattung des Metroon* (Olympische Forschungen 19; New York: De Gruyter, 1991); also discussed in S. R. F. Price, *Rituals and Power: The Roman Imperial Cult in Asia Minor* (Cambridge: Cambridge University Press, 1984) 160–61.

[41] Ἡλῆοι Θ[εοῦ] υἱοῦ Καί[σαρος] | Σεβαστοῦ Σωτ[ῆρος τῶν Ἑλ] | λήν[ω]ν [τ]ε καὶ [τῆς οἰκου | μέ]ν[ης] πά[σ]η[ς ...]. The Greek is taken from Hitzl, *Die Kaiserzeitliche Statuenausstattung,* 22; see also discussion in Koester, *Cities of Paul*, "Olympia: Metroon and Fountain of Regilla: Statue: Torso of Augustus."

oikoumenē ("inhabited world"). Also discovered at the site of the Metroon was an over life-size (2.1 m) statue of Claudius as Zeus, replete with eagle and (now missing) scepter, and signed by two Athenian sculptors (Fig. 2).[42] It can be better understood in light of the more complete statue of Claudius as Jupiter, a dedication of the people of Lanuvium (Fig. 3).[43] In Olympia, Greek *paideia* was put to work to re-present Roman power geographically (from Greece to the rest of the inhabited world) and religiously. Claudius was pious, but he was also Zeus; Augustus was savior and son of God. The thin line between the Roman emperor's role in conquering and in saving the Greeks and the entire *oikoumenē* is erased.

Susan Alcock has interpreted Roman-period Athens as an example of a "memory theater" where Romans used a key space for Greek *paideia* and cultural prestige and literally built their own presence into it; certain "memories" of ancient events, persons, and spaces were highlighted, and their juxtaposition with new building projects gave both old and new different rhetorics and meanings.[44] So too Olympia embodied a centuries-long conversation about the prestige of classical Greek culture and the desire of various kingdoms and elites to associate their nations, their cultures, and themselves with this prestige. In a similar move, as we shall see, early Christian apologists built their own texts into the preexisting edifices of Homer, Plato, Euripides, and others, to critique them and to associate with their cultural prestige, sometimes simultaneously.

The Fountain of Regilla and Herodes Atticus

While, according to tradition, portions of Olympia were nicely wooded, the site of the games themselves would have been hot, dry, and eye-straining bright in the summers. Olympia was a site in need of a fantastic fountain.[45] In the

42 Hitzl, *Die Kaiserzeitliche Statuenausstattung*, 38–56, 67–70 on this statue and those of Agrippina, Titus, and two headless statues, perhaps of Vespasian and Flavia Domitilla, from the Metroon, and pp. 122–23 on an ancient repair of the Claudius statue; Koester, *Cities of Paul*, "Olympia: Metroon and Fountain of Regilla: "Statue: Claudius as Zeus."

43 On the complex issues of the gods at Lanuvium, see, e.g., Clifford Ando, *The Matter of the Gods: Religion and the Roman Empire* (Berkeley: University of California Press, 2008) 108–9.

44 See, e.g., Susan E. Alcock, "The Reconfiguration of Memory in the Eastern Roman Empire," in Susan E. Alcock et al., eds., *Empires: Perspectives from Archaeology and History* (Cambridge: Cambridge University Press, 2001) 334–35; and her *Archaeologies of the Greek Past*, esp. 54 n. 29. See also the discussion of the Athenian agora in Chapter 3.

45 See Lucian's story of the dry location and the wandering Peregrinus, who critiques the fountain and its benefactor while guzzling the water; Peregrinus also reverses himself the next year in a speech and praises its benefactor (*De morte Peregr.* 19–20). Pausanias passes over the fountain without mention, as he so frequently does with Roman-period monuments. See William Hutton, *Describing Greece: Landscape and Literature in the* Periegesis *of Pausanias* (Cambridge: Cambridge University Press, 2005) 41–82; Ian Rutherford, "Tourism and the Sacred: Pausanias and the Traditions of Greek Pilgrimage," in Susan Alcock et al., eds.,

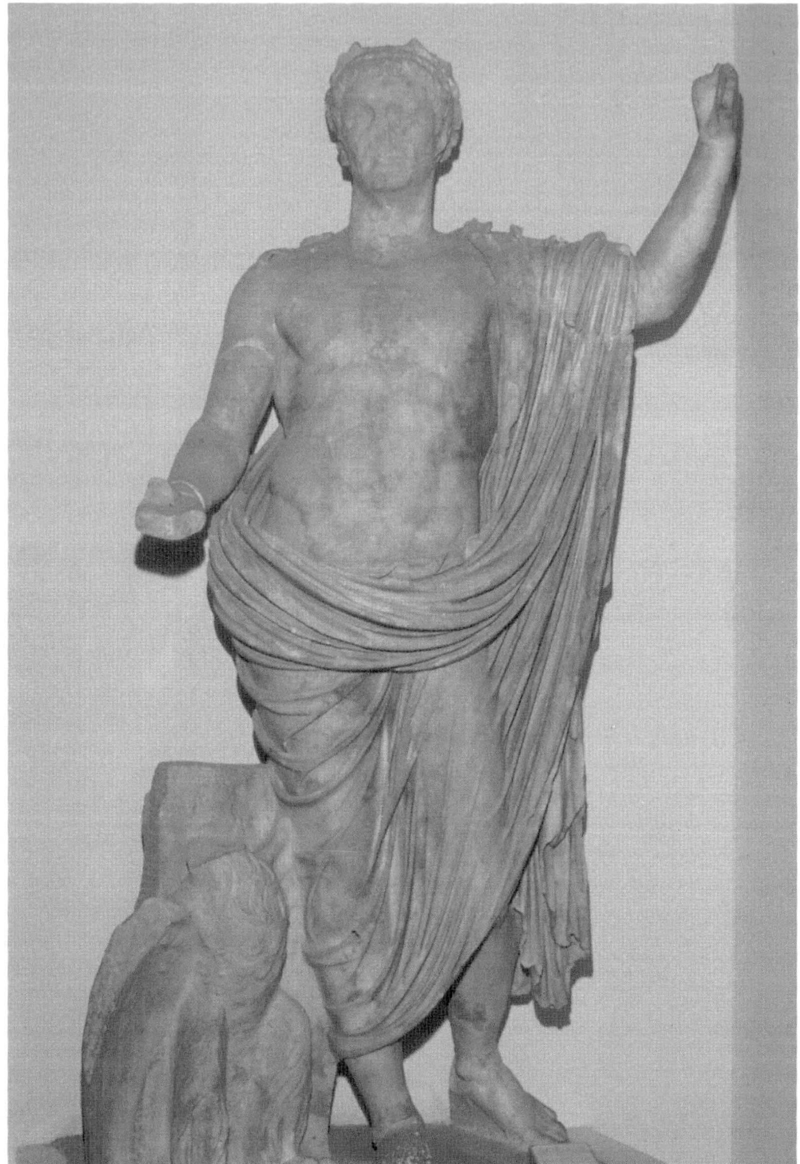

2. Claudius as Zeus/Jupiter from the Metroon. Olympia Museum. Courtesy of Fortress Press and Helmut Koester (*Cities of Paul: Images and Interpretations from the Harvard New Testament Archaeology Project*). © The President and Fellows of Harvard College. All Rights Reserved.

second century, just to the west of the row of temple treasuries, sprawled over part of the foot of the Hill of Kronos, Herodes Atticus and his wife Regilla built such a fountain. It was roughly in alignment with the treasuries' dipteral façades

Pausanias: Travel and Memory in Roman Greece (Oxford: Oxford University Press, 2001) 40–52. For a reading of Pausanias's travel narrative as "imaginative geography" see in the same volume Jaś Elsner, "Structuring 'Greece': Pausanias's *Periegesis* as a Literary Construct," 4.

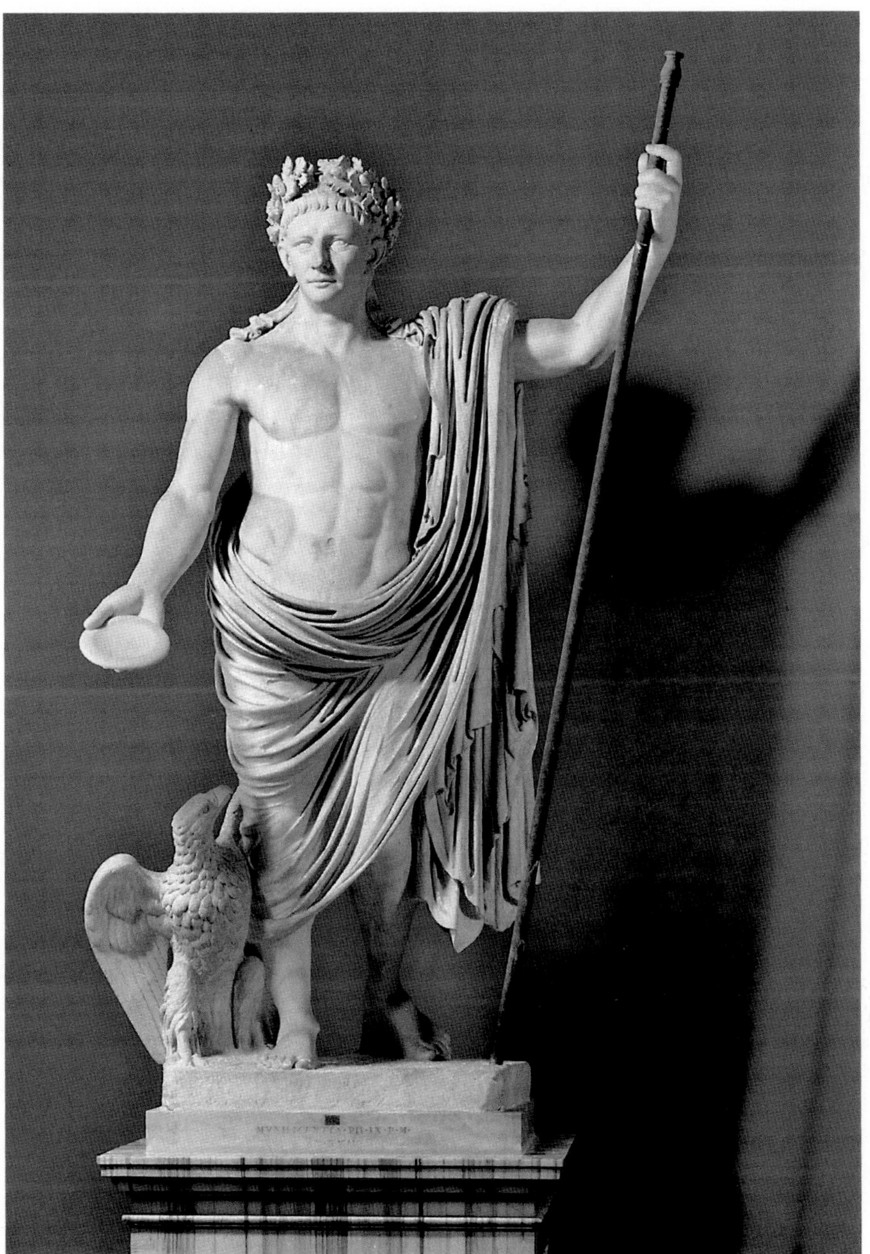

3. Claudius as Jupiter. Museo Pio Clementino, Vatican Museums, Vatican State. Scala/Art Resource, NY.

and on the same alignment as the Metroon; its western edge was a few meters from the eastern façade of the archaic Heraion (see again Fig. 1). The fountain slid into the extant plan and alignment of the ancient buildings and other monuments of Olympia. Yet with its sophisticated waterworks and its imposing size – it towered over the ancient Temple of Hera, states Susan Walker – it also made a loud statement.[46] The monumental fountain commissioned by the wealthy Regilla and her husband Herodes Atticus offers an intriguing case of how one might *visually* address the emperors and at the same time communicate certain ideas about the value of Greek *paideia* as well as Roman *pietas* ("piety" or "religious duty").[47]

Herodes Atticus was one of the most famous sophists of the second century CE, a student of oratory in Athens, which was of course *the* famous center of Greek culture,[48] and a teacher of the emperors Marcus Aurelius and Lucius Verus. His fame derives in part from Philostratus's lavish treatment. The author who coined the term "Second Sophistic" in his *Lives of the Sophists* also described Herodes as the "the tongue of the Greeks" (*Vit. soph.* 2.598); according to Philostratus, Herodes was described by no less than Hadrian, who also performed his funeral oration, as the "emperor of words" (2.586).[49] At his estate in Loukou on the Peloponnesos many classicizing statues have been discovered; Herodes, it is no surprise, was a connoisseur and art collector of the sort that Tatian would despise.[50] Herodes was depicted as the quintessential *pepaideumenos* or educated man.[51]

46 Susan Walker, "Roman Nymphaea in the Greek World," in Sarah Macready and F. H. Thompson, eds., *Roman Architecture in the Greek World* (London: The Society of Antiquaries of London, 1987) 61: "The nymphaeum towered over the ancient Temple of Hera, its crude gaudy statues and coloured marble revetment blanching the little treasuries on the terrace to the east."

47 It was not the only such statement, nor the only such one produced in a woman's name: The monumental gate of Plancia Magna at Perge in modern-day Turkey offers another intriguing example. See Haluk Abbasoğlu, "The Founding of Perge and its Development in the Hellenistic and Roman Periods," in David Parrish, ed., *Urbanism in Western Asia Minor: New Studies on Aphrodisias, Ephesos, Hierapolis, Pergamon, Perge, and Xanthos* (Portsmouth, RI: Journal of Roman Archaeology, 2001) 173–88, esp. 178–79; Mary Boatwright, "Plancia Magna of Perge: Women's Roles and Statue in Roman Asia Minor," in Sarah Pomeroy, ed., *Women's History and Ancient History* (Chapel Hill, NC: University of North Carolina Press, 1991) 249–71.

48 In a *Prolegomena* preserved among works of Aelius Aristides there is mention that Herodes held a chair of rhetoric in Athens in 167. Jennifer Tobin, *Herodes Attikos and the City of Athens: Patronage and Conflict under the Antonines* (Amsterdam: Gieben, 1997) 51.

49 Whitmarsh, *Greek Literature in the Roman Empire*, 105.

50 On Herodes at Loukou, see Appendix II of Tobin, *Herodes Attikos*, esp. pp. 337–53; George Spyropoulos, *Drei Meisterwerke der griechischen Plastik aus der Villa des Herodes Atticus zu EVA/Loukou* (New York: Peter Lang, 2001); see also mention in Andrew Stewart, "Baroque Classics: The Tragic Muse and the *Exemplum*," in James I. Porter, ed., *Classical Pasts: The Classical Traditions of Greece and Rome* (Princeton, NJ: Princeton University Press, 2006) 136. These sculptures included a portrait of Antinoos, an over life-size portrait of Commodus, and a fragment of Menelaos carrying the dead Patroklos. On Tatian, see pp. 241–47.

51 Whitmarsh, *Greek Literature in the Roman Empire*, 107; Whitmarsh argues that Philostratus subtly critiques this wealth and power.

Herodes was as wealthy as a king.[52] Philostratus takes pages to list Herodes' benefactions.[53] Even if Philostratus exaggerates Herodes' virtues, epigraphic and archaeological evidence demonstrates the geographical scope, variety, and expense of his benefactions and those of his family, including his father and grandfather.[54] In her study, Jennifer Tobin refers to archaeological evidence of Herodes' benefaction of over 200 statues and approximately twenty-five new buildings or renovations. Over 150 inscriptions remain that name him, and his euergetic impact was felt from Italy to Albania to Greece to Turkey.[55]

Herodes Atticus is not only the son of Atticus, but also the child of the region of Attica. Many of Herodes' benefactions were directed toward the cities of Attica; like Hadrian before him Herodes was also interested in making Athens a jewel of Greek *paideia*, set within the sparkling chains of empire.[56] Even if Herodes' family was famously embroiled in Athenian politics and at times hated by the Athenian populace, Herodes' benefactions in Athens were plentiful. They included the famous Odeion on the south slope of the Acropolis, dedicated to his wife Regilla, and the Panathenaic Stadium just south of the Olympieion complex completed by Hadrian, among others.[57]

We find evidence of Herodes and his family not only in Athens but also in Olympia. The fountain there was dedicated by his wife Regilla, a priestess of Demeter and famous in Roman circles: "Appia Annia Regilla Atilia Caucidia Tertulla . . . was a member of a family of senatorial and patrician status, with numerous consuls and other high government officials among her remote and recent ancestors."[58] The fountain was probably finished in the early 150s, before her mysterious death in ca. 161; she was likely murdered by Herodes.[59]

52 Tobin, *Herodes Attikos*, 14–22. See Philostratus *Vit. soph.* 2.555 on the conflict with Antoninus Pius regarding his misspending of funds in Alexandria Troas. On Marcus Aurelius's mediations to the Athenians on Herodes' behalf, see James H. Oliver, *Marcus Aurelius: Aspects of Civic and Cultural Policy in the East* (Hesp. Supp. 13; Princeton, NJ: American School of Classical Studies at Athens, 1970). Herodes is a private citizen who continues the legacy of an emperor like Hadrian; see Walker, "Roman Nymphaea in the Greek World," 62.

53 See, e.g., Philostratus *Vit. soph.* 2.551–52, which also mentions Herodes taking up Nero's ambition to cut through the Isthmus of the Peloponnesus.

54 See Tobin, *Herodes Attikos*, esp. appendix I.

55 Ibid., 10.

56 On Hadrian and Athens, see Chapter 3.

57 Philostratus claims that the Athenians wittily and bitterly "said the Panathenian stadium was well named, for it was built from [funds] from which all the Athenians were robbed" (*Vit. soph.* 2.549). Tobin, *Herodes Attikos*, 173, 177–84 and also her "Some New Thoughts on Herodes Atticus's Tomb, His Stadium of 143/44, and Philostratus VS 2.550," *AJA* 97 (1993) 81–89.

58 Sarah Pomeroy, *The Murder of Regilla: A Case of Domestic Violence in Antiquity* (Cambridge, MA: Harvard University Press, 2007) 13, passim.

59 For the date of the fountain, see Renate Bol, *Das Statuenprogramm des Herodes-Atticus-Nymphäums* (Olympische Forschungen 15; Berlin: Walter De Gruyter, 1984) 100 who says that 149 CE is the earliest possible date for the design and beginning of construction. On Regilla's murder, see Philostratus *Vit. soph.* 2.555–56; Pomeroy, *The Murder of Regilla*.

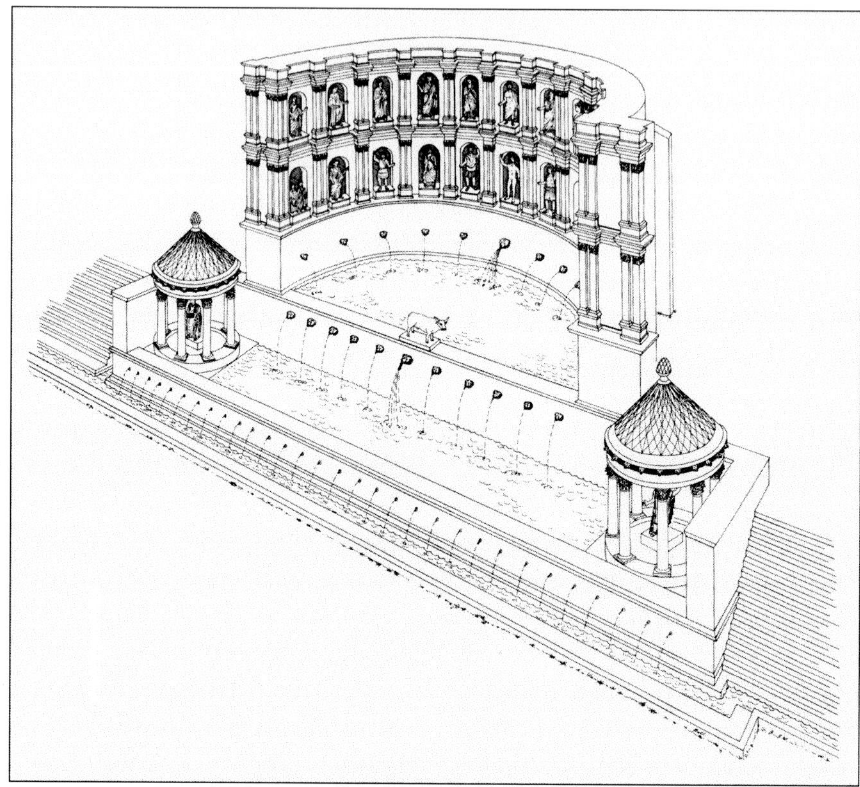

4. Reconstruction of the Fountain of Regilla and Herodes Atticus. Reconstruction by Renate Bol, *Das Statuenprogramm des Herodes-Atticus-Nymphaeum*. By permission of Renate Bol.

Regilla dedicated a grand double-tiered fountain surmounted by two storeys of sculpted figures – at least twenty-two portraits – in a hemicycle façade (Fig. 4). According to Renate Bol's reconstruction, Herodes' family was above, garbed in Roman and in one case in Greek dress, flanking a draped statue of Zeus. On the lower register were statues of the imperial family of Hadrian and Antoninus Pius, together with their wives and at least seven children, including Marcus Aurelius and Lucius Verus, flanking a nude Zeus. Unlike Herodes and his male family members, the emperors and mature boys wore cuirasses, which "marked the members of the imperial family as the . . . ultimate defenders of the Empire."[60]

The imperial family and that of Herodes and Regilla were differentiated in two ways: They stood on different levels, and there were slight variations in the profiles of the statue bases.[61] The viewer would not have seen significant differences in the portrayal of the two families, however. The two levels "talked" to

[60] R. R. R. Smith, "Cultural Choice and Political Identity in Honorific Portrait Statues in the Greek East in the Second Century A.D.," *JRS* 88 (1998) 76.

[61] Bol, *Das Statuenprogramm*, 50, passim.

each other insofar as the figures of Zeus and the husbands, wives, and children were "arranged horizontally to parallel and shadow a 'corresponding' figure of the imperial family."[62] We can consider this a many-sided conversation. Although the fountain was dedicated by Regilla, and represented her family, the imperial family, and Zeus, the statues were a gift from the citizens of Elis.

While most of the members of Regilla's and Herodes' families wore the Roman toga (civilian garb), at least one wore a "Greek civilian tunic-and-himation suit (in the 'officiating' type, with right arm extended, holding a patera)." According to R. R. R. Smith's interpretation of the monument, this was likely Herodes himself, who could take for granted his Roman connections and so did not need to signal them with the toga, but could emphasize his Greek identity instead.[63] Just as Christian apologists performed Greek *paideia*, so too Regilla and her husband Herodes Atticus, famous for his abilities in Greek rhetoric, embedded some signs of Greek culture into a building project that proclaimed the family's simultaneous Greek and Roman ethnicities, that addressed the family's relationship with Rome, and that was also located in a key site of Greek religion and ritual.

The fountain was a civic benefaction, providing water and a cool place to sit; it was also an ethnic statement that linked Greek culture and Roman power. In addition, the fountain made a statement about piety. A bull in Pentelic marble (Fig. 5), 1.6 m long and .7 m high, would have been located centrally at the monument's visual center, according to Bol's reconstruction (see again Fig. 4). The inscription on the bull declared Regilla a priestess of Demeter and dedicated the site to Zeus. The inscription reads in simple, archaizing terms, and the choice of a bull signals sacrifice to and piety before the highest god, Zeus.[64] Of course that highest god was already assimilated nearby, in the old Metroon, to Augustus and to Claudius.

What kind of imperial address was conducted here in the fountain? And what statements were made about religion and culture? What was the rhetorical effect of juxtaposing the family of Regilla and Herodes Atticus with the Antonines? The emperors address the gods in offering sacrifice and indeed assimilate to them, becoming the highest of the ancient Greek pantheon, as

62 Smith, "Cultural Choice and Political Identity," 76.

63 Smith speculates that perhaps it is Herodes himself, who in wearing the himation, a "lower ranking" costume in comparison with the toga, expresses "*pietas* to his father [whose statue then wears the toga], and in the logic and context of the monument is able to juxtapose his Greek himation as being on an equal footing with the Roman togas of his father and father-in-law" (ibid., 77).

64 The inscription across the body of the marble bull reads "Regilla, priestess of Demeter, [dedicates] the water and its surrounding structures to Zeus." Bol, *Das Statuenprogramm*, 1 and plate 1; Koester, *Cities of Paul*, "Olympia: Metroon and Fountain of Regilla: Fountain of Regilla: Dedicatory Inscription." The architrave inscription is extremely fragmentary (Bol, *Das Statuenprogramm*, 111–12).

5. Bull with dedicatory inscription. Olympia Museum. Courtesy of Fortress Press and Helmut Koester (*Cities of Paul: Images and Interpretations from the Harvard New Testament Archaeology Project*).

we saw in the statue of Claudius. The emperors and the family of Herodes and Regilla engage in pious performance; the emperor Hadrian, for example, stands tall (2.30 m when reconstructed) and cuirassed and eternally pours libations from a *patera*, or shallow offering dish (Fig. 6).[65] Like the apologists, who address the emperors, perform Greek *paideia*, and think about what true piety is, this fountain "talks" about empire, power, *paideia*, and religion. It does so in a location, as we have seen, that is a crossroads of global travel and communication; Olympia is a key site to publish news, from the classical period through Alexander the Great and on.

The "conversation" between the imperial family and that of Herodes Atticus did not only exist in stone. Herodes had tutored Marcus Aurelius and Lucius Verus, and Philostratus offers the story of the famous case in Sirmium in 174 when Herodes was forced to defend himself before Marcus Aurelius against the Athenians' charge of tyranny. He did so poorly and left in a frenzy. According to Philostratus, Marcus Aureius said, "Defend yourselves, Athenians (Ἀπολογεῖσθε, ἔφη, ὦ Ἀθηναίους), even if Herodes does not allow it" (*Vit. soph.* 2.561).[66] Marcus Aurelius used the language of *apologia*, and the

[65] Bol, *Das Statuenprogramm*, 151–53 and plates 15–17 for a detailed description and photographs.

[66] See the larger passage at *Vit. soph.* 2.559–63; Tobin (*Herodes Attikos*, 1–2) begins her book with this story, as does Millar, *The Emperor in the Roman World*, 3–9. The Greek edition is C. L. Kayser, *Flavii Philostrati opera*, vol. 2. (1871; reprinted Hildesheim: Olms, 1964).

6. Hadrian with *patera*. Olympia Museum. Courtesy of Fortress Press and Helmut Koester (*Cities of Paul: Images and Interpretations from the Harvard New Testament Archaeology Project*).

Athenians' defense won. Marcus was convinced of the Athenians' plight (and suspicious of Herodes' former dealings with Lucius Verus) and ruled against his former teacher. The *Lives of the Sophists* says that, after the incident at

Sirmium, Herodes addresses Marcus Aurelius: "Doing an experiment to see whether the emperor was harsh toward him on account of what had happened in the court, he [Herodes] sent him a letter, which was not an *apologia* but an accusation" (2.562). Herodes protested that while he sometimes used to receive multiple letters a day from the emperor, now he received none. Marcus Aurelius offered a tempered reply, saying that he hoped he had not offended Herodes in chastising the "crimes of some of your household," and asking Herodes to initiate him into the Eleusinian mysteries. "Such," concludes Philostratus, "was the *apologia* of Marcus, and thus benevolent and powerful" (2.563). We know from epigraphic evidence as well as literary that Marcus likely defended his friend and former teacher to the Athenians, encouraging them to allow Herodes' return to the city.[67] Herodes needed to defend himself before the Athenians; Emperor Marcus Aurelius benignantly defended himself against Herodes' accusations regarding a distance that had grown between the two.

The Fountain of Regilla takes part in this exchange of defenses, and is itself an *apologia* on many levels. Although it was likely complete at the time of Regilla's death, given the inscription naming her as donor, its very presence defends against the charge that Herodes murdered Regilla. The Nymphaion also defends the idea that the family of Herodes Atticus is intimate with the imperial family, despite strains such as a possible argument with Antoninus and the sure trouble that Herodes experienced not only with the Athenians but also with Marcus Aurelius. It defends the idea that the imperial family is proximate to the divine; that the families of the emperor and of Herodes are linked not only by blood (Regilla was, after all, related to Faustina the Elder) but also by some mysterious relation of wealth and Greek *paideia*. It is a monument that in its apologetic nature might remind the later viewer that Marcus, too, defended and apologized for Herodes before the Athenians.

III. APOLOGETICS AND CHRISTIANNESS

The Fountain of Regilla and Herodes Atticus shows the complexity of ethnic identity, expressions of piety, and relations of power in the second century, issues that writers like the early Christian apologists engage. Yet scholars still often seek to interpret Christian texts in binary terms: Are the so-called apologists heroes of Christianity, defining and defending it in the face of Roman persecution? Are they the sordid assimilators of Christianity, tempted by Greek culture and Roman power to distort Christianity's pure essence? Was early Christianity tainted or buoyed up by the Greek ethnic-cultural identity that was the mark of the educated person of the second century?

[67] *IG* II^2 3606, discussed in Oliver, *Marcus Aurelius*, 34.

Several scholars famed for their studies of early Christianity in general and early Christian apologetics in particular show key issues at stake in defining apologetics. Adolf von Harnack's *History of Dogma* offers the following subtitles under the topic of apologetics: "Fixing and Gradual Secularization of Christianity as a Church" and "Fixing and Gradual Hellenization of Christianity as Doctrine."[68] The terms are instructive. "Secularization" and "Hellenization" imply that something has happened to the essence of Christianity; the apologists offer a transition between the revelation at Christian origins and the continuing centuries of speculation about and interpretation of that revelation. Apologists try "to explain Christianity to the cultured world," writes Harnack.[69] He continues: "The theses of the Apologists finally overcame all scruples in ecclesiastical circles and were accepted by the Graeco-Roman world, because they made Christianity *rational* without taking from, or adding to, its traditional historic material."[70]

In the 1950s, Johannes Quasten's *Patrology* explained that while the apostolic fathers write for an in-group, for the "guidance and edification of the faithful,"[71] "with the Greek Apologists the literature of the Church addresses itself for the first time to the outside world and enters the domain of culture and science."[72] Quasten like Harnack thus categorized apologetics as Greek and as a rational defense to outsiders. Yet Quasten defended the "Greek Apologists"

[68] "Fixirung [*sic*] und allmähliche Verweltlichung des Christenthums als Kirche" and "Fixirung [*sic*] und allmähliche Hellenisirung des Christenthums als Glaubeslehre": Adolf von Harnack, *Lehrbuch der Dogmengeschichte* (3 vols.; Freiburg/Leipzig: J. C. B. Mohr, 1894) 1.319, 455. For the English translation, see Adolf von Harnack, *History of Dogma* (trans. from the 3rd German edition by Neil Buchanan; 7 vols. in 4; Gloucester, MA: Peter Smith, 1976) section 2.2.4. In *Die Überlieferung der griechischen Apologeten des zweiten Jahrhunderts in der alten Kirche und im Mittelalter* (*The Transmission of the Greek Apologists of the Second Century in the Ancient Church and in the Middle Ages*) (Leipzig: J. C. Hinrichs, 1882), Harnack provides detailed information regarding the manuscripts and transmission history of a variety of texts often characterized as apologetic, including the *Apologies* of Quadratus and Aristides, texts predicated on Aristo of Pella's work, works that bear Justin's and Athenagoras's names, Tatian's *To the Greeks*, the writings of Apollinarius of Hierapolis, Melito of Sardis, and Miltiades, and Theophilus's *To Autolycum*. The third volume contains Oscar v. Gebhardt's short book *Der Arethascodex Paris. Gr. 451*.

[69] Harnack, *History of Dogma*, 169–70.

[70] Ibid. While the "Gnostics" "meddled" with the tradition, the conservativism of the apologists won out, according to Harnack. For apologists embracing tradition and revelation, see Harnack, *History of Dogma*, 173; for Christians and Gnostics, p. 174; for Christian use of Jewish apologetics, p. 175. Christian apologists were heroes of a rationalistic translation of Christianity that resulted in triumph: Christianity became the "religion of the spirit, of freedom, and of absolute morality" as it accorded with reason and overthrew all polytheism (pp. 171, 177). On Harnack's place within a late nineteenth- and early twentieth-century discussion on the essence of Christianity and the use of historical method to find that essence, see Lori Pearson, *Beyond Christianity: Ernst Troeltsch as Historian and Theorist of Christianity* (HTS 58; Cambridge, MA: Harvard University Press, 2008) chap. 1.

[71] Quasten, *Patrology*, 1.186.

[72] Ibid.

against the taint of Greekness.[73] While Harnack understood Greekness to render Christian teachings more rational and comprehensible, Quasten asserted, "We may speak therefore of a Christianization of Hellenism but hardly of a Hellenization of Christianity."[74] For him, syncretism was a one-way street.

Henry Chadwick in his 1967 *The Early Church* is less concerned than Quasten about the philosophical qualities of so-called apologists. Chadwick implies that early Christianity differed from Judaism insofar as Christianity resisted Roman rule and kept among its communities a "revolutionary" spirit.[75] "There is no reason to think that the early Christian movement was ever a political revolution *manqué*, or that the history of the Church can be told in terms of bourgeois leaders taking over a proletarian uprising and diverting it into innocuous other-worldly mysticism," he writes in a frustrated and dismissive tone, disturbed, perhaps, by Weberian-style ruminations on the development of Christianity, in which charismatic origins are routinized into institution. Chadwick presents a Christianity ambivalent in its attitudes towards government,[76] presumably retaining within itself not only defense but also the possibility of revolution. The apologists do not represent a fall from grace.[77]

In more recent work, too, we find that the definition of Christian apologetic literature is both broad and unstable. Recent collections such as *Apologetics in the Roman Empire* and Pouderon and Doré's *Les apologistes chrétiens et la culture grecque* reveal that different scholars have vastly different definitions of apologetic.[78]

[73] Ibid., 1.188.

[74] Ibid., 1.187.

[75] Chadwick does not have a separate chapter dedicated to apologetic, but includes a section "The Defence of the Faith" within a chapter titled "Expansion and Growth." He writes (*The Early Church* [Baltimore, MD: Penguin, 1967] 69): "The paradox of the church was that it was a religious revolutionary movement, yet without a conscious political ideology; it aimed at the capture of society throughout all its strata, but was at the same time characteristic for its indifference to the possession of power in this world.... The future lay within the programme first announced by Justin Martyr, by which the Church would make common cause with Platonic metaphysics and Stoic ethics."

[76] Ibid., 73; quotation is from p. 72.

[77] Karl Barth in his 1956 *The Doctrine of the Word of God: Prolegomena to Church Dogmatics* ([repr. Edinburgh: T&T Clark, 1975] 333) wrote: "When we read the apologetics of the second and third centuries, can we altogether avoid the painful impression that what we have here – as though the persecuted can only regard themselves as spiritually undeserving of the external pressure brought to bear on them – is, on the whole, a not very happy, a rather self-righteous, and at any rate a not very perspicacious boasting about all those advantages of Christianity over heathen religion which were in themselves incontestable but not ultimately decisive? In these early self-commendations of Christianity a remarkably small part is played by the fact that grace is the truth of Christianity." In this amusing quotation, we see that for Barth, the unhappy apologists are a corruption of true religion, true belief, true grace, true Christianity.

[78] Bernard Pouderon and Joseph Doré, eds., *Les apologistes chrétiens et la culture grecque* (Paris: Beauchesne, 1998). In Edwards et al., eds., *Apologetics in the Roman Empire*, apologetic is largely understood as a Christian phenomenon; only two of its ten chapters deal with non-Christian sources. The volume's introduction offers a working definition ("defence of a cause or party supposed to be of paramount importance to the speaker") even as the editors admit that some of its authors resisted the terminology of apologetic (p. 1).

Encyclopedia and dictionary entries by scholars eminent in the field who are forced to define apologetics label it weakly as "a study of the 'art of persuasion' employed by early Christians" or define it in terms of "reason."[79]

In dictionaries and encyclopedias of early Christianity, apologetics is most often defined as defensive behavior on several fronts: against Jews, pagans, the Roman Empire, and other Christians.[80] One can hardly think of anyone in the world who is left out of the prosecutorial role. Not only do apologetic Christians resist everyone: Almost all of Christian literature is apparently also apologetic in such entries. A typical list of apologetic literature in introductory volumes or in dictionary or encyclopedia entries includes sections of 1 Corinthians and 1 Peter, Acts, Hebrews, the *Epistle of Barnabas*, the *Dialogue between Jason and Papiscus* attributed to Aristo of Pella, indeed all *adversus Iudaeos* tracts (writings against the Jews), various testimonia of scripture gathered to demonstrate Christian supersession over Judaism, some of John Chrysostom's homilies, Quadratus, Aristides, Justin's *Apologies*, Tatian's *To the Greeks*, Athenagoras's *Plea*, Theophilus's *To Autolycus*, the lost apologies of Melito and Apollinaris of Hierapolis, the *Epistle to Diognetus*, and the earliest Latin works that include Tertullian (*To the Nations, Apology, To Scapula*) and Minucius Felix's *Octavius*, Clement of Alexandria's *Exhortation*, Origen's *Against Celsus*, Eusebius's *Preparation for the Gospel*, Theodoret's *Cure of the Greek Maladies*, and Augustine's *City of God*.[81] All this literature apparently takes part in a clear Christian development towards some rational *telos* or end.

In trying to define apologetic, scholars have worked hard to map boundaries of religion, culture, and power in the ancient world. But as we have seen, apologetics is a modern category – and an ill-defined one – not an ancient genre attribution. The definitions of apologetic discussed above reify the categories of Christians, Jews, and pagans, despite work in the last decades to finesse our usual categories of "Christian," "Jew," and "pagan." Recent work by scholars like Daniel Boyarin, Denise Buell, and Karen King shows, however, that those of us who study early Christianity have too often adopted ancient labels without attending to the ways in which such ethnic–religious markers were rhetorical constructions. That is, early Christian uses of terms such as Greek, Roman, Jew, Christian, orthodox, and heretic were precisely

[79] For the former definition, see A. J. Droge, "Apologetics, NT," in David N. Freedman, ed., *The Anchor Bible Dictionary* (New York: Doubleday, 1990) 1.302–7; for the latter, H. Gamble, "Apologetics," in Everett Ferguson, ed., *The Encyclopedia of Early Christianity* (New York: Garland, 1990) 65–71.

[80] Droge, "Apologetics, NT."

[81] Gamble, "Apologetics." For Gamble, pagan writers both popular and philosophical emerge as the cause of Christian apologetics (e.g., Lucian, Fronto, Galen, Celsus, Porphyry, Julian); but see the reversal of the term in Clifford Ando's article on Julian as a pagan apologist ("Pagan Apologetics and Christian Intolerance in the Age of Themistius and Augustine," *JECS* 4.2 [1996] 171–207).

constructions, inventions of borderlines in a time of blurred boundaries.[82] Writers like Harnack, Quasten, and Chadwick, as well as the writers defining early Christian apologists in dictionaries, encyclopedias, and survey material on early Christianity, know this. Nevertheless, their statements about early Christian apologists usually posit some Christian essence that is changed in some way by contact with the surrounding culture or that resists the influence of various "others."

This contact of Christianity with the surrounding culture is usually interpreted using one of two models. The first model reads the apologists as a synthesis of Christianity and Hellenism that launches Christianity's degeneration: It posits some pure originary Christian essence that is subsequently polluted by the surrounding culture. The apologists, with their addresses to emperors and Greeks, are blamed for taking early steps toward such pollution. But the second model is problematic as well. It implies that as Christianity moves from East to West over time it becomes less connected with a "barbarian," particular, and Jewish past and more integrated into universal and philosophical Greek (Western) *paideia*. Implicit in this perspective is the idea that the dominant, productive strain of early Christianity is found in the apologists, who were in communication with and who appealed to emperors and to philosophical Greeks. Prophecy, apocalyptic, and the martyrdoms would eventually cease as Christianity came to be seen as the *telos* of empire – both its end and its perfection – and as Christianity would take up and transform Greek *paideia*.[83]

CONCLUSIONS

Early Christian writings that are labeled as apologetic take part in and emerge from the world of Regilla's Fountain, which itself materially manifests an *apologia* or defense. At stake in the Olympia fountain were many elements that we also find in Christian apologetic writings. The display of Greek and Roman ethnicities at the fountain is matched by the question of where Christians belong within Greek history and space; Herodes is displayed in terms of Greek

[82] See especially Karen King, *What is Gnosticism?* (Cambridge, MA: Belknap Press of Harvard University Press, 2003), and her "Which Early Christianity," in Susan Ashbrook Harvey and David G. Hunter, eds., *The Oxford Handbook of Early Christian Studies* (Oxford: Oxford University Press, 2008) 66–84; Buell, *Why This New Race?*; Daniel Boyarin, *Dying for God: Martyrdom and the Making of Christianity and Judaism* (Stanford: Stanford University Press, 1999), and his *Border Lines: The Partition of Judaeo-Christianity* (Philadelphia: University of Pennsylvania Press, 2004); see also Shaye J. D. Cohen, *The Beginnings of Jewishness: Boundaries, Varieties, Uncertainties* (Berkeley: University of California Press, 1999); Judith Lieu, *Neither Jew nor Greek? Constructing Early Christianity* (London: T & T Clark, 2002) and her *Christian Identity in the Jewish and Graeco-Roman World* (Oxford: Oxford University Press, 2004).

[83] See Laura Nasrallah, *An Ecstasy of Folly: Prophecy and Authority in Early Christianity* (HTS 52; Cambridge, MA: Harvard University Press, 2003) 1–26.

paideia, and in apologists we find Christian articulations of Greek *paideia*. In both the Fountain of Regilla and Herodes and in early Christian writings we learn about the relation of imperial power to the elites of the empire, or those who wished to be given the same rights as elites; at the fountain we find a connection between piety and wealth and the divinization of humans, and in the so-called apologists, too, we find discussions of such themes. It is in the context of a monument like the Fountain of Herodes and Regilla that we can better understand early Christian writings labeled as apologetic as broadly engaged in defensive tactics amid the broader cultural and political wars of their day.

Modern scholarship has not offered a clear or adequate definition of apologetic and scholars' lists of apologetic texts are largely governed by assumptions about community boundaries and situations of power in the early and high Roman Empire. Moreover, ancient texts on rhetoric do not immediately help to elucidate the genre of what we are reading when we approach so-called apologies. Plato's *Apology* certainly casts a long and influential shadow over the Greco-Roman world, but while early Christians frequently invoked Socrates as a way of figuring their own oppression and response, they did so in a variety of ways that cannot easily be clustered under the one category. Rather than being a generic term from antiquity or an organic literary phenomenon arising from Christian persecution, the category of apologetic may emerge from the taxonomic impulses of seventeenth-century European scholars, struggling in the context of the rise of Protestantism and the clash of religion and science.

Yet many of the texts that are called Christian apologies *do* have something in common. As J. Rendel Harris resignedly said in 1891 as part of his translation of the Syriac version of Aristides, "almost all the Apologies that are known to us are painfully alike."[84] By this I think that he meant that many of them seem to have a checklist of obligatory elements: a section of the nature and unity of God, on the Logos, on the morality of Christians, on ridiculous Egyptian worship of animals, on the silliness of polytheism – adulterous and ever multiplying divinities that lead to similar bad behavior among humans. What Harris does not say is that although many so-called Christian apologies have these elements *de rigeur*, we find them too in non-Christian sources of the time. As Dale Martin has discussed so well in *Inventing Superstition*, many in antiquity were engaged in debate over what constituted *superstitio*, or, to put it in Greek terms, over the true meaning and translation of *deisidaimonia* in the ancient world: Is *deisidaimonia* to be understood as proper pious reverence, or as superstitious fear of the gods?[85] What really motivates piety?

[84] J. Rendel Harris, *The Apology of Aristides on Behalf of the Christians: From a Syriac Manuscript Preserved on Mount Sinai* (1891; Piscataway, NJ: Gorgias Press, 2004) 1.

[85] Dale Martin, *Inventing Superstition: From the Hippocratics to the Christians* (Cambridge, MA: Harvard University Press, 2004).

What if, instead of using the category of apologetic to map Christian versus Jewish versus "pagan" identity, we were to envision apologetic texts on a different stage, engaged in a different drama? What if we were to read some so-called Christian apologies as taking part in and taking advantage of a broader conversation, such as that we have glimpsed in Olympia and especially at the Fountain of Regilla? The traditional divisions of pagan-Jew-Christian have obscured possible alliances between those of high status who engaged in a culture war about the value of Greek *paideia* in the high Roman Empire. They have obscured the possibility that Christian apologists do not define Christianity against paganism or Judaism as much as they define Christianity against certain *kinds* of other ethnic and religious practices.[86] Christian "apologies" engage larger, cross-cultic and cross-ethnic conversations about the nature of true religion and right ritual. It is to this topic, and to the placement of Christian writers among others on the map of the Roman Empire, that we turn.

[86] Regarding "Christian *paideia*" or "*paideia* of the Lord," see Jaeger, *Early Christianity and Greek Paideia*, 24–26.

CHAPTER TWO

WHAT IS THE SPACE OF THE ROMAN EMPIRE? MAPPING, BODIES, AND KNOWLEDGE IN THE ROMAN WORLD

In the late 1960s, African American children in Boston were asked to draw maps of their neighborhood, near the old Mission Hill housing project. The housing project, largely white at the time, took up a large part of their hand-drawn maps, but was figured in various ways as a big blank: a no-man's land, a topography absent of marks or monuments.[1] The streets around it, as well as schools, restaurants, and stores, were often carefully and clearly articulated, but the housing project itself was an open, unmarked rectangle. Recent critical geographers have been interested in the way "people's spatial behaviour is shaped by the hills and valleys of the invisible information and environmental stress surfaces over them."[2] Landscape and the built environment of the city are not neutral, but have their own rhetoric, exerting influence on the bodies of those who move through them. Moreover, humans map and interpret space, understanding the limits of their known world through the movements of their particular bodies, which are marked by gender and race.

1 See Peter Gould and Rodney White, *Mental Maps* (1974; 2nd ed.; Boston: Allen and Unwin, 1986) 14–17; maps are on pp. 16–17.

2 Gould and White, *Mental Maps*, 108; Ruth M. Van Dyke and Susan E. Alcock, "Archaeologies of Memory: An Introduction," in their edited volume *Archaeologies of Memory* (Malden, MA: Blackwell, 2003) 5–6; see also the methodological interventions of Blake Leyerle, "Landscape as Cartography in Early Christian Pilgrimage Narratives," *JAAR* 64 (1996) 119–43.

The idea of humans rendering abstract space into concrete place is not new,[3] nor is the concept of a city's perils or of configuring fear as a topographical blank. Subjects of the Roman Empire talked about urban decay, speculated on the limits of the *oikoumenē gē*, or "inhabited world," and knew the danger of not knowing where one was.[4] We find the idea that ignorance about geography can lead to danger in Strabo's early first-century CE *Geography*, which seeks to persuade the reader of the utility of geography for states and commanders, among others. Using the examples of the Romans against the Parthians, as well as the Germans and the Celts, Strabo writes: "In marshes, inaccessible roads, and deserts the barbarians carried on a *topomachia*, and in [the minds of] the ignorant [Romans] they made the far off to be near and concealed the roads and the resources for food, and the rest" (*Geog.* 1.1.17). *Topomachia* literally means a "battle of place," or, as Horace Jones translates it, "guerilla warfare."[5] According to Strabo, geography serves the needs of empire (preventing *topomachia*, for instance) at the same time that the spread of empire leads to more empirical knowledge of geography and, presumably, the pushing back of barbarian boundaries.[6] Knowledge, space, and imperial power are intertwined.

3 David Harvey, "From Space to Place and Back Again," in his *Justice, Nature and the Geography of Difference* (Cambridge, MA: Blackwell, 1996) 291–326. See the cautionary words of Henri Lefebvre on the term "space" in his *The Production of Space* (trans. Donald Nicholson-Smith; Oxford: Blackwell, 1991) esp. 1–27; Edward Soja, *Postmetropolis: Critical Studies of Cities and Regions* (Oxford: Blackwell, 2000).

4 Regarding geography and space in the Roman world, see esp. Claude Nicolet, *Space, Geography, and Politics in the Early Roman Empire* (Ann Arbor: University of Michigan Press, 1991), originally published in 1988 as *L'inventaire du Monde: Géographie et politique aux origines de l'Empire romain*. Other important recent work includes Clifford Ando, *Imperial Ideology and Provincial Loyalty in the Roman Empire* (Berkeley: University of California, 2000) esp. 320–35; Colin Adams and Ray Laurence, *Travel and Geography in the Roman Empire* (New York: Routledge, 2001); Richard Talbert and Kai Brodersen, eds., *Space in the Roman World: Its Perception and Presentation* (Münster: Lit Verlag, 2004); James S. Romm, *The Edges of the Earth in Ancient Thought: Geography, Exploration, and Fiction* (Princeton, NJ: Princeton University Press, 1992); Katherine Clarke, *Between Geography and History: Hellenistic Constructions of the Roman World* (Oxford: Oxford University Press, 1999); Indra McEwen, *Vitruvius: Writing the Body of Architecture* (Cambridge, MA: MIT Press, 2003) 16–31. Some scholars of New Testament and Early Christianity have recently used geography and mental mapping as a framework for analysis: e.g., Loveday Alexander, "Mapping Early Christianity: Acts and the Shape of Early Church History," *Interpretation* 57.2 (2003) 163–75 and her "'In Journeyings Often': Voyaging in the Acts of the Apostles and in Greek Romance," in C. M. Tuckett, ed., *Luke's Literary Achievement* (Sheffield: Sheffield Academic Press, 1995) 17–39; Judith Perkins, "Social Geography in the *Apocryphal Acts of the Apostles*," in Michael Paschalis and Stavros A. Frangoulidis, eds., *Space in the Ancient Novel* (Groningen: Barkhuis, 2002) 118–31.

5 See also Strabo *Geog.* 16.4.22. The Greek edition is A. Meineke, *Strabonis geographica* (1877; 3 vols.; repr. Leipzig: Teubner, 1969). Strabo, *The Geography* (LCL; 8 vols.; trans. Horace L. Jones after J. R. S. Sterrett; Cambridge, MA: Harvard University Press, 1960–70) 1.37. See McEwen, *Vitruvius*, 10, 16 on Vitruvius, Augustus, and knowing the world.

6 Among Alexander the Great's workers were two road measurers who recorded distances between stopping places and described geography, soil, flora, and fauna (O. A. W. Dilke, *Greek and Roman Maps* [Baltimore, MD: Johns Hopkins University Press, 1998] 29); see also Strabo *Geog.* 2.1.9 and book 15.

Strabo tries to sell his audience on the importance of geography and of his *Geography* by pointing to the danger of ignorance and the power of knowing one's place in the *oikoumenē*.[7]

Writings in the Roman period that are labeled as geographies, like Strabo's, may contain some or all of the following: ethnographic writing; lists of cities' longitudes and latitudes; descriptions of topography; land itineraries and merchants' accounts of voyages; speculations on the relationship between mapping the heavens, especially the zodiac, and the terrestrial regions governed by those heavens. Such "geographical thinking" thrived not only in geographies proper, but in a variety of texts and genres in the first and second centuries CE, like that of a first-century merchant traveling the Erythrean Sea or the fantastic voyages of Greek novels.[8] Those who used this kind of thinking often offer complex pictures of the world, folding issues of ethnicity, *paideia* or culture, language and dialect, politics and power into descriptions or *ekphraseis* of locations.

The literature of the first and second centuries CE often turns to Odysseus as a model. The wanderer builds up cultural credentials, whether you are Paul as depicted by Luke, Apollonius as depicted by Philostratus, Socrates turning exile to his advantage in Dio, or Lucian meditating upon the fatherland. Yet these constructions and self-constructions of traveling teachers emerge from a context of struggles over provincial and metropolitan identities under colonial conditions. Postcolonial critics' discussions of the hybrid identities of subject elites keeps our eyes open to something analogous in antiquity, something we see in Justin, Tatian, and Lucian: the negotiation of authoritative (Greek) culture under conditions of (the Roman) empire, and simultaneous resistance and assimilation to this *paideia*.[9]

7 On itineraries and fear in ancient Greek literature, see also François Hartog, *Memories of Odysseus: Frontier Tales from Ancient Greece* (1996; trans. Janet Lloyd; Edinburgh: Edinburgh University Press, 2001) 88: "Designed as it was to produce an inventory, a *periplous* held the void (blank spaces) in horror." Regarding Strabo, see also Hartog's p. 92; Dilke, *Greek and Roman Maps*, 62–64; and esp. Nicolet, *Space, Geography, and Politics*, 8.

8 For a merchant's itinerary see Lionel Casson, *The Periplus Maris Erythraei. Text with Introduction, Translation, and Commentary* (Princeton, NJ: Princeton University Press, 1989). For a reading of Pausanias's travel narrative as "imaginative geography" see Jaś Elsner, "Structuring 'Greece': Pausanias's *Periegesis* as a Literary Construct," in Susan Alcock et al., eds., *Pausanias: Travel and Memory in Roman Greece* (Oxford: Oxford University Press, 2001) 4. Nicolet states: "This geography (representation through discourse, description, an account of a voyage, or an itinerary and geometric conceptualization) also comes with a cartography, or rather, it is cartography. In antiquity the same words specify *discourse* and *drawings*" (*Space, Geography, and Politics*, 4). For more on cartography and for a survey of geographical literature from the classical to the Roman period, see Dilke, *Greek and Roman Maps*. Regarding Greco-Roman novels depicting a "world without Rome," see Simon Swain, *Hellenism and Empire: Language, Classicism, and Power in the Greek World AD 50–250* (Oxford: Clarendon, 1996) chap. 4; quotation from p. 109.

9 See Homi Bhabha, *The Location of Culture* (New York: Routledge, 1994). On state control of space and on resistance to that control, see, e.g., Lefebvre, *Production of Space*, 23. See also the speech of Socrates to the Romans in Dio *Or.* 13. 31–37.

One aspect of geographical thinking is the evaluation of the relative locations and importance of cities, and the tracing of real and imaginary routes between them.[10] From the new conditions of the Roman Empire emerged complex mental mappings like those of Vitruvius, who addresses his *De architectura* to Augustus.[11] As we saw in the introduction, Vitruvius centers the map on Italy and the Roman people: "The populations of Italy partake in equal measure of the qualities of both north and south, both with regard to their physiques and to the vigor of their minds, to produce the greatest strength. . . . Thus the divine intelligence established the state of the Roman People as an outstanding and balanced region – so that it could take command over the earthly orb" (*De arch.* 6.1.11).[12]

Yet geographical thinking is unstable, shifting even within the same text. In the same passage, Vitruvius celebrates the man who is shipwrecked, the universal traveler: "An educated person is the only one who is never a stranger in a foreign land, nor at a loss for friends even when bereft of household and intimates. Rather, he is a citizen in every country" (6.preface.2).[13] Vitruvius offers two maps. One map of the world centers on Rome; the other has no center but is traced by the universal traveler, citizen of everywhere, his particular body traveling with *paideia* in hand. Although many of these mappings do consider Rome and Italy to be central in the space of the world, such geographical thinking cannot be simplistically conceived in terms of periphery and center, even if mappings such as Vitruvius's and Strabo's are products of and implements for imperial (or proto-imperial) rule.

The first goal of this chapter is to complicate the model of center and periphery that has often been used to talk about the Roman Empire or about Greeks and barbarians in the ancient world. Justin, Tatian, and Lucian do not merely contrast Rome and their marginal, eastern homeland. Justin, Tatian,

[10] Consider Claudius Ptolemy's *Geography* and *Almagest*.

[11] On Vitruvius between Greek and Roman precedents, see Andrew Wallace-Hadrill, *Rome's Cultural Revolution* (Cambridge: Cambridge University Press, 2008) chap. 4; on the relationship between Vitruvius's *corpus* and Augustus's body and power, see McEwen, *Vitruvius*.

[12] ET Vitruvius, *Ten Books on Architecture* (trans. Ingrid D. Rowland; commentary and illustrations by Thomas Noble Howe; New York: Cambridge University Press, 1999) 77; see also McEwen, *Vitruvius*, 156–62. Architecture, geography, cosmography, and ethnicity are all part of the same complex of problems; see also *De arch.* 6.1.12. Arguments like Vitruvius's presage Herder's and others debates over *Volk* and land in eighteenth and nineteenth centuries. On Herder, autochthony, and hybridity, see Robert Young, *Colonial Desire: Hybridity in Theory, Culture and Race* (New York: Routledge, 1995) 36–43. For more on climate/region and ethnic identity, see, e.g., Hartog, *Memories of Odysseus*, 138–39.

[13] ET Rowland, 75; McEwen, *Vitruvius*, 148–54. Citizenship and displacement are discussed often in literature of the first and second centuries; one example is Paul's statement in Phil. 3:20: "But our citizenship is in the heavens" (ἡμῶν γὰρ τὸ πολίτευμα ἐν οὐρανοῖς ὑπάρχει) and its *Nachleben* in early Christian writings. Regarding elite males and exile, see Tim Whitmarsh, "'Greece Is the World': Exile and Identity in the Second Sophistic," in Simon Goldhill, ed., *Being Greek under Rome: Cultural Identity, the Second Sophistic and the Development of Empire* (Cambridge: Cambridge University Press, 2001) 269–305.

Lucian, and others are educated travelers like the shipwreck victim Vitruvius describes. They are engaged in travel between cities and in attaining the authority that such cosmopolitanism lends; they weigh the metropolitan claims of cities like Athens or Jerusalem or even Hierapolis – according to Lucian in *On the Syrian Goddess*, a site to which he has gone as a pilgrim, in his home territory of Assyria. They sketch mental maps of the world, sometimes centered on an invented Greece, an imagined Athens, a real Rome, or an idealized barbarian land.

In the last chapter I suggested that one important way to read earliest Christian apologies is in light of the culture wars of the so-called Second Sophistic. The second goal of the present chapter is to remap the traditional scholarly approach. This approach usually frames Justin and Tatian in terms of Christian apologetic, understanding them to assert boundaries between Christianity and Hellenism; it also interprets Justin as central to Christian apology and Tatian as angrily at its margins. I instead read both authors alongside the non-Christian Lucian as traveling points on a broader map, engaging the theological-philosophical issues of their day. Not only do all three construct their travels through rhetoric; their rhetorical constructions of these travels also give authority to their arguments, guarantee their experience, and signal something about their place within the fluidity of Greek identity and the seeming solidity of Greek *paideia* in the Roman world.[14]

Scholars have attended to issues of geography and space in the writings of Greeks and Romans. But insufficient attention has been paid to the same topic among Christians in the Roman Empire, despite the fact that Christianity has long been depicted as thriving because of cities and travels between them,[15] and despite the fact that Christians lived in a world where discussions of geography were widely prevalent. Thus, the third goal of this chapter is to take up and nuance the themes of cities, travel, and geography, addressing the broadest spaces of the Roman Empire. I bring together a kind of "map" of the various

[14] Discussing Parmenides and Lucian, Tim Whitmarsh writes: "Rather than confining him to his native land, *Paideia* offers him access to the whole world; and, in particular, access to the centre, Rome. Education offers a relocation from the parochial to the universal, from the particular to the general" (*Greek Literature and the Roman Empire: The Politics of Imitation* [Oxford: Oxford University Press, 2001] 124); of course, this image could be used of Justin and Tatian as well; see Timothy J. Horner, *Listening to Trypho: Justin Martyr's Dialogue Reconsidered* (Leuven: Peeters, 2001) 73–83. Mark S. Burrows mentions, too, the possible connection between Tertullian's satirical writing and Lucian's: "Christianity in the Roman Forum: Tertullian and the Apologetic Use of History," *VC* 42.3 (1998) 210, 221–22. On the idea of fluidity, see the work of Denise Kimber Buell, who argues that early Christians partook in the racializing discourse of Greco-Roman antiquity, in part by rhetorically deploying the rhetoric of the fluidity and fixity or race or ethnicity: "Race and Universalism in Early Christianity," *JECS* 10.4 (2002) 429–68, esp. 436–38; and *Why This New Race? Ethnic Reasoning in Early Christianity* (New York: Columbia University Press, 2005).

[15] For one example, see Wayne Meeks, *The First Urban Christians: The Social World of the Apostle Paul* (1983; 2nd ed.; New Haven, CT: Yale University Press, 2003).

ethnē ("nations") dominated by Rome, found in Aphrodisias, with the travel discussions and rhetoric of bodily vulnerability of two Christian writers, Justin and Tatian, and a non-Christian compatriot, Lucian.

I. TRAVELING MEN: LUCIAN, TATIAN, AND JUSTIN

Justin, Tatian, and Lucian, all writing in Greek and all responding in various ways to the prestige of Greekness in the second-century Roman Empire, offer similar stories about themselves. They are philosophers (or at least truth-seekers) from the eastern ranges of the empire, struggling with what it means to be a rhetor, sophist, and/or philosopher in the Roman Empire. As with Vitruvius's shipwrecked man, their *paideia* renders them universal travelers of sorts. Justin not only famously constructs himself as a philosopher, but also does not challenge the appellation of sophist when it is applied to him.[16] Tatian describes himself as "having played the sophist" (*Ad Graec.* 35.1); he also criticizes those who are attracted to the *glossomania* of the philosophers rather than a "serious investigation after the truth."[17] In multiple writings, such as *A Double Accusation*, Lucian toys with his (and his characters') roles as rhetors and philosophers.

All three also present their philosophical quests by drawing upon a common *topos* of the time: that of the truth-seeker who wanders the philosophical marketplace,[18] seeing the shortcomings of various teachers. Justin presents himself as having progressed through Stoic, Peripatetic, Pythagorean, and finally Platonist philosophy, but he only became a philosopher as his spirit was set on fire with an "affection for the prophets, and for those who are friends of Christ" (*Dial. Tryph.* 8.1–8.12).[19] Tatian too asserts that he "participated in

[16] Justin *Dial. Tryph.* 3.3. Φιλόλογος οὖν τις εἶ σύ, ἔφη, φιλεργὸς δὲ οὐδαμῶς οὐδὲ φιλαλήθης, οὐδὲ πειρᾷ πρακτικὸς εἶναι μᾶλλον ἢ σοφιστής; "Therefore are you some philologist, he said, who is not at all industrious or a truth-lover, nor does he attempt to be a man of action, but rather a sophist?" The Greek edition is Miroslav Marcovich, *Iustini Martyris Dialogus cum Tryphone* (Berlin: De Gruyter, 1997).

[17] Tatian *Ad Graec.* 3. My translations are aided by Molly Whittaker, ed. and trans., *Tatian Oratio ad Graecos and Fragments* (Oxford: Clarendon, 1982), and I follow her section divisions (originally Goodspeed's). The Greek edition is Miroslav Marcovich, *Tatiani Oratio ad Graecos* (Berlin: De Gruyter, 1995).

[18] See Arthur Darby Nock, *Conversion: The Old and the New in Religion from Alexander the Great to Augustine of Hippo* (1933; repr. Baltimore, MD: Johns Hopkins University Press, 1998) 107–22; Erwin R. Goodenough, *The Theology of Justin Martyr* (Jena: Verlag Frommansche Buchhandlung, 1923) 59–62; and esp. Tessa Rajak, "Talking at Trypho: Christian Apologetic as Anti-Judaism in Justin's *Dialogue with Trypho the Jew*," in Mark Edwards et al., eds., *Apologetics in the Roman Empire: Pagans, Jews, and Christians* (Oxford: Oxford University Press, 1999) 64–66. The *topos* of the truth-seeker wandering various philosophical schools may be modeled on Socrates' testing out the *sophoi* in Plato's *Apology*; see also Dio *Or.* 13.

[19] For another promenade of philosophers, albeit in a different style, see Tatian *Ad Graec.* 2.

mysteries and tested cults" and rejected them in favor of "barbarian writings" (*Ad Graec.* 29.1). From reading Lucian, we would think that everyone in the second century was running around in philosophical drag, claiming serious interest in philosophy and dressing the part, but really in love with money and fame.[20] All guarantee the rightness of the truth to which they have come by offering *ekphraseis* or descriptions which remind the reader of the authenticity of their travels and the certitude of what they learned through autopsy – seeing with their own eyes.[21]

All three also critique common cult practices of the time:

> If anybody sacrifices, they [the gods] all have a feast, opening their mouths for the smoke and drinking the blood that is spilt at the altars, just like flies. . . . Then too they [humans] erect temples, in order that the gods may not be houseless and hearthless, of course; and they fashion images in their [human] likeness. . . . Those who offer victims . . . deck the animal with garlands . . . ; then they bring it to the altar and slaughter it under the god's eyes, while it bellows plaintively – making, we must suppose, auspicious sounds, and fluting low music to accompany the sacrifice! Who would not suppose that the gods like to see all this? And although the notice says that no one is to be allowed within the holy-water who has not clean hands, the priest himself stands there all bloody, just like the Cyclops of old, cutting up the victim, removing the entrails, plucking out the heart, pouring the blood about the altar, and doing everything possible in the way of piety. (*De sacr.* 9–13)[22]

Reading this without attribution, one might guess that it was written by Tatian or some other Christian satirist bitter about surrounding religious practices.[23] But it comes from the pen of Lucian, who mocked the various Mediterranean rituals and cults that claimed to produce true piety. If we were to read Justin and Tatian merely as Christian apologists, we would miss this larger context of debate over Greek education, Greco-Roman myths, true piety, and the panoply of cult practices around the Mediterranean.[24]

20 See Lucian *Reviv.*; *Icaromenippus* 275–77; *Ver. hist.* 1.5.

21 On the connection between travel and *theōria* or seeing, see Hartog, *Memories of Odysseus*, 90–91, 112. On *ekphrasis* (narrative description) and autopsy, see Simon Goldhill, "The Erotic Eye: Visual Stimulation and Cultural Conflict," in Goldhill, ed., *Being Greek under Rome*, 154–94; J. L. Lightfoot, "Pilgrims and Ethnographers: In Search of the Syrian Goddess," in Jaś Elsner and Ian Rutherford, eds., *Pilgrimage in Graeco-Roman and Early Christian Antiquity: Seeing the Gods* (Oxford: Oxford University Press, 2005) 333–52; Loveday Alexander, *The Preface to Luke's Gospel: Literary Convention and Social Context in Luke 1.1–4 and Acts 1.1* (Cambridge: Cambridge University Press, 1993) 34–39.

22 ET *Lucian Works* (LCL; 8 vols.; trans. A. M. Harmon; Cambridge, MA: Harvard University Press, 1960) 3.165–69.

23 See, e.g., Justin *1 Apol.* 4–5.

24 Rebecca Lyman, "The Politics of Passing: Justin Martyr's Conversion as a Problem of 'Hellenzation,'" in Kenneth Mills and Anthony Grafton, eds., *Conversion in Late Antiquity and the Early Middle Ages: Seeing and Believing* (Rochester, NY: University of Rochester Press, 2003) 43–44.

I have called Justin, Tatian, and Lucian Vitruvian men because their stories echo Vitruvius's account of the shipwrecked traveler who needs only *paideia* to fit into foreign country or household. But I want too to conjure up Leonardo da Vinci's famous drawing of the perfectly balanced man, inscribed within a circle, as well as the source which the drawing interprets: Vitruvius's *De architectura* and its comments about the ideal symmetry of the human body and the analogy of this body to architectural measure.[25] Several disciplines, from religion to critical geographical theory to feminist theory, open our eyes to the way in which space is understood and geographical understanding is developed from particular bodies. Jonathan Z. Smith, discussing geography, puts it well: "It is the relationship to the human body, and our experience of it, that orients us in space, that confers meaning to place. Human beings are not placed, they bring place into being.... Place is best understood as a locus of meaning."[26] We shape our maps and orient ourselves through our bodies, and Justin's, Tatian's, and Lucian's particular bodies – with their natal ethnicities asserted, yet supplemented by Greek *paideia* – are represented as tracing the geography of the empire in various ways.[27]

Thinking with and beyond Vitruvius, we can see that the human body is a site from which an understanding of space emerges, but that it is also a measure for defining the architectures, cities, and the spaces surrounding the body. As we saw in the introduction, Vitruvius suggests that altars and gods be placed at various heights in relation to the human body in order to effect awe and worship (*De arch.* 4.5–4.9). Humans are transformed by the rhetoric of given places and by their movements through space. And as feminist scholars have stressed, the body is itself a space open to use and penetration, subject to mapping, with borders that are discrete yet penetrable.[28] Justin, Tatian, and Lucian are elite males who are concerned both with their approaches to cities,

[25] See Vitruvius *De arch.* 3.1, esp. section 9.

[26] Jonathan Z. Smith, *To Take Place: Toward a Theory in Ritual* (Chicago: University of Chicago Press, 1987) 27–28; this emerges in a discussion of Kant. For a succinct overview of the concept of space in the history of philosophy, see Lefebvre, *Production of Space*, 1–2; this is followed by a strenuous critique of postmodern uses of the term "space." Smith elsewhere reminds us of the importance of geography to the study of religion, as in his "What a Difference a Difference Makes" (in Jacob Neusner and Ernest S. Frerichs, eds., *"To See Ourselves as Others See Us": Christians, Jews, "Others" in Late Antiquity* [Chico, CA: Scholars Press, 1985] 3–48) regarding Greco-Roman understandings of geography and Christopher Columbus. Regarding ritual and geography, see also David Frankfurter, "Introduction: Approaches to Coptic Pilgrimage," in his edited volume *Pilgrimage and Holy Space in Late Antique Egypt* (Leiden: E. J. Brill, 1998) esp. 13–18.

[27] This concept of the body's movement through space has also been developed by Soja and Lefebvre, mentioned earlier (see n. 3 above), as well as Smith's *To Take Place*. See also Michel de Certeau, *The Practice of Everyday Life* (trans. Steven Rendall; Berkeley: University of California Press, 1984); and Heidi J. Nast and Steve Pile, "Introduction, MakingPlacesBodies," in their edited volume *Places through the Body* (New York: Routledge, 1998) 1–6.

[28] See Elizabeth Wilson, *The Sphinx in the City: Urban Life, the Control of Disorder, and Women* (Berkeley: University of California Press, 1992); Dolores Hayden, *The Power of Place: Urban Landscapes as Public History* (Cambridge, MA: MIT Press, 1995).

gods, and altars, and with how the borders of their bodies and minds are formed by Greek *paideia* and the Roman Empire to which they are subject – that is, with their potential feminization as they are vulnerable to pressures from without.[29] Recent scholarly analysis of hybridity and ambiguity, of assimilation and negotiation under the conditions of empire, helps us to read Justin's, Tatian's, and Lucian's mental mappings and their deployment of ethnic, cultic, and local categories as part of colonial conditions under the Roman Empire.[30]

In the sections that follow, I shall read Justin and Tatian – the latter, I will argue, is not as lugubrious as has been thought – alongside Lucian, who is a much deeper theologian than scholars have recognized.[31] All three are from the eastern parts of the empire, toying with barbarian identity as well as Greekness, mentally mapping the *oikoumenē*, simultaneously in terms of its geography, its ethnicities, and its authoritative locations of knowledge. They draw on the long tradition, studied by scholars like François Hartog and Arnoldo Momigliano, of Greek concerns about alien or barbarian wisdom and thus anxiety about what constitutes Greek identity and knowledge.[32] Their works construct maps of the relative epistemic topography of the Roman Empire, pointing out the high points of true *paideia* in different locations. The writers present themselves as authoritative bodies which, having toured the Roman Empire, can guarantee the truth of their evaluations by autopsy and *ekphrasis*. They also present themselves as bodies subject to potential danger.

Lucian

At the center of many of his dialogues, Lucian, born between 115–125 CE in Samosata,[33] constructs a Syrian character who is a truth-teller. Both as himself

[29] On male bodies and concerns about integrity and penetrability, see, for example, Jennifer A. Glancy, "Boasting of Beatings (2 Corinthians 11:23–25)," *JBL* 123.1 (2004) 99–135.

[30] Rebecca Lyman ("The Politics of Passing") also offers an excellent discussion analyzing Justin in terms of hybridity and postcolonial theory. See also her "Hellenism and Heresy: 2002 NAPS Presidential Address," *JECS* 11.2 (2003) 209–22.

[31] There are only few brief linkings of Tatian and Lucian in modern scholarship. See, e.g., Kathy L. Gaca, *The Making of Fornication: Eros, Ethics, and Political Reform in Greek Philosophy and Early Christianity* (Berkeley: University of California, 2003) 224 n. 10; Peter Lampe, *From Paul to Valentinus: Christians at Rome in the First Two Centuries* (Minneapolis, MN: Fortress, 2003) 289 n. 19; Molly Whittaker, "Tatian's Educational Background," in Elizabeth Livingstone, ed., *Studia Patristica*, vol. 13: *Papers Presented to the Sixth International Conference on Patristic Studies Held in Oxford 1971, Part II: Classica et Hellenica, Theologica, Liturgica, Ascetica* (Berlin: Akademie-Verlag, 1975) 57–59; Lyman, "The Politics of Passing," 40 (On Justin and Lucian); see also J. L. Lightfoot, *Lucian On the Syrian Goddess* (Oxford: Oxford University Press, 2003) 203.

[32] Hartog, *Memories of Odysseus*; Arnoldo Momigliano, *Alien Wisdom: The Limits of Hellenization* (Cambridge: Cambridge University Press, 1975); Guy G. Stroumsa, *Barbarian Philosophy: The Religious Revolution of Early Christianity* (WUNT 112; Tübingen: Mohr Siebeck, 1999).

[33] Swain, *Hellenism and Empire,* 298–99. On the complexity and hybridity of Lucian's identity, see esp. Whitmarsh's excellent *Greek Literature and the Roman Empire*, 248–301; Jaś Elsner, "Describing Self in the Language of Other: Pseudo (?) Lucian at the Temple of Hierapolis" in

and speaking in character, he performs an identity as a Syrian who is a rhetor, a master of Greek oratory and Greek *paideia* performing and writing in the cities of the Mediterranean basin.[34] As we shall see, Lucian is like Justin in his admiration of Greek philosophy and rhetoric, and like Tatian in his impulse to use and satirize Greekness.[35] Here I deal only briefly with a few works from Lucian's wide corpus, focusing on his discussion and depiction of three cities, and their relative epistemic values: the city of Hierapolis within his homeland of Assyria, Athens, and Rome.

Although elsewhere in his writings he appears as the character of the Syrian, in *On the Syrian Goddess*, Lucian assumes an autobiographical tone: "I myself that write am an Assyrian."[36] Lucian maps Hierapolis, a city to which he has gone as pilgrim in his natal area of Assyria, as the center of the sacred and holy.[37] It is also the place that literally holds a part of him, a lock of hair that he placed in the city's main sanctuary, in obedience to local tradition (*De dea Syr.* 60). Moreover, the city is a kind of macrocosm of Lucian's hybrid identity and literary impulses:[38] *On the Syrian Goddess* itself is written not in his normal

Goldhill, ed., *Being Greek under Rome*, 123–53. See also Tim Whitmarsh, "Varia Lucianea," *CR* 53.1 (2003) 75–78.

[34] See Gleason, *Making Men*, and R. Bracht Branham, *Unruly Eloquence: Lucian and the Comedy of Traditions* (Cambridge, MA: Harvard University Press, 1989) 1–4 on oratorical performance. On defining Lucian as a sophist, see R. Bracht Branham, "Introducing a Sophist: Lucian's Prologues," *Transactions of the American Philological Association* 115 (1985) 237–43. Regarding Lucian and oral performance, see Christopher Jones, *Culture and Society in Lucian* (Cambridge, MA: Harvard University Press, 1986) 12–14. For a reading of Lucian using postcolonial and feminist theory, see Rosa Cornford Parent, "Mapping Identity in the Lucianic Corpus" (Ph.D. dissertation, Department of Classics, University of Southern California, 2000). Lucian discusses his own career turn in *The Dream*, or *Lucian's Career*, which depicts Sculpture and *Paideia* competing over him in a dream, and his choice to attach himself to *Paideia*. In this work he admits that it is *Paideia* that allows him to travel and to see the map of the world from on high, literally: On her chariot "I was carried up into the heights and went from the East to the very West, surveying cities and nations and peoples, sowing something broadcast over the earth like Triptolemus" (Lucian *Somn.* 15; ET Harmon, 3.229). The barbarian Lucian claims that he cannot remember what he sowed, only the applause of those over whose heads he flew. But with this image Lucian/the main narrator signals that he carried something like Triptolemus's corn, a sign for cultivation and civilization in Greek literature. The emperor Claudius and his wife Agrippina were also depicted as Triptolemus and Ceres.

[35] On the limits and usefulness of a term like "satire" in relation to the poly-generic Lucian, see Whitmarsh, *Greek Literature and the Roman Empire*, 247–53.

[36] Lucian *De dea Syr.* 1; ET Lightfoot, 249; see also *My Native Land*. All translations are from Lightfoot's translation and edition of Lucian *On the Syrian Goddess*.

[37] "These are the ancient and great sanctuaries of Syria. But as many of them as there are, none seems to me to be greater than those in the Holy City, nor any other temple holier, nor any country more sacred" (*De dea Syr.* 10; ET Lightfoot, 253).

[38] For a similar reading, see Elsner, "Describing Self" in Goldhill, ed., *Being Greek under Rome*, 123–53. Lucian's description of cults in Syria points to a hybridity of religions and identities that occurred in the second-century Roman world: "There is another large temple in Phoenicia, one that belongs to the Sidonians. As they themselves say, it is Astarte's – I myself think that Astarte is Selene – but as one of the priests told me, it belongs to Europa the sister of Cadmus" (*De dea Syr.* 4; ET Lightfoot, 249). On attempts to map deities of one

Atticizing Greek but with a "Pseudo-Ionism" that echoes Herodotus and draws on the association of the Ionian dialect as the "language of ethnography."[39] Speaking of the city's central cult, located on a hill in the middle of the city (28), Lucian says that "many stories were told, of which some were sacred, some manifest, some thoroughly mythological, and others were barbarian, of which some agreed with the Greeks. I shall relate them all, but by no means accept them all" (11).[40] Lucian does not foreclose on competing stories or multiple scenarios of origins, but instead includes four possible accounts of the temple's foundation (1–16).

This ambiguity and hybridity is woven into the very characters who are key to one of the holy city's stories of origin (19–25), which include a castrated man who helped in the building of the temple and whose statue stands there "in the shape of a woman but still in the clothing of a man" (26).[41] Even the image of Hera in the sanctuary "appears to be of many forms" and "has something of Athena and Aphrodite and Selene and Rhea and Artemis and Nemesis and the Fates" in her many attributes (32).[42] Lucian mentions another statue that "has no shape of its own, but bears the forms of the other gods. It is called the standard (σημήϊον) by the Assyrians themselves, who have not given it a name of its own, nor have they anything to say about its place of origin and form" (33).[43] This city of pilgrimage in Lucian's homeland is a theme park of hybridity.

Elsewhere in his corpus, Lucian's mappings again involve cities and ethnicities. He is interested in how Syrians, for example, survive in Athens, and how Greek identity performs in Rome. The former situation is played out in *The Dead Come to Life*.[44] Here Parrhēsiadēs, literally "of free speech," is

ethnic group onto those of another, see Clifford Ando, *The Matter of the Gods: Religion and the Roman Empire* (Berkeley: University of California Press, 2008) chap. 3.

39 Lightfoot, *On the Syrian Goddess*, 91–158, esp. 91–92. Lucianic authorship of this piece has been questioned, but Simon Swain has convincingly argued that the piece is Lucian's (*Hellenism and Empire*, 304–7; Lightfoot, "The Authorship of *De Dea Syria* Revisited" [in *On the Syrian Goddess*, 184–208]; see discussion of this issue, as well as Lucian's *ekphrasis*, in Jaś Elsner, *Roman Eyes: Visuality and Subjectivity in Art and Text* [Princeton: Princeton University Press, 2007] 12, 18–26; see also Jones, *Culture and Society in Lucian*, 41). Lucian talks about a desire to imitate Herodotus in his *Herodotus* or *Aetion*.

40 ET Lightfoot, 253.

41 ET ibid., 265. Lucian tells the story of Stratonike, a queen who falls for Combabos, the king's architect, who castrates himself to escape blame for seduction. The story offers an etiology for ongoing sexual ambiguity in the city: "This sort of love exists in the Holy City and still endures today: women desire galli and galli go mad for women, but no one is jealous and they believe the thing to be entirely sacred" (*De dea Syr.* 22; ET Lightfoot, 263).

42 ET ibid., 269. The statue also embodies in its materials, which include precious stones "sent by Egyptians, Indians, Aethiopians, Medes, Armenians, and Babylonians."

43 ET ibid., 271.

44 *The Dead Come to Life* performs a situation so often associated with Christian apologetic: trial and defense. The theme is also evidence in *The Double Indictment*, which is set in Athens, on the Areopagus. A rhetor, only called "the Syrian," is called up to trial for having offended

a stand-in character for Lucian.[45] Questioned by the character Philosophy about his fatherland, Parrhēsiadēs replies: "I am Syrian, Philosophy, from the banks of the Euphrates. But what of that? I know that some of my opponents here are just as foreign-born as I.... Yet as far as you are concerned it would make no difference even if a man's speech were foreign, if only his way of thinking were manifestly right and true" (*Reviv.* 19).[46] The setting is the Athenian acropolis, where piety (Parrhēsiadēs prays to Athena Polias) and prosecution can coexist; all the old prestigious Greek philosophers gather in Athens to judge the Syrian Parrhēsiadēs. The evocation of a judicial setting in which Greek *paideia* is central to the trial is similar to Christian apologists' writings. In both the form and the content of *The Dead Come to Life*, where the main character ventriloquizes the arguments of philosophers like Plato and Diogenes, Lucian the Syrian writer demonstrates that the Syrian Parrhēsiadēs is able to perform Greek *paideia*. He in fact defends philosophy against those who are merely costumed philosophers: "in beard, I mean, and walk and garb" (*Reviv.* 31).[47] Athens itself is depicted as a magnet for every kind of philosophical fakery,[48] for those who claim to be interested in philosophy but instead are lured by wealth. Lucian often jokes about the confusion between true and false philosophy that results from the fact that any man – even the unphilosophical – can dress up with a long beard and mantle to look like a philosopher, a costume we also find in Justin's *Dialogue with Trypho*.

While *The Dead Come to Life* depicts Athens simultaneously as the *polis* of true philosophy and of fake philosophy, *Nigrinus*, set in Rome, offers a less ambivalent picture of Athens. It begins, in effect, by measuring in terms of true *paideia* the distance on the map between Rome and Athens. Lucian writes, "The talk began with praise of Greece and of the people of Athens." Athens is here praised not as a magnet of false philosophy, but as the ultimate philosophical and pedagogical city. When the nouveau riche enter, according to *Nigrinus*, Athenians gently correct by mocking displays of wealth, and

both Rhetoric and Dialogue – the real offence, it seems, is the hybridizing of genres and the bringing of humor into dialogues. Regarding genre-mixing in Lucian, see esp. Whitmarsh, *Greek Literature and the Roman Empire*, 249, passim.

45 On the slipperiness of Lucian's personae, see Whitmarsh, *Greek Literature and the Roman Empire*, 250–53.

46 ET Harmon, 3.31. *The Dead Come to Life* claims to respond to complaints about *Philosophies for Sale*. Lucian also treats the theme of philosophy, the city of Athens, and the foreigner in his discussion of Anacharsis in *The Scythian* – a work in which, according to Hartog, Lucian himself is working out issues of *paideia* and patronage (*Memories of Odysseus*, 114).

47 ET Harmon, 3.47; see similar language in Justin *1 Apol.* 4.

48 See especially the account of the second part of the trial, where "philosophers" are lured for judgment by the promise of gifts.

"disciplining" with "public education."[49] Those who love wealth and power, states the philosophical Nigrinus, should live in the city, presumably Rome, "for every street and every square is full of the things they cherish most, and they can admit pleasure by every gate – by the eyes, by the ears and nostrils, by the throat and reins. Its everflowing, turbid stream widens every street... and sweeps the flooded soul bare of self-respect, virtue, and righteousness" (*Nigrinus*).[50] The geography of the city and the individual body are conflated so that urban and philosophical ills are one: Literal and philosophical sewage streams through both city and person. The city itself is a perfect testing ground for the philosopher, since it is so full of temptations, from food to races to philosophical lecture-rooms which are mere "factories and bazaars."[51]

Rome is not only a center for dangers, temptations, and potential pollutions; it is also the site of a kind of voluntary slavery for philosophers hawking Greekness.[52] This is something of which Tatian too accuses the Greeks or those who claim Greek identity through *paideia*,[53] although he does not locate the compromised philosophers in Rome: "You established rhetoric through injustice and dishonesty, selling your freedom of speech for a wage" (*Ad Graec.* 1.3).

Some scholars understand the Roman Empire to have generously incorporated and given voice to a figure like Lucian.[54] While it is difficult to reconstruct Lucian's reception by the Roman elite, he hints that his rhetorical self-formation occurs in a particular imperial market that was less generous than consuming of others' talents. While *The Dead Come to Life* mocks those who are costumed as philosophers, *On Salaried Posts in Great Houses* implies that Lucian is precisely that: a costumed philosopher for hire. The text maps Rome as a site for ethnic hierarchy and humiliation. The client-philosopher

[49] Lucian *Nigrinus*; ET Harmon, 1.113. For more on Rome and Lucian, see Whitmarsh, *Greek Literature and the Roman Empire*, chap. 5, especially for a discussion of the complexity of Lucian's construction of Rome in *Nigrinus* and its pair, the *Apology*, in which Lucian somewhat apologizes for his critique of the patronage system (291–93; and 265–79).

[50] ET Harmon, 1.117. See Juvenal *Sat.* 3.62–65 on the River Orontes (from Syria) polluting the Tiber with its language, customs, music, and prostituted girls.

[51] ET Harmon, 1.125.

[52] Voluntary entry into a salaried post for a rich patron leads only to servitude: "Remember never again... to think yourself free or noble. All that – your pride of race, your freedom, your ancient lineage – you will leave outside the threshold, let me tell you, when you go in after having sold yourself into such servitude" (*De merc.* 23; ET Harmon, 3.449).

[53] On *paideia* allowing for a claim to Hellenic identity, see Jonathan Hall, *Hellenicity: Between Ethnicity and Culture* (Chicago: University of Chicago Press, 2002) 223–26; see also Whitmarsh, *Greek Literature and the Roman Empire*.

[54] "It marks a certain degree of cultural self-confidence when a system such as the Roman Empire can not only incorporate 'foreigners' like the Gallic eunuch Favorinus or the Syrian 'barbarian' Lucian among its major Greek writers but can also give the 'other' a critical voice in commenting on its own customs and attitudes" (Jaś Elsner and Joan-Pau Rubiés, "Introduction," in their edited volume *Voyages and Visions: Towards a Cultural History of Travel* [London: Reaktion, 1999] 10–11). See also Swain, *Hellenism and Empire*, 329.

seeking a patron is "subordinate to a doorman with a vile Syrian accent" (*De merc.* 10).[55] Lucian's joke hints at his own vulnerability as a Syrian, who perhaps masked an accent and marketed *paideia* in various venues. Not only is the Syrian doorman superior, but the patron's unphilosophical friends also complain about the new client, saying, "It is only these Greeks who have the freedom of the city of Rome. And yet, why is it that they are preferred to us? Isn't it true that they think they confer a tremendous benefit by turning wretched phrases?" (*De merc.* 17).[56] Lucian points to the ways in which the patron buys or "collects" the philosopher: "As you have a long beard, present a distinguished appearance, are neatly dressed in a Greek mantle, and everybody knows you for a grammarian or a rhetorician or a philosopher . . . it will make people think him [the patron] a devoted student of Greek learning and in general a person of taste in literary matters. So the chances are, my worthy friend, that instead of your marvelous lectures it is your beard and mantle that you have let for hire" (*De merc.* 24).[57] Eventually, Lucian claims, the philosopher will become a slave, part of a Roman-owned collection, one among many performers for the rich Roman patron, juxtaposed perhaps with "an Alexandrian dwarf who recites Ionics" (*De merc.* 23).[58] As Whitmarsh puts it, "The theatricalization of Greek *paideia* – the requirement that it be subsumed into the competitive and patronal structures of display required by Rome's power-pyramid – is one of the most enduring objects of his vituperation."[59] The bearded philosopher's borrowed identity and Attic dialect are tchotchkes of *paideia* for the wealthy, upwardly mobile Roman.

Lucian uses geographical thinking to toy with the claims of different cities in the Roman Empire to be the center of the world. When Rome is at the center, it is shown to be a city mapped as analogous to a hungry and excreting body, with gateways that welcome pleasures and roads that run with sewage. Rome is ravenous, collecting Greekness and other oddities. When Athens is the center of Lucian's map, it is shown to be a haunt of those who claim to be true philosophers and rhetoricians, but are lacking; even a Syrian can show them up. Rome and Athens also hold within them hybrid possibilities, but this mixing is presented as hierarchical, abusive, dangerous. Hierapolis, in contrast, is depicted as an important site within Lucian's homeland of Assyria, which holds a bit of Lucian and which is a pious center for every sort of hybridity and ambiguity.

[55] ET Harmon, 3.431.
[56] ET ibid., 3.441.
[57] ET ibid., 3.455.
[58] ET ibid., 3.459.
[59] Whitmarsh, *Greek Literature and the Roman Empire*, 253–57, quotation at 257; see also p. 280 on how this work maps power and the Roman house; see also pp. 123–24 regarding Lucian's "autobiography," *The Dream*.

Tatian

Nobody likes Tatian. Eusebius, citing Irenaeus, says that Tatian introduced the "blasphemy" of Encratism.[60] Jerome labels him the "patriarch of the Encratites"; Epiphanius concurs.[61] Even those who more recently than the fourth or fifth century have worked intimately enough with Tatian to edit his work offer judgments like this: "The harshness and obscurity of his style seem to mirror his arrogant and intransigent personality."[62] Tatian is famed and maligned for at least three things: first, for his *Diatessaron*, a gospel harmony; second, for being the founder of Encratism, which is understood as heresy; and third, for the bitterness of his late-second century *To the Greeks* – the only of Tatian's works to survive in nearly complete form. But the first two accusations are historically questionable, and the last is a matter of interpretation.[63] Tatian is often characterized as Justin Martyr's slightly crazed student, vicious and brutal in his rhetoric.[64] Both are understood as early apologists for Christianity who struggled with the question of how to fit Christianity and Hellenism together, but Justin is depicted as offering higher apologetic to the empire and the possibility of the assimilation of Christianity and Hellenism. Tatian, with his vitriol against Greekness, is seen as the failed path that Christianity did not pursue.

This reading of Tatian does serious injustice to the passion and humor of *To the Greeks*. Tatian's over-the-top critique of the Greeks draws upon satirical conventions of his time and participates in ongoing culture wars about connoisseurship in the Roman Empire – connoisseurship not only of works of art,

60 Eusebius *Hist. eccl.* 4.29.3. Later, Eusebius is more positive in his representation of Tatian, lumping him with Justin, Miltiades, Clement, and others who speak of Christ as God (5.28.4). It is important to note that even Eusebius considers Tatian's *To the Greeks* (and, incidentally, his *Diatessaron*) to be useful and appropriate (4.29.7).

61 Jerome *In ep. ad Tit.*, praef; cited in Whittaker, *Tatian Oratio ad Graecos and Fragments*, 83. Epiphanius calls the Encratites "those who have succeeded Tatian" (*Pan.* 47.1.1).

62 Whittaker, *Tatian Oratio ad Graecos and Fragments*, xiv–xv. But see her statement: "Tatian is not an Oriental with an inferiority complex; the differentiation is one of culture, not of race" ("Tatian's Educational Background," 59). For scholarship that takes Tatian himself more seriously and that contextualizes those heresiologists who treat him, see Naomi Koltun-Fromm, "Re-imagining Tatian: The Damaging Effects of Polemical Rhetoric," *JECS* 16.1 (2008) 1–30. See also Emily J. Hunt, *Christianity in the Second Century: The Case of Tatian* (New York: Routledge, 2003).

63 Leslie W. Barnard ("The Heresy of Tatian – Once Again," *JEH* 19.1 [1968] 1–10) reads Tatian's detractors uncritically and seeks to secure a timeline of the evolution of Tatian's "heretical" thought – that is, his Encratism – and the writing of his *To the Greeks*. Others read Tatian as tainted by his "Oriental" background; for a critique of this, see Lampe, *From Paul to Valentinus*, 290. On dating, see G. W. Clarke, "The Date of the Oration of Tatian," *HTR* 60 (1967) 123–26, who argues that *To the Greeks* may not be as late as 177 CE, R. M. Grant's dating. See Chapter 6 for a discussion of Kathy Gaca's opinion of Tatian.

64 E.g., Barnard, "The Heresy of Tatian – Once Again." For ancient accounts, see Irenaeus *Adv. haer.* 1.28.1.

but also of certain kinds of ethnicity and knowledge.[65] Scholars have debated whether Tatian's late second-century work is a protreptic and a kind of calling card for Tatian's teaching.[66] If we read Tatian in light of contemporaneous writers like Lucian, his near-contemporary and fellow Easterner, we can see that Tatian mixes genres and performs Greekness – he has a full repertoire of philosophical and cultural references – in order to subvert the contemporary cultural valuation of Greekness and praise barbarian (Christian) identity.

Because it is hard to hear the sound of play in cultures different from our own, Tatian's wicked humor has gone unrecognized.[67] But he does signal that what he said may or should be taken as a joke. At a crucial moment in his argument, when Tatian has explained his tour of Greek cult and his "conversion" to Christianity, he turns to his inscribed audience and says, "To you, the Greeks, what else can I say but do not revile your betters, nor, if they are called barbarians, take this as an occasion for a joke" (*Ad Graec.* 30.1–30.2).[68] In *To the Greeks*, vocabulary of jokes and laughter is used often; we know from Lucian that irony, joking, and satire can reveal a bitter truth. In Tatian's work, the joke is on the Greeks, since he mocks their famed philosophers and customs through quick, devastating character sketches and illustrations.[69] Lucian wrote two different pieces about Anacharsis, the Scythian who signaled so much about barbarian identity, barbarian wisdom, and barbarian hunger for Greek philosophy. Tatian, too, throws this tradition in the face of the "Greeks" (ἄνδρες Ἕλληνες) whom he addresses. Tatian makes himself into a kind of

[65] On Tatian's education, see Lampe, *From Paul to Valentinus*, 285–90, esp. 287–88. On Tatian as a sophist, see Whittaker, "Tatian's Educational Background," 57.

[66] Michael McGehee ("Why Tatian Never 'Apologized' to the Greeks," *JECS* 1 [1993] 143–58) has argued that *To the Greeks* is a *protreptikos*, advertising to students Tatian's philosophical stance and rhetorical skills. Molly Whittaker too understood it as hortatory, but pointed to a different audience: "his main concern is to urge pagan readers to leave the error of their ways in order that they may turn to the truth" (*Tatian Oratio ad Graecos and Fragments*, xv). Robert Grant argued that Tatian's oration takes the form of a "*logos syntaktikos* or 'farewell discourse' to the culture of Greece and Rome"; but instead of offering praise, as one usually would, Tatian instead inverts praise into ψόγος ("vituperation") ("Five Apologists and Marcus Aurelius," *VC* 42 [1988] 12).

[67] Cicero states that "all . . . who tried to teach anything like a theory or art of this matter [humor] proved themselves so conspicuously silly that their very silliness is the only laughable thing about them. That is why I think this accomplishment cannot possibly be imparted by teaching" (*De or.* 2.54.217–18; ET in *Cicero De oratore, Books 1–2* [LCL; trans. E. W. Sutton and H. Rackham; Cambridge, MA: Harvard University Press, 2001] 359). On humor, rhetoric, and Lucian, see also R. Bracht Branham, "Authorizing Humor: Lucian's *Demonax* and Cynic Rhetoric," *Semeia* 64.1 (2001) 33–48.

[68] On Tatian's "conversion," see Laura Nasrallah, "The Rhetoric of Conversion and the Construction of Experience: The Case of Justin Martyr," in E. J. Yarnold and M. F. Wiles, eds., *Studia Patristica 18: Papers Presented at the Fourteenth International Conference on Patristics Studies Held in Oxford, 2003* (Leuven: Peeters, 2006) 467–74.

[69] Elsewhere, Tatian seems to instruct his audience on which parts of his speech are funny and which are not; see, e.g., *Ad Graec.* 17.1, amid many references to laughter and joking (e.g., 1.3, 2.3, 3.1, 17.1).

misunderstood Anacharsis: "You, who don't curse the Scythian Anacharsis now, also shouldn't be indignant at being educated by those who follow a barbarian code of laws" (12.5). Both Lucian and Tatian try on different barbarian roles in their play with Greek *paideia*.

Tatian discusses not only his homeland and the travels he has made, but also maps the relative values of knowledge in these regions.[70] The overlap between ethnic identity, geographical thinking, and knowledge becomes clear at important moments in his text, at the beginning and end. Tatian ends *To the Greeks* in this way: "I have set these things in order for you, Greeks – I, Tatian, a philosopher in the region of the barbarians, born in the land of the Assyrians, but educated (παιδευθείς) first in your learning and second in what I now announce that I preach" (42.1). The first lines of Tatian's *To the Greeks* read: "Do not maintain a totally hostile attitude toward barbarians, men of Greece, nor resent their teachings. For which of your own practices did not have a barbarian origin?" (1.1). He then displays his knowledge about the true genealogies of arts that the Greeks claim as their own: The Phrygians Marsyas and Olympus taught them flute-playing, Etruscans taught sculpture, Egyptians taught about history (1.1–2).

Tatian begins his *To the Greeks* by ossifying the categories of Greek and barbarian, and then immediately questions the same in order to show the impure genealogy of Greek language itself. Taking up the long tradition of discussing "barbarian" or foreign influences on Greek knowledge, Tatian shows that Greekness itself is a fiction, a miscegenation. Greek language appropriates words from other languages and dialects from other cultures.[71] Greek itself is made up of multiple dialects: Dorians differ from Attic speakers, Aeolians from Ionians. What is strangest – literally most out of place, most no-place of all (ἀτοπώτατον) – is that those who consider themselves Greeks have mixed with expressions that are not "akin" (τὰς μὴ συγγένεις ὑμῶν ἑρμηνείας) (1.3)[72] – that are not genetically Greek, so to speak.

In this passage on Tatian's apprehension of truth, Tatian's introductory themes of the false pretensions of Attic purity and the "arrogant and crazy talk" of pseudo-philosophers[73] arise again and lead to a kind of climax: the story

[70] Tatian directly engages geographical theories of the time, in a passage where he points to the superior knowledge of the (barbarian) prophets (*Ad Graec.* 20.2–3). See Lampe's list of the geographers to whom Tatian alludes (*From Paul to Valentinus*, 429).

[71] Strabo, too, admits that Greek language appropriates others' terms; see *Geog.* 14.2.28. See also his intriguing comment (in a different context) about mixing and a "third race" in 14.5.25. See also Eran Almagor, "Strabo's *Barbarophonoi* (14.2.28 C 661–63): A Note," *Scripta Classica Israelica* 19 (2000) 133–38.

[72] He precedes this by saying that he doesn't know "whom I must call a Greek" in light of so many regional variations in Greek (*Ad Graec.* 1.3).

[73] Ibid., 3.3, where we find again a pun on *philopsophos* ("lover of inarticulate sound"). While Justin applies the term to Crescens (see p. 72), Tatian here contrasts it explicitly with (true) philosophers.

of Tatian's own philosophical choices. In a crucial passage about his own "conversion," Tatian reverses the pattern of his introduction. He attacks philosophers first, and then turns to the related issue of language.[74] He accuses his inscribed audience of constructing itself by its relationship to words, and of engaging in verbal imperialism. "Stop your triumphal procession of another's words," he insists. The word θριαμβεύοντες conjures up a ritual parade of prisoners and spoils of war: verbal pillaging. "Stop decorating yourselves with feathers that aren't your own, as if you're a jackdaw!" he says, using an image of linguistic pretension that also appears in Lucian.[75] He goes on to point at current trends in Greek education (27.1; cf. 19) – and, in particular, trends in rhetoric – as the root cause of tragic and comedic misunderstandings of the truth.[76]

Tatian adopts the voice of the traveler or ethnographer.[77] In the second century, Pausanias's tour of Greece imitated Herodotus, celebrated classical culture, and constructed Greek identity in the face of Roman imperialism, ignoring many recent changes to the landscape.[78] Like Pausanias, but with a twist, Tatian offers a brief tour of the empire and beyond. Greeks avoid intercourse with their mothers; Persians think it is a good idea. Barbarians avoid pederasty, but Romans herd children together; Tatian is not impressed

74 Ibid., 25–26. See 1–2 for the opposite ordering of argument. For Tatian, philosophy and language are linked.

75 Tatian continues: "Why do you assert that wisdom is yours alone? . . . The grammarians have been the origin of your nonsense. . . . You are puffed up with opinions, but you are humiliated by misfortunes; you abuse beyond reason figures of speech. . . . Why do you get ready for a war of letters? Why, like boxers, do you strike together their pronunciations through Athenian stammerings, when it's right to speak more naturally? For if you atticize but aren't an Athenian, tell me why don't you 'doricize'? Why does it seem to you that one [dialect] is more barbarian, while the other is more satisfactory for communication?" (ibid., 26.2–4).

76 Tatian mocks Greek myths and superstitions and especially critiques what we might call "ancient pluralism." Tatian employs the language of the courtroom to condemn the pluralism that undergirds "their" legislation: what is shameful to some is considered good to others, and as many legal positions exist as do cities, yet all is tolerated (Διὰ τοῦτο καὶ τῆς παρ' ὑμῖν κατέγνων νομοθεσίας, ibid., 28.1). Claudius Ptolemy, the second-century CE geographer and astronomer famous for his cool mathematical calculations of the cosmos, also wrote the *Tetrabiblos*, which he calls "astronomical prognostication," and we might call astrology. His references both to customs and to the effect of the fixed stars and planets upon various ethnicities are similar to Tatian's characterizations of various nations. See, e.g., *Tetrabiblos* 4.10; see also Clement *Paid.* 1.7; Lucian *De sacr.* 5. For more on legal diversity and injustice in the Roman Empire, see Chapters 4 and 5.

77 On this theme, see Hartog, *Memories of Odysseus*; Elsner and Rubiés, "Introduction," 10–11, 15; Whitmarsh, "'Greece Is the World': Exile and Identity in the Second Sophistic," 269–305.

78 Jaś Elsner, "Pausanias: A Greek Pilgrim in the Roman World," *Past and Present* 135 (1992) 3–29. See also James I. Porter, "Ideals and Ruins: Pausanias, Longinus, and the Second Sophistic," in Alcock et al., eds., *Pausanias: Travel and Memory in Roman Greece*, 63–92; and Ian Rutherford, "Tourism and the Sacred: Pausanias and the Traditions of Greek Pilgrimage," in the same volume (pp. 40–53).

by the diversity. His cultic tourism left him cold: He claims that he partook in mysteries, like so many of the elites of his time, and that he tested the cults (which he claims were organized by the effeminate and androgynes), and what he found was Zeus Latiaris and Artemis of Ephesus enjoying human gore and blood, and demons inspiring wrongdoing (28–29.1). Tatian found truth not in this tour of Greek cults but in "barbarian writings" (that is, the Jewish scriptures). He was persuaded by the "unaffected nature of the words" and by the "artlessness of the things which they said" (29.2). These barbarian writings offered clarity of language and philosophical thought, characteristics that he mocks the Greeks for lacking.[79] In this section, Tatian twice uses the word *planē* to mark the Greek error in which he had participated (29.1, 2). *Planē* means "error" but also "wandering" or "roaming." Tatian's very travels were the source of error; back in Assyria, he found simple and true philosophy.

In *To the Greeks*, Tatian also deploys the rhetorical technique of *ekphrasis*. Pausanias and Lucian, among others, describe statues and buildings in detail, in part to demonstrate the scope of their knowledge and the power of their rhetoric to recreate in skilled words the skilled lineaments of artwork.[80] Tatian's *ekphrasis*, however, does not celebrate aesthetics. His list and his descriptions of statues focus on sculptures of females and famous figures which exemplify not the art and grace of Greece, but its shames. All the women described have engaged in some questionable activity, according to Tatian, usually of a sexual sort; other figures described are "memorials of evil" (34.1).[81] "Our" women, in contrast, are chaste, Tatian asserts. Tatian follows and guarantees the truth of this *ekphrasis* by returning to the theme of his own travels and by focusing on the city of Rome.[82]

> I set forth these things, not having learned them from another, but having haunted much of the earth. I played the part of the sophist, using your goods. I met with much art and many ideas. Finally, having spent time in the city of the Romans, I thoroughly learned about the varied statues that they brought back from you as theirs. For I do not try, as is the custom of many, to strengthen with others' opinions my own, but I

[79] See also Justin *Dial. Tryph.* 7–8, where Justin was moved to embrace Christianity as true philosophy not by reading the prophets, but by their mere mention. See also Tatian's critique of grammarians and of misuses of language in *Ad Graec.* 26.

[80] See Jaś Elsner, *Art and the Roman Viewer: The Transformation of Arts from the Pagan World to Christianity* (Cambridge: Cambridge University Press, 1995). On Lucian's anxieties about art and *ekphrasis*, see Gregory W. Dobrov, "The Sophist on His Craft: Art, Text, and Self-Construction in Lucian," *Helios* 29.2 (2002) 173–92; see also the discussion on pp. 120–21.

[81] See *Ad Graec.* 33–34.

[82] Ancient authors claim that Tatian settled in Rome and founded a school there (Irenaeus *Adv. haer.* 1.28.1) before returning home, perhaps to found his own school (Epiphanius *Pan.* 1.3.46). See Koltun-Fromm, "Re-Imagining Tatian," 1–2. For more discussion of this passage and connoisseurship, see Chapter 6.

> wanted to compile a record of all these things which I myself directly apprehended. . . . Therefore, saying goodbye to Roman arrogance and Athenian nonsense – incoherent teachings – I sought after what you say is a barbarian philosophy. Don't scorn our *paideia* nor busy yourself with a quarrel directed against us, full of nonsense and coarse jesting, saying, "Tatian is instituting anew barbarian doctrines, over and above the Greeks and the countless mass of those who philosophize!" (35.1)

Tatian asserts that he has played the part of the sophist; he affirms his personal experience through repeated travel (ἐπιφοιτήσας). He also offers a particularly biting comment "to the Greeks": He learned Greek *paideia* and Greek patrimony by visiting Rome, where one can find Greek statuary, now spoils of war. Tatian maps the Roman Empire as a site of relative appropriations and valuations of kinds of knowledge. Rome has robbed Greece of its culture, but it is the barbarians' edges of the world, with their simple and truthful knowledge, which should be its center.

Tatian mocks the conventions of contemporary travel or ethnographic literature. He presents himself, among others, as a traveler in the culturally elite realms of the Roman Empire. He frames the equivalent of a "Grand Tour" of his time not in terms of a description of piety, history, cult, aesthetics, but in terms of cultic oddities and shame, insult and comparison. Tatian's travels, whether in his imagination or in reality, have allowed him to see how language, philosophy, geography, and *paideia* are conjoined. "What is the benefit of Attic style and sorites of philosophers and plausabilities of syllogisms and measurement of the earth and positions of stars and courses of the sun? For to be engaged in such investigation is the work of one who frames his own teachings as law" (27.3). For Tatian, language, philosophy, and terrestrial and astronomical cartographies are linked, part of one system of *paideia*.

Throughout, Tatian's focus is on the Greek *paideia* and identity that some elite Romans adore and seek to appropriate, and which Greek elites configure and market for their own and others' consumption. Like his contemporary Lucian, among others, Tatian meditates upon Greekness in part in order to mock it, but he does so while using its tools and themes with great sophistication. In Tatian's mental mapping, Rome is important both as the guarantor of the authenticity of Tatian's view and as a scavenger city, location of the prizes of Greek cultural identity. But Tatian inverts the traditional importance of travel to Rome – with the prestige and higher speaking fees that this trip often yielded to a rhetor or teacher[83] – and concludes his work by asserting Assyrian identity and the joys of philosophizing among the barbarians.

[83] Hartog, *Memories of Odysseus*, 193.

Justin

Justin, writing in the mid-second century, begins both the *First* and the *Second Apologies* by marking Rome as the center of his mental map, in terms of its political and philosophical importance. In the first lines of Chapter 1 we read the beginning of the *First Apology*, which addresses Antoninus Pius, Marcus Aurelius, Lucius Verus, the sacred Senate and all the Romans. Justin then introduces himself: "I, Justin, the son of Priscus and grandson of Bacchius, from the city of Flavia Neapolis in Syria Palestine, have made this address and petition on behalf of those of every race who are unjustly hated and abusively threatened, myself being one of them."[84] Thus, unlike Lucian and Tatian, whose critiques of Rome are scathing, and whose geographical thinking tends to center on their barbarian home, Justin's *Apologies* emphasize Rome's centrality. He appeals to Roman claims to tolerance and addresses himself to Rome as one of its provincial elites, speaking the common language of Greek, of privileged philosophy, and of Roman subject-hood.[85]

In both of his *Apologies*,[86] Justin had marked Rome as the center of his mental map. But in the *Second Apology* Rome is also the site where a Christian woman "does violence to herself" (βιαζομένη ἑαυτήν) by remaining with her abusive non-Christian husband in the hopes of persuading him to amend. Not only that, but she is forced into court proceedings when her husband accuses her of being a Christian. Her appeals to the emperor for time to prepare a defense ultimately result in the arrest (and imprisonment and punishment) of three others (her teacher, and two Christian bystanders), in a kind of domino effect of witness to Christianity. Lucius, one of the arrested, addresses the prefect: "Your judgment is not fitting to the Emperor Pius, nor to the philosopher, Caesar's son, nor to the sacred senate!" (*2 Apol.* 2.16).

With the story of this Christian woman, Justin offers a sharp exemplum of *apologia* within his own defense. Yet Justin avoids critiquing the emperors

[84] Justin *1 Apol.* 1.1. My translations were aided by Leslie W. Barnard, *St. Justin Martyr: The First and Second Apologies*. New York: Paulist, 1997). The Greek edition is Miroslav Marcovich, *Iustini Marturis Apologiae Pro Christianis* (Berlin: De Gruyter, 1994).

[85] In doing so, Justin participates in a long tradition of provincial Greek-speaking elites who address themselves to Rome, such as Polybius, Josephus, and Aelius Aristides. Rebecca Lyman has argued in the context of her larger discussion of the creation of "orthodoxy": "Justin's intellectual hybrid reflected his own attempt as a Christian provincial and a philosopher to portray universal truth within the cultural traditions of the second century" ("Hellenism and Heresy," 220; see also 221). Athenagoras *Leg.* 1, 6, 37 presents a similar appeal to the Roman imperial family's piety and policies of toleration. See Chapters 4 and 5 for further discussion.

[86] The actual audience of Justin's *Second Apology*, probably written between 150 and 155 CE as an appendix to the *First Apology*, is elusive, but it has the same inscribed audience as the *First Apology*, and makes brief reference to its audience as the Romans and the emperor. Marcovich, *Iustini Marturis Apologiae Pro Christianis*, 1–10; Eric Osborn, *Justin Martyr* (Tübingen: Mohr [Siebeck], 1973) 10–11; but see Goodenough, *Theology of Justin Martyr*, 84–87.

directly by putting his assessment in Lucius's mouth. Similarly, by using the phrase "she does violence to herself," Justin points to Rome as a location of violence, but avoids directly accusing the city and its citizens of effecting violence. Yet, in the *First Apology*, Justin directly states that "the rulers should give their decision in obedience, not to violence and tyranny, but to piety and philosophy" (Justin *1 Apol.* 3.2).[87]

Unlike Tatian and Lucian, Justin takes up Roman imperial propaganda about the emperor's household as philosophical, pious, and peaceful, and places Rome at the center of his plea that the empire live up to its own claims. But elsewhere in the *Apology*, it becomes clear that the very claim to philosophy can itself become a cause for violence in Rome, given the ongoing culture wars that have real political effects. "I too," Justin writes, ". . . expect to be plotted against and fixed to the stake, by some of those I have named, or perhaps by Crescens, that *philopsophos* and *philokompos*, lover of noise and din" (*2 Apol.* 3.1).[88] Justin himself is a lecturer who has made the "Roman voyage." According to Hartog, only by making this voyage "could renown and prestige be won: Higher fees could then be charged by a professor or a lecturer, and a greater social and political role could be exercised, in particular as an (effective) intercessor on behalf of one's native city."[89] Having traced the world from Neapolis in Syria through (perhaps) Asia Minor and into Rome, Justin's own experienced and cultured body is able to offer up an authentic tour of knowledge, but nonetheless is vulnerable. Lucian presented himself (or the client-philosopher) as subject to the vagaries and corruptions of life in Rome; so too Justin, but in a more extreme way. Justin himself maps Rome not only as a site of demons and exorcisms and intra Christian conflict, but also as the dangerous site of philosophical battles and disputes between the likes of himself and Crescens.[90]

The defiant Christian response which Justin offers in the *Apologies* addresses civil injustice, yet implicitly praises the imperial family and Senate, and confirms Rome's central place on the map: a location where violence is possible and likely, but where redress and justice are sought. Ashis Nandy asks, "Has the dominant idea of metropolitan civility, grounded in the vision of the European

[87] ὁμοίως δ' αὖ καὶ τοὺς ἄρχοντας μὴ βίᾳ μηδὲ τυραννίδι, ἀλλ' εὐσεβείᾳ καὶ φιλοσοφίᾳ ἀκολουθοῦντας τὴν ψῆφον τίθεσθαι. In the same passage Justin alludes to Plato's *Republic*, to the ideal city where rulers are all philosophers; see Marcovich, *Iustini Marturis Apologiae Pro Christianis*, 35.

[88] Justin may allude to himself as a kind of Socrates in *2 Apol.* 3, where he says that he thoroughly examined Crescens and found that Crescens knew nothing.

[89] Hartog, *Memories of Odysseus*, 193.

[90] On Crescens see *2 Apol.* 11.4 (also Tatian *Ad Graec.* 19.1; Eusebius *Hist. eccl.* 4.16.8–9). According to Justin, Rome is also the site of demons and exorcisms; it is the site of intra-Christian conflict, given that the Roman senate (so says Justin) has erected a statue to Simon, whom they believe to have been Christian, but whom Justin understands to be a heretic (*1 Apol.* 56).

Enlightenment, itself been in league with that hidden record of violence?"[91] The question can be fruitfully applied to antiquity as well. In the *Apologies*, which map Rome as center, Justin legitimates Rome's metropolitan status and claims to civility, but also hints at a "record of violence" found there.

The *Dialogue with Trypho*, in contrast, offers a different mental map. This is due in part to the fact that the *Apologies* take the form of an appeal and a direct address, while the *Dialogue* uses the conventions of a philosophical dialogue. It is also due to different implied audiences. The *Apologies* at least claim for their audience non-Christians in Rome, while the *Dialogue* imitates Plato's dialogues, and has no clearly inscribed audience.[92] The *Dialogue* asserts and constructs a Christian identity apart from Judaism. This Christian identity is universal, not particular; it is certainly not attached to the present Jerusalem, lately taken over and renamed Aelia Capitolina after the Bar Kochba revolt during the reign of Hadrian.[93] The *Dialogue*'s mental mapping is more complex than that of the *Apologies*, in part because of the *Dialogue*'s complicated allegorical interpretation of the Jewish scriptures. Justin deftly moves between mental maps of actual and allegorical locations; geographies and ethnic markers become fluid expressions. For example, while in the *Apologies* the categories of barbarian and Christian sometimes overlap, the *Dialogue*'s one significant use of the term "barbarian" rejects the characterization of Christians as barbarians, and thus as a people mapped in a particular region, rather than a people who

[91] Ashis Nandy, *Time Warps: Silent and Evasive Pasts in Indian Politics and Religion* (New Brunswick, NJ: Rutgers University Press, 2002) 219.

[92] For a good framework for reading such dialogues, and a discussion of Justin's Trypho, see Andrew Jacobs, "Dialogical Differences: (De-)Judaizing Jesus' Circumcision," *JECS* 15.3 (2007) 297–304. Most hypothesize that the *Dialogue* is written for Christians or for proselytes who are wavering between Christianity and Judaism. Regarding the debate on audience for *Dialogue with Trypho*, see Graham N. Stanton, "'God-Fearers': Neglected Evidence in Justin Martyr's *Dialogue with Trypho*," in T. W. Hillard et al., eds., *Ancient History in a Modern University*, vol. 2: *Early Christianity, Late Antiquity and Beyond* (Grand Rapids, MI: Eerdmans, 1998) 43–52; Graham N. Stanton, "Justin Martyr's *Dialogue with Trypho*: Group Boundaries, 'Proselytes' and 'God-Fearers'," in Graham N. Stanton and Guy G. Stroumsa, eds., *Tolerance and Intolerance in Early Judaism and Christianity* (Cambridge: Cambridge University Press, 1983) 275–78; Rajak, "Talking at Trypho," 75–80; Judith Lieu, *Image and Reality: The Jews in the World of the Christians in the Second Century* (London: T & T Clark, 1996) 104–9 (she calls it a "bridge" audience). Marcovich states, "It is for such a group of *Gentiles leaning towards Judaism* that the treatise is *primarily* intended" (*Iustini Martyris Dialogus cum Tryphone*, 64–65). Timothy Horner argues that a historical dialogue (and the voice of Trypho) can be reconstructed from the text (*Listening to Trypho*).

[93] In *1 Apol.* 31 Justin presents Bar Kochba as persecuting Christians; thus Justin places Christians alongside Romans as those who suffered from the revolutionary. On Justin's rhetoric of Christian universality and Jewish particularity, see Denise Kimber Buell, "Rethinking the Relevance of Race for Early Christian Self-Definition," *HTR* 94.4 (2001) 465, and her "Race and Universalism in Early Christianity," esp. 462–68. See also chap. 3 of her *Why This New Race?* Daniel Boyarin sees a debate over the Logos as the key to analyzing the *Dialogue with Trypho*; see his *Border Lines: The Partition of Judaeo-Christianity* (Philadelphia: University of Pennsylvania Press, 2004) chap. 2, esp. 37–41.

transcend the bounds of *ethnos* and region.[94] "But we are not only a people (*laos*) but also a holy people, as we have already shown: 'And they will call it a holy people, because it has been redeemed by the Lord' (Is 62:12). Therefore <not only> are we not a people to be despised, nor a barbarian tribe nor such as the nations of the Carians or Phrygians, but 'God has chosen us' . . . ." (*Dial. Tryph.* 119.4). Justin argues that Christians must be understood as God's "holy people" mentioned in prophecy. As Denise Buell has shown, Justin in the *Dialogue* maps Christians as a new Israel that is not geographically conceived, but rather is understood as infusing all places/nations.[95] At the same time, Justin uses the scriptures of Israel to insist that it was foretold that the real Syria Palestine and especially its metropolis of Jerusalem would burn, consumed by God's justified violence, not Roman injustice.

Although elsewhere in his writings his family identity and homeland in Neapolis in the region of Syria Palestine emerge (*1 Apol.* 1.1), in the *Dialogue*, especially in contrast to the Jew Trypho, Justin rises as the consummate universal Greek, a philosophical everyman. Trypho, his interlocutor (who, of course, speaks through Justin's voice) greets Justin as a philosopher because of Justin's dress.[96] Trypho's Jewish identity is mapped in a few brief strokes: "I am a Hebrew of the circumcision; having fled the ongoing war, I am spending time in Greece, and mostly in Corinth" (*Dial. Tryph.* 1.3). These point to Trypho's location slightly off-center: a Jew from the war-ravaged province of Palestine,[97] philosophically located not quite at the center of Greek thought, but slightly to the west, in Corinth, an ancient rival of Athens, which Rome razed and reestablished as a colony. Justin in contrast is not introduced with simple identity markers paralleling those of Trypho, as he might have been: The text could read "a Christian, son of Priscus, lately in Neapolis" – that is, something similar to what he offers in his *First Apology*

[94] See in contrast *1 Apol.* 5.4; 7.3; esp. 46.3 where philosophical models are set in parallel: the "barbarian" Abraham, Ananias, and other figures from the Jewish scriptures are juxtaposed to the "Greeks" Socrates and Herakleitos.

[95] Buell, *Why This New Race?*, 98–115.

[96] The beginning of the *Dialogue* also alludes to Socratic techniques of questioning, and contains a reference to Homer (J. C. M. van Winden, *An Early Christian Philosopher: Justin Martyr's Dialogue with Trypho Chapters One to Nine. Introduction, Text and Commentary* [Leiden: E. J. Brill, 1971] 22).

[97] Regarding problems in Judea, see also *Dial. Tryph.* 9. Judea as a real location is mentioned only *sotto voce*: as the group moves from one section of the colonnade to another to sit, Trypho turns to a companion to mention the war in Judea; in his introduction of himself, Trypho mentions having escaped the "ongoing war" (1.3). See Shelly Matthews's "The Need for the Stoning of Stephen," in Shelly Matthews and E. Leigh Gibson, eds., *Violence in the New Testament* (New York: T & T Clark International, 2005) 124–39, which discusses a situation analogous to Justin's construction of Trypho: Luke-Acts' construction of Jews as other and barbarous in the story of the stoning of Stephen; see also her *Perfect Martyr: The Stoning of Stephen and the Making of Gentile Christianity in Acts* (Oxford: Oxford University Press, forthcoming).

(1.1). Instead, he offers a long conversion story, which expands upon Trypho's first impression of him (or Vitruvius's ideal shipwreck victim) as cloaked in such a way that markers of ethnic origin or ritual affiliation fall away, with only the identity of philosopher remaining (*Dial. Tryph.* 1–9).[98]

The *Dialogue* asserts Justin's universal appeal, while it ties Jews intimately to Jerusalem and its environs. Jerusalem is not just another city, but it is the quintessential city over time, "God's holy mountain" of Zion, where Jesus Christ will appear again and will reign for a thousand years (80–81, 85). Justin also depicts Jerusalem as the city from which persecution of Christians has recently emerged: "Having selected certain men from Jerusalem, you then sent them into all the earth to say that an atheistic heresy of Christians has appeared" (17.1). Thus, he implies, Jerusalem is also now a site of violent destruction. Justin adopts scriptures about the Babylonian destruction of Jerusalem in order to talk about the city's destruction by the Romans, except that he attributes this destruction to God, not human empire. I quote the famous passage about circumcision marking Jews for abuse, which uses the spatial language of boundaries or demarcation: "The circumcision from Abraham, according to the flesh, was given for a sign, so that you should be marked off (ἀφωρισμένοι) from other nations and from us, and so that you alone might suffer now the things which you justly suffer, and so that your lands might become deserts . . . and no one of you should go up into Jerusalem" (16.2).[99] Roman imperial involvement in this violence is not recognized; the word "Rome" does not even appear in the *Dialogue*.

The *Dialogue* maps a world where violence is located on the edge, in a region that was once center: the ruined Jerusalem and weakened Syria Palestine. Eusebius historicizes the dialogue, placing it in Ephesus, but I think that Justin is deliberately vague in locating his interaction with Trypho. The *Dialogue* offers a generic stage set for acting out Greek traditions of philosophy: a covered colonnade (1.1), and later, some stone benches (9.3); so too Justin wears a philosophical costume. Throughout his corpus, Justin alludes to Plato

[98] See Nasrallah, "The Rhetoric of Conversion." Attempts to find a concrete historical and geographical setting for this event of "conversion" (e.g., Oskar Skarsaune, *The Proof from Prophecy: A Study in Justin Martyr's Proof-Text Tradition: Text-Type, Provenance, Theological Profile* [Leiden: E. J. Brill, 1987] 245–46) miss the fact that the image of the philosophical seeker is a *topos* of antiquity. Note Rajak's astute observation that "the narrative has to be set up in such a way as to pull the participants into the ambit of philosophy. The Jew is attracted by Justin's garb, and thus Trypho is temporarily constructed as 'one of us'" ("Talking at Trypho," 64).

[99] Part of this passage is a quotation from Is. 1:7. See also *Dial Tryph.* 25–26, 40, 108. See, however, Graham N. Stanton on the "moderate tone of the *Dialogue* as a whole" ("Other Early Christian Writings: 'Didache,' Ignatius, 'Barnabas,' Justin Martyr," in John Barclay and John Sweet, eds., *Early Christian Thought in its Jewish Context* [Cambridge: Cambridge University Press, 1996] 188); Demetrios Trakatellis, "Justin Martyr's Trypho," *HTR* 79 (1986) 297.

and appeals to the story of Socrates' life and death in order to muse on the persecution of Christians and his own role as a philosopher. While Justin's *Apologies* constructed a map focused on Rome, the *Dialogue* asserts no place. Jerusalem burns on its margins, but a philosopher like Justin cannot be tied down to one place.

II. THE SEBASTEION IN APHRODISIAS

At the beginning of this chapter, we learned that the second century was a particularly rich time in "geographical thinking." Such thinking of course predates Justin, Lucian, and Tatian. We find particularly powerful evidence of it at the time of the shift from Roman Republic to the Roman Empire. At this time, in the center of Rome itself were posted maps, such as that of Agrippa in the Porticus Vipsania, which publicly displayed the *oikoumenē* and the regions that Rome had conquered (Pliny *Nat. hist.* 3.2.17).[100] The inscription of Augustus's *Res gestae* is said to have been displayed nearby in Rome on two bronze tablets at Augustus's mausoleum; since it is known through Greek and Latin inscriptions found in Asia Minor, we can say it had "international" publication. This text about Augustus's *pietas* and productive deeds is defined in terms of geography: It is "a copy of the acts of the deified Augustus by which he placed the whole world under the sovereignty of the Roman people (*orbem terrarum imperio populi Rom*[*ani*] *subiecit*)" (1).[101] The text is literarily structured in terms of geography, moving from Augustus's deeds and benefactions in Rome outwards to describe his impact upon the world. At least fifty-five locations are listed, framed within a rhetoric of expansion, peace, and salvation:[102] "Wars, both civil and foreign, I undertook throughout the world, on sea and land, and when victorious I spared all citizens who sued for pardon. The foreign nations (τὰ ἔθνη/*externas gentes*) which could with safety be pardoned I preferred to save rather than to destroy."[103]

Nearby, within the Portico of the Nations, were *simulacra omnium gentium* ("images of all the peoples"), according to Servius.[104] From Tacitus and Cassius

[100] Although this map does not survive, it is described in two sources and perhaps depicted in a third, the Hereford world map in which Caesar (or Augustus) is "shown enthroned, decreeing the survey of the world" (James M. Scott, "Luke's Geographical Horizon," in David W. J. Gill and Conrad Gempf, eds., *The Book of Acts in Its First Century Setting*, vol. 2: *The Book of Acts in Its Graeco-Roman Setting* [Grand Rapids, MI: Eerdmans, 1994] 488).

[101] For the Greek and Latin see *Res Gestae divi Augusti* in *Velleius Paterculus Compendium of Roman History; Res Gestae divi Augusti* (LCL; trans. Fredrick Shipley; New York: G. P. Putnam's Sons, 1924).

[102] Scott, "Luke's Geographical Horizon," 489–91.

[103] *Res gest.* 3; ET Shipley, 348. For a discussion of representations of conquered *ethnē* in the Roman Empire, see Ando, *Imperial Ideology*, 296–320.

[104] R. R. R. Smith, "*Simulacra Gentium*: The *Ethne* from the Sebasteion at Aphrodisias," *JRS* 78 (1988) 72; see Servius *Ad Aen.* 8.271.

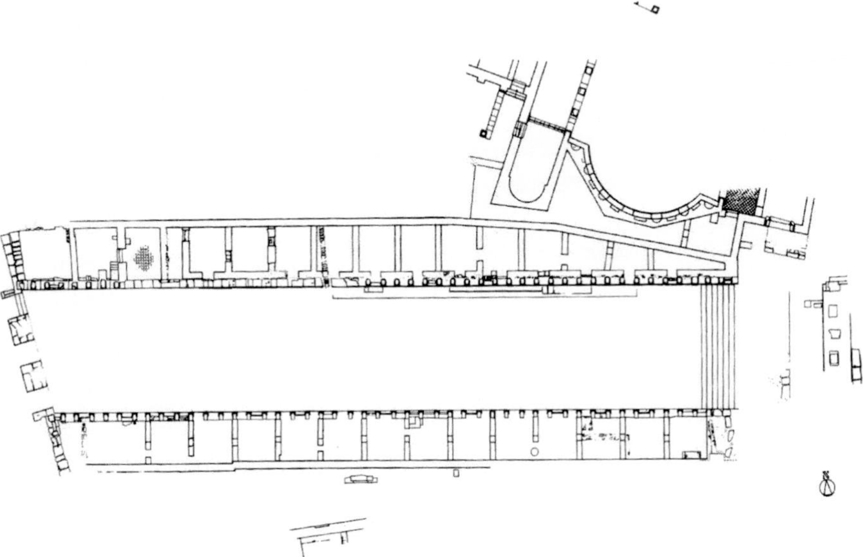

7. Plan of Sebasteion, Aphrodisias. By permission of R. R. R. Smith ("The Imperial Reliefs from the Sebasteion at Aphrodisias").

Dio we learn of a group of bronze statues of *ethnē* ("nations"), attired in native dress, carried in Augustus's funeral.[105] We know of triumphal processions of prisoners of war – subject peoples, now slaves to Rome and its empire – paraded publicly, bound, through the streets.[106] In this case, bronze images clustered behind Augustus's corpse as it moved in funeral procession. These were not bound and captured, but the miniaturization and idealization and sort of synecdoche of subject peoples. All the nations, free yet not free, followed the father of the empire.

Such depictions of Roman power over the nations were not limited to Rome or to Italy or even to propaganda paid for by the Roman emperors. Nor were they limited to expressing geography through maps or descriptions in words. We find geographical thinking visually expressed in the second century in monuments such as the Parthian Monument in Ephesus or the Temple of Hadrian in Rome, where provinces and nations are represented as personifications. The best preserved example of such visual geographies, however, is a monument from the Julio-Claudian period.

The Sebasteion at Aphrodisias (Fig. 7) in present-day Turkey now stands largely in ruins, although reconstruction of parts of the monument has begun. Entering through a *propylon* or gate, one's eyes would be drawn through the narrow processional space (14 m by 90 m) to the temple at the end

[105] While Tacitus only mentions titles of nations, Cassius Dio supplies "there followed all the subject *ethnē* attired in native dress, represented by bronze *eikones* [images]" (56.34.3); see also Tacitus *Ann.* 1.8.4, discussed in Smith, "*Simulacra Gentium*," 74.

[106] Mary Beard, *The Roman Triumph* (Cambridge, MA: Belknap, 2007).

8. Sketch of Sebasteion, Aphrodisias. By permission of R. R. R. Smith ("The Imperial Reliefs from the Sebasteion at Aphrodisias").

(Fig. 8).[107] Two long *stoai* or colonnaded halls towered over the viewer on both sides, lending an almost "interior" feeling to the space, a uniquely Roman configuration of space and of temple placement, reminiscent of some imperial *fora* in Rome.[108] On one's right, the second storey of the south portico depicted in sculptured relief gods and emperors; on its first storey one would see scenes from Greek mythology. To the left, the north portico depicted allegories (and perhaps emperors) on the second storey, and the series of *ethnē* on the first storey.[109] These two porticoes pointed toward the end of the sanctuary, a temple dedicated to Aphrodite (the goddess of both the city and the Julio-Claudian family), the *theoi sebastoi* (the "divine emperors," in this case, the Julio-Claudian imperial family), and the *dēmos* or people of Aphrodisias. Two wealthy local families paid for the complex.[110]

[107] Smith, "*Simulacra Gentium*," 50.

[108] See R. R. R. Smith, "The Imperial Reliefs of the Sebasteion at Aphrodisias," *JRS* 77 (1987) 93–94 on this space functioning as a "funnel," unlike Greek sanctuaries where the *naos* or temple is usually in center of complex.

[109] Smith, "*Simulacra Gentium*," 51, passim.

[110] Smith, "The Imperial Reliefs," 88. Inscriptions indicate that the complex was probably begun under Tiberius and finished under Nero (Smith, "*Simulacra Gentium*," 51). One family paid for the propylon and north portico, the other for the south portico and temple. The northern portico and propylon are dedicated to "Aphrodite, the Theoi Sebastoi, and the Demos." The southern portico is dedicated to "Aphrodite, an uncertain divinized emperor or empress (Livia?), Claudius, and the Demos." The dedication of the temple itself is uncertain; the inscription as it stands only mentions Aphrodite, the Theoi Sebastoi, and the Demos" (Smith, "Imperial Reliefs," 90). To understand better provincial elites making such donations that linked them to Rome, see S. R. F. Price, *Rituals and Power: The Roman Imperial Cult in Asia Minor* (Cambridge: Cambridge University Press, 1984); and Ando, *Imperial Ideology*, esp. chap. 8.

9. Augustus by land and sea. Relief from the Sebasteion, Aphrodisias. New York University Excavations at Aphrodisias.

From the north portico only two allegories survive, *Hēmera* and *Okeanos*, Day and Ocean. These imply a larger series which would have included at least Earth (to match Ocean) and Evening or Night (to match Day). These allegorical depictions were a way of marking the boundaries of the Roman world. The winds of empire blow from Rome to Aphrodisias, off Okeanos that bounds the known world, from the edge of earth where Day begins to the boundary lands where it sets.[111] Across from such images, the now-ruined south portico held a relief of a naked Augustus striding forward (Fig. 9). On the left is a figure of earth, offering a cornucopia. On the right is a sea figure with a ship's rudder.[112] Backed by the blowing veil, energetically moving from

[111] Smith, "*Simulacra Gentium*," 77.

[112] "He receives a cornucopia from an earth figure to the left and a ship's steering oar from a sea figure on the right." Smith, "Imperial Reliefs," 104.

land to sea, Augustus is offered the riches of the cornucopia and the right to safe forward travel (with the oar proffered by the fish-legged sea). In return he "guarantees the produce of the land (cornucopia) and the navigability of the sea (rudder)."[113] As Smith states, "Combined, the allegories and the *ethne* stated that the Roman empire extends from furthest west to furthest east, from the rising to the setting sun, from Day to Night, bounded only by Ocean."[114]

Also on the north portico were depictions of various *ethnē*, the nations of the Roman Empire. "The surviving *ethnos* reliefs show single, standing, draped women, all well differentiated by costume, attributes, and posture," Smith writes.[115] To depict the provinces as female is typical, based upon both grammar and convention. But it is not neutral: as women were considered passive land to be used (fields to be plowed, in the metaphor of sex for reproduction), so also the provinces. Some *ethnē* (which included Judea) were likely bound; at least one that remains has her hands tied together.[116] The statuary nations at Aphrodisias celebrate empire's reach and allow one to grasp visually the broad geographical victories of the Roman Empire.[117] As Smith puts it: "The members so far could be understood as including a range of different parts of the Augustan empire, thus: some from the civilized centre (the Greek islands, Egypt), some from beyond the frontier illustrating the effective reach of imperial power (Dacians, Bosporans, Arabs), and many or most from the periphery, defining the Romanized side of the frontier (the northern and western *ethne*). This is something similar to the categories of the *Res Gestae*, chs. 26–33: some 'recovered,' some defeated, some 'pacified' (= Romanized)."[118] The effect of this iconography, even in a metropolitan center far from Rome, is to bedazzle by a profusion of obscure names and peoples, about whom the people of Aphrodisias likely had never heard; it is also to "sum up the victories and frontier advances of a whole reign," but by depicting a "peaceful incorporation."[119]

Yet this "peaceful incorporation" is belied by the panels in the upper storey of the south portico, which depict scenes of imperial victory and of gods and emperors (and, as we shall continue to see throughout this book, the difference between human and divine is often blurred at this time).[120] In these, various

[113] Ibid., 106.

[114] Smith, "*Simulacra Gentium*," 77.

[115] Smith, "Imperial Reliefs," 96; Smith notes possible parallels: Pompey's theater (with its 14 *nationes*); the Porticus ad Nationes; Augustus's funeral (i.e., its bronze statues); the forum of Augustus, which had *tituli* of conquered peoples; the altar of Augustus at Lugdunum, which was decorated with sixty *ethnē*.

[116] Smith, "*Simulacra Gentium*," 60.

[117] Ibid., 70, 75.

[118] Ibid., 59.

[119] Ibid., 71; "it seems clear that in the Sebasteion the selection of outlandish peoples was meant to stand as a visual account of the extent of the Augustan empire, and by the sheer numbers and impressive unfamiliarity of the names, to suggest that it is coterminous with the ends of the earth" (p. 77).

[120] Smith, "Imperial Reliefs," 97.

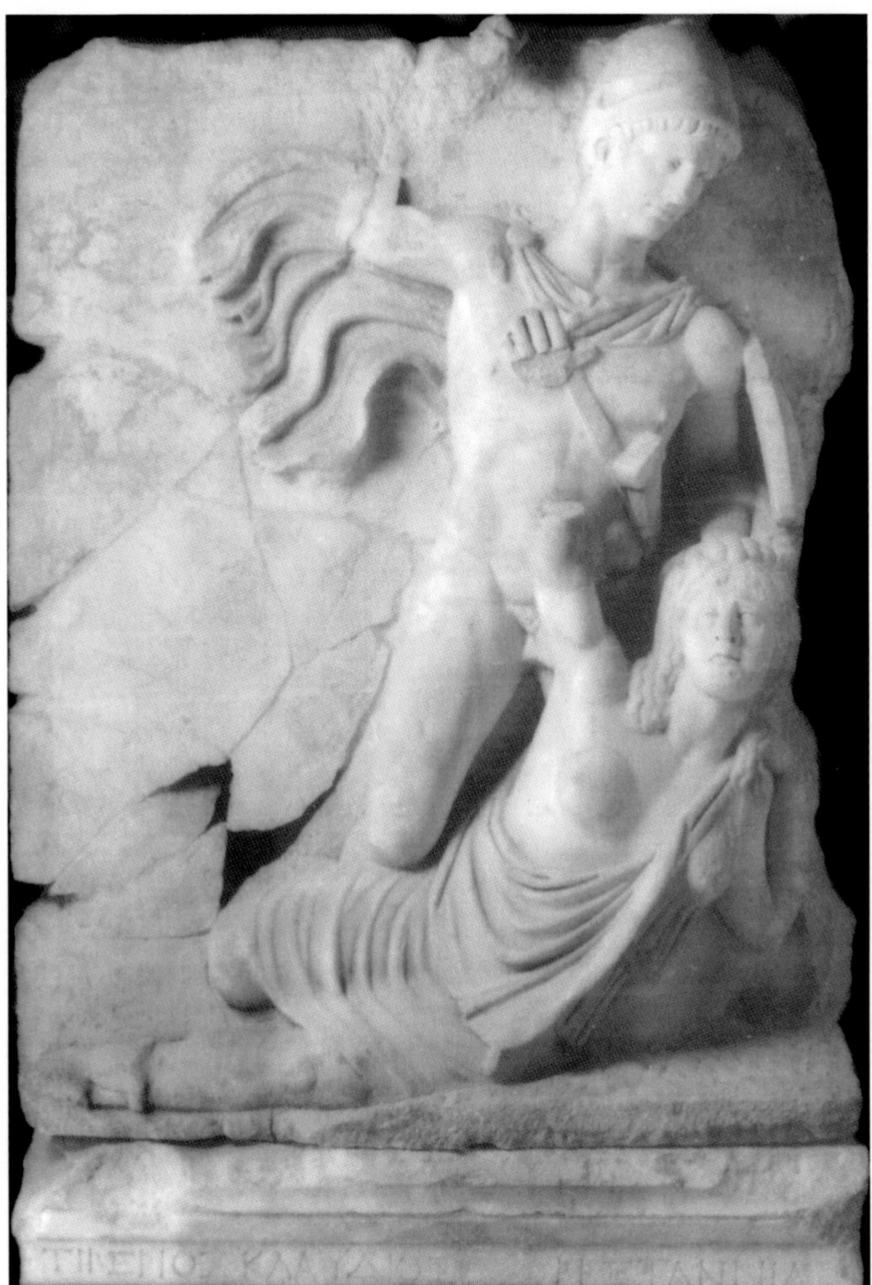

10. Claudius subduing Britannia. Relief from the Sebasteion, Aphrodisias. New York University Excavations at Aphrodisias.

ethnē are depicted as women violently subjugated, as in a scene of Claudius subjugating Britannia (Fig. 10) or Nero subjugating Armenia.[121] Whether in the Augustan period or the Hadrianic, Smith argues, similar iconography was used: Monuments from both periods "reflect a continuing ambivalence in

[121] Ibid.

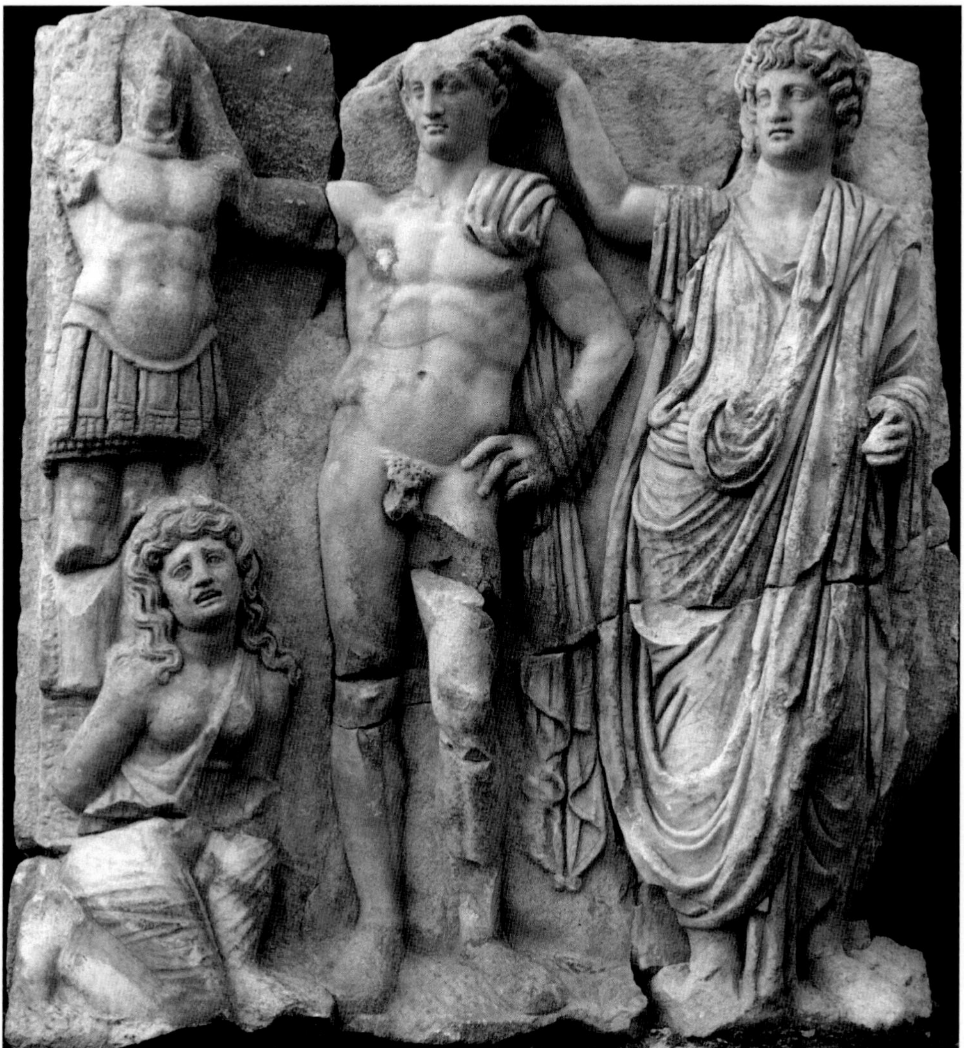

11. Imperator with Roman people or Senate. Relief from the Sebasteion at Aphrodisias. New York University Excavations at Aphrodisias.

Roman thinking about the nature of their empire. Was it a series of conquests or a family of equal partners? Both, they liked to think."[122] These scenes – allegories, triumphs, *ethnē* – can also be read as pedagogical. The figures of the *ethnē* are inscribed with names to teach about Rome's far-flung powers; and the concatenation of allegories of Day and Ocean, personifications of the provinces, mythological scenes, and imperial conquering offer a message that geographical control is justified and sacralized, even if it is sometimes (proudly) depicted as violently gained. This is true not only because the architectural complex of the Sebasteion finds its *telos* in a temple, but also on a relief (Fig. 11)

[122] Smith, "*Simulacra Gentium*," 77.

in which the emperor stands casually over a female captive, her face twisted in pathos, who kneels in front of the trophy which marks her ineffective attempts at self-defense. The Roman people or Senate, personified and standing alongside the emperor, sanction or crown this effort.[123]

The colonnades of the Sebasteion at Aphrodisias form an embrace propelling the viewer forward toward the *theoi sebastoi*, the venerable gods who are the pious emperors. That this architectural plan gathers the nations and encourages the Aphrodisian viewers onward to their own goddess Aphrodite, distant relative of the emperors, and to the emperors *as* gods is not accidental.[124] The two *stoai* antiphonally proclaim the extent of the inhabited world and the Julio-Claudian family's control over it.

CONCLUSIONS

What did the spaces of this world look like? The Sebasteion at Aphrodisias engages geographical thinking and helps to make sense of second-century provincial traveling men's rhetoric of the vulnerability – the feminization – of their bodies within the inhabited world. Even more, it highlights the vulnerability of female and enslaved bodies, and how the use and abuse of those bodies was sanctioned by extant systems of domination and their claims to piety.

Justin, Tatian, and Lucian are Vitruvian men in two senses. They remind us of Vitruvius's shipwrecked traveler, at home everywhere in the world with only *paideia* in hand. They rhetorically construct themselves as wandering truth-seekers from the empire's eastern ranges, struggling with their quests for truth in their common cultural context, and questioning the value of Greek *paideia* even as they have mastered it. Yet they are also Vitruvian men in that their bodies, which contain the perfect symmetry of their mastery of Greek *paideia*, become the measure by which they map the world. Because of their proximity to or embracing of barbarian identity, they are vulnerable in the Roman world: In the city of Rome, Justin and Lucian especially are vulnerable to real violence and to violence done to certain kinds of knowledge, and Tatian depicts Greeks as vulnerable to the city of Rome's appropriation of their cultural patrimony. As we learned in the previous chapter, scholars have generally understood apologetic as a Christian (or perhaps Jewish and Christian) phenomenon that offers some resistance either to Hellenism or to the Roman Empire or to both. This chapter has instead used a framework

[123] Smith, "Imperial Reliefs," 113ff. See also relief of an empress, perhaps Livia, sacrificing (plate XXII).

[124] Smith, "*Simulacra Gentium*," 77 reads this viewer as acquiescing: "The new *ethne* reliefs illustrate the Aphrodisians' identification with Roman world rule and their determination to leave no iconographic means untried to represent it."

of geographical thinking to place Justin's and Tatian's references to travel and cities within the broader cultural context of the so-called Second Sophistic, rather than marginalizing them as Christian apologists. I am trying to shift the scholarly map: Justin and Tatian should not be sequestered into the questionable category of Christian apologetic, but instead should be read as engaged in broader cultural conversations, in which Lucian represents one satirical and strong voice. These writings take part in a struggle within (and against) the Roman Empire, whose conquests occurred not only through military means, but also through an uneven policy of tolerance that rewarded and at times demanded assimilation. We have also seen that Justin, Tatian, and Lucian teach us about one use of the sign "barbarian" under this Roman Empire: the person who has mastered Greekness and yet is ambivalent about that mastery.

The model of center and periphery which is often used to talk about the Roman Empire is inadequate for interpreting Lucian, Justin, and Tatian, whose writings show the ambiguous and complicated ways in which cities like Rome, Athens, and the barbarian homeland are mapped. Key to their rhetorical constructions of important cities – Jerusalem, Rome, Athens, Hierapolis – is the issue of the dangers of travel, both to body and mind. But these writers do not so much fear *topomachia* in the blank spaces of the map as they question what cities or regions of the inhabited world are (falsely) named as centers of knowledge. In the works of Justin, Tatian, and Lucian, the usual valuation of Greek *paideia* under the high Roman Empire is challenged. Rome is portrayed as complicit in a sometimes violent consumption of purchased *paideia* and of enslaved goods – both statuary bodies and real, live philosophers' bodies. According to all three, out of (As)syria, coded as barbarian, may come a purer, simpler knowledge. In the chapters that follow, we turn to Athens and then to Rome to see what claims to *paideia* and piety lie there.

PART TWO

INTO THE CITIES

CHAPTER THREE

WHAT INFORMS THE GEOGRAPHICAL IMAGINATION? THE ACTS OF THE APOSTLES AND GREEK CITIES UNDER ROME

"THIS WAS NOT DONE IN A CORNER," ASSERTS PAUL IN THE ACTS OF THE Apostles, speaking about the ideas and origins of his movement (Acts 26:26).[1] In this brief sentence Luke's geographical imagination spills from Paul's mouth. Paul has just explained his own travel from Damascus to Jerusalem and throughout Judea and to the Gentiles, echoing Luke's understanding that "the Way" moves through the entire *oikoumenē* or inhabited world, eclipsing Jerusalem. And as he utters these words, Paul himself stands on the cusp of his final journey; after this he will be sent from Caesarea (where he had arrived from his Jerusalem imprisonment) to Rome. "This was not done in a corner." Luke's economical assertion, placed in Paul's mouth, leads us to wonder: In the midst of Roman power and claims to possess the *oikoumenē* – claims manifest literarily and in the built environment – how did some early Christian communities imagine the space of the world? As we asked in the last chapter: What kind of geographical thinking did they engage?

Scholars have long noted that there is something peculiarly geographical about Luke-Acts. Luke refers to Christianity as "the Way" (ἡ ὁδός), and the canonical Acts' story of Christianity is restless and urban.[2] Judea and Jerusalem

[1] All New Testament translations are RSV, unless otherwise noted; sometimes I have modified them slightly. The Greek is from the twenty-sixth edition of Nestle-Aland's *Novum Testamentum Graece*.

[2] Loveday Alexander, "Mapping Early Christianity: Acts and the Shape of Early Church History," *Interpretation* 57.2 (2003) 163–75, and her "'In Journeyings Often': Voyaging in the Acts

were eclipsed in Justin's *Dialogue with Trypho*; in Acts, Christianity is propelled from the margins of empire and the center of Judaism, Jerusalem, to the center of the empire, Rome.[3] The characters in Acts constantly make their way between cities, moving throughout the *oikoumenē* and producing a kind of Christian empire parallel to Roman rule.

This chapter argues that Paul's travels to Greek cities in the latter half of Acts, and the geography of Acts more generally, are best understood in light of contemporaneous political and cultural discourses about Greek cities under Rome. Moreover, through its account of Paul's deeds and speeches in key sites like Lystra, Thessalonikē, Philippi, and Athens, Acts articulates a theological vision of how Christianity and its notion of one, true God, can fit within a "pluralistic" empire and its notions of ethnic difference. To use the terminology of postcolonial criticism, Acts mimics the logic of empire without shading into mockery; it seeks to find a place for "the Way" within a system of Roman domination.[4] It does so with a Greek twist of the sort that the Roman Empire fostered and even invented. In the midst of the so-called Second Sophistic, the movement that cherished all things classically Greek, the philhellenic emperor Hadrian founded the Panhellenion, centered in Athens, a coalition that fostered diplomacy among putatively Greek city-states. The Panhellenion encouraged various cities' inventions of genealogies and myths that established their cities as solidly Greek in race as well as unified in piety, cult, and political outlook under Athens *and* Rome. In Acts, Paul's travels, especially to cities in the Greek East, resonate with the logic and functions associated with the creation and promotion of city leagues.[5] The author of Luke-Acts, likely writing in a city of the Greek East such as Antioch or Ephesus, configures a Christianity that fits within the superior aspects of Greek culture and cities under the Roman Empire.

of the Apostles and in Greek Romance," in C. M. Tuckett, ed., *Luke's Literary Achievement* (Sheffield: Sheffield Academic Press, 1995) 17–49. See also James M. Scott, "Luke's Geographical Horizon," in David W. J. Gill and Conrad Gempf, eds., *The Book of Acts in Its First Century Setting*, vol. 2: *The Book of Acts in Its Graeco-Roman Setting* (Grand Rapids, MI: Eerdmans, 1994) 483–544. Hans Conzelmann brings together the topic of geography with Luke-Acts in *The Theology of St. Luke* (1961; trans. Geoffrey Buswell; Philadelphia: Fortress, 1982).

3 Conzelmann, *The Theology of St. Luke*; see also Alexander, "Mapping Early Christianity," 166. This reading of Acts is true even if Luke and Acts were early transmitted separately (see Andrew Gregory, *The Reception of Luke and Acts in the Period before Irenaeus* [WUNT 2.169; Tübingen: Mohr Siebeck, 2003] 353), since Acts too moves from Jerusalem to Rome. On the eclipsing of Jerusalem see Richard I. Pervo, "My Happy Home: The Role of Jerusalem in Acts 1–7," *Forum* n.s. 3.1 (2000) 31–55, esp. 38.

4 Homi Bhabha, *The Location of Culture* (New York: Routledge, 1994), esp. 86–101. For a postcolonial analysis of Luke-Acts, see Virginia Burrus, "The Gospel of Luke and the Acts of the Apostles," in R. S. Sugirtharajah, ed., *A Postcolonial Commentary on the New Testament Writings* (New York: T & T Clark, 2007) 133–55. On reading Luke-Acts' theology within the socio-politics of the Roman Empire, see Philip Esler, *Community and Gospel in Luke-Acts: The Social and Political Motivations of Lucan Theology* (Cambridge: Cambridge University Press, 1987) esp. 1–2.

5 Other resonances include diaspora and the ingathering of God's people in second Isaiah: David Pao, *Acts and the Isaianic New Exodus* (WUNT 2.130; Tübingen: Mohr Siebeck, 2000).

The discourse of Greek cities under Rome in which Hadrian's Panhellenion partakes intertwines with Acts – especially Acts' depiction of Paul – in four principle ways. First, Hadrian like other emperors traveled the Mediterranean basin, making benefactions and binding cities more closely into the Roman Empire, sometimes by encouraging them to create links of *homonoia* ("harmony" or "concord") with each other. Moreover, embassies moved between key cities in the second century, whether the ambassadors were orators or officers of the Panhellenion. So also the cities that Paul traveled in the canonical Acts can be seen as a kind of Christian civic league, produced by Paul's gospel and his ambassadorial role.

Second, like Hadrian and, as we shall see, Aelius Aristides, Acts deployed commonly available discourses about civic identity, ethnicity, kinship, and correct religion. This second-century conversation relied on a long history of the use of rhetoric of ethnicity, myths of origins, concerns about civic leagues and *homonoia*. This is a form of "ethnic reasoning," Denise Buell's term for the deploying of arguments about fixed and fluid identity in the service of constructing peoplehood.[6] With its idea of being part of "God's race" or offspring (Acts 17:28–29) and with its development of a Christian geographical imagination that embraces the entire *oikoumenē*, Acts engages such ways of thinking.

Third, Greek cities under Rome in the first and second centuries often served as "memory theatres."[7] We have already seen this phenomenon in second-century Olympia; there, as elsewhere, Greek cityscapes changed under Rome, but cities were not usually razed or completely transformed. Rather, the recent stood next to the ancient, giving the appearance of mutually affirming religious values, ethnic identity, and certain ideas of aesthetics and *paideia*. So also Luke-Acts produces a Christian memory theater by juxtaposing materials ancient (such as the Septuagint) and recent, locations exotic (Malta and Lystra) and central (Athens, with all of its culture).

Finally, the cities to which Paul travels in Acts produce a Christian parallel to the cities that comprised the Panhellenion. Luke's depiction of Paul's travels emerges from this discursive setting and similarly constructs in narrative a kind of pan-Christian alliance, tying cities to one of Acts' key founders of

6 Acts does not describe Christians as a new or third "race" or people (*genos*, *ethnos*, or *laos*), language found elsewhere in the second century, the implications of which Denise Kimber Buell skillfully treats in *Why This New Race? Ethnic Reasoning in Early Christianity* (New York: Columbia University Press, 2005) esp. 2–4. Nonetheless, these texts highlight "the rhetorical situations in which early Christian texts use ideas about peoplehood to communicate and persuade readers about Christianness" (p. 2). By crafting Christian communities as a league of cities unified by common (divine) origins, kinship, and worship, Acts offers an example of Christian ethnic reasoning.

7 See, e.g., Susan Alcock, *Archaeologies of the Greek Past: Landscape, Monuments, and Memories* (Cambridge: Cambridge University Press, 2002) 54 n. 29.

Christianity. Just as the Panhellenion links together cities that recall or create archaic Greek origins, so Luke uses the story of Paul travelling between cities in order to provide a foundation myth for Christianity.

Exploring Lukan depictions of Paul's city travels underscores an influential early Christian "political theology," to borrow Allen Brent's term.[8] Acts, embedded within a world negotiating relations between Greeks, Romans, and "barbarians," creates a story of the origins of a Christian city league that might be comprehensible and attractive to Rome, and in its logic offers seeds for a Christian empire that resembles the Roman Empire.[9]

I. PLACING ACTS

Acts presents a Christian geography that conforms to the geographical thinking of the Roman Empire, but it does so via the prestige of Greek *paideia* and of second-century Greek city leagues. We learned in the last chapter that many writers in the first and second centuries bolstered their discussions of similar topics with sophisticated vocabulary, good atticizing writing, and allusions to Greek classical writers and ancient myths. They frequently offered eye-witness travel accounts, as we saw in Tatian's *To the Greeks*, in order to authenticate their insights into *paideia*, empire, civic and ethnic identity, and correct religiosity.[10] Visual manifestations of such discussions of space and ethnicity are evidenced in the Aphrodisias's Sebasteion or the "publication" of the *Res gestae*, as we have seen. Luke-Acts is not the only evidence of a text concerned with geography, the spaces of empire, the status of cities and nations under Rome, and the role of Greek language and culture under Rome. To understand Luke's approach to space and politics, we must place Luke-Acts in the context of the so-called Second Sophistic, the archaizing movement, often Roman-sponsored, that celebrated Greekness.[11] To exaggerate: First- and second-century Rome

8 Allen Brent, *The Imperial Cult and the Development of Church Order* (Leiden: E. J. Brill, 1999) 76.

9 Of course, at the time of the writing of Luke-Acts, Christianity had negligible political and cultural powers compared with the Roman Empire. On Roman universalism, see, e.g., François Bovon, "Israel, the Church and the Gentiles in the Twofold Work of Luke," in his *New Testament Traditions and Apocryphal Narratives* (trans. Jane Haapiseva-Hunter; Allison Park, PA: Pickwick, 1995) 82–87. He concludes: "Lucan universalism was neither accommodation to Rome nor a polemic against Rome. But it could become either of these" (p. 87).

10 Loveday Alexander explores Luke's use of the unusual word *autopsis*, which is often used for "medical and geographical" information (*The Preface to Luke's Gospel: Literary Convention and Social Context in Luke 1.1–4 and Acts 1.1* [Cambridge: Cambridge University Press, 1993] 34–39).

11 On the Panhellenion and the Second Sophistic, see Ilaria Romeo, "The Panhellenion and Ethnic Identity in Hadrianic Greece," *Classical Philology* 97.1 (2002) 21–40. Regarding second-century Christian apologists and the Second Sophistic, see Rebecca Lyman, "Hellenism and Heresy: 2002 NAPS Presidential Address," *JECS* 11.2 (2003) 209–22, esp. 212–16; see also Tim Whitmarsh, *Greek Literature and the Roman Empire: The Politics*

produced Greek identity – at least certain strands of it. It was in this environment that Luke strove to represent a new Christian "Way" that is similar to Roman-period Greek city alliances.

Acts has long been labeled a "history," as by Henry J. Cadbury in the early twentieth century and Martin Dibelius in the mid-twentieth century.[12] The stakes of this classification are high. Even if scholars who argue that Luke was a historian recognize the extent to which ancient history involved the fabrication of speeches, the classification of "history" can bring hopes for an objective, true account.[13] Others, recognizing Luke-Acts' theological and perhaps even political stakes, have returned to the tradition from 1721 onward of labeling Luke-Acts as "apologetic" literature.[14] Thus, Luke-Acts is often understood as an appeal to Roman authorities for tolerance, or even, as Marianne Bonz argues, as an imitation of Roman epic, offering a foundational story for the early Christian church along the lines of Virgil's *Aeneid*.[15]

The genre of Luke-Acts is controversial; scholars' conclusions are informed by their views on Lukan theology in relation to the Roman Empire, on the one hand, and Judaism, on the other. What is important is that Luke-Acts is a second-century document[16] that strives toward a literary Greek, shows

of Imitation (Oxford: Oxford University Press, 2001) esp. chap. 2; and Glenn Bowersock, *Greek Sophists in the Roman Empire* (Oxford: Clarendon, 1969).

12 Henry J. Cadbury, *The Making of Luke-Acts* (2nd ed.; London: S.P.C.K., 1958) 132–39; Martin Dibelius, *The Book of Acts: Form, Style, and Theology* (ed. K. C. Hanson; Minneapolis, MN: Fortress, 2004) 1–86, who says, "It is distinguished from the New Testament and many other early Christian writings by its literary character, and from the work of the historians by what we may call a theological purpose" (p. 3). Marianne Palmer Bonz discusses both in *The Past as Legacy: Luke-Acts and Ancient Epic* (Minneapolis, MN: Fortress, 2000) 1–5. Most scholars read the preface and Luke-Acts as something like history. See, e.g., David Balch, who disagrees with Alexander: "ΜΕΤΑΒΟΛΗ ΠΟΛΙΤΕΙΩΝ: Jesus as Founder of the Church in Luke-Acts: Form and Function," in Todd Penner and Caroline Vander Stichele, eds., *Contextualizing Acts: Lukan Narrative and Greco-Roman Discourse* (Atlanta: SBL, 2003) 140–42; see also Todd Penner, *In Praise of Christian Origins: Stephen and the Hellenists in Lukan Apologetic Historiography* (New York: T&T Clark, 2004) esp. 260–61, for whom Acts adheres to the model of (Jewish apologetic) historiography.

13 See, e.g., Bonz's assessment of Cadbury in *The Past as Legacy*, 2.

14 See Esler's survey of scholarship from 1720 on (*Community and Gospel*, 205–7). Henry Cadbury dates the origins of the identification of Luke as apologetic to C. A. Heumann's 1721 *Bibliotheca Bremensis*; Cadbury himself argued that "Luke's expressed purpose is ἀπολογία" and that Theophilus was likely an official who did not sympathize with Christianity, but whom Luke sought to convince ("The Purpose Expressed in Luke's Preface," *The Expositor* 21 [1921] 437). More recently, see Gregory Sterling (*Historiography and Self-Definition: Josephos, Luke-Acts, and Apologetic Historiography* [Leiden: E. J. Brill, 1992] 393). Penner employs the term "apologetic historiography" in *In Praise of Christian Origins*. Esler (*Community and Gospel*, 16) dubs Luke-Acts a literature of "legitimization" rather than "apologetic."

15 Bonz, *The Past as Legacy*. I do not treat the entire debate over Luke-Acts's genre, such as its relation to the Greek novel. See Richard I. Pervo, *Profit with Delight: The Literary Genre of the Acts of the Apostles* (Philadelphia: Fortress, 1987) and his *Acts: A Commentary* (Hermeneia; Minneapolis, MN: Fortress, 2008) 14–18.

16 The dating of Luke-Acts is debated. Luke and Acts are not well attested until Irenaeus and the Muratorian Canon (François Bovon, "The Reception and Use of the Gospel of Luke in the

knowledge of Greek historiographical practices, and may even hint at larger aims for Christianity. The topics Luke-Acts wrestles with and Christianizes indicate a deep involvement in cultural crises of the time.[17] Moreover, since before the days of Ferdinand Christian Baur, it has been clear that the writer was a unifier, seeking to bring together what Baur, for example, considered to be the Petrine and Pauline sides of Christianity.[18] Luke-Acts crafts a universalizing narrative of Christian identity that would be attractive or at least comprehensible to philosophical and political minds of the time. Acts retrospectively portrays a community that shared its goods in a philosophical way and whose leaders, although *agrammatoi* ("uneducated"), offered lengthy and sophisticated speeches. Such speeches drew upon the exotic (to Roman eyes) past of the people of Israel, yet also spoke to the philosophical themes of the one God and true piety, key topics of the second century. History, novel, or epic are all insufficient labels for Acts. The attempt to fix its genre does not take into account the genre hybridity of this time period, and often misses the fact

Second Century," in Craig Bartholomew et al., eds., *Reading Luke: Interpretation, Reflection, Formation* [Grand Rapids, MI: Zondervan, 2005] 379–400; see also Hans Conzelmann, *Acts of the Apostles: A Commentary on the Acts of the Apostles* [Hermeneia. Philadelphia: Fortress, 1987] xxx–xxxii). Gregory is cautious to insist that this does not mean that Luke or Acts were not circulating previously (Gregory, *The Reception of Luke and Acts*, 4–5 n. 11; see his conclusion that we cannot know if Justin used Acts; pp. 317–21). There is no firm evidence for others' knowledge of Acts until ca. 185 CE. While our current data remains inconclusive, many recent scholars argue that Luke-Acts in its present form emerged in the second century to resist Marcion's appropriation of Luke and Paul. See John Knox, *Marcion and the New Testament: An Essay in the Early History of the Canon* (Chicago: University of Chicago Press, 1942) 114–39; Joseph B. Tyson, *Marcion and Luke-Acts: A Defining Struggle* (Columbia: University of South Carolina Press, 2006). J. C. O'Neill in the early 1960s placed Luke-Acts to approximately 115–130 CE (*The Theology of Acts in its Historical Setting* [London: S.P.C.K., 1961] 1–63), as have more recent scholars like Shelly Matthews (*Perfect Martyr: The Stoning of Stephen and the Making of Gentile Christianity in Acts* [Oxford: Oxford University Press, forthcoming]); Christopher Mount (*Pauline Christianity: Luke-Acts and the Legacy of Paul* [Leiden: E. J. Brill, 2002]), Richard I. Pervo (*Dating Acts: Between the Evangelists and the Apologists* [Santa Rosa, CA: Polebridge, 2006] 5).

17 Conzelmann, *Acts*, xxxv; Alexander, "In Journeyings Often," 38–39. See David Balch, "Comparing Literary Patterns in Luke and Lucian," *The Perkins School of Theology Journal* 40.2 (1987) 39–42; Burrus, "Luke-Acts," 144–47. Loveday Alexander challenges those who equate Luke with the famous writers of the so-called Second Sophistic. The Greek of Luke-Acts, while smoother than the *koinē* of other New Testament documents, does not attain to the prose of Dio of Prusa or Aelius Aristides. Alexander concludes that rather than Thucydidean-style historiography, the preface is the kind of preface that "scientific" or technical handbooks had (*The Preface to Luke's Gospel*, 102; for her critique of Luke's Greek, see chap. 8). See also Cadbury, *The Making of Luke-Acts*, 114, 213–38. But we do not need such a literarily sophisticated Luke-Acts to say that the text engages themes of the so-called Second Sophistic.

18 F. C. Baur, *Paul: The Apostle of Jesus Christ* (1873; 2 vols. in one; Peabody, MA: Hendrickson, 2003). See also Joseph B. Tyson, "From History to Rhetoric and Back: Assessing New Trends in Acts Studies," *Luke, Judaism, and the Scholars: Critical Approaches to Luke-Acts* (Columbia, SC: University of South Carolina Press, 1993) chap. 2, esp. p. 27, and his "The Legacy of F. C. Baur and Recent Studies of Acts," *Forum* n.s. 4.1 (2001) 125–44; and Penner, *In Praise of Christian Origins*, 8–14.

of Acts' participation in a larger second-century debate about the formation of ethnic and religious identity.

To understand more deeply issues regarding Greek ethnicity and Roman power in this period, it is helpful to turn to a famous, sophisticated, if perpetually ill, rhetor. Aelius Aristides' geographical rhetoric encompasses both Greek cities and the Roman Empire.[19] Aristides is from the Greek East, as Luke probably is; he is writing at the same time as Justin. Exploring his thought allows us to see an aspect of Roman "geographical thinking" which celebrates Greekness (as did Hadrian's policies) and illumines Luke's geographical imagination.

In his famous *Roman Oration*, perhaps given in the city in 155 CE,[20] Aelius Aristides celebrates Rome's geography. The empire surpasses all previous empires in size; it is not only extensive but also harmonious, perfect, unmarred by incursions from other lands; it is "the chorus of the civilized world."[21]

> When were there so many cities on continents or on the seas, or when have they been so thoroughly adorned? Who then ever made such a journey, numbering the cities by the days of his trip, or sometimes passing through two or three cities on the same day, as it were through avenues? Therefore those former men are not only greatly inferior in the total extent of their empires, but also where they ruled the same lands as you, each people did not enjoy equal and similar conditions under their rule, but to the tribe which then existed there can be counterpoised the city which now exists among them (ἀλλ' ἔνεστι τῷ τότε ἔθνει πόλιν ἀντιστῆσαι τὴν ἐν αὐτῷ νῦν). And one would say that those had been kings, as it were, of deserts and garrisons, but that you alone are rulers of cities. (*Roman Oration* 93)[22]

This brief exclamation makes remarkable claims: Under Roman rule there were more and better organized cities; the roads and seaways were like a grand, new, broad avenue allowing quick travel through cities; the Romans

[19] Greg Woolf's discussion applies to Greek cities as well: "Culture could thus offer Gauls a chance to enter the empire of friends. What of the empire of cities? That aspect of the empire can be thought of as a complex hierarchy of privileges and statuses, communal as well as individual. . . . The key question then is how far was cultural capital convertible into privileged places in that hierarchy?" (*Becoming Roman: The Origins of Provincial Civilization in Gaul* [New York: Cambridge University Press, 1998] 63–64).

[20] See P. Aelius Aristides, *The Complete Works* (trans. Charles Behr; 2 vols.; Leiden: E. J. Brill, 1981) 2.373–74 n. 1 for an introduction to the *Roman Oration*.

[21] Aelius Aristides *Roman Oration* 29–31 (quotation at 31); ET James H. Oliver, *The Ruling Power: A Study of the Roman Empire in the Second Century after Christ through the Roman Oration of Aelius Aristides* (1953; repr. Philadelphia: The American Philosophical Society, 1980) 898. Richard L. Rohrbaugh's "The Pre-industrial City in Luke-Acts: Urban Social Relations" unfortunately does not treat archaeological evidence regarding first-century cities (in Jerome H. Neyrey, ed., *The Social World of Luke-Acts: Models for Interpretation* [Peabody, MA: Hendrickson, 1991].

[22] ET modified from Behr, 2.94.

brought *isonomia* ("equal rights") to each city, allowed for each *ethnos* to express itself with true civic status, and disregarded the preferential treatment offered by previous empires.

According to Aristides, Rome is not only superior with regard to geography and justice; it is also the meta-city to which the entire *oikoumenē* or inhabited world is a suburb.[23] In this role Rome supervenes traditional ethnic, geographical, and linguistic boundaries: "You sought its [citizenship's] expansion as a worthy aim, and you have caused the word Roman to be the label, not of membership in a city, but of some common nationality . . . for the categories into which you now divide the world are not Hellenes and Barbarians. . . . The division which you substituted is one into Romans and non-Romans. To such a degree have you expanded the name of your city" (*Roman Oration* 63).[24] In a speech directed to Romans, Aristides shifts the ethnic and geographical map from Greek/barbarian to Roman/non-Roman.[25] Rome is a postmetropolis, collecting previous identities and expanding its name.[26]

Not only does Aristides note Rome's geographical extension or the city's role as an urban center to the entire *oikoumenē*, he also conceives of the Roman Empire as a kind of league of cities in the ancient Greek mode, with Rome as its *hēgemōn* ("leader"):[27] "Now all the Greek cities rise up under your leadership, and the monuments which are dedicated in them and all their embellishments

[23] "What another city is to its own boundaries and territory, this city is to the boundaries and territory of the entire civilized world" (*Roman Oration* 61; ET Oliver, 901). Compare with Commodus's configuration of Rome as ἀθάνατον εὐτυχῆ κολωνίαν τῆς οἰκουμένης in 192 CE. Olivier Hekster explains the title this way: "making Rome the 'immortal, fortunate colony of the whole earth' also implied that . . . all the inhabitants of the realm could take symbolic 'possession' of the civilized world" (*Commodus: An Emperor at the Crossroads* [Amsterdam: Gieben, 2002] 95).

[24] ET Oliver, 902.

[25] Admittedly, such writers often seek to trouble the Greek/barbarian binary, elevating "barbarian" wisdom. See Chapter 2; see also, e.g., Dio *Or.* 36; Lucian *Demon.* and *Anach.*; and esp. Aelius Aristides' *Panathenaic Oration.* On this topic see also Arnaldo Momigliano, *Alien Wisdom: The Limits of Hellenization* (New York: Cambridge University Press, 1975); Guy G. Stroumsa, *Barbarian Philosophy: The Religious Revolution of Early Christianity* (Tübingen: Mohr Siebeck, 1999).

[26] This claim chafes against contemporary writers who employ the Greek/barbarian binary, as even Aristides himself does elsewhere. Aristides presents the Roman Empire as an innocent *synekism*: in Edward Soja's definition, "the economic and ecological interdependencies and the creative – as well as occasionally destructive – synergisms that arise from the purposeful clustering and collective cohabitation of people in space" (*Postmetropolis: Critical Studies of Cities and Regions* [Malden, MA: Blackwell, 2000] 12). Aristides celebrates that all have united to help Smyrna after the earthquake of the late 170s CE, including Rome, the Greek *ethnos*, and "all the races, which comprise our Asia" (*Or.* 20: "A Palinode for Smyrna," 18; ET Behr, 2.17). See also Aristides *Or.* 23: "Concerning Concord."

[27] Oliver, *The Ruling Power*, 879–84. This is no surprise given Aristides' ideology of concord and rhetoric elsewhere; see *Or.* 23.5–7, a speech key to his interpretation of cities and competition for imperial cult temples in Asia Minor, and see S. R. F. Price, *Rituals and Power: Roman Imperial Cult in Asia Minor* (Cambridge: Cambridge University Press, 1984) 153–55.

and comforts redound to your honor like beautiful suburbs.... Taking good care of the Hellenes as of your foster parents, you constantly hold your hand over them, and when they are prostrate, you raise them up. You release free and autonomous those of them who were the noblest and the leaders of yore...." (*Roman Oration* 94, 96).[28] Earlier in the speech, Aristides had explicitly linked the Roman Empire to the prestigious, if conflict-ridden, Greek past by arguing that its empire surpasses even Athenian, Spartan, and Theban attempts at hegemony.[29] Aristides makes Rome homologous and superior to Greek city-states that had their own expansive powers and colonies, and he borrows their long tradition of kinship language. He also configures the relationship between the Roman Empire and Greek cities as one of adoptive kinship. One might expect such adoption to benefit the "child" – here, Rome. Yet Aristides focuses on how the child aids its parents, hinting at the decrepitude of the Greek world that is passing away, its genes to be carried on by the Romans.[30]

Rome was thus an empire of cities, for Aristides. Cities, however, were also possible sites of resistance to empire.[31] The *polis* and discourses of the *polis* were intimately connected with Greek democracy; they revived traditions and memories of the power and prestige of the city-state, and stories of free debates and *parrhēsia* ("free speech") in these cities' assemblies. Thus the city contained the possibility of resistance to empire or at least of changing allegiances depending upon the fortunes of a given claimant to the *imperium*. At times in the early Roman Empire, the power of some cities was restricted for this reason.[32]

Rome exercised its influence over independent and non-independent cities, all potentially rebellious, in explicit and subtle ways. The Roman Empire held cities spread out like small, diverse jewels, faceted with memories of past great deeds, with famed cultural objects – buildings, sculpture, well-known festivals. The cities' systems of civic engagement, *bouleutēria* ("council houses") and *ekklēsiastēria* ("assembly houses"), were knotted into the grid of the streets.

28 ET Oliver, 905. The language of foster parenting is found also in the *Panathenaic Oration* where the "men of Athens" are the "common foster fathers" of all who claim Greek identity (1).

29 Aristides *Roman Oration* 43–57.

30 On the *topos* of a succession of empires or of aging in ancient historiography, see Arnaldo Momigliano, *Essays in Ancient and Modern Historiography* (Middletown, CT: Wesleyan University Press, 1977) 189.

31 Aristides may hint at this in *Or.* 23.46 ("Concerning Concord"): "They reduced the king, *who equated his empire with that of Zeus, to such fear and humility that he leaped from his throne* and went off in flight from land to land" (my emphasis; ET Behr, 2.35). This comment on Persia seems to point to Roman emperors who equate themselves with the highest god.

32 Christopher P. Jones, *Kinship Diplomacy in the Ancient World* (Cambridge, MA: Harvard University Press, 1999) 106–7. On vibrant, debating city assembles under the Roman Empire, see Anna Miller, "The Body of Christ as *Demos*: Democratic Discourse of the *Ekklesia* in 1 Corinthians" (Ph.D. dissertation, Harvard University, Committee on the Study of Religion, 2007).

Rome chained and clustered these cities together into empire, in the words of Aristides.[33] The memories of cities' past greatness were mobilized on behalf of Rome and individual cities. Cities also served as key arenas in which native elites could attract the attention of the empire, and in which imperial power, especially in the creation and performance of imperial cult, could be manifest.[34] Such cities could be honored with imperial benefactions, such as the right to build a temple for the imperial cult (neokorate or "temple warden" status), or the status of "free and autonomous," an important change in tax status.[35] The politics and religion of such interactions were inseparable; in the *Roman Oration* Aristides connects Rome's rule over the preexisting chaos with Zeus's rule after the "strife, confusion, and disorder" of the Titans (99, 103).

II. THE PANHELLENION

The rule of Hadrian, among other emperors, stimulated the processes that Aelius Aristides celebrates two decades later: The power of the Roman Empire made the inhabited world safe and navigable for the celebration and spread of Greekness and Greek *paideia*. Although the precise origins of the Panhellenion are unclear, in 131 or 132 Hadrian seems to have founded this league of cities headed by Athens. This is the same year that he made his third visit to Athens and presided over the dedication of the Olympieion, or Temple of Zeus Olympios, there.[36] In that precinct, Hadrian was closely associated with Zeus.[37] In present times, bases that once held statues of Hadrian, dedicated by

33 Aristides uses a variety of metaphors for connections between cities; for the image of bats clustering like beads or links, see *Roman Oration* 68. See also *Or.* 17.10 ("Smyrnean Oration"): "Proceeding from west to east, you go from temple to temple and from hill to hill, along a single avenue which is fairer than its name.... The city itself... takes one's breath away through three spectacles most fair, nor can one find a place where he might rest his eyes. Each object attracts him, like the stones in a variegated necklace" (ET Behr, 2.3).

34 After Price's *Rituals and Power* it is impossible to ignore the mutually affirming back-and-forth of the imperial family with urban elites in the Greek East (see, e.g., pp. 247–48); on this topic see also Clifford Ando, *Imperial Ideology and Provincial Loyalty in the Roman Empire* (Berkeley: University of California Press, 2000). See also Jones, *Kinship Diplomacy*; Ursula Kampmann, "*Homonoia* Politics in Asia Minor: The Example of Pergamon," in Helmut Koester, ed., *Pergamon: Citadel of the Gods* (HTS 46; Harrisburg, PA: Trinity Press International, 1998) 387–93.

35 On city status under Rome, see Maud W. Gleason, "Greek Cities under Roman Rule," in David S. Potter, ed., *A Companion to the Roman Empire* (Malden, MA: Blackwell, 2006) 228–49; A. H. M. Jones, *The Greek City from Alexander to Justinian* (Oxford: Oxford University Press, 1940). On cities and neokorate status, see Price, *Rituals and Power*, and Steven Friesen, *Twice Neokoros: Ephesus, Asia, and the Cult of the Flavian Imperial Family* (Leiden: E. J. Brill, 1993).

36 A. S. Spawforth and Susan Walker, "The World of the Panhellenion. I. Athens and Eleusis," *JRS* 75 (1985) 79.

37 On inscriptions to Hadrian Olympios, see Helmut Koester, ed., *Cities of Paul: Images and Interpretations from the Harvard New Testament Archaeology Project* (CD-Rom; Minneapolis, MN: Fortress, 2005) "Athens: Inscription to Hadrian Olympios." On the association of Trajan with Zeus Eleutherios, see Antony E. Raubitscheck, "Hadrian as the Son of Zeus Eleutherios," *AJA* 49.2 (1945) 128–33.

a vast range of cities, have been found in the precinct of the Olympieion.[38] Nearly 100 altars have been found in Athens more generally that name Hadrian as "savior and founder." Surviving inscriptions suggest that Athens thrived especially under him and his successor Antoninus Pius.

The Panhellenion was well known – Clement in his *Exhortation* at one point uses the vocative to address "Panhellenes" (*Prot.* II 34.1), perhaps a reference to that institution or its roots in the past – and its scale is surprising.[39] While it was formerly thought that the Panhellenion met in the Olympieion's precinct, most scholars now think that it occupied a large building of Hadrianic date.[40] This basilica had interior measurements of ca. 64 m by 30 m; perhaps accommodating 700 people or more, it was two and one-thirds times larger than the Curia at Rome, which accommodated approximately 300 senators.[41]

The Panhellenic league consisted of at least twenty-eight cities: eleven in Achaia, ten in Asia, five in Crete and Cyrene, one each in Macedonia (Thessalonikē) and Thrace (see Fig. 12).[42] The second century was distinguished

38 Anna Benjamin, "The Altars of Hadrian in Athens and Hadrian's Panhellenic Program," *Hesp.* 32.1 (1963) 57–86.

39 The Panhellenion is known only from a few literary sources: see Cassius Dio 69.16 (epitome). Pausanias (*Descr.* 18.9) refers to a temple of Hera and Zeus Panhellenios but not to a Panhellenion. Our main information for the Panhellenion is epigraphic. Fifty-four inscriptions are known; most are from Greece, but some are from Asia Minor, Italy, and Libya (Spawforth and Walker, "Panhellenion. I," 79). James H. Oliver, *Marcus Aurelius: Aspects of Civic and Cultural Policy in the East* (Hesp. Supp. 13; Princeton, NJ: American School of Classical Studies at Athens, 1970) originally collected the inscriptions; Spawforth and Walker in "Panhellenion. I" and a subsequent article ("The World of the Panhellenion. II. Three Dorian Cities," *JRS* 76 [1986] 88–105) add a few more. Which inscriptions have been found and where are to some extent matters of chance; thus, assertions about the Panhellenion are always provisional.

40 See Spawforth and Walker, "Panhellenion. I," 92–98, esp. fig. 2. Located to the east of the Roman agora and Hadrian's library, this building is usually identified as the "temple of all the gods" mentioned by Pausanias. Christopher P. Jones hypothesizes that the sanctuary may have been at Eleusis ("The Panhellenion," *Chiron* 26 [1996] 36). Alternatively, it may have been located in an as-yet partially unexcavated building just northwest of the Stoa of Attalos.

41 Spawforth and Walker, "Panhellenion. I," 70. The Panhellenion's office holders seem mostly to have been wealthy Roman citizens, some of equestrian or senatorial rank (pp. 84–87.) Those called Panhellenes – not leaders, but regular participants – seem to have been more of a social mix, and not necessarily Roman citizens, although enrolled among them was Herodes Atticus, the fabulously wealthy Athenian sophist (p. 88).

42 Mary Boatwright, *Hadrian and the Cities of the Roman Empire* (Princeton, NJ: Princeton University Press, 2000) 147. Seminal in the study of Hadrian in Athens and the Panhellenion is Paul Graindor, *Athènes sous Hadrien* (Cairo: Imprimerie Nationale, Boulac, 1934). We do not know whether Hadrian assigned involvements in the Panhellenion or whether cities appealed to be participants. On the question of who proposed the Panhellenion, see Romeo, "The Panhellenion," 21–40; James H. Oliver, "Hadrian's Reform of the Appeal Procedure in Greece," *Hesp.* 39.4 (1970) 332–36. On Cyrene, Hellenization, and Hadrian's Panhellenion, see P. M. Fraser, "Hadrian and Cyrene," *JRS* 40.1–2 (1950) 77–90; James H. Oliver, "New Evidence on the Attic Panhellenion," *Hesp.* 20.1 (1951) 31–33; J. A. O. Larsen, "Cyrene and the Panhellenion," *Classical Philology* 47.1 (1952) 7–16; and esp. Joyce Reynolds, "Hadrian, Antoninus Pius and the Cyrenaican Cities," *JRS* 68 (1978) 111–21.

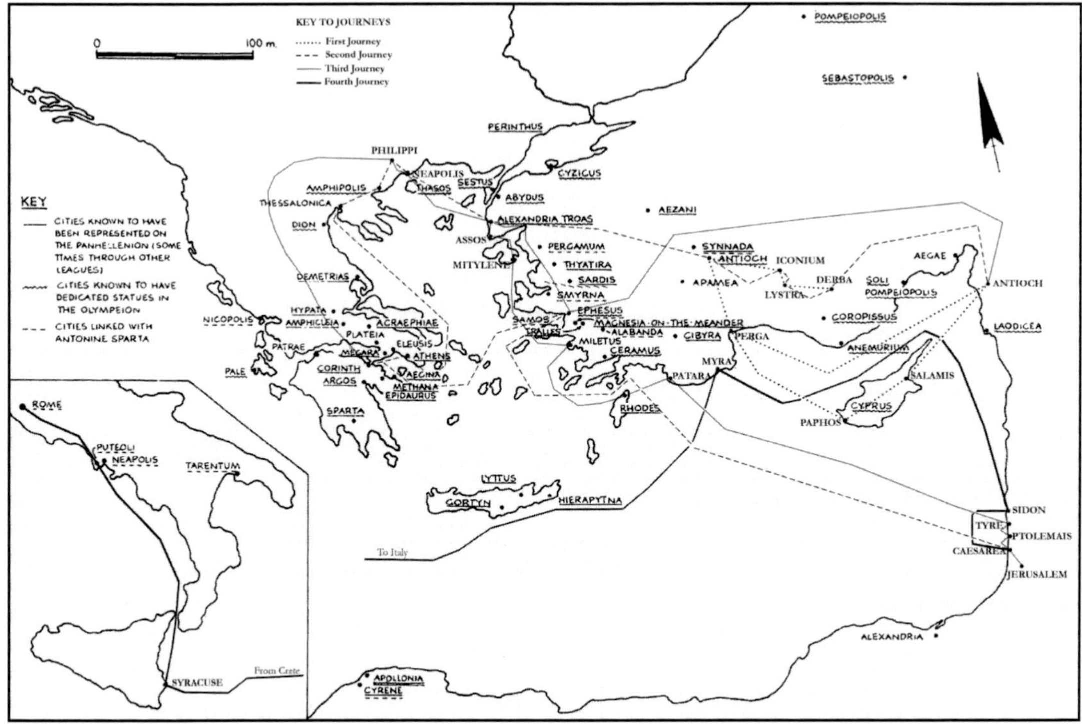

12. Paul's travels (according to Acts) and the cities of the Panhellenion. Figure courtesy of Daniel Hawkins, Nan Hutton, Mikael Haxby, and the staff of Information Technology Services at Harvard Divinity School, and modeled on Spawforth and Walker, "Panhellenion. I," 80 fig. 1.

by sharp rivalries between cities, but also by alliances forged by cult, festivals, gifts, culture, and political strategizing. The Panhellenion was like those ancient leagues that still in the second century carried some power, psychic or real, such as the Delphic Amphictyony, which Hadrian also supported, or the *koinōn* of cities of Asia.[43] Hadrian likely established or accepted the Panhellenion for manifold reasons, including the practical desire to reduce the number of embassies seeking his attention by encouraging cities to send joint embassies.[44]

The Panhellenion brought various cities' representatives to Athens to engage in cultic, cultural, and diplomatic activities; it also may have acted as a court.[45]

[43] Hadrian may have developed the Panhellenion because he could not do what he wished with the Delphic Amphictyony (Romeo, "The Panhellenion," 24–25). See Oliver, *Marcus Aurelius*, 92–93.

[44] On overwhelming embassies, see pp. 26–27 and Spawforth and Walker, "Panhellenion. I," 83. On cities jockeying for new civic status under the Roman Empire and on *humanitas* (that is, civilization in contrast to past wild barbarity) as a criterion of inclusion, see Woolf, *Becoming Roman*, esp. 64–67.

[45] Spawforth and Walker, "Panhellenion. I," 83–84. The associations with imperial cult are evident from a statue base set up in Thessalonikē in honor of the emperor Pius; for the Panhellenion's function as a court, see Eusebius *Hist. eccl.* 4.26.10.

Panhellenic impulses overtook cities as close to Athens as Corinth and as far as Laodicea and Cyrene. Two inscriptions in particular tell us what was required to join the Panhellenion. An inscription regarding the acceptance of Magnesia on the Maeander and a dedicatory inscription from the Phrygian city of Kibyra, not far from modern Burdur, Turkey, refer to three elements: their cities' Greek ancestry, their histories of good relations with Rome, and Hadrian's benefactions.[46] The Kibyrian inscription references Zeus Soter, an unusual epithet which is elsewhere linked to Hadrian.[47] Beginning on the third line of the inscription, Kibyra defines itself as

> Ἡ Κιβυρατῶν πόλις ἄποικος Λ[υδῶν οὖσα καὶ]
> συγγενὶς Ἀθηναίων καὶ φι[λ . . . . καὶ]
> αὐτὴ τοῦ κοινοῦ τῆς Ἑλλάδος [ἐν ταῖς μάλιστα]
> ἐνδόξοις οὖσα καὶ μεγάλαις [τῆς Ἀσίας πόλε]
> σιν διά τε τὸ γένος Ἑλληνι[κόν . . .]
>
> The city of the Kibyrians, being a colony of Lydians and
> kin and friend of the Athenians, . . . and
> the same city (belongs to) the *koinōn* of Greece, being among
> those cities of Asia quite highly reputed and great
> on account of their Greek race . . .[48]

The inscription from Magnesia on the Maeander, also in Asia Minor, is found on a fine piece on marble with regularly carved letters (but a break on its left side). This inscription is more elaborate in its genealogical rhetoric:

> [- – – – – – ψήφισ]μα τὸ γένομενον ὑπὸ τῶν Πανελλήνων
> [ἐπειδὴ Μάγνητες οἱ] πρὸς τῷ Μαιάνδρῳ ποταμῷ ἄποικοι
> [μὲν ὄντες Μαγνήτων] τῶν ἐν Θεσσαλίᾳ, πρῶτοι Ἑλλήνων
> [δὲ καὶ διαβάντες εἰ]ς τὴν Ἀσίαν καὶ κατοικήσαντες, συνα
> [γωνισάμενοι ἐκτενῶς] πολλάκις Ἴωσι καὶ Δωριεῦσι καὶ τοῖς ἐ
> [πὶ τῆς Ἀσίας ταὐτοῦ γ]ένους Αἰολεῦσι, τιμηθέντες καὶ ὑπὸ
> [τῆς συγκλήτου τῆς Ῥω]μαίων . . .
>
> . . . a measure passed by the members of the Panhellenion.
> When the Magnesians were settlers by the Maeander River,

[46] Spawforth and Walker, "Panhellenion. I," 82.

[47] This epithet is found at a round temple mimicking the Pantheon at the Asklepios cult site at Pergamon; Hadrian was the benefactor of this temple. Christian Habicht, *Altertümer von Pergamon*, III.3, *Die Inscriften des Asklepieions* (DAI; Berlin: De Gruyter, 1969) 11–14. An inscription refers to Hadrian with many epithets, including Olympios and Panhellenios (pp. 30–31). On second-century control of cult space at Pergamon, see Alexia Petsalis-Diomidis, "The Body in Space: Visual Dynamics in Graeco-Roman Healing Pilgrimage," in Jaś Elsner and Ian Rutherford, eds., *Pilgrimage in Graeco-Roman and Early Christian Antiquity: Seeing the Gods* (Oxford: Oxford University Press, 2005) 183–218.

[48] Oliver, *Marcus Aurelius*, 95–96. I start my translation on line 2 of the inscription, which continues for four to five more lines, discusses relations with Rome, and refers to the "God Hadrian."

> they were of the Magnesians in Thessaly, the first of the Greeks
> who also crossed over into Asia and colonized it,
> often eagerly fighting alongside the Ionians and Dorians and those
> Aiolians of this race in Asia, honored also
> by the Senate of the Romans . . .[49]

As Spawforth and Walker write, the idea of "fabricat[ing] Greek pedigrees" is known as early as the Hellenistic period in the eastern Mediterranean.[50] In the second century, as Buell's work shows, both fixed and fluid explanations of race were employed. Sometimes *genos* ("race"), *laos* ("peoplehood"), or *ethnos* ("nation, ethnicity, nationality") were defined in terms of blood and genealogy; at other times, in terms of the acquisition of Greek *paideia*.[51] We find hints of such thinking in Aristides, who in his *Panathenaic Oration* links Athens with the cities opposite in Asia Minor, but also proclaims: "For no one would be proud to have Pella or Aegae as his country; there is no Greek who would not wish to have been born an Athenian rather than a citizen of his own city. Not only do private citizens prefer Athens in this way, but also in the case of cities, those which have been actually founded from here and by you would rather boast that they descend from you than possess power equal to yours; and the others go about seeking somehow to trace themselves back to you" (334).[52] Panhellenic identity was founded on ancient mythic links to Hellenic (particularly Athenian) identity; distant communities were ethnically linked at the earliest, most mythical of stages. It did not matter if connections were, from a modern viewpoint, fabricated.[53]

These participants were oriented through the Panhellenion not only to the traditions of Athenian *paideia* and toward Hellenic identity, however invented, but also toward Rome. Christopher Jones has argued that scholars have understood the Panhellenion mainly as a diplomatic United Nations, ignoring its

[49] See ibid., 94–95 and plate 7. I begin my translation on line 3 of the inscription, which continues in four more lines to discuss further Magnesian relations with Rome and the imperial family.

[50] Spawforth and Walker, "Panhellenion. I," 82; "Panhellenion. II," 95. See also Romeo, "The Panhellenion," 26 on the Hadrianic Panhellenion returning to a fourth-century BCE concept of *genos*; Jones, *Kinship Diplomacy*, esp. 110–11.

[51] See Buell, *Why This New Race?*, esp. 35–62. On Greekness, see, e.g., Jonathan Hall, *Hellenicity: Between Ethnicity and Culture* (Chicago: University of Chicago Press, 2002); Benjamin Isaac, *The Invention of Racism in Classical Antiquity* (Princeton, NJ: Princeton University Press, 2004); on Romanness, see Emma Dench, *Romulus' Asylum: On Roman Identities from the Age of Alexander to the Age of Hadrian* (Oxford: Oxford University Press, 2005). On shifting definitions of race with regard to the Panhellenion, see Romeo, "The Panhellenion," esp. 32–37.

[52] ET Behr, 1.68. For other examples of such "ethnic reasoning" (Buell's term), see *Or.* 24.5 ("To the Rhodians: Concerning Concord") and *Or.* 17.5 ("The Smyrnaean Oration [I]").

[53] As in the case of cities like Aizanoi in Phyrgia, or Sardis, which entered the Panhellenion; Romeo, "The Panhellenion," 29–31.

cultic focus. He asserts that "the most certainly attested activity of the Panhellenes is the cult of the emperors," since inscriptions which describe the *archōn* or leader give him the title of "*archōn* of the Panhellenion, priest of the god Hadrian Panhellenios, and *agōnothetēs* ["director of the games"] of the Great Panhellenia."[54] An inscription in Pergamon depicts Hadrian as "Emperor Caesar Trajan Hadrian Sebastos Olympios Panhellenios, savior and benefactor of all of his own *oikoumenē*,"[55] not only declaring Hadrian's political power and marking his connection with the Panhellenion, but also conflating him with Zeus Olympios, the ultimate savior and benefactor.

Collective definitions of ethnicity and race are often grounded in civic ties, real and imagined, forged through a history of colonization as well as through inventions of myths, claims to kinship, and especially religious practice.[56] Hadrian's Panhellenion encouraged Greek cities to continue producing these political, religious, and mythical stories in the service of producing a cultivated, cultured Roman Empire. At the same time, Greeks actively used Roman interest in Greekness in order to secure their own positions. As we shall see more clearly in the third part of this chapter, there is a homology between the Panhellenion and Luke-Acts. Luke-Acts produces a Christianity rooted in the civic ties forged through Paul's travels. It is not necessarily interested in establishing links between cities – it offers no exhortations that those in Philippi should help those in Derbe, for instance. Rather, the geographical imagination of Luke-Acts uses Paul's travels to establish etiological myths for the Christianness of cities, at the same time as it tells a geographical tale of Christianity's movement from Jerusalem to Rome via Greece and its *paideia*.

Hadrian, Ethnicity, and True Religion

The emperor Hadrian (117–138 CE) was a prodigious traveler who marked the cities of his empire by the monuments he left there and by the monuments that locals dedicated to celebrate his visits.[57] His reign is characterized by concerns about the cities of his empire, Greek identity, and proper (archaizing) religion,[58] themes he shares with the writer of Acts. For his philhellenism, Hadrian was mockingly called *Graeculus*, "little Greek."[59] Hadrian

54 Jones, "The Panhellenion," 32.

55 Habicht, *Die Inscriften des Asklepieions*, 30–31 regarding the statue base for Lucius Verus, Hadrian's adopted son (Inv. 1932, 26).

56 Buell, *Why This New Race?*, esp. chap. 1.

57 William L. MacDonald and John A. Pinto, *Hadrian's Villa and Its Legacy* (New Haven: Yale University Press, 1995) 13–23; Fergus Millar, *The Emperor in the Roman World (31 BC–AD 337)* (Ithaca, NY: Cornell University Press, 1992) 28–40. Boatwright demonstrates that "during Hadrian's twenty-one-year reign more than 130 cities received, in all, more than 210 marks of his favor" (*Hadrian*, 15).

58 "Hadrian was famed for almost perversely archaistic predilections" (Boatwright, *Hadrian*, 13).

59 *Hist. Aug. Hadr.*, 1.5; *Epit. de Caes.* 14.2.

purchased and reconfigured Greek identity (among other identities, such as Egyptian), marrying *Romanitas* and Greek *paideia*, whether in his initiation into the Eleusinian mysteries and his gifts to that cult,[60] in his vast benefactions to Athens, or in his own villa in Tivoli, in which he collected art and reproduced architecture, especially Greek, from around the empire.[61]

In uniting Greek practice and Roman power, Hadrian sought to define proper religion and piety.[62] Hadrian's interest in religion extended past the cult practices that were the purview of the Panhellenion and past Athens. Religious sites made up "his most frequent single type" of benefaction; one-third of all known Hadrianic architectural and engineering donations were to temples, shrines, or (cult-associated) tombs; at least eleven temples or shrines associated with imperial cult also received Hadrian's benefactions.[63] Boatwright concludes that Hadrian contributed to a "wide spectrum of religious structures, appealing to many different people."[64] This was at a time when Christian and non-Christian intellectuals debated what exactly constituted right religion. "Pagan monotheism" was part of the culture of the day, and some even suggested it might be best to set aside traditional religious practices and the embarrassing notions of gods who engaged in questionable moral activities.[65] Before and after Hadrian's reign, Christians and pagans alike challenged traditional practices of sacrifice and making images of the gods. Lucian, writing a few decades after Hadrian's great benefactions, mocks sacrifices (and the idea that true gods would need bloody, smoky offerings, as we have seen).[66] Luke, as we shall see, distills narrative scenes, like that at Lystra, which engage in

[60] Eleusis, linked to Athens by tradition and by the sacred way, was the famous home of the mysteries of Demeter and Persephone into which Hadrian was inducted perhaps in 124/5 (Boatwright, *Hadrian*, 100); see Jones, "The Panhellenion," 29–56. Regarding Eleusis's importance, see Aelius Aristides *Or.* 22 ("The Eleusinian Oration").

[61] See MacDonald and Pinto, *Hadrian's Villa*: Tivoli became the best of the empire *in nuce*, with key sculptures and buildings from around the *oikoumenē* reproduced there.

[62] Oliver (*The Ruling Power*, 892) argues that Aristides' *Roman Oration* envisions Hadrian's Panhellenion, celebrating the "exhilaration felt by the Greek cities . . . upon the establishment of the Panhellenion and upon the announcement of its program and of the aspirations of that *basileus euergetes* and citizen of Athens, the emperor Hadrian, *restitutor libertatis*." Behr (e.g., *Complete Works*, 1.447, n. 548) critiques Oliver for this association of the *Panathenaic Oration* with Hadrian and the Panhellenion.

[63] Boatwright, *Hadrian*, 127–40; quotation at p. 28. Benjamin, "The Altars of Hadrian," 57.

[64] Boatwright, *Hadrian*, 142.

[65] E.g., Plutarch *De superstitione*; Varro *De rustica* which no longer exists but Augustine discusses it in *De civitate dei*; Cicero *De natura deorum*. Some texts argue that stories of the gods are better understood as allegories for the forces of nature, and that one true God rules over all things, but one should still practice ancestral religions. See Harold W. Attridge's meticulous "The Philosophical Critique of Religion under the Early Empire," *ANRW* II.1 (1978) 45–78; Robert M. Grant, *Gods and the One God* (Philadelphia: Westminster, 1986) 75–83; and esp. Polymnia Athanassiadi and Michael Frede, "Introduction," in their edited volume *Pagan Monotheism in Late Antiquity* (Oxford: Clarendon, 1999) 7–10; and in the same volume Frede, "Monotheism and Pagan Philosophy in Later Antiquity," 46–57.

[66] See p. 57 and Lucian *Iupp. trag.* 3.

a similar critique of a certain kind of *deisidaimonia*, "religiosity" or "superstition," that impels the inhabitants to want to honor and to sacrifice to Paul and Barnabas. In the midst of this second-century debate over what constituted true religion and religious practice, Hadrian promoted religion on multiple and contradictory levels. He echoed the interest some elites had in restoring ancient glories, at the same time that others were offended by ancient glories and their bloody, embarrassing forms of sacrificial cult.[67]

Except for Rome, Athens was the city where Hadrian spent the most time.[68] His lavish benefactions in Athens, including those surrounding the creation of the Panhellenion, made second-century Athens more "classically" Greek than it had been in the first century. Hadrian thereby created a strong context for his Panhellenion to meet regularly and celebrate ritually once every four years. His benefactions towards cults that he considered proper to Greek and Roman identity also helped to define true religion and proper ethnicity. Indeed, with Hadrian, we can speak about "Greco-Roman" identity.

What Has Athens To Do with Rome?

The Athenians responded to Hadrian's presence and attentions; he had been a citizen there and even held its archonship before he assumed the *imperium*. At the time of his first visit in 124/5, Hadrian was honored by a statue on the Altar of the Eponymous Heroes in the Athenian agora and an addition of a tribe named *Hadrianis*.[69] These interactions between Hadrian and Athenians crystallize a particular moment in Roman-Greek relations. The idea of Romans as barbarians[70] was publicly effaced as Rome bought into Greece's cultural capital and traditions. The reality of Athenian and Greek subordination to Rome was veneered with new buildings and benefactions, most of which quote from Greece's classical period in their architectural form and decoration.

Even before Hadrian, Athens was familiar with building projects sponsored by Roman emperors and Roman citizens (not to mention other kingdoms), although the scale of Hadrian's building projects was unprecedented. From the second century BCE to the second century CE, Romans reconfigured significant spaces within Athens, including parts of the ancient agora. To build in the agora where Socrates had walked, where Athenian democracy thrived,

67 Perhaps for this reason we find contradictory comments about Hadrian in *Sib. or.* 8. Hadrian was a kind of Julian before-the-fact, reviving an archaizing form of religion that many elites found distasteful.

68 Boatwright, *Hadrian*, 144.

69 James H. Oliver, "Athenian Citizenship of Roman Emperors," *Hesp.* 20.4 (1951) 346–49; Boatwright, *Hadrian*, 144–45, esp. n. 3.

70 See, e.g., Vitruvius *De arch.*; see François Hartog, *Memories of Odysseus: Frontier Tales from Ancient Greece* (1996; trans. Janet Lloyd; Edinburgh: Edinburgh University Press, 2001) 163–97; Dench, *Romulus' Asylum*, 93–151.

and through which Athena was processed in festival, was to insert oneself into this theater of cultural and political memories. Susan Alcock puts it this way: "The Agora has been taken as a superb architectural equivalent to the antiquarian tendencies of the Second Sophistic."[71] That is, the impulses of the time were not limited to literary texts. In the Athenian agora, the Romans inscribed themselves materially, quoting from and engaging with its ancient "texts." In the first and second centuries CE, the open triangular region marked by the Stoa of Zeus and the Metroon on one side, the Middle Stoa to the south, and the Panathenaic Street on the west became busy with buildings. Probably from the time of Augustus into the second century, a fifth-century BCE "itinerant temple" of Ares – that is, a Greek temple from the classical period – was moved from an unknown location and (re)built in the center of the agora, as indicated by Roman builder's marks on older building materials. Since Ares was not an especially popular god, "specifically Roman interests" may have spurred the choice of this temple and its relocation – namely, that because Gaius Caesar associated himself with Ares/Mars, the Athenians made Ares a focus of the agora.[72]

Thus, various locations within Athens came to serve as "memory theaters": "spaces which conjured up specific and controlled memories of the past through the use of monuments, images, and symbols, spaces which served to remind communities at large of just who they were by drawing on who they had been."[73] These spaces juxtaposed ancient monuments with new benefactions. Those who walked these spaces would have noticed something about relations between Rome and Greece, about the nature of true religion, about the proper acting out of cult. So also, we can think of Acts as a space filled with objects ancient and new, with stories of Greeks, Romans, and barbarian others jostling for place on its pages.

III. TRAVELING BACK TO ACTS

In the example of the changed cityscape of Athens under Rome we see an abundant recollection of the past and the display of architectural citation, as Romans imitated ancient building techniques and details. Similarly, Luke-Acts

[71] Much of the information here is derived from Alcock, *Archaeologies of the Greek Past*, 36–98 (quotation on p. 51); see also John Camp, *The Archaeology of Athens* (New Haven, CT: Yale University Press, 2001). Price shows that this can be read as "a system of exchange" in the "relationship between subject and ruler," no matter who requested the innovations (*Rituals and Power*, 53–77).

[72] Alcock, *Archaeologies of the Greek Past*, 55.

[73] Susan E. Alcock, "The Reconfiguration of Memory in the Eastern Roman Empire," in Susan E. Alcock et al., eds., *Empires: Perspectives from Archaeology and History* (Cambridge: Cambridge University Press, 2001) 334–35.

collects extant sources and creates a literary memory theater for early Christianity, where past stories are newly used, transformed, and embedded into the narrative.[74] Of course this is true too for a text like Matthew, which uses the sayings source Q, Mark, and other materials, and with a strong redactor's hand creates its own literary architecture. But Luke is more explicitly a bricoleur of sources, from places known and unknown, as was the tradition of Hellenistic and Roman historians. The preface that serves both the gospel and Acts (Luke 1:1–4), and Acts' brief recapitulation (Acts 1:1–2), authorizes Luke-Acts precisely by positioning it in relation to past narratives:

> Inasmuch as many have undertaken to compile a narrative (διήγησιν) of the things which have been accomplished among us, just as they were delivered (παρέδοσαν) to us by those who from the beginning were eyewitnesses (αὐτόπται) and ministers of the word, it seemed good to me also, having followed all things closely for some time past, to write an orderly account for you, most excellent Theophilus, that you may know the truth concerning the things of which you have been informed. (Luke 1:1–4)

Luke's narrative supersedes these other sources, the text implies, because of its power to collect and arrange; his style incorporates and paraphrases works from the past.[75] Moreover, the worth of Luke's sources is guaranteed by their connection to tradition (signaled by παρέδοσαν) and by the eyewitness quality (αὐτόπται) of the accounts.[76]

We can picture the text of Luke-Acts like the city of Athens. The long text is studded with the architectures of earlier materials – "itinerant temples," fit into the landscape. The language of Luke-Acts in places mimics the Septuagint, giving it an archaizing and authoritative patina.[77] One wanders Acts' stories, sensing but not clearly seeing the seams of the narrative.[78] The "we"

[74] On Acts' use of sources and "rewriting the past," see Penner, *In Praise of Christian Origins*, 247–61 and esp. Cadbury, *The Making of Luke-Acts*, e.g., 139, 155–93; see also Pervo, *Dating Acts*, 12–14.

[75] Cadbury, *The Making of Luke-Acts*, 155–209; Bonz, *The Past as Legacy*, 87 on Luke's "hint of dissatisfaction with the work of his predecessors."

[76] Cadbury, *The Making of Luke-Acts*, 22–23.

[77] There are many studies of "Septuagintalisms" in Luke-Acts, e.g., Pervo, *Dating Acts*, 31–35; Cadbury, *The Making of Luke-Acts*, 122–26 on Luke's language and his more detailed treatment in *The Study and Literary Method of Luke* (HTS 6; Cambridge, MA: Harvard University Press, 1920) 1–72; J. de Zwaan, "The Use of the Greek Language in Acts," and William Clarke, "The Use of the Septuagint in Acts," in F. J. Foakes-Jackson and Kirsopp Lake, eds., *The Beginnings of Christianity: Acts of the Apostles* (5 vols.; London: MacMillan, 1920–33) 2.30–65, 66–105; for a philological comparison of Luke-Acts with Second Sophistic writers, see de Zwaan, pp. 37–38.

[78] See, e.g., Jacques Dupont, *The Sources of the Acts: The Present Position* (trans. K. Pond; London: Darton, Longman & Todd, 1964) 166–67; Cadbury, *The Making of Luke-Acts*, 49–75.

narrative, for example, which suddenly appears and disappears,[79] stands up like an architectural wonder in the narrative setting.

Luke is also interested in unity, in juxtaposing his diverse sources and narratives, as well as his own redactional activities, into a coherent memory theater, on the one hand, and into a coherent geography, on the other. Like Aristides, Luke uses universalizing rhetoric to draw diverse members into *concordia* or *homonoia*, even if these terms are never used. We find this harmony in Acts 2:44 and 4:32 as well as in the smoothing over of the conflict between "Hebrews" and "Hellenists" in Acts 16. Acts 10–11 presents the inclusion of Gentiles with a great emphasis on the term *koinos*: on discerning correctly what is "common" and permissible food, thus creating the grounds for a larger community (Acts 10:14, 15, 28; 11:8–9).[80] Acts 15's story of the council held at Jerusalem gently washes over controversies, instead presenting an easily accomplished unity on issues of Gentile inclusion and apostolic authority.[81]

The Panhellenion linked Greek cities together in part through imagined links to mythic Greek identity. Acts 15:21 offers a similar logic: The passage addresses what legal requirements those "Gentiles who turn to God" are required to keep, and thus the potential for new ethnic-religious lines, as Gentiles are affiliated with ancient Israel. It concludes: "For from early generations Moses has had in every city (ἐκ γενεῶν ἀρχαίων κατὰ πόλιν) those who preach him, for he is read every Sabbath in the synagogues." The minimal requirements for Gentile inclusion – abstaining from the pollution of idols (τῶν ἀλισγημάτων τῶν εἰδώλων), *porneia*, what is strangled, and blood – are bolstered by a claim that Moses was available to cities for generations, and that Gentiles dwelling in cities must merely restore the ancient connection to become part of the city league of "the Way."

This section is immediately followed by an official embassy. Men from the council repair with Paul and Barnabas to Antioch with a letter: "To the brothers and sisters from the nations, greeting" (Acts 15:23). In the aftermath of the council in Jerusalem, we are assured of the unity of the program. Even as Paul and Barnabas split from each other, even as Paul takes on Timothy as a travel companion, the hearer is reassured that "as they went through the cities, they handed on to them (παρεδίδοσαν) the teachings to guard, which had

[79] Stanley E. Porter, "Excursus: The 'We' Passages," in Gill and Gempf, eds., *The Greco-Roman Setting*, 562.

[80] Acts 21:28 engages in a deliberate irony: Paul, having brought Greeks into the Jerusalem temple, is accused by "the Jews from Asia," who cry out, "'Men of Israel, help! This is the man who is teaching people everywhere against the nation and the law and this place; moreover he also brought Greeks into the temple, and he has defiled (κεκοίνωκεν, literally, "made common") this holy place."

[81] Paul himself of course presented things otherwise, referring for instance acrimoniously to "false brothers and sisters" (Gal. 2:4) in Jerusalem.

been adjudicated by the apostles and elders in Jerusalem. And so the assemblies were strengthened in the faith and increased in number each day" (Acts 16:4–5). Παρεδίδοσαν signals the handing down of authoritative knowledge and is the same verb used to authorize Luke's own work (Luke 1:2); the teachings continue safely from generation to generation and from place to place. Acts depicts the leaders of "the Way" wending around the Mediterranean basin with no fracture or division.

Acts 2

In Acts, Jerusalem appears as already the superseded (it competes with Antioch for importance[82]) but still mythical central city of the league. Just as Athens at the center of the Panhellenion was eclipsed by the reality of the true power of Rome, Jerusalem for Luke is eclipsed and insignificant compared to Rome, toward which Paul is headed. Yet Acts begins in Jerusalem. Acts 2:1–13 has been a passage of key importance in scholars' theories of Luke's relations to empire. This passage offers a vision of Pentecost where tongues descend upon each of the disciples and all present hear them speaking in disparate languages. Embedded within the story of these tongues is a list of regions of the world.

> Now there were dwelling in Jerusalem Jews, devout men from every nation under heaven (ἀπὸ παντὸς ἔθνους τῶν ὑπὸ τὸν οὐρανόν). And at this sound the multitude came together, and they were bewildered, because each one heard them speaking in his own language. And they were amazed and wondered, saying, "Are not all these who are speaking Galileans? And how is it that we hear, each of us in our very own language, that into which we were begotten? Parthians and Medes and Elamites and residents of Mesopotamia,[83] Judea and Cappadocia, Pontus and Asia, Phrygia and Pamphylia, Egypt and the parts of Libya belonging to Cyrene, and visitors from Rome, both Jews and proselytes, Cretans and Arabians, we hear them telling in our own tongues the mighty works of God." (Acts 2:5–11)

In the story we find Luke's dream of instant translation, the hope that myriads can come together and understand simultaneously and effortlessly the "mighty works of God."

Acts presents us with this international list of Jews, a diaspora called back home for Shavuot. But why these particular peoples? What is the importance

[82] See discussion in Balch, "ΜΕΤΑΒΟΛΗ," 164, 185–86.

[83] During Trajan's reign Mesopotamia was made a province; see vol. 11 of *Cambridge Ancient History*: Alan Bowman et al., eds., *The High Empire, A.D. 70–92* (2nd ed.; Cambridge: Cambridge University Press, 2000) 125. Thanks to Rangar Cline for this information.

of this story, coming as it does roughly in the middle of Luke-Acts, a fulcrum from the ministry in Judea, the Galilee, and environs to the edges of the earth? Gary Gilbert has usefully organized scholarly opinions of this episode in Acts 2 into four camps: Some scholars say the passage derives from ancient astrological lists;[84] others that it derives from lists of locations of Jews in diaspora; others that it draws from the table of nations and the story of the tower of Babel in Genesis 10–11 (a story with its own message about language and unity); and still others that Luke draws from Jewish prophecies about the eschatological ingathering of diaspora Jews.[85]

Acts 2's geographical vision is also temporal; it offers an image of kingdoms of the world that were great at different historical periods. Listing these disparate empires together produces a movement not only through space but also through time, from the Parthians to the Romans. Moreover, it echoes and corrects the disaster of Babel: In Acts 2, languages are miraculously different yet comprehensible. The scattering of the Babel episode is reversed. The Jews of the diaspora, the devout of the world, are gathered together. From its beginning, Acts inscribes some idea of the entire *oikoumenē*, whether that idea is derived primarily from antiquarian geographical-astrological texts or from a text like Genesis 10's table of nations – or some mix of the two.

Nearly everyone agrees that Acts' geographical thinking has something to do with the Roman Empire.[86] Many conclude that Acts' geography mimics but subverts the Roman idea of *basileia* or kingdom. Gilbert argues that Luke-Acts "offers . . . the tools to dismantle the ideological foundation upon which Rome has built its empire."[87] Alexander concludes: "It is precisely this itinerant role that defines the apostles (and Paul) in Acts, and I would suggest that this provides a vital key to understanding Luke's cartography of early Christianity" that offers a "loose-knit dynamic network rather than either a centralized hierarchy or a congeries of disconnected congregations."[88] Balch argues that Luke's Asian historiography "acculturates and Romanizes early Christianity," but he also asserts that "the Christian missionaries from the East subverted

[84] See Stefan Weinstock, "The Geographical Catalogue in Acts II, 9–11," *JRS* 38.1–2 (1948) 43–46.

[85] Gary Gilbert, "The List of Nations in Acts 2: Roman Propaganda and Lukan Response," *JBL* 121.3 (2002) 500–1. For a comprehensive treatment of interpretations of Acts 2, see Scott, "Luke's Geographical Horizon," 483–544; see also Bonz, *The Past as Legacy*, 99–101 on those who read Acts 2 as Luke's reworking of the Sinai epiphany.

[86] See, e.g., Conzelmann, *Acts*, xlvii; idem, *The Theology of St. Luke*, 137–38.

[87] Gilbert, "The List of Nations," 529. See also Brent, *The Imperial Cult*, 101–23 who understands Luke-Acts not as revolutionary but as "contra-culture" – that is, it borrows from the political propaganda of the Roman Empire in order to correct its terms. See also Todd Penner, "Civilizing Discourse: Acts, Rhetoric, and the Declamation of the *Polis*," in Penner and Vander Stichele, eds., *Contextualizing Acts*, 102.

[88] Alexander, "Mapping Early Christianity," 171.

Western, European, Roman values."[89] Bonz concludes that the catalog reconfigures Judea on the theological world map: The inclusion of various nations denies "Judea's pride of place. It is henceforth just one among the nations."[90]

We see here that scholars tend to understand that Luke-Acts depicts a Christian *basileia* that is unlike Rome's. The Christian *oikoumenē* is peaceful and unified, characterized by universal acceptance, with no trace of hegemony. Even in earliest Christianity, however, such rhetoric of universalism was carefully and strategically employed, often to argue for Christian inclusivity over and against Jewish particularity.[91] In order to make Christianity more appealing in light of Jewish uprisings against Rome, Acts sacrifices Jews, molding the community of "the Way" into a form of religion that looks less foreign and more pious to a philosophical, Hellenized Rome.[92] Present-day Jews become the angry mob, such as that which stones Stephen, while the epic Jews of the past are made into the forerunners of "the Way," as Shelly Matthews argues.[93] While Jerusalem is the city of the origins of "the Way" (if not of the term "Christian," a privilege given to Antioch [Acts 11:26]), Stephen declares its obsolescence early on. False witnesses before the Sanhedrin argue that Jesus had claimed he would destroy the temple and Mosaic customs (Acts 6:13–14). In reply, Stephen uses Jewish scripture itself (Is 66:1) to argue that, despite the temple of Solomon, the highest God does not live in houses made with human hands (Acts 7:47–50). For philosophical reasons Luke can erase the significance of the temple in Jerusalem in his narrative of the years before the temple's destruction; this conveniently allows him to erase Jerusalem as

89 Balch, "ΜΕΤΑΒΟΛΗ," 187; he goes on: "God speaks Septuagintal Greek (not Attic) and Jesus teaches leaders to serve as slaves (i.e., a radical reorientation of traditional Greco-Roman values). God does not favor one ethnic group.... [T]he geographical movement in Luke's story (from Asia to Europe, from east to west) is thus indicative of larger ideological agendas: the Jordan River muddies the imperial Tiber" (pp. 186–87). Acts 2 is much discussed in missiological and Pentecostal circles: e.g., H. Wagenaar, "Babel, Jerusalem, and Kumba: Missiological Reflections on Genesis 11:1–9 and Acts 2:1–13," *International Review of Mission* 92 (2003) 406–32; G. J. Leeper, "The Nature of the Pentecostal Gift with Special Reference to Numbers 11 and Acts 2," *Asian Journal of Pentecostal Studies* 6.1 (2003) 23–38; Amos Yong, "As the Spirit Gives Utterance: Pentecost, Intra-Christian Ecumenism, and the Wider Oikoumenē," *International Review of Mission* 92 (2003) 299–314.

90 Bonz, *The Past as Legacy*, 106, 111; quotation at p. 106.

91 Buell, *Why This New Race?*, esp. 44–77, 59–62, 78–93, 138–65.

92 For a similar, perhaps contemporaneous, strategy, see Justin's *Dialogue with Trypho*.

93 Shelly Matthews, "The Need for the Stoning of Stephen," in Shelly Matthews and E. Leigh Gibson, eds., *Violence in the New Testament* (New York: T & T Clark, 2005) 124–39; Shelly Matthews, "Clemency as Cruelty: Forgiveness and Force in the Dying Prayers of Jesus and Stephen," *Bib. Int.* 17 (2009) 118–46, and her *Perfect Martyr*; Lawrence Wills, "The Depiction of the Jews in Acts," *JBL* 110 (1991) 631–54; Richard I. Pervo, "Meet Right – and Our Bounden Duty," *Forum* n.s. 4.1 (2001) 57–60. Bonz (*The Past as Legacy*, 94, 128) underscores the competition between Lukan communities and communities of the Jewish diaspora.

well. In addition to erasing Jerusalem's significance and painting modern Jews as a mob, Luke-Acts drains its sources of clues of Christian conflict with Rome, such as the arrest and execution of John the Baptist, and leaves Paul at the end enjoying what sounds like a comfortable and safe house arrest (long puzzling to scholars) under Roman care.

Paul in Lystra and Athens: Confusing Humans and Gods

The issue of space and geography continues to be addressed throughout Acts. The term *ekklēsia*, found as a self-designation for community even in Paul's earliest letter, is the same one used for political assemblies in Greek cities and recalls the rich debates and struggles of such institutions and their traditions of deliberative discourse. Yet Luke-Acts only retains the plural *ekklēsiai* in one place; otherwise, the "assemblies" are reduced to a singular.[94] In crafting this unity Acts reminds us of the league of cities under Rome that Aristides celebrates. Aristides, frequently using the term *koinos*, described Rome as a lead city to an empire that looked more like a civic league than a conquering force;[95] he celebrated the ease of moving throughout empire, city to city, "as on an avenue." In urban planning, Rome's influence was "literally woven through the city like a thread" by the *cardo* or *decumanus*, and this tie to the center was again marked by milestones that "reminded the traveler of the center of the empire."[96] Travelers were guided by the routes into the nodes of cities and knotted into the system of the Roman Empire. Luke-Acts represents Paul as such a traveler.[97]

The cities to which Paul travels repeatedly are in the same regions where many of the cities of the Panhellenion were, not to mention cities with statues and altars of Hadrian (see Fig. 12).[98] Having emerged from their days in the east, Paul and his companions head to the heartland of ancient Greece and its

[94] Acts 16:5 is the only plural amid twenty-three uses of the term *ekklēsia*.

[95] See discussion in Oliver, *Ruling Power*, 889.

[96] Paul Zanker, "The City as Symbol: Rome and the Creation of an Urban Image," in Elizabeth Fentress, ed., *Romanization and the City* (Portsmouth, RI: Journal of Roman Archaeology, 2000) 27; the quotation is from p. 29. See also Clifford Ando, *The Matter of the Gods: Religion and the Roman Empire* (Berkeley: University of California Press, 2008) 118.

[97] In the 1950s, Cadbury focused the question of Luke and empire on Paul: "What mixed names and backgrounds have the people that Paul meets! . . . Such a world needed a universal religion and a missionary who could be 'all things to all men.'" Paul, then, becomes for Luke and for Cadbury the quintessential servant of the "great commission" to "go into all the world and preach the gospel." He is the universal man, binding together the Roman Empire under a Christian sign. Henry J. Cadbury, *The Book of Acts in History* (New York: Harper & Brothers, 1955) 28–29; regarding Acts 2 he writes, "In many ways his was already 'one world'" (p. 14). See also Robert Tannehill, "Paul Outside the Christian Ghetto: Stories of Intercultural Conflict and Cooperation in Acts," in Theodore W. Jennings, ed., *Text and Logos: The Humanistic Interpretation of the New Testament* (Atlanta: Scholars Press, 1990) 247.

[98] Benjamin, "The Altars of Hadrian," 57–86.

colonies in Asia Minor, powerful cities of the second century CE and of the mythic Greek past. They return again and again, as if on political embassies, to these cities.[99] Even before the council in Jerusalem, Paul and Barnabas had been commissioned in Antioch to travel, and covered the territory of Seleucia, Cyprus (Salamis and Paphos), Perge (in Pamphylia), Pisidian Antioch, Iconium, Lystra, Derbe, Lystra again, Iconium, Pisidian Antioch, Pamphylia again, Attalia, and Antioch. A pattern is developed throughout Acts: Acts 13 describes this back and forth travel, and after the council of Acts 15 the story is repeated, as if to affirm the linking of these and other cities under the care of Paul and his companions.

Many of Luke's scenes of Paul's travels serve as narrative distillations of issues of ethnicity, proper practice of religion, *paideia*, and relations with Rome – that is, some of the precise issues raised in writings of the so-called Second Sophistic. In the midst of Paul's travels, several locations stand out because they are the settings of longer narratives about Paul's interactions with "natives." These stories are narrative forms of theorizing theology and politics. Luke takes part in a debate over what is proper religion and what practices are efficacious, at a time when Hadrian and others also discuss religion explicitly, with words, and implicitly, with benefactions for festivals and cultic practice.

The account of Paul and Barnabas at Lystra spoofs tendencies to misapprehend humans as gods, tendencies we saw in Olympia with Claudius depicted as Zeus: "And when the crowds saw what Paul had done, they lifted up their voices, saying in Lykaonian, 'The gods have come down to us in human form!' (οἱ θεοὶ ὁμοιωθέντες ἀνθρώποις κατέβησαν πρὸς ἡμᾶς)" (Acts 14:11). In their native tongue, in their backwater town, the Lystrans ignorantly manifest confusion between gods and humans that many would say was rampant throughout the empire. The cities that Luke and his first readers traveled housed imperial cult and contained statuary of humans representing themselves as gods, as well as gods in human form whose faces sometimes resembled members of the imperial family. They also sometimes conducted executions where criminals were made to represent the gods.[100]

While Acts turns the Lystran's misunderstanding into a joke, writers like Justin and Athenagoras take up the theme raised here in more philosophical tones, arguing about the nature of the creator versus the created or mocking (alongside their pagan contemporaries) the myths of gods busying themselves among humans in more or less admirable and sexually avaricious ways. Luke makes a similar, briefer argument about true piety and correct religion in sparkling narrative form. The scene commences with Paul's healing miracle and includes a priest of Zeus who wants to make sacrifice for the incarnate

[99] Bovon, "Israel, the Church and the Gentiles," 92–95 reads this as pastoral "fortifying."

[100] On such confusion in representation and the executed criminal as demi-god, see Chapter 5; for more on theomorphy and statuary, see Chapters 6–7.

Zeus and Hermes (Acts 14:8–18).[101] As the priest of Zeus offers animals for sacrifice and garlands for celebration, marching out of the city toward the temple of Zeus, Paul and Barnabas weep at this pious misunderstanding. "'We ourselves are humans, similar and subject to the same laws as you!' ... And saying these things they barely stopped the mobs from sacrificing to them" (Acts 14:15, 18). Here we find another joke. The ignorant mobs for once are not violent but over-adulatory, like the crowds Lucian depicts happily gathered for Peregrinus's praise and immolation, as he becomes a god.[102]

Dean Béchard argues that Paul's speech to the people of Lystra matches his speech to the Athenians. The story of Lystra marks Paul's interaction with rustics, not urban sophisticates.[103] Paul's speech to the Athenians, as Dibelius and others have argued, marks his interaction with Greek culture.[104] Acts 14 and Acts 17 contrast rural and native, barbarian and the epitome of Greece. But in both, the line between human and divine and the nature of true religion are misapprehended and critiqued.

Luke's depiction of Paul in Athens is the "climax of the book."[105] Athens symbolizes philosophical significance even under Rome, and Paul's speech from the Areopagus takes place not just on a high place topographically in the city, but a high place of cultural values. Standing on the Areopagus, the very ancient site of the Athenian *ekklēsia* or assembly – of ancient judgment and knowledge – Paul thoroughly critiques Greek *deisidaimonia*: "I see that you are in every way very *deisidaimonesterous*" (κατὰ πάντα ὡς δεισιδαιμονεστέρους ὑμᾶς θεωρῶ, Acts 17:22). The Revised Standard Version translates this "very religious," but "very superstitious" – fearing the gods in a way that completely misapprehends the divine – is also a legitimate translation. Plutarch, for instance, discusses *deisidaimonia* as a dangerous inclination to conduct cultic rites out of fear of the gods.[106]

In Athens, Luke-Acts foregrounds issues of religion and its truly philosophical practice. Paul, placed on a hill above the agora (Acts 17:3), acts as philosopher to address other philosophers. Even before the time of Hadrian's great benefactions, and certainly thereafter, we can imagine an Athens crowded with temples, altars, buildings, and statuary, including statuary that blurs the

[101] Dean Philip Béchard, *Paul Outside the Walls: A Study of Luke's Socio-Geographical Universalism in Acts 14:8–20* (Rome: Editrice Pontificio Istituto Biblico, 2000) 376.

[102] Lucian *De mort. Peregr.*; on mobs and Acts, see Wills, "The Depiction of the Jews," and Matthews, "The Need for the Stoning." See Amy Wordelman, "Cultural Divides and Dual Realities: A Greco-Roman Context for Acts 14," in Penner and Vander Stichele, eds., *Contextualizing Acts*, 205–32, esp. 228–29. There is a play on the word *lykon*, wolf, in this passage; elsewhere too Luke alludes to Jews being like wolves (Luke 10:3; Acts 20:29) (Wordelman, p. 228).

[103] Alexander, "In Journeyings Often," 35.

[104] Dibelius, *The Book of Acts*, 95–133; Bechard, *Paul Outside the Walls*, 255–53. Lucian's *Double Accusation* too uses the Areopagus as a setting of judgment.

[105] Dibelius, *The Book of Acts*, 95. See also Werner Jaeger, *Early Christianity and Greek Paideia* (Cambridge: Belknap, 1961) 11–12.

[106] See discussion on p. 192.

human and divine.[107] Paul's horror at Lystran religiosity was linked to the people's confusion between human and divine: "The gods have come down to us in the likeness of humans (ὁμοιωθέντες ἀνθρώποις)!" cried the people when they saw Paul's miracle, as we have seen. *Homoiōthentes* (the passive of the verb ὁμοιόω is defined "to be made like, to become like") recalls terms which are often used for statuary and image-making that imitate real life, on the one hand, and Genesis 1's language of human creation, on the other, where God decides to make humans in God's "image and likeness."[108]

So also in Athens, Paul is described as provoked in his spirit when he sees "the city full of idols (κατείδωλον)" (17:16). In the cultural context of the ancient Mediterranean, where gods look like humans and humans like gods in the statuary of cities and temples, Acts presents a Paul who is offended because neither backwater Lystra nor cosmopolitan Athens draws proper lines between god and humans. Paul's speech insists that God does not "dwell in shrines made by human hands, nor is God served by human hands, as though in need of something" (17:24b–25a). The frantic restoration and building efforts of someone like Hadrian are misdirected: They miss the true nature of the divine.

Acts uses Athens as a stage setting[109] for Paul's philosophical critique of Greek religion. Conzelmann's commentary notes that Paul's speech is not unusual in light of past and present Greek philosophical thought.[110] Acts sets this speech on the Areopagus, that ancient site of judgment and community deliberation. Pushed there by the crowd that surrounds him, Paul states:

> [God] made[111] from one every nation of humans to dwell upon all the face of the earth, having delimited the prescribed times and the fixed boundaries of their dwelling place, to seek God, if indeed they should touch him and find him. And yet [God] is not far from each one of us,

[107] Acts 17:17 depicts Paul as "in the synagogue with the Jews and the devout persons and in the market place (*agora*) every day." Since Acts draws broad painterly strokes, and since Epicureans and Stoics haunt this particular agora (see v. 18), which seems to be near the Areopagus, I think Acts 17:17 conjures the philosophically engaged ancient agora. See also Halvor Moxnes, "'He saw that the city was full of idols,' (Acts 17:16): Visualizing the World of the First Christians," in Halvor Moxnes et al., eds., *Mighty Minorities? Minorities in Early Christianity: Positions and Strategies* (Oslo: Scandinavian University Press, 1995) 107–31.

[108] LSJ s.v. ὁμοιόω. For other Greek and Latin vocabulary for statuary, see Peter Stewart, *Statues in Roman Society* (Oxford: Oxford University Press, 2003) 19–45. See Gen. 1:26–27, and, e.g., J. Maxwell Miller, "In the 'Image' and 'Likeness' of God," *JBL* 91.3 (1972) 289–304.

[109] Conzelmann, *Acts*, 146–48.

[110] Plutarch cites the Stoic Zeno's argument that one should not build temples of the gods; Seneca and Pseudo-Heraclitus also argued that the divine is to be consecrated within each human (according to the first) or in all the world (according to the second). Plutarch *Moralia* 1034b: "It is a doctrine of Zeno's 'not to build temples of the gods'; all the above are cited in Conzelmann, *Acts*, 141. See also, e.g., Lucian *Sacr.* 11.

[111] I follow Conzelmann's argument that ἐποίησεν governs both κατοικεῖν and ζητεῖν (*Acts*, 142). Ernst Haenchen (*The Acts of the Apostles* [Philadelphia: Westminster, 1971] 523), emphasizes that ἐποίησεν echoes the ποιήσας of verse 24 and is thus a "recapitulation of the creation account."

for "in God we live and move and have our being"; as even some of your poets have said, "For we are indeed his offspring." Being then God's offspring, we ought not to think that the divine is like gold, or silver, or stone, a representation by art and human conception.[112]

ἐποίησέν τε ἐξ ἑνὸς πᾶν ἔθνος ἀνθρώπων κατοικεῖν ἐπὶ παντὸς προσώπου τῆς γῆς, ὁρίσας προστεταγμένους καιροὺς καὶ τὰς ὁροθεσίας τῆς κατοικίας αὐτῶν ζητεῖν τὸν θεόν, εἰ ἄρα γε ψηλαφήσειαν αὐτὸν καὶ εὕροιεν, καί γε οὐ μακρὰν ἀπὸ ἑνὸς ἑκάστου ἡμῶν ὑπάρχοντα. ἐν αὐτῷ γὰρ ζῶμεν καὶ κινούμεθα καὶ ἐσμέν, ὡς καί τινες τῶν καθ' ὑμᾶς ποιητῶν εἰρήκασιν τοὺ γὰρ καὶ γένος ἐσμέν. γένος οὖν ὑπάρχοντες τοῦ θεοῦ οὐκ ὀφείλομεν νομίζειν χρυσῷ ἢ ἀργύρῳ ἢ λίθῳ, χαράγματι τέχνης καὶ ἐνθυμήσεως ἀνθρώπου, τὸ θεῖον εἶναι ὅμοιον. (Acts 17:26–29)

The passage is a tour de force, combining allusions to Greek poets with the story of creation in Genesis 1–2, and weaving together abstract geographical and temporal thinking with the hard built environment of statues of gold, silver, and stone. In verse 28, the phrase "in God we live and move and have our being" borrows from the Cleanthes' third-century BCE *Hymn to Zeus*: "For it is right for all mortals to address you: / for we have our origin in you, bearing a likeness to God, / we, alone of all that live and move as mortal creatures on earth."[113] In the phrase "for we are also his offspring," scholars have long seen the influence of Aratus's *Phaenomena*.[114]

In this speech Luke's Paul also combines the topic of creation – how God "made from one every nation of humans" with the question of "what the divine is like" (τὸ θεῖον εἶναι ὅμοιον), or not: The divine is not like the images produced by humans. The speech articulates one primary and one secondary theological point: First, it tries to establish proper human relations with the divine, and, second(arily), proper human relations with each other. I use the term "relations" deliberately since Acts employs the terminology of *genos*, which can also be translated "race" and which, as we have seen, is a key term in establishing kinship.[115] Humans and the divine are indeed alike: The Septuagint version of Gen. 1:26 states, "God said, 'Let us make a human according to our image and likeness (κατ' εἰκόνα ἡμετέραν καὶ καθ' ὁμοίωσιν).'" The Areopagus speech hints that the nature of the similarity

[112] The term χάραγμα has connotations of an impression, inscription, or stamp.

[113] Lines 3b–5: Johan C. Thom, *Cleanthes'* Hymn to Zeus: *Text, Translation, and Commentary* (Tübingen: Mohr Siebeck, 2005) 52.

[114] Line 5: τοῦ γὰρ καὶ γένος εἰμέν. For the Greek see Aratos, *Phénomènes* (2 vols.; text, trans., comm. Jean Martin; Paris: Les belles letters, 1998) 1.1. Aratus was also cited by the Hellenistic Jewish Aristobulus before Luke-Acts (Eusebius *Praep. evang.* 13.12); Clement *Strom.* 14.101 also uses Aratus. See Cadbury, *The Making of Luke-Acts*, 122 n. 10.

[115] See Buell, *Why This New Race?*, e.g. 29–33. The language of *genos* reminds us of the same terminology in the Kibyran Panhellenion inscription (τὸ γένος Ἑλληνι[κόν]).

between God's image and humans does not extend to representing gods by human images or to thinking of God as having human needs. In the Lystran episode, we saw the theme that humans are not to be confused with gods; Paul and Barnabas are not Hermes and Zeus. In the speech in Athens, we see the inverse: God is not like humans: humans cannot make images of the divine or build homes/shrines for it.[116]

What is the "one" from which this impartial God "made the world," in the terms of Acts 17? Conzelmann suggests Adam; we can go further and suggest that from Adam until Babel, all peoples were one, united at least by language (ἐξ ἑνὸς πᾶν ἔθνος ἀνθρώπων).[117] From this one proliferate many nations. Terminology of boundary-making (*horizō*, *horothesia*, *prostassō*) fills the passage. *Kairoi* ("fixed times") and *horothesiai* ("prescribed boundaries") refer "to the epochs in the histories of the nations and to their national boundaries" and "'periods and boundaries.'"[118] Each human *ethnos*, derived from an original "one," moves outward to its proper place in time and space.

Thus in Acts 17 we see a God who is Panhellenios and more. Luke employs logic similar to that of Hadrian's Panhellenion, inventing a story of origins that links together various cities under the banner of a Christian nation (*ethnos*) and a unified church (*ekklēsia*). Luke does not recover an ancient mythic past but molds one that will serve Christian empire in due time. Although the Roman Empire allowed (to some extent) the worship of multiple gods – the shrines and representations to which Paul refers – Luke through Paul communicates a vision of the world where one God commands all, everywhere (τὰ νῦν παραγγέλλει τοὶς ἀνθρώποις πάντας πανταχοῦ μετανοεῖν, Acts 17:30b). Thus the God that Paul describes in Athens as the one true God repeats and expands the God of Acts 2. In Acts 2, Jews of "every nation" are able to hear in their own language; in Acts 17, Luke's imperial God, communicating through Paul's always threatened but invulnerable body, commands all people, of all nations, to repent and submit, even as he insists that all are ultimately one in origin, mythically and primordially linked.

In Athens, the heart of Hadrian's projects, Paul offers a religious option that draws on the rhetoric, traditions, and literature of ancient Greece. He recalls the glories of ancient Greece, but also announces God's command and impending judgment on the *oikoumenē*. Roman imperial command, judgment, and reign over the world, as well as Roman imperial claims to be and to represent the divine, are paltry in the face of Paul's God.

[116] The passage repeats a logic already legitimized twice by Peter in Acts 10–11: "Truly I understand that God is not partial, but in every nation (*ethnos*) one who fears God and practices justice is acceptable to God" (Acts 10:34–35).

[117] Buell, *Why This New Race?*, 78–84, 138–65.

[118] For Dibelius, *kairoi* refer to seasons and a "philosophy of nature" (*The Book of Acts*, 97–101).

Paul in Thessalonikē and Philippi: Sedition against Rome?

But does this mean that Acts presents a vision of a kingdom of God that stands over and against the Roman Empire? No. In its depiction of Paul in Thessalonikē and Philippi, Acts both preserves and denies traces of a politically seditious Christianity. Acts instead appeals to the logic of Greek cities under Rome, on the one hand, and to the logic of philosophical conversations about the nature of true worship, on the other, in order to construct a Christianity that hybridizes neatly with Rome.

Paul has already traveled through the eastern rim of the Mediterranean, shifting from Antioch to Cyprus to Jerusalem and back. Paul then travels extensively in various parts of Asia Minor; being prevented by the "Spirit of Jesus" (16:7) from travel in the province of Asia proper, he is called to Macedonia in a dream. There, in the heartland of Alexander the Great's empire, where Rome exerted its influence through means such as the Panhellenion, Paul and his cohort are labeled "the ones who have stirred up the inhabited world" (οἱ τὴν οἰκουμένην ἀναστατώσαντες, Acts 17:7). Specifically, they stir up the *oikoumenē* by "acting against the decrees of Caesar, saying that there is another king, Jesus." In other words, Paul and company are accused (even in absentia, as in Thessalonikē), of political sedition.

What comes of these accusations of treason? Nothing, in the end, because Acts carefully constructs a "Way" that is not seditious toward Rome.[119] In Philippi, Paul and Silas encounter a girl with a Pythian spirit, who declares that the two are servants of the Most High God. Thus even a "pagan" slave, economically and pneumatically exploited by human and divine, proclaims the truth of monotheism and the identity of Paul and Silas as the one God's representatives (16:16–40). When Paul and Silas are thrown into prison for exorcising the girl (and thus, according to her owners, destroying their tool for money-making), Paul refuses an offer of quiet release. With their Roman citizenship, he insists, they should not be so humiliated, and thus Rome comes to the rescue of these cultured travelers. In the episode just before this, Paul's strident claim to Roman citizenship gets Silas and him shown Philippi's city gate (16:35–40). Acts thus retains traces of understandings of Paul as a political seditionary who stands against Rome but it overwrites these traditions. Paul is a master of escape and acquiescence, whose nearly invulnerable body uses imperial roadways and seaways in no way especially offensive to the empire. Paul slips off safely, under threat of Jewish violence, not Roman judicial proceedings.

[119] Esler, *Community and Gospel*, 202–25.

CONCLUSIONS

As the Romans embellished ancient buildings in the Athenian agora and inserted their own, so also Luke-Acts produces a "memory theater," invoking the language of the Septuagint, monumental traditions regarding the earliest Jesus movement, and retelling again and again the epic of the people of Israel, reconfiguring its literary spaces for a new (Christian) Israel.[120] Luke's narrative and his map of the *oikoumenē* contain significant shards of the past. Acts is a product of and participant in the culture wars of the so-called Second Sophistic: It crafts a story of a city league formed by the ambassadorial presence of Paul; it looks back to the first generation of the Jesus movement and to the ancient traditions of Israel.

Many of Acts' speeches can be read as mini-epics: short recountings of the *mythos* of the people of Israel. As Esler has argued, Luke-Acts draws on this ancestral religion in order to "assuage doubts which Roman members of Luke's community might have entertained as to the political implications of Christianity."[121] A religion that has such deep ancient ties, as did so many other religions under the Roman Empire, must be a proud and legitimate community. Acts presents a vision of a new Christian identity. This Christian identity is moored in prestigious ancient Israelite traditions; it is the rightful inheritor of these stories of salvation and of God's activity in the world. In placing into Peter's and Paul's mouths stories of the ancient people of Israel who traced their relations to God into the very distant past, Luke does something analogous to the cities of the Panhellenion that were encouraged to invent complex genealogies to establish their metropoleis as solidly Greek in race.[122]

Reading Acts in light of Hadrian's Panhellenion provides a fresh vantage point from which to see the debate over Acts' "apologetic" stance and Roman ideology. Prevailing explanations for Luke's geographical vision have moved toward the magnetic poles of these questions: Did Luke's geographical vision imitate Roman geography to support or to undermine it? Or was Luke's geographical vision a quotation of Jewish eschatological traditions, and if so, did it move toward the inclusion of all peoples into the people of God? Luke-Acts maps Paul's movement through the Roman *oikoumenē* and produces a Christian *oikoumenē* in turn. Paul's travels, in particular, build up a list of cities – an ancient Christian coalition. The Panhellenion, a Roman-sponsored Greek ethnic coalition, fostered diplomacy among Greek city-states. It also called for

[120] See Bonz, *The Past as Legacy*, 26.

[121] Esler, *Community and Gospel*, 216; see also chap. 5 in which he argues that Luke presents Christians, not Jews, as the inheritors of Moses.

[122] On similar ethnic reasoning, see Buell, *Why This New Race?*, 4, 85–90.

pious practice that bound diverse cities to the Roman Empire and the imperial family. Similarly, Acts tells the story of a Christianity that is comprehensible to and even in ways imitative of the Roman Empire. In Acts, Paul's travels produce a kind of pan-Christian league echoed in the Panhellenion. Luke-Acts makes its claims about a universal Christian geography using short, action-filled stories. We turn now to Justin's long address, written in Greek purportedly to the Roman imperial family, Senate, and people of Rome, which tries to place Christians safely in the spaces of empire.

CHAPTER FOUR

WHAT IS JUSTICE? WHAT IS PIETY? WHAT IS *PAIDEIA*? JUSTIN, THE FORUM OF TRAJAN IN ROME, AND A CRISIS OF *MIMĒSIS*

IN LITERATURE, ARCHITECTURE, AND EVEN ON COINAGE, THE ROMAN IMPERial family repeatedly claimed its commitment to and even embodiment of justice and piety. Justin's *Apologies*, which are addressed to the Roman emperors, the Senate, and the Roman people, contest such claims. This chapter shows how Justin's arguments about correct philosophy and religious practice (that is, topics usually treated by theologians) and about imperial power (that is, topics usually treated by historians) make sense in relation to imperial claims about culture, religiosity, and power, claims we have already seen in the emperor Hadrian's support of the Panhellenion. In the face of such representations of Roman imperial justice, piety, and even godhood, Justin struggles to define true religion and he debates the nature of true justice. Justin asks: How can one properly align the word (or name) and the thing it represents?

That Justin, who mentions Roman judicial persecution of Christians, would resist Rome is no surprise. That his resistance would be complex and sly, in the manner of a colonized elite speaking in the language of the dominant voice, is also no surprise. What is surprising and interesting is to see how *both* Justin *and* the Roman emperors work hard to define justice, *paideia*, and proper religious thought and practice. They do so from different positions of power and with different means and force of persuasion; we should not allow the passage of time to flatten all rhetoric onto a page so that we forget differences in the power to effect one's rhetoric. Yet even if Justin and the imperial family are not engaged in an equal dialogue, they are participants in a common debate or struggle over how piety, *paideia*, and justice intertwine.

The guiding theme for this chapter is *mimēsis*. This term is key to understanding Justin's arguments in the *Apologies*, and it is a word that is often used in antiquity and the present to discuss the making of images, or artistic endeavors more generally. Although the Greek *mimēsis* is usually translated "imitation," it has a broader range of meanings. Stephen Halliwell has argued that the modern term that best conforms to the Greek *mimēsis* is "representation."[1] In the *Republic* Plato seems to reject the mimetic work of artists because such *technē* is at third remove from the true Form. Painters or sculptors do not produce the Form of a *klinē* or reclining couch, nor even a couch, but a mere representation of the couch (*Resp.* 10.595c–598d). Although there were different conceptions available in the second century and beyond, including the idea that some artisans produced images not by the mechanics of sense perception but through a divinely inspired inner vision, the making of images was still often treated as derivative and deceptive, sheared off from the power of the thing itself.[2]

Pliny tells the famous story of how *mimēsis* in painting or image-making can become a contest of deception: The birds fly to eat the grapes that Zeuxis has painted; but Zeuxis begs Parrhasius to draw up the curtain in order to see his painting, when the curtain *is* the painting (Pliny *Hist. nat.* 35.36.65). Writers of the so-called Second Sophistic produced *ekphraseis* or narrative descriptions that claimed merely to index an image with weak words, but then clearly competed with and sought to supersede the image that the writer describes.[3] Kallistratos offered this *ekphrasis* of a marble statue standing in a cave in Egypt: "You could have seen the veins standing out as though they were filled with a

1 Stephen Halliwell, *The Aesthetics of Mimesis: Ancient Texts and Modern Problems* (Princeton, NJ: Princeton University Press, 2002); see also the review by David Konstan, "The Two Faces of *Mimesis*," *The Philosophical Quarterly* 54.215 (April 2004) 301–08.

2 See Clifford Ando, *The Matter of the Gods: Religion and the Roman Empire* (Berkeley: University of California Press, 2008) 21–58 on ancient and modern debates about idols and representation, on the one hand, and the *interpretatio Graeca* and *interpretatio Romana* (the identification of the Greek and Roman pantheons), on the other; see esp. pp. 28–31 on Plato. See Shadi Bartsch, *Actors in the Audience: Theatricality and Doublespeak from Nero to Hadrian* (Cambridge, MA: Harvard University Press, 1994) on emperors, theatricality, and the complexities of representation. See Halliwell, *The Aesthetics of Mimesis*, 7–14 on eighteenth-century definitions of *mimēsis* and aesthetics, as well as ancient ones.

3 See, for example, Lucian *The Hall*; Philostratos *Imagines*; and the *Tabula of Cebes*. For discussion of the complexity of the above-mentioned passage, and how this story self-consciously plays with criteria of naturalism, see Stephan Bann, *The True Vine: On Visual Representation and the Western Tradition* (Cambridge: Cambridge University Press, 1989) 27–40. See Jaś Elsner, *Art and the Roman Viewer: The Transformation of Art from the Pagan World to Christianity* (Cambridge: Cambridge University Press, 1997) 19–27, passim, and his *Roman Eyes: Visuality and Subjectivity in Art and Text* (Princeton, NJ: Princeton University Press, 2007) 1–26 on naturalism and representation discussed in ancient texts and theorized in ancient art. See the brilliant work of Peter Stewart, *Statues in Roman Society: Representation and Response* (Oxford: Oxford University Press, 2003) chap. 6.

sort of breath, the Satyr drawing the air from his lungs to bring notes from the flute, the statue eager to be in action, and the stone entering upon strenuous activity – for it persuaded you that the power to blow the flute was actually inherent in it, and that the indications of breathing was the result of its own inner powers – finding a way to accomplish the impossible" (*Descr.* 422K).[4] The pen is more powerful than the brush or chisel, or at least the writer plays with that idea. The writer claims to represent faithfully the process of viewing, even if words are inadequate, he claims, to the task. The joke, of course, is that we readers can never know if the power of the word did supersede the image; usually, all we have is the *ekphrasis*.

Such questions about representation are especially urgent in a culture where words and images fight for prominence, where human and divine are blurred in statuary, and where the god or goddess and his or her statue are referred to by the same term. Pausanias refers to some statues not as "an Artemis" or "the statue of Artemis," for example, but as "Artemis" herself. As Richard Gordon has pointed out, translators are uncomfortable with what they feel to be a (primitive?) confusion of the god or goddess with his or her statue. "It is we who introduce the concept of 'representation,' where Pausanias says, 'they are . . . .'" Gordon rightly points to the fact that modern interpreters are more exercised than were our ancient sources about whether a thing *is* or *represents* a god; in his words, "people believed simultaneously that statues were gods and that they were not."[5] Yet many ancient writers played with the trope of the confusion between a statue and the thing it represented; early Christian writers like Justin turn this conversation toward a critique of the deception involved in *mimēsis*.

Justin, in applying *mimēsis* and its cognate terms not only to image-making but also and especially to the creative activities of *daimones* ("spirits" or "demons") in the world, draws on a century-long discourse that links *mimēsis* and deceptive power. He also alludes to contemporaneous writings where the power of the word seems, at least, to trump the power of images. Justin's use of the vocabulary of *mimēsis* is aimed at both artisans and the power of *daimones*. It draws from and activates the negative understanding of *mimēsis* as deception, on the one hand, and the rich ancient discussion of the power of

[4] "Eis Satyron"; ET *Philostratus, Imagines: Callistratus, Descriptions* (LCL; trans. Arthur Fairbanks; New York: Putnam, 1931) 379; see Elsner, *Roman Eyes*, esp. 3–11; Stewart, *Statues in Roman Society*, 189–90.

[5] Richard Gordon, 'The Real and the Imaginary': Production and Religion in the Graeco-Roman World," *Art History* 2 (1979) 5–34; quotations at pp. 7–8 and 16; Gordon rightly shows how those of lower status ("popular") are critiqued in sources ancient and modern for confusing the real and its representation. See also Elsner, *Roman Eyes*, 11, 22–26. On labile representations of the gods in names and images, see Ando, *The Matter of the Gods*, 43–58, esp. p. 57. For the slipperiness of Greek and Roman terminology involving statues, see Stewart, *Statues in Roman Society*, 19–45.

representation, on the other. Justin makes his arguments in an environment in which Roman culture is also mimetic, literally reproducing or emulating Greek literature and famous Greek sculptures and images.

In this chapter, I argue that Justin uses a vocabulary of *mimēsis* or imitation to expose and criticize what he considers a multi-layered crisis of representation. The emperors make claims about themselves, taking on names and labels that are false; at the same time, their representatives in the courts name or constitute Christians in a way that does injustice and violence to Christians. Images represent gods, and these images (and gods) are false and deceptive. Moreover, *daimones* have rigged all of religion in order to confuse humanity into practices and beliefs that look right, but are not. The *daimones* understood the nature of the true religion to come, Christianity, but only dimly. Nevertheless, they made sure that the myths and religious practices of all who preceded Christianity would proleptically imitate Christian stories and practices. In doing so, they wished to deceive humanity into thinking that Christianity was a derivative representation of religion, rather than the original truth. There is, for Justin, much problematic *mimēsis* in the world.

I also use the theme of *mimēsis* to think about Justin's own positioning within the ethnic, cultural, and religious systems of valuation of the second century. Postcolonial critics, especially Homi Bhabha, have used the terms *mimēsis* and mimicry to think about the colonized subject under empire. Such terms, as we shall see, help us to think about how Justin crafts himself in his writing. Throughout the *Apologies*, Justin plays with the rhetoric of the sameness of Christianity with surrounding religious and philosophical practice; that is, we might think of him as a mimic. He defines himself as an ethical, law-abiding colonial subject from an edge of empire, who speaks for all races who are "unjustly hated and abusively threatened" (*1 Apol.* 1.1).[6] He does so in Greek, with clear training in philosophy and rhetoric and with a fair number of exempla from ancient Greek culture. Roman imperial claims to justice and true piety – claims made manifest throughout the empire by elites who served as priests and priestesses of imperial cult, as governors and magistrates – were productive for Christian theological thinking, stimulating Christians to sharpen their own definitions, which often re-presented or mimicked Roman arguments and reformed them for Christian purposes. Thus, Justin establishes similarity, but sometimes uses it to highlight difference.

This chapter moves in three steps. In the first part, we glimpse the Column of Trajan, located in the Forum of Trajan in Rome. Through this we see one important instance of Roman imperial claims about piety, justice, and power, manifest in the cityscape of Rome. The second part moves to the

[6] See discussion in Rebecca Lyman, "Hellenism and Heresy: 2002 NAPS Presidential Address," *JECS* 11.2 (2003) 209–22, esp. 214–18.

literary texts of the *Apologies*, showing that Justin's address to the emperors shows that the emperors and imperial justice are not what they seem. Justin elaborates a world that is in crisis due to *mimēsis* or representation. The making of images of the gods, on the one hand, and the activities of *daimones* in the world, on the other, fill this world with deceptions.

The third part of the chapter brings the reader back to the Forum of Trajan, a key site where the Roman imperial family articulates itself in relation to institutions of *paideia*, or culture/education (the library of Trajan), justice (the Basilica Ulpia), and piety or religion (the temple of the divinized Trajan, among other objects). These are the sort of architectural and artistic claims to *paideia*, justice, and piety among which many second-century Christians would have lived and moved and had their being. I bring together the Justin and Forum of Trajan not to assert that Justin walked there, although this is possible, since he spent time in Rome.[7] Rather, I treat the Forum of Trajan and Justin's *Apologies* as two roughly contemporaneous "texts" that shed light on each other because both participate in a similar discourse, manifest in words and images, of justice, religion, culture, and power in the spaces of the Roman Empire.

1. THE COLUMN OF TRAJAN

The Column of Trajan rises more than 40 m (131 ft) to celebrate the emperor Trajan's military victories over the "barbarian" Dacians in 101–102 and 105–106 CE (Fig. 13).[8] Dedicated by the Senate and People of Rome in 113, paid for by the booty from the Dacian wars, the monument is embedded within the Forum of Trajan, which is itself embedded within a series of imperial fora at the heart of Rome.

Although the Column of Trajan still stands – it survived as a platform for a statue of St. Peter – the surrounding Forum is largely ruined, known only through literary sources and archaeologists' reconstructions, its reconstructions still debated. Yet what remains shows that the architecture, the juxtaposition of buildings, the sculptures, and the inscriptions of Trajan's complex would have been thick with messages of Roman power, piety, *paideia*, and justice. So too is the column within it.[9] The base of the column alone, set on a

7 Peter Lampe, *From Paul to Valentinus: Christians at Rome in the First Two Centuries* (Minneapolis, MN: Fortress, 2003) 260.

8 For more on the column and its immediate surroundings, see James E. Packer, *The Forum of Trajan in Rome: A Study of the Monuments in Brief* (Berkeley: University of California, 2001) 72–77.

9 Against those who think that Hadrian remodeled the column, James E. Packer ("Report from Rome: The Imperial Fora, a Retrospective," *AJA* 101.2 [1997] 320) talks about the column as part of the original master plan. The Dacian Wars are also memorialized in the trophy of Trajan in Adamklissi with "provincial art"; for discussions of this monument see Diana Kleiner, *Roman Sculpture* (New Haven, CT: Yale University Press, 1992) 230–32;

13. View of the Column of Trajan, Rome. DAIR 67.913.

travertine foundation, is 6.155 m high.[10] A relief of a jumble of weaponry typical of the Dacians and their allies the Roxolani decorates it.[11] Shields with delicate scrollwork and varied designs lie under fine mail armor; axes tumble near the helmets of the defeated. All these are piled on each other like an enormous thrift bin for warfare. On the front façade, the weapons are tucked under an inscription, carried by two winged Victories, that honors Trajan, referring to the emperor as the "son of the deified."[12] Even without lifting

and esp. Florea Bobu Florescu, *Monumentul de la Adamklissi* (Bucharest: Editura Academiei Republicii Populare Romine, 1959).

[10] The column stood within a narrow rectangular Corinthian peristyle measuring 25 by 20.20 m. Filippo Coarelli (*The Column of Trajan* [trans. Cynthia Rockwell; Rome: Editore Colombo in collaboration with the German Archaeological Institute, 2000] 26; Packer, *The Forum of Trajan in Brief*, 72–77. For an analysis of building materials and the process of the construction of the column, see Lynne Lancaster, "Building Trajan's Column," *AJA* 103.3 (1999) 419–39.

[11] James E. Packer, *The Forum of Trajan in Rome: A Study of the Monuments* (2 vols.; Berkeley, CA: University of California, 1997) 1.4–5; regarding the column base, which is made from eight large blocks of Luna marble in four courses, see 1.113–20. See also Coarelli, *The Column of Trajan*, 21, 25–26. Frank Lepper and Sheppard Frere, *Trajan's Column: A New Edition of the Cichorius Plates* (Glouchester: Alan Sutton, 1988) reprints the late nineteenth-century photographs of Conrad Cichorius (from casts done for Napoleon III). Regarding modern emperors' interest in the column, see Paul Zanker's preface in Coarelli, *The Column of Trajan*, vii–viii.

[12] The inscription reads: "The Senate and Roman People [dedicate this column] to the emperor Caesar, son of the deified Nerva, Nerva Trajan, Augustus, Germanicus, Dacicus, Pontifex Maximus with tribunician power for the seventeenth time, commander-in-chief for the sixth time, consul for the sixth time, father of his country in order to declare how deep were

one's eyes higher to the column itself, the theological message of victory and power – wonder wrought through technology and art – is clear. The capital is a 56-ton monolithic block.[13] Raising one's eyes above it, one would glimpse a five-meter high gilded-bronze statue of Trajan, a crown to the column's rhetoric.[14]

In 117, after the immolation of Trajan's body (and the celebration of his divinization and flight to heaven),[15] Trajan's ashes were placed into the base of the column; the empress Plotina's ashes would be set there too.[16] The column was in part a monument to Trajan's apotheosis.[17] The temple to the deified Trajan stood just to the north,[18] associating tomb with triumph. In 128 the complex was completed when the emperor Hadrian dedicated the temple to his deified predecessor. The Column of Trajan was surrounded not only by the temple and its pious message but also by the Basilica Ulpia, a hall for conducting law and justice, and by the Greek and Latin wings of the library to its east and west, signs of *paideia* (Fig. 14). The Column of Trajan, as well as elements of the larger forum of which it was a part, was at its time an innovation.[19]

Like a strip of papyrus wrapped counterclockwise into a spiral twenty-three times, the Column offers the story of the Dacian wars and the glory of

the rock and earth excavated for these great works" (Packer, *The Forum of Trajan*, 1.117). The column contained 185 steps punctuated by 43 windows that lit the inner stair. See Penelope J. E. Davies, "The Politics of Perpetuation: Trajan's Column and the Art of Commemoration," *AJA* 101.1 (1997) 41–65, who thinks that a viewer's movement around the Column was part of a forced funeral ritual; even if her argument is wrong, the idea of a circumambulation of the column as a kind of ritual compulsion of the viewer's body is interesting.

13 Coarelli, *The Column of Trajan*, 26; the total weight of the column alone was over 1100 tons (Lancaster, "Building Trajan's Column," 419). Regarding the production of wonder in the viewer, see Ammianus Marcellinus (16.10, 15–16) regarding a visit of Constantius II (cited in Coarelli, *The Column of Trajan*, 3).

14 Coarelli, *The Column of Trajan*, 26–27; see also Packer, *The Forum of Trajan*, 1.120.

15 See, e.g., the depiction of the apotheosis of Titus on the Arch of Titus in Rome (Fig. 18) or the apotheosis of Antoninus Pius and Faustina the Elder.

16 Coarelli, *The Column of Trajan*, 15–16.

17 Paul Zanker, "Das Trajansforum in Rom," *AA* 4 (1970) 533. The puzzle of the column is that it is so difficult to "read": the architecture around it does not easily allow the viewer to move around the column to follow its story; see Coarelli, *The Column of Trajan*, 27; Richard Brilliant, *Visual Narratives: Storytelling in Etruscan and Roman Art* (Ithaca: Cornell, 1984) 96–98.

18 James E. Packer and Roberto Meneghini debate where the Temple of Trajan was placed in the Forum; see James Packer and John Burge, "TEMPLUM DIVI TRAIANI PARTHICI ET PLOTINAE: A Debate with R. Meneghini," *JRA* 16, no. 1 (2003) 109–36.

19 By 180 CE the emperor Commodus had imitated his forebear in erecting a similar column for his father, Marcus Aurelius. See Rachel Kousser, "Conquest and Desire: Roman *Victoria* in Public and Provincial Sculpture," in Sheila Dillon and Katherine E. Welch, eds., *Representations of War in Ancient Rome* (Cambridge: Cambridge University Press, 2006) 218–43; Brilliant, *Visual Narratives*, 114–15.

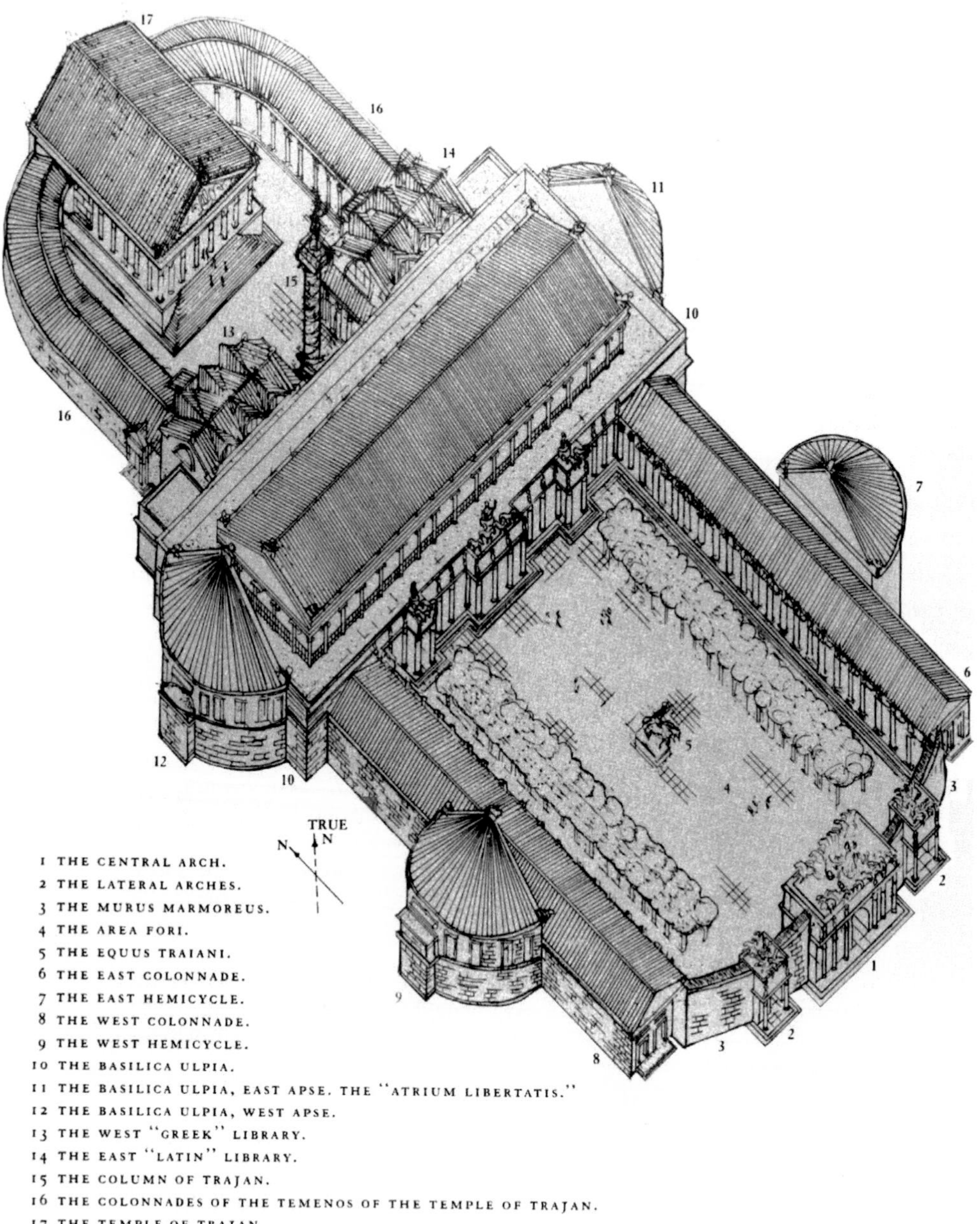

14. Reconstruction of Forum of Trajan, Rome. By permission of J. E. Packer.

Trajan in approximately 155 scenes, with more than 2500 figures; unwound, it would display 200 meters of "text."[20] Metallic objects such as small weapons

[20] Coarelli picks up Stzygowski's old hypothesis of the column as an "illustrated *volumen*" despite its current unpopularity in scholarly circles (*The Column of Trajan*, 11). Regarding the winding of the images and the number of scenes and figures, see p. 27; Brilliant, *Visual Narratives*, 90–92.

punctured the relief, the marble was left slightly rough lest sunlight on it dazzle the eyes and render the column even more illegible.[21] Its message was militaristic, but not brutal, like its immediate successor, the Column of Marcus Aurelius. Trajan's column makes statements about Roman triumph but also about Roman order, control, and piety. Amid the banalities of war preparation – the column depicts the mechanics of moving men, cutting timber, and building fortifications – and war itself, the gods occasionally appear to approve human labors.[22] Only a quarter of the column's scenes represent battles, and while Trajan is represented fifty-nine times on the column, he is never presented in battle. More often, he is shown in *adlocutio* scenes (where he addresses his troops) or in the act of sacrifice. According to Coarelli, this emphasizes "the emperor's function as a supreme commander, the stolid prime mover of the entire bellicose machine, a tranquil and rationalizing force in an otherwise chaotic reality."[23] In addition, the reliefs of the column that do depict the Dacians in war (as well as the sculptures of male Dacians used as pseudo-caryatids in the architecture throughout the Forum) are aesthetically compelling. They might lead the viewer to be fascinated with the "barbarian" Dacians and even to feel pathos in the face of their defeat.[24] Such victims were worthy of Rome's might.

Scenes of piety balance and enforce the message of Roman power manifest through war and decapitations. If at one point the severed heads of Dacian males are proudly thrust forward toward Trajan (Fig. 15), more often we find the rhetoric of well-ordered Roman *pietas* and willingness to welcome

[21] Coarelli, *The Column of Trajan*, 27. The height of the relief and the figures increasing from the bottom of the column to the top (relief: 0.89 m to 1.25 m; figures: 0.60 m to 0.80 m). Although some think that the reliefs may have been painted, Conti has argued that no such traces have ever been noted; she instead points to the variety of tools used to work its surface, including a curved rasp, a flat chisel, a roundel, and running drills. The relief was not polished with pumice. Cinzia Conti, "The Restoration of Trajan's Column (1981–1988)," in Coarelli, *The Column of Trajan*, 245–49.

[22] See, e.g., Coarelli, *The Column of Trajan*, plates 11–15. The personified river god of the Danube appears at the start of the Column, and later Jupiter appears, hurling a thunderbolt against the Dacians.

[23] Brilliant, *Visual Narratives*, 97–99. Coarelli notes that there are eight *adlocutio* scenes, eight sacrifice scenes, and many representations of men at work building battlements or traveling to war (Coarelli, *The Column of Trajan*, 27). See, however, the analysis of Natalie Boymel Kampen ("Looking at Gender: The Column of Trajan and Roman Historical Relief," in Donna Stanton and Abigail Stewart, eds., *Feminisms in the Academy* [Ann Arbor: University of Michigan Press, 1995] 60), who carefully shows the "emperor's remove from violence": he is usually "at least one compositional unit away from the actual bloodshed," and the artisans use walls, trees, and reverse the emperor's direction of movement in relation to the battle scene in order to keep him apart from the violence. Kampen argues that this visual rhetoric keeps Trajan as an exemplar of *moderatio*, *humanitas*, and manly reserve.

[24] On the depiction of barbarians as *pathos*-inspiring, see Tonio Hölscher, *The Language of Images in Roman Art* (trans. A. Snodgrass and A. Künzl-Snodgrass; Cambridge: Cambridge University Press, 2004) 27–34; see the analysis of the depiction of Decebalus, the Dacian leader, in Kampen, "Looking at Gender," 63.

15. Roman soldiers proffer severed heads of Dacians to the Emperor Trajan. Relief from Column of Trajan, Rome. DAIR 41.1455.

barbarians. In one scene, Dacian men (Figs. 16 and 17), their beards, long hair, and heavy cloaks marking them as non-Roman, stand with their children at the edge of a city. Their arms are outstretched in welcome and supplication; we can see the creases of their gesturing hands. Once in the city, Trajan offers a libation, pouring from a *patera* (a broad, shallow dish for pouring offerings) as a flute player stands behind and to the emperor's right. From the top register of the relief we know that an impressive animal sacrifice is to follow. Four bulls await, each held by strong-armed men nude to the waist. Below, crowds of Romans and Dacians join together, Dacian women bringing up the rear, one veiled woman holding a baby, the children gesturing. All participate in the moment of piety. The relief communicates the idea that this war brings peaceful ceremony and is accompanied by right religious festival, and the next generation is there as witness, to attest to it in the future. Those in Rome

16. Adventus and sacrifice scene, part 1. Relief from Column of Trajan, Rome. DAIR 89.558.

17. Adventus and sacrifice scene, part 2. Relief from Column of Trajan, Rome. DAIR 89.559.

who look closely at the column learn about the clemency and piety of the emperor, the resolution of war in the distant provinces, and the self-control of the Roman army.[25]

We shall return in the third part of this chapter to the Forum of Trajan. I begin with the Column of Trajan because even a glance at it – its setting, embedded between a basilica of justice and a temple to the deified emperor, literally in the middle of the Latin and Greek libraries of Trajan; and its rhetoric of piety, ethnic identity, and Roman might – allows us to see the discourse in which Justin's *Apologies* participate. That the Dacian defeat is both a cause for celebration and something pathos-inspiring also allows us to see how such Roman propaganda contained within itself seeds for viewers' many and differing interpretations.

II. JUSTIN'S *APOLOGIES*

As we learned in Chapter 2, Justin was one of the traveling men of the empire and a full participant in the debates over *paideia* and ethnic identity in the so-called Second Sophistic. He states that his home city is Flavia Neapolis (modern-day Nablus) in Syria Palestine.[26] His *Dialogue with Trypho*, in which Justin constructs and trumps a Jewish interlocutor,[27] mentions the Bar Kochba revolt of 132–135, which results in the takeover of Jerusalem by Rome and its renaming as Aelia Capitolina; in *1 Apol.* 31 he asserts that Bar Kochba persecuted Christians. He writes in the shadow cast by Jewish resistance to Rome in 66–73 in Palestine and in 115–117 in Cyrenaica, Egypt, and Rome, and at a time when Christianity was often perceived as an aberration from or a heresy of Judaism. In fact, Justin has been called an inventor of heresy, since he works to construct a Christianity different from contemporaneous Jewish and Christian communities.[28]

[25] Dillon discusses the Column of Marcus Aurelius and its depiction of women with children as "synecdoche for the entire community, for a people and their future" ("Women on the Columns of Trajan and Marcus Aurelius and the Visual Language of Roman Victory," in *Representations of War*, 246–62; quotation at 262); Kampen, "Looking at Gender."

[26] Syria Palestina is the name given to the regions formerly called Judea after Hadrian's subjection of Jerusalem (Erwin R. Goodenough, *The Theology of Justin Martyr* [Jena: Verlag Frommansche Buchhandlung, 1923] 57); this renaming may have been intended to diffuse the force of the term "Judea" and thus "Jew" (*Ioudaios*).

[27] See Laura Nasrallah, "The Rhetoric of Conversion and the Construction of Experience: The Case of Justin Martyr," in F. Young et al., eds., *Studia Patristica: Papers Presented at the Fourteenth International Conference on Patristic Studies Held in Oxford 2003* (Leuven: Peeters, 2006) 467–74; Andrew Jacobs, *Remains of the Jews: The Holy Land and Christian Empire in Late Antiquity* (Stanford, CA: Stanford University Press, 2004) 27–32, and his "Dialogical Differences: (De-)Judaizing Jesus' Circumcision," *JECS* 15 (2007) 291–335.

[28] See esp. Justin *Dial. Tryph.* 16, 130–32. Daniel Boyarin, *Border Lines: The Partition of Judaeo-Christianity* (Philadelphia: University of Pennsylvania Press, 2004), and also his *Dying for*

Justin's writings indicate that he lived in Rome for a time and there fought with the philosopher Crescens. This rivalry, it is often claimed, led to his death;[29] the implication is that Crescens exposed Justin as a Christian philosopher at a time when being a Christian was a dangerous thing. Justin himself offers Christians' courage at death as one explanation for his attraction to Christianity (*2 Apol.* 2–3); he also mentions the tortures suffered by Christians (*Dial. Tryph.* 110). The *Martyrdom of Justin and His Companions*, a work of questionable historical value, picks up this thread. It depicts Justin as a philosophical teacher who lived and taught above a bath complex in Rome and died for his troubles.[30] For those who knew the martyrdom story and also read or heard read Justin's own *Apologies*, the issues of justice, piety, culture, philosophy, and articulations of Christian identity already found in the *Apologies* would be intensified by the poignant "memory," whether legendary or real, of a Justin who witnessed in a court in Rome that he was a philosopher and a Christian, and was martyred for it.

Like other philosophers of the day, Justin, in his *Apologies* of 150–155 CE, throws himself into the debate over right theological thinking and religious practice, fully participating in the cultural economy (displaying Greek rhetorical skills, for example, or demonstrating a knowledge of philosophy, cult practice, and myths), and resisting what he sees as the travesty of how piety and atheism are defined at the time. He does so in part to criticize imperial claims to good judgment, to being lovers of *paideia*, and to being pious. Instead, Justin declares one, true God (and that God's Logos). It is God's imperial right to judge.

As he elaborates the themes of justice, piety, and *paideia*, Justin asserts that a crisis of representation exists in the Roman Empire. This crisis manifests itself in two ways. First, imperial justice and imperial claims to philosophical, cultural, and pious behaviors and attitudes are a sham; the imperial family's self-representation is a lie. Second, *daimones* in the world have labored to make Christianity *seem* derivative.[31] The *daimones*, Justin argues, knowing what

God: Martyrdom and the Making of Christianity and Judaism (Stanford, CA: Stanford University Press, 1999) esp. 22–41. On Justin as the inventor of heresy see Alain Le Boulluec, *La notion d'hérésie dans la literature greque, IIe–IIIe siècles* (2 vols.; Paris: Etudes augustiniennes, 1985) 1.110 and more generally 1.36–90; and Daniel Boyarin, "Justin Martyr Invents Judaism," *CH* 70.3 (2001) 427–61, esp. 438–40.

29 Tatian *Ad Graec.* 19.1 = Eusebius *Hist. eccl.* 4.16.8–9. Epiphanius *Pan.* 46.1 talks about Justin's death at thirty years during the reign of Hadrian, although this date is probably wrong (Leslie William Barnard, *St. Justin Martyr: The First and Second Apologies* [New York: Paulist Press, 1997] 3).

30 See Harlow Gregory Snyder, "'Above the Bath of Myrtinus': Justin Martyr's 'School' in the City of Rome" (*HTR* 100.3 [2007] 335–62) for an attempt to place Justin within Rome, based upon remaining evidence of Roman baths. See Herbert Musurillo, *The Acts of the Christian Martyrs* (Oxford: Clarendon, 1972) xix–xx regarding different recensions of the martyrdom.

31 See also Lyman, "Hellenism and Heresy," 216–17.

would come, proleptically constructed gods, myths, rituals, and philosophical attitudes that look like Christianity and seem to predate Christianity, but are historically secondary to Christianity, and differ from it.

Names and Deeds: Justin Introduces Himself, the Emperors, and the Mock Court

In the first phrases of his *First Apology*, as we have seen, Justin invokes and evokes as his readers the Roman imperial family, while he presents himself as a provincial subject of empire.

> To the Emperor Titus Aelius Hadrianus Antoninus Eusebes [i.e., Pius] Augustus; and to his son Caesar Verissimus the Philosopher; and to Lucius the Philosopher,[32] the natural son of Caesar[33] and the adopted son of Pius, a lover of *paideia*; and to the sacred Senate, with the whole People of the Romans, I, Justin, the son of Priscus and grandson of Bacchius, from the city of Flavia Neapolis in Syria Palestine, have made this address and petition on behalf of those of every race who are unjustly hated and abusively threatened, myself being one of them.
>
> Αὐτοκράτορι Τίτῳ Αἰλίῳ Ἀδριανῷ Ἀντωνίνῳ Εὐσεβεῖ Σεβαστῷ, καὶ Καίσαρι Οὐηρισσίμῳ υἱῷ φιλοσόφῳ, [καὶ Λουκίῳ φιλοσόφῳ, Καίσαρος φύσει υἱῷ καὶ Εὐσεβοῦς εἰσποιητῷ, ἐραστῇ παιδείας,] ἱερᾷ τε συγκλήτῳ καὶ δήμῳ παντὶ Ρωμαίων, ὑπὲρ τῶν ἐκ παντὸς γένους ἀνθρώπων <θεοσεβῶν>, ἀδίκως μισουμένων καὶ ἐπηρεαζομένων, Ἰουστῖνος Πρίσκου του Βακχείου, τῶν ἀπὸ Φλαουίας Νέας πόλεως τῆς Συρίας Παλαιστίνης, εἷς αὐτῶν <ὤν>, τὴν προσφώνησιν καὶ ἔντευξιν πεποίημαι.[34]

Justin's *Apologies* – which we should understand as related documents, composed only a few years apart and directed toward the same audience – inscribe as addressees Antoninus Pius, Marcus Aurelius, Lucius Verus, and the Sacred

[32] There is a problem with this line in the Arethas codex. We know from 2 *Apol.* 2.47–48 that Antoninus Pius and Marcus Aurelius are certainly addressed in the *Apologies*, and throughout the Roman emperors (rather than the people or the Senate, who are mentioned separately, e.g., at *1 Apol.* 56.2) are the main addressees. The first lines of Justin's *First Apology* are taken from Eusebius *Hist. eccl.* 4.12; according to Robert M. Grant (*Greek Apologists of the Second Century* [Philadelphia: Westminster, 1988] 52), Eusebius had access to better materials than the Arethas codex. See the apparatus in Miroslav Marcovich, *Iustini Martyris Apologiae Pro Christianis* (Berlin: De Gruyter, 1994) 31; see also esp. the edition and apparatus of Johannes Otto, *Corpus apologetarum Christianorum saeculi secundi* (9 vols.; Wiesbaden: Sändig, 1851–1969) 1.2–3 for a detailed discussion. Gustav Volkmar, "Die Zeit Justin's des Märtyrers, kritisch untersucht," *Theol. Jahr.* 14 (1855) esp. 234–83 discusses text critical problems and imperial titles in an attempt to fix the date of the *First Apology*. He also concludes that the phrase καὶ Λουκίω φιλοσόφου Καίσαρος . . . υἱῷ καὶ Εὐσεβοῦς εἰσποιητῷ, ἐραστῇ παιδείας is an interpolation (p. 261).

[33] I.e., the natural son of L. Aelius Caesar, whom Hadrian appointed as a successor, but who never reached the throne.

[34] *1 Apol.* 1.1. Unless otherwise noted, I use the Greek edition of Miroslav Marcovich, *Iustini Martyris*; and unless otherwise noted, all translation are mine; see also the translation of Barnard, *St. Justin Martyr: The First and Second Apologies*.

Senate and Roman people.[35] Justin uses the emperors' own epithets of "piety" (*eusebeia* in Greek, *pius* in Latin, applied to Antoninus Pius) and "philosophy" or "philosophical" (applied to Marcus Aurelius). He also refers to Lucius as both philosopher and "lover of *paideia*."[36]

Scholars have often defined apologetic as minority speech directed toward powerful outsiders[37] – as speech directed towards emperors, provincial governors, Jews, or "the nations." Recent work has questioned, however, whether early Christian writings were indeed headed to the emperors as petitions or pamphlets. What is clear is that texts like Justin's were immediately used in Christian communities; for example, Athenagoras likely borrows from Justin, and Eusebius collates these writers and their texts into his history of Christianity. Many readers and hearers in the earliest reception of the apologies knew that they or their communities were not the imperial family or the Greeks purportedly addressed. They knew that the judicial or ambassadorial setting constructed by the text was not enacted in their reading or hearing of it.

Even if the imperial family was not discussing Justin's recent prose address over their luxurious meal of quail and cuttlefish, addressing the emperors allows Christian writers to call the emperors into being, just as – so they claim – the imperial system of justice calls Christians into being by accusing them of crimes based upon the "name alone."[38] Justin (and, as we shall see, Athenagoras) constructs himself and those on behalf of whom he writes as subjects of the empire's rhetoric of tolerance and reality of exclusion.[39] From the beginnings of their respective treatises, both Athenagoras and Justin do nothing unexpected in this initial claim of subject-hood or in their evocation of titles that the emperors allowed to be applied to themselves, epithets that packed cultural and religious punch. The usual form of a *proemium* includes the name of the writer and the addressee, including his or her titles. Terms like "pious," "philosophical," "lover of culture" were often chosen by the imperial family,

35 Already in the seventeenth century scholars realized that the two apologies are integrally related, with the second presupposing some of the information offered in the first. The *Second Apology* is an appendix or supplement to the first, which was published in ca. 150 (Marcovich, *Iustini Martyris*, 10–11). For fuller discussion and debate, see Marcovich, *Iustini Martyris*, 1–10; Eric Osborn, *Justin Martyr* (Tübingen: Mohr [Siebeck], 1973) 10–11; in opposition to these, see Goodenough, *The Theology of Justin Martyr*, 84–87. *2 Apol.* 1 addresses "the Romans" as well as the emperors; *2 Apol.* 2.47–48 refers to Antoninus Pius and Marcus Aurelius. Each oration has a rhetorical unity, including perorations for each (Marcovich, *Iustini Martyris*, 3–9).

36 Athenagoras uses similar language: "To the Emperors Marcus Aurelius Antoninus and Lucius Aurelius Commodus, conquerors of Armenia and Sarmatia, and above all philosophers" (*Leg.* 1.1).

37 See esp. Grant, *Greek Apologists*, 9.

38 See discussion of the genre of so-called apologies in Chapter 1.

39 On the issue of Christian intolerance in the writings of G. E. M. de Ste. Croix, and a summary of recent scholarship on the topic, see Joseph Streeter, "Introduction: de Ste. Croix on Persecution," in G. E. M. de Ste. Croix, *Christian Persecution, Martyrdom, and Orthodoxy* (eds. Michael Whitby and Joseph Streeter; Oxford: Oxford University Press, 2006) 4–8, 30–32.

celebrated as expansions of their titles, and displayed by means of architecture, statuary, or coinage.[40] But what *is* piety, and its opposite, atheism? What *is* true philosophy, and its opposite: those who garb themselves as philosophers but are charlatans, incorrect practitioners? What is true *paideia* or culture, that matrix for philosophical thought? The emperors themselves, because of their traditional yet, to Justin's eye, hubristic epithets, become terms under debate.

Justin appeals to Roman claims to tolerance, speaking the common language of Greek, of privileged philosophy, and of Roman subject-hood. Justin also addresses himself to Rome as one of its beleaguered provincial elites, who takes up the standard for others.[41] He writes not an *apologia* but an "address and petition" (τὴν προσφώνησιν καὶ ἔντευξιν πεποίημαι) "on behalf of those of every race who are unjustly hated and abusively threatened, myself being one of them" (1.1).[42] Thus his rhetoric both acknowledges his particular identity (son of Priscus, grandson of Bacchius, from Flavia Neapolis in Syria Palestine), and subsumes and erases this identity into a universal mission.[43] Justin admits his provincial origins, asserts his cultured right to speak, and critiques Roman claims to tolerance or what we might call cultural diversity.[44] Justin and other Christian apologists often reject such claims because, they

[40] See Carlos Noreña, "The Communication of the Emperor's Virtues," *JRS* 91 (2001) 146–58; for a later period, see Michael Peachin, *Roman Imperial Titulature and Chronology, A.D. 235–84* (Amsterdam: Gieben, 1990). See Olivier Hekster, "Coins and Messages: Audience Targeting on Coins of Different Denominations?" 20–35 in Lukas De Bois, Olivier Hekster, et al., eds., *The Representation and Perception of Roman Imperial Power. Proceedings of the Third Workshop of the International Network Impact of Empire (Roman Empire, c. 200 BC–AD 476)* (Amsterdam: Geiben, 2003). See also Marcus Aurelius's *Meditations.*

[41] In doing so, Justin participates in a long and continuing tradition of provincial/Greek elites who address themselves to Rome, such as Polybius, Josephus, and Aelius Aristides. "Justin's intellectual hybrid reflected his own attempt as a Christian provincial and a philosopher to portray universal truth within the cultural traditions of the second century" (Lyman, "Hellenism and Heresy," 220; see also 221).

[42] Grant, *Greek Apologists*, 54 notes that one term that Justin uses for his writing, *prosphōnēsis* or address, is the same term the rhetorician Menander applies to a "speech of praise to rulers spoken by an individual." On the debate regarding apologists and speeches of praise, see esp. William R. Schoedel, "In Praise of the King: A Rhetorical Pattern in Athenagoras," in Donald F. Winslow, ed., *Disciplina Nostra: Essays in Memory of Robert F. Evans* (Cambridge, MA: Philadelphia Patristic Foundation, 1979) 69–92. Grant also notes (p. 54) that Justin uses the term *enteuxis*, petition, and *exēgēsis*, explanation. See also Lampe, *From Paul to Valentinus*, 268, who finds legal terms in Justin.

[43] As Goodenough puts it, Justin does not give "decisive information about his race." His father's name (Priscus) is Latin; his grandfather's (Bacchius) is Greek, so his ancestors may have been Greek, or Roman colonists. Goodenough, *The Theology of Justin Martyr*, 57. Goodenough and more recent writers like Grant (*Greek Apologists*, 50), attribute to Justin a Samaritan origin, but Otto refuted this in his 1851 edition of Justin's writings (*Corpus apologetarum Christianorum*, 1.6 n. 5). On Justin's rhetoric of race and Christian universalism, see discussion in Chapter 2 earlier and esp. Denise Kimber Buell, *Why This New Race? Ethnic Reasoning in Early Christianity* (New York: Columbia University Press, 1995) 78–80, 141–42.

[44] Such a stance has resonances with Bhabha's discussion of the modern colonized subaltern: "From that shadow . . . emerges cultural difference as an *enunciative* category; opposed to relativistic notions of cultural diversity, or the exoticism of the 'diversity' of cultures" (Homi Bhabha, *Location of Culture* [New York: Routledge, 1994] 60).

argue, Roman respect for such institutions and practices is quixotic.[45] Justin presents himself as a colonial subject who insists upon his provincial origins and identity, as well as his right to address those at the center of the empire.

At the same time, Justin's first lines can be read in light of postcolonial criticism as a form of *mimēsis*. Justin constructs himself as the Roman Empire's shadow figure, someone who is "almost the same, but not quite."[46] On the one hand, he is culturally different: He is part of the diversity emerging from the *oikoumenē*'s borders, and he aligns himself with the "oppressed of every race" within the empire. On the other hand, through his skill at Greek and knowledge of cultured arguments, Justin configures himself as a Hellenizing philosopher.

It is an irony that scholars have debated whether Justin and others like him *either* were Christians at heart, play-acting at Hellenism to gain converts *or* were Greek at heart, muddying the pure baptismal waters of Christianity with Greek philosophy. Such modern scholars echo ancient accusations of fake philosophical cloaking. Lucian, for instance, repeated the old joke of the dirty, bearded, ragged man who seemed to others to be a philosopher, but was a charlatan. To ask about the authenticity of Justin's Christian *or* Greek identity misses the point of how fluidly the rhetoric of ethnicity and religion operated in the Roman world, as we have seen in the last chapters. Greek *paideia* and even Greek ethnicity can be bought or borrowed through correct training and use of language, or the invention of genealogies by those cities joining the Panhellenion. Justin's *mimēsis* encompasses his various rhetorical positionings as Greek, philosophical, educated, Christian, baptized, interpreter of Jewish scripture.

In the very first pages of the *Apology*, Justin turns to the emperors for judgment. Yet just after these introductory words, Justin obliquely criticizes

45 See, e.g., Athenagoras *Leg.* 14. On tolerance and diversity as a matter of Roman policy, see Ando, *The Matter of the Gods*, 95–148.

46 "Then colonial mimicry is the desire for a reformed, recognizable Other, *as a subject of a difference that is almost the same, but not quite*. Which is to say, that the discourse of mimicry is constructed around an *ambivalence*; in order to be effective, mimicry must continually produce its slippage, its excess, its difference" (*Location of Culture*, 86). Rebecca Lyman uses Homi Bhabha's concept of the hybrid to elucidate Justin, and uses Bhabha's comment that the hybrid "intervenes in the exercise of authority" (Lyman, "Hellenism and Heresy," 216, quoting Bhabha, *Location of Culture*, 114.) With the term "hybrid," Lyman rightly seeks to break the old impasse; yet we must be careful to refine our use of the term hybridity, since it could well apply to the emperor Hadrian, a Spanish provincial philhellenic Roman emperor. See Rebecca Lyman, "The Politics of Passing: Justin Martyr's Conversion as a Problem of 'Hellenization,'" in Kenneth Mills and Anthony Grafton, eds., *Conversion in Late Antiquity and the Early Middle Ages: Seeing and Believing* (Rochester, NY: University of Rochester Press, 2003) 34–54; esp. 37–38 on the subversive potential of hybridity; pp. 38, 40 on "an indeterminacy of religion and culture in Roman Hellenism itself" (quotation at p. 40). On the problems of the term "hybridity" for postcolonial criticism, see Robert Young, *Colonial Desire: Hybridity in Theory, Culture, and Race* (New York: Routledge, 1995), esp. 1–28. As it is used in postcolonial criticism, "hybrid" implies some sort of resistance or, to use Bhabha's language, intervention "in the exercise of authority." While Justin may resist Roman imperial misuse of justice, he does so in the service of his own "exercise of authority," which involves authorizing Christians over and against Jews.

the emperors. Armed with the force of the *logos*, which can be read, depending on the audience, as the Logos that is Christ or as Reason in the world, Justin offers a one-two punch using the terminology of truth:

> Reason (ὁ λόγος) dictates that those who are truly pious and philosophers should honor and desire truth alone, declining to follow the opinions of the ancients, if those be bad. For the wise *logos* not only dictates that the lover of truth, even if death is threatened, should not follow those who do and teach something unjustly, but also that s/he should choose to say and to do just things. Therefore you [who are called][47] pious and philosophers and guardians of justice and lovers of *paideia*, listen in every way! If you even are, let it be shown! For we have come forward to speak, not flattering you through these writings or addressing you just for the sake of it, but demanding that a judgment be made according to a precise and closely examined study – that you not be held fast by a preconception or the desire to please superstitious people or by an irrational impulse or long continuing, prejudicial rumor, so that you cast a vote against yourselves. For we have reckoned that we ourselves are not at all able to suffer some evil except we be judged workers of evil or determined to be wicked. You are able to kill, but not to harm. (2.1–4)

Justin here pairs piety and philosophy three times, once in the titles of the emperors, once in musing on reason, piety, philosophy, and truth (the first line of the quotation above), and again immediately thereafter, when he brings together a second-person address and the imperial titles with this issue of truth: "Therefore you [who are called] pious and philosophers and guardians of justice and lovers of *paideia*, listen in every way!" Justin appeals to the emperors to be what they say they are. Apuleius's *Apologia* – his defense against charges of magic – is contemporaneous with the writings of Justin and refers to a statue of the emperor present and watching in court.[48] By evoking the presence of the emperors and by using terms of crime and judgment, Justin conjures a court setting. In the readers' or hearers' minds, such a setting involves simulacra – statues – of the emperors, further intensifying Justin's play with the theme of imperial representation.

[47] ὅτι λέγεσθε is deleted by Stephanus as a gloss (Marcovich, *Iustini Martyris*, 33), but even absent this phrase, the meaning remains: The addressees, who in the construction of the *Apology* are the emperors, are called "pious and philosophers and guardians of justice and lovers of *paideia*." The term "guardians of justice" (φύλακες δικαιοσύνης) recalls the language of Plato's *Republic*.

[48] Apuleius *Apol.* 85; so too Severianus of Gabala *In Cosmogoniam* 6.5, written ca. 400 and quoted in Ando, *Imperial Ideology*, 233–34; see also Ando's discussion of imperial portraits and their dissemination and power (pp. 206–73); see Jaś Elsner, *Imperial Rome and Christian Triumph: The Art of the Roman Empire AD 100–450* (Oxford: Oxford University Press, 1998) 54–58. See also Eric Varner, *Mutilation and Transformation:* Damnatio Memoriae *and Roman Imperial Portraiture* (Leiden: E. J. Brill, 2004) esp. 1–12 on the power of imperial images and the impulse to destroy them.

Justin seeks to make the rulers whom they claim to be: "Rulers should cast their vote, again, by neither violence nor tyranny, but following piety and philosophy" (3.2). But Justin also quickly reverses the term of the court and challenges the idea that it is Christians who are really on trial. Justin has suggested that if the emperors are persuaded by rumor or false accusation – distracted from "due process" – their votes against Christians will somehow reverse "so that you cast a vote against yourself" (2.3). While it is the subjects' responsibility to allow a proper inspection and to offer a full narrative of their deeds, it is "your" task – the imperial task – to be good judges. If the emperors do not act justly, once they have learned about Christians, they are inexcusable or indefensible before God.[49]

Christians are misrepresented by Roman courts, insofar as they are judged by the "name alone" with no reference to the deeds which constitute the name, according to Justin. Justin puns, as Christians often did, on the homophone in Greek between *chrēstos*, which means "excellent," and "Christian":[50] "Therefore the surname of a name is judged to be neither good nor bad, apart from the deeds which underlie the name. Otherwise, as far as [one would know] from what our name indicates, we would be *chrēstotatoi*, 'most excellent'" (4.1). Christians are excellent for the Roman Empire. They pay their taxes quickly (17.1) and if judged guilty of some real crime, they will willingly submit to Roman law and be condemned.[51]

On the Name

Among the Greeks, one can claim the name "philosopher" even if one merely dresses the part (*1 Apol.* 4, 7); the "barbarians" are stuck with the label even if they are wise (*1 Apol.* 7).[52] Some Christians, Justin later admits, are like the so-called philosophers: They dress themselves in the name "Christian" while displaying none of the virtues associated with Christianity.[53] In such a context, what does a name mean, and why are Christians judged on account of it?

From literature other than Justin's *Apologies* or Athenagoras's *Embassy* we know stories of Christians accused in court based upon the name alone.[54] In

[49] Αναπολόγητον γὰρ λοιπὸν μαθοῦσιν <ὑμῖν>, ἢν μὴ τὰ δίκαια ποιήσητε, ὑπάρξει πρὸς θεόν, *1 Apol.* 3.5.

[50] This is due to the itacisms of the second century and beyond. *1 Apol.* 12 explains that "Christians" comes from the name Jesus "Christ."

[51] Athenagoras *Leg.* 2; Justin *1 Apol.* 4. Later, Justin will hint that sedition toward empire and a refusal to submit to Roman law undergird accusations against Christians: he states that the kingdom for which "we" hope is not a human one (*1 Apol.* 11).

[52] On this *topos*, see Arnaldo Momigliano, *Alien Wisdom: The Limits of Hellenization* (Cambridge: Cambridge University Press, 1975); Guy G. Stroumsa, *Barbarian Philosophy: The Religious Revolution of Early Christianity* (WUNT 112; Tübingen: Mohr Siebeck, 1999).

[53] *1 Apol.* 26, directed especially against Marcion; see also *1 Apol.* 58.

[54] On martyrdom as a means of forging "racial, civic, and national identities," see Buell, *Why This New Race?*, 52–59, quotation at p. 53. My reading of erasure of identity through the

the correspondence between Pliny, governor of Bithynia, and the emperor Trajan (ca. 112), Pliny queries whether one can arrest Christians on the basis of the "name itself, if it is without crimes, or if crimes consistent with the name are punishable."[55] The theme of the name "Christian" as an offense to Roman power appears in other early Christian literature. In the *Acts of the Scillitan Martyrs*, which claims to be an account from 17 July 180, the group's insistence upon the name Christian, and their refusal to honor Caesar, lead to persecution. The pagan governor Saturninus plaintively asserts that "we too are a religious people, and our religion is a simple one,"[56] trying to convince the group to turn away from the name. Yet Vestia states, "I am a Christian" (*Christiana sum*). Secunda offers: "What I am, that I hope to be" (*quod sum, ipsud uolo esse*), asserting the already and not yet of Christian identity. Twice, Speratus asserts: "I am a Christian" (*Christianus sum*) and we learn that all agreed with him, despite the punishments to come. In the end, they are beheaded, as the text puts it, *pro nomine Christi*, for the name of Christ.[57]

Similarly, the early third-century *Martyrdom of Perpetua and Felicitas* offers a play on the inextricable connection between the person and her sign or name, "Christian." The Christian Perpetua converses with her non-Christian father, who is trying to convince her to recant and to leave prison.

> "'Father,' said I, 'do you see this vase here, for example, or water pot or whatever?'
>
> 'Yes, I do', said he.
>
> And I told him: 'Could it be called by any other name than what it is?' (*Numquid alio nomine uocari potest quam quod est?*)
>
> And he said: 'No.'

assertion of the name "Christian" is influenced by her analysis. On martyrdom and spectacle, see Elizabeth Castelli, *Martyrdom and Memory: Early Christian Culture Making* (New York: Columbia University Press, 2004) chaps. 3–4; see esp. pp. 112–17 on apologists' polemics against spectacle.

55 *Nomen ipsum, si flagitiis careat, an flagitia cohaerentia nomini puniantur, Ep.* 10.96. The edition is Selatie Edgar Stout, *Plinius, Epistulae: A Critical Edition* (Bloomington: Indiana University Press, 1962). On Pliny's letters as a "representation of how *humanitas* is to be manifested in the government of an eastern province," see Greg Woolf, *Becoming Roman: The Origins of Provincial Civilization in Gaul* (Cambridge: Cambridge University Press, 1998) 68. See the discussion of Robert M. Grant ("Sacrifices and Oaths as Required of Early Christians," in Patrick Granfield and Josef Jungmann, eds., *Kyriakon: Festschrift Johannes Quasten* [2 vols.; Münster: Verlag Aschendorff, 1970] 1.12–17), who does not see such stories as constructions of Christian identity, but from them tries to index what Christians were required to do to escape condemnation in such judicial situations.

56 *. . . et nos religiosi sumus et simplex est religion nostra.* The edition and translation are from Musurillo, *The Acts of the Christian Martyrs*, 86–87. See also Cicero *Har. resp.* 19 on the superiority of Roman piety, and Ando, *The Matter of the Gods*, 120–48.

57 There may be echoes of the canonical Acts, with its references to miracles done "in the name of Jesus."

> 'Well, so too I cannot be called anything other than what I am, a Christian.'
>
> At this my father was so angered by the word 'Christian' that he moved towards me as though he would pluck my eyes out." (3.1–3)[58]

Again, when the procurator Hilarianus asks if she is a Christian, Perpetua replies, "I am a Christian" (6.4).

So also from the *Acts of the Martyrs of Lyons and Vienne*, we find the example of Sanctus who "held his ground against them with such resistance that he did not even tell his own name, or the race or the city whence he was, nor if he were slave or free, but to all questions he replied in the Roman language, 'I am a Christian.' This he conceded for name and city and race and for everything else, again and again. The nations (*ta ethnē*) heard no other sound from him" (Eusebius *Hist. eccl.* 5.1.20). All ethnic and status markers disappear[59] as Sanctus – he embodies his name, "holy" – becomes the essence of Christianity. He becomes totally Christian not only by his name or by his insistent "I am a Christian" but also because he manifests Christ's sufferings in himself: "His poor body was a witness to the things that had come to pass: it was entirely wound and bruise, shriveled and degraded, outside the human form. In it, Christ, suffering, brought to perfection great glories" (5.1.23).[60] Taking on Christ in one's body or in name is a crime: Attalus was paraded with a placard in Latin that stated, "This is Attalus, the Christian" (5.1.44); when asked while being roasted alive "what name God has, he replied, 'God has not a name as a human has'" (5.1.52).[61] While God has no name, the witness has no name but that of Christian; the martyr's entire self stands for Christ. The Christian becomes the sign – the *onoma* – of Christ.

A range of early Christian martyrdom traditions express the danger of the name Christian, on the one hand, and the willingness of the martyr to subsume every aspect of his or her identity to it, on the other. To every query about race or ethnicity (*genos*) and name and city, Sanctus replied, *Christianus sum*. In their insistence on foregrounding "Christian" as their ethnic identity and religious practice, with their bodies and voices these martyrs are depicted as engaging questions about Roman justice, true piety, the grounds of ethnic

58 ET Musurillo, *The Acts of the Christian Martyrs*, 109.

59 This disappearance calls to mind the pre-Pauline baptismal formula in Gal. 3:28.

60 The line between Christ and the Christian blurred in Sanctus's body, or, as Eusebius later records, in the body of the female slave Blandina who is hung on a stake in the shape of a cross. Blandina "had put on that great and invincible athlete, Christ" (*Hist. eccl.* 5.1.42), herself becoming Christ.

61 The theme of God's namelessness appears also in Justin's work; he distinguishes between the name (*onoma*) and the "address" (*prosrhēsis*), insisting that "God" is not really a name, but marks a "thing hard to explain" (*2 Apol.* 6.3).

affiliation, and Christian identity.[62] Christians represent other Christians, who are on the edge of death, as enacting and engaged in a semiotic debate of the utmost importance.

The Name and Speech–Acts

Justin asserted that the emperors as judges can go wrong in their casting of a vote "if they are misled by the superstitious and the irrational" (*1 Apol.* 2.1–4). That is, if they are misled by *atheotēta*, the atheism of which Christians are accused, the ritual of judgment will boomerang, and the emperors will cast a vote against themselves. Justin thus subtly asserts his role as both defendant and judge. Moreover, a text like Justin's provides a case of rhetorical infelicity; even more, of a deliberate misfire, to borrow from the thought and terminology of J. L. Austin's *How to Do Things with Words*. This is because the *Apologies* appear to be written to the emperor and his family, but are certainly received within another audience, a Christian one. The audience is doubled: The imperial family is invoked, but the more likely readers are Christians. Moreover, the court setting is evoked by Justin's appeal to the emperors, and it is reversed, since he asserts that there is a court higher than the imperial one.

Judith Butler's reading of Austin and analysis of the relation between words and acts provides a framework to read portions of Justin's *Apologies*.[63] Justin, and others before and after him, as we have seen, protests the signification of Christians whereby they are judged by name and not deed. The name becomes an act that is punishable. Austin and Judith Butler after him have been concerned about the relation between word and deed; they are interested in "the illocutionary speech act which is itself the deed that it effects."[64] Especially in the context of new legal regulations in the United States regarding "gays in the military," Butler asks: When can speech *be* a violent deed? – that is, when and what can a word *effect*?[65]

[62] On language of erasure and the idea of shifting race or affiliation, see Buell, *Why This New Race?*; on "Christians as an alternative ethnopolitical grouping to Roman imperial classifications" in the *Acts of the Scillitan Martyrs*, see p. 58. Elizabeth Castelli discusses such Christian texts as "counterscripts" that turn Roman violence to Christian advantage (*Martyrdom and Memory*, 122; see also 104–33).

[63] J. A. Austin, *How to Do Things with Words* (2nd ed.; ed. J. O. Urmson and Marina Sbisà; Cambridge, MA: Harvard University Press, 1975); Austin's speeches were originally given in 1955. On court-sanctioned violence, see Judith Butler, *Excitable Speech: A Politics of the Performative* (New York: Routledge, 1997) esp. 43–69. Butler is concerned with a variety of situations in which an image or a word is legally understood to be an act: pornography, racial slurs, and other hate speech.

[64] Butler, *Excitable Speech*, 3. This topic of efficacious speech and the connection between speech and deed is relevant to the study of ritual practice; see Talal Asad, *Genealogies of Religion: Discipline and Reasons of Power in Christianity and Islam* (Baltimore, MD: John Hopkins University, 1993) 55–79.

[65] Butler, *Excitable Speech*, 18. Aspects of Butler's analysis of new legal regulations in the United States regarding "gays in the military" provide a useful analogy for the analysis of Christian

The ritual space of the courtroom calls Christians into being by naming them, but then it also accuses Christians of effecting injury by their very name. Thus at the beginning of Justin's *Second Apology* we find Justin's account of a courtroom that is almost laughable in the arbitrariness of its "justice." As we saw in Chapter 2, Justin speaks of a Christian woman who decides to separate from her non-Christian husband because of his many vices. He brings against her the accusation of being a Christian, but she receives a stay of judgment from the emperor while she arranges her affairs. In the mean time, her husband turns his anger toward her teacher, Ptolemaeus: "He persuaded a centurion . . . to seize Ptolemaeus and to ask him only this: if he is a Christian" (*2 Apol.* 2.10–11). When Ptolemaeus, a "lover of truth," confesses to the name Christian, he is called up by the governor Urbicus and asked the same question and only that question: "If he was a Christian" (*2 Apol.* 2.13). Lucius, a bystander, piqued by the "unreasonable judgment," also comes forward as a Christian, as does a third man. They are all in the end sentenced and punished, according to Justin's story.[66] These Christians like the emperors, presumably, love truth and justice, but they are punished for it.

"Linguistic injury appears to be the effect not only of the words by which one is addressed but by the mode of address itself, a mode – a disposition or conventional bearing – that interpellates and constitutes a subject," writes Butler.[67] Justin too is concerned with the mode of address. As Justin (and, as we shall see, Athenagoras) represents it, this concern with the force of names or words in a judicial contest is not merely an arcane crisis of language, something that might result in a judicial slap on the wrist. Two kinds of performative speech are implied. The first is that being named "Christian" alone effects judicial consequences. The second is that judicial speech under the right conditions

claims that they are accused based upon the "name alone" or the "name itself." In both cases, to call oneself by name is to perform an illegal act. Butler encourages us to consider the puzzling matter of "how it is that a term or the proclamation of an identity might be understood discursively to carry or cause an injury."

[66] See Margaret Y. MacDonald, *Early Christian Women and Pagan Opinion: The Power of the Hysterical Woman* (Cambridge: Cambridge University Press, 1996) 205–13.

[67] Butler's topic here is the effect of pornography and hate speech (*Excitable Speech*, 2). Butler defines interpellation as "an address that regularly misses its mark, it requires the recognition of an authority at the same time that it confers identity through successfully compelling that recognition. . . . The mark interpellation makes is not descriptive, but inaugurative" (p. 33). She points out the underlying logic of Althusser's idea of interpellation: that a subject is constituted only in relation to his or her guilt before the law (Louis Althusser, "Ideology and the Ideological State Apparatuses: Notes towards an Investigation," in *Lenin and Philosophy and Other Essays* [trans. Ben Brewster; New York: Monthly Review Press, 2001] 106–26). On interpellation, see also Judith Butler, "Conscience Doth Make Subjects of Us All," *Yale French Studies* 88 (1995) 6–26, esp. 6–11 on the divine power of naming and baptism. Clifford Ando uses Althusser's concept of interpellation to discuss the Roman legal system in *Imperial Ideology and Provincial Loyalty in the Roman Empire* (Berkeley: University of California Press, 2000), e.g., at p. 212.

has effects. These effects, according to Butler, mask their own violence, the violence of the legal system.[68]

The narrative conceit of Justin's *Apologies* or of other ancient stories of the "name alone" is that to declare the name "Christian" is to resist the Roman court or mob. This speech-act is "insurrectionary," to use Butler's term.[69] When one uses the name, one knows the punishing effect this speech-act will generate; one knows that for the unjust judicial process, the name enacts atheism and thus treason, since to refuse to worship the gods was to endanger the piety and thus the safety of the state. Thus early Christian writings labeled as apologetic often assert "linguistic injury" as the precondition of their writing. Christians have been "interpellated": They have been called into being by the ritual force of the judicial system. Justin asserts that two wrongful acts of naming have taken place. First, Christians are named not according to their deeds, which are (according to the homophonic pun) excellent. Second, he calls into question imperial claims to piety, philosophy, and love of culture or *paideia*, claims that are often made concrete by the direct *naming* of an emperor with an epithet. What makes his *Apologies* even more interesting is the issue of naming in which Justin himself engages. Justin's actual audience is likely quite different from the audience he names in the *Apologies*. That is, the Christians who heard or read Justin's writings are not the emperors, Senate, or even the Roman people to whom the writings are addressed. Justin's *Apologies* judge Roman imperial claims to piety, philosophy, and justice in a Christian court.

A Higher Court

The beginning of Justin's *First Apology* grounds his petition in what seem to be straightforward judicial terms: Justin appeals the questionable rulings of various courts throughout the empire. But Justin does more than this. He suggests that another court will sit in judgment of the imperial family. That is, Justin uses the emperors' claims to represent or embody (to be the sign of) piety and justice in order to show the slippage between these names and the emperors who adopt them, on the one hand, and in order to point to true piety and true justice, on the other. He exposes this crisis of representation in order to set out what he sees as the truth of the situation.

Justin articulates the charges that have been brought against Christians: "Hence we have even been called atheists." In the judicial setting he conjures, he accepts the terms of the initial accusation: "We agree that we are atheists with regard to such so-called gods" (*1 Apol.* 6.1). But for Justin, these so-called

[68] Athenagoras states this judicial danger even more clearly than Justin: "The penalty imposed by our persecutors does not aim [only] at our goods, nor the shame at our honor, or the harm at some other lesser matters, . . . but at our bodies and souls, once we are bankrupt" (*Leg.* 1.4).

[69] See Butler, *Excitable Speech*, 160.

gods are really demons, and the criminal charge of atheism against Christians recalls for him the philosophically and unjustly killed Socrates. Christian religiosity, according to Justin, is directed toward the God who is "the truest and father of justice and self-control (σωφρωύνης) and of all virtues" (6.1). In a time when the emperor makes claims about his godhood and his fathering of the empire, Justin's naming God as father of justice and philosophical self-control shows up the falsity of imperial claims to the same.

To strengthen further his case against the emperors, Justin also uses past oracles, embedding his criticisms of imperial "justice" within the voices of others. We see this in a passage where Justin's quotation of LXX Psalm 2 can be read as addressed directly to the Roman imperial family, since the Psalm uses the second person plural to address "kings" or "emperors": "And now, emperors, understand; all who judge the earth, be educated [or "be disciplined," παιδεύθητε]. . . . Embrace knowledge (παιδείας), lest the Lord be angry, and you be destroyed from the just way, when his anger is kindled quickly. Blessed are all who trust in him" (*1 Apol.* 40.16–19).[70]

According to Aristotle, past oracles are especially useful proofs because they cannot have been biased by the contemporary situation.[71] Justin uses the unbiased and weighty voices of the past prophets and their statements about piety, justice, and *paideia* to bolster his arguments and to address the injustice of empire. The ancient tones of the Psalmist offer the same advice that Justin wishes to. Moreover, the passage he selects uses *paideia* and its verbal form; using the Psalm, Justin emphasizes that emperors need *paideia*, rather than already possessing it. The reader is reminded of imperial claims to culture and justice – Lucius is called a "lover of *paideia*" – at the beginning of the *First Apology* (1.1).

Justin also directly warns his inscribed audience of a divine court that sits in judgment. He cajoles and almost threatens the emperors into effecting justice in the court:

> Everywhere we try before all others to pay tributes and property taxes to those appointed by you, as we have been taught by him. . . . [Then follows the Jesus saying: "Give therefore to Caesar the things that are Caesar's, and to God the things that are God's."] For this reason we worship God alone, but respecting all other things, we serve you happily, agreeing with emperors and rulers of humans and praying that along with imperial power, you also be found to have sober reasoning.

70 Καὶ νῦν, βασιλεῖς, σύνετε παιδεύθητε πάντες οἱ κρίνοντες τὴν γῆν. Δουλεύσατε τῷ κυρίῳ ἐν φόβῳ καὶ ἀγαλλιᾶσθε αὐτῷ ἐν τρόμῳ. Δράξασθε παιδείας, μήποτε ὀργισθῇ κύριος, καὶ ἀπολεῖσθε ἐξ ὁδοῦ δικαίας, ὅταν ἐκκαυθῇ ἐν τάχει ὁ θυμὸς αὐτοῦ. Μακάριοι πάντες οἱ πεποιθότες ἐπ᾿ αὐτόν. Elsewhere, Justin uses the second-person plural to remind the emperors of their involvement in controlling Jewish territory and in the destruction of the temple (*1 Apol.* 32). On this idea of "doublespeak" to emperors, see Bartsch, *Actors in the Audience*, esp. chap. 4.

71 Aristotle *Rhet.*, esp. 1.15.13, "On Witnesses."

> But if you pay no heed to both our prayers and our setting forth all things clearly, we will be harmed not at all, we believe; but rather, we have also been persuaded that each, according to the worth of his or her deeds, will pay a price through eternal fire and receive judgments even according to the proportion of powers which s/he were demanded from the word of God, as Christ declared, saying, "To whom God gave much, much also will be demanded from him or her" (cf. Luke 12:48).
>
> Pay attention to the end of each of the previous emperors: they died a death common to all, which, if it came without sensation, would be unexpected luck for all the unjust. (*1 Apol.* 17.1–18.1)

Outside of Justin's mock court with the emperors stands a greater courtroom: a divine court and a divine judgment with painful consequences. This is reinforced clearly at the end of the *First Apology*: "We foretell to you that you will not escape the coming judgment of God, if you continue in injustice" (68.2).

Mimēsis, *Images, and* Daimones

On every level of his writing, Justin is thinking about *mimēsis* and crises of representation; he is exposing a world where attempts at imitation of virtues or of the divine often result, he claims, in a tragic misunderstanding. We have already seen that Justin outlines two representational crises. First, the emperors claim to be pious and philosophical; they are not, but he enjoins them to be so. Second, in a crazy world where anyone dressed in the right clothes can appear to be a philosopher, Christians are accused on the basis of their name alone, with no investigation of the deeds attached.

As we progress further into Justin's *Apologies*, we find that his writings detail another representational crisis: that of the mimetic powers of humans and especially of *daimones*. Quotidian "pagan" ritual and philosophical teachings are confused imitations of true religion – that is, of Christianity – that are actually demonic. *Daimōn* is often a neutral term in Greek, referring to a "spirit" or "divinity,"[72] but Justin presents *daimones* as skewing the world and

[72] See, e.g., Everett Ferguson, *Demonology of the Early Christian World* (New York: Edwin Mellen, 1980) 33–67. Although Justin's naming of the gods as *daimones* is polemical, in using the term Justin takes part in a larger and fairly neutral debate about how gods and spirits worked in the cosmos. We hear something similar in the second century writer Maximus of Tyre, who in a speech about Socrates' *daimonion* (his spirit or *genius*) argues that Homer refers to Athena as a *daimonion*. From here Maximus moves to ask: "But Homer's daemonic power is not a single entity, nor one that associates with just one individual in only one set of circumstances for only trivial purposes. It takes many forms and intervenes on many occasions, under many names, in many shapes, and with many different voices. Do you accept this to some degree, and believe in the existence of Athena, Hera, Apollo, Strife, and all the other Homeric *daimones*?" Maximus of Tyre *Or.* 8.5–6; ET M. B. Trapp, *The Philosophical Orations* (Oxford: Oxford University Press, 1997) 73. Plutarch's *On the Obsolescence of Oracles*

aborting justice. People driven by "irrational passion and lashing from evil demons" (5.1) do not perceive who Christians really are. The *daimones* are named gods because they inflict terror and fear: "But those who were seized by fear and did not know the *daimones* to be bad named them gods, and called each by the name which each among the *daimones* had set for itself" (5.2). That is, the *daimones* operate precisely contrary to true religiosity, as religion or piety would be philosophically defined at the time. Plutarch states, for example, that the emotions, and in particular fear of the gods, spur one not to piety but to its perverted simulacrum, an obsession with ritual that emerges from superstition. *Deisidaimonia* contains within it etymologically the idea of fearing the spirit realm.[73] The mind of the superstitious person renders the gods similar to the wicked *daimones* of which Justin speaks. As Plutarch puts it, "You see what kind of thoughts the superstitious have about the gods; they assume that the gods are capricious, unfaithful, changeable, vengeful, cruel, suspicious. As a result, the superstitious person must both hate and fear the gods" (*De superst.* 170E).[74]

Justin draws on the philosophical prestige of Socrates, the epitome of ancient Greek thought, and equates Christian identity with Socrates, in fact making Socrates a Christian.[75] Justin argues that Socrates, that anonymous Christian, to use Karl Rahner's term, tried to bring to light demonic machinations. Because he taught that the so-called gods were merely *daimones*, the *daimones* made sure that he was judged and executed as denying the gods and as impious (ὡς ἄθεον καὶ ἀσεβῆ, 5.3).

The *logos*/Logos – the word can be understood generally to mean "reason," or to mean Christ as Logos, for Christians – revealed the truth to the Greeks through Socrates and others, argues Justin; among the barbarians, the

(*Mor.* 417D) asks: Do the gods themselves actually demand bloody sacrifice? (See also Lucian *De sacr.* 9). No, according to one interlocutor; it is evil spirits who make such demands. Elsewhere, the *daimones* who guard or order the oracular site are described more neutrally as departing or returning, taking with them the power of the oracle (418D). See Ferguson, *Demonology*; and Arthur Droge, *Homer or Moses? Early Christian Interpretations of the History of Culture* (Tübingen: Mohr [Siebeck], 1989) 54–57. Thus while Justin may be influenced by the *Book of the Watchers* and the idea of fallen angels and their demonic progeny, as Annette Yoshiko Reed argues ("The Trickery of the Fallen Angels and the Demonic Mimesis of the Divine: Aetiology, Demonology, and Polemics in the Writings of Justin Martyr," *JECS* 12.2 [2004] 141–71, esp. 143–45), he is also engaging in an ongoing discussion with "pagans" about gods, demi-gods, and *daimones*. His understanding of the φαῦλοι δαιμόνες is thus not a "radical indictment of Greco-Roman culture" (Reed, "The Trickery of the Fallen Angels," 159) that is external to that culture, even if other aspects of his argument may be.

73 See Dale Martin, *Inventing Superstition: From the Hippocratics to the Christians* (Cambridge, MA: Harvard University Press, 2004) 1–35, 93–108, 125–39; see also Reed, "The Trickery of the Fallen Angels," 141–71; see also her *Fallen Angels and the History of Judaism and Christianity: The Reception of Enochic Literature* (New York: Cambridge University Press, 2005) chap. 5.

74 *Mor.* 170E; ET Plutarch *Moralia* (LCL; trans. Frank Cole Babbitt; 16 vols.; repr. Cambridge, MA: Harvard University Press, 2002) 2.489 with some modifications.

75 See the pamphlet by Adolf von Harnack, *Sokrates und die alte Kirche* (Berlin: G. Schade, 1900).

Logos – that is, as Christ – revealed itself directly.[76] Thus Justin renders the accusation that Christians are impious and atheists as a new variation of the old condemnation of Socrates. Christians are the new height of classical Greek courage, philosophical depth, and integrity: "Those who have lived by aid of the *logos* were Christians, even if they were considered atheists, as, for instance, among Greeks, on the one hand, Socrates and Herakleitos and those similar to them; among barbarians, on the other, Abraham and Ananias and Azarias and Misael[77] and Elias and many others, whose deeds and names we decline to recount now, since they are known" (46.3). Justin Christianizes not only Socrates and Herakleitos, great ancient Greek philosophers, but also the patriarch of Judaism, Abraham, the young men thrown into the fiery furnace for resisting the command to worship their king, and the prophet Elias. A Christian is a Socrates, and Socrates a Christian; for Justin, Abraham was not only a common father of Jews and Christians, but indeed a Christian before his time. What some see as atheism is in others' eyes the essence of resistive piety, whether on the part of Socrates or on the part of the men in the fiery furnace.

For Justin, those who strive to live according to the Logos in any age – Stoics (Herakleitos and Musonius come in for special mention), Socrates, and others – take part in some measure of Christian identity (cf. *2 Apol.* 8, 10). Who knew? Justin re-presents the world in a way few would expect, precisely drawing those from every "race" who are oppressed and rendering them Christians before the fact: The best of the Greeks and the best of the "barbarians" (that is, Jews) become part of the Christian *genos* or race. In Roman eyes, present-day Christians are atheists because they do not worship the *daimones* who are mere simulacra of gods; yet, Justin asserts, Christians are not atheists because they worship the Creator of all things (*1 Apol.* 13.1).

Justin first links the *daimones* explicitly with mimetic activity early in his treatise in a section that discusses images. "We do not honor with many sacrifices and wreaths of flowers those whom humans – forming them and setting them in sanctuaries – have given the name 'gods.' Therefore we know them to be soulless and dead things, which do not have the form of god – for we do not consider god to have such a form, which some say have been represented

[76] Justin borrows this argument from Stoicism; the Stoics tended to think that "the λόγος was present in its purest form at the beginning of the world" (Glenn W. Most, "Cornutus and Stoic Allegoresis: A Preliminary Report," *ANRW* II.36 [1989] 2020, citing M. Pohlenz, *Die Stoa. Geschichte einer geistigen Bewegung* [Göttingen: Vandenhoeck and Ruprecht, 1948] 97). From this grew a conviction about the special wisdom of the ancients, which led to "the expectation that they must have expressed correct (i.e., Stoic) philosophical views; and the fact that, on the surface, they seemed not to do so at all, will have led quickly to the strategy of unearthing these views at a deeper level," that is, in allegorical readings (Most, "Cornutus," 2021).

[77] The last three names are from Dan. 1.7 in its apocryphal supplement; see note by Barnard in his translation: Justin Martyr, *The First and Second Apologies*, 159–60 n. 296.

(μεμιμῆσθαι) for the purpose of honor[ing god]. We know them to have both the names and the forms of these evil *daimones* who have appeared" (*1 Apol.* 9.1). Things cannot be judged on the name alone, as Justin so often argues; if one glances beneath the signifier "gods," whether that signifier is in language or in image, one finds something other than the truly divine.

Not only are the so-called gods actually just *daimones*; these gods are also wrongly represented in material form. Thus the crisis of divine representation occurs on the level of language and image. Justin draws on the common philosophical idea that the divine (defined as immaterial) and the material world belong in different ontological categories. God does not have a form of the sort that is manifest through such material objects; in fact, God is "of unspeakable glory and form" (10.1). Like so much polemic of the time, both Christian and non-Christian, Justin discusses the busy labors of making a god, the materiality of the objects from which the divine emerges and the brutal mechanics of "boiling and cutting and smelting and beating matter" into a god (9.1). Such gods are often recycled, Justin continues in a serious and subtly satirical tone; they are often made out of "dishonorable vessels" (9.2). By this Justin activates an inventory of stories of low vessels rendered from former statues and rich metals, and the satirical tradition regarding humans who claim to be powerful and even divine. Juvenal, for example, recounted with glee the destruction of images of Sejanus: "Now the fires hiss; now, in bellows and forges, the head which was worshipped by the people burns, and remarkable Sejanus cracks. Then out of that face which was second in all the world are made little pitchers, basins, pans, chamberpots" (*Sat.* 10.62–64).[78] The raw materials out of which such gods were crafted were just that: material, corruptible, needing care as true divinity did not, or should not (*1 Apol.* 10.1).[79] The transformation from raw material to god is not the result of a numinous process; it is a mere change of form. "And often from dishonorable vessels, through craft changing and giving [them] form with respect only to their shape, they name [them] gods" (9.2).[80] Such human-effected metamorphosis

[78] I slightly modify the translation of *Juvenal and Persius* (ed. and trans. Susanna Morton Braund; LCL; Cambridge, MA: Harvard University Press, 2004) 370–71. On mutilation of images more broadly, see Varner, *Mutilation and Transformation*; Harriet I. Flower, *The Art of Forgetting: Disgrace and Oblivion in Roman Political Culture* (Chapel Hill: University of North Carolina Press, 2006).

[79] Paul Corby Finney, *The Invisible God: The Earliest Christians on Art* (New York: Oxford University Press, 1994) 47–53 on "hylotheism"; Robin Jensen discusses Justin in *Face to Face: Portraits of the Divine in Early Christianity* (Minneapolis, MN: Fortress, 2005) 71–73.

[80] καὶ ἐξ ἀτίμων πολλάκις σκευῶν, διὰ τέχνης τὸ σχῆμα μόνον ἀλλάξαντες καὶ μορφοποιήσαντες, < . . . > θεοὺς ἐπονομάζουσιν. The translation is awkward because an object or phrase seems to be missing from the text. H. Stephanus supplies ἀνθρώπων εἰκόνας before the word μορφοποιήσαντες; after the same word, Marcovich supplies instead ἀνδριάντας ποιήσαντες.

of a god is, in Justin's opinion, both irrational and an affront to god (ἐφ' ὕβρει τοῦ θεοῦ, 9.3).

Justin's comments on the making of god(s) out of matter are paired with a play on the terminology of *mimēsis*. Artisans engage in a mimetic enterprise (9.1), but Justin offers a better one: "We have been taught and we have been persuaded and we believe that God accepts only those who represent (μιμουμένους) the good things that are characteristic of God – self-control (σωφροσύνην) and justice and love of humanity (φιλανθρωπίαν) and such things as are proper to God, who is called by no given name" (10.1). *Mimēsis* should consist not in carving or molding statues; instead, an imitation of divine attributes – and not the thunderbolt or eagle of Jupiter (see again Fig. 3), but the virtues of the one true God – constitutes the productive and pious imitation of the unnamable divine.[81]

Justin names virtues that are not only associated with the divine, but with philosophers and also with the purportedly philosophical, pious, and beneficent imperial household. *Sōphrosunē* – often translated "moderation," "self-control," or "prudence" – is a key philosophical value especially for elite males; justice, as we have already seen, is a quality that the emperors claim to possess; *philanthrōpia* is that quality of generosity on which the subjects of the empire often relied for the upkeep of their cities and even sometimes for grain and other more urgent needs. The pursuit of virtue in the ancient world is gendered, with women who obtain philosophical heights often depicted as courageous or manly exceptions to their sex. Justin points to the amazing *sōphrosunē* of Christians as evidence of Christianity's success: Christian women and men, and Christians from all races, retain their purity and self-control (15.1, 15.6–7). The implication is that if Christianity can render even women and barbarians (or non-Greeks) philosophical, then it is the true philosophy.

Sameness and Difference

For Justin, the whole of myth – that is, foundational stories – and religious practice is cast into doubt and open to misinterpretation because of deceptive *mimēsis*. Justin addresses his readers directly: "For we caution you: guard yourselves lest the *daimones* whom we have previously accused should deceive (ἐξαπατήσωσιν) you and should turn you away from conversing with and comprehending the things we say (for they are struggling to have you as slaves and servants)" (14.1).[82] Demonic enslavement can afflict even those who seem most free from slavery and servitude: the emperors.

[81] For a direct critique of rulers crafting images of themselves as gods in Plutarch, see pp. 174–75; see also Justin *1 Apol.* 21; *2 Apol.* 4 on imitating God's nature.

[82] On this as imperial critique, see Elaine Pagels, "Christian Apologists and the 'Fall of the Angels': An Attack on Roman Imperial Power?" *HTR* 78.3/4 (1985) 306.

Justin must caution against deceit because part of the problem of the world is that Christian teachings, stories, and rituals look so *similar* to those in the world that surrounds them. He cites the Sibyl, Hystaspes, and Stoic philosophers on the end of the world, and then defensively asks:

> If, therefore, we say some things which are similar to claims made by your honored poets and philosophers, and other things that are both better and more divine, and we alone offer proof, why are we unjustly hated beyond all others? For when we say that all things have been ordered and have come into being by God, we seem to speak the teaching of Plato; when we say that there is a conflagration, we seem to speak the teaching of Stoics. When we say that the souls of the unjust are punished in sensation, existing even after death, but those of the excellent have been delivered from punishments to live well, we seem to say the same things as poets and philosophers. When we say that we must not worship the works of human hands, we declare the same things as the comic Menander and those who say these things. For they declare that the creator is greater than what has been made. (20.3–5)

Justin declares sameness to the cults and practices around him even as he seeks to articulate some kind of difference. Even Christian stories sound suspiciously similar, as Justin freely admits. With the story of the Logos born without sexual union, "we say nothing new," since some stories of the sons of Zeus were similar (21.1).[83] The implication is this: Christian myths are like your myths; thus, it is incorrect to see us as different and atheistic and to haul us to court.

Yet the stories of the sons of Zeus, Justin argues, are more fabulous and disturbing than Christian stories: "And such sorts of deeds are narrated of each of the so-called sons of Zeus – there is no need to tell those who know – except that these have been written for the purpose of the advantage and exhortation of those who are being educated (ἐκπαιδευομένων). For all think that it is good to be imitators (μιμητάς) of the gods" (21.4–5; see also *2 Apol.* 12). Justin points out that these stories are the foundation for education/*paideia*; from rhetorical handbooks we know the extent to which imitation of classics was fundamental to the educational system of the day. Yet these stories of the sons of Zeus are not truly beneficial and their imitation leads nowhere good. Aspects of your *paideia*, Justin implies, are corrupt. In the critique he launches, he adopts the logic of "pagan" piety: "Put away from the self-controlled soul (σωφρονούσης ψυχῆς) such a thought concerning gods, as that Zeus, even the very commander and begetter of all, is (according to them) both a parricide and has come forth from such a father [i.e., his father is also a parricide], who has

[83] On Justin's strategies of articulating sameness, see Reed, "The Trickery of the Fallen Angels," 164–68; see also Lyman, "The Politics of Passing."

yielded to love of evil and shameful pleasures, coming to Ganymede and many adulterous women, and his children continued in similar deeds. But, as we have already said, the evil *daimones* did these things" (21.5–21.6).[84] Justin slips into the skin of the pious Greek and seems to champion Zeus's divine integrity.

Justin plays with the rhetoric of sameness: Christians are the same as pious, cultured peoples, people with *paideia.* The beginning of the *Second Apology* as it now stands directly appeals to the "Romans" and aligns Christians with Romans, insisting that Justin's arguments are composed "on your behalf, who are of the same feelings and are brothers and sisters (even if you are ignorant and do not want to be [our brothers and sisters] on account of what you consider to be high rank)" (*2 Apol.* 1.1). But here the rhetoric of sameness functions to point to a little bitter difference. Justin insists that on some points Christians teach the same things as non-Christian poets and philosophers (*1 Apol.* 20.4–5);[85] Christian rituals are often the same as Greek ones (e.g., *1 Apol.* 61–62 on water rituals); even the idea of the Logos is nothing new, given the Greek teachings about sons of Zeus (*1 Apol.* 21.1). But Christian teachings are also different insofar as Christians are better, closer to the ideal, and even prior in historical time. Christians are different because demons overheard the prophets, had a sense of what was to come, misunderstood it, and began to disseminate in the world misrepresentations of a truth that would later be manifest clearly in the world[86]: "They, hearing what was said through the prophets, did not understand accurately, but as ones who err, imitated the things said about our Christ" (*1 Apol.* 54.4).[87]

Mimicry is occurring, Justin argues, but not in the direction that most might argue. Christians have not stolen Greek philosophy; Christians have not mimicked Jews or stolen their scriptures; Christians have not imitated pagan ritual, creating a ceremony with bread and wine that looks suspiciously like the goings-on in the cult of Mithras.[88] Rather, Plato knew and misunderstood

[84] See parallel argument in *2 Apol.* 5.5, nicely discussed by Reed, "The Trickery of the Fallen Angels," 160–61.

[85] Of course, Justin refers to "good" philosophers, not like the Cynic-influenced Crescens, who attacks Justin and calumniates Christians. See *2 Apol.* 3. There are hierarchies of philosophy, too, and Justin tries to align Christians as much as possible with Platonism. See also *Dial. Tryph.* 1–9; Nasrallah, "The Rhetoric of Conversion."

[86] See also Reed, "The Trickery of the Fallen Angels," 164–71.

[87] Ὅτι δὲ καὶ ἀκούοντες τὰ διὰ τῶν προφητῶν λεγόμενα οὐκ ἐνόουν ἀκρίβῶς, ἀλλ' ὡς πλανώμενοι ἐμιμήσαντο τὰ περὶ τὸν ἡμέτερον Χριστόν, διασαφήσομεν.

[88] *1 Apol.* 66. *1 Apol.* 62 discusses demonic rites of sprinkling with water and of removing shoes as imitations of Moses. Justin provides exempla for this thesis in *1 Apol.* 54–67. For example, Moses is "older than all historians" (compare Tatian *Ad Graec.* 40.1) and told of a ruler who "'will be the expectation of the nations, binding his foal to a vine, washing his robe in the blood of a vine' (Gen. 49.10d–11). Therefore, the *daimones*, hearing these prophetic words, said Dionysos had become a son of Zeus, and handed down the tradition that he was the

the prophecies, not understanding in the *Timaeus* that the X (*chi*) placed in the universe is the cross (*1 Apol.* 60). Justin bursts out in frustration: "*We* therefore do not think the same things as others, but all of them speak, imitating our teachings" (Οὐ τὰ αὐτὰ οὖν ἡμεῖς ἄλλοις δοξάζομεν, ἀλλ' οἱ πάντες τὰ ἡμέτερα μιμούμενοι λέγουσι, 60.10). Even Jews read their own texts wrongly, and thus scripture belongs to the Christians. In order to make these arguments about justice and about sameness and difference, however, Justin stands before the Roman imperial family and judges two groups: Jews, whose sufferings in the aftermath of the Bar Kochba revolts were a matter of divine justice, and whose very existence destabilizes Christian attempts to *be* a new Judaism; and those of low status, whose dirty rituals are not piety but its opposite: superstition and irrational fear of the gods.[89] Justin minimizes Christian differences with mainstream philosophical and pious culture at the same time that he asserts Christian superiority by insisting that Christians are more authentic, more pure, more original.

Justin elsewhere asserts with regard to his own attraction to Christian philosophy: "I confess that I both pray for and with all my resources struggle to be found a Christian, not because Plato's teachings are different from Christ's, but because they are not similar in every way – nor are the teachings of others, the Stoics and the poets and the historians" (*2 Apol.* 13.2).[90] On the one hand, all who acted according to reason (*logos*), not even understanding that

discoverer of the vine (and they have placed on record that wine is among his mysteries), and they taught that he, having been rent into pieces <rose again and> was lifted into heaven" (*1 Apol.* 54.6). ("Rose again" [ἀναστῆναι καὶ] is a conjecture, but a fuller passage including mention of "resurrection" is found in *Dial. Tryph.* 69.2. See Marcovich, *Iustini Martyris*, 109.) The reading of Genesis becomes even more complex: the foal mentioned in Genesis, the foal ridden by Jesus towards his death in Jerusalem, and Bellerophon and Pegasus become linked in a "sophisticated exercise in midrashic intertextuality" (Jon Levenson, email correspondence, 7/07). The argument about Plato learning from Moses is a typical one in Jewish and then Christian literature. See, e.g., Tatian's chronography, and much earlier in Jewish sources, especially Alexandrian. See also Droge, *Homer or Moses?*, 45–47, 59–65, 91–96; Momigliano, *Alien Wisdom*, 113; and Stroumsa, *Barbarian Philosophy*, 41.

[89] See *1 Apol.* 30–53 for Justin on prophecy and Jewish misreadings of scripture, as well as *Dial. Tryph.* On "textual communities" and varieties of Jews, as well as Christians, defining themselves based on their interpretations of scripture, see Judith Lieu, *Christian Identity in the Jewish and Graeco-Roman World* (Oxford: Oxford University Press, 2004) chap. 2. The pagan Celsus, in his ca. 175 *Alēthēs Logos* or *True Doctrine* (known to us through quotations of it in Origen's *Contra Celsum*) will reverse the terms of Justin's argument and say that Christians are imitating both Jews and pagans; they are a new sect derivative from the philosophical prowess and ritual acts of others. Some think that Celsus's *True Doctrine* is written in dialogue with Justin's *Apologies*. See discussion in Droge, *Homer or Moses?*, 72–81; see also Carl Andresen, *Logos und Nomos: die Polemik des Kelsus wider das Christentum* (Berlin: De Gruyter, 1955) who concludes that Celsus wrote his text after reading Justin.

[90] See Nasrallah, "The Rhetoric of Conversion"; see also Reed, "The Trickery of the Fallen Angels," 162–63.

logos is manifest in the Logos who is Christ, are Christians before the fact of Christianity, or at least "whatever therefore was said that was good by anyone, it belongs to us Christians" (*2 Apol.* 13.4; see also 8, 10). But here also are the limits to Christian sameness. Christian philosophy is "higher than all human philosophy" (*2 Apol.* 15.3). And while the *daimones* borrowed from Christian truth to fabricate myth, they never took up the image of the crucifixion (*1 Apol.* 55).

Elaine Pagels has argued that Justin's cosmology, in which the entire world is mapped by the *daimones*' mimetic plan, is a clear statement of resistance to the emperors, aligning them explicitly with the *daimones*.[91] We do find what can be read as critiques of the emperors, for example, in Justin's statement that "many among you turned from violent and tyrannical acts" toward Christian rejection of anger and embracing of longsuffering (*1 Apol.* 16.4). Yet we can refine Pagels' insight: Justin represents the emperors as pawns in the demonic game. Despite their claims to *paideia*, philosophy, and piety, the emperors are ignorant and deluded. They are certainly not divine, despite imperial cult and even merely imperial self-representations in coinage and statuary that assert imperial divinity in every metropolitan center. Justin slyly points this out: "Because you are human, they [law-breakers] act unjustly, knowing that it is possible to escape your notice" (*1 Apol.* 12.3). Because they are his primary addressees in the *First Apology*, every reference to the audience's ignorance critiques the emperors too. "But if you too, just like the mindless, honor customs before truth, do what you are able: but rulers who honor opinion rather than the truth have just as much power as bandits in a wilderness," Justin bursts out in quick disgust (12.4), before he goes on to threaten such powerful rulers with a more kingly ruler than they.[92] Despite their claims to philosophy and piety, the emperors, who claim to be lovers of truth, need to be warned to guard against demons; these kings stand in danger of becoming their "slaves and servants" (14.1).

The emperors need to be reminded to "pay attention to the end of each of the previous emperors: they died a death common to all" (18.1). Justin makes this statement in the face of visually manifest claims of imperial apotheosis, as in the eagle-winged Titus, in the crown of his memorial arch in Rome (Fig. 18).[93]

[91] Pagels, "Christian Apologists," 301.

[92] Justin's (imperial) audience is inscribed as ignorant and in need of Justin's persuasive powers: "But although we know that it is not easy to change a soul that is immediately arrested by ignorance, we are eager to add a few small things for the purpose of persuading those who are lovers of truth" (*1 Apol.* 12.11).

[93] This is probably a memorial arch completed by Domitian, since there was a triumphal arch in the Campus Martius already for Titus's victory in the Jewish War. See Robin Haydon Darwall-Smith, *Emperors and Architecture: A Study of Flavian Rome* (Bruxelles: Latomus, 1996) 80.

18. Apotheosis of Titus. Arch of Titus, Rome. DAIR 79.2393.

Titus soars up, presumably from his funeral pyre, over the depictions of his own triumphal entry on a chariot back into Rome from the Jewish wars, on the one side, and the celebratory and degrading procession of spoils from the Jerusalem temple, on the other.[94] Justin mentions such imperial claims to divinity explicitly: "And what of the dead emperors, whom you consider worthy to be deified eternally, and you bring forward someone swearing that s/he has seen the incinerated Caesar mount upward from the fire into the heavens?" (21.3).[95] As we shall see in the conclusion, Justin also argues that all images of the emperors as gods are displayed under the sign of the cross.

[94] See Darwall-Smith, *Emperors and Architecture*, 166–8.

[95] Καὶ τὶ γὰρ τοὺς ἀποθνῄσκοντας παρ' ὑμῖν αὐτοκράτορας, <οὓς> ἀεὶ ἀπαθανατίζεσθαι ἀξιοῦντες <λέγοντα> καὶ ὀμνύντα τινὰ προάγετε ἑωρακέναι ἐκ τῆς πυρᾶς ἀνερχόμενον εἰς τὸν οὐρανὸν τὸν κατακαέντα Καίσαρα; See also Justin's mockery of the divinization of Hadrian and Antinoos at *1 Apol.* 29.

III. JUSTICE, PIETY, AND *PAIDEIA* IN THE FORUM OF TRAJAN

We have already begun to see that the second century is a time of crises of *mimēsis* or representation, crises that have to do with ethnicity, *paideia*, piety. Does one call oneself Greek? Philosophical? Roman? Barbarian? Cultured? Who is really pious, and who denies the gods, and can the person who denies the gods do so precisely because s/he is pious? Who has the right to give a name, and how does a name do its representational work, or not? Is a given image a god or a human? An elite or an emperor? This crisis over representation was exposed visually through statuary and other images; for Justin it was manifest in a justice system more interested in names than deeds, and in emperors who claimed to be philosophical and pious but whose actions manifested something else entirely.[96] To understand more deeply Justin's crisis of *mimēsis*, we turn back to the Forum of Trajan in Rome, where we find representations of imperial *pietas*, *clementia* ("forebearance"), *iustitia* ("justice"), and even images of the emperors' gracious reception of ambassadors, a role that Justin takes on literarily.[97]

Relatively little of the Forum of Trajan still exists, and the exact reconstruction of its scant elements is a matter of debate among archaeologists and architectural historians. What is important to my argument is that, from the fragments that undeniably remain, we can discover how the forum borrows iconographic vocabulary from the Roman and Greek past to make points about the greatness of the present and its continuity with and authorization in past culture and greatness.[98] The Forum of Trajan in Rome brings together the rhetoric of justice, power, knowledge, triumph, and piety – a convergence of typical metropolitan architectural and sculptural rhetorics to which Christian writers might respond.

Given its date and location, Justin may have visited the Forum of Trajan. I chose it not for this reason, however, but because it offers two important innovations in imperial fora that make it exemplary of the sort of discourse of imperial power to which Justin and others respond. The first innovation in this forum, with which we began this chapter, is its column, depicting Trajan's military successes. The second is the insertion of a basilica – a hall of justice – within its space.[99]

[96] The philosophical discussion about words and their representative power had started long earlier, for example with Plato's *Cratylus*. For a discussion of that text see Chapter 5.

[97] On this topic generally, see, e.g., Paul Zanker, *The Power of Images in the Age of Augustus* (Ann Arbor: University of Michigan Press, 1988); S. R. F. Price, *Rituals and Power: Roman Imperial Cult in Asia Minor* (Cambridge: Cambridge University Press, 1984); and Ando, *Imperial Ideology*.

[98] Hölscher, *The Language of Images in Roman Art*, chaps. 7–8.

[99] As Packer writes, "Roman sources agree that the Forum of Trajan and the Basilica Ulpia, the great law court that was its most famous building, were among the most important monuments of imperial Rome" (*The Forum of Trajan*, 1.xxiii).

The Forum's Surroundings

James E. Packer has offered a reconstruction of the forum that allows us to imagine key elements of the forum and their relation to each other.[100] The Forum of Trajan in Rome was the last in a series of "grandiose imperial fora."[101] It was begun by Domitian, continued by Trajan (and by his architect Apollodoros), and completed under Hadrian. It seems to complete and organize the other fora, quoting in particular from the architectural proportions of the Forum of Augustus. In doing so it makes an explicit link between Trajan's rule and Augustus's *pietas* and *pax*.[102] Probably pushing aside the markets that had previously been there, and ingeniously relocating them onto terracing on the Quirinal Hill,[103] Trajan and Apollodorus of Damascus "apparently consciously conceived of the Forum of Trajan as the triumphant climax in the series of imperial fora."[104]

[100] See Packer and Burge, "TEMPLUM DIVI TRAIANI, 109–36; regarding the challenge of interpreting the careless 1930s Fascist era excavations of the imperial fora, and for a review of efforts since, see Packer, "Report from Rome," 307–30. James E. Packer, "Trajan's Forum Again: The Column and the Temple of Trajan in the Master Plan Attributed to Apollodorus (?)," *JRA* 7 (1994) 163–82; Roberto Meneghini, "Templum Divi Traiani," *BullCom* 97 (1996) 47–88; Roberto Meneghini and Riccardo Santangeli Valenzani, *I Fori Imperiali Gli scavi del Comune di Roma (1992–2007)* (Rome: Viviani, 2007) 83–113.

[101] Packer, *The Forum of Trajan*, 1.3. By the time of Domitian, there were three fora in this area: Caesar's, completed by Augustus; the Forum of Augustus; and the so-called Temple or Forum of Peace built by the Flavian emperor Vespasian. Domitian's Forum Transitorium (also called the Forum of Nerva, for the emperor who completed it) united the Flavian "Temple" of Peace to the south with the Forum of Augustus to the north. Before his death, Domitian also initiated the enormous forum that would become the Forum of Trajan. Regarding the Forum Transitorium and its message of domesticity and the limitation of female authority, see Eve D'Ambra, *Private Lives, Public Virtues: The Frieze of the Forum Transitorium in Rome* (Princeton, NJ: Princeton University Press, 1993).

[102] The Flavians had to negotiate both Nero's popularity and the memory of his excesses; they also groped to develop propaganda and traditions continuous with the grandeurs of the Julio-Claudian house, that asserted the right and strength of the *gens Flavia*, especially after the memory of the civil war of 68 and the year when three different men claimed the status of emperor. See Darwall-Smith, *Emperors and Architecture*.

[103] William MacDonald, *The Architecture of the Roman Empire* (2 vols.; New Haven, CT: Yale University Press, 1982–86) 1.76–79. Packer, "Report from Rome," 313, discusses how the macellum was also leveled for the Forum Transitorium.

[104] Packer, *The Forum of Trajan*, 1.260; Packer, "Report from Rome," 327. This "conversation" with other fora existed at multiple levels, including the small scale of the materials: "The pavonazzetto, giallo antico, africano, and cipollino that typified all the fora also emphasized their close architectural ties" (Packer, "Report from Rome," 327–29). On a larger scale, Packer reads the Forum of Trajan as a repetition and magnification of Vespasian's "Temple of Peace." Apollodorus also took the length of the court in front of the Temple of Peace (400 Roman feet) and used it as a "grand measurement that determined the proportions of his various buildings" (Packer, *The Forum of Trajan*, 1.261). So also the proportions of the Temple of the Deified Trajan may correspond to those of the Temple of Mars Ultor built in the Forum of Augustus.

Some of the messages of the fora and especially of the Forum of Trajan – the social, economic, and technological forces that allowed it to exist at all – are articulated not only by the buildings but also by the space, materials, and labor necessary to achieve them. First, a macellum or marketplace may have been destroyed to free this space; its move into the new Market of Trajan to the east displaced and resettled merchants and workers.[105] The forum articulates imperial power over labor, from the labors of the famous architect Apollodoros of Damascus[106] to those humbler workers who laid the brickwork of the substructures[107] to those workers displaced by the forum. Second, the forum was "marble-laden" at a time when much building was in brick. The building materials themselves – white marble, Phrygian pavonazzetto, Egyptian gray granite, Numidian giallo antico[108] – communicated the power of the imperial family over quarries across the *oikoumenē* and brought the empire's commodities home to Rome. Finally, the forum transformed the cityscape of Rome. The new market rose thirty-five meters above the forum's pavement, equivalent to the height of Trajan's Column. From its high terrace one could have a splendid view of the forum and much of Rome.[109] An inscription on the base of the Column of Trajan celebrates "how deep were the rock and earth excavated for these great works," a reminder that the column and its environs expressed not only military power and imperial piety, but also the ability of the emperor and his workers to mold Roman topography to their will.[110]

Moving through the Forum of Trajan

The Forum itself (see again Fig. 14), as one moved from south to north, included a monumental gate, porticoes, and the Basilica Ulpia, which was a judicial court; behind that, the Greek and Latin wings of the Library of Trajan embraced on the east and west a courtyard containing the Column of Trajan. Just past this courtyard, to the north, was the Temple of the Deified

[105] But see Lancaster, "Building Trajan's Column," about a road that underlies the area, and the free space in the northern part of the forum.

[106] See MacDonald, *The Architecture of the Roman Empire*, 1.129–35.

[107] There was a danger in such work, too: Juvenal *Sat.* 33.257–260: "Here's the great trunk of fir-tree swaying along on its wagon, and look, another dray behind it, stacked high with pine-logs, a nodding threat over the heads of the crowd. If that axle snapped, and a cartload of marble avalanched down on them, what would be left of their bodies?" quoted in Lancaster, "Building Trajan's Column," 437; the translation she uses is Juvenal, *The Sixteen Satires* (trans. P. Green; Harmondsworth: Penguin Books, 1967).

[108] Numidia is in present-day Tunisia. The latter two materials are used in the libraries (Packer, *The Forum of Trajan in Brief*, 79), among other places.

[109] MacDonald, *The Architecture of the Roman Empire*, 1.78, 90–93.

[110] See Coarelli's theory that the height of the column duplicates the height of the hill that had formerly been there; he argues that the unusual inscription regarding the excavation reflects the "trauma" of the removal of the hill, and the community's memory of this change (*The Column of Trajan*, 4–7). Against this idea, however, see the summary by Lancaster, "Building Trajan's Column," 421.

19. The central arch of the main gate into the Forum of Trajan. Aureus, reverse. By permission of J. E. Packer.

Trajan. To code the forum in terms of the themes of this chapter, one walked from justice (basilica) to *paideia* (libraries) to piety (temple). Throughout, from the materials of construction themselves to the statues of Dacian captives, the message of Roman imperial power was also clear.

With the Forum of Augustus behind and the Forum of Caesar to the south, one would enter the Forum of Trajan's central triumphal arch, which was aligned with and likely mirrored the central porch of the Basilica Ulpia.[111] Immediately upon entering the forum, one was reminded of the victory of Trajan and the *pathos* of the conquered. Numismatic evidence indicates that this gate had four columns placed upon substantial pedestals; behind and between these intercolumniations, placed within the wall of the gate, were four aediculae that held statues (Fig. 19); above these were *imagines clipeata*, busts emerging from circular shields. Packer hypothesizes that above the

[111] "The Central Arch appears on the reverses of Trajanic gold and bronze coins (aurei and sestertii)" (Packer, *The Forum of Trajan in Brief*, 54); see also Darwall-Smith, *Emperors and Architecture*.

20. Dacian captives. In re-use on the Arch of Constantine, Rome, Italy. Art Resource, NY.

free-standing columns of the gate were sculptures of Dacian males (Fig. 20).[112] These caryatid-like figures, their captive bodies seeming to bear the weight of the architecture,[113] also likely occurred along the east and west colonnades of the Forum in two types. Some had their arms "crossed below the waist, symbolizing captivity," and others had their arms "folded across the chest in a gesture of mourning."[114] The central arch of the gate was surmounted by a massive amount of statuary, likely gilt in bronze. The charioteer in the *seiugis* ("six-horse chariot") that stood atop the gate was probably Trajan. Trophies stand over the second and fourth bays of the arch. (They look like stick-figures in the coinage.)

The main gate thus offers a powerful introductory message of imperial triumph and barbarian subjugation. As one entered the gate (Fig. 21), or if one stood in the upper gallery of the East or West Colonnade, that message would

[112] For discussion of atlantes and the gate, see Packer, *The Forum of Trajan in Brief*, 55.

[113] Marc Waelkens ("From a Phrygian Quarry: The Provenance of the Statues of the Dacian Prisoners in Trajan's Forum at Rome," *AJA* 89.4 [1985] 650) points out that none of the preserved heads "shows any trace of a real supporting function," although the many fragments of the cornice of the entablature hint that the captives' heads just below seemed to support this cantilevering part of the architecture.

[114] Waelkens, "From a Phrygian Quarry," 645. Six statues of Dacians of the captive type were re-used in the Arch of Constantine; see Fig. 20. For a catalog of statues of the Dacians, see Zanker, "Das Trajansforum," 499–544, esp. 506–12.

21. Restored view. The Forum of Trajan, Rome. By permission of J. E. Packer.

be reinforced: The statue of Trajan atop the Column of Trajan hovered over the Basilica Ulpia.[115] Moving into the courtyard, past the east and west colonnades and past an equestrian statue of Trajan, one would approach the Basilica Ulpia (Fig. 22), an unusual addition to an imperial forum. The nave measured 169 m by 22 m,[116] and the enormous building was a space for decisions regarding justice. Even at the turn of the fourth to the fifth centuries, "slaves still gained their freedom in the Atrium Liberatis."[117] Above the colonnade of the south side of the Basilica one would see more Dacian captives appearing to support the architecture, perhaps an irony or a warning to slaves about to gain freedom.[118]

Moving through the Basilica Ulpia, one entered a courtyard formed by the libraries, the basilica, and the temple, with the Column of Trajan in its

[115] As one entered through the gate, one would look across a wide expanse with the equestrian statue of Trajan in the middle, surrounded by gardens and other statuary. See Packer, *The Forum of Trajan*, 1.96 or *The Forum of Trajan in Brief*, 60; on the form of this statue, deduced in part from numismatic evidence, see Zanker, "Das Trajansforum," 508–10; Zanker concludes that the equestrian statue was one where the horse stood calmly, rather than a depiction of Trajan crushing a Dacian underfoot of a rearing horse. See also Davies, "The Politics of Perpetuation," 64. On either side, the intercolumniations of the east and west colonnades would likely have been punctuated with statues (Packer, *The Forum of Trajan in Brief*, 60–69).

[116] MacDonald, *The Architecture of the Roman Empire*, 2.114.

[117] Packer, *The Forum of Trajan*, 1.9 refers to Sidonius Apollinaris *Carmina* 2 ("To Anthemius") 544–45.

[118] On the location of these statues on the Basilica Ulpia, see Waelkens, "From a Phrygian Quarry," 649. The statues of the Dacian captives, which serve as pseudo-caryatids, echo the caryatids of the Forum of Augustus, which themselves are copies of the "maidens" of the Erechtheion in Athens.

22. Forum of Trajan. East-west section reconstruction. By permission of J. E. Packer.

middle. Past these, the Temple of Trajan is squeezed into its forum but still would have provided a climax to a space full of rich rhetoric about power, religion, knowledge, and justice.[119] What is likely its dedicatory inscription reads in part: "The Emperor Trajan Hadrian Augustus, son of the deified Trajan Parthicus, grandson of the deified Nerva . . . by decree of the Senate [dedicates this temple] to his deified parents, Trajan Parthicus and Plotina."[120] The temple announces the imperial family's divinity.

While this temple was piously completed by Trajan's successor, Hadrian, the double libraries just before it were completed in Trajan's own time. They contained Greek volumes on one side, Latin on the other,[121] and demonstrated imperial support of *paideia* in both languages, and the importance of Greek culture, even if the Greeks were a conquered people. Trajan's own *Dacica*, his account of the wars in Dacia, along the lines of Caesar's own war record, the *Commentarii de bello Gallico*, was likely contained within the libraries. Imperial knowledge and mastery were also evidenced in the very center of the library complex in the Column of Trajan at its center, which likely echoed Trajan's written account of the war.[122] Thus the column was surrounded by *paideia* on two sides in the form of the libraries, by justice to the south, and by claims to piety and the emperor's godhood to the north side.[123]

The Forum of Trajan did not only conjure thoughts of Trajan's death and deification, although such rhetoric clustered especially at its northern end.[124]

[119] The location of this temple remains a subject of intense debate between Packer and Meneghini. See Roberto Meneghini, "The Temple of the Deified Trajan," in Coarelli, *The Column of Trajan*, 250–54 and Packer and Burge, "TEMPLUM DIVI TRAIANI."

[120] The structures were double-storied; inside, a two-storey Corinthian colonnade ended in a space which likely contained well over life-sized statuary, "perhaps of Trajan and Minerva," on the west side. Packer, *The Forum of Trajan in Brief*, 80.

[121] Packer, *The Forum of Trajan in Brief*, 78.

[122] Coarelli, *The Column of Trajan*, 11–14; Packer, *The Forum of Trajan*, 1.119. See Brilliant, *Visual Narratives*, 103–6 for a formal analysis of Caesar's texts on the Gallic wars alongside the visual rhetoric of the Column.

[123] Coarelli, *The Column of Trajan*, 16–18.

[124] The column and surrounding reliefs refer "both to the emperor's victorious power and to his eventual victory over death in apotheosis." Davies, "The Politics of Perpetuation,"

It was not a static site of imperial propaganda in architecture and statuary, but a dynamic location for imperial performances of *philanthrōpia* and euergetism. It was a chief official judicial center of Rome. It was here that Hadrian burned the official records of debts owed to the state, here too Marcus destroyed tax records and adorned the forum with statues, including one to his tutor Marcus Frontus. Here Commodus handed out *congiaria* or imperial donations to the needy and presided in the Basilica Ulpia, in the east apse known as the *atrium libertatis*. In this forum, new laws were posted and *summi viris* or public heroes were honored with statues. The Forum of Trajan was a location for the public display of imperial *philanthrōpia* and justice.[125]

The triumphs of Trajan celebrated in the forum presented a form of justice – the very sort of justice that Justin contests. In the Forum of Trajan, we see depictions of barbarian Dacians, captive in the architecture between deified emperors, beautiful and pathos-evoking, standing under bronze military standards. Walking in the forum, one's eyes would nearly have been pierced by all the weaponry – the military trophies, as well as the *quadriga* and two *biga* which surmounted the building, a statue of Trajan, right arm raised in salute, likely above it all. Thus in the heart of *the* city of the empire, the capital of empire,[126] we find a concatenation of rhetoric, materially expressed, of imperial power, justice, and piety – all under signs of imperial violence.

War and the "Temple of Peace"

These messages are not unique to the Forum of Trajan, of course. War, triumph, and booty could be a source of propaganda and authority, whether with power of the Roman Empire over subject provincial peoples depicted in Aphrodisias's Sebasteion, the Dacian Wars celebrated in Trajan's Forum, or Vespasian's nearby "Temple" of Peace.[127] We briefly turn to the latter so that we can understand how the emperors wove together peace and violence, culture and conquering, in their rhetoric, and how Justin's writing

48; Zanker, "Das Trajansforum," 532–33. Davies follows Paul Zanker in arguing that the iconography throughout the Forum has funereal resonances. See also Brilliant (*Visual Narratives*, 102) regarding the Column's emphasis on Trajan and its impact on the viewer: "The column may be understood as a permanent form of epic theater, reproducing faraway things and events and bringing them closer, both spatially and experientially, to an audience. That audience, in turn, never loses sight of Trajan."

[125] *Hist. Aug. Comm.* 2.1.

[126] Recall how Aristides describes Rome as the urbs to which all the rest of the *oikoumenē* is mere suburb, discussed on pp. 94–95.

[127] Darwall-Smith, *Emperors and Architecture*, 56, discusses the fact that although today the space is referred to as the Temple or Forum of Peace, Josephus calls it a *temenos* and Pliny and Suetonius use the term *templum*. The organization of the space is unusual; this and the lack of archaeological remains make interpretation of it challenging. See her discussion on pp. 58–68.

contains traces of this logic. The acts of war often resulted in cultural borrowing and display of the sort that Justin and our other sources both protest and foster.

Josephus, a former general of the Jewish War of 66–73, later in the employ of the Flavian imperial family, writes in the last quarter of the first century about the triumphal procession held by Vespasian (and Titus and Domitian) in Rome after the Jewish War. The distant land is re-presented within Rome through display of its people, animals, gods, sacred objects, legal documents, and through images of the war itself.[128] This *thriambos* ("triumphal procession") contained objects of many sorts, including statues (*agalmata*) of the gods who had been conquered in Babylonia. These are described by their size, their *technē* ("craft"), and the expense and preciousness of the material used to construct them (*Bell. Jud.* 7.124–136). Also paraded were golden objects from the Jerusalem temple and a copy of the Jewish law, as well as seven hundred men "choice in greatness and beauty of body" (7.118). Captives moved past, for whom any "ill-usage of body" was concealed with rich garments (7.138). In the procession were also "stages" or "scaffolds" (πήγματα) that represented the events of the war – slaughter, city walls overcome, blood and supplication, temples on fire and houses pulled down. The conquering general posed with each of these massive scenes (7.139–148).

The spaces of the conquered land were constructed again in the political-religious moment of the triumphal procession. The emperors solemnly process in purple and laurel; Vespasian covers his head and delivers prayers; sacrifice is performed to the (statues of the) gods set up outside the gate. This celebration of triumph seems to guarantee purity and to represent stability. But the event also inspired *pathos*. The fact of Roman triumph over those conquered lands, peoples, and gods, could evoke in the viewer of each object or person a crisis with regard to representation. Are the conquered images of gods representations of true gods? Are the bodies under those beautiful robes healthy or wounded, their "ill-usage" hid? At the images of war, should one feel *pathos* for the suffering, or triumph because of the victory, or both? Is the emperor or general who piously presides over it all god, or godlike, in this triumph? Speaking about the *triumphator* who is dressed to look like Jupiter in the parade, Mary Beard asks: "For what could be more appropriate in Roman religious terms than to set the triumph, and the general-as-actor, at the heart of a play which broaches such major problems of representation? Or, to put it the other

[128] In my interpretation of Josephus, I have been influenced by Mary Beard's discussion of the Roman triumph and her mention of the *pathos* it may have inspired ("The Triumph of the Absurd: Roman Street Theater," in Catharine Edwards and Greg Woolf, eds., *Rome the Cosmopolis* [Cambridge: Cambridge University Press, 2003] 21–43, and her *The Roman Triumph* [Cambridge, MA: Belknap, 2007]).

way round, what could be more appropriate than using the conventions of the triumph as a peg and a prompt for debating those problems? The hermeneutical question that is at stake here (both in the drama and the procession) is: how *can* you ever tell the difference between 'being,' 'playing,' or 'acting,' god?"[129]

The several days of the triumphal process affirm the geographical reach of the empire within Rome itself. But this act of representing or containing parts of a distant eastern province extends further. With Vespasian's "Temple of Peace," the capital comes to contain for all time some part of the conquered land. After having listed many riches taken from the East, and having detailed the events (including the pious prayers) of the parade, Josephus concludes:

> After these triumphs and the surest establishment of the leadership of the Romans, Vespasian determined to build a sanctuary space (τέμενος) of Peace. It was finished exceedingly quickly and was greater than all human conception. For using a marvelous expense of wealth, he also already equipped it with ancient masterpieces of painting and sculpture. For all things were collected and displayed in that shrine, which people once wandered around the entire *oikoumenē* to view.... Here he placed also the golden worked objects from temple of the Jews; he held his head high on account of these. But he guarded their law and the purple curtains of the sanctuary, which were stowed away in the palace buildings. (7.158–162)

Pliny's *Natural History*, too, refers to this phenomenon of the Vespasianic "museum," praising Vespasian for publicly displaying that which Nero had hidden away in his palace.[130] Cicero, writing against Verres, critiques those who plunder local goods for their private benefit and thus simultaneously engage in acts of connoisseurship, greed, and impiety.[131] In the midst of this long-standing discussion about cultural inheritance, both Josephus and Pliny

[129] Beard, "The Triumph of the Absurd," 43. The drama to which she refers is Plautus's *Amphitruo*.

[130] "And among the list of works I have referred to all the most celebrated have now been dedicated by the emperor Vespasian in the Temple of Peace and his other public buildings; they had been looted by Nero, who conveyed them all to Rome and arranged them in the sitting-rooms of his Golden Mansion." Pliny *Nat. hist.* 34.84; ET Pliny, *Natural History* (10 vols.; LCL; trans. H. Rackham et al.; Cambridge, MA: Harvard University Press, 2003) 9.189, 191. The Porticus Octaviae was another sort of open-air museum with works on public view (see Pliny *Nat. hist.* 34.31, 35.114; Darwall-Smith, *Emperors and Architecture*, 65).

[131] E.g., Cicero *Verr.* 2.1.59; 2.4.101; Pliny *Nat. hist.* 34.16.34 regarding Metrodorus of Scepsis who "reproached us with having taken by storm the city of Volsinii for the sake of the 2000 statues which it contained" (ET Rackham, 9.153). On this topic more generally, see Margaret M. Miles, *Art as Plunder: The Ancient Origins of Debate about Cultural Property* (Cambridge: Cambridge University Press, 2008).

imply that Vespasian corrected Nero's error and made *paideia*, both Greek and exotic, broadly available for viewing.[132]

Modern scholars struggle to define this "Temple of Peace." Its architecture is unusual, and its functions also cross categories that we usually keep distinct: the museum and the temple. The objects within and around the temple were valued for their sacrality, their aesthetic worth, and their marking of Jewish defeat and Roman victory. Justin as a proponent of the newly emerging "Christianity" does not have material power over Jews. Nonetheless, his use of Jewish scriptures and Greek philosophical materials also takes objects of aesthetic, sacral, and cultural worth and re-displays them, rendering their message different. Just as the Roman emperors owned all things in the *oikoumenē*, so also Justin "owned" such artifacts as he was Greek by virtue of his *paideia* and Jewish by virtue of his cult, since ethnicity is malleable and can be accrued in antiquity by affiliation, education, and conversion.[133]

CONCLUSIONS

In the Upper Tembris Valley in Phrygia in 1926, Sir Christopher Cox found a headless statue carved from marble, buried to its knees in quarry chips. The left leg was broken off to the knee. It was dressed in "barbarian" clothing, one arm folded across the chest. Marc Waelkens has identified this fragment as a never-completed statue of a Dacian prisoner from the Forum of Trajan in Rome. The sculpture was "in an advanced stage of work"; it had even been worked with a fine pointed chisel.[134] Some flaw in the marble probably prevented the sculptors from finishing the conquered Dacian and shipping it to Rome.

The Upper Tembris Valley is far from Rome and far from Dacia. The flawed captive there marked imperial power over quarries, but also something more. The story of Roman power was communicated not only through rumors of the wars in Dacia, but also concretely through the order that this Dacian be

[132] David Noy ("Rabbi Aqiba Comes to Rome: A Jewish Pilgrimage in Reverse?" in Jaś Elsner and Ian Rutherford, eds., *Pilgrimage in Graeco-Roman and Early Christian Antiquity* [Oxford: Oxford University Press, 2005] 373–86) suggests that ancient Jews may have traveled to Rome in a kind of "Jewish pilgrimage in reverse" to see the cult objects from the Jerusalem temple. See also Ra'anan Boustan, "The Spoils of the Jerusalem Temple at Rome and Constantinople: Jewish Counter-Geography in a Christianizing Empire," in Gregg Gardner and Kevin L. Osterloh, eds., *Antiquity in Antiquity: Jewish and Christian Pasts in the Greco-Roman World* (Tübingen: Mohr Siebeck, 2008) 334–41.

[133] Buell, *Why This New Race?*; Caroline Johnson Hodge, *If Sons then Heirs: A Study of Kinship and Ethnicity in Paul's Letters* (Oxford: Oxford University Press, 2007); Jonathan Hall, *Hellenicity: Between Ethnicity and Culture* (Chicago: University of Chicago Press, 2002).

[134] Waelkens, "From a Phrygian Quarry," 644.

carved, through the expropriation of luxurious stones from imperial mines, through the labor of shipping, moving, hoisting, and affixing such sculptures and stones. The message of Roman might was communicated to laborers – less skilled quarriers and skilled sculptors – at this far reach of the empire, who would replicate the message through their sculptures.[135]

Justin's *Apology* is another trace of a different sort of reaction to imperial power and its power to constrain the representation of an *ethnos* – in this case, Christians rather than Dacians. Justin argues that Christianity is foundational and original to whatever is truly pious or philosophical. In the context of her larger discussion of the creation of "orthodoxy," Rebecca Lyman states that "Justin's intellectual hybrid reflected his own attempt as a Christian provincial and a philosopher to portray universal truth within the cultural traditions of the second century."[136] We can refine this idea by saying that Justin does so by playing to Roman valuation of Greek culture and by appropriating the best of Jewish tradition and re-displaying it as Christian. He claims that only Christians truly understand Jewish scriptures.[137] Under colonial conditions, and interested in the mimetic powers of *daimones* as well as the mimesis of artisans who sculpt gods, a writer like Justin imitates the dominating moves of empire, even as he reflects back to the empire its claims to justice and its right to name, and reverses the terms of the transaction. As Justin, among others, asserts these various ethnic-religious positions, he often trades upon extant hierarchies in order to shore up his own position. Women and those of low status, we shall not be surprised to find in Justin and elsewhere, are pawns in a Christian game that mimics the standards and patterns of the existing hegemony: *Theirs* are corrupt; *ours* are exemplary and philosophical.[138] Moreover, in the *Dialogue with Trypho*, Justin shores up Christian identity on the backs of Jews; he accuses them of ignorance, sedition against Rome, and of actively trying to subvert Christianity.[139]

Throughout the *Apologies*, Justin argues about representation and reverses the usual argument about *mimēsis*: that Christians are merely mimicking non-Christian cult, whether the cult of Judaism or of Mithras or of something else.

[135] On labor and especially slave labor in Roman period quarries, see F. H. Thompson, *The Archaeology of Greek and Roman Slavery* (London: Duckworth, 2003) 136–43; for insight into the work of sculptors, see Peter Rockwell, *The Art of Stoneworking: A Reference Guide* (Cambridge: Cambridge University Press, 1993).

[136] Lyman, "Hellenism and Heresy," 220, 221; see Justin *1 Apol.* 14.

[137] Reed, "The Trickery of the Fallen Angels," 169–70.

[138] For more on the rhetoric of Christian women as philosophical, see pp. 243–44.

[139] See Chapter 2; Reed, *Fallen Angels*, 166–70. There has been a long scholarly tradition of seeing the contact between Justin and his (real or literarily constructed) Jewish interlocutor Trypho as irenic. See, e.g., Demetrios Trakatellis, "Justin Martyr's Trypho," *HTR* 79 (1986) 287–97, who emphasizes the gentlemanliness of the conversation; see also Judith Lieu, *Image and Reality: The Jews in the World of the Christians in the Second Century* (London: T & T Clark, 1996) 103 on "the largely favorable presentation of Trypho."

Justin argues instead that the mimics are Jews and those who follow religious cults other than Christianity, and even the emperors themselves, whenever they merely claim to be just without effecting the sort of justice that is readily available in the divine court. Justin rhetorically constructs an imperial court to judge Christians, appealing to the emperor's piety, philosophy, religiosity, and justice. But just as Christian cult supersedes pagan cults, so also a divine court trumps the emperors. Justin's last words in the *Second Apology* remind the reader – his inscribed reader, the emperors – of all these themes: "Our teachings are not shameful, in accordance with sober judgment, but are higher than all human philosophy. . . . And therefore we shall stop, since we did as much as we could, and, in addition, prayed that all people altogether should be deemed worthy of the truth. Therefore, you too should judge righteous deeds in a manner worthy of piety and philosophy, for your own sakes!" (*2 Apol.* 15.3–5).[140]

Treatment of the apologists has often devolved to the question of whether Christians successfully adopt the philosophical language of Hellenism – that is, whether they take their Christian essence and properly cloak it in terms more attractive to elites of any stripe. Instead of trying to find the Christian essence of someone like Justin, we should look at Christians as multilingual subjects under a widespread, complex, and far-reaching colonial rule. Christians claim that the Roman courtroom with its rituals calls them into existence at the same time that it seeks to annihilate them. "Sticks and stones can break my bones but words will never hurt me," says the children's chant. Words – names – can do violence. Yet, in Butler's words, "to take up the name that one is called is not simple submission to prior authority, for the name is already unmoored from prior context, and entered into the labor of self-definition. . . . Insurrectionary speech becomes the necessary response to injurious language, a risk taken in response to being put at risk, a repetition in language that forces change."[141] The rituals of the courtroom mask the violence of its proceedings and the power that it wields over those who come before its judgment. Justin's *Apologies* mimic the controlled setting of the courtroom in order to point out the uncontrolled violence that Christians suffer and the possibilities for controlled and obfuscated violence that the emperors could enact; the *Apologies* mimic ritual in order to criticize it.

[140] Οὐκ ἔστι δὲ ἡμῶν τὰ διδάγματα κατὰ κρίσιν σώφρονα αἰσχρά, ἀλλὰ πάσης μὲν φιλοσοφίας ἀνθρωπείου ὑπέρτερα. . . . Καὶ παυσόμεθα λοιπόν, ὅσον ἐφ᾽ ἡμῖν ἦν πράξαντες καὶ προσεπευξάμενοι τῆς ἀληθείας καταξιωθῆναι τοὺς πάντῃ πάντας ἀνθρώπους. Εἴη οὖν καὶ ὑμᾶς ἀξίως εὐσεβείας καὶ φιλοσοφίας τὰ δίκαια ὑπὲρ ἑαυτῶν κρῖναι. This quotation also emerges in the context of arguments against other Christian groups (Simon, for example, although there may be a text problem here; see Marcovich, *Iustini Martyris*, 159) and other philosophies and sects with which Justin does not want to be associated.

[141] Butler, *Excitable Speech*, 163.

Yet there is collateral damage in Justin's system. Justin's rhetoric sets up not only Jews, but also the artisan and those of low status, for critique and humiliation before his purported Roman and surely Christian readers and hearers. Justin's critique of statuary uses a *topos* that appears frequently in later Christian texts: that of the artisan who hammers and planes, cuts and crafts a god. Justin elevates the mockery of cult statues to a new level in his assertion that the artisans are impure: "They also ruin the young slave girls who are their co-workers. What sheer stupidity, that [you say] that people who are licentious should make and alter gods for the purpose of worship, and that [you] establish such people as guards of the sacred things, there where they are dedicated, not comprehending that it is unlawful even to think or to say that humans could be guardians of gods" (*1 Apol.* 9.4–5). Justin uses status markers – the stupidity and pollution of the simple artisan dallying with his low status female cohorts – and in doing so appeals to an elite audience.[142] When Justin and others appeal to those of low status within their midst, it is precisely to show that Christianity elevates such people to a higher cultural standard of philosophical knowledge and virtue.[143] Similarly, Justin's student Tatian accuses Greeks and the Romans who have stolen their statuary of admiring and learning from lewd sculptures of lecherous, unethical women, while real, fleshly Christian women are chaste and exemplary.

What is the force of such an argument about statuary in texts that purport to be speeches or writings to emperors? As we have seen, the city of Rome was filled with imperial building projects and claims to the justice, culture, and piety *and* divinity of the imperial family. In this context, to critique statuary and its proliferation is also to critique imperial participation in the same, whether in the form of imperial benefactions that aided in temple building and renovations, or imperial investment in and agreement for temple building and the erection of statues for their own cults or for the cults of their families – the sorts of things we have just seen in Rome and Olympia. We might think that there is no link between Justin's image of lusty artisans carving statuary, quoted above, and the imperial household, which might fund such statuary. Yet elsewhere in the *Apology*, Justin criticizes imperially sponsored images quickly but directly. He argues that the emperors themselves use the sign of the cross, not knowing its true meaning. The sign of the cross is found everywhere – in the mast, in the plough, in the human body standing with arms extended, and even in the form of standards and trophies of the Roman government: "But the symbols you use make clear the power of this form [the cross], such as are on *vexilla* ("military ensigns") and trophies, which accompany your processions everywhere. By these signs you display signs of rule and power,

[142] See also Aristotle *Pol.* 1260a–b regarding the similarities between artisans and slaves.
[143] See Tatian *Ad Graec.* 32–33, discussed on pp. 243–46.

even if you do not know that you do this. And you dedicate images of your deceased emperors by this form, and you name them gods by inscriptions" (*1 Apol.* 55.6–8).[144] We can imagine the bronze trophies on the Basilica Ulpia in Trajan's Forum – or we can imagine Justin imagining them. Little do the Romans know that Justin has made Christian the sign that bears the message of imperial godhood and military triumph. Justin theorizes Roman religion in such a way that Roman triumph is effectively conducted under the sign of the cross, under the sign of Christianity.

[144] Καὶ τὰ παρ' ὑμῖν δὲ σύμβολα τὴν τοῦ σχήματος τούτου δύναμιν δηλοῖ, <οἷον τὰ τῶν> οὐηξίλλων καὶ τῶν τροπαίων, δι' ὧν αἵ γε πρόοδοι ὑμῶν πανταχοῦ γίνονται· τῆς <γὰρ> ἀρχῆς καὶ δυνάμεως τὰ σημεῖα ἐν τούτοις δεικνύντες, εἰ καὶ μὴ νοοῦντες, τοῦτο πράττετε. καὶ τῶν παρ' ὑμῖν ἀποθνῃσκόντων αὐτοκρατόρων τὰς εἰκόνας ἐπὶ τούτῳ τῷ σχήματι ἀνατίθετε καὶ θεοὺς διὰ γραμμάτων ἐπονομάζετε.

PART THREE

HUMAN BODIES AND THE IMAGE(S) OF GOD(S)

CHAPTER FIVE

HOW DO YOU KNOW GOD? ATHENAGORAS ON NAMES AND IMAGES

THROUGHOUT THE BOOK WE HAVE BEEN ASKING WHAT CLAIMS REGARDING ethnicity, *paideia*, piety, and power are made through words and images. How are people represented? How do they represent themselves? And who, gently or not so gently, points to the gap between the thing and its representation? The city squares of the Greek East were crammed with statuary of gods and elites. From the coin in your pocket – if you were so lucky – to the sculptures that gazed down on you in the temple or the agora, emperors and elites made statements about their piety, their knowledge of culture, and their likeness to the gods.[1]

The Christian writer Athenagoras enters into this landscape. He lives in a world where a woman at death is depicted as a naked Aphrodite/Venus, as we shall see in Chapter 7, and where emperors are gods before they die and are depicted as rising to the heavens at death, as we have already seen. Athenagoras's *Embassy*, purportedly addressed to the emperors, reverses the terms of the visual argument that seeks to overwhelm anyone who walks the public spaces of empire: that humans, including the emperors, are or are becoming gods.

1 See Clifford Ando, *Imperial Ideology and Provincial Loyalty in the Roman Empire* (Berkeley: University of California Press, 2000) 209–32 on the ideology of such images and the fact that "there existed a demonstrable popular belief that officials of the government or even the emperor himself oversaw the production and distribution of its images" (p. 212).

Both Justin and Athenagoras, as they address the imperial family, call the emperors to task for their inability *to be what they are named*. That is, Justin and Athenagoras protest a poor match between the name or the noun (*to onoma*)[2] and the thing that it represents. Justin exposed the power of "the name" in the ritual context of the courtroom and evoked a larger court and a divine judge who would evaluate the emperors and their claims to philosophical and cultural prowess, to piety, and to justice.

Athenagoras's *Embassy* takes a different approach. It deploys philosophical-grammatical debates of his day to expose an ongoing crisis of representation in the second-century Roman world. The *Embassy*, which claims to address the emperors Marcus Aurelius and his son Commodus, argues that names and images alike are being "usurped" or "occupied" (*epibateuein*). It is best understood as an extended philosophical argument on the slippage between signs, both linguistic and visual, and the things that they are supposed to represent in the second-century Roman world. Athenagoras offers a more subtle philosophical debate than Justin, grounded in part in the vocabulary of contemporaneous debates about grammar and the "criterion of truth," an epistemological struggle over the means by which one determined if something were true and sought true *epistēmē*, or knowledge.[3]

This chapter continues the discussion of crises of representation in the second century by situating Athenagoras's *Embassy* among ancient debates about what words and images are and what they do. I argue that the *Embassy* consistently persuades the audience – purportedly the emperors themselves – to ask: What is the connection between the names the emperors take for themselves ("pious" or "philosophical"), and the emperors themselves, especially their deeds? What is the connection between an image, especially a statue, and the thing that it claims to re-present naturalistically? One does things not only with words, to pick up Austin's language and turn it back again, but also, of course, with material objects.[4]

2 *To onoma* has many possible translations, especially in Stoic epistemology. See, e.g., Diogenes Laertius 7.58, and other passages discussed in A. A. Long and D. N. Sedley, *The Hellenistic Philosophers* (2 vols.; Cambridge: Cambridge University Press, 1987) 1.198, passim. Volume 1 provides translations and commentary of the principal sources, and volume 2 provides the original language and further commentary. My citations will contain the chapter number and the entry letter, followed by volume and page numbers.

3 See Abraham J. Malherbe, "The *Supplicatio Pro Christianis* of Athenagoras and Middle Platonism" (Ph.D. dissertation, Harvard University, 1963) 17 on Albinus's and Athenagoras's searches for *epistēmē* in their writings. On larger issues of epistemology versus faith as a key difference between Roman religion and Christianity, see Clifford Ando, *The Matter of the Gods: Religion and the Roman Empire* (Berkeley: University of California Press, 2008). Although I disagree with this thesis, Ando's treatment of representational heterogeneity is excellent; see chap. 3.

4 On representation, see pp. 120–22; see also Richard Gordon, "The Real and the Imaginary: Production and Religion in the Graeco-Roman World," *Art History* 2 (1979) 25–28. Regarding J. L. Austin, see pp. 140–42.

Athenagoras's may sound like an arcane argument, fit mainly for genteel academics haunting salons, discussing grammar and semiotics. Athenagoras does deliberately demonstrate his familiarity with the grammatical-philosophical debates of the educated elite, and he blames unphilosophical thinking on a non-Christian "multitude."[5] He asserts a Christian philosophical approach that can hold its own among those who had already questioned representation in names and images; he shoulders up to those who had long before rejected bloody sacrifice and had a cleaner, more unitary idea of the divine. Yet the debate about the function and force of words in the ancient world was not arcane or limited to philosophical salons: Christians claimed that they were dragged into courts on the basis of "the name alone," as we saw in the previous chapter.

This chapter will argue that Athenagoras's arguments, like Justin's, are elucidated when we place him within the material culture of the Roman Empire. Within the structure of my book, this chapter moves us from the broad space of the inhabited world and from the spaces of the city to engagement with particular statuary bodies. The first part of this chapter focuses on one sculpture (among many such images) that renders more comprehensible Athenagoras's argument about crises of representation: the half-length portrait of Commodus as Herakles, now in the Capitoline Museum in Rome. Athenagoras directly addresses Commodus, and although the *Embassy* probably predates the portrait, an investigation of this particular image helps us to understand the sorts of discourses of godhood and imperial power that were roiling at Athenagoras's time. Herakles himself is a particularly and famously ambivalent sign: the man who is also a god, straining between heroic and divine status, tragic and lifted up, a murderer and a hero. What did Herakles invoke? We know that not only emperors and elites took on his form, representing themselves with his attributes, but that convicted criminals too were forced to die in public spectacles by self-immolation as if they were acting out his labors and spectacular death.

The second part of the chapter then turns to Athenagoras's *Embassy*. Many scholars have seen this work as contradictory and disorganized. I demonstrate that the issue of representation is the key to finding in the *Embassy* a consistent and organized argument. The entire treatise bends toward the issue of names and images of humans and of gods, and how misrepresentations are rife in the language and visual culture of the time. In teasing out Athenagoras's logic, this chapter points to previous discussions in this book of the "landscape of having to repeat" and of the claims made regarding justice, piety, and power in the Forum of Trajan and in Justin's judgment of similar imperial

[5] Malherbe, "The *Supplicatio*," 59; see also p. 48; on blaming the populace for ignorant treatment of images, see Gordon, "The Real and the Imaginary," 8–11.

representations. But it also points forward: The *Embassy*'s sustained discussion of statuary prepares us to turn in later chapters to Tatian and Clement of Alexandria, who also engage in the debate over how images, especially statuary, function to persuade, what sorts of knowledge they produce, and what they truly represent.

I. "THIS GOLDEN ONE, THIS HERAKLES, THIS GOD"[6]: COMMODUS AND HERAKLES

Ancient literary sources – and often modern scholarship – insist on the emperor Commodus's insanity, violence, and extreme behaviors.[7] Ancient literature depicts Commodus as obsessed with gladiatorial competition and charioteering, as well as with portraying himself as the god Herakles or various other gods in these and other settings. Coins and statuary too depicted a pious and god-like or divine Commodus, who had a preference for Herakles.[8] Legends on coins from 190–192 CE have a portrait of Commodus and read HERCULI COMMODIANO, and later HERCULI ROMANO AUGUSTO.[9] When the phrase *Hercules Commodianus* appears on coins from his reign, one is unsure whether Commodus or Herakles is represented in both the image and in the inscription: The point is that both are intended and united.[10]

Plutarch, writing a century before Commodus's reign, had said, "Therefore justice is the aim of law, but the law is the work of the ruler, and the ruler is the image of the God who rules all things (ἄρχων δ' εἰκὼν θεοῦ τοῦ πάντα κοσμοῦντος), who needs no Pheidias or Polykleitos or Myron forming (him), but he renders himself in the likeness of God through virtue and makes the statue that is best and most appropriate to divinity to be seen (ἀλλ' αὐτὸς αὑτὸν εἰς ὁμοιότητα θεῷ δι' ἀρετῆς καθιστὰς καὶ δημιουργῶν ἀγαλμάτων

6 Cassius Dio 72.16.1.

7 Christopher Hallett (*The Roman Nude: Heroic Portrait Statuary 200 BC–AD 300* [Oxford: Oxford University Press, 2005] 253): "In particular the emperor's assumption of divine titles, like 'Hercules Romanus Augustus,' and his desire to have himself represented in the *habitus* of Hercules, is regarded as a straightforward symptom of his megalomania and his despotic nature." Olivier Hekster (*Commodus: An Emperor at the Crossroads* [Amsterdam: Gieben, 2002] 88): "Commodus's emphasis on his superhuman status went hand in hand with a further change in imperial self-representation. But it may simply have been the moment in which the emperor finally went insane." Commodus is the first explicitly dynastic Roman emperor, rather than one who gained his position through adoption. Athenagoras alludes to this in his closing lines, affirming the justice of this arrangement (*Leg.* 37.2); see Hekster, *Commodus*, 30.

8 On a medallion of 190/1 CE an unusual bearded Sol likely depicts Commodus as Sol. See Marianne Bergmann, *Die Strahlen der Herrscher: Theomorphes Herrscherbild und politische Symbolik im Hellenismus und in der römischen Kaiserzeit* (Mainz: von Zabern, 1998) 247; Hekster, *Commodus*, 100.

9 Hekster, *Commodus*, 104–5; Eric Varner, *Mutilation and Transformation:* Damnatio Memoriae *and Roman Imperial Portraiture* (Leiden: E. J. Brill, 2004) 137–38.

10 Hallett, *The Roman Nude*, 245. See Hekster, *Commodus*, 109 regarding the six new Hercules types in the years 190–92, compared to only one new Jupiter type (Defensor).

τὸ ἥδιστον ὀφθῆναι καὶ θεοπρεπέστατον)" (*Ad princ. inerud.*).[11] Plutarch maintains that the imperial goal is to become a god of sorts, but urges that this status and representation should occur by the chisels of virtue rather than a commission or a copy of an ancient, prestigious Greek statue. Therefore, it is not only a Christian like Athenagoras who critiques those who make false claims to divinity and false self-presentations as just and virtuous.

Although we only have Cassius Dio's writings on Commodus through the hand of a late epitomizer, the text reads as if written by Commodus's contemporary, the senator Cassius Dio himself.[12] He says that Commodus's love of Herakles and of himself was so excessive that it led to overt resignifications: "Indeed, he actually cut off the head of the Colossus [of Nero], and substituted for it a likeness of his own head; then, having given it a club and placed a bronze lion at its feet, so as to cause it to look like Hercules, he inscribed on it, in addition to the list of his titles which I have already indicated, these words: 'Champion of secutores; only left-handed fighter to conquer twelve times (as I recall the number) one thousand men' " (72.22.3).[13] In the literary imagination, at least, Commodus's self-representation as great athlete and god is mocked. The famous Colossus of Sol – purportedly 120 meters high in bronze, which was to have been placed in the *Domus Aurea*, Nero's Golden Palace, with Nero's own face on it – is no longer Sol or even Nero, but Commodus-Herakles.[14] Over more than a century, from arrogant emperor to delusional emperor, slight changes in portraiture and attributes can shift a statue from a god to a human (who is a god).

[11] *Mor.* 780E–F; ET *Plutarch's Moralia* (LCL; 16 vols.; trans. Harold North Fowler; Cambridge, MA: Harvard University Press, 1969) 10.59 with some modifications. The passage continues: "Now just as in the heaven god has established as a most beautiful image of himself the sun and the moon, so in states a ruler 'who in God's likeness / Righteous decisions upholds' (Homer *Od.* xix 109. 101), that is to say, one who, possessing god's wisdom, establishes, as his likeness and luminary, intelligence in place of scepter or thunderbolt or trident, with which attributes some rulers represent themselves in sculpture and painting, thus causing their folly to arouse hostile feelings, because they claim what they cannot attain. For God visits his wrath upon those who imitate (τοῖς ἀπομιμουμένοις) his thunders, lightnings, and sunbeams, but with those who emulate his virtue and make themselves like unto his goodness and mercy, he is well pleased" (780F–781A; ET 10.61).

[12] Cassius Dio was a senator and contemporary of Commodus, but of the section of his *Roman History* covering Commodus, only the eleventh-century epitome of monk Ioannes Xiphilinus remains. In the rhetorically bombastic *Scriptores Historiae Augustae*, probably written at the end of the fourth century, Commodus is said to be fond of seeing himself as a god on earth; he frequently donned the attributes of Herakles in public (*Hist. Aug. Comm.* 14.8). Hekster, *Commodus*, 4–5.

[13] ET *Dio's Roman History* (LCL; trans. Earnest Cary on the basis of Herbert Foster; 9 vols.; Cambridge, MA: Harvard University Press, 1970–87) 9.117. See also Cassius Dio 72.18.2, in which Commodus drinks sweet wine from a cup shaped like a club.

[14] On colossus of Nero see Hallett, *The Roman Nude*, 178–79 and esp. Bergmann, *Die Strahlen der Herrscher*, 190–94. See, however, R. R. R. Smith's caution that Bergmann is too accepting of the literary sources ("Nero and the Sun-God: Divine Accessories and Political Symbols in Roman Imperial Images" [a review of M. Bergmann, *Die Strahlen der Herrscher*], *JRA* 13.2 [2000] 532–42).

The Ambivalence of Herakles

Commodus chose a complicated signifier. Even absent a *Herakleid*,[15] we learn that Herakles is an ambivalent sign. Herakles, born of Zeus and a mortal mother, is powerful: As an infant he strangled the snakes Hera sent to his bed and as a man he completed the twelve labors assigned him. Herakles is feminized. He is enslaved to Omphale and to Hera and he is sometimes literally clothed in women's dress; he is at the same time hyper-masculine, mad and powerful in his rages. As Nicole Loraux writes, "Ever since Homer, the primary ambivalence of Herakles resides in the fact that the powerful hero of many exploits is inseparable from the hero who struggles, who is reduced to helplessness, to that *amēkhania* from which, in Homer and Aiskhylos, Athena and even Zeus come to save him at the last minute."[16] These stories did not languish in obscurity but are frequently portrayed in reliefs and other images available in the cityscapes of the Roman Empire.[17]

[15] Karl Galinsky, "Herakles in Greek and Roman Mythology," in Jaimee Pugliese Uhlenbrock, ed., *Herakles: Passage of the Hero through 1000 Years of Classical Art* (New Rochelle, NY: A. D. Caratzas and Annandale-on-Hudson, NY: Edith C. Blum Art Institute, Bard College, 1986) 19–22.

[16] Nicole Loraux, "Herakles: The Super-Male and the Feminine," in David Halperin et al., eds., *Before Sexuality: The Construction of Erotic Experience in the Ancient Greek World* (Princeton, NJ: Princeton University Press, 1990) 21–52, quotation at p. 24; regarding a funerary portrait of a Roman woman as Omphale wearing Herakles' lion skin, see Natalie Boymel Kampen, "Omphale and the Instability of Gender," in Natalie Boymel Kampen et al., eds., *Sexuality in Ancient Art: Near East, Egypt, Greece, and Italy* (Cambridge: Cambridge University Press, 1996) 233–46.

[17] See Raimond Wünsche, ed., *Herakles Herkules* (München: Staatliche Antikensammlungen und Glyptothek, 2003); and Uhlenbrock, ed., *Herakles*. On Herakles among Christian apologists and in Stoic philosophy, see Robert Grant, *Gods and the One God* (Philadelphia: Westminster, 1986) 68–69. Herakles is the traveler to the western edge of the earth, to the eponymous "Pillars of Herakles." In Lucian's madcap *True History*, self-admittedly a "true lie," on an island even further west than the Pillars of Herakles are footprints and an inscription about Herakles and Dionysos (Lucian *Ver. hist.* 1.4; discussed in Aristoula Georgiadou and David H. J. Larmour, *Lucian's Science Fiction Novel* True Histories*: Interpretation and Commentary* [Leiden: E. J. Brill, 1998] 1–9). Spoofing both Herodotus's account (4.82) of a big-footed Herakles and the gigantic-ness of Herakles and his deeds in the second-century imagination, Lucian writes, "Proceeding some three stades from the sea through the wood, we saw a certain *stēlē* (memorial marker) that had been made of bronze, and had been written upon with Greek letters, faint and rubbed out. The *stēlē* said, 'Until these [places] Herakles and Dionysos have reached.' There were also two footprints upon the rock nearby, one the size of 100 feet, the other less than that. It seemed to me that the one of Dionysos was the smaller; the other of Herakles. We worshiped, therefore, and went onward" (*Ver. hist.* 1.7; my translation modifies Lucian, *Works* [LCL; trans. A. M. Harmon; 8 vols.; Cambridge, MA: Harvard University Press, 2000] 1.255). Lucian also points to another far reach of the world when he mentions a Celtic image, perhaps a painting, of Herakles. This Herakles is old, bald, wrinkled, and blackened, although he can be recognized by his attributes, the familiar lion's skin, club, and quiver. This Herakles' tongue is pierced; from it, a chain forged with amber and gold links runs to the ears of a great crowd that is dragged behind him. A Celt, conveniently standing nearby, explains the image in beautiful Greek: the Celts identify Herakles with

Commodus was not the only one who chose in representations to blur himself with Herakles. So did other elites. An early third-century Roman man, pudgy around the chin, with a face slightly sad and shy, is depicted at 2.06 meters high as the hero Herakles, likely for his funerary monument (Fig. 23).[18] He stands fully, frontally nude, contrapposto, the lion's head high upon his neck, and the front paws knotted on his sternum so tightly that they cannot dangle. His left arm catches up the remainder of the lion's skin and his right hand delicately holds the club more like a torch than a weapon. A wild boar runs by his feet, in front of a tree trunk; the necessary marble supports are rendered as part of Herakles' story, alluding to his task of bringing to Erystheus alive the Erymanthian boar. While this sculpture is unusual, it is not the only non-imperial Herakles.[19]

23. Man as Herakles. Palazzo Barberini, Rome. DAIR 77.1730.

The form of Herakles can be donned by emperors and elites; but it can also be a far more ambivalent sign. Tertullian, in the late second or early third century, talks about a criminal executed in the form of Herakles.

eloquence. For the playful orator Lucian, true power lies in the tongue; his words are nuggets of gold and amber that bind the audience to him: "We consider that the real Heracles was a wise man who achieved everything by eloquence and applied persuasion as his principal force" (Lucian *Heracles*; ET Harmon, 1.67). In Lucian's Celtic Herakles, force, power, and words are linked. Herakles plays in ten thousand places, lovely and horrible in his many forms. For a terrifying Herakles who accepts human sacrifice, see Pliny *Nat. hist.* 36.4.39.

18 Henning Wrede, *Consecratio in formam deorum: vergöttlichte Privatpersonen in der Römischen Kaiserzeit* (Mainz: von Zabern, 1981) cat. no. 126 (pp. 240–41). The statue's provenance is unknown; it dates to ca. 230 CE and is now located in Rome in the Palazzo Barberini.

19 See also Wrede, *Consecratio in formam deorum*, cat. no. 122 (p. 239), and a grave monument from Tunis in cat. no. 127 (pp. 241–42), where the face of an older, balding man emerges flatly from the lion's-head hood.

> Then, again, when the likeness of a god is put on the head of an ignominious and infamous wretch, when one impure and trained up for the art in all effeminacy, represents a Minerva or a Hercules, is not the majesty of your gods insulted, and their deity dishonored? Yet you not merely look on, but applaud. You are, I suppose, more devout in the arena, where after the same fashion your deities dance on human blood, on the pollutions caused by inflicted punishments, as they act their themes and stories, doing their turn for the wretched criminals, except that these, too, often put on divinity and actually play the very gods. We have seen in our day a representation of the mutilation of Attis, that famous god of Pessinus, and a man burnt alive as Hercules. We have made merry amid the ludicrous cruelties of the noonday exhibition, at Mercury examining the bodies of the dead with his hot iron; we have witnessed Jove's brother, mallet in hand, dragging out the corpses of the gladiators. (*Apol.* 15.1)[20]

Tertullian begins by protesting theater masks, including those of Minerva and Hercules, and the indeterminate gender of the actor. The polymorphy or unstable signification of the actor becomes a means by which to vilify the deities portrayed by that actor. Herakles arises again a few lines later, when Tertullian makes the quick, horrific reference to a "man burnt alive as Hercules" in the arena.

We can ask whether this is merely Tertullian's calumnious rumor against those who are not Christians, since the *Apology* aims to critique others' religious practices and to decry persecution of Christians. Kathleen Coleman, however, has found other examples of those who were considered criminals being forced to play out a mythological or historical narrative, with real death at the end of the scene. Another immolated Herakles appears in an epigram of Lucilius from the reign of Nero (*Anth. Pal.* 11.184):

> Ἐκ τῶν Ἑσπερίδων τῶν τοῦ Διὸς ἦρε Μενίσκος
> ὡς τὸ πρὶν Ἡρακλέης χρύσεα μῆλα τρία.
> καὶ τί γάρ; ὡς ἑάλω, γέγονεν μέγα πᾶσι θέαμα
> ὡς τὸ πρίν Ἡρακλέης ζῶν κατακαιόμενος.
> Out of the Hesperidean garden of Zeus Meniskos –
> Like Herakles before him – lifted three golden apples.
> And for what? When he was caught, he became a great spectacle for all;
> Like Herakles before him, he was completely burned alive.[21]

20 ET ANF; see also Tertullian *Ad nat.* 1.10.47 and *Apol.* 15.4–5. Kathleen Coleman begins her "Fatal Charades: Roman Executions Staged as Mythological Enactments," *JRS* 80 (1990) 44–73 with Tertullian's reference to a criminal executed in the form of Herakles; see also pp. 55, 60. Regarding imitation of the gods in theatrical spectacle, see also Tatian's critique (pp. 240–41). On the blurring of representation and reality in the theater, and especially Nero's appearances on stage, see Shadi Bartsch, *Actors in the Audience: Theatricality and Doublespeak from Nero to Hadrian* (Cambridge, MA: Harvard University Press, 1994) chap. 2.

21 The Greek is from Coleman, "Fatal Charades," 60; I have modified her translation slightly.

As Coleman explains, because Zeus and the emperor were often associated with each other, it is possible that Meniskos was burned alive for stealing apples from the garden of Nero's *Domus Aurea*.[22]

Among the many versions of Herakles' life, we know that the hero dies, immolated at first by the robe given to him by his wife Deianeira and then finally, as the robe torturously wraps tighter around his body, at his own request on Mount Oeta. Athena in the gods' mercy plucks him out of the flames; he is presumably purified and divinized. Read in light of Herakles' story, the criminal's end as recorded in Lucilius's epigram seems to be not punishment but the working out of a narrative: How can anyone intervene to stop something that has already happened again and again in myth? The cruel trick for the burning criminal is that there is no Athena to save or divinize him.

Even dreaming about Herakles – or dreaming about his representation in statuary – was an ambivalent thing, according to Artemidorus, the second-century writer of the *Oneirokritikon*, or *Interpretation of Dreams*. In a section on what dreaming of the gods or their images means, Artemidorus first offers these thoughts on Herakles: "Seeing Heracles himself or a statue of him is auspicious for all those who govern their lives by sound moral principles and who live in accordance with the law, especially if they have been treated unjustly by others. For when he lived among men, the god always came to the defense of those who had been treated unjustly and he avenged them." Then, as we would expect from Artemidorus's dream world and the figure of Herakles, things get more complicated.

> Thus, if a man dreams that he spends time with the god and assists him in his work or shares his meals with him or wears the same clothes or receives from the god his lion skin, his club, or any other weapon, this dream has been observed to be inauspicious and bad for all men. And I myself have come to the same conclusion after long experience. It is both fitting and logical that these things should not mean good luck. For the life that Heracles led is the one that he imparts to the dreamer, and the life that he led when he lived among men was a life full of trials and misery, although he himself was very famous and esteemed. Frequently the dream signifies that a man will find himself in situations similar to those that the god was in when he was carrying these weapons. (*On.* 2.37)[23]

Through these stories, we have met Herakles the mighty, the orator, the traveler, the demi-god, the god, and the criminal. Even if Athenagoras or

[22] Ibid., 61.

[23] ET Artemidorus, *The Interpretation of Dreams* (trans. Robert J. White; Torrance, CA: Original Books, 1975) 119.

any "ordinary viewer"[24] did not see one of the exact images discussed above, s/he would have known the stories of Herakles and would have known of the phenomenon of becoming Herakles.

Commodus as Herakles

Commodus is unique for the amount of blame heaped upon him for representing himself as Herakles, but he is not unique in choosing this demi-god for himself. Previous rulers had represented themselves as Herakles, from Alexander the Great onward.[25] Seneca's *Hercules Furens* may have been an attempt to provide both philosophical direction to Nero and an *apologia* for an emperor whose mad shifts and claims to divinity were as dangerous as those of Herakles, whose anger led him to kill his wife Megara and their children.[26] Martial described a temple to Herakles built by Domitian and located on the Via Appia, where Herakles' statue had Domitian's features.[27] Trajan, Hadrian, and Antoninus Pius used imagery of Herakles long before Commodus did,[28] and although Commodus's father Marcus Aurelius did not use images of Herakles often,[29] Commodus's co-emperor Lucius Verus did.[30]

[24] See, e.g., John R. Clarke, *Art in the Lives of Ordinary Romans: Visual Representation and Non-Elite Viewers in Italy, 100 BC–AD 315* (Berkeley: University of California Press, 2003) 1–13 for method and cautions.

[25] For an overview of uses of Herakles among a variety of rulers, see Harald Schulze, "Vorbild der Herrschenden. Herakles und die Politik," in Wünsche, ed., *Herakles Herkules*, 344–65. See also Olivier Hekster, "Propagating Power: Hercules as an Example for Second-Century Emperors," in Louis Rawlings and Hugh Bowden, eds., *Herakles and Hercules: Exploring a Graeco-Roman Divinity* (Swansea: Classical Press of Wales, 2005) 205–21.

[26] Eleanor OKell, "*Hercules Furens* and Nero: The Didactic Purpose of Senecan Tragedy," in Rawlings and Bowden, eds., *Herakles and Hercules*, 185–204.

[27] In Martial's poetry, Domitian's and Herakles' deeds become confused (9.64.1–2; see also Hallett, *Roman Nude*, 239). Moreover, in the *aula regia* or main audience hall of Domitian's Palatine palace were found two statues of dark green stone. They represent Dionysos and Herakles and may have been depicted alongside other statues of gods and white marble statues of the Flavian family. See discussion in Diana Kleiner, *Roman Sculpture* (New Haven, CT: Yale University Press, 1992) 181–84. See also Statius *Silvae* 3.1 ("The Hercules of Pollius Felix at Surrentum") and 4.6 ("The Hercules Statuette of Novius Vindex"): "There it was and then [at Vindex's, for dinner] that I learned of a thousand shapes of bronze and antique ivory and of false bodies in wax, ready to speak. For who would ever rival Vindex' eyes in recognizing the hands of old masters and restoring its maker to an untitled statue. . . . Amid all this the guardian spirit of the temperate board, Amphityron's son, took my heart captive in fond love. Long as I looked, he left my eyes unsatisfied. Such was the dignity of the work, the majesty confined in narrow limits. A god he was, a god!" ET Statius, *Works* (LCL; trans. D. R. Shackleton Bailey; 3 vols.; Cambridge, MA: Harvard University Press, 2003) 1.283.

[28] Hekster, "Propagating Power," 205–8; regarding Hadrian, see Hallett, *The Roman Nude*, 253.

[29] Hekster says Marcus Aurelius never used images of Herakles for himself (*Commodus*, 91) but see Cornelius Vermeule, "Herakles Crowning Himself: New Greek Statuary Types and Their Place in Hellenistic and Roman Art," *JHS* 77.2 (1957) 283.

[30] Hekster, *Commodus*, 91.

On the reverse of a bronze medallion, the emperor Commodus and Herakles are presented as facing and contemplating each other.[31] Commodus is depicted as the sacrificing magistrate, veiled and tilting the *patera* over an altar. The emperor is slimmer than the buff Hercules, whose type we know better from the statue of the Farnese Hercules found in the baths of Caracalla,[32] but the two communicate across the altar: Herakles leans in on his club, waiting for the sacrifice. Commodus, contrapposto, mirrors him; the *patera* nearly touches his lion's skin and so by means of religious ritual the connection between the two is strengthened.

"This golden one, this Herakles, this god": Cassius Dio mocks Commodus's self-representations. The half-length portrait of Commodus as Herakles at the Capitoline Museum is particularly important for our discussion because of its rarity, given the order to destroy Commodus's images, its exquisite execution, and the symbolic punch it packs into a less than full-length figure (Fig. 24).[33] The piece probably dates to 191–192 CE, late in Commodus's reign.[34]

The portrait was discovered in 1874 in a cryptoporticus of the Horti Lamiani on the Esquiline. After Commodus's condemnation, the statue was stored on imperial grounds in an underground hall with other statuary from various time periods.[35] Commodus was found near two male tritons who likely held a *parapetasma* – a high, stiff curtain arching over his head, as we saw in several reliefs from Aphrodisias.[36] The sculpture itself is of marble; the base, which is likely also ancient, is from a brownish alabaster; together they are 1.33 m high. It is in nearly perfect shape.[37]

The portrait blends Commodus's identity "with that of the god to an unprecedented degree."[38] Commodus's head, skin glowing with a fine-sheened

31 Vermeule, "Herakles Crowning Himself," 295, plate III, 12.

32 See Miranda Marvin, "Freestanding Sculptures from the Baths of Caracalla," *AJA* 87.3 (1983) 374–84, esp. 355–63.

33 Robin Jensen discusses this statue in relation to early Christian writings (*Face to Face: Portraits of the Divine in Early Christianity* [Minneapolis, MN: Fortress, 2005] 66).

34 Kleiner, *Roman Sculpture*, 275–77. Regarding another, similar statue see Anne-Marie Leander Touati, "Commodus Wearing the Lion Skin: A 'Modern' Portrait in Stockholm," *Opuscula Romana* 18.7 (1990) 115–29, who argues that this image of Commodus with a lion skin tightly around his head: "is either a copy of unusually high fidelity of an at present lost ancient Commodus head, or an ancient head which has been overworked by a modern restorer" (p. 120).

35 Varner, *Mutiliation and Transformation*, 140–41.

36 While its original location is unknown, it was likely displayed in a public place. See Klaus Fittschen and Paul Zanker, *Katalog der römischen Porträts in den Capitolinischen Museen und den anderen kommunalen Sammlungen der Stadt Rom* (2 vols.; Mainz: von Zabern, 1983) 1.88 for a sketch of the reconstruction of the statuary ensemble.

37 Ibid., 1.87–88 (cat. no. 78); see also the list of fourteen similar portraits on pp. 86–87. Restorations of the statue are minimal. According to Varner (*Mutilation and Transformation*, 140–41) they include sections of the lion skin, the index, middle, and little finger of the right hand, and sections of shield. Also missing is one of the Amazons at the base.

38 Hallett, *The Roman Nude*, 253.

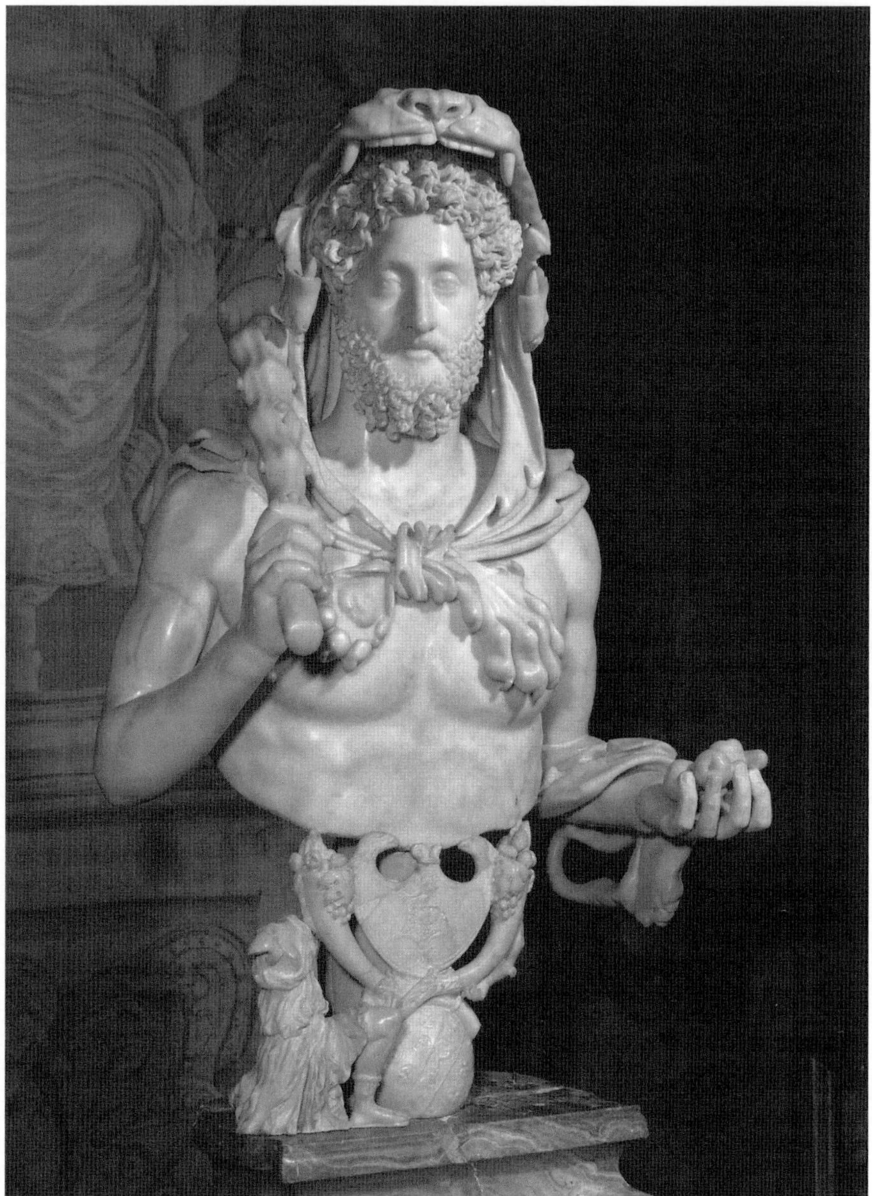

24. Half-length portrait of Emperor Commodus as Herakles. Excavated on the Esquiline in Rome, 1874. Musei Capitolini, Rome, Italy. Erich Lessing/Art Resource, NY.

patina, is draped with a high, huge lion's head. Commodus's hair and beard are vibrantly curly. His eyes, pupils precisely inscribed, look impassively toward the right, in the direction in which he could best swing his club, if he wanted to bother. The lion's paws are knotted in the Herakles knot around Commodus's sternum, one paw up and one down, claws visible. His right hand loosely grasps the knotted wooden club, which is propped casually on his shoulder. In his left hand are three apples. Kleiner interprets the message: "Commodus . . . through Hercules's deed of fetching the apples of the Hesperides, has acquired *virtus* and immortality."[39] These stolen apples will lead to glory, not the punishing immolation we learned about earlier.

As important as the portrait is what surrounds it. The marble image of Commodus sits atop an elaborately carved brownish alabaster base.[40] At its peak is an Amazon pelta topped by two eagles' heads; this is flanked on either side with overflowing cornucopias. The cornucopias are balanced upon a small perfect globe: the cosmos, banded by small carvings of the zodiac. According to Robert Hannah, its depiction of Taurus, Capricorn, and Scorpio likely signals the constellations dominant in the month of October, a month significant to Commodus for many reasons: his share in the Parthian triumph on 12 October 166, when he was named Caesar; his acquisition of the title Germanicus on 15 October 172; his official acknowledgement in Rome as emperor on 22 October 180. Moreover, Commodus had renamed the month of October after Herakles.[41] Next to the globe, one leg kneeling, the other foot on the ground, is a small, now fragmentary Amazon, originally likely balanced by another on the right.[42] The message blooms vertically upward: The cosmos sustains Commodus and he protects and rules it; he emerges from the bounties of the earth and sustains them; the double-headed eagle empire is his; he embodies divine or demi-divine masculinity, putting the *vir* into *virtus*.[43]

A Proliferation of Signs

Cassius Dio sketches a name- and image-obsessed Commodus:

> He actually ordered that Rome itself should be called Commodiana, the legions Commodian, and the day on which these measures were voted Commodiana. Upon himself he bestowed, in addition to a great many other names, that of Hercules. Rome he styled the "Immortal, Fortunate Colony of the Whole Earth"; for he wished it to be regarded as a settlement of his own. In his honour a gold statue was erected of a thousand pounds weight, representing him together with a bull and a cow. Finally, all the months were named after him, so that they were enumerated as follows: Amazonius, Invictus, Felix, Pius, Lucius, Aelius,

39 Kleiner, *Roman Sculpture*, 277.

40 Varner, *Mutilation and Transformation*, 140–41.

41 Robert Hannah, "The Emperor's Stars: The Conservatori Portrait of Commodus," *AJA* 90.3 (1986) 337–42, esp. p. 341.

42 See Cassius Dio below and 72.20.2 on Commodus's use of an epithet relating to the Amazons.

43 "The pelta and kneeling Amazon," writes Kleiner, "refer to Rome's barbarian enemies, over which Commodus has triumphed and has brought peace and prosperity, symbolized by the cornucopiae, to the empire (seen in the orb)" (Kleiner, *Roman Sculpture*, 277).

> Aurelius, Commodus, Augustus, Herculeus, Romanus, Exsuperatorius. For he himself assumed these several titles at different times, but "Amazonius" and "Exsuperatorius" he applied constantly to himself, to indicate that in every respect he surpassed absolutely all humankind superlatively; so superlatively mad had the abandoned wretch become. And to the senate he would send messages couched in these terms: "The Emperor Caesar Lucius Aelius Aurelius Commodus Augustus Pius Felix Sarmaticus Germanicus Maximus Britannicus, Pacifier of the Whole Earth, Invincible, the Roman Hercules, Pontifex Maximus, Holder of the Tribunician Authority for the eighteenth time, Imperator for the eighth time, Consul for the seventh time, Father of his Country, to consuls, praetors, tribunes, and the fortunate Commodian senate, Greeting." Vast numbers of statues were erected representing him in the form (*schēmati*) of Hercules. (Cassius Dio 72.15.2)[44]

Even if other emperors too take on names for themselves and re-form themselves into gods, Commodus's representations, according to Dio, are excessive and ridiculous; to state the obvious, the passage is funny. Commodus's name is everywhere, used to re-signify place and time; juxtaposed with other names, his name takes on the characteristics or attributes of those names. The hyperbolic profusion of imperial titles reminds us of how Justin and Athenagoras take up imperial titles to address the emperors, and thus reflect back the emperors' own representations.

Commodus's representations and their destruction exemplify the dangerous impermanence of signs in the Roman Empire at the time of Athenagoras. Commodus would suffer *damnatio memoriae* after his death, and then just as rapidly a rehabilitation and deification four years later under Septimius Severus. In the time between, some of his images would be destroyed.[45] In some reliefs of the benefactions and leadership of Marcus Aurelius, carved for a now no-longer extant triumphal arch, Commodus was carefully chiseled away (Fig. 25).[46] A scene of triumph celebrates Marcus Aurelius's victory over the Sarmatian and German tribes in 176; Athenagoras mentions the victory over Sarmatia at the beginning of his text. In this relief, Commodus's absence

[44] ET Cary, 9.103, 105 (slightly modified). The passage continues (72.20.2): "But of the populace in general, many did not enter the amphitheatre at all, and others departed after merely glancing inside, partly from shame at what was going on, partly also from fear, inasmuch as a report spread abroad that he would want to shoot a few of the spectators in imitation of Hercules and the Stymphalian birds" (ET Cary, 9.113).

[45] *Damnatio memoriae* is a modern term for the ancient practice of defacing statues and other images and rubbing out portions of inscriptions. See Hekster, *Commodus*, 137–62 and Varner, *Mutilation and Transformation*, 138–39.

[46] For a discussion of the reliefs and the debate about the Arch of Marcus Aurelius, see Varner, *Mutilation and Transformation*, 142–46.

25. Triumph Scene. Relief from the Arch of Marcus Aurelius. Palazzo dei Conservatori, Rome, Italy. Nimatallah/Art Resource, NY.

is marked by a suddenly smooth background, a space a little wider than normal aesthetics would demand, and an inconsistency in the façade of the Temple of Fortuna behind the chariot. Victory's arm is poised to plant a wreath – now erased – on the head of no one. Ghostly fillets of the disappeared wreath flutter on the column behind.[47] Many of the images celebrating Marcus Aurelius's reign later would be reused in the Arch of Constantine, so that Commodus's absence was convenient, and Marcus became a Constantine – yet another instance of transformation and transmutation in representation. Athenagoras lived at a time when the forces of the Roman Empire threatened not only goods or honor; the "loss, disgrace . . . and harm" extended to "bodies and souls" (*Leg.* 2.3). This was always and especially true of those of lower and marginal status, such as Christians and slaves, whose bodies could be scarred with punishments. The empire was full of the destruction and transformation of bodies and images of bodies, and not even the emperors were safe from (statuary) harm.

We have seen several who don the cloak of Herakles, presumably to assimilate his strength and might to themselves and to re-present themselves as a divinized hero and a demi-god. Yet Herakles expressed something else as well, something which Commodus presumably did not want to evoke. In a section where Athenagoras considers a Euhemeristic argument that the gods were once kings and humans, he also writes about Herakles. He first quotes a passage from the *Odyssey*, which talks about Herakles' "monstrous actions" in killing "Iphitos while he was a guest in his household."[48] Herakles is the subject of the couplet: "'Merciless, who did not respect the vengeance of the gods or the table / at which they partook, but then even killed him,' that is, killed Iphitus. It is fitting that such a person should go mad, fitting that he light a pyre and burn himself to death" (*Leg.* 29.1). Athenagoras uses Homer to expose Herakles as one who did not respect the gods, who did not respect human traditions of the guest-host relationship, and who was subject to madness and death. What did Herakles invoke? Many things, clearly, if his image was used not only for emperors and elites, but also for convicted criminals in public spectacles, forced to act out the labors and death of Herakles.

II. ATHENAGORAS

For the epitomizer of Dio Cassius, Commodus's sin lay in his ridiculous and multiple self-representations as a Greek clothed in Indian goods, as a Mercury (72.17.3–4) and as a Herakles (72.16.1). Athenagoras likely does not have the benefit of hindsight as did Dio, or the knowledge of Commodus's

[47] See Kleiner, *Roman Sculpture*, 288, 291–94. Eleven panels still exist; eight are in the attic of the north and south sides of the Arch of Constantine in Rome; three are in the walls of the Museo del Palazzo dei Conservatori. In appropriating these reliefs, Constantine sought to associate himself with the "good" reign of Marcus Aurelius; see discussion in Richard Brilliant, *Visual Narratives: Storytelling in Etruscan and Roman Art* (Ithaca, NY: Cornell University Press, 1984) 119–22.

[48] Homer *Od.* 21.26–7; ET Richmond Lattimore, *The Odyssey of Homer* (New York: Harper Perennial, 1965) 310.

condemnation by the Senate in 193 upon Commodus's assassination. Yet Athenagoras does write during Commodus's reign, penning his *Embassy* to the emperors amid the representations of Commodus, of imperial families before him, and of elites from around the empire. The arguments in Athenagoras's *Embassy* loop back to the issue of representation, especially the failure of the imperial family to align correctly their claims to truth, philosophy, justice, and piety with their actions.[49]

Who Athenagoras was, why he wrote his *Embassy*, its actual audience: all of these very basic data are difficult to grasp. It is amusing that for a text concerned with naming and representation, we possess so little information about the author, the audience, and the reasons for writing the *Embassy*.[50] The *inscriptio* of the manuscript as found in the Arethas codex, from which all other versions derive, demonstrates the problem of determining Athenagoras's identity. It is in the hand of the scribe Baanes and reads: "By Athenagoras the Athenian, philosopher, Christian. Embassy concerning Christians" (ἀθηναγόρου ἀθηναίου φιλοσόφου χριστιανοῦ | πρεσβεία περὶ χριστιανῶν).[51] The scribe offers us Athenagoras the Athenian, philosopher and Christian. But even this information, which Baanes presumably copied from another manuscript, may be incomplete. Athenagoras's writing, proper, begins not with

49 I leave aside *On the Resurrection* since it is not addressed to the emperors and its authorship is debated. Robert Grant argues that it represents a later debate against Origen's ideas of the resurrection ("Athenagoras or Pseudo-Athenagoras," *HTR* 47.2 [1954] 121–29); William Schoedel, "Introduction," in Athenagoras, *Legatio and De Resurrectione* (trans. William R. Schoedel; Oxford: Clarendon, 1972) xii, regards it to be dissimilar to the *Embassy*. (It is Schoedel's Greek edition that I cite, and his translations have aided my own.) Leslie W. Barnard argues against Grant and Schoedel (*Athenagoras: A Study in Second Century Christian Apologetic* [Paris: Beauchesne, 1972] 28–31), and Bernard Pouderon too thinks it is authentic (*D'Athènes d'Alexandrie: Études sur Athènagore et les origines de la philosophie chrétienne* [Québec: Presses de l'Université Laval and Louvain: Editions Peeters, 1997] 71–144).

50 All manuscripts of the *Embassy* are apographs of the Arethas codex – that is, they all copy from it. This was originally the insight of Adolf von Harnack (*Die Überlieferung der griechischen Apologeten des zweiten Jahrhunderts in der alten Kirche und im Mittelalter* [Leipzig: J. C. Hinrichs, 1882] 86–88, discussed in Miroslav Marcovich, *Athenagoras Legatio pro Christianis* [New York: de Gruyter, 1990] 17). For a discussion of the various manuscripts and conversation about the correct title of the piece, written before Harnack's insight, see Johannes Otto, *Corpus Apologetarum Christianorum saeculi secundi* (9 vols.; Wiesbaden: Sändig, 1851–1969) 7.xi–lxxv, esp. lxii–lxxv (VII. De inscriptione et aetate Supplicationis).

51 See Otto, *Corpus Apologetarum Christianorum*, 7.xiii: this reading is from the Arethas codex (*Parisinus gr.* 451) fol. 322,b. In his Prolegomena (7.lxii–lxv), Otto discusses small variations in the title over various manuscripts and the significance of the use of the term φιλοσόφου. Ἀθηναίου is missing from the Angelicus and Bodleianus 1 manuscripts. Everyone who has studied the manuscript of *Parisinus gr.* 451, from which all other texts of Athenagoras derive, comments that both the *notarius* or scribe Baanes and Arethas, the archbishop of Caesarea (Cappadocia) for whom he wrote, used similar brown ink and a nearly identical hand, with the latter "correcting" (sometimes incorrectly) the work of the scribe (Marcovich, *Athenagoras*, 17). The *subscriptio* to the *Embassy* is in the bishop Arethas's hand and reads, with disregard for orthography, ἀθηναγόρυ πρεσβεῖα ("the embassy of Athenagoras") (Marcovich, *Athenagoras*, 17).

himself but his addressees:[52] "To the emperors Marcus Aurelius Antoninus and Lucius Aurelius Commodus, conquerors of Armenia and Sarmatia, and, above all, philosophers." The names employed and the information about what they had conquered indicates that the text was likely written by 176 or 177 CE; by 17 March 180 Marcus was dead and Commodus had assumed the name Marcus Aurelius Commodus Antoninus.[53]

We have little information about Athenagoras apart from the text contained in the Arethas codex. This lack of information invites speculation. Baanes in his *inscriptio* offers an Athenian, philosophical, and Christian Athenagoras. The fifth-century Christian historian Philip of Side dramatically (and fictively) filled out Athenagoras's intellectual legacy, describing him as the first to head a school in Alexandria, and making Clement of Alexandria his disciple and Pantainos, the disciple of Clement, Athenagoras's intellectual grandson.[54] Who

[52] In a marginal note, Arethas writes to the effect that although the manuscript has a sort of title, its beginning is in fact incomplete, lacking the name of the sender and the greeting. The *Embassy*, it seems, may have been transmitted to Arethas and Baanes with a fragmentary beginning. See Otto, *Corpus Apologetarum Christianorum*, 7.1 n. 2. The addressees are in the dative. The normal conventions of the day, "so and so to someone else, greetings," are half missing, according to Schoedel, "Introduction," xii. On standard epistolary beginnings to prefaces, see Loveday Alexander, *The Preface to Luke's Gospel : Literary Convention and Social Context in Luke 1.1–4 and Acts 1.1* (Cambridge: Cambridge University Press, 1993). P. Lorraine Buck points out that there is no reason to expect an epistolary form at the beginning of an embassy or speech ("Athenagoras's *Embassy*: A Literary Fiction," *HTR* 89.3 [1996] 221).

[53] This phrase has caused much debate regarding the date of the writing of the *Embassy*; see Schoedel's summary: "M. Aurelius dropped the title 'victor of Armenia,' after the death of his adoptive brother, L. Aurelius Verus, in A.D. 169; and Commodus never had it. Schwartz therefore suggested that 'victors of Germany' be read instead; Harnack suggested expunging the phrase as an interpolation; and Johannes Geffcken welcomed the confusion as evidence of the unreliability of the salutation (*Zwei griechische Apologeten* [Leipzig: B. G. Teubner, 1907]). But Giovanni Porta has shown that in unofficial papyri and inscriptions 'victor of Aremania' *was* a title used of M. Aurelius after the death of L. Verus and that it was also given to Commodus" ("Introduction," xi–xii). See Giovanni Porta, "La dedica e la data della *Πρεσβεία* di Atenagora," *Didaskaleion* 5.1–2 (1916) 53–70. See also Varner, *Mutiliation and Transformation*, 136.

[54] This differs from Eusebius's account, where Pantainos is Clement's teacher and Athenagoras is not mentioned at all (Schoedel, *Legatio*, ix). See, however, Pouderon, who argues that Philip does indicate that Athenagoras was in Athens, and who also argues that Philip is right in placing Athenagoras as the first head of a school in Alexandria (*D'Athènes d'Alexandrie*, 29–30). Philip, preserved in a fourteenth-century manuscript, is also unusual in thinking that Athenagoras addresses Hadrian and Antoninus (Schoedel, *Legatio*, ix). Other than Philip of Side, the only early evidence for Athenagoras comes from Methodius (d. 311), who alludes to the *Legatio* (24.4) and identifies its author as Athenagoras; Epiphanius's and Photius's attestations depend on Methodius (ibid., ix). Scholars usually dismiss Philip of Side's evidence (Timothy Barnes, "The Embassy of Athenagoras," *JTS* 86.1 [April 1975] 113). W. H. C. Frend in his *Martyrdom and Persecution in the Early Church: A Study of a Conflict from the Maccabees to Donatus* (Oxford: Blackwell, 1965) 285–86 places Athenagoras in Asia Minor but he leaves the question of Athenagoras's location open in his *The Rise of Christianity* (Philadelphia: Fortress, 1984) 241–43. See also Barnard, *Athenagoras*, 15–17 regarding Athenagoras's mention of camels (*De res.* 12), which leads Barnard to conclude that Egypt, rather than Greece or Asia Minor, is a likely location for Athenagoras's life and writing.

Athenagoras was or claimed to be is also a matter of debate for modern scholars. Frustrated by those who assert that apologists writing to emperors engaged in "an empty formality of an elaborate pretence," Timothy Barnes has argued that Athenagoras did write his text as an embassy to the emperors,[55] and that he may have delivered the speech in Athens in 176, when Marcus Aurelius and Commodus were both there after they had been initiated into the Eleusinian mysteries.[56] Pouderon, less interested in the precise location of the address, still takes seriously the evidence from Philip of Side and other summaries of earliest church history to argue that Athenagoras moved from an academy in Athens to head the one in Alexandria.[57]

The strength of Athenagoras's philosophical rhetoric produces a desire to pin him to a date and a place – to place him precisely within the culture wars of his time. It makes a good story: A Christian scholar who melds Christianity and philosophy moves from intellectual center to intellectual center, from Athens to Alexandria, marking the success of Christian philosophy in both famous Greek cities and stopping along the way to talk to the emperors. Both locations represent neat imaginings after the fact.[58] We cannot know whence precisely he wrote, although it is likely that he worked from some Greek-speaking metropolis interested in philosophy.

As the identity of the author has been debated, so too has the content and purpose of the text. Athenagoras's *Embassy* has often been mined for phrases about the resurrection, for early hints of trinitarian thinking, for a muted but insistent threat of Christian persecution, to give a few examples. Schoedel has argued that the *Embassy* expresses a doctrine of God culminating

55 On embassies and *apologiai*, see Barnes, *The Embassy*. Regarding Athenagoras specifically, see William R. Schoedel, "In Praise of the King: A Rhetorical Pattern in Athenagoras," in Donald Winslow, ed., *Disciplina Nostra: Essays in Memory of Robert F. Evans* (Cambridge, MA: The Philadelphia Patristic Foundation, 1979) 69–90, and esp. his "Apologetic Literature and Ambassadorial Activities," *HTR* 82.1 (1989) 55–78, esp. 70–78. While Schoedel tries to understand Athenagoras's *Embassy* in light of the performance of speeches to the emperors, Buck ("Athenagoras's *Embassy*: A Literary Fiction," 209–26) characterizes the *Embassy* as a literary fiction, yet she ignores the important forensic elements of Justin's or Athenagoras's texts (p. 215).

56 We recall this from Herodes' famous brawl with Marcus Aurelius in Sirmium in 174, presumably healed by the time of Marcus Aurelius and Commodus's entry, with Herodes Atticus's participation, into the mysteries in 176. See Chapter 1 and Barnes, "The Embassy," 111–14; Robert Grant, *Greek Apologists of the Second Century* (Philadelphia: Westminster, 1988) 100; Fergus Millar understands Athenagoras's text to have been delivered before the emperors in ca. 177, although he allows it might be a "literary fiction" (*The Emperor in the Roman World [31 BC–AD 337]* [Ithaca, NY: Cornell University Press, 1992] 564; see also Marcovich, *Legatio*, 1; Gustave Bardy, *Athénagore: Supplique au sujet des chrétiens* [SC; Paris: Éditions du Cerf, 1943] 12–16). Buck, "Athenagoras's *Embassy*: A Literary Fiction," 217–20 rightly criticizes the attempt to pinpoint a face-to-face meeting between Athenagoras and the emperors.

57 Pouderon, *D'Athènes d'Alexandrie*, 29–30.

58 In *Leg.* 6.2 Athenagoras states that he uses doxographies, or philosophical handbooks that collected the opinions of the great philosophers of classical antiquity, a common practice in antiquity. Schoedel, "Introduction," xx; Barnard, *Athenagoras*, 41–42.

in trinitarian theology, although explicitly trinitarian thought emerges only once (*Leg.* 10.1–5) and is immediately surpassed by Athenagoras's admission that there are even more who belong in this discussion of divinity, namely, angels and ministers of God.[59] Barnard plumbs the *Embassy* for information about some of the traditional categories of systematic theology.[60] Some scholars in contrast have argued that Athenagoras's thought is too chaotic to deserve close analysis. We find such an opinion in one of Athenagoras's main interpreters. Schoedel argues that "[Athenagoras's] train of ideas is not always clear, and his command of materials is not secure."[61] Yet he also states that "[Athenagoras's] organization of materials is orderly. His style is Atticistic. Despite weaknesses in structure, the *Plea* [i.e., the *Embassy*] projects an atmosphere of the 'refinement' sought after by devotees of the 'second sophistic.'"[62]

Even if Schoedel is ambivalent about Athenagoras, he is right to place Athenagoras within the discourses of the so-called Second Sophistic, where philosophy and rhetoric blended and where Greek *paideia* was attractive, even and sometimes especially to the Roman emperors, as we have learned. Moreover, Malherbe, Schoedel, and Barnard, who have attended most to the study of Athenagoras, all rightly explicate his engagement with Middle Platonic philosophy.[63] Yet, unlike these scholars, who find Athenagoras's prose chaotic, I argue that questions about names and images – in particular, the names and images of the gods – are key to and organize his *Embassy*. Athenagoras uses Greek grammatical-philosophical debates to think about representation in the context of the Roman Empire and in the midst of a contemporaneous theological debate about nature of piety and atheism.[64]

59 Regarding trinitarian elements, see Schoedel, "Introduction," xviii.

60 Barnard, *Athenagoras*.

61 Schoedel, "Introduction," xv.

62 Ibid., xviii–xix. See also Geffcken, *Apologeten*, 163; 163–75 discuss Athenagoras's style and presentation.

63 Beginning with his unpublished 1963 dissertation and extending through several articles on Athenagoras, Malherbe carefully reads the entire *Embassy* against Albinus's admittedly later handbook on philosophical treatises to show that Athenagoras engages in a precise way in contemporaneous philosophical thinking and writing. Malherbe mentions scholarly allegations that Athenagoras was not a real philosopher or a real Christian in his useful summary of his dissertation: "The Structure of Athenagoras, 'Supplicatio pro Christianis,'" *VC* 23 (1969) 1. On Athenagoras's philosophical orientation in Middle Platonism, see also Barnard, *Athenagoras*, 44–51, who also outlines Aristotelian and Stoic influences.

64 Schoedel complained of a weak structuring of the *Embassy* and then added in a note that "too many 'footnotes' get into the text, and Athenagoras has trouble fully integrating some materials (such as his discussion of the 'names' of the gods)" (Schoedel, "Introduction," xix n. 30). Schoedel thus consigns to a footnote what I would argue is the core of Athenagoras's argument. Athenagoras focuses on the question of how god or gods should be represented in language and images. Malherbe understands Athenagoras to have organized at least part of his *Supplicatio* in correspondence with the philosophical trends of the day, where physics, ethics, and dialectic or logic were often treated in turn, as they were in Albinus's *Didaskalikos*, to which Malherbe compares Athenagoras's writing ("The Structure of Athenagoras," 1–20).

Athenagoras's Argument: The Proemium

The address and the *proemium* (1–3) of the *Embassy* introduce the reader to the topic of a crisis of representation in language and in imagery, touching on terms and themes dexterously woven through the rest of the text. Although Athenagoras will not name the emperors again, by using the second-person plural and the vocative "emperors," he, like Justin, renders the entire *Embassy* a direct address to the emperors: "To the emperors Marcus Aurelius Antoninus and Lucius Aurelius Commodus, conquerors of Armenia and Sarmatia, and, above all, philosophers (τὸ δὲ μέγιστον φιλοσόφοις)." In his first words, the quick phrase, "above all, philosophers," points to one of the key issues of the text. The emperors take for themselves the name "philosophical," but are they? How does this claim to philosophy, so visibly manifest in Marcus Aurelius's life and Stoic-influenced philosophical writings, for instance, translate into treatment of Christians and other subjects of the empire? Schoedel argues that Athenagoras wrote a panegyric, saluting the emperors with titles reminding the reader of their victories, emphasizing their *paideia* and philosophical understanding, and offering an "articulation of the imperial idea [that] also serves as an appeal to the emperor to become what he is."[65]

In leisurely and sophisticated Greek, the first two chapters of the *Embassy* lay out the issues of the text. The opening words of the *proemium* read: Ἡ ὑμετέρα, μεγάλοι βασιλέων, οἰκουμένη: "your very own *oikoumenē*, great emperors" (1.1). The *oikoumenē* – which is often translated the "inhabited" or "known world"– sustains a diversity of customs, laws, and ancestral traditions, according to Athenagoras. Indeed, the Roman emperors consider it "impious and unholy" (ἀσεβὲς καὶ ἀνόσιον) not to believe in a god (1.2). Athenagoras's statement hints at imperial self-representation. Commodus would be represented on coins and in statuary as pious and religious, literally; by 182 he took on the title *Pius*, in part to associate himself with past emperors who did so, such as Antoninus. By 187 CE, coins emphasize "a connection between the emperor's *pietas* and traditional religiosity"; the legend AUCTOR PIETATIS is matched with a depiction of *Pietas* sacrificing.[66]

Yet Athenagoras begins to erode subtly the imperial claims that he had politely parroted just a few lines earlier, namely, claims to be philosophical and to sustain religion. According to Athenagoras, the emperors support piety because belief in a god leads to fear of the divine and thus to avoidance of

[65] Schoedel, "In Praise of the King," 90; Schoedel uses Menander Rhetor to argue that Athenagoras's writing is a sort of panegyric to the king (69–90; esp. 76, 83, 90).

[66] From the beginning of his reign until 184, *Providentia deorum* is depicted on his coins of many denominations, communicating Commodus's destiny to rule. By late 182 CE he takes on the title *Pius*; by 185 he adds *Felix*, perhaps in connection with the celebration of ten years of rule, or perhaps to signal the gods' special care for him. Hekster, *Commodus*, 92–98.

doing wrong (ἵνα τῷ πρὸς τὸ θεῖον δέει ἀπέχωνται τοῦ ἀδικεῖν, 1.2). In *De superstitione*, Plutarch says that those who do good merely out of fear of the gods are *unphilosophical*: "The name (*onoma*) itself [i.e., *deisidaimonia*] reveals that superstition is an emotional opinion and a notion that produces fear, utterly humiliating and crushing a person. The person thinks that there are gods, but that the gods cause pain and harm" (*De superst.* [*Mor.* 165B]).[67] Such persons, Plutarch goes on to say, "are persuaded by bronze-workers and sculptors and modelers in wax: those who make anthropomorphic images of the gods, and they fashion such images and equip them and worship them. But they look down on philosophical and political men, who demonstrate the high holiness of god, with his goodness and greatness of thought and favor and care" (*De superst.* [Mor. 167E]). The superstitious, not the truly pious, according to Plutarch, engage in frenzied and paranoid rituals to stave off the wrath of the gods; they are spooked by representations. For Athenagoras, the emperors, by supporting religion in order to sustain fear of the gods and thus lawful behavior, misunderstand true piety and act impiously.

Athenagoras extends the issue of proper names to his own people by discussing *onoma* without mentioning the name or word itself: "But to us – and do not be misled, as is the majority, by hearsay – is incurred hatred on account of the name. But names are not worthy of hatred, but injustice is worthy of judgment and punishment" (1.2).[68] In this odd introduction of "us" Christians, Athenagoras seems to postpone for several lines the name – that is, "Christian" – in order to focus on the fact that it is the deed that should be analyzed, and the congruence of the name with the deed.[69]

Athenagoras moves quickly in his next sentence to perform this very move of setting side by side the name and the deed, saying, "For that reason all people, amazed at your meekness and civility and peaceful stance towards all and love of humanity, enjoy *isonomia* ('equality before the law') as individuals; the cities have a share of equal honor according to their worthiness; and the entire *oikoumenē* enjoys a deep peace because of your wisdom" (1.2). The disjunction between imperial claims to civility and benefaction and the reality

[67] My translation from ET Plutarch *Moralia*.

[68] ἡμῖν δέ, καὶ μὴ παρακρουσθῆτε ὡς οἱ πολλοὶ ἐξ ἀκοῆς, τῷ ὀνόματι ἀπεχθάνεται· οὐ γὰρ τὰ ὀνόματα μίσους ἄξια, ἀλλὰ τὸ ἀδίκημα δίκης καὶ τιμωρίας.

[69] Eduard Schwartz brackets this sentence, with a note discussing how it should instead be read after the sentence where Athenagoras first uses the term "Christians" (1.8) (*Athenagorae libellus Pro Christianis, Oratio de Resurrectione Cadaverum* [Leipzig: J. C. Hinrichs, 1891] 2). It is true, as Schwartz notes, that there is a grammatical problem here; there is no real subject to the verb ἀπεχθάνεται: "for us" ἡμῖν likely corresponds to the "we who are called Christians" ἡμεῖς δὲ οἱ λεγόμενοι Χριστιανοί, who awkwardly only appear five lines later. Schoedel and Marcovich also mark it as parenthetical in their texts. Schoedel even writes in a note (*Legatio*, 3 n. 4): "Although Athenagoras is not always well organized, he seems incapable of having written so dislocated a passage." But this phrase is dislocated only if one does not recognize the underlying logic of Athenagoras, who delays the name itself.

of Christian persecution on account of the name is sharpened by the sentence that follows. Athenagoras states that Christians, although the most pious and righteous concerning the divine and "your kingdom" (1.3), are not given this *isonomia* and peace. Indeed, not only their property and civic standing but also their "very bodies and souls" are threatened by those who take them to court "only because of our name" (1.3–4). Athenagoras calls the emperors to attention: "If the charge stops short at our name," the emperors must react: "It is your task as mighty, humane, and learned kings to bring to an end by law the abuse we suffer" (2.1).[70] The later writings collected under the name Menander Rhetor insist that an ambassador's speech should emphasize the ruler's *philanthrōpia* and mercy.[71] Athenagoras does this, but he also challenges the emperors to live out this imperial beneficence.

Athenagoras like Justin persists with a pun that reveals that he is engaging larger grammatical-philosophical issues of what words do: "No name by itself and through itself is considered either evil or good (*chrēston*); on account of the evil or good underlying them [the names], it seems that the deeds are bad or good" (2.2).[72] The term *chrēston*, because of itacism, would have sounded like "Christian." Athenagoras employs this etymological play alongside technical grammatical-philosophical language: *onoma* ("noun" or "name") and *hypokeimenos* ("something that underlies, is foundational, or subordinate to something else").[73]

"How could our name make us wicked?" Athenagoras asks (2.4). Philosophers are judged not for their name but for the guilt presumably proceeding from their deeds; so too should Christians – who are also philosophers – be fairly judged. Athenagoras concludes by directly addressing the emperors:

> I need, as I begin to defend our doctrine, to beg [you], greatest emperors, to listen equitably to us, and not to be prejudiced, carried off by the common and irrational rumor – to beg you to turn your love of learning and love of truth toward our speech.
>
> (ἀναγκαῖον δέ μοι ἀρχομένῳ ἀπολογεῖσθαι ὑπὲρ τοῦ λόγου δεηθῆναι ὑμῶν, μέγιστοι αὐτοκράτορες, ἴσους ἡμῖν ἀκροατὰς γενέσθαι καὶ μὴ τῇ

[70] See also *Leg.* 2.2: "For it is not consonant with your justice that others who have received a charge of wrongdoing should not be punished before they are examined, while among us the name [alone] of those who are being examined prevails against justice. Those who sit in judgment do not search out if the one who has been picked out has done something wrong, but abuse [him] in respect to the name as [if it were] a crime."

[71] See p. 24. See the discussion of Menander's content as a model for Athenagoras in Schoedel, "In Praise of the King" and his "Apologetic Literature and Ambassadorial Activities," 56. See Aristides *Or.* 18 ("A Monody for Smyrna") and *Or.* 19 ("A Letter to the Emperors concerning Smyrna").

[72] οὐδὲν δὲ ὄνομα ἐφ' ἑαυτοῦ καὶ δι' αὐτοῦ οὐ πονηρὸν οὐδὲ χρηστὸν νομίζεται, διὰ δὲ τὰς ὑποκειμένας αὐτοῖς ἢ πονηρὰς ἢ ἀγαθὰς ἢ φλαῦρα ἢ ἀγαθὰ δοκεῖ. For Justin's similar play on the name Christian, see p. 137.

[73] See LSJ, s.v. ὑπόκειμαι esp. II.9.

κοινῇ καὶ ἀλόγῳ φήμῃ συναπενεχθέντας προκατασχεθῆναι, ἐπιτρέψαι δὲ ὑμῶν τὸ φιλομαθὲς καὶ φιλάληθες καὶ τῷ καθ' ἡμᾶς λόγῳ. (*Leg.* 2.6)

Athenagoras's language of necessity (ἀναγκαῖον), of defense, of impartiality and judicial hearing all reinforce a sense of urgency and lead at the end of the *proemium* to the *stasis* ("statement of position"). This articulation of the key issues of the text reveals that Athenagoras will treat accusations leveled against Christians; these accusations involve atheism (ἀθεότητα), Thyestean feasts (cannibalism), and Oedipean unions (incest) (3.1).

Although Athenagoras claims he will address all these charges, he focuses mainly on the accusation of atheism (4.1–30.4), weaving it together with the themes of the *proemium*. These questions about the gods – how their names and deeds align; how their images are connected to their realities, whether Christians are atheists with regard to divinity or not – pervade the majority of the text. The topic of atheism, theology, and godhood is punctuated by his frequent appeals to the emperors. Thus, Athenagoras never lets his reader forget that many of the key themes raised in his *proemium* are not abstract, but involve the emperors, imperial justice and power, and imperial claims to godhood like the one we have just seen in Herakles-Commodus. Where is justice? What is true piety? What is good philosophy? Who is a god? What is the connection between the name or title of an emperor and what he is?[74]

Grammar and Theology

Athenagoras thus wrote and was read in a cultural context where Christians were aware of the power and danger of naming. We have already seen in the previous chapter the evidence that some Christians were accused on account of the "name alone." Christians represent other Christians who are at the edge of death as engaged in a semiotic debate of the utmost importance: Their identities, their bodies, and their lives were at stake.

Justin's concerns about *mimēsis* or representation were focused not only on how the emperors (mis)represented themselves, but also on the production of a divine court that trumped the imperial court, on the one hand, and the explanation of demonic imitations of Christianity that intended to confuse people about what was true religion, on the other. Athenagoras engages the issue of representation from a different angle, focusing on the grammatical-philosophical debates of the ancient world. Like other philosophers of his time, Athenagoras is engaged in seeking the "criterion of truth"; according

[74] As we might expect from the study of Justin in the previous chapter, Athenagoras will later call God "the great judge" and will remind the reader that no one will escape that God's judgment (12.1–2).

to Malherbe, he "[rejects] an unacceptable theory of knowledge in language deriving from Middle Platonism."[75] Philosophers of the day engaged the epistemological question of how humans know what is true, and how humans can evade the potentially deceptive turns of sense perception and language.[76]

"Ancient linguistic thinking was essentially semantically oriented," writes Ineke Sluiter of ancient grammarians. "Ancient students of language virtually always considered language as an instrument for conveying meaning."[77] This intimacy between questions of grammar and philosophy is evident in a range of ancient writers. Plato's *Cratylus* begins with Hermogenes introducing the problem of naming to Socrates and other interlocutors. In it we find the sort of debate that is the conceptual backdrop for Athenagoras and his contemporaries:[78] "Cratylus, whom you see here, Socrates, says that everything has a right name of its own, which comes by nature, and that a name is not whatever people call a thing by agreement, just a piece of their own voice applied to the thing, but that there is a kind of inherent correctness in names, which is the same for all, both Greeks and barbarians" (383A–B).[79] Socrates uses his famous method to wheedle out of Hermogenes how precisely language works. Is the name or *onoma* related somehow by nature to the thing it represents, or are names mere social conventions? Does the name "give access to essences"?[80] The dialogue partners of the *Cratylus* conclude together that if

75 Abraham J. Malherbe, "Athenagoras on the Pagan Poets and Philosophers," in Patrick Granfield and Josef A. Jungmann, eds., *Kyriakon: Festschrift Johannes Quasten* (2 vols.; Münster: Verlag Aschendorff, 1970) 1.219. On the idea of the "criterion of truth," see, e.g., John Rist, *Stoic Philosophy* (Cambridge: Cambridge University Press, 1969) chap. 8; A. A. Long, "Ptolemy on the Criterion: an Epistemology for the Practising Scientist," and the translation and edition of Ptolemy's *Kriterion* in Pamela Huby and Gordon Neal, eds., *The Criterion of Truth* (Liverpool: Liverpool University Press, 1989) 179–230.

76 See Malherbe, "The *Supplicatio*," 15–18, on the pursuit of *epistēmē* in Athenagoras and other philosophical writers.

77 Ineke Sluiter, *Ancient Grammar in Context: Contributions to the Study of Ancient Linguistic Thought* (Amsterdam: Proefschrift Vrije Universiteit, 1990) 2. I am grateful to Catherine M. Chin, whose "Origen and Christian Naming: Textual Exhaustion and the Boundaries of Gentility in *Commentary on John* 1," *JECS* 14 (2006) 407–36 led me to these sources on ancient grammar; see also her *Grammar and Christianity in the Late Roman World* (Philadelphia: University of Pennsylvania Press, 2008).

78 Malherbe, "The *Supplicatio*," 30–31.

79 The translation is Plato, *Euthyphro, Apology, Critio, Phaedo, Phaedrus* (LCL; trans. Harold North Fowler; repr. Cambridge, MA: Harvard University Press, 1995) 7. Timothy Baxter summarizes the importance of the *Cratylus*: "The more general philosophical aim of the dialogue was to demonstrate that Greek thinkers and poets had consistently put too much trust in names, implicitly regarding them as surrogates for the things they named.... To show the extent of this fallacy and to refute it required a thorough examination of names, which Socrates duly carried out.... Seen in this light, the etymologies are not an irrelevant and tedious interlude, but a vigorous attack on a tendency in Greek (and not only Greek) thought to overvalue names" (*The Cratylus: Plato's Critique of Naming* [Leiden: E. J. Brill, 1992] 184). For Latin etymologizing, see Varro *De ling.* 5 and discussion in Ando, *Matter of the Gods*, 53–57.

80 Baxter, *The Cratylus*, 54.

a name is a kind of instrument, then an artisan must have "worked" or crafted the name: The *onomatourgos* or the *nomothetēs* – the "name-worker" or "law-giver" – "is of all the artisans among humans the rarest" (389A).[81] The user of the name, and in particular the dialectician, is then the best superintendent of the work of the lawgiver and judge, whether in Greece or abroad (390C–D).

We find such speculation about names and how language works in other later ancient philosophical conversations, also. As with the *Cratylus*, hypotheses regarding the origin of human language become an important foundation upon which to build hypotheses about current uses of language.[82] The first-century Jewish writer Philo of Alexandria, whose Middle Platonic combination of Stoic and Platonic philosophy was influential for Christians in Alexandria, discusses naming.[83] When God allowed Adam to name creatures, the process went perfectly: "For the native reasoning power in the soul (τῆς λογικῆς φύσεως ὑπαρχούσης ἐν ψυχῇ) being still unalloyed, and no infirmity or disease or evil affection having intruded itself, he received the impressions made by bodies and objects in their sheer reality (τὰς φαντασίας τῶν σωμάτων καὶ πραγμάτων ἀκραιφνεστάτας λαμβάνων), and the titles he gave were fully apposite (εὐθυβόλους ἐποιεῖτο τὰς κλήσεις), for right well did he divine the character of the creatures he was describing, with the result that their natures were apprehended as soon as their names were uttered (ὡς ἅμα λεχθῆναί τε καὶ νοηθῆναι τὰς φύσεις αὐτῶν)" (*De opif. mund.* 150).[84] For the Stoics, according to Ineke Sluiter, "language was originally in perfect rational order, i.e., there was a direct and simple mimetic relationship between the form

81 ET Fowler, 25.

82 Epicurus (*Letter to Herodotus* 75–76) states: "Thus names too did not originally come into being by coining (ὅθεν καὶ τὰ ὀνόματα ἐξ ἀρχῆς μὴ θέσει γενέσθαι), but humans' own natures underwent feelings and received impressions (καὶ ἴδια λαμβανούσας φαντάσματα) which varied peculiarly from tribe to tribe, and each of the individual feelings and impressions caused them to exhale breath peculiarly, according also to the racial differences from place to place. Later, particular coinings were made by consensus within the individual races" (Long and Sedley, *The Hellenistic Philosophers*, 19A [1.97 and 2.98]). Lucretius 5.1028 offers this: "It was nature that compelled the utterance of the various noises of the tongue, and usefulness that forged them into the names of things" (*at varios linguae sonitus natura subegit/mittere et utilitas expressit nomina rerum*) (19B [1.97 and 2.99]). See also Origen *Contra Celsum* 1.24 (= SVF 2.146) quoted in Long and Sedley, *The Hellenistic Philosophers*, 32J (1.192): "The foregoing matter is beset by the profound and mysterious issue of the nature of names. Are names, as Aristotle [*De interpretatione* 1] holds, the product of convention? Or, as the Stoics believe, of nature, the primary sounds being imitations of the things of which the names are said? This is the basis on which they introduce some elements of etymology."

83 Annewies van den Hoek, "The 'Catechetical School of Early Christian Alexandria and Its Philonic Heritage," *HTR* 90.1 (1997) 59–87.

84 ET Philo, *Works* (LCL; trans. F. H. Colson and G. H. Whitaker; 10 vols.; Cambridge, MA: Harvard University Press, 1971) 1.119. But see the rejoinder to this sort of thinking in Lucretius 5.1028–90: "So to think that someone in those days assigned names to things, and that that is how men learnt their first words, is crazy" (Long and Sedley, *The Hellenistic Philosophers*, 19B [1.97]) or Diogenes of Oenoanda 10.3.11–5.15 (19C [1.98]).

of words and their meaning."[85] Since then, words have been "corrupted," "alienated from their origins because of letters having disappeared or changed place."[86] According to Philo, Adam named creatures in a paradise of perfect language.

In this passage from Philo we also see some of the terminology and concepts of the debate over present language and its origin: the question of the soul's reasoning power in relation to perception, the issue of how impressions or mental images (*phantasiai*) are made by bodies and things (*sōmata* and *pragmata*), the relation between the mental understanding and the speech produced (*lechthēnai*). In Stoic and other philosophical discussions in the Greek language, we find various terms other than *onomata* used to talk about the origins and functioning of language.[87] Sextus Empiricus provides a good example of both Stoic definitions and the larger issue at stake:

> There was another disagreement among philosophers [concerning what is true]: some took the sphere of what is true and false to be 'the signification' (περὶ τῷ σημαινομένῳ), others 'utterance', and others 'the process that constitutes thought'. The Stoics defended the first opinion, saying that three things are linked together, 'the signification', 'the signifier', and 'the name-bearer'. The signifier is an utterance, for instance, 'Dion'; the signification is the actual state of affairs revealed by an utterance, and which we apprehend as it subsists in accordance with our thought,

[85] Sluiter, *Ancient Grammar*, 18.

[86] Ibid., 18–19. In this Stoic understanding, naming was a kind of onomatopoetic enterprise that arose naturally among various races and nations. Etymological study allows humans to backtrack to purity, to understand the original form and thus true meaning of a word. Of course, such etymologizing also freed these philosophers from defending the literal stories of the gods, with their questionable morality. Instead, they could allegorize the names of the gods into elements and qualities, as we shall soon see in Athenagoras's critique. See Chin, "Origen and Christian Naming," 412 on Cornutus and Heraclitus and etymology; see p. 413: "Origen, like other grammarians, inclines toward a theory of natural correspondence between words and their meanings, and uses etymology and allegory to uncover that correspondence; he further subscribes to a theory of the ultimate rationality of language, and in a Christian sense, to a theory of the immanence of the *logos*."

[87] Diogenes Laertius explains that "utterance and speech are different (διαφέρει δὲ φωνὴ καὶ λέξεις), because vocal sound is also an utterance but only articulated sound is speech. And speech is different from language. . . . Furthermore, saying is different from voicing (διαφέρει δὲ καὶ τὸ λέγειν τοῦ προφέρεσθαι). For utterances are voiced but it is states of affairs (τὰ πράγματα) which are said – they are, after all, actually sayables (τὰ λεκτά)" Diogenes Laertius 7.57 in Long and Sedley, *The Hellenistic Philosophers*, 33A [1.195 and 2.196]. Regarding Stoic ideas about this proliferation of grammatical terms and the potential imprecision of language, see David Blank and Catherine Atherton, "The Stoic Contribution to Traditional Grammar," in Brad Inwood, ed., *The Cambridge Companion to the Stoics* (Cambridge: Cambridge University Press, 2003) 318. Diogenes Laertius too, regarding the Stoics and their idea that the wise man is a dialectician, says that "in regard to the 'correctness of names' (περὶ τ᾽ ὀνομάτων ὀρθότητος), the topic of how customs have assigned names to things (or, better for our purposes, deeds: ὅπως διέταξαν οἱ νόμοι ἐπὶ τοῖς ἔργοις), the wise man would have nothing to say" (Diogenes Laertius 7.83 [= SVF 2.130], in Long and Sedley, *The Hellenistic Philosophers*, 31C [1.184 and 2.187]).

> whereas it is not understood by those whose language is different[88] although they hear the utterance; the name-bearer is the external object, for instance, Dion himself. Of these, two are bodies – the utterance and the name-bearer; but one is incorporeal – the state of affairs signified and sayable, which is true or false. (*Adv. math.* 8.11–12)[89]

The *lekta* or "sayables" – the incorporeal that stands between the thing itself (Dion, in this case, with his body) and the utterance of the thing (the soft body of the utterance which hits the ear)[90] – must "subsist in accordance with a rational impression" (*phantasia logikē*). It is through dialectic reasoning that the truth of the opinion that arises from the *lekta* must be evaluated.[91]

We have made our way quickly through a thicket of grammatical debate in order to understand better that a complex philosophical conversation about words and meaning forms the context of Athenagoras's thought. In the sections that follow, I return to the *Embassy*, showing how discussion of crises of representation (in words and images) threads through the remainder of the treatise.

Atheism and Piety "in the presence of philosopher-kings"

As we recall, Athenagoras's main goal in the *Embassy* is to defend Christians against the charge of atheism. Chapters 4.1–16.4 represent Athenagoras's first extended argument in response to accusations of atheism, and he begins his argument by distinguishing god and matter (ὕλη). Athenagoras's first exemplum brings us neatly back to Herakles and questions of piety and representation. Athenagoras defends Christians by saying that they are not like Diagoras who, according to various Christian and non-Christian writers, chopped up a wooden image of Herakles to cook his food (4.1). That is, rather than seeing in a wooden *xoanon* ("primitive image") Herakles the god, Diagoras discovered a useful piece of firewood.[92] Does this pragmatic act demonstrate knowledge of what a thing truly is, or atheism? While Athenagoras presumably supports chopping up an idol, he also states that Christians are unlike Diagoras because Diagoras said that there is no god. Christians are not atheists, he insists, but subtle philosophical people who "distinguish God from matter" (4.1).

88 Literally, "the barbarians."

89 ET Long and Sedley, *The Hellenistic Philosophers*, 33B (1.195–96).

90 See also Epicurus *Letter to Herodotus* 46–53 on a similar materialist approach to hearing: "Hearing too results from a sort of wind traveling from the object which speaks, rings, bangs, or produces an auditory sensation in whatever way it may be. This current is dispersed into similarly-constituted particles" (Long and Sedley, *The Hellenistic Philosophers*, 15A [1.73]).

91 On *phantasia logikē* see, e.g., Diogenes Laertius 7.63 in Long and Sedley, *The Hellenistic Philosophers*, 33F (1.196 and 2.199). See also Chin's assessment of tensions in the Stoic theory of language ("Origen and Christian Naming," 414–17).

92 Diagoras is an example elsewhere: Clement puts him in the same category as the likes of Euhemeros (*Prot.* IV 2); Tatian makes a brief reference to him (*Ad Graec.* 27.1).

The story of Diagoras launches a section that grapples with representation (5.1–6.4). As Malherbe says, Athenagoras discusses both poets and philosophers in order to determine their relative success or failure in using a dialectic method for "attain[ing] knowledge of God."[93] The topic is the names of the gods and the connection between these names and their substances/essences (οὐσίαι); to put it in other terms, what are the "underlying things" (ὑποκείμενα πράγματα) to which these names refer? If "poets and philosophers were not thought atheists for what they knew about god," why should Christians be? Athenagoras starts with a fragment from Euripides:[94]

> Do you see the boundary-less ether of the heights
> And its encircling of the earth in its damp folds?
> Consider this to be Zeus; believe *this* is god.

Euripides, Athenagoras then immediately argues, "was at a loss over those who are unscientifically (ἀνεπιστημόνως) named gods, according to a common preconception" (5.1).[95] Athenagoras follows with a bitter critique, saying, "[Euripides could discern] neither the substances thought to underlie the gods – substances of which the word god happened to be predicated ('Regarding Zeus, what Zeus is, I do not know, except by rumor'), nor that their names were predicated on underlying things (for if the substances of things do not underlie them, is there anything more to them than their names?); but [he discerned] him [Zeus] from his [Zeus's] works, seeing the appearances of indistinct intellectual things" (5.1–2). Athenagoras, like other philosophers of the time, seeks to affirm philosophically what he knows of the divine. He accuses Euripides of lacking a secure epistemology; Euripides derives his knowledge of the divine only from the *effects* of the divine in works and appearances. The

93 Malherbe, "Athenagoras on the Poets and Philosophers," 214. Elsewhere, Malherbe puts it differently: "This philosophical investigation is for Athenagoras concerned with the names of the pagan gods, who are criticized on the basis of the relation of the names to the essence and the accidents of the beings to whom they are applied" ("The *Supplicatio*," 10). Such concerns, Malherbe points out, are alive in Plato's discussion of words and names, as well as the first-century CE philosophical text, Albinus's *Didaskalikos*. On philosophical-theological conceptions of names in Valentinus and Antony, and the danger of misnaming and deceit, see David Brakke, *Demons and the Making of the Monk: Spiritual Combat in Early Christianity* (Cambridge, MA: Harvard University Press, 2006) 17–19.

94 Athenagoras is in good philosophical and satirical company in citing these lines: "This fragment (Nauck fr. 941) is also cited by Heraclitus, by Cicero [*De nat. deo.* 2.25.65] and by Lucian [*Iupp. trag.* 41]" (Barnard, *Athenagoras*, 40).

95 Malherbe, "Athenagoras on the Poets and Philosophers," 215; "The *Supplicatio*," 34–40: "His discussion of the names of the gods is thus an elaboration of ἐπὶ μὲν κατὰ κοινὴν πρόληψιν ἀνεπιστημόνως ὀνομαζομένων θεῶν" (p. 39). Baxter, summarizing Socrates' position in the *Cratylus*, gives us a philosophical context for reading Athenagoras: "Socrates always separates name and thing, copy and original, and stresses that the former is derivative of the latter, warning the reader thereby of the dangers that lie in 'fixing' the mimetic values or meanings of names. For by doing that one risks taking the name as more secure a reference point than the named" (*The Cratylus*, 85).

names of gods were found to have nothing underlying them, while the essence or substance of god remained elusive.

Athenagoras's larger point in this section is that God is one, and God is apart from and above matter. To think anything else is impious.[96] He drags out proofs of the oneness of god from a range of philosophers and poets – Sophocles, Philolaus, Lysis, Optimus, Plato, Aristotle, and finally the Stoics.[97] Since he had started by depicting the Roman Empire as tolerant of all gods and supportive of a proliferating religious diversity, this insistence on the oneness of god can be read either as sharp critique of such proliferation, or as philosophical one-upmanship: Athenagoras, a Christian, stands with the philosophical elite to remind the emperors of the oneness of God.[98]

That the Roman Empire and its policies are implicated in Athenagoras's demand for (true) pluralism and in his discussion of monotheism becomes clear when Athenagoras splices asides to the emperors into his discussion of the oneness of God. "I know that even as you outdo all in respect to comprehension and the might of your kingdom, so also you conquer all in (your) accurate understanding of all *paideia*" (6.2). This confluence of the vocabulary of might, conquering, and knowledge is not coincidental. To the educated emperors Athenagoras then offers this argument: Plato is no atheist; neither are we. Athenagoras quotes Plato as an authority and guiding light for the Christian pursuit of the knowledge of God, and in doing so points to the limits of that knowledge and to the limits of speaking about – using names for – the divine: "To discover, then, the maker and father of all is work, and, having discovered him, it is impossible to declare him to all" (6.2, quoting Plato *Tim.* 28c).[99] So also, Athenagoras's later assertions about God as unseen and known only by the mind imply the folly and stupidity of those who found both busy imagistic cityscapes and representations of the imperial family to be divine. He says, "Therefore, [to think] this is not to be atheists: It has been, I think, sufficiently demonstrated that we bring forward a god who is uncreated and eternal and *unseen* and impassible and incomprehensible and infinite, *comprehensible only by mind and word*, surrounded by light and beauty and spirit and indescribable might, by which God has created the entirety which is organized and ruled by his *logos*" (10.1, my emphasis). Although Athenagoras

96 See esp. 5.2–6.4; at 8.1–9.3 the argument turns from doxography to a philosophical investigation of whether there might be "two or more gods from the beginning," which is then bolstered by quotations from the prophets. Again, the knowledge of the emperors is simultaneously assumed and questioned, in this case with regard to the Jewish scriptures (9.1).

97 In doing so he demonstrates his own philosophical prowess, even if he admits to using *doxographia*, or collections of quotations and proofs (6.2).

98 On the ridiculousness of the gods' proliferation, see Cotta's speech in Cicero *De nat. deo.* 3.16ff; see also Ando, *Matter of the Gods*, chap. 3.

99 See the discussion of this passage from Plato in Malherbe, "The *Supplicatio*," 69–70; on Plato's authority in Athenagoras see also his pp. 79–84.

had praised the intelligence and cultural knowledge of the emperors, he will (again) call these into question later by asking that the emperors not be "borne along by low and irrational opinion" (11.1, echoing 2.6). As he writes he becomes blunter about the purpose of the *Embassy*: "that you may know the truth" (11.1), something that "lovers of truth," as he had earlier called the emperors (2.6), presumably should know already.[100]

Athenagoras's fight with those who accuse Christians of being atheists and immoral, as well as with the so-called philosophical emperors, is grounded in the philosophical approaches to language and truth discussed earlier. In an unfortunately lacunose text, Athenagoras explains, "Since this teaching [*logos*; Athenagoras has just quoted early Christian sayings] has come into hearing with a great cry, permit [me] to lift up with freedom of speech (ἐπὶ παρρησίαν) what is being defended, as in the presence of philosopher-kings! For who either of those who solve syllogisms and eliminate ambiguities and clarify etymologies, or of...[101] the homonyms and synonyms and [logical] propositions and what is the subject and what is the predicate... profess to render their followers happy through these and (other) such teachings..." (11.3). Even if the text is partially missing at a significant point in Athenagoras's railing against grammarians and philosophers, the reader can see his point: Such people claim to provide happiness but have no ethical underpinning from which to teach their followers. They embody the rupture between what is said and what exists in reality; "they are the ones who have made the matter to be the *technē* of words and not the display of deeds" (11.3).

Christian communities, Athenagoras admits, are made up of those who are common and artisans and old women. Despite their lack of philosophical education, such Christians do better than the emperors in correctly aligning word and deed: "They do not call to mind words (λόγους), but they show forth good deeds...; they give to those who ask and they love their neighbors as themselves" (11.4). Unlike the masses who constantly distort philosophy, Athenagoras's low-status Christians represent the reverse of the philosophical crisis Athenagoras has been treating in Greco-Roman philosophy and among the emperors themselves.

The Material Gods

Athenagoras had mentioned the *xoanon* of Herakles at the beginning of his argument against the accusation that Christians are atheists, and he later returns to the topic of gods and matter. The majority of those who accuse Christians

[100] See also how Athenagoras bullies the emperors about prophecy (*Leg.* 7.3).

[101] Schwartz (*Athenagorae*, 12) notes a lacuna here; according to Gesner, we should add διδασκόντων, which would supply "of those who teach" (Schoedel, *Legatio*, 24). For a similar complaint about Atticisms and syllogisms, see Tatian *Ad Graec.* 27.3.

of atheism, he states, bring forward two pieces of evidence: Christians do not sacrifice and they do not follow the cities' gods. Athenagoras quickly dismisses the one accusation using arguments common at the time: The truly divine does not desire the blood and gore of sacrifice but instead "bloodless sacrifice" and "rational worship" (τὴν λογικὴν . . . λατρείαν, 13.4; cf. Rom 12:1).[102]

Athenagoras also points out that it is irrational to accuse Christians "of not also following the same gods as do the cities" (13.1), since the very people who launch such accusations disagree with each other over the gods.[103] The diversity of gods of the empire became a matter of mockery for Christians. Athenagoras goes on to say, "If we then are impious because we do not worship in common with these people, then all races are impious: for all do not follow the same gods" (14.3).[104]

The religious and political strategy of the Roman Empire was to tolerate others' gods, to assimilate them to more familiar gods, and even, at times of war, through the rite of *evocatio* to call such gods over to one's own side. Christians were not the only ones to mock this situation of what we might today call relativism, when it was not providing them with tolerance and protection. Lucian, too, writes satirically, "The Scythians offer sacrifice to a scimitar, the Thracians to Zamolxis, a runaway slave who came to them from Samos, the Phyrians to Men, the Ethiopians to Day, the Cyllenians to Phales, the Assyrians to a dove, the Persians to fire, and the Egyptians to water. And while all the Egyptians in common have water for a god, the people of Memphis have the bull, the people of Pelusium a wild onion, others an ibis or a crocodile, others a dog-faced god or a cat or a monkey. Moreover, taking them by villages, some hold the right shoulder a god and others, who dwell opposite them, the left; others, half a skull, and others an earthen cup or dish. Isn't that matter for laughter?" (*Iupp. trag.* 42).[105] Christians, refusing to worship the same gods as some people of the empire, sometimes discuss

[102] Athenagoras makes such statements at a time when non-Christians were also questioning the efficacy and appropriateness of sacrifice. We recall that Hadrian's revival of old-time religions may have met with skepticism from the philosophical elite who were turning to a pagan monotheism that honored the one true God, other gods as manifestations of these, and that turned away from bloody sacrifice (pp. 102–3).

[103] This argument reprises Athenagoras's introductory statement (1.1–2); see Ando, *Matter of the Gods*, chaps. 3–6.

[104] Tatian makes a similar complaint in a more legal framework: "Why, Greeks, do you wish for civic governments to clash in a fight with us? And if I do not wish to avail myself of the customs of some, why should I be hated as if I am the most foul, polluted thing? The emperor orders me to pay taxes; I'm ready to produce" (*Ad Graec.* 4.1). He later expands: "Because of this I also condemn your legislation. For there is a need for all to have one, common government. But now there are as many kinds of cities as there are also codes of laws, so that what is shameful among some is excellent among others" (*Ad Graec.* 28.1).

[105] ET Harmon, Lucian, *Works*, 2.155. See also Tatian *Ad Graec.* 28.1–29.1 for another satirical comment on religious diversity.

the ridiculousness of the diversity of cults at the time, but they also expose the limits of Roman tolerance. Who can bear to tolerate those who insist on religious difference and the incommensurability of various religious beliefs and practices?

While Athenagoras has so far addressed more philosophical-grammatical questions about the gods and their representation in names, he here turns to accuse "the many" (οἱ πόλλοι) of confusing matter and divinity. He offers a deliberately absurd argument: "For if matter and God are the same – two names for one thing – we are impious, if we do not think the gods to be stones and wood, gold and silver" (15.2). With the aside "two names for one thing," Athenagoras pushes the grammatical-philosophical debate to the point of ridiculousness: Can *hylē*, matter, and *theos,* god, both signify the same thing?[106] The ensuing sections turn to the topic of representation in images, in which Athenagoras says, "The masses, since they are not able to discern what matter is from what god is, and how great is the difference between them, approach images made of matter; on their account are we also to go to and to worship statues – we who differentiate and distinguish the unbegotten and the begotten, being and that which is not being, the intellectual and the sensible, also giving the proper name to each of them?" (15.1).[107] Athenagoras thus moves from a crisis of representation in the linguistic realm – names do not correspond to what they represent – to a crisis of representation in the imagistic realm – images by their very material nature cannot represent the divine. Plutarch had already argued a similar point, as we recall; only the superstitious are persuaded to worship images that have been crafted and fashioned. Following a Middle Platonic line, Athenagoras insists that creator and creation are different; even the artisan is superior to the clay or wood or stone with which s/he works: "How can I call these things gods which I know are human craftsmanship?!" (16.5).

With that question, Athenagoras shifts his discussion from the philosophical to the historical. He argues that god and matter are completely different things, the one imperishable and the other perishable, and that an investigation of history also reveals the origins in time of the names and images of the gods. They have no eternal existence. "It is necessary when defending my case to supply more precise arguments also concerning the names (περὶ τῶν ὀνομάτων), that they are recent, and concerning the images (περὶ τῶν

[106] When is one thing equivalent to another, and through what philosophical "dialectic" (διαίρεσις), or division and resolution, can this be discerned? See Malherbe, "The *Supplicatio,*" 40–41.

[107] ἐπεὶ οἱ πολλοὶ διακρῖναι οὐ δυνάμενοι, τί μὲν ὕλη, τί δὲ θεός, πόσον δὲ τὸ διὰ μέσου αὐτῶν, προσίασι τοῖς ἀπὸ τῆς ὕλης εἰδώλοις, δι᾽ ἐκείνους καὶ ἡμεῖς οἱ διακρίνοντες καὶ χωρίζοντες τὸ ἀγένητον καὶ τὸ γενητόν, τὸ ὂν καὶ τὸ οὐκ ὄν, τὸ νοητὸν καὶ τὸ αἰσθητόν, καὶ ἑκάστῳ αὐτῶν τὸ προσῆκον ὄνομα ἀποδιδόντες, προσελευσόμεθα καὶ προσκυνήσομεν τὰ ἀγάλματα;

εἰκόνων), that they have come into being yesterday or the day before, so to speak. But *you* know these things even more notably [than I] since among all and beyond all you are acquainted with the ancients" (17.1). Orpheus, Homer, and Hesiod – people so recent we know their names – "are those who made for the Greeks a genealogy of the gods, also giving names and distributing honors and crafts [to them] and signifying their forms (εἴδεα αὐτῶν σημήναντες)" (17.2).

Athenagoras moves from literary inventions of the gods to material, artisanal ones; he recounts the history of molding, painting, and the making of statuary. "So short, then, is the time since the introduction of images and the occupation with statues that it is possible to name the artisan of each god" (17.4).[108] A list of statues and their sculptors follows, to prove his point. This list has two effects. First, it displays the sort of Greek cultural information that was treasured under Rome: the names and forms of famous ancient sculptures, including the Aphrodite of Knidos, whom we shall investigate in Chapter 7. Although Athenagoras's list is brief, it reminds the reader of the more extensive catalogue in Pliny the Elder, who is interested in the mechanics of the production, collecting, and circulation of ancient statuary and images.[109] Second, Athenagoras's list demonstrates his superiority to the seduction of the symbolic capital of the time. He is not drawn in by connoisseurship or by worship, and for him these statues of the gods are not timeless and eternal aesthetic objects. Athenagoras implicitly concedes that statues are theological statements,[110] yet he rejects what they say.

Where others see beautiful objects worthy of reproduction, collection, and worship, Athenagoras sees philosophical bankruptcy and intellectual absurdity, the impiety of rendering the divine in time and space and matter. "If then they are gods, why were they not so from the beginning? Why are they more recent than those who have made them? Why did they need humans and craft in order to come into being? They are earth and stones and matter and overwrought craft (περίεργος τέχνη)" (17.5). In making this statement Athenagoras engages in right naming. Images made from matter are not signs of actual gods. They are what they are: earth and stones, bent and formed through no agency of their own, but by particular humans in particular times.

[108] ὁ μὲν δὴ χρόνος ὀλίγος τοσοῦτος ταῖς εἰκόσι καὶ τῇ περὶ τὰ εἴδωλα πραγματείᾳ, ὡς ἔχειν εἰπεῖν τὸν ἑκάστου τεχνίτην θεοῦ.

[109] Athenagoras *Leg.* 17.3 on the origins of line-drawing, painting, and relief modeling has parallels in the long treatment of the origins of images in Pliny *Nat. hist.* 35.43.151 (portraits), 35.5.15 (painting), 35.44.153 (plaster); Athenagoras mentions the "Corinthian girl" as had Pliny before him (see discussion of the origins of images in Chapter 6). See also Giuseppe Botti, "Atenagora quale fonte per la storia dell'arte," *Didaskaleion* 4 (1915) 395–417.

[110] On connoisseurship see esp. Chapter 6. See Geffcken, *Apologeten*, 193–96 regarding Athenagoras seeking to impress his readers; regarding symbolic capital, see Gordon, "The Real and the Imaginary," esp. 16–23; in his terms, "making is the process of literally reifying knowledge; it is an act of translation" (p. 21).

Yet Athenagoras concedes that some philosophically minded people might say that he is not fair. Athenagoras has been arguing as if everyone thinks that statues of the gods are somehow διοπετές – fallen from heaven, Zeus-given, imbued with divine power[111] – rather than a representation deliberately produced for the aid of memory and worship. But there are other perspectives:

> Now some say that these are only images, but that the images exist in reference to gods, and that the processions by which they approach them [i.e., the gods] and the sacrifices offered up to them and that exist for them are because there is no other way than this to approach the gods ("the gods are dangerous when they appear visibly" [Homer *Il.* 20.131]). And as evidence that this is so, they furnish proof of the activity of some images (εἰδώλων). Bearing this in mind, let us examine the power in the names.
>
> I beg you, greatest absolute rulers, before the speech begins, to excuse the one who presents[112] true arguments. For it does not fall to me to condemn images (εἴδωλα). (18.1–2)[113]

Athenagoras's last statement, assuring the emperors that he has no axe to grind, is delicately put. Yet given his preceding, hard-hitting philosophical arguments about the gods and images, and especially given the argument that follows, it becomes clear that in the busy cityscapes of the empire, Athenagoras would have criticized nearly every image he encountered as a representational misfire, including and perhaps especially those images sponsored by the Roman imperial family.

In the passage just cited, Athenagoras quickly slips from the "activity of some images" to "power in the names." Both images and names misrepresent, for Athenagoras. In Greek *theologia* – theology, or, in Athenagoras's use of the term, mythology[114] – ridiculous accounts of the gods' generation expose that they have come into being and thus that they are perishable and not divine (18–19). "There is no disagreement between myself and the philosophers," he brags; he aligns himself with Platonic thought that declares this sort of notion of the gods to be stupid (19.2). The very idea of the "bodies of the gods" exposes the absurdity of the popular theology that emerges from the

[111] See also Acts 19:35.

[112] παρέχω in the middle voice can be used of an ambassador representing someone or something in his or her own person (LSJ s.v. παρέχω, BII), further attesting to the ambassadorial *topos* that drives Athenagoras's *Embassy*.

[113] The gods seen in and of themselves are *chalepoi*: "hard to bear" or dangerous. Athenagoras quotes this from Homer, but the terminology was also used in later epistemological debates. Φαίνεσθαι ἐναργεῖς, "to appear visibly," hints at philosophical use of the term *enargeia* to signal clear, distinct, or true perception of a thing or what is "self-evident." See, e.g., Epicurus *Letter to Herodotus* 82 and Diogenes Laertius 10.33 in Long and Sedley, *The Hellenistic Philosophers*, 17D–E (1.17–18).

[114] On Athenagoras's use of the term *theologia*, see esp. this passage (18–20) and Malherbe, "Athenagoras on the Pagan Poets and Philosophers," 216.

poets' error (22.1). He hints at his earlier pun about excellent Christians, asking what is remarkable or good (χρηστόν) about the gods' behavior. They have monstrous, horrifying forms and sometimes their bodies are battered – castrated, devoured. The "forms of their bodies" (αἱ διαθέσεις τῶν σωμάτων) hardly help one to believe that these are gods (20.4).

In a culture rife with manifestations of gods' bodies (and, as we have seen and shall see, of bodies of men and women, imperial and non-imperial, who look to be gods), Athenagoras mocks divine bodies. He chooses not to highlight the familiar and aesthetically pleasant sculptures and images of the time, such as the geometrically sculpted torso of Herakles or the well-fed stomach and rounded breasts of Aphrodite. Rather, he points to gods who are beastly-formed (θηριόμορφοι, 20.5) and monstrous. His references to the hideous form of gods also allows him to talk about the multiplicity of images that are supposed to refer to one god; in doing so he can hint again at an ongoing crisis of representation.[115] Tatian, as we shall soon see, is also disgusted at what he claimed were the monstrosities and licentiousness of the sculptures of the Greeks he found in Rome.[116] But the gods' bodies that Athenagoras describes are also pathetically vulnerable, in fleshly form (σαρκοειδεῖς) and subject to the passions and also to the wounds of body and soul (21.1–3).[117] These very ideas, Athenagoras insists, are "impious nonsense" (21.4).

Even if someone were to try philosophically to weasel his or her way out of Athenagoras's argument (don't many philosophers agree, after all, about the danger of the poets and their influence upon the common and ignorant?), Athenagoras would attack the next defense s/he might offer of the gods and their representations. To defend the gods against Athenagoras's arguments, someone might turn to the Stoic idea that the names of the gods represent abstract concepts and that the stories and names of the gods are best understood allegorically. Athenagoras recounts the arguments: Zeus sounds like *zeousa*, that which seethes; Hera like *aēr* or air, Poseidon like *posis*, a drink (22.4).[118] To allegorize the gods into elements helps to erase their embarrassing misdeeds,

[115] For a similar critique, see Theophilus *Ad Autolycum* 1.10; Clement *Prot.* II 28.1–3, and overview of Greek philosophical approaches to the topic in Robert Grant, *Gods and the One God*, 75–83.

[116] See pp. 243–48.

[117] Athenagoras is aware of the danger that his argument be turned back on Christianity, given its incarnated, crucified God. He hints at the problem with this sentence: "and if God takes on flesh according to a divine dispensation, is he necessarily a slave of lust?" Unfortunately, this sentence is immediately preceded by a lacuna (Schwartz, *Athenagorae*, 25).

[118] Similar arguments arise in the *Cratylus*, although Socrates frames them in terms of humans giving names to the gods (400D–404A). What transpires are extreme wordplays: for example, "Poseidon" may derive from *desmos podōn* (a bond of his feet) or from *eidotos polla* (knowing many things), or he may have been connected with earthquakes (*ho seiōn*) (402E–403A). The possibilities are endless.

the accounts of their pain and even their slavery, as these are recounted in poems and myths (22.1). Against this etymological sleight-of-hand, or "natural" argument (22.8), Athenagoras insists that even these allegorized "gods" are trapped in the realm of the changeable and material and not at all divine. Against the Stoic concept that the gods are material, Athenagoras takes the Platonist line of argument, insisting of those who try to justify the myths: "But they fail to obtain to the greatness of God and they are not able to glimpse it by reason (for they do not have an affinity with the heavenly realm). They have fused themselves with the forms of matter; having fallen, they have made into gods (θεοποιοῦσιν) the changeable nature of the elements" (22.12). The attempt to deal with the names of the gods by allegorizing them using ancient grammatical-philosophical arguments about etymology merely binds the gods again into the material world and exposes the bankruptcy of this philosophical vision.

Athenagoras must cope with yet another objection to his argument, which he places in the mouths of his audience and thus in the mouth of the emperors. "Therefore you, who exceed all in intelligence, may say: 'What, then, is the reason that some of the images (εἰδώλων) are active, if they are not gods, to whom we set up statues (ἀγάλματα)? For it is not likely that images that are soulless and incapable of motion would be powerful in themselves without something moving [them].' Indeed, we ourselves do not deny that in some places, cities, and nations certain actions occur in the name of images. But if some have been benefited, and again others have been harmed, we do not at all consider the gods to be those who effected these things in either case" (23.1–2). Vacillating between terminology of images as statues and images as idols, Athenagoras admits the power of some statues to benefit and to harm their supplicants, a reality that seems to contradict his argument that these representations are matter bound and philosophically idiotic. If some statues are powerful and efficacious, could it be that these signifiers of the gods successfully represent the gods?

Athenagoras summarizes his own past arguments: "We have examined with precision (ἐπ' ἀκριβὲς ἐξητάκαμεν) the reason you consider the images (τὰ εἴδωλα) to have might, and who might be activating [them], usurping (ἐπιβατεύοντες) their names" (23.2; see also 26.2). By now we have seen the verb *epibateuein* applied to both names and images: Signifiers are being usurped, and Athenagoras wishes to get to the source of the problem, lest some think that these images – these material objects which nonetheless are somehow active, energetic – are truly gods or conduits of the gods.

To solve this puzzling problem of efficacious statues, Athenagoras turns first to philosophers and their cosmologies as his witnesses. Thales discusses gods, demons, and heroes; Plato too has an idea of an uncreated God and other beings, called *daimones*, which God created. Christians, Athenagoras explains, also believe that many powers exist: There is God, and the Son (the Logos), the Spirit, and "other powers which have a connection with matter and through it" (24.2). Christians agree that *daimones* exist. Athenagoras mentions dangerous angels who sound like the Watchers of *1 Enoch*, those who "fell from heaven" and haunt air and earth but cannot attain the higher heaven. The *daimones* are the "souls of the giants" who have descended from "the ruler of matter and its forms" (25.1–5).[119] Athenagoras writes, "These *daimones* that we have been discussing are also those who drag people to the images; they stick close to the blood of the sacrificial animals and lick them up. The gods who please the crowd (τοῖς πόλλοις) and who give their names (ἐπονομαζόμενοι) to these images, as is known from their story, were once humans. The activity of each of these is proof that the *daimones* are usurping the names" (26.1).

Athenagoras sounds like Plutarch, who is aware that deceptive *daimones* can haunt the Delphic shrine (*De defect. orac.* 10, 14–16 = *Mor.* 414F, 417C–418E), or Lucian, who satirizes human practices that cast the gods as hungry, disgusting, and human-dependent. In the face of Epicurean philosophy and questions about the gods' powerlessness over fate, Lucian's Zeus worries: "We cannot make light of the danger if men are going to take his [Epicurus'] word for this: our temples will have no wreaths, our wayside shrines no savoury steam, our wine-bowls no drink-offerings, our altars will be cold, and in short there will be a general dearth of sacrifices and oblations, and famine will be rife" (*Bis acc.* 2).[120] Elsewhere, Zeus is accused: "You are carried off by pirates even as we are, and plundered by temple-robbers, and from very rich become very poor in a second; and many have even been melted down before now, being of gold or silver; but" – and here the speaker, Kyniskos, cuts to the quick, implying that Zeus is subordinate to fate – "of course they were fated for this" (*Iupp. conf.* 8).[121] Zeus had earlier called Kyniskos one of the "abominable sophists" (6); there were many of the so-called Second Sophistic who needled the gods.[122] The future of religion is at stake, and the crisis is in part the fault of philosophers and sophists like Athenagoras, who question the gods' *pronoia* or providence, and then the gods' very existence (*Iupp. trag.* 16–17).

For Athenagoras, statues that seem to be efficacious and to indicate truly divine power do not point to the reality of the god represented, but to a

[119] Annette Yoshiko Reed, *Fallen Angels and the History of Judaism and Christianity: The Reception of Enochic Literature* (New York: Cambridge University Press, 2005) 152.

[120] ET Harmon, 3.89; see also Lucian *De sacr.* 9–13.

[121] ET Harmon, 2.71, 73. On Zeus's unwillingness to prevent the robbery-shearing of his own golden locks at Olympia, see *Timon* 3.

[122] *Iupp. trag.* 19; see also 25. Elsewhere, Lucian has a speaker impudently hint that Zeus might be dead, referring to the Cretan tradition of a tomb on their island – a tradition enjoyed by Christians as well. See Athenagoras *Leg.* 30.3.

deep crisis of representation. Athenagoras's argument regarding *daimones*, as we have seen in the last chapter, is not uniquely Christian. Maximus of Tyre, Plutarch, and others discussed the role of *daimones* in the world; Maximus concluded that the so-called gods were really *daimones* who served under God, while Plutarch offered a variety of opinions on the role of *daimones* in oracles. Athenagoras does detective work to demonstrate that the statues' powers do not prove the truth of the named gods, but the dangerous reality of *daimones*. He turns to statues (*andriantes*) of Neryllinus ("a man of our own time"; *Leg.* 26.3) in Troy and Alexander and Proteus in Parium. The statues of Neryllinus beautify the city as "public monuments," presumably standing among other statues of benefactors and civic elites scattered through the city. "One of them, however," Athenagoras continues, "is thought both to give oracles and to heal the sick, and because of these things the Trojans sacrifice to the statue and gild and crown it" (26.3). So too, public sacrifice and festivals are conducted for the statues of Alexander and Proteus (26.4).

What is the source of the activity and power of these statues? Is it the "substance of the material" (τῆς ὕλης ἡ συστάσις, 26.5)? No, Athenagoras argues, referring to a typical story that reminds the reader of the true nature of images: The king Amasis has a bronze foot basin made into his own image. Whether it functions for humble use or is cast as a king, bronze is bronze. Moreover, Neryllinus, whose image heals, was not even able to heal himself when he was alive and ill (26.5). Thus the power of these statues lies in the weakness of some human souls, which are easily deluded because they have no sound criterion of truth and believe what they *think* they perceive.

Athenagoras makes his argument about the deceit of these "active" statues using the grammatical-philosophical vocabulary of his day: "Therefore, these movements of the soul, which are irrational and based in what *seems* to be, bring to birth an image-crazed state in the mental imagination" (αἱ οὖν ἄλογοι αὗται καὶ ἰνδαλματώδεις τῆς ψυχῆς κινήσεις εἰδωλομανεῖς ἀποτίκτουσι φαντασίας, 27.2). My infelicitous translation highlights what other translators have not: Athenagoras talks here not of "fantasy," a frequent translation, but of *phantasia*, a philosophical term better rendered "mental imagination." Athenagoras highlights the cognitive process whereby something presents itself to the mind or consciousness, and the mind or consciousness then evaluates the truth of this perception – or should.[123] Athenagoras places the blame for misunderstanding statues squarely on the soul, which does not "contemplate the truth" (ἀθεώρητος δὲ τοῦ ἀληθοῦς) but readily "receives upon itself the impressions of false opinions" (ἐναποσφραγίσηται ψευδεῖς περὶ αὐτῆς δόξας,

[123] As we shall see on pp. 227–28, Cicero (*Or.* 9–11) and Philostratus (*Vit. Ap.* 6.19) discuss sculptors who through *phantasia*, and not through any copying of a model or person before them, produce truly sublime (god-inspired) art.

27.2). The soul is like soft wax stamped from without by things it thinks are real, but are illusory.[124]

The *daimones*, associated with matter and thus hungry for blood and fat, "are human-deceivers. Taking hold of these movements, produced by false opinions, in the soul of the majority, they usurp (ἐπιβατεύοντες) their mental imagination (φαντασίας); they supply a flood into their thoughts, as if it were the images and statues which did so" (27.2). Earlier, Athenagoras had applied the term for occupying or usurping (*epibateuein*) when he insisted that he would investigate those who usurped the "names" of gods (23.2, 26.2). Here, we have Athenagoras's answer and judgment: It is the evil *daimones* who doubly usurp, illegitimately taking on both names and images. They take on the names of gods *and* they occupy some statues, making these statues active and powerful.

Athenagoras offers a final argument: "It is perhaps necessary, after what has been said above, to speak a little concerning the names" (28.1). The Egyptians are the ones from whom the names of Greek gods have originated, and they themselves say that the gods were named after the first kings of the land, in part out of "ignorance of true piety" and in part out of gratefulness to the kingly families (28.3). Athenagoras argues that the temples of the gods were formerly the tombs of elites (28.7). Egyptian priests admit, Athenagoras says, that it was out of piety and honor that the first Egyptian kings and queens came to be considered gods (28.3). Others perhaps were originally, carelessly called gods because of their strength (like Herakles) or their skill (like the healing god Asklepios) (30.1).

Through confusion and the mists of history, humans became gods, Athenagoras argues, picking up the old argument made famous by Euhemeros and frequently employed in the second-century debate about religion and piety. And – Athenagoras here digs at very contemporary Roman culture – some are called gods for other reasons, such as fear. "Thus even Antinoos by the philanthropy of your ancestors towards their subjects, happened to be thought a god" (30.2). In such an open text to the emperors, the term *philanthrōpia* is a sharp critique. On the one hand, in highlighting how the imperial family presented itself as kindly toward all, full of benefactions, and like the gods in its love of humanity, Athenagoras employs the rhetorical techniques of speaking to an emperor, such as we find distilled in Menander Rhetor.[125] On the other hand, the etymology of *philanthrōpia* reminds the reader that Antinoos becomes divine through the emperor Hadrian's benefaction, through Hadrian's own very human love, rendered to a human.

[124] See Malherbe, "The *Supplicatio*," 34 on *epistēmē* versus *doxa*; see Gordon, "The Real and the Imaginary," 27: "As paradoxes, divine representations are jokes, threats to the process of miscognition."

[125] Malherbe, "The *Supplicatio*," 119, on the term *philanthrōpoi*; Menander Rhetor 423 (*Presbeutikos*; the "Ambassador's Speech").

CONCLUSIONS

Athenagoras ends his proof finally, audience exhausted, with the argument that "we are not atheists" (30.6).[126] Athenagoras concludes with another direct appeal to the emperors, requesting their assent for his arguments, affirming that they should be what they say they are, and even perhaps rendering them quasi-Christians as he puns on the word *chrēstoi*. "But you – you who are altogether in every way, by nature and *paideia*, excellent (χρηστοί) and moderate and humane and worthy of the empire – nod your royal head to my resolution, since I have showed that [we are] pious and mild and chastened in soul" (37.1). Christians pray for the emperors' reign and succession and wish to lead a "quiet and peaceable life" (cf. 1 Tim 2:2).

While Schoedel found Athenagoras disorganized and Malherbe thought that Athenagoras's "apologetic" stance produced a lack of systematic thought in his writing,[127] I have argued that once one understands Athenagoras's key concern – crises over representation and the relation between essence and name or image – the arrangement of the treatise falls into place, and the premise of writing this theological-philosophical piece as an embassy or a defense becomes clear. Osiris, Herakles, Asklepios, and others: The idea that any of them is divine is a joke (28.10–29.4). Statements like these, in the face of a long tradition of emperors associating themselves with Herakles, and as Commodus's representations as Herakles crescendo, function to critique the Roman imperial family's impious religious displays and concepts.

Athenagoras writes in a world where a man at death can look like Herakles, a woman at death is a naked Aphrodite, an unjust emperor can wield Herakles' club, and an emperor's lover can look like Silvanus or Bacchus or Apollo, as Antinoos did. In questioning the origins of the names of gods, and in connecting their temples with tombs, Athenagoras argues that all who die cannot really be gods, even if they are called divine. Antinoos has died; Zeus has a tomb on Crete; the ashes of Trajan, tucked into the base of his column, lie close to the temple where he is honored as god. In the midst of this busy world of images, Athenagoras uses the Euhemeristic argument that the gods were once human, aligning himself with a major strand of philosophical thought at the time. He also reverses the terms of the visual argument that forces itself upon anyone in the public spaces of empire: that the humans, including the emperors, are becoming gods. For Athenagoras, these so-called gods are false. They are nothing but humans who have become blood-thirsty, deceptive *daimones*.

[126] Athenagoras makes short work of the accusations of "godless banquets and sexual unions." He appeals again directly to the emperors "whose wisdom is greater than that of all others" (31.3) and who thus are aware of the ethics of those who are regulated by God: Christians too are blameless in their actions; their bodies are pure.

[127] Malherbe, "The *Supplicatio*," 136.

Athenagoras is not the only one to mock the misrepresentation of the divine in images and names, nor is he the funniest. Lucian too argues that statues of the gods and indeed the gods themselves are utterly powerless. And Athenagoras would not be the first or last Christian to engage in a debate about names and the larger theme of representation. We have already seen Justin's grappling with the topic, and we turn next to Tatian's.

CHAPTER SIX

WHAT DO WE LEARN WHEN WE LOOK? (PART I) IMAGES, DESIRE, AND TATIAN'S *TO THE GREEKS*

THE *PAIDAGŌGOS* IS A SLAVE, OFTEN DESCRIBED AS GREEK, WHO LED THE children of the elites to school and back home. In this chapter and the next, I shall discuss images as pedagogical not only because I treat ancient discussions of what Roman-period images of the bodies of humans and gods teach, but also because I discuss Greek objects that were purchased, stolen, replicated, interpreted, and displayed by Roman elites. These anthropomorphic images – images of humans, often as gods, or gods as humans – are like the enfleshed and owned *paidagōgos*: Both statue and slave are simultaneously objects and persons, or like persons.

Statues take the viewer by the hand and try to lead her or him somewhere. "In a landscape of having to repeat," images, particularly Greek or Hellenizing statuary bodies, are thus like the Greek *paidagōgos*'s body: far from home, enslaved, leading the eyes in various ways to learn about Greek *paideia* through the lens of Roman domination. At the same time, Greek images stolen and copied by Rome demonstrate that the colonized may have some kind of superiority and power to lead or even to enslave the viewer with iconographic power. Just as the Greek language was the *koinē* or common language of elites in the eastern portion of the Roman Empire, so also Greek images, from classical to Hellenistic, were the semantic foundation of much of Roman iconography.[1]

[1] Tonio Hölscher, *The Language of Images in Roman Art* (trans. A. Snodgrass and A. Künzl-Snodgrass; Cambridge: Cambridge University Press, 2004) esp. 86–118; Hölscher shows how Greek styles from different time periods are deployed in the same Roman work in order to

Postcolonial critics have explored how colonized lands and peoples are often simultaneously objects of desire and disgust for the colonizers. Fears of miscegenation mixed with the realities of transgressive desire and violence against subject peoples, who were sometimes enslaved as a result of empire and whose bodies were thus objects or tools available for sexual use.[2] What makes the second century particularly complicated is that, unlike nineteenth-century Europeans and North Americans discoursing about "primitive" races, Romans often demonstrated, by their purchasing power and by the way they educated themselves and their children, that Greek culture – which they had conquered – was superior to and more desirable than their own.[3] As Horace famously wrote even in the first century BCE, "Captive Greece conquered her savage captor."[4] Internal critique of Roman decadence often implicated Greece as a corruptor of solid Latin, or even barbarian, values. Thus we shall not be surprised in this chapter and the next to find a complicated mix of desire and disgust, nor to discover that contemporaneous Christian literature similarly uses a rhetoric of desire and disgust to talk about Greek images taken or copied by Romans.

In the previous two chapters, we saw that Justin and Athenagoras were less engaged with particular objects of art than they were concerned to demonstrate

offer different meanings regarding piety, military might, or other themes. Scholars debate how successful the Romans were at bringing a Hellenistic aesthetic to various provinces. Jane Webster analyzes Roman influences on the iconography of Britain in the first few centuries using a framework of "creolizing" to analyze the possibilities of complex mixing of iconography, rather than offering a top-down model of Greco-Roman norms clamping down on Celtic cult representations ("Creolizing the Roman Provinces," *AJA* 105.2 [2001] 209–25). See the reaction to Webster's earlier work in Miranda Green, "God in Man's Image: Thoughts on the Genesis and Affiliations of Some Romano–British Cult Imagery," *Britannia* 29 (1998) 17–30. For a broader discussion of these problems of method and the term "Romanization," see Greg Woolf, *Becoming Roman: The Origins of Provincial Civilization in Gaul* (Cambridge: Cambridge University Press, 1998) esp. 6–7, 15–16.

2 In making this statement, I am not trying to erase the differences between the Roman Empire and European colonization or slavery in the Americas. There are, however, similarities in structures of domination and in the use of enslaved/subject bodies. Robert J. C. Young, *Colonial Desire: Hybridity in Theory, Culture, and Race* (New York: Routledge, 1995) esp. chap. 1 on obsessions about hybridity and miscegenation; Anne McClintock, *Imperial Leather: Race, Gender, and Sexuality in the Colonial Context* (New York: Routledge, 1995), esp. 47–48 on the control of women's bodies and the importance of sexual purity for "breeding a virile race of empire-builders" and chap. 2 "'Massa' and Maids: Power and Desire in the Imperial Metropolis"; Franz Fanon, *Black Skin White Masks* (trans. Charles Lam Markmann; New York: Grove Press, 1967) 41–82 explores the issue from the perspective of black desire for whiteness.

3 See Peter Stewart, *Statues in Roman Society: Representation and Response, Oxford Studies in Ancient Culture and Representation* (New York: Oxford University Press, 2003) 224–31 on Roman connoisseurship and anxieties about effeminacy of Greek culture; Jaś Elsner, *Roman Eyes: Visuality and Subjectivity in Art and Text* (Princeton, NJ: Princeton University Press, 2007) 49–66.

4 *Graecia capta ferum victorem cepit.* Horace *Ep.* 2.1.156. See also Juvenal *Sat.* 3.60–61: "I cannot stand a Greekified Rome" (ET Juvenal, *Satires* [trans. Susanna Morton Braund; LCL; Cambridge, MA: Harvard University Press, 2004] 171).

the dirty materiality of manufacturing the "gods." They were especially concerned to show how images, words, and the act of naming could result in representational crises for Christians and others in the Roman Empire. Still, they too sought to persuade their inscribed audiences to transform their collective eye and to engage some different way of interpreting the world in which they lived and moved and had their being.[5]

The early Christian texts to which we turn in this chapter and the next, Tatian's *To the Greeks* and Clement's *Exhortation*, do not claim to address the imperial family, but "the Greeks" or the "Panhellenes." They try to persuade and train their audiences toward a certain set of responses to images in the cityscapes of the Roman Empire. Clement and others thus seek through rhetoric to reform and re-form vision. In addition, they present connoisseurship as a moral problem born of a mix of wrong attitudes towards ethnicity and culture, desire and philosophy, and the divine itself. We shall explore how early Christians and their contemporaries articulated the rhetorical function of the (non-Christian) image and how they encouraged a certain way of seeing, or scopic regime. For them and for others, the idea of the image as pedagogical – the question of how and to what ends an image leads the viewer – begs a prior epistemological question. How does or should one view, very literally: through the eye or through the mind? In a culture where often sense perception was considered inferior to noetic or mental perception, but sight was often considered superior among the senses, what were the mechanics of viewing and how should the eye be trained? David Freedberg has written: "People are sexually aroused by pictures and sculptures; they break pictures and sculptures; they mutilate them, kiss them, cry before them, and go on journeys to them; they are calmed by them, stirred by them, and incited to revolt. They give thanks by means of them, expect to be elevated by them, and are moved to the highest levels of empathy and fear. They have always responded in these ways; they still do."[6] This is precisely what worries Tatian and Clement.

Tatian and Clement argue that the eye itself should become Christianized, interrupting certain messages of power and sex and ethics that (Christians say) Greco-Roman images mean to "say." Although Christian "apologists" are often defined as different from or resisting their cultural context, and as prurient and horrified at images and their erotic power, Clement and Tatian are very like some of their contemporaries. Regardless of cultic or ethnic affiliation, many were concerned about the act of making and viewing images, especially images of the divine, and how these images might aid in or distract

[5] Jaś Elsner asks: "How does the act of looking at art condition and create the identity of individuals?" (*Art and the Roman Viewer: The Transformation of Arts from the Pagan World to Christianity* [Cambridge: Cambridge University Press, 1995] 19).

[6] David Freedberg, *The Power of Images: Studies in the History and Theory of Response* (Chicago: University of Chicago Press, 1989) 1.

from true piety. A great variety in thought distinguishes these writers, and even Tatian and Clement differ from each other. Tatian reclaims the term barbarian as a badge of pride for Christians as he mocks Greek images collected by the Romans. Clement articulates a Christian *paideia* that looks very much like the best of Greek *paideia*. Yet they both fully engage Greek *paideia* and throw themselves into the midst of the culture wars over true *paideia* and true piety, offering their analysis of the dangers and misuses of the images that surround them – educated, traveling men – in the cityscapes of the Roman Empire, in Alexandria, Athens, and beyond to Syria.

Not only do Tatian and Clement critique images in a way similar to their non-Christian counterparts; they also similarly trade on issues of status and gender hierarchy in their time in order to make their arguments. It is not surprising in the cultural context of the ancient Mediterranean that they argue that ethical perversion and deformation often occurs when viewing statues of women, nor is it surprising that Christian women's virtue becomes the foil to such "pagan" perversion. As part of their polemic, Tatian and Clement emphasize the feminine quality of statuary bodies, especially those of goddesses: They are material, passive, vulnerable to the gaze and to physical abuse. Writers like Clement and Tatian resist being enslaved to the Greek or Hellenizing images in which the Romans traded. But they do so by trading upon the dominant kyriarchal logic available at the time. They treat the statues almost like slaves, objects for purchase, viewing, and derision.[7]

Scholarship traditionally has focused on the elite male as the financer and intended viewer of images in the Roman period; he is the connoisseur. Scholars recently have challenged the idea that we should be interested only or primarily in this viewer,[8] and have also encouraged us to think about how

[7] Kyriarchy is Elisabeth Schüssler Fiorenza's term to signal the overall system of mastery or lordship (*kyrios*) that functions at every level of Roman society; see, e.g., Elisabeth Schüssler Fiorenza, *But She Said: Feminist Practices of Biblical Interpretation* (Boston: Beacon Press, 1992) 37.

[8] Elsner, *Art and the Roman Viewer*; Natalie Boymel Kampen, "Epilogue: Gender and Desire," in Ann Olga Koloski-Ostrow and Claire L. Lyons, eds., *Naked Truths: Women, Sexuality, and Gender in Classical Art and Archaeology* (New York: Routledge, 1997) 273; Simon Goldhill, "The Erotic Eye: Visual Stimulation and Cultural Conflict," in Simon Goldhill, ed., *Being Greek under Rome: Cultural Identity, the Second Sophistic and the Development of Empire* (Cambridge: Cambridge University Press, 2001) 154–94; John R. Clarke, *Art in the Lives of Ordinary Romans: Visual Representation and Non-Elite Viewers in Italy, 100 B.C.–A.D. 315* (Berkeley: University of California Press, 2003). On seeing differently, see, e.g., feminist art historian Linda Nochlin, *Bathers, Bodies, Beauty: The Visceral Eye* (Cambridge, MA: Harvard University Press, 2006) 15: "For there is history, of course: the corporeal eye, the visceral eye – all eyes are located not merely in bodies but in historically specific bodies and can thus be viewed within a history of representation and a history of practices, a social history, in short, that can thicken up our responses." The question of the diversity of viewers raises as many hermeneutical troubles as any written text.

other viewers might resist the persuasive powers of an image.[9] Thus this chapter and the next are driven by the implicit question of how multiple viewers might have (multiply) interpreted an image, and the question of how bodies are differentially treated in the Roman world – that is, how the enslaved body, the female body, and the barbarian body were passive objects of desire and use, whether enfleshed or in stone and bronze.[10]

Arjun Appadurai, in his edited volume *The Social Lives of Things: Commodities in Cultural Perspective*, has proposed that "we regard luxury goods" – and from Cicero to Constantine and beyond we can regard sculptures and images collected by those in power in the Roman Empire as luxury items – "as goods whose principal use is *rhetorical* and *social*, goods that are simply *incarnated signs*. The necessity to which *they* respond is fundamentally political."[11] We should think of *things* as having biographies or careers, says Appadurai. We also hear in his insight echoes of Pierre Bourdieu's idea of cultural capital.[12] Connoisseurship is a political and social act; when it works well, both objects and their possessors are elevated as embodying culture and knowledge. In this chapter, and even more in the next, we shall trace the biographies of various Greek sculptures (originals or copies) and how their stories are alternatively held up as the apex of culture or reviled as the worst of ethical depravity masquerading as culture.[13]

In Chapter 7, we shall turn to the Aphrodite of Knidos and to Clement on viewing and desire. In the present chapter I trace one ancient discourse about

9 See, e.g., Natalie Boymel Kampen, "Gender Theory in Roman Art," in Diana E. E. Kleiner and Susan B. Matheson, eds., *I, Claudia: Women in Ancient Rome* (Austin, TX: University of Texas Press and New Haven, CT: Yale University Art Gallery, 1996) 14, 20.

10 On a Marxist turn in art history away from connoisseurship and toward production and material conditions, and on the limits of such a method, see Richard Gordon, "The Real and the Imaginary: Production and Religion in the Graeco-Roman World," *Art History* 2 (1979) 5–7. See Elizabeth Spelman, "Who's Who in the Polis," in her *Inessential Woman: Problems of Exclusion in Feminist Thought* (Boston: Beacon, 1988) and discussions of the sex-gender system in the Greek and Roman world, which operated along the binary of active and passive: Bernadette J. Brooten, *Love between Women: Early Christian Responses to Female Homoeroticism* (Chicago: University of Chicago Press, 1996) and Michel Foucault, *The History of Sexuality*, vol. 2: *The Use of Pleasure* (trans. Robert Hurley; New York: Vintage Books, 1990) esp. 187–225.

11 Arjun Appadurai, "Introduction: Commodities and the Politics of Value," in Arjun Appadurai, ed., *The Social Life of Things: Commodities in Social Perspective* (1986; repr. Cambridge: Cambridge University Press, 2003) 38, his emphases; see also p. 27 on art and archaeology collections. Appadurai draws attention to the "conditions under which economic objects circulate in different *regimes of value* in space and time" (p. 4).

12 See esp. Pierre Bourdieu, "The Forms of Capital," translated by Richard Nice, in J. G. Richardson, ed., *Handbook of Theory and Research for the Sociology of Education* (New York: Greenwood, 1986) 241–58; this is a translation by Richard Nice of the original 1983 essay "Ökonomisches Kapital, kulturelles Kapital, soziales Kapital."

13 On connoisseurship in the ancient world, see Jeremy Tanner, *The Invention of Art History in Ancient Greece: Religion, Society and Artistic Rationalization* (Cambridge: Cambridge University Press, 2006) 205–302.

the origin of images, a discourse relevant for Aphrodite, goddess of love: that humans first produced portraits out of longing and desire. We then turn to Tatian and his concerns with spectacle, sculptures, and connoisseurship.

I. WHAT AN IMAGE DOES

Early Christians are often characterized as aniconic, as having inherited from Judaism a hatred of images, especially images of the gods. Yet, as we shall see, Christians are not the only ones to question the pedagogical and theological value of image-making.[14] When Christians of the second century discuss such images and image-making, especially images of the gods, they do not sound happy. We see this in the focal texts of this book. In the Acts of the Apostles, Luke presents a Paul who comes to Athens and is immediately offended, "seeing that the city was full of idols" (Acts 17:16). We recall that Justin in the mid-second century writes, "We do not honor with many sacrifices and wreaths of flowers those whom humans – forming them and setting them in sanctuaries – have given the name 'gods.' Therefore we know them to be soulless and dead things, which do not have the form of God (for we do not consider God to have such a form, which some say have been represented for the purpose of honor[ing God]); we know them to have both the names and the forms of these evil *daimones* who have appeared" (*1 Apol.* 9.1). Athenagoras adds, with a muck-raker's tone, "It is these demons who drag people to the images. They engross themselves in the blood from the sacrifices and lick all around them" (*Leg.* 26.1). Clement of Alexandria, we shall see, gives the lurid scene of barbarians who torture and kill their captives by binding them together to corpses until both rot. So also, he argues, the living are bound by superstition to wood and stone statues until both rot away together.[15] He later takes a different approach, citing ancient zoological experiments in which dolls and toys were handed to monkeys, who somehow knew that they were not real: "Such stinging madness did the arts (αἱ τέχναι) create by their fraudulent artifice in those who are senseless. . . . You have become even worse

[14] For a fuller discussion of Philo, creation, and the *eikōn*, see Laura Nasrallah, "The Earthen Human, the Breathing Statue: The Sculptor God, Greco-Roman Statuary, and Clement of Alexandria," in Konrad Schmid and Christoph Riedweg, eds., *Beyond Eden: The Biblical Story of Paradise [Genesis 2–3] and Its Reception History* (FAT II; Tübingen: Mohr Siebeck, 2008) 110–40. For an overview of reactions to "art and idolatry" among pagans, Christians, and Jews, see Robin Jensen, *Face to Face: Portraits of the Divine in Early Christianity* [Minneapolis, MN: Fortress, 2005] 4–100.

[15] "This wicked tyrant and serpent . . . has bound together with a wretched chain of superstition stones and wood and statues and some such idols, indeed, as it is said, bringing the living to bury them together [with the statues and idols], so that both also are destroyed together" (*Prot.* I 7.4).

than monkeys, since you devote yourselves to stone and wood and gold and ivory sculptures and paintings" (*Prot.* IV 58.1).

Scholars have often argued that Christians condemn images, especially images of the gods, because of Jewish tradition and scripture.[16] In the Septuagint, the form in which most early Christians writing in Greek would have accessed Jewish scriptures, the second commandment of the Decalogue against the making and worship of images reads: "You shall not make for yourself an image or any likeness (εἴδωλον οὐδὲ παντὸς ὁμοίωμα), of such as in the heaven above or in the earth below or in the waters which are under the earth. Do not kneel before these nor worship them. For I am the Lord your God." This command has a double force. On the one hand, one is not to worship such objects; on the other hand, it seems that the very act of creation – of making something *similar* – might be seen as disturbingly competitive to God.[17]

Ancient Jewish prophets pick up and expand upon this tradition, and early Christian writers draw from such writings. Recent discoveries and new methodologies have revealed, however, that Judaism in antiquity was not universally aniconic.[18] As we might expect, ancient Jewish reactions to images were varied and complex. For example, in the Mishnah, *M. Abodah Zarah* 3:1 begins with the statement "All images are prohibited," which is immediately nuanced in a variety of ways, with a clear concern regarding the image that is worshipped. This passage and its saying, "But the Sages say: Only that is forbidden which bears in its hand a staff or a bird or a sphere," have often been read as an interdiction of images particularly connected with imperial cult, specifically, representations of the emperor as Jupiter (with his attributes of the eagle, the scepter, and often the globe).[19] Elsewhere in *M. Abodah Zarah*, it seems that use or interaction with images that had been or could be considered idols is permitted.[20] In other rabbinic literature, there is mention of

16 For an overview of these arguments and an assessment of some ancient art and, even more, of modern political and theological investments in the debate over Jewish and Christian art, see Jaś Elsner, "Archaeologies and Agendas: Reflections on Late Ancient Jewish Art and Early Christian Art," *JRS* 93 (2003) 114–24.

17 See Gen 1:26–27, in which God makes the human in God's "image and likeness." Sculptors of naturalistic anthropomorphic forms thus duplicate God's power and activity. On the dangers of Daedalus's creativity, see Gordon, "The Real and the Imaginary," 8–10, passim.

18 On the politics of declaring ancient Judaism aniconic, see Steven Fine, *Art and Judaism in the Greco-Roman World: Toward a New Jewish Archaeology* (Cambridge: Cambridge University Press, 2005) 47–56.

19 ET Herbert Danby, *The Mishnah* (London: Oxford, 1933) 440. I limit myself to discussion of the Mishnah, rather than including also the Babylonian and Jerusalem Talmuds on *Abodah Zarah*, since the *terminus ad quem* of the Mishnah is earlier, likely in the third century. On idolatry, see also *M. Sanhedrin* 7:6.

20 *M. Abodah Zarah* 3:2, 3:7, 4:4–5; see also Seth Schwartz, "The Rabbi in Aphrodite's Bath: Palestinian Society and Jewish Identity in the High Roman Empire," in Goldhill, ed., *Being Greek under Rome*, 358.

Jewish families making images of their family members, even masks or likenesses after death, as did the Romans.[21]

Thus even within *M. Abodah Zarah*, we find debate and nuance. In a later passage of the tractate we encounter the famous story of Rabbi Gamaliel, who is questioned about his taking a bath in "Aphrodite's bathhouse." His reply is that "I came not within her limits; she came within mine!" (3:4). Aphrodite was an "adornment for the bath"; people urinate before her image.[22] Since she is not treated as a god, Rabbi Gamaliel's proximity to her does not constitute a contradiction of the commandments.

Contrary to one movement in scholarship today, Seth Schwartz has argued that the rabbis whose stories we read in the third-century Mishnah were not like their Greco-Roman contemporaries. Rabbi Gamaliel's reference to Aphrodite as purely decorative would not have made sense to Gamaliel's contemporaries; Schwartz goes so far as to call it a "radical misinterpretation of Greco-Roman paganism."[23] First-century Jerusalem, Schwartz reminds us, was an aesthetically strange place in the Roman world. At its center was a massive temple complex like those of Artemis at Ephesus or Athena and Zeus at Pergamon, but, unlike those busy precincts, the Jerusalem temple was devoid of images. By the second and third centuries, however, Judea had been "de-judaized," and the city, refounded as Aelia Capitolina, was full of shrines and images.[24] The rabbis, Schwartz argues, did not assimilate smoothly and easily to this new imagistic world in which they lived, but instead as a minority voice offered ways to live with images and idols that "*functioned* as accommodation."[25]

Yet other contemporaneous Jews reacted in a different way, purchasing "sarcophagi, gold glasses, and other artistic products from the same workshops as those that catered to pagans and Christians," as Leonard Rutgers summarizes in his study of material realia and Roman Jews of the third and fourth centuries CE.[26] Many of the sarcophagi had "decorative frameworks and iconographical

[21] See the discussion of *Mekilta de rabbi Ishmael*, tractate *Pisha* 13 and tractate *Besallah* 8 in Yaron Eliav, "Roman Statues, Rabbis, and Graeco-Roman Culture," in Yaron Eliav and Anita Norich, eds., *Jewish Literatures and Cultures: Context and Intertext* (Providence, RI: Brown Judaic Studies, 2008) 99–115.

[22] ET Danby, 440. Schwartz, "The Rabbi in Aphrodite's Bath," 337–41.

[23] Schwartz, "The Rabbi in Aphrodite's Bath," 357; see also 346, 355–60.

[24] Ibid., 335. See also discussion of Philo's *Legatio ad Gaium* and *In Flaccum* in Chapter 7.

[25] Ibid., 359, his emphasis. See, however, Eliav, "Roman Statues," who argues instead that the rabbis were responding to already extant Greco-Roman distinctions between consecrated and non-consecrated statues.

[26] Leonard Victor Rutgers, *The Jews in Late Ancient Rome: Evidence of Cultural Interaction in the Roman Diaspora* (Leiden: E. J. Brill, 1995) 262; see also 77–79 on the methodological problems of distinguishing pagan and Jewish sarcophagi in the catacombs of Rome. For more of an overview, see his *The Hidden Heritage of Diaspora Judaism* (2nd ed.; Leuven: Peeters, 1998) 45–96 on the Jewish catacombs in Rome.

motifs that are either neutral or plainly pagan."[27] We cannot merely dismiss such images as elements of pagan iconography that would have been "spiritualized" and drained of their pagan religious meaning, as Erwin Goodenough suggested.[28] Later Jewish iconography from Byzantine Palestine becomes even more difficult to explain away: Some ancient synagogues were full of images of the zodiac, of birds, even of prophets and patriarchs.[29]

Thus, in whatever ways early Christian reactions to images were informed by Jewish responses, as certainly they were, Judaism of the first and second centuries had set no one clear path along which Christians proceeded. Moreover, as soon as Christians had enough funds to produce images, some did. It is also clear that Christians from the very start used commonly available images and applied their own meanings to them. According to Clement – the very Clement who talks about rotting away with your idols – a signet ring picturing a ship, properly understood, can be a Christian symbol (*Paid.* 3.11). Anyone interpreting the archaeological record finds it hard to distinguish a Christian image from a Jewish or a pagan one in the Roman world precisely because Christians were not necessarily different in their customs, their philosophy, their use of objects and symbols – in all those small acts that historians scrutinize to fix boundaries or mark identity in antiquity.[30]

The Origins of Images

Literature of the first century BCE and the first two centuries CE and beyond offers various tales of the origins of naturalistic representation. This literature takes part in a centuries-long and widespread conversation about how images began and what purpose they serve or what pedagogy they inculcate. By

[27] Rutgers, *The Jews in Late Ancient Rome*, 79. Note his description here of a sarcophagus in which the clipeus is specifically commissioned by a Jewish buyer and contains a menorah; however, the rest of the sarcophagus is "pre-fabricated" or merely typical of the workshop, so that the menorah is flanked and supported by two Victories.

[28] Erwin R. Goodenough, *Jewish Symbols in the Greco-Roman Period* (New York: Pantheon Books, 1953).

[29] The frescoes of the synagogue at Dura Europos, with a *terminus ante quem* of 267 CE, provide the best example, but we find figural iconography also in Palestine in the Byzantine period. See Lee I. Levine, *The Ancient Synagogue: The First Thousand Years* (2nd ed.; New Haven, CT: Yale University Press, 2005) 210–49. We find a variety of evidence of Jewish iconography, some of very poor quality, in diaspora synagogues, but these are often difficult to date. See also mention of the idea of Jewish aniconism and bibliography cited in C. Kavin Rowe, "New Testament Iconography? Situating Paul in the Absence of Material Evidence," in Annette Weissenrieder et al., eds., *Picturing the New Testament: Studies in Ancient Visual Images* (Tübingen: Mohr Siebeck, 2005) 290.

[30] Elsner, "Archaeologies and Agendas," 114–28; Ross Kramer, "Jewish Tuna and Christian Fish: Identifying Religious Affiliation in Epigraphic Sources," *HTR* 84.2 (1991) 141–62; on common workshops that produced goods for multiple religious/ethic groups, see Rutgers, *The Jews in Late Ancient Rome*. On Christians producing images, see Tertullian's harsh critique in *De idol.* 6.

addressing the question of why one makes an image in the first place, these texts help us to understand ancient ideas about what an image is supposed to *do* to a person. If in the sections that follow the reader is unsure for a moment whether a writer is Christian or Jewish or neither, I shall have successfully made one of my points: A variety of religious texts offer etiologies that link the creation of images with desire and longing.

As we know, human and divine forms in the ancient Mediterranean world were blurred, since humans were depicted as gods and goddesses, and the gods and goddesses were depicted as having human bodies (admittedly usually of the most excellent sort). In such a world of "naturalistic" imagery, many of our writers slip easily between discussing images of gods and images of humans.[31]

Those who write about the origins of representation often say that naturalistic images of human bodies begin because of absence and are bound up with human *pathos*.[32] Pliny famously offers the origins of portraits in clay, "Modelling portraits from clay [were] first invented by Butades, a potter of Sicyon, at Corinth. He did this owing to his daughter, who was in love with a young man (*quae capta amore iuvenis*); and she, when he was going abroad, drew in outline on the wall the shadow of his face thrown by a lamp. Her father pressed clay on this and made a relief, which he hardened by exposure to fire with the rest of his pottery" (*Nat. hist.* 35.43.151).[33] Clay portrait reliefs emerge out of love, desire, and absence between a young woman and a young man. Artistic collaboration between daughter and father results in a naturalistic representation that is the product of (and perhaps produces) love and longing.

So also in both the *Wisdom of Solomon* and Minucius Felix's *Octavius*, separated by more than a century yet engaged in a common theme over the years, absence and grief spur not only the production of images but also the improper confusion of human and divine bodies. The *Wisdom of Solomon* was written in Greek, likely in first-century BCE Alexandria, and is perhaps influenced by the rhetoric and imagery of the Augustan period.[34] In the midst of strenuous

31 On such blurring in language and image, see Gordon, "The Real and the Imaginary," 5–16.

32 See also Deborah Steiner, *Images in Mind: Statues in Archaic and Classical Greek Literature and Thought* (Princeton, NJ: Princeton University Press, 2001) chap. 4. See also A. A. Donohue, *Xoana and the Origins of Greek Sculpture* (Atlanta: Scholars Press, 1988) esp. 13–32 and 175–231.

33 ET Pliny, *Natural History* (trans. H. Rackham et al.; LCL; Cambridge, MA: Harvard University Press, 1952) 373. Athenagoras mentions this story of the Corinthian girl and origins of relief modeling (*Leg.* 17.3). This is, of course, only one of many stories of the origins of various plastic arts in Pliny (see *Nat. hist.* 35.5.15 on the origins of painting and 35.44.153 on the first plaster likeness of a human being made from life). See Robert Rosenblum, *Transformations in Late Eighteenth Century Art* (Princeton, NJ: Princeton University Press, 1967) 21 and fig. 16 regarding Joseph Wright's painting of this scene in his "Corinthian Maiden" (1782–84).

34 David Winston dates the text after the Roman conquest of Alexandria in 30 BCE and likely to the reign of Gaius (Caligula) (37–41 CE); *Wisdom* would then be sparked by tensions surrounding the Alexandrian pogrom and riots against Jews in 38 BCE (*The Wisdom of Solomon. A New Translation with Introduction and Commentary* [Garden City, NY: Doubleday, 1979] 20–23). He characterizes the author as "a learned and thoroughly Hellenized Jew"

critique of the use and worship of images,[35] the writer of this Jewish text argues that "the conception of idols is the beginning of fornication, and their discovery is life's ruin"[36] and then offers this poignant story:

> A father, consumed with untimely grief, made an image of the child so swiftly taken. He honored as god what was once a human corpse, and handed down to those in his household mysteries and initiation rites. Then, strengthened by the passage of time, the impious custom (τὸ ἀσεβὲς ἔθος) was maintained as law, and at the command of monarchs (τυράννων) carved images were worshiped. When people, because they lived at a distance, were unable to honor them in person (ἐν ὄψει), they formed an image of the distant sight (τὴν πόρρωθεν ὄψιν ἀνατυπωσάμενοι), and made a visible image of the honored king, so that by their eagerness they might flatter the absent one as though present. Then the ambition of the artisan impelled even those who did not know the king to intensify their worship. For the artisan, perhaps wishing to please the ruler, skillfully forced the likeness to take more beautiful form, and the multitude, attracted by the charm of the workmanship, now considered as an object of worship (σέβασμα) the one who only lately had been an honored human. (*Sap.* 14:15–20)[37]

Naturalistic representation emerges simply at first, from grief over the death of a child. Images for the *Wisdom of Solomon* serve as replacements for what is absent, whether the absent one is a longed-for child or a powerful king.[38] The

whose philosophical inclination and emphasis on Sophia, and Wisdom, make him/her similar to the contemporary Philo (pp. 3–4). The *Wisdom of Solomon* is rhetorically classified as a *logos protreptikos* or exhortatory discourse (p. 18), and thus is generically similar to the focal texts for this chapter and the next, Tatian's *To the Greeks* and Clement's *Exhortation*. There is a general consensus about the Greek philosophical context of the *Wisdom of Solomon*; see John Collins, *Jewish Wisdom in the Hellenistic Age* (Louisville, KY: Westminster/John Knox, 1997). See also Paul Corby Finney, *The Invisible God: The Earliest Christians on Art* (New York: Oxford University Press, 1994) 27.

35 *Sap.* 13:1–15:19. This passage is preceded by a critique of nature worship and a lambasting of the practices of making statues and images, which also mentions the very material origins of such practices. The arguments are like those that we find in early Christian sources. See also *Sap.* 13:10, 13–16, 18.

36 Ἀρχὴ γὰρ πορνείας ἐπίνοια εἰδώλων, εὕρεσις δὲ αὐτῶν φθορὰ ζωῆς. *Sap.* 14:12; ET Winston, *The Wisdom of Solomon*, 269 (slightly modified). The Greek edition is *Sapientia Salomonis, Septuaginta* vol. 12.1 (ed. Joseph Ziegler; Göttingen: Vandenhoeck and Ruprecht, 1962).

37 My translation. Regarding honoring a dead child, Winston's commentary cites inscriptions which indicate the honoring of an eight-year old child as a hero in Smyrna in the second century CE, and child of four who is honored as a tutelary god at Smyrna (*The Wisdom of Solomon*, 275); note also the child Euephenēs who is honored with a heroon in Philippi in the mid third century BCE.

38 See also Severianus of Gabala *In Cosmogoniam* 6.5: "Since the emperor cannot be present everywhere, it is necessary to set up a portrait of the emperor at tribunals, in marketplaces, at meetings, and in theaters. In fact, a portrait must be present in every place in which a magistrate acts, so that he might sanction whatever transpires" (quoted in Clifford Ando, *Imperial Ideology and Provincial Loyalty in the Roman Empire* [Berkeley: University of California Press, 2000] 233).

artisan colludes in the process by making the image beautiful and seductive so that not only the thing itself inspires worship, but also the aesthetics of its representation. As the dead human comes to be worshiped as a god, so also an image rendered from grief (the polemic of the text insinuates a death mask or mummy portrait)[39] somehow transforms into legally required worship of images and into the honoring of monarchs even in their absence. Winston, who prefers an early first-century date for the text, thinks that this king may be understood as a Roman emperor.[40] As tenderly stated as the *Wisdom of Solomon* is, the idea that grief produces art is a well-known *topos* of the ancient world. We read of other such image-producing griefs. For example, in Apuleius's *Metamorphoses* a woman has an image of her husband made in the likeness of Liber, "unto which she rendered divine honors and services, so that she grieved herself even by her consolation" (*Met.* 8.7).[41] In the previous chapter we have seen evidence of the human-turned-god in the man depicted as Herakles in his funerary monument; in the next chapter we shall see more examples in memorials that depict the deceased as Aphrodite/Venus. In an age where some statues were painted, such depictions would have imitated life, and deliberately confused the differences between dead stone, living (or dead) humans, and gods and goddesses.

The debate over religion in the perhaps third-century Latin *Octavius* – a conversation between two Christians and a non-Christian – is provoked by an image. The non-Christian Caecilius, walking with his friends and passing a statue of the god Serapis, blows it a kiss (2). The Christian Octavius is angered, and argues that, for friendship's sake, he and his Christian friend should not allow Caecilius – the name puns on the Latin for "blind" – to continue in his ways without a fight. Octavius's statement contains a thinly veiled insult: The statues of gods are merely (stumbling) stones. "It is not for a good man, brother Marcus, to leave a person who has clung to you at home and in the forum to skulk thus in dark obscurity in this blindness of the ignorant multitude, that you should allow him in the brightness of day to fasten onto stones, however molded and anointed and crowned [they are]."[42] In his response

39 Regarding ancestral masks, see Pliny *Nat. hist.* 35.2.4–5.

40 For Winston, the term *sebasma* recalls the Greek title for Augustus, *Sebastos* (*The Wisdom of Solomon*, 279).

41 Translated and discussed in Winston, *The Wisdom of Solomon*, 276–77. There are many references to falling in love with statues and images, e.g., Pliny *Nat. hist.* 36.4.38: "Formerly too there were statues of the Muses of Helicon by the temple of Prosperity, and a Roman knight, Junius Pisciculus, fell in love with one of them, according to Varro, who incidentally was an admirer of Pasiteles, a sculptor who was also the author of a treatise in five volumes on the World's Famous Masterpieces" (ET Pliny, *Natural History* [LCL; trans. D. E. Eichholz; Cambridge, MA: Harvard University Press, 1962] 31). See also the discussion of Pygmalion and others on pp. 281–84.

42 Minucius Felix *Oct.* 3.1. I consulted the Latin of Bernhard Kytzler, ed., *M. Minuci Felicis Octavius, Bibliotheca Scriptorium Graecorum et Romanorum Teubneriana* (Leipzig: B. G. Teubner,

to this critique, Caecilius downplays the images of the gods. He insists that Rome has conquered the world precisely because of its support of all the gods and its piety (6.2–3) and because of the presence of the gods within temples and shrines (7.5).[43] In turn, the Christian Octavius explains the origin of images in a way similar to the *Wisdom of Solomon* (and may, in fact, borrow from it): "Likewise and assuredly, our ancestors, heedless, credulous, in ignorant simplicity, also believed with respect to the gods. While religiously revering their kings, while desiring to see in images those who had died, while passionately wishing to keep their memory in statues, sacred objects were fashioned, objects which had been (originally) adopted for consolation" (*Oct.* 20.5). Statues were originally created as an aid to memory and as an evocation of those who were founders, virtuous, or worthy of memory in some way. In a misunderstanding that grew through time, this aid to memory became an object of worship. Thus the *Octavius* as well as the *Wisdom of Solomon* understands divine images in terms of Euhemerism, the ancient Greek idea that the gods are nothing more than great humans of the past.

In these three stories of the origins of images – the Corinthian girl, the bereaved parent, the credulous ancestors – some emotion or *pathos* spurs the production of images; desire, absence, and even death are intertwined with representation. In other texts from antiquity as well, seeing and desire are intimately linked, even when death and absence are not involved. To address more fully the cultural possibilities in antiquity for training the eye, it is important to take a step back and investigate some theories of the mechanics of viewing, and how these are intertwined with desire.

What You See and What You Get: Theorizing Vision

"Schools of thought on optics in antiquity adhered to versions of several theories that we might roughly characterize as bounded on one end by extramission, on the other by intromission. Throughout, however, the common denominator seems to have been the tactile quality of 'seeing,'" says Shadi Bartsch in a helpful summary.[44] We learn of intromissionist theory especially from the writings of Epicurus and Lucretius, who argued that objects emitted tiny particles (*eidōla* in Greek; *simulacra* in Latin) that reached the eye.[45] These "films"

1982) 2 and made reference here and elsewhere to the translation of Rudolph Arbesmann in *Tertullian Apologetical Works and Minucius Felix Octavius* (Washington, D.C.: Catholic University of America Press, 1962).

43 See also Cicero *Har. resp.* 19 and Clifford Ando, *Matter of the Gods: Religion and the Roman Empire* (Berkeley: University of California Press, 2008) 135–48.

44 Shadi Bartsch, *The Mirror of the Self: Sexuality, Self-Knowledge, and the Gaze in the Early Roman Empire* (Chicago: University of Chicago Press, 2006) 3.

45 Ibid., 59–60. See the variation on this theory in Lucretius 4.722–822; the films that come off of objects can mix in the air, thus producing in the eye Centaurs and other hybrid images.

were thus tactile objects that entered the viewer. Extramissionist theories see "the eye as an active agent that emitted rays or a visual current toward the object of perception," an idea stated most clearly in Hipparchus, who speaks of the rays of the eyes as a kind of hand, grasping external objects.[46]

Stoics talk instead about *pneuma* ("spirit") that strikes the pupil, stamping an impression of the object onto the eye. This perception is then communicated to the *hēgemonikon* or governing part of the soul.[47] This philosophical stance is recast in novelist form in the second-century romance of Achilles Tatius's *Leucippe and Clitophon*: "The pleasure of the gaze, sliding into the eyes, is seated in the chest. It eternally draws in the lover's image, which is impressed upon the soul's mirror and molds anew its form. The emanation of the beautiful, drawn by the erotic heart, through unseen rays impresses down [in the soul] a shadow" (5.13).[48] Images impress something on you; they can literally reform the eye. Seeing can even be a kind of sexual intercourse:[49] "And do you not know what a thing it is that the lover be seen? This pleasure is greater than doing the deed. For the eyes, reflecting each other, take an impression of images of bodies as in a mirror. But the efflux of beauty, flowing through them [the eyes] into the soul, has a certain intercourse by means of emanation; and it is a bit of an intercourse of bodies. For it is a new embrace. But *I* predict that you will do the deed soon" (*Leucippe and Cliptophon* 1.9).[50] As Goldhill has pointed out, and as we shall see more in the next chapter, Clement agrees with the logic of Achilles Tatius: Both describe looking as a kind of copulation.[51] Knowledge from the eye was potentially dangerous. One could literally be struck by what one saw and could also be deceived by what one saw, especially in a culture producing illusionistic and naturalistic images.[52]

These questions about the mechanics and disciplining of viewing are part of an ongoing and longstanding ancient philosophical debate that asked: What

[46] Bartsch, *Mirror of the Self*, 62. Hipparchus is quoted in Aetius 4.13.8–12.

[47] Ibid., 65. Regarding theories of seeing, also see Goldhill, "The Erotic Eye," and esp. Gerard Watson, "Discovering the Imagination: Platonists and Stoics on *phantasia*," in John Dillon and A. A. Long, eds., *The Question of 'Eclecticism': Studies in Later Greek Philosophy* (Berkeley: University of California Press, 1988) 208–33; Gerard Watson, *Phantasia in Classical Thought* (Galway: Galway University Press, 1988).

[48] The Greek edition is that of Ebbe Vilborg, *Achilles Tatius: Leucippe and Clitophon* (Stockholm: Almqvist and Wiksell, 1955). My translation and interpretation is aided by John J. Winkler's in Bryan P. Reardon, *Collected Ancient Greek Novels* (Berkeley: University of California Press, 1989) 239 and by Goldhill's translation and discussion of this passage "Erotic Eye," 178. Regarding the ability of the eyes to reflect shame or dejection, see Plutarch *Mor.* 528E–F, discussed in Simon Swain, "Polemon's *Physiognomy*," in Simon Swain, ed., *Seeing the Face, Seeing the Soul: Polemon's Physiognomy from Classical Antiquity to Medieval Islam* (Oxford: Oxford University Press, 2007) 141.

[49] See also Bartsch, *Mirror of the Self*, 67–83.

[50] See discussion in Goldhill, "The Erotic Eye," 169.

[51] Tertullian seems to adopt the same ideas of optics as a rhetorical strategy against virgins with unveiled heads seeing and being seen in *On the Veiling of Virgins*.

[52] See Elsner, esp. "Ways of Viewing," 16–17 in *Art and the Roman Viewer*. For a Stoic-influenced Christian defense of the eye and sense perception, see Tertullian *De an.* 17.

is the best sort of seeing? Perceptions gained through the senses, even the highest sense, vision, were often considered to be of less epistemic value than perceptions gained through the exercise of the "vision" of the *nous* ("mind") in contemplation.[53] An anecdote from the third-century *Life of Apollonius* by Philostratus illustrates my point, using as examples Pheidias, the famous Greek sculptor of the Olympian Zeus, whom we shall meet in Dio's "Olympian Oration," and Praxiteles, the famous sculptor of the Aphrodite of Knidos. On a visit to India, the Greek philosopher and miracle-worker Apollonius insults one of his hosts, Thespesion, by asking about the images of the gods that he sees, which "seem to honor irrational and dishonorable animals rather than gods." Thespesion bitterly jokes that "Pheidiases and Praxiteleses, surely, went up into heaven and, taking an impression of the forms of the gods, made these by art – or, was there some other thing that prescribed their sculpture?" (*Vit. Ap.* 6.19).[54] Apollonius insists in opposition that the work of such sculptors was not a product of *mimēsis*, but of *phantasia* – not of imitation or representation, but of imagination.[55] Through *mimēsis*, according to Apollonius, one is limited to what has been seen, but through *phantasia* one has access to the unseen, "through reference to what really is" (*Vit. Ap.* 6.19).

This slight comment signals a larger conversation about the connection between famous sculptors, their works, and the theological imagination. Against Thespesion's slight, Apollonius argues that some sort of insight rather than simple sight – something special with regard to the theological imagination – makes possible the work of a sculptor like Pheidias. We find evidence of this longstanding conversation in a text like Cicero's *Orator* 8–9, from which Philostratus may have borrowed:

> This cannot be perceived by eyes or ears or any sense: we grasp it only through thinking (*cogitatione tamen et mente complectimur*). For example, in the case of the statues of Phidias, the most perfect of their kind which we can see, and in the case of the paintings mentioned, we can, in spite of their beauty, imagine something more beautiful. That great sculptor

[53] Watson, "Discovering the Imagination," 208–33.

[54] My translation after Philostratus, *The Life of Apollonius of Tyana* (LCL; 2 vols.; ed. and trans. Christopher P. Jones; Cambridge, MA: Harvard University Press, 2005) 2.155. Apollonius goes on: "Doubtless if you envisage the shape of Zeus, you must see him together with the heaven, the seasons, and the plants, as Phidias ventured to do in his day. If you are planning to portray Athena, you must think of armies, intelligence, the arts, need how she sprang from Zeus himself. But if you create a hawk, an owl, a wolf, or a dog, and bring it into your holy places instead of Hermes, Athena, or Apollo, people will think animals and birth worth envying for their images, but the gods will fall far short of their own glory." Thespesion insists that Apollonius has missed the point: "They make these forms symbolic and suggestive, since in that way they seem far more venerable." ET Jones, 2.157.

[55] Of course, these are rough definitions of contested philosophical words from antiquity; see discussion in Chapter 5. For more on definitions of *phantasia*, see Watson, "Discovering the Imagination," 214–17 and Tanner, *The Invention of Art History*, 283–88 on *phantasia* as a rational process.

> Phidias, while shaping the image (*formam*) of Jupiter or Minerva, did not keep looking at some person from whom he drew the likeness, but in his own mind (*in mente*) there dwelt a surpassing vision of beauty; at this he gazed, and, fixed on this, he directed his art and hand to the production of a likeness of it. Accordingly, as there is something perfect and surpassing in the case of sculpture and painting, with the vision of which in the mind there are associated in the process of imitation those things which are never actually seen (*cuius ad cogitatam speciem imitando referuntur ea quae sub oculos ipsa non cadunt*), so with our minds we conceive the ideal of perfect eloquence (*sic perfectae eloquentiae speciem animo videmus*), but with our ears we catch only the copy. These patterns of things are called *ideai* ["forms"] by Plato.[56]

The passage compares the epistemic process of producing good art – the best art, the chryselephantine Greek standard even under Rome – to the process of producing "perfect eloquence." In both Philostratus and Cicero's *Orator*, the artisan engages in a special epistemic process. S/he goes beyond the reaches of the eye to the mind's eye to produce his or her[57] image of the gods.

This language of *phantasia* and *mimēsis*, as well as the language of vision and desire that we found in *Leucippe and Clitophon* and other texts discussed above, show that a great deal of ancient texts treating the topic of vision, images, and knowing and seeing the divine echo the ideas of Plato's *Phaedrus*.[58] The *Phaedrus*, with its unusual celebration of a fourth kind of madness that leads to knowledge of the divine, uses the image of a winged soul and the language of vision and *eros*. Socrates speaks in the voice of Stesichorus, son of Euphemus ("pious or auspicious speech"), from Himera ("Desire"), in order to argue against the idea that the lover's madness should be avoided (244A). Thus the *Phaedrus* like the *Symposium* treats the intersection of (erotic) love and the quest for true knowledge, which is the quest for the truly divine.

Socrates offers the process of that quest *in nuce*: "For a human being must understand a general conception formed by collecting into a unity by means

[56] Watson, "Discovering the Imagination," 211–12; he makes the connection to Philostratus. I use his translation, which is a modification of *Cicero. Brutus; Orator* (LCL; trans. H. M. Hubbell; Cambridge, MA: Harvard University Press, 1939) 311–13. See his notes regarding text critical problems, and see p. 226 regarding similar discussions in Seneca the Elder (*Contr.* 10.5.8) and Seneca the Younger (*Ep.* 65.4ff). Both deny that Pheidias or an artist sees an object before his or her eyes; Seneca the Younger explicitly states that the artist instead sees what Plato describes as an *idea*. See also Andrew F. Stewart, *Art, Desire, and the Body in Ancient Greece* (Cambridge: Cambridge University Press, 1997) 19–23.

[57] E.g., Pliny *Nat. hist.* 35.40.147 discusses women painters.

[58] Even in the second century this was a foundational text for thinking about how one could know the divine; as Bartsch has shown, the vocabulary of the *Phaedrus* appears in Achilles Tatius's *Leucippe and Clitophon*, in Plutarch, and in Philostratus as they express their ideas on the erotics of seeing (Bartsch, *Mirror of the Self*, 78–79). For more on this passage in light of early Christian discussions of prophecy and madness, see Laura Nasrallah, *An Ecstasy of Folly: Prophecy and Authority in Early Christianity* (HTS 52; Cambridge, MA: Harvard University Press, 2003) chap. 1.

of reason the many perceptions of the senses; and this is a recollection of those things which our soul once beheld, when it journeyed with God and, lifting its vision above the things which we now say exist, rose up into real being" (249C).[59] This person, asserts Socrates, is "called a lover (ἐραστής)" (249E) and is regarded as mad because "when he sees the beauty on earth, remembering the true beauty, feels his wings growing and longs to stretch them for an upward flight, but cannot do so, and, like a bird, gazes upward (βλέπων ἄνω) and neglects the things below" (249D).[60] Socrates speaks of the practice of contemplating or viewing images, by which one comes to understand the beauty and brightness of the heavenly forms of such things as justice (*dikaiosunē*) and self-control (*sōphrosunē*) (250B).

Tatian's terminology indicates that he may know the *Phaedrus* or its ideas. Although he clearly asserts that the soul is not pre-existent (*Ad Graec.* 6.2) and thus would reject the idea that humans have some *anamnēsis* ("recollection") of Beauty, he shares with Plato's *Phaedrus* an understanding of the poignant struggle of the soul in the world. He describes the world as that which "yet draws us down." "For the wings of the soul are perfect spirit, which the soul cast away because of sin, fluttering like a chick and falling to earth. Having shifted from heavenly intercourse (συνουσίας), it longed for partnership with inferiors" (20.2).[61] Tatian, unlike Justin, is no explicit champion of Plato or Socrates as an anonymous Christian before his time. Yet Tatian's idea of the soul builds upon the famous image of the winged soul and offers a Christian improvisation: a soul that does not preexist but that still longs for the divine; a soul that is similarly caught in the lower realms; a soul that through the prophets – rather than through the mysteries, contemplative practice, or the *anamnēsis* Socrates discusses – races back to its "ancient kinship" (20.6). As we shall see, Tatian argues in the same breath that Christians are deeply philosophical *and* that they reject the sort of desire that is taught through seeing statues. Tatian speaks in a world where seeing and desire can lead to philosophical perfection, because correctly directed desire and vision can help humans to recover their longing for divine realities.

Images and the Theological Imagination: Cicero, Dio, and Maximus of Tyre

One ancient argument is that the origins of images lay in human desire to produce mimetically what is absent; this mimetic image then becomes an object of worship. Several writers of the Roman period follow this idea that images stand in for the absent one, in this case a god. They discuss the theology

59 ET Plato, *Euthyphro, Apology, Critio, Phaedo, Phaedrus* (LCL; trans. Harold North Fowler; Cambridge, MA: Harvard University Press, 1995) 481.

60 ET ibid., 483.

61 For more regarding Tatian's idea of the soul, see *Ad Graec.* 12–13.

of images, asking in particular how images are adequate or not adequate to piety and true religion. These conversations – Cicero, Dio of Prusa, and Maximus of Tyre will be representatives – tend to use famous ancient Greek sculptures as touchstones.[62] The debate focuses not on art or sculpture in general, but on particularly famous *Greek* sculpture and its power in the cultural economy of the first century and beyond; thus the theological controversy over images is intertwined with issues of ethnic hierarchy and cultural commoditization.

In around 105 Dio of Prusa, a traveling orator to many of the cities of the Roman Empire, and, if he is to be believed, an advisor to an emperor, composed an oration delivered in Olympia.[63] As we learned in Chapter 1, Olympia on the Greek Peloponnesos is the site of Pheidias's famous chryselephantine statue of Zeus and the temples to Zeus and Hera. The quadrennial Olympic Games occurred there, and it was a prime center of ancient Panhellenic cultural identity, revived in importance under Rome. In his oration Dio conjures not only the statue of Zeus, but also its fifth-century BCE sculptor Pheidias.

Dio's initial question is a philosophical one: Where do humans gain their conceptions of the divine?[64] The speech asserts that there are four things that teach about the gods. Nature itself is the prime teacher; poets/mythologers also teach; so do lawgivers; and so do those who make images of the gods, although their images are often crafted on the basis of what the poets and mythmakers say. Rough sketches, line drawing with blended colors, stone-carving, wooden images, bronze-casting, wax-mouldings – according to Dio, all are fit media for material theologizing (*Or.* 12.44).[65] Dio then offers a list of famous

[62] Regarding the power of images and *ekphrasis*, see pp. 120–21 and, for example, the second-century CE *Tabula of Cebes*: "The explanation [of the painting] carries with it an element of danger (ὅτι ἐπικίνδυνόν τι ἔχει ἡ ἐξήγησις)" (3.1, edition and translation of John T. Fitzgerald and L. Michael White, *The Tabula of Cebes* [Chico, CA: Scholars Press, 1983]).

[63] Christopher P. Jones, *Kinship Diplomacy in the Ancient World* (Cambridge, MA: Harvard University Press, 1999) 138 gives a date of ca. 101; see also p. 53. Elsewhere, too, Dio is concerned with images and their use, e.g., *Or.* 31 ("To the Rhodians"), which discusses the reuse of statues and the recarving of honorary inscriptions.

[64] On Dio's life and evocation of a civic setting for many of his speeches, see Simon Swain, "Dio's Life and Works," in his edited volume *Dio Chrysostom: Politics, Letters, and Philosophy* (Oxford: Oxford University Press, 2000), esp. 5. For Dio as for so many others in antiquity, poetry/*mythos* and image-making are connected. Both attempt to craft – the one from words, the other from stone or other materials – an image of the gods. Thus Dio states that the image of Zeus in Olympia is "of all the statues on earth, the most beautiful and the most god-beloved" (*Or.* 12.25), and that the sculptor Pheidias took his cue from Homer's description of Zeus. Dio's discussion of how Homer's words produced in his soul the *enargeia* ("clarity") to produce a statue demonstrates the extent to which the visual is dependent upon the rational word, at least for Dio, an "orthodox Stoic" (Tanner, *The Invention of Art History*, 286–87). Cf. Cicero *De nat. deo* 3.16f, which recounts Cleanthes' account of the four ways that humans gain ideas of the gods; this account does not include images.

[65] Dio is careful to assert that all sorts of artisans provide sources for our conceptions of the divine (*Or.* 12.44).

Greek artists.[66] According to Dio, these artisans chose to represent the divine, not the commonplace, and in doing so they filled the public with "a many and varied conception concerning the spiritual" (πολλῆς . . . ὑπονοίας καὶ ποικίλης περὶ τοῦ δαιμονίου, 12.45).[67] Dio conjoins the adjectives *pollē* ("many," "much") and *poikilē* ("various") to the singular *hyponoia* ("thought," "conception") of the people. This tension between the potential multiplicity and variety of the imagination and the unity or uniformity of a conception of the divine underlies Dio's decision to put the sculptor Pheidias on trial.

Dio sets the scene with rhetorical gusto, multiplying his authorial voice by *prosōpopoiia*, the practice of speaking through other characters' voices. He conjures up "someone" who will question the long-dead Pheidias; also conjured are Pheidias himself and a "general court of the Peloponnesians" (κοινὸν δικαστήριον ξυμπάντον Πελοποννησίων, 12.49–50).[68] When Pheidias is addressed, he is praised for how his famous image of Zeus *strikes* or amazes a viewer (ἐκπλήξειε, 12.51). The verb *plēttō* has the connotation of striking or stamping an object, such as a coin. The effect of Pheidias's statue, according to Dio, is that the bulls dragged forward to be sacrificed, catching a glimpse of it, go willingly; savage animals are subdued and gladdened; distressed humans too forget the fear and difficulty of human life.[69] Seeing *does* something to the viewer, whether beast or human; the eye is impressed with the image of Zeus, and the viewer transformed by the vision of it.

But then the accusations against Pheidias begin. I quote at length because the passage is extraordinarily rich in its treatment of the topic of the imagination, as well as in its address of the central question of how one knows the gods:

> Did you make a form appropriate to and a shape worthy of the nature of God when you used a delightful material (ὕλῃ τε ἐπιτερπεῖ), showing forth a beauty and greatness that surpassed the form of a man (ἀνδρός

[66] In doing so Dio demonstrates *paideia* and his identity as *pepaideumenos theatēs*, an educated viewer, among the *pepaideumenoi* (*Or.* 12.43) whom he addresses. On these terms see Goldhill, "The Erotic Eye," 157–58.

[67] My translations of Dio have been aided by Dio Chrysostom, *Discourses 12–30* (LCL; trans. J. W. Cohoon; 1939; repr. Cambridge, MA: Harvard University Press, 2001) 24–87.

[68] Dio plays on the theme of Hellenic unity in cult and ethnicity, a theme that, as we have seen in Chapter 3, Romans actively appropriate and encourage.

[69] Dio *Or.* 12.51–52. See also Pausanias *Descr.* 5.11.9: "I know that the height and breadth of the Olympic Zeus have been measured and recorded; but I shall not praise those who made the measurements, for even their records fall short of the impression made by a sight of the image. Nay, the god himself according to legend bore witness to the artistic skill of Pheidias. For when the image was quite finished Pheidias prayed the god to show by a sign whether the work was to his liking. Immediately, runs the legend, a thunderbolt fell on that part of the floor where down to the present day the bronze jar stood to cover the place" (ET Pausanias, *Description of Greece* [LCL; 5 vols.; trans. W. H. S. Jones and H. A. Ormerod; Cambridge, MA: Harvard University Press, 2000] 2.443). See also what follows, about the care of the ivory statue with olive oil. On this holding together of the concepts of statue-as-object and statue-as-god, see Gordon, "The Real and the Imaginary," 16.

> τε μορφήν), and besides its being in man's form, you made its attributes (τἄλλα) as you made it? We investigate these things now. . . . For in former days, when we knew nothing with certainty, we each formed his or her own idea, each according to his or her ability and nature picturing and dreaming [the gods]. If there were somehow certain small or weak likenesses by ancient artists, we would neither quite believe them at all, nor pay attention to them. But you by the might of craft first conquered and brought together Greece, then others, by this sign (φάσματι); you created something more than human and magnificent, so that it was not easy for those who saw it to hold any other opinion. (12.52–53)[70]

Pheidias is prosecuted on three counts. First, did he indeed make the right decision in his choice of materials (chryselephantine, that is, gold and ivory, bolstered by a cypress wood core)? Second, did he choose rightly in making the statue in a man's form and with the "other things" – that is, attributes – it has? Third, and most interesting, by his skill and by the beauty and power of his image did Pheidias rob humans of a rich imagination of the divine?

Pheidias defends himself, insisting that it is better to have some "shrine or image of the gods" than none (12.60). He ultimately defends his material manifestations of the gods by appealing to the connections between images of the gods and the piety directed towards them. "On account of the inclination to the spiritual (τὸ δαιμόνιον), a mighty *eros* exists within all humans to honor and to worship the divine, approaching and touching with persuasion, sacrificing and crowning [it]" (12.60–61). Just as stories of the origin of images from Pliny, the *Wisdom of Solomon*, and Minucius Felix posit the creation of images as a result of longing and absence, so too Pheidias explains: "For just as infant children artlessly [ἀτεχνῶς is a deliberate pun on the *technē* or craft of artisans] have a terrible yearning and desire for father or mother when they have been torn away from them, and they stretch out their hands often while they are dreaming to those who are not present, thus also humans do to the gods, justly loving them on account of both their benefaction and kinship, eager to be with and to associate with them in every way" (12.61). Images are a poignant second-best to presence. They are a childish grasping after absence. From absence, desire and longing emerge, and these are satisfied or stoked by some representation – of a lover gone to travel, of a beloved child who has died, or of a god. One implication of this theological debate is that it is not only Pheidias's chryselephantine masterpiece, but also his choice to represent the god in human form, that constrains the theological imagination. Similarly, as we have seen in the *Wisdom of Solomon* and Minucius Felix's *Octavius*, when

[70] The Greek edition is J. von Arnim, *Dionis Prusaensis quem vocant Chrysostomum quae exstant omnia* (2 vols.; 1893–96; repr. Berlin: Weidmann, 1962).

people first made images of humans, the human form was quickly understood to stand in for the divine (or the divine was understood to be manifest in human form).

Dio defends Pheidias (or has him defend himself) in the midst of a broader debate about images and their potentially deceptive powers to ruin true piety, stretching back to Plato and forward to the second century. In the first century BCE, Cicero engaged this question in multiple ways, condemning the robbery and expatriation of images in his *Verrine Orations*, even as he wrote with nervous eagerness to his own antiquities dealer in Athens, requesting the perfect art objects for his villa.[71] Cicero's *De natura deorum* is a philosophical dialogue that includes multiple viewpoints on imagining and then imaging the gods. The Epicurean speaker, Velleius, offers this: "But if the human figure surpasses the form of all other living beings, and god is a living being, god must possess the shape which is the most beautiful of all; . . . it follows that the gods possess the form of man. Yet their form is not corporeal, but only resembles bodily substance; it does not contain blood, but the semblance of blood (*Nec tamen ea species corpus est, sed quasi corpus, nec habet sanguinem, sed quasi sanguinem*)" (*De nat. deo.* 1.48–49).[72] Velleius's gods are statues. This description of the anthropomorphic gods prefigures later *ekphraseis* of statuary that entranced the reader with narrative descriptions of statues that looked like they had just taken a breath, the veins pulsing on their necks.[73]

Velleius's interlocutor, Cotta, immediately pursues this question of divine bodies and statuary. Cotta knows that Velleius's philosophical statement about the nature of the gods is found everywhere physically manifest in images; he even refers to the Venus of Cos (1.75). Cotta also knows that Velleius spouts jargon, "'It is not body but a semblance of body,'" he quotes Velleius, scoffing. "I could understand what this supposition meant if it related to waxed images or figures of earthenware, but what 'a semblance of body' or 'a semblance of blood' may mean in the case of god, I cannot understand; nor can you

71 Cicero especially criticizes Verres because he uses the public goods of the Sicilians not for the public good of Rome but for his own private luxury. Margaret M. Miles, *Art as Plunder: The Ancient Origins of Debate about Cultural Property* (New York: Cambridge University Press, 2008) 105–51; Miranda Marvin, "Copying in Roman Sculpture: The Replica Series," 161–88 in Eve D'Ambra, ed., *Roman Art in Context* (Englewood Cliffs, NJ: Prentiss-Hall, 1993). Her appendix includes Cicero's letters concerning finding and purchasing images.

72 ET Cicero, *De Natura Deorum; Academica* (LCL; trans. H. Rackham; reprinted Cambridge, MA: Harvard University Press, 2000) 49.

73 Part of the art critical game of the second century and beyond was that one's ability to describe the living, breathing qualities of a given image added not only to the image's own prestige but also to the idea that author's *ekphrasis* can come to supersede the image itself. See Elsner, *Art and the Roman Viewer*, 15–155; Stephen Bann, *The True Vine: On Visual Representation and the Western Tradition* (Cambridge: Cambridge University Press, 1989) 27–40 on the possibility of *ekphrasis* as a deliberate language of excess which marks the defect of language in comparison to image.

either, Velleius, or you won't admit it" (1.71).[74] Cotta insists that, whatever this nonsense means, the practice of image-making is at base a bit deceitful. "Was there ever any student so blind as not to see that human shape has been thus assigned to the gods either by the deliberate contrivance of philosophers, the better to enable them to turn the hearts of the ignorant from vicious practices to the observance of religion, or by superstition, to supply images for men to worship in the belief that in so doing they had direct access to the divine presence?" (1.77).[75] Every animal, states Cotta, prefers its own species; every person dreaming of a goddess pictures her with the form and attributes that s/he knows from her or his homeland.[76] These images are convenient ways to grasp the gods, fabricated for the ignorant and superstitious, but they are nothing more.[77]

The second-century Maximus of Tyre, whose inclinations are more philosophical and Platonizing than those of Cicero or Dio, reminds us that those who stretch toward images of the gods are like children – perhaps the abandoned children that Dio's Pheidias mentioned, perhaps the infantilized ignorant that Cicero discusses. "In just the same way, divinity in its own nature has no need of statues and dedications; but humanity, an utterly feeble species that lies as far from the divine as heaven from earth, contrived them as symbols through which to preserve the gods' names and their reputations. People whose memories are strong, and who can reach straight out for the heavens with their souls and encounter the divine, may perhaps have no need of images" (*Or.* 2.2).[78] For Maximus, images of the gods are like the faint outlines that teachers draw to guide the pupil's hand as s/he learns letters. They are "for a class of children" in order to help humans to find a "kind of pathway to recollection (πρὸς ἀνάμνησιν)" (2.2). The gods do not need statues; humans

[74] ET Rackham, 69; see also *De nat. deo.* 1.71–75.

[75] ET Rackham, 73, 75. The passage continues: "These notions moreover have been fostered by poets, painters and artificers, who found it difficult to represent living and active deities in the likeness of any other shape than that of man. Perhaps also man's belief in his own superior beauty, to which you referred, may have contributed to the result."

[76] Cicero *De nat. deo.* 1.81; ET Rackham, 79: "Very likely we Romans do imagine god as you say, because from our childhood Jupiter, Juno, Minerva, Neptune, Vulcan, and Apollo have been known to us with the aspect with which painters and sculptors have chosen to represent them, and not with that aspect only, but having that equipment (*ornatu*), age, and dress. But they are not so known to the Egyptians or Syrians, or any almost of the uncivilized (*barbaria*) races." On this diversity of the gods, see Ando, *Matter of the Gods*, chap. 3.

[77] The Stoic viewpoint, offered by Lucilius Balbus, is concerned with the power of seeing among the senses. "Nothing is more difficult than to divert the eye of the mind from following the practice of bodily sight," he mourns; "uneducated people and those philosophers who resemble the uneducated to be unable to conceive of the immortal gods without setting before themselves the forms of men" (*De nat. deo.* 2.45; ET Rackham, 165, 167).

[78] ET Maximus, *The Philosophical Orations* (trans. M. B. Trapp; New York: Oxford University Press, 1997) 18. The Greek edition is Michael B. Trapp, ed., *Maximus Tyrius Dissertationes* (Leipzig: Teubner, 1994).

do.[79] Again, viewers who appreciate rather than resist images are depicted as of lower *paideia* and status than the writers themselves. The writers understand that the divine is best known through the mind, and that images in satisfying the eye can dim the mind's eye. As we saw earlier in Justin's *Apology*, images and their creation are often associated with those of low status and even low morals, with those who misunderstand the nature and power of signs.[80]

So should one make images, if they are second best? Why do humans use the material world to try to know, intellectually, the divine (ἐπιθυμούντες μὲν αὐτοῦ τῆς νοήσεως, 2.10)? Maximus concludes his oration by echoing what we have already seen in Plato's *Phaedrus*: the connection between *eros*, vision, and the pursuit of divine truth. "This very thing is the pathos of lovers, to whom the forms of [their] darlings are the sweetest thing for sight; sweet in recollection is also a lyre and a javelin or a seat or a running track, or simply anything that effects the memory of the beloved.[81] Why then does it remain to me to examine and to lay down the law about images? Let them know the divine race; let them only know it. If the *technē* of Pheidias aroused the Greeks to the memory of God, if the honor rendered to animals roused the Egyptians, and others a river and others fire, I am not upset at the diversity. Let them only know, let them only love, let them recollect!" (2.10).[82] Maximus realizes the power of images to rouse people to passions and actions and is sympathetic to this poignant situation.

Maximus brings us full circle. We began this section with several texts that suggested that images originated from human longing for the absent lover, the lost child, the revered ruler. A long thread of discussion, from the first-century BCE *Wisdom of Solomon* to the second-century CE Maximus and beyond, understands images as pedagogical. They lead people towards the gods who are dangerous when visible, according to Athenagoras.[83] One prominent discourse threaded through several centuries also understands images to satisfy human longing and desire for the visibly absent human or divine. Images are inextricably linked with *eros* and absence.

79 The world is such that "no race, Greek or foreign, seafaring or landsmen, nomadic or urban, can bring itself to dispense with establishing some kind of symbols for the honour they pay their gods" (*Or.* 2.9; ET Trapp, 23).

80 See p. 167 see also Gordon, "The Real and the Imaginary," 10: ". . . a continuous series of metaphors and antitheses registering the ambiguous status of the art object (and especially sculptures and painted figures) suggests to me a 'deliberate' refusal on the part of the majority in the ancient world to take the 'sensible' way out adopted by different philosophical traditions, particularly Platonism and Stoicism: the development of a theory of the imagination."

81 Trapp notes in his edition that Maximus echoes Plato *Phaedo* 73D.

82 My translation after Trapp.

83 "The gods are dangerous when they appear visibly": Athenagoras *Leg.* 18.1 quoting Homer *Il.* 20.131; see discussion on p. 205.

II. TATIAN, SPECTACLE, AND CONNOISSEURSHIP

By providing this overview of ancient discussions of the origins of images in absence and desire, the tactile qualities of seeing, and concerns over how images affect the theological imagination of viewers, I have set a broad context within which to understand Christian writers' discussions of images. What does an image do? What does it evoke; what does it teach? What happens, tactilely, when we see a god? Do statues or images effectively stand in for the thing we truly desire? Are these famous (classically Greek) images a commodity that restricts the theological imagination?

We have already met Tatian, Justin's student, who wrote between the 150s and 170s. *To the Greeks*, his only writing to survive in full, may date to the late 170s.[84] In it, he called himself "a philosopher among barbarians, born in the land of the Assyrians, educated (παιδευθείς) first in your things, second in those which I now profess to proclaim" (*Ad Graec.* 42.1).[85] Tatian asserts his training in Christian, not Greek, *paideia* or education.[86] On the cultural map of the Roman Empire, he places Christians not among the Greeks, as did his teacher Justin, but remakes Christian identity by proudly locating himself among the barbarians. He implies that he is a sort of new Anacharsis, that Scythian barbarian whom the ancient Greeks considered a paragon of wisdom, and he insists that he should be taken at least as seriously as an "oracular oak," alluding to the ancient oak of Dodona, the movement of whose leaves was thought to offer oracles.[87] Surely Tatian, the barbarian Assyrian, who is at least human, might be on par with a waving tree. Here and throughout we should recognize Tatian's quick tongue and sharp wit, rather than accusing him of

[84] R. M. Grant, "The Date of Tatian's Oration," *HTR* 46.2 (1953) 99; idem, *Greek Apologists of the Second Century* (Philadelphia: Westminster, 1988) 112–15. Grant associates the tone of Tatian's writing with the martyrdoms at Vienne and Lyon in 177, as well as the imperial donation in 176 of four professorships of philosophy and one of rhetoric at Athens. See also G. W. Clarke, "The Date of the Oration of Tatian," *HTR* 60.1 (1967) 123–26.

[85] On the use of the term "Assyrian" rather than "Syrian," see Grant, *Greek Apologists*, 115, who notes that Lucian too calls himself Assyrian in *De Dea Syria*.

[86] On a later concept of Christian *paideia*, see Werner Jaeger, *Early Christianity and Greek Paideia* (Cambridge: Belknap, 1961) 86–102.

[87] *Ad Graec.* 12.4: "You who do not curse the Scythian Anacharsis, now too do not be so indignant that you cannot learn from those who follow a barbarian law-code (βαρβαρικῇ νομοθεσίᾳ)." See also Lucian, *The Scythian*. My translations are aided by Molly Whittaker, *Oratio ad Graecos and Fragments* (New York: Clarendon, 1982). The Greek edition is Miroslav Marcovich, *Tatiani Oratio ad Graecos; Theophili Antiocheni ad Autolycum* (Berlin: De Gruyter, 1995), who relies primarily on Eduard Schwartz's edition; I do not use his numbering system, however, but Whittaker's (originally Goodspeed's). There are four extant manuscripts of Tatian's text; all are likely apographs from a missing portion of the Arethas codex (Marcovich, *Tatiani*, vii, 1–4); Emily J. Hunt, *Christianity in the Second Century: The Case of Tatian* (New York: Routledge, 2003) 2. For a list of Arethas's additions to the text of Tatian, see Eduard Schwartz, *Tatiani Oratio ad Graecos* (Leipzig: J. C. Hinrichs'sche Buchhandlung, 1888) 44–47.

angry ranting, as so many scholars have.[88] Tatian, in his critique of Greek *paideia* and art, and his implied critique of Roman interest in them, positions himself as a satirical outsider looking in, as did Lucian.[89]

It is perhaps because Tatian positioned himself as an outsider that he is so marginal in the study of early Christianity. He is most famous for having (perhaps) written the *Diatessaron*, a synopsis of the four gospels in Syriac popular for centuries, despite its eventually losing to the four-gospel canon.[90] He was also accused of extreme views regarding sex and the body, views which some might argue affected his perception of Greek spectacle and statuary. Clement of Alexandria said that Tatian considered even marital sex to lead to corruption, and quotes a now-lost work where Tatian discussed Paul's statement in 1 Corinthians 7 that it is better to marry than to burn (with passion) (*Strom.* 3.12).[91] Irenaeus criticizes Tatian for teaching against eating animal food and for rejecting marriage; Jerome names Tatian "founder of the Encratites," someone committed to extreme control of the flesh, or, as Kathy Gaca puts it, "sexually alienated." Gaca, Irenaeus, and Jerome are unfair. In the text that does remain to us, *To the Greeks*, Tatian's emphasis on Christian purity and self-control is one along a range of common Christian arguments that demonstrate – literally, bodily manifest – the philosophical nature and self-control of its adherents.[92]

88 R. M. Grant, "The Heresy of Tatian," *JTS* 5.1 (1954) 63 uses the phrase "violent polemic." Regarding Tatian's section on mythology and astrology, Grant states, "Tatian's discussion is intemperate, incomplete, and poorly arranged" (*Greek Apologists*, 121). Gerald Hawthorne ("Tatian and His Discourse to the Greeks," *HTR* 57.3 [1964] 162) states, "The tone of the Discourse is violently hostile, harshly dogmatic." For a new understanding of Tatian, which questions his authorship of the *Diatessaron* and shows how he was used in intra-Christian debates, see Naomi Koltun-Fromm, "Re-Imagining Tatian: The Damaging Effects of Polemical Rhetoric," *JECS* 16.1 (2008) 1–30.

89 On Tatian's use of ethnic categories and his similarities to Lucian, see Chapter 2. On Tatian as part of the sophistic movement, and for a truly remarkable analysis of his rhythm and style, see Aimé Puech, *Recherches sur le Discours aux Grecs de Tatien, suivies d'une traduction française du Discours avec notes* (Paris: F. Alcan, 1903) 2, 16–26; see also 31–36 on stylistic problems and solecisms.

90 William Petersen, "Tatian's Diatessaron," in Helmut Koester, *Ancient Christian Gospels: Their History and Development* (Valley Forge, PA: Trinity Press International, 1990) 403–30, Koltrun-Fromm, "Re-Imagining Tatian," 18.

91 Clement also accused Tatian of following Valentinian Gnostic ideas, and hints that Tatian drove a wedge between the god of the Old Testament and the New, like Marcion. On the idea of Tatian as influenced by Valentinianism, see Grant, "The Heresy of Tatian," 64–67 and a refutation in Hunt, *Christianity in the Second Century*, 20–51.

92 Irenaeus *Adv. haer.* 1.28.1; Jerome *In amos* 2.12; *In ep. ad Tit.* praef; *In ep. ad Gal.* 6.8. See Molly Whittaker, "Tatian's Educational Background," in Elizabeth Livingstone, ed., *Studia Patristica*, vol. 13: *Papers Presented to the Sixth International Conference on Patristic Studies Held in Oxford 1971, Part II: Classica et Hellenica, Theologica, Liturgica, Ascetica* (Berlin: Akademie-Verlag, 1975) 82–83. Kathy Gaca, in her analysis of Christian responses to sexuality in the ancient world, assumes that this calumny regarding Tatian as Encratite is a fact (*The Making of Fornication: Eros, Ethics, and Political Reform in Greek Philosophy and Early Christianity* [Berkeley: University of California Press, 2003] chap. 8). But many Christians were accused by later

Tatian begins his speech "to the Greeks" with a critique of pretensions of Greekness and throughout he displays his knowledge of Greek *paideia* even as he challenges it. This is true of nearly all of our texts of focus: Athenagoras, Justin, and Clement at length criticize Greek cult and the incoherence of various Greek philosophical arguments about religion and the gods. Tatian is unusual because he starts by attacking the Greek language itself, which was considered one of the glories and markers of Greek culture in the Roman period. As Simon Swain puts it, "Atticism – the use of a classicizing form of Greek – was socially significant for a very simple reason: one had to have the social leisure and economic stability to educate oneself sufficiently to be able to command the vocabulary and grammatical structures that distinguished Atticism from ordinary Greek. Thus linguistic purism in this period is a sign of elite solidarity and speaking the correct language was a way of . . . demonstrating rapport/camaraderie with fellow members of the upper classes."[93] Certainly other non-Christian contemporaries also mocked the pretensions of the Atticizing Greek popular in their day. In Pseudo-Lucian's *The Consonants at Law*, the letter sigma takes the letter tau to court for stealing words; the story thus satirizes the antiquarian preference in this period to use the conventions of classical, Attic Greek rather than to accept language's evolution, which had replaced the double tau with a double sigma (note Dio's use of *plēttō* above!). Lucian talks about provincials who correctly ape Atticizing Greek and are thus marketable rhetorical teachers in Rome; he also satirizes the effeminate, low-born, shameless rhetor who by his arrogance, appearance, and fifteen to twenty words of Attic Greek impresses an audience.[94]

Clearing the smoke and removing the mirrors, Tatian argues that Greek language, culture, and identity are not unitary and superior but are constituted by pillaging from other ethnicities: "Stop your triumphal procession (θριαμβεύοντες) of another's words," he insists (26.1). "Triumphal procession" conjures up a ritual parade of prisoners and spoils of war of the sort that Josephus described after the Jewish War. Tatian accuses the Greeks of verbal pillaging and even linguistic connoisseurship or collecting: "Stop decorating yourselves with feathers that aren't your own, as if you're a jackdaw!" (26.1).

writers of being part of some or the other heretical sect; see Koltun-Fromm, "Re-imagining Tatian," for a careful exposition of what we can know about Tatian from his own writing, instead of the calumnies of heresiological writing.

93 Swain, "Polemon's *Physiognomy*," 142.

94 See *Rhet. praec.* 16; see also 11ff where the guide to the quick route to Rhetoric is described this way: "Even if you had your eyes shut, and he should come and speak to you, opening that Hymettian mouth, and letting loose the customary voice, you discover that he is not like us 'who eat of the fruit of the glebe' [Homer *Il.* 6.142] but some unfamiliar apparition (φάσμα), nurtured on dew or ambrosia" (ET Lucian, *Works*, 4.149, 151, with slight modifications). Eventually we find that this guide up the path to the lady Rhetoric is himself born of an Egyptian slave and a seamstress mother (24). Lucian's wicked satire continues, with a description of an effeminate guide who insists on leaving behind all shame and moderation (15).

Instead of the Romans conquering, dragging away the war prizes of Greek statuary, Tatian depicts the Greeks hauling in the booty of various other nations, material and linguistic, and enriching themselves not by their "indigenous" arts but by prizes stolen from others. Tatian exposes the game. Greek language, one of the basic markers of Greek culture, is not unitary, despite claims made to common genealogies and mythic origins – claims of the sort that we saw in Hadrian's Panhellenion. Those who purchase "Greekness" buy a sham product: a bricolage language, culture, and ethnicity produced for a particular market. We know from Cicero and others of the Roman penchant for collecting and copying or emulating Greek antiquities; we know too about Roman tendencies, even before the technical period of empire, to take statuary and other arts as booty from the Greeks. Tatian thus slyly implicates the Romans in his critique of the Greeks. They, like the Greeks, have "decorated themselves with feathers that aren't their own"; in triumphal processions and places like the "Temple of Peace" they have displayed their acquired, famed cultural objects, as we saw in Josephus's writings.[95] The Romans too have been duped into purchasing the cultural commodity of unified "Greekness," as well as the prized goods of "barbarian" nations.

Thus, like Clement's *Exhortation*, a slightly later text that also has been understood to address Greeks, Tatian's *To the Greeks* focuses on a critique of Greek culture but in doing so thoroughly implicates the Romans who have literally bought into this *paideia*. His examples of depravity even extend to the Roman emperors. In the midst of his argument against *daimones* who deceive and gods who can metamorphize into animals and monsters, Tatian swipes at the very human Antinoos, the emperor Hadrian's lover, who somehow upon his death became a god or transformed into a new Ganymede, Zeus's own wine-pourer and beloved. "How is it that the dead Antinoos, a beautiful young man, received a shrine in the moon? . . . Why have you robbed my God? Why do you dishonor God's creation?" (10.2). In addressing his treatise to the Greeks, Tatian also speaks to all involved in the new production of Greek culture, even Romans, and even and especially Hadrian with his economic support of antiquarian Greek cult and his deification of his lover. Unlike Athenagoras, who blamed theological misunderstandings on the lower-status masses, Tatian locates cultural and religious corruption among elite connoisseurs who fancy Attic Greek and classical and Hellenistic sculpture.[96]

95 See pp. 162–63.

96 We find a similar argument, differently stated, in Pliny, who complains about the debasing of what we might call realistic portraiture precisely because of connoisseurship. While images used to conjure the ancestors, with wax masks of their faces carried in procession and displayed in the home, now "they prize the likeness of strangers," he insists, "while as for themselves they imagine that the honour only consists in the price, for their heirs to break up the statue and haul it out of the house with a noose. Consequently nobody's likeness lives and they leave behind them portraits that represent their money, not themselves" (*Nat. hist.* 35.2.5; ET Rackham, 263, 265).

Tatian at the Theater

Tatian, like other authors we have seen, offers the typical argument about how ridiculous it is to believe in gods who are matter: "How can I declare wood and stones as gods?" (4.2). Tatian too is concerned with the issue of form and reality, of representation and truth. Tatian brings together critique of *panēgyreis* or religious-civic festivals with a critique of mis-representation. "I saw a certain man many times," Tatian begins, "and when I saw him, I was amazed and, after being amazed, I was disdainful of how he deceived: He is one person inwardly but outwardly he is what he is not" (22.1). (Why Tatian was viewing this actor frequently if he was so contemptuous of spectacle is a question that remains unanswered.) I deliberately translate awkwardly to show the double-edged sword of some of Tatian's description of this actor: "He was exceedingly delicate and softly enervated in all kinds of ways, and he flashed his eyes, he also twisted his hands around and through a clay mask he expressed madness/was possessed by a *daimōn*, and became at one time like Aphrodite, then like Apollo. He was a one-man prosecutor for/betrayer of all the gods, the epitome of piety/superstition, doing slander to the heroes, an expounder/actor of murders" (22.1).[97] Tatian uses the representational instability of language to mimic the effect of a spectacle that does not teach and edify, but confuses. What is real and what is false? What does it mean that the actor is the epitome of *deisidaimonia*, a word used to mean either piety or superstition? In a world of masks Tatian protests false representations that mislead the young and allow for public obscenities – for entertainment that is not entertaining, or religious festivals that are not at all pious.

Spectacle and statuary are joined in literal ways in the ancient world. We can think of the story of the three thousand statues for the temporary *scaenae frons* (scene building). Or we can picture a variety of other theaters and *odeia* ("lecture or performance halls") such as that of Herodes Atticus at Athens, similarly busy with *aediculae* framing statues, usually of the imperial family and prominent citizens, as well as with reliefs, often of mythical scenes of the gods and heroes.[98] The architecture of the *scaenae frons* contained representations;

[97] Εἶδόν τινα πολλάκις, καὶ ἰδὼν ἐθαύμασα καὶ μετὰ τὸ θαυμάσαι κατεφρόνησα <κατανόησας> πῶς ἔσωθεν μέν ἐστιν ἄλλος, ἔξωθεν δὲ ὅπερ οὐκ ἔστι ψεύδεται· ἁβρυνόμενον σφόδρα καὶ παντοίως διακλώμενον, καὶ τοῦτο μέν τοῖς ὀφθαλμοῖς μαρμαρύσσοντα, τοῦτο δὲ [καὶ] τὼ χεῖρε λυγιζόμενον καὶ διὰ πηλίνης ὄψεως διαμονῶντα, καὶ ποτὲ μὲν ὡς Ἀφροδίτην, ποτὲ δὲ ὡς Ἀπόλλωνα <παρα>γινόμενον· ἕνα κατήγορον <ὄντα> πάντων τῶν θεῶν, δεισιδαιμονίας ἐπιτομήν, διάβολον ἡρωϊκῶν πράξεων, φόνων ὑποκριτήν. See Lucian *Reviv.* 31ff regarding a shape-shifting "womanish" actor playing characters such as Theseus and Herakles.

[98] Pliny *Nat. hist.* 36.114; see further discussion Stewart, *Statues in Roman Society*, 1–2, 118–56. See also, e.g., Jennifer Ferol Trimble, "The Aesthetics of Sameness: A Contextual Analysis of the Large and Small Herculaneum Woman Statue Types in the Roman Empire," (Ph.D. dissertation, Department of Classical Art and Archaeology, University of Michigan, 1999) 27–30 on statuary and hierarchy in theaters.

of course representations were the business onstage as well, with actors and pantomimes wearing masks.[99]

In this environment, Tatian takes offense not only at the actor's effeminate gestures, but also at his ability to be sometimes Aphrodite and sometimes Apollo. Thus, just as statues might try to capture the character of a human or represent the divine, humans too in theatrical performances were mimetic. The actor could represent both sexes, could represent the gods, could *be* a god, and could be praised by the audience for this ability to metamorphosize.[100] Each aspect of this offends Tatian. Such spectacle is pedagogical, Tatian asserts, and what, really, are you supposed to learn from this character? These are foul words, obscene gestures, adultery, and wickedness which "your daughters and sons view" (22.2).

"All the world is a stage"; representational confusion extends past the theater.[101] As Tatian (and others, including Lucian) complains, philosophers dress the part and claim to have no needs, but are gluttons for pleasures (25.1). The Attic Greek that is the coin of the realm for philosophers, sophists, and the elites, the essence of Greekness, is revealed to be merely foreign words led in procession masquerading as autochthonous talent (26.1). Just as Tatian opposes the linguistic triumphal procession of Greek, so also he lives in a world of imagistic triumphalism. In Simon Goldhill's terms, "both the circulation of images – statues of Antinous by Hadrian, say – and the spectacle in performance – games sponsored by the elite in Rome and throughout the provinces, for example – construct a regime in and through which authority, status, positions are negotiated in the field of the visual."[102] And, Tatian would say, so also truth is negotiated in the field of the visual.

Tatian's Grand Tour

Tatian addresses this issue of representation not in the context of an appeal to Roman judicial tolerance, as Justin and Athenagoras did, but specifically in the context of culture wars. After speaking about statuary in *To the Greeks*, he states, "Therefore I set these observations down not from second-hand knowledge, but I haunted much of the earth and played the sophist, toying

[99] See, e.g., Eckart Köhne and Cornelia Ewigleben, eds., *Gladiators and Caesars: The Power of Spectacle in Ancient Rome* (Hamburg: Museum für Kunst und Gewerbe and London: British Museum Press, 2000) fig. 129.

[100] See Dio's critique of the Alexandrians who love the theater (pp. 270–71).

[101] See Mary Beard, "The Triumph of the Absurd: Roman Street Theater," in Catharine Edwards and Greg Woolf, eds., *Rome the Cosmopolis* (Cambridge: Cambridge University Press, 2003) 34–43 on theater and confusion about representation. Tatian moves from a critique of acting to one of gladiatorial spectacles (*Ad Graec.* 23.2).

[102] Goldhill, "The Erotic Eye," 159. See also Elsner, *Art and the Roman Viewer*; Stewart, *Statues in Roman Society*; Christopher A. Frilingos, *Spectacles of Empire: Monsters, Martyrs, and the Book of Revelation* (Philadelphia: University of Pennsylvania Press, 2004).

with your goods. I set this forth having met with much art and ideas, but finally I spent time in the city of the Romans and learned thoroughly the varieties of statues that they took away from you as theirs. For I did not try, as is the custom of the majority, to empower myself with others' opinions, but I wished to put in order a record of all these things I myself have made from direct apprehension" (35.1).[103] Tatian guarantees the truth of his insights by stating that he is an eye-witness; his discussion of statuary is hard-won from long travels, not a mere catalog ungrounded in experience.[104] Moreover, Tatian punctures the pride of his constructed interlocutors, the *andres Hellēnes* ("Greeks"), by casually pointing out that what he knows of Greek culture, he knows from Rome.[105] I have already mentioned Cicero's *Verrine Orations*, which criticize Roman appropriation of indigenous patrimony and specifically Verres's stealing of cultural artifacts; Cicero also claims that foreigners in Rome wept as they recognized pieces taken from their homeland.[106] Moreover, this is a landscape that repeats. In an empire crowded with images and statuary bodies, Greek goods, whether stolen or repeated in casts and copies, were available for Roman consumption. Indeed, Greek images ceased to *be* Greek and became

[103] Ταῦτα μὲν οὖν οὐ παρ' ἄλλου μαθὼν ἐξεθέμην, πολλὴν δὲ ἐπιφοιτήσας γῆν, καὶ τοῦτο μὲν σοφιστεύσας τὰ ὑμέτερα, τοῦτο δὲ τέχναις καὶ ἐπινοίαις ἐγκυρήσας πολλαῖς, ἔσχατον δὲ τῇ Ῥωμαίων ἐνδιατρίψας πόλει καὶ τὰς ἀφ' ὑμῶν ὡς αὐτοὺς ἀνακομισθείσας ἀνδριάντων ποικιλίας καταμαθών. Οὐ γάρ, ὡς ἔθος ἐστὶ τοῖς πολλοῖς, ἀλλοτρίαις δόξαις τἀμαυτοῦ κρατύνειν πειρῶμαι, πάντων δὲ ὧν <ἂν> αὐτὸς ποιήσωμαι τὴν κατάληψιν, τούτων καὶ τὴν ἀναγραφὴν συντάσσειν βούλομαι.

[104] On autopsy in the ancient world, see, e.g., Jaś Elsner, "Describing Self in the Language of Other: Pseudo (?) Lucian at the Temple of Hierapolis," in Goldhill, ed., *Being Greek under Rome*, 123–53; and esp. François Hartog, *Memories of Odysseus* (trans. Janet Lloyd; Edinburgh: Edinburgh University Press, 2001). The position of Tatian's argument about travel and statuary in the middle of a section on the antiquity of Christianity is odd. See the outline of Martin Elze, *Tatian und seine Theologie* (Göttingen: Vandenhoeck and Ruprecht, 1960) 52, who calls it an excursus. On the integrity of this passage within Tatian, see R. C. Kukula, *'Alterbeweis' und 'Künsterkatalog' in Tatians Rede an die Griechen* (Vienna: self-published, 1900) esp. 17–19 and his brief commentary of the same year: R. C. Kukula, *Tatians sogenannte Apologie* (Leipzig: Teubner, 1900). Puech is in agreement with Kukula that the passage usually called the "catalogue of artists" is a deliberate interruption of the flow of the narrative, a technique borrowed from rhetorical tradition (*Recherches sur le Discours aux Grecs de Tatien*, 35).

[105] Grant argues that the stolen objects are "primarily from Athens" (*Greek Apologists*, 118), although he does not clarify how we could know this. On the idea of making pilgrimage elsewhere to see your own patrimony, see David Noy, "Rabbi Aqila Comes to Rome: A Jewish Pilgrimage in Reverse?" in Jaś Elsner and Ian Rutherford, eds., *Pilgrimage in Graeco-Roman and Early Christian Antiquity: Seeing the Gods* (Oxford: Oxford University Press, 2005) 374–85.

[106] Cicero *Verr.* 2.1.59: "For a large number of persons from Asia and Achaia, who happened at the time to be in Rome serving on deputations, beheld in our Forum the revered images of their gods that had been carried away from their own sanctuaries, and recognizing as well the other statues and works of art, some here and some there, would stand gazing at them with weeping eyes." ET Cicero, *The Verrine Orations* (LCL; 19 vols.; trans. L. H. G. Greenwood; New York: G. P. Putnam's Sons, 1927) 7.183. Miles, *Art as Plunder*; Bettina Bergmann, "Greek Masterpieces and Roman Recreative Fictions," *HSCP* 97 (1995) 91.

thoroughly Roman, interpretations of Greek *paideia* proudly signed by the Roman artists who (re)made them.[107] But Tatian with the word *anakomizein* ("to bring back" or "to take away") leaves no doubt that these are indeed stolen goods – and here the knife drives deeper – "from you."

From his travels, Tatian claims to have gained hard-won but despicable knowledge. Just as he has already questioned why certain stories of the gods' adulteries and injustices should be embodied and re-presented in myth and song, so also Tatian questions why the Greek sculptures that he has seen are considered powerful and culturally valued. What, he wonders, in the "social lives of things" would have led to *these* objects being aesthetically valued by "Greek" culture (no matter how he deconstructs that culture at the same time) and culturally valued by the Romans?

This Greek sculptures listed in Tatian's own, guaranteed eyewitness catalog show that Greek *paideia* is monstrous. Most of the sculptures discussed depict women.[108] In the few cases when the names of sculpture of men are included, Tatian describes ones who are extreme or monstrous: Aristodemos's sculpture of Aesop, the hunchback and hideous slave and philosopher (and truth-teller), and Polyneikes and Eteokles the fratricides. "Certainly the tyrant Phalaris is also quite renowned, who feasted upon not-yet-weaned children. . . . The people of Akragas feared to look at the face of the aforementioned, on account of his cannibalism, but those care for *paideia* boast that they have seen him through his image" (34.1). Tatian suggests how we *should* see the image: We should take on the eyes of the population of Akragas, who knew to fear it. He seeks to undermine the connoisseur's approach to the image by equating "culture" and the monstrous.

Tatian's comments on statuary are launched as part of an argument that he is having with "the Greeks" and their *paideia*. He emphasizes that "we" do not have cultured adherents, but women, youngsters, and the poor. These, however, have become philosophical by the teachings they are freely offered (32.1–3); famous Greek heroes are in contrast embarrassingly unphilosophical. Tatian continues, "I am eager to prove from the things you consider to be honorable that our customs are self-controlled (σωφρονεῖ), while yours come close to real madness" (33.1).[109]

Tatian rests the bulk of his argument against Greek statuary upon the bodies, real and sculpted, of women. Lysippus made a bronze of the poet Praxilla;

[107] On copying and emulation, see the discussion and bibliography on pp. 5–6. On signing, see, e.g., Bergmann, "Greek Masterpieces," 103.

[108] Kukula argues that at the end of *To the Greeks* Tatian offers both a chronology and a section on "art criticism" as proofs of Christian truth against paganism (*'Altersbeweis' und 'Künstlerkatalog,'* 14).

[109] See Gaca, *The Making of Fornication*, 235–39, who overstates the case and argues that Tatian hated Greek gods, especially Aphrodite, and sexual activity in general; see, however, Hunt, *Christianity in the Second Century*, 64.

Silanion sculpted "Sappho the *hetaira*" (33.1). "I want to speak about these women [i.e., statues of women he has just discussed] so that you may not think that what we do is strange, and, comparing [our] way of life by viewing [it], you may not scoff at the women who philosophize among us" (33.2). Tatian begins his criticism by pointing to the kind of women that have been sculpted, and the uselessness of the deeds that won them celebrity or commemoration. Praxilla's poetry is worthless despite her bronze statue; Sappho was not only a courtesan (*hetaira*) but also "a whore, a love-mad little woman, and she is praised for her licentiousness. But all our women are self-controlled and modest, and the virgins at the distaffs speak utterances concerning God, more worthy of serious attention than *your* girl. On this account you should be ashamed; you should seek to be disciples of [our] women, but you scoff at those women who take part in government together with us and with the gathering along with them" (33.2–3).[110] Tatian uses vocabulary associated with politics and schools to underline the philosophical nature of "our" women. What is the image of the sculpted Sappho supposed to teach, compared to the fleshly and breathing bodies of virtuous Christian women, Tatian challenges? The former might have claims to ecstatic poetry, but the latter offer serious (ecstatic and prophetic, we can assume) utterances about God.

Tatian's critique continues, highlighting the "specialities" or gifts of other women memorialized in sculpture. His emphasis on their monstrous sexuality is not primarily an argument about sex itself, although it is clear that Tatian, Justin, and others are proud of Christian philosophical self-control against *eros*. Tatian and Justin can use and allude to Platonic philosophy without succumbing to the *Phaedrus*'s dangerous conflation of vision, erotic love, and the pursuit of true knowledge.

Tatian's emphasis on the celebration of women's monstrous sexuality in Greek sculptures is an act of cultural criticism on two fronts. First, Tatian criticizes Greek women (and women are often the litmus test of cultural morality) and the cultural product of statuary (Greek objects so highly valued by Romans). Second, the status and connoisseurship of the *pepaideumenos theatēs* or educated viewer is called into question.

> Why is Glaukippe brought forward by you as a sacred object, who bore a monstrous child as her image (εἰκών) shows, which is cast in bronze by Nikeratos son of Euktemonos, an Athenian by race? For if she was

[110] καὶ ἡ μὲν Σαπφὼ γύναιον πορνικὸν ἐρωτομανές, καὶ τὴν ἑαυτῆς ἀσέλγειαν ᾄδει· πᾶσαι δὲ αἱ παρ' ἡμῖν σωφρονοῦσι, καὶ περὶ τὰς ἠλακάτας αἱ παρθένοι τὰ κατὰ θεὸν λαλοῦσιν ἐκφωνήματα, σπουδαιότερον τῆς παρ' ἡμῖν παιδός. Τούτου χάριν αἰδέσθητε, μαθηταὶ μὲν ὑμεῖς τῶν γυναίων εὑρισκόμενοι, τὰς δὲ σὺν ἡμῖν πολιτευομένας σὺν τῇ μετ' αὐτῶν ὁμηγύρει χλευάζοντες. *Gunaion* means wifey or weak woman. Gaca, *The Making of Fornication*, 237 translates this way: "Sappho, the sex-mad and cheap little whore." The Greek verb ἐκφωνέω also has a sense of crying out, perhaps in prophetic ecstasy. Sappho is a sore spot for Tatian, perhaps because she was considered an inspired poet, even as Christian women engaged in ecstatic speech were questioned regarding their inspiration.

> pregnant with an elephant, what cause was there for Glaukippe to enjoy public honor? Praxiteles and Herodotos made Phyrne the courtesan for you, and Euthykrates wrought Panteuxida in bronze after she was seized by a rapist. Deinomenes through his *technē* rendered Besantida the queen of the Panionians to be memorialized, because she conceived a black child. And I myself condemn Pythagoras for setting Europa upon a bull, and you, who have honored Zeus's accuser on account of his [Pythagoras's] *technē*. And I ridicule the skill of Mikon, who made a calf and, upon it, a Victory, because, by seizing the daughter of Agenor, it obtained a prize of adultery and lack of self-control. Why did Herodotos the Olynthian craft Glykera the courtesan and Argeia the lyre-player? Bryaxis set up Pasiphae; whose licentiousness you memorialize; and you all but prefer that such women exist now. A certain Melanippe was wise. Because of this, Lysistratos sculpted her, but you do not believe that there are wise women among us. (*Ad Graec.* 33.3–4)

The list continues, wending its way to the woman who had thirty children,[111] Ares seducing Aphrodite, and various prostitutes who had been memorialized in art. It concludes: "Why on account of Leochares have you honored Ganymede the man-woman, as if you had a worthwhile possession, and also a certain armleted woman that Praxiteles made?" (34.3). Thus Tatian closes by highlighting two images charged with great power and rhetorical force in the Roman Empire: that of Ganymede (often associated with the emperor Hadrian's lover, Antinoos),[112] and that of the Knidian Aphrodite, sculpted by Praxiteles. Tatian completes his invective by comparing the pedagogical effect of the long, foregoing list of sculptures to two famous sex manuals (34.3). These images lead the viewer not toward philosophical desire and self-knowledge, but toward illicit, obscene, unproductive desire.

With disgust, Tatian ends his musings on sculpture with the passage cited above, in which he drives home to the Greeks that he knows these works of art from "the city of the Romans" (35.1). "Saying goodbye both to the boasting of the Romans" – boasting, we can imagine, about these fantastic collections of objects – "and to the nonsense of the Athenians – their incoherent teachings – I sought after what is, according to you, barbarian philosophy" (35.1). Tatian maps the world according to ethnicity: the Romans, the Athenians, and barbarian philosophy. The citizenries of Rome and Athens

[111] For a possible source for Tatian or a common tradition, see Pliny *Nat. hist.* 7.3.34: "Pompey the Great among the decorations of his theatre placed images of celebrated marvels . . . ; among them we read of Eutychis who at Tralles . . . who had given birth 30 times, and Alcippe who gave birth to an elephant" (ET Rackham, 2.529). On similar rhetoric regarding women's bodies at another time period, including an account of a woman who prolifically produced rabbits rather than children, see Lisa Forman Cody, *Birthing the Nation: Sex, Science, and the Conception of Eighteenth-Century Britons* (New York: Oxford University Press, 2005).

[112] Ganymede and Zeus feature in Plato *Phaedrus* 255b in a discussion of erotic love and the "route to self-knowledge" (Bartsch, *The Mirror of the Self*, 80).

become synecdoches for the kinds of acquisitive power and knowledge that Tatian rejects; the umbrella term "barbarian," so broad as to be meaningless as an ethnic marker, is nonetheless what Tatian prefers.[113] By choosing this, he situates Christian philosophy as distinct and different from the *paideia* and power exercised by Greece and Rome.[114]

Tatian is coy; if you do not know the discussions of his day you miss his rhetorical jab at famous statuary and at the Roman Empire. The Knidian Aphrodite is not named as such, in an age in which her image proliferated. Instead, Tatian alludes to her twice, mentioning Phryne, the *hetaira* who was Praxiteles' model, and an "armleted woman." He doubly denies the statue's divinity: She is a courtesan model, and only a woman with jewelry.

CONCLUSIONS

What is the social life of a statue, and what cultural and real status is associated with it? Can a god be a commodity? Lucian's *Zeus the Tragedian* starts with a crisis in religion and then uses cult statues to embody this tragedy. Zeus mourns: "The circumstances of the gods are as bad as they can be, and, as the saying goes, it rests on the edge of a razor whether we are still to be honoured and have our due on earth or are actually to be ignored completely and count for nothing" (*Iupp. trag.* 3).[115] To address this tragic situation, the gods are called together in *ekklēsia*, an assembly, the term usually translated "church" in New Testament writings. The order in which they should sit is unclear (7): Should a heavy gold piece which is poorly worked sit in a better seat than the perfect bronzes of the ancient Greek sculptors Myron and Polykleitos, and the famed marble sculptures of Pheidias and Alkamenes?

Because Zeus determines that gold must have precedence, traditional Greek deities are shoved to the back. Hermes, organizing the *ekklēsia* at the Pnyx, calls, "Come to the front seats, then, you of gold. It is likely, Zeus, that none but foreigners will occupy the front row, for as to the Greeks you yourself see what they are like, attractive, to be sure, and good looking and artistically made, but all of marble or bronze, nevertheless, or at most in the case of the very richest, of ivory with just a little gleam of gold, merely to the extent of being superficially tinged and brightened, while within even these are wood, and shelter whole droves of mice that keep court inside. But Bendis here

[113] Grant (*Greek Apologists*, 116) also rightly notes that Tatian's special attack on Athenians stands in contrast to the sort of oration in praise of a city that we find in Aelius Aristides' "Panathenaic Speech."

[114] As Martin Elze argues, Tatian's *To the Greeks* argues for Christianity's godliness, antiquity, and unity in contrast to the diversity, relative novelty, and impiety of Greek religions (*Tatian und seine Theologie*, 34–40).

[115] ET Harmon, 2.95.

and Anubis over there and Attis beside him and Mithras and Men are of solid gold and heavy and very valuable indeed" (8).[116] The "gold-snouted" Anubis is placed in front of Poseidon, to the latter's horror.[117] The gods are commodities, and for Lucian it is the foreign gods, newfangled products of far flung ethnicities, that are now wealthy and making their way to the most honored seats in the famed old Athenian assembly-site. "Not all of them understand Greek, Zeus," points out Hermes (13).[118] But even if they do not all have the same *paideia*, the gods gather with the same concerns: They have no power when the Fates are spinning the world's outcome. Their statues are mere objects or commodities, valued for their material substance by robbers, or for their cultural worth by connoisseurs or poseurs. Lucian hints that this is the end of religion.

Christians and non-Christians of Tatian's day talked about the various theological and cultural problems raised by statues, especially statues of the gods. While Tatian is not alone in his criticism, his catalog provides a glimpse of his troubling criteria regarding what constitutes the monstrous and immoral: prostitutes, poets, pregnancies by rape, the bearing of a "black child."[119] Athenagoras writes of a representational crisis where words and images are usurped; Justin presents artisans as low status, and thus the gods that are products of their hands as even lower. Tatian holds up Greek sculpture as leading to a different sort of crisis. Such sculpture, so valued that the Romans have taken it as booty, *does* something to the viewer. The act of viewing is a pedagogical moment, but in looking at these sculptures one learns about the improper blurring between human and divine, about the monstrous and the licentious. These images want to draw you in, Tatian fears. They want to encourage you toward *mimēsis*, and the Christian eye must resist both their ethics and their claims to be culture, to represent *paideia*. It is not the unphilosophical, impious masses who are the trouble, as Athenagoras had thought. According to Tatian, the connoisseurs of culture lead to ethical depravity.

Tatian presents himself as a barbarian cultural critic who from his simple and clear position can see how connoisseurship breeds a senseless and elitist cultural hegemony. Whether you are gathering Attic Greek words for your precious vocabulary or visiting a collection of Greek objects in Rome, Tatian argues, you are duped. Second-century Greekness is not natural or pure, but a product of a certain moment and of Roman power to promote and to buy the

[116] ET Harmon, 2.103.

[117] Lucian stands alongside Christians in satirizing Egyptian cult's worship of animals (τὸν κυνοπρόσωπον τοῦτον). See especially his *Deorum concilium*, in which the gods assemble and evaluate who among them is truly a resident alien or stranger.

[118] ET Harmon, 2.109.

[119] On the topic of color and blackness in antiquity, see especially Gay L. Byron, *Symbolic Blackness and Ethnic Difference in Early Christian Literature* (London; New York: Routledge, 2002).

products of a given ethnicity. Tatian, for all his Greek language and learning, claims that he opts out of the system.

Gaca says that "Aphrodite is Tatian's devil," but that is an exaggeration; she is one among many *daimones* threatening Christians and others.[120] Tatian mentions Aphrodite as part of his concerns about female, monstrous, and extreme bodies and the *paideia* they teach. We now turn to Clement of Alexandria and others who use the statuary bodies of the Aphrodite of Knidos to frame their theological and cultural criticism.

[120] Gaca, *The Making of Fornication*, 240. The Projecta casket, which depicts a Christian woman as Venus at her toilet, later makes a very different statement about Christianity's relationship to *eros*.

CHAPTER SEVEN

WHAT DO WE LEARN WHEN WE LOOK? (PART II) APHRODITE AND CLEMENT OF ALEXANDRIA

FROM THE HELLENISTIC PERIOD ON, PRAXITELES' SCULPTURE OF THE Aphrodite of Knidos appears frequently in life-size, over life-size, and miniature reproductions; she is also much discussed in literary sources. She is an object – a sculpture or figurine or painted image – that duplicates and spreads in the Roman Empire. This object, in her many iterations, has complex lives and biographies. The sculpture of the Aphrodite of Knidos inhabits several categories simultaneously, categories one would think to be contradictory: She is a goddess, she is a woman, and she is enslaved in marble or terracotta or stone. She is a goddess whose body is "worn" by Roman matrons commemorated her form, with their own portraits, in funerary statues. She is human in appearance and is a human insofar as she is rumored to have been modeled on Phryne, courtesan lover (*hetaira*) of the sculptor Praxiteles. What does it mean to duplicate and to trade in such a body or *sōma*, a term also used in the Roman period for a slave?[1] When we study the proliferation of sculptures in the second century, especially variations on the Aphrodite of Knidos in stone and the many condemnations and celebrations of her in contemporaneous literary texts, what can we make of the exchange value or price of this goddess, or this human, or this object?[2]

[1] See Rev 18:13; LSJ s.v. σῶμα II.2.

[2] Igor Kopytoff, "The Cultural Biography of Things: Commoditization as Process," in Arjun Appadurai, ed., *The Social Life of Things: Commodities in Social Perspective* (1986; repr. Cambridge: Cambridge University Press, 2003) 64–91. Kopytoff's concerns about slavery and

We learned in the previous chapter that Arjun Appadurai has proposed that "we regard luxury goods as goods whose principal use is *rhetorical* and *social*, goods that are simply *incarnated signs*. The necessity to which *they* respond is fundamentally political."[3] In the same volume, Igor Kopytoff challenges the reader to apply to things "questions similar to those one asks about people: What, sociologically, are the biographical possibilities inherent in its 'status' and in the period and culture and how are these possibilities realized? Where does the thing come from and who made it? What has been its career so far, and what do people consider to be an ideal career for such things?"[4]

The idea of tracing the biographies or careers of *things* drives this chapter. That very statement blurs the line between human and thing, since biographies are usually considered the purview of humans alone. Kopytoff states that this "conceptual polarity of individualized persons and commoditized things is recent and, culturally speaking, exceptional."[5] In antiquity, people were commoditized through slavery; they still are today. In the economy and sculptural practices of the second century, the "polarity of . . . persons and commoditized things" is collapsed in both statue and slave: Both look human, stand on a pedestal, and are in danger of becoming things subject to connoisseurship, evaluation, and purchase. According to Aristotle and others, the slave in antiquity was both human and thing (*ktēma, res*); so too statues of anthropomorphic gods and theomorphic humans blurred the line between human and thing.[6] Aristotle had stated that "nature wishes to render different the bodies of the free and of slaves"; if all in the world worked as it should, slaves (who are humans of lower rationality, tipping toward the animal) would demonstrate their status in their bodies, yet some slaves have bodies that are like "images of

objects extends to "the transfer and organs and ova and the development of surrogate motherhood" (86), concerns that highlight the materiality and embodiment of those acts under Aphrodite's jurisdiction in the ancient world.

3 Arjun Appadurai, "Introduction: Commodities and the Politics of Value," in Appadurai, ed., *The Social Life of Things,* 38, his emphases; see also 27 on art and archaeology collections. Appadurai draws attention to the "conditions under which economic objects circulate in different *regimes of value* in space and time" (4).

4 Kopytoff, "The Cultural Biography of Things," 66.

5 Ibid., 64. See also Pierre Bourdieu, "The Forms of Capital," in John G. Richardson, ed., *Handbook of Theory and Research for the Sociology of Education* (New York: Greenwood, 1986) 241–58. For an example of Kopytoff's principle worked out elegantly in relation to images from India, see Richard H. Davis, *Lives of Indian Images* (Princeton, NJ: Princeton University Press, 1997) 6–8.

6 Aristotle defines a slave as "one who is a human being belonging by nature not to himself but to another is by nature a slave, and a person is a human being belonging to another if and if being a man he is an article of property, and an article of property is an instrument for action separable from its owner" (*Pol.* 1254a; ET Aristotle, *Politics* [LCL; trans. H. Rackham; London: William Heinemann and New York: G. P. Putnam's Sons, 1932] 19). Consider also discussion of contemporary human bodies as commodities in the global market in J. D. Wacquant and Nancy Scheper-Hughes, eds., *Commodifying Bodies* (London: Thousand Oaks, 2002).

gods" (*Pol.* 1254b). The status of person, slave/thing, or god is not immediately legible through the human body.

Another slippage between thing and person occurs because of the rhetorical power of anthropomorphic sculpture. Images with their persuasive power have a kind of human power of communication, even while their materiality might be associated with slavery and the status of an object. In the words of Natalie Boymel Kampen,

> On the one hand, we can argue that the Roman object is like the conquered or the enslaved or Woman. We might say that things are feminized to the extent that they are possessable. . . . And further, if we imagine that the object is in some ways feminized, then the very act of Roman looking can be understood as active and possessing and thus a manly one.
>
> On the other hand, we can argue that the object also addresses, attracts, or even dominates the viewer, and so the viewer, desiring or manipulated by the objects, is possessed by it.[7]

This chapter engages "in doing the biography of a thing" and in plumbing the paradox of a sculpture that is simultaneously object, human, and goddess. It does so by tracing the sculpture of the Aphrodite of Knidos through a narrow slice of her life, and by investigating how she and her powers of persuasion are depicted.

I. THE KNIDIAN APHRODITE AND HER AFTERLIFE

As we saw in the last chapter, Tatian is concerned with the Knidian Aphrodite; as we shall see later in this chapter, so is Clement, and like Tatian he questions what such images are meant to teach. Kathy Gaca sees Tatian as a contentious and marginal figure among early Christian writers. Yet, she asserts, "On one major point, as we will see, the church fathers endorse the ideas of Tatian. . . . They abhor Aphrodite. . . . The encratite argument of Tatian and his followers . . . reawakens our awareness of Aphrodite's once formidable sexual presence."[8] As I have argued, Gaca's characterization of Tatian as "sexually alienated" and encratistic is hardly fair. Much of our information about Tatian is gleaned from his ancient detractors, and Tatian inhabits a world where sexual self-control is valued. But Gaca correctly points to the power of Aphrodite in the second-century world. She thereby also reminds us of the Christian and larger philosophical struggle to think about what the self and body should and

7 Natalie Boymel Kampen, "Gender Theory in Roman Art," in Diana E. E. Kleiner and Susan B. Matheson, eds., *I, Claudia: Women in Ancient Rome* (Austin, TX: University of Texas Press and New Haven, CT: Yale University Art Gallery, 1996) 20.

8 Kathy L. Gaca, *The Making of Fornication: Eros, Ethics, and Political Reform in Greek Philosophy and Early Christianity* (Berkeley: University of California Press, 2003) 222–23.

could be, and how that ideal might best be achieved, whether in relation to Aphrodite and *eros* or not.

Among the many ancient representations of Aphrodite,[9] this chapter focuses on a particularly famous and sexually fraught one, the Aphrodite of Knidos. Praxiteles' original creation, set up in the mid-fourth century BCE in Knidos, is lost.[10] From the late Hellenistic period, representations of her in literature and imagery proliferate across the Mediterranean; Kristen Seaman offers a catalog of 200 representations of the Knidia, and these are limited to images that conform to "the statue's main features as depicted on Knidian coinage . . . : a naked woman who covers her *aidos* with one hand and holds drapery that reaches to a pot in the other."[11] The Knidia is found on Roman-period coins; over life-size for cultic and other public display; she is found in miniatures for household worship and in reliefs.[12] Praxiteles' mid-fourth century BCE

[9] The goddess Aphrodite, known to the Romans as Venus, appears in many iconographic forms in the second century. The goddess also becomes popular in the stories and form of Venus Genetrix, in myth the *progenetrix* of the Julio-Claudian imperial line through Aeneas and thus in a way the mother of the Roman Empire. Christine Mitchell Havelock, *The Aphrodite of Knidos and Her Successors: A Historical Review of the Female Nude in Greek Art* (Ann Arbor: University of Michigan Press, 1995) categorizes seven types of ancient Aphrodites. On the Aphrodite of Aphrodisias, see the catalog and analysis of Lisa Brody, *The Aphrodite of Aphrodisias* (Mainz: von Zabern, 2007); on the martial Venus, see Rachel Kousser, "Sensual Power: A Warrior Aphrodite in Greek and Roman Sculpture" (Ph.D. dissertation, New York University, 2001). On the use of the Knidian Aphrodite in portraits of Roman matrons, see Eve D'Ambra, "The Calculus of Venus: Nude Portraits of Roman Matrons," in Natalie Boymel Kampen and Bettina Ann Bergmann, eds., *Sexuality in Ancient Art: Near East, Egypt, Greece, and Italy* (Cambridge: Cambridge University Press, 1996) 222; Eve D'Ambra, "Nudity and Adornment in Female Portrait Sculpture of the Second Century AD," in Diana E. E. Kleiner and Susan B. Matheson, eds., *I, Claudia II : Women in Roman Art and Society* (Austin, TX: University of Texas Press, 2000) 103. On depictions of imperial women as Aphrodite/Venus, see Susan E. Wood, *Imperial Women: A Study in Public Images, 40 B.C.–A.D. 68* (Leiden: E. J. Brill, 1999) esp. 119–20; J. Aymard, "Vénus et les impératrices sous les derniers Antonins," *Mélanges d'archéologie et d'histoire* 51 (1934) 178–96. See also James Rives, "Venus Genetrix outside Rome," *Phoenix* 48.4 (1994) 294–306.

[10] There is a great deal of Roman art historical discussion of the original form. For a survey of some of what has been at stake in such discussion (with regard to shame, nakedness, and the female body), see Havelock, *The Aphrodite of Knidos*, 40–54, 69–73. I do not engage question of the original form of the statue but focus on its Roman-period manifestations.

[11] Kristen Seaman, "Retrieving the Original Aphrodite of Knidos," *Rend.* 9.15 (2004) 531–32, 534–35 (quotation at the latter); Alain Pasquier, "Les Aphrodites de Praxitèle," in Alain Pasquier and Jean-Luc Martinez, eds., *Praxitèle* (Paris: Musée du Louvre, 2007) 130–201. Wiltrud Neumer-Pfau counts more than 100 replicas of this type in marble. Wiltrud Neumer-Pfau, "Die nackte Liebesgöttin: Aphroditestatuen als Verkörperung des Weihlichkeitsideals in der griechisch-hellenistischen Welt," in Hans G. Kippenberg, ed., *Approaches to Iconology* (Leiden: E. J. Brill, 1985) 208.

[12] See Seaman, "Retrieving the Original," 535. Regarding coins, see, e.g., Havelock, *The Aphrodite of Knidos*, 11–12, 64; regarding miniatures and reliefs, see, e.g., 56–57, 66–67, 104ff. Maj in the mid-twentieth century counted 33 copies of Medici and 101 of Capitoline (B. J. Felletti Maj, "'Afrodite Pudica': Saggio d'arte ellenistica," *Archeologia Classica* 3.1 [1951] 61–65).

sculpture of the nude Aphrodite of Knidos thus haunts the Roman period in multiple forms, in images, and in literature. So also in the modern era, forms of this sculpture have been replicated (as in Hiram Powers's *The Greek Slave*) and understood paradoxically as the quintessence of the female and as a degradation of the female.[13]

Art historians generally date the origins of the female monumental nude to the Greek sculptor Praxiteles, and nearly everyone agrees that his Aphrodite of Knidos was something new and powerful in the mid-fourth century BCE.[14] On the one side of the interpretive divide regarding the Knidia we have scholars like Andrew Stewart and Kenneth Clark who interpret her as the height of female beauty, as nude rather than shamefully naked,[15] as informed by "geometrical discipline" rather than the "bulging body" of previous representations of women. Such analysis is often built on implicit connoisseurship not only of art but also of female bodies more generally.[16] On the other we find Nancy Salomon, for example, who argues that Praxiteles' "configuration" of the Knidia gives form to "the continued and incessant idealization of female humiliation in the Western tradition from ca. 340 BCE to the present."[17] Both sides of the art historical coin deal explicitly or implicitly with the eroticism or desirability of the Knidia.

The debate over the Knidia runs from antiquity to today. What is she meant to *do* to you? And what has been done to her? Sexual arousal is usually seen

[13] On discussions of the Knidos in the modern period, see the brief comment in Seaman, "Retrieving the Original," 532–33; on Hiram Powers's *Greek Slave* and the Aphrodite of Knidos, see Laura Nasrallah, "The Knidian Aphrodite in the Roman Empire and Hiram Powers's *Greek Slave*: On Ethnicity, Gender, and Desire," in Laura Nasrallah and Elisabeth Schüssler Fiorenza, eds., *Prejudice and Christian Beginnings: Investigating Race, Gender, and Ethnicity in Early Christian Studies* (Minneapolis, MN: Fortress, 2009) 51–78.

[14] Havelock, *The Aphrodite of Knidos*, 1–2.

[15] Andrew Stewart argues that whereas previous Greek sculptors took the male form as canon and imaged females as mutated men, Praxiteles took seriously female bodies and in doing so inaugurated a "new representational orthodoxy" (*Art, Desire, and the Body in Ancient Greece* [New York: Cambridge University Press, 1997] 104). Clark's distinction between nakedness and nudity (Kenneth Clark, *The Nude: A Study of Ideal Art* [London: J. Murray, 1956]) has influenced scholars of Roman art like Andrew Stewart and Christopher Hallett. See also Lynda Nead, *The Female Nude: Art, Obscenity, and Sexuality* (New York: Routledge, 1992) 14–15.

[16] Clark's evaluation is founded in uninvestigated criteria connected to his notions of status and sex: one statue of a woman is a "stocky little peasant"; another painting of female bodies is "almost comically unideal" (*The Nude*, 112, 115; see also 130). Havelock offers a strange *apologia* for the Knidia: "One is justified in writing rhapsodies about the Doryphoros' marvelous equilibrium. But the Knidia deserves no less" (*The Aphrodite of Knidos*, 18; see also 21).

[17] Nanette Salomon admits that "each reiteration of the *pudica* pose" (through the Renaissance and into the present) has a meaning specific to its context. But she also thinks that there is an "accrued force of their collective strength" ("Making a World of Difference: Gender, Asymmetry, and the Greek Nude," in Ann Olga Koloski-Ostrow and Claire L. Lyons, eds., *Naked Truths: Women, Sexuality, and Gender in Classical Art and Archaeology* [New York: Routledge, 1997] 197–99).

as an improper response to art, yet Aphrodite, the goddess of love and by the Roman period, of marriage too, invites such winking speculation in the second-century CE debate over the Knidia's erotic aftereffects and her (erotic) courtesan prototype.[18] Art historians' debates over the meaning of this "modestly" nude statue, whether it represents Aphrodite or women as Aphrodite (and is there a difference?), allow us to glimpse the complicated gender politics of interpreting the Knidia not only in the second century, but even in recent debates among art historians. The Aphrodite of Knidos is a vanishing point on the horizon. Her original Praxitelean form – and Praxiteles himself – are as elusive as the historical Jesus. The Knidia is, of course, a beautiful sculpture, but she also becomes a paradigm or form in which the intersection of gender, ethnicity, and the boundary between thing, human, and divine are culturally and religiously negotiated.

Aphrodite at Knidos

While the original sculpture no longer exists, stories about it do. One, recounted by Pliny, says that Praxiteles made a version that was clothed and one that was unclothed; he offered both for sale. The people of Kos, who had the first choice, chose the modest version, but theirs faded from the imagination as everyone preferred the Knidian nude. Pliny also states that King Nikomedes wanted to buy the statue from the Knidians in exchange for debt forgiveness, but the Knidians rejected the offer (*Nat. hist.* 36.4.21). Stories of the Knidia's origins employ terms of buying and selling; they emphasize the statue's commodity value.[19]

The original Knidia[20] is said to have been naked except for a hairband and a jeweled armband. She was made of marble, either Parian or Pentelic, depending upon which source one reads, and parts of the statue may have been gilded and tinted.[21] Next to her was a small pot, from which she was likely lifting up drapery, perhaps after having washed herself from the foam of the sea. Legend says she had stopped in Knidos during her travels from Paphos, where she was born from the foam of the severed genitals of Kronos, cast into the sea, to Greece. She holds a hand over her genitalia; some versions also

[18] On the eros of one setting of Aphrodite, see Rachel Kousser on the setting of the Venus of Melos in the gymnasium, among ephebes ("Creating the Past: The Vénus de Milo and the Hellenistic Reception of Classical Greece," *AJA* 109.2 [2005] 227–50).

[19] Richard Gordon, "The Real and the Imaginary: Production and Religion in the Graeco-Roman World," *Art History* 2 (1979) 22–28; Havelock, *The Aphrodite of Knidos*, 87.

[20] See Seaman, "Retrieving the Original," 537–57.

[21] Havelock, *The Aphrodite of Knidos*, 11–16; Stewart, *Art, Desire, and the Body*, 96–106. Much art historical labor has been spent on trying to determine from the multiple later forms of the Knidian Aphrodite what Praxiteles' original sculpture may have looked like; see Havelock, *The Aphrodite of Knidos*, 40–41, 49–54.

have her shielding her breasts with her other arm. In some versions, her head is turned in profile, as if surprised in the act of bathing.[22]

Questions about the Knidia's original form are fraught with ideological issues concerning whether she is ashamed or proud of her nudity, whether she is caught surprised in the act of bathing or stands plainly naked, and whether subsequent interpretations – Roman "copies" – are coy devolutions from Praxiteles' original. The Capitoline Venus, a second-century piece in Parian marble, provides an example of the sort of statue of the Knidia that one might have encountered in the Roman world (Figs. 26 and 27). We find another example of the Knidia in the over-life-size (2.24 m), second-century Campo Iemini Aphrodite of Parian or Thasian marble currently in the British Museum (Fig. 28).[23] The answer to the question of the Knidia's original form is often a product of the interpreter's ideology and is more a modern concern than an ancient one. As Kristen Seaman writes: "... the ancient world was not interested in maintaining fidelity to one original or even to a particular variant when copying.... This recategorization [of her bathing furniture] thus suggests that the persistent belief in a fourth-century original and a later variant must be seriously questioned if not entirely dismissed."[24] While Seaman focuses here on the Knidia's "bathing furniture," the point holds more generally.

A probable setting for the original Aphrodite has been found in Knidos, at the archaeological site on a jutting peninsula in western Turkey, south of the Turkish city of Bodrum and the Greek island of Kos. It seems that a round temple stood in Knidos even in the second century CE, within which Praxiteles' sculpture may have been displayed.[25] The site was popular and expanded over time, with a Roman-period building edging up to the older monopteros. That the site had a cultic function seems clear: At least according to Love's cursory excavation reports, a monumental altar existed just in front of the monopteros.[26] But the site was also a kind of tourist center. At Hadrian's

22 See Havelock, *The Aphrodite of Knidos*, 28, 36.

23 See a full discussion of the Capitoline Aphrodite in Wiltrud Neumer-Pfau, *Studien zur Ikonographie und gesellschaftlichen Funktion hellenistischer Aphrodite-Statuen* (Bonn: R. Habelt, 1982) 62–116. See also discussions in Havelock, *The Aphrodite of Knidos*, 74; *LIMC* II.1.52; Pasquier and Martinez, *Praxitèle*, 146–47. The Campo Iemini Venus has its own interesting history as a commodity; she was once prized by Italians and the Prince of Wales alike, but then was consigned to the basement of the British Museum since she was judged a mere Roman copy. See Ilaria Bignamini, "The 'Campo Iemini Venus' Rediscovered," *The Burlington Magazine* 136 (1994) 548–52.

24 Seaman, "Retrieving the Original," 550.

25 Ibid., 558–59. Pliny *Nat. hist.* 36.20 and Pseudo-Lucian *Erotes* 13–14 are used to reconstruct the ancient temple. See Havelock, *The Aphrodite of Knidos*, 58–63 on the setting at Knidos.

26 A statue base with a fragmentary inscription, dated by its lettering to the third or second century BCE, hints at the words "Praxiteles" and "naked"; Iris Cornelia Love, "A Preliminary Report on the Excavations at Knidos, 1970," *AJA* 76.1 (1972) 72. These excavation reports, however, are full of problems. Regarding the Roman building and altar, see Iris Cornelia Love, "A Preliminary Report on the Excavations at Knidos, 1972," *AJA* 77.4 (1973) 413–24.

26. Capitoline Venus (front). Musei Capitolini, Rome, Italy. Alinari/Art Resource, NY.

27. Capitoline Venus (back). Musei Capitolini, Rome, Italy. Scala/Art Resource, NY.

palace complex in Tivoli not only Aphrodite was copied, which we might expect, but also the monopteros from Knidos.[27]

Pseudo-Lucian and the Knidia

In the second century CE, in the middle of a book on the nature of love, Pseudo-Lucian facetiously describes a visit to the shrine of Praxiteles' Aphrodite of Knidos.[28] Thus the repetition of the Knidia occurs not only at Hadrian's Tivoli or in the many statues of her that proliferated around the empire, but also in literature of the time. It is worth recounting the scene in the *Erotes* in detail because through it we see that the statue and its story were so famous that they become an object of satirical thinking on the nature of love. Moreover, the story reveals both the power and the vulnerability of the stone goddess.

The scene is this: Three friends make their way through the city of Knidos, amused by its potters crafting erotic and obscene pottery figurines, and approach the shrine of the Knidia. They move admiringly through the luxuriant garden-*temenos* that surrounds the temple, with its well-placed benches where "the city mob together truly makes a festival" for Aphrodite, as they *aphrodisiazontes*, perhaps best translated "are acting lustfully" (*Erotes* 12). (There is no end of winks and ribald elbowing in the *Erotes*.) They enter the temple itself.

> Therefore, in the midst [of the temple] the goddess is set up – a most beautiful work of art of Parian stone – smiling a little, arrogantly and with a laughing grin. But her beauty is entirely uncovered; she has been stripped naked of any covering clothing, except insofar as with one hand she imperceptibly covers her shame. The artisan's *technē* was truly so powerful that the very hard and powerful nature of the stone was conspicuous on every limb. Charikles [who prefers the love of women], at least, raving and frenzied, shouted out something. "Most happy," he said, "of the gods was Ares, since he was enchained on account of her," and, at the same time, running up, he kissed her with importunate lips, stretching out his neck as far as he was able. Kallikratidas [who prefers the love of man] who stood by in silence, marveled in his mind. (13)

The three men ask to see the goddess from behind (see again Fig. 27). Ushered through the locked back door by the temple attendant, the Athenian

[27] Hadrian's complex at Tivoli includes a kind of miniaturization of the "best" of the empire. See William Lloyd MacDonald and John A. Pinto, *Hadrian's Villa and Its Legacy* (New Haven, CT: Yale University Press, 1995). Regarding other copies of this temple, see Nigel Jonathan Spivey, *Understanding Greek Sculpture: Ancient Meanings, Modern Readings* (New York: Thames and Hudson, 1996) 183–84.

[28] See Judith Mossman, "Heracles, Prometheus, and the play of genres in [Lucian]'s *Amores*," in Simon Swain et al., eds., *Severan Culture* (Cambridge: Cambridge University Press, 2007) esp. 146: "many of the literary techniques employed are utterly typical of Lucian himself; if this work is by an imitator, (s)he was a very skilful one."

28. Campo Iemeni Venus. British Museum, London. © The Trustees of the British Museum.

Kallikratidas, who had been impassive, bored, and confused by this woman/goddess, has a new reaction: "He closely observed the boyish parts of the goddess, when suddenly he shouted out, much more frenzied than Charikles, 'Herakles, such harmony of the back; how bounteous the flanks; what a handful to embrace! How the well-contoured flesh of the buttocks is arched, neither set against its bones, leaving it too thin, nor the fattiness spread out in excessive bulk.... Such a Ganymede poured sweeter nectar for Zeus in heaven!'" (14). Kallikratidas shouted while tears ran from Charikles' eyes. But then all three noticed a stain on the goddess's thigh, which the speaker originally concluded was a black mark in the marble, which Praxiteles skillfully made sure was located in less visible place on the sculpture.[29] But this was not a flaw in the marble, the temple attendant explained. "She said that a young man from a not insignificant family (but his deed rendered him nameless) came habitually, over and over, to the sacred precinct with a wretched *daimōn* [within him] to love the goddess passionately, wearing away every day in the sanctuary. In the beginning it had the appearance of a ritual of a pious man (δεισιδαίμονος).... Sitting all day long just opposite the goddess, he fixed the glances of his eyes straight upon her. His unintelligible whisperings and lover's accusations were described thoroughly by means of a stolen conversation" (15). He wrote on walls and scratched into trees messages of his love for Aphrodite; "he honored Praxiteles as equal to Zeus" (16). He dedicated everything in his home to the Knidia. One "night that cannot be spoken of" (ἀρρήτου νυκτός), he slipped into the chamber and had his chance. He left a stain of semen on her thigh, and then threw himself into the sea, whence Aphrodite had come (16).[30]

The statue made them do it. It provoked the young man's passionate love, lustful deed, horrible rape.[31] It provoked Charikles' dash and kiss and tears; it provoked Kallikratidas's ode to Aphrodite's eternal bottom. These men approached the goddess/statue and touched her. Nicole Loraux writes, "Aphrodite incarnates the immediacy of realized desire, the very image of 'love made flesh.'"[32] As Pseudo-Lucian says, the artisan triumphed over the hard

[29] Spivey, *Understanding Greek Sculpture*, 181 discusses Foucault's interpretation and the sexual ambiguity of the Knidia. On this passage, see Simon Goldhill, *Foucault's Virginity: Ancient Erotic Fiction and the History of Sexuality* (Cambridge: Cambridge University Press, 1995) 103–9.

[30] There are also allusions to the story of a young man who fell in love with the Knidia in Lucian *Eikones* 4 and Pliny *Nat. hist.* 36.4.21.

[31] On the vulnerability of Aphrodite's body, see Clement *Prot.* II 36.1; see also Lucian *Iupp. conf.* 8 on the gods' wounds and enslavement. See also Nicole Loraux, *The Experiences of Tiresias: The Feminine and the Greek Man* (Princeton, NJ: Princeton University Press, 1995) 223–24. On seeing and potentially violating power, see David Fredrick, "Introduction: Invisible Rome," in his edited volume, *The Roman Gaze: Vision, Power, and the Body* (Baltimore, MD: Johns Hopkins University Press, 2002) 1–3, passim.

[32] Loraux, *The Experiences of Tiresias*, 197.

stone (12). And yet there is the danger of seeing Aphrodite's statuary body naked and soft, something for which she punishes mortals mortally.[33] Praxiteles and those after him (and presumably before, although art historians treat him as a starting point for such nudity) chose a challenging theological route. As Andrew Stewart puts it, "To have her [Aphrodite] stand naked in public forever was a highly charged decision that carried with it large consequences and needed to be handled with considerable tact."[34]

The Knidia and the Ancient Gaze

The theme of transgressive sexual arousal clings to the Knidian Aphrodite. This is inevitable for Aphrodite, the goddess of love, with all her myths of her illicit connections, most famously, as Homer sings it, her being discovered in adultery with Ares (*Od.* 8.256–369). Still, the Knidia – or, better, different proliferations of what may have been Praxiteles' statue – becomes a particularly powerful sign, a commodity around which to organize one's thought about illicit love, desire, and what beauty can do to the viewer.

The rumor-mongering started in the Hellenistic period, and Phryne, Praxiteles' *hetaira* ("courtesan lover" or perhaps "high-class prostitute"), was at the center of speculation.[35] The Roman-period stories that circulated about Phryne have to do with her beauty, her nudity, and her forwardness. The early third-century CE writer Athenaios tells the story of her walking naked into the sea at the Eleusinian festival; from this image of her loosening her hair, Apelles painted his Aphrodite Anadyomene (13.590–591). Along with Athenaios, the second or third century epistolary inventions of Alciphon use an old trope and claim that her naked breasts transformed the opinion of an Athenian jury in her favor (*Ep.* 4.4). Alciphron also crafts a letter that Phryne writes to Praxiteles; in it, Phryne toys with the theological implications of Praxiteles' use of her as a model for Aphrodite, and her statuary appearance at a sanctuary to Eros at Thespiai. She writes, "Do not fear. For you have achieved such an all-beautiful thing [*chrēma*, a term used for products or goods], such as no one, indeed, has ever yet seen of all things worked by human hands; you have set up your very own *hetaira* in a sacred precinct. For I stand in the midst, by Aphrodite and Eros, both yours. Do not begrudge me the honor. For those who gaze at me sing praises to Praxiteles, and because I have come about out

33 Consider the blindness of Teiresias, effected by Zeus when Teiresias saw Aphrodite naked, or the myth of Actaeon, the hunter who was torn apart by his own dogs after he accidentally stumbled upon Artemis bathing naked in a pool. Stewart (*Art, Desire, and the Body*, 100) discusses the general theme of the danger of seeing the gods.

34 Ibid., 100.

35 Her very name describes what she is, since this name was used for prostitutes in Athens from the classical period on (Havelock, *The Aphrodite of Knidos*, 43, citing Aristophanes *Ecclesiazusae*). For a summary of some of the texts regarding Phryne see pp. 42–49.

of your craft, the Thespians did not hold me in ill repute but set me up in the midst of gods." Phryne continues, we can imagine, in breathy tones: "One thing is yet lacking in your gift: that you come to me, so that we may lie with each other in the sacred precinct. For we may not defile the gods whom we ourselves have created" (*Ep.* 1.1).[36]

These "letters" by Alciphron succinctly capture several issues regarding statues of the gods that are also articulated in other Christian and non-Christian writers. First, there is the issue of the sculptor and the statue's very human production. Phryne praises Praxiteles' art and glancingly compares his statues with those that are truly godsent, not crafted by human hands. She thus signals a larger conversation about the role of the artisan as god-like, on the one hand; we are reminded of the Knidian statue's frustrated human lover, who thinks Praxiteles equal to Zeus (Pseudo-Lucian *Erotes* 16). On the other, Phryne's words signal a conversation about the impossibility of truly divine statuary; Clement, as we shall see, works hard to date and historicize all statuary as clearly the humble work of human hands, so that none can claim that an image tumbled from heaven. Second, Alciphron's "letter" from Phryne raises the issue of the blurring between human and divine in Praxiteles' statue. Phryne hints at the nasty rumors that swirl around a *hetaira* who models as goddess when she says that the Thespians do not hold her in ill repute (οὐκ ἀδοξοῦσί μοι). She acknowledges the blur between human and divine with her statement that she has been set up in the midst of gods, between the divine figures of Aphrodite and Eros. Clement among others would shudder at this blatant joking about the slide between human and divine in statuary. Clement himself combines these themes and another connection of Aphrodite with prostitution: "For the Cypriot islander Kinyras may never persuade me, he who dared to transfer the lewd orgies for Aphrodite from night to day, because he was ambitious to deify a prostitute of his city" (*Prot.* II 13.4).[37]

Finally, Phryne's sexual come-on to Praxiteles to join her in the *temenos* or sacred precinct itself confirms the worst fears of Clement and others about art. Alciphron satirically channels Phryne as a self-confident hussy, happy to see herself among the gods, believing she belongs within the sacred precinct, praising Praxiteles for his godlike ability to create, and even inviting him to sexual relations within sacred space. Uncontrolled sexual desire inspired *technē*

[36] The Greek edition is M. A. Schepers, *Alciphronis rhetoris epistularum libri iv* (1905; repr. Leipzig: Teubner, 1969).

[37] See Pliny *Nat. hist.* 35.37.119 on Arellius, who used his mistresses as models for his paintings of goddesses. In my translations of the *Exhortation* I found helpful Clement of Alexandria, *Exhortation to the Greeks: The Rich Man's Salvation to the Newly Baptized* (1919; LCL; trans. G. W. Butterworth; repr. Cambridge, MA: Harvard University Press, 2003). The Greek edition is Clément d'Alexandrie, *Le Protreptique* (SC; ed. Claude Mondésert; Paris: Cerf, 1949).

or art, and art and desire are inextricably linked and can even lead to the gods' pollution.

The Knidia and Roman Portraits

What the Knidia means is debated in the literary sources that talk about her image and its creation, but she is also debated in the variety of monuments that reproduce this image. Knowing what we do now about the Knidian Aphrodite and her statuary and literary proliferation in the Roman period, how can we understand her appearance in Roman-period portraits, many of which seem to have been funerary monuments?

Sometimes the famed Aphrodite becomes a Roman matron. The body of Aphrodite is used as a kind of "costume," to use the terminology of Larissa Bonfante,[38] on which is placed a portrait head of a Roman woman. One example of the Capitoline type reinterpreted is imposing (Fig. 29), well over life-size (1.91 m).[39] She would have had a small Eros beside her. She probably dates to the late Flavian period and was found at a villa near Lake Albano; she may be Marcia Furnilla, a wife of the emperor Titus.[40] Her aging, drawn face and fierce Flavian hairstyle juxtapose incongruously with her rounded but youthful form.[41] Her shoulders round, making her Aphrodite body seem even slimmer (perhaps her high hair adds to the effect), and she covers both her genitalia and her breasts. She is not the only one. An even more imposing example (2.14 m) comes from the environs of Santa Croce in Gerusalemme in Rome (Fig. 30). This better-preserved sculpture retains a young Eros gazing upward, and elaborate drapery held before the *pubes* and draped snugly around the right leg, behind the statue, and over the left arm.[42] The detailed sculpture and linearity of the drapery contrast with and call attention to the softness and smoothness of the flesh. Both statues covered their genitalia, as did all versions of the Knidian Aphrodite. The late Flavian model also semi-conceals

[38] Larissa Bonfante cited in Eve D'Ambra, "The Calculus of Venus," 219. For another example in a *kline* form, see Eve D'Ambra, "The Cult of Virtues and the Funerary Relief of Ulpia Epigone," *Latomus* 78.2 (1989) 392–400.

[39] Henning Wrede, *Consecratio in formam deorum: vergöttlichte Privatpersonen in der römischen Kaiserzeit* (Mainz: von Zabern, 1981) 306–08 (no. 292); his footnote on the topic of similar portraits which he cannot consider runs to over a page in small type. See also Christopher Hallett, *The Roman Nude: Heroic Portrait Statuary 200 BC–AD 300* (Oxford: Oxford University Press, 2005) 201; D'Ambra, "The Calculus of Venus," 223–27.

[40] See Diana E. E. Kleiner, *Roman Sculpture* (New Haven, CT: Yale University Press, 1992) 178.

[41] See, e.g., Wrede, *Consecratio in formam deorum*, 308 (no. 292); D'Ambra, "Nudity and Adornment," 101.

[42] Wrede, *Consecratio in formam deorum*, 313–14 (no. 306); see also Hallett, *The Roman Nude*, 199–202.

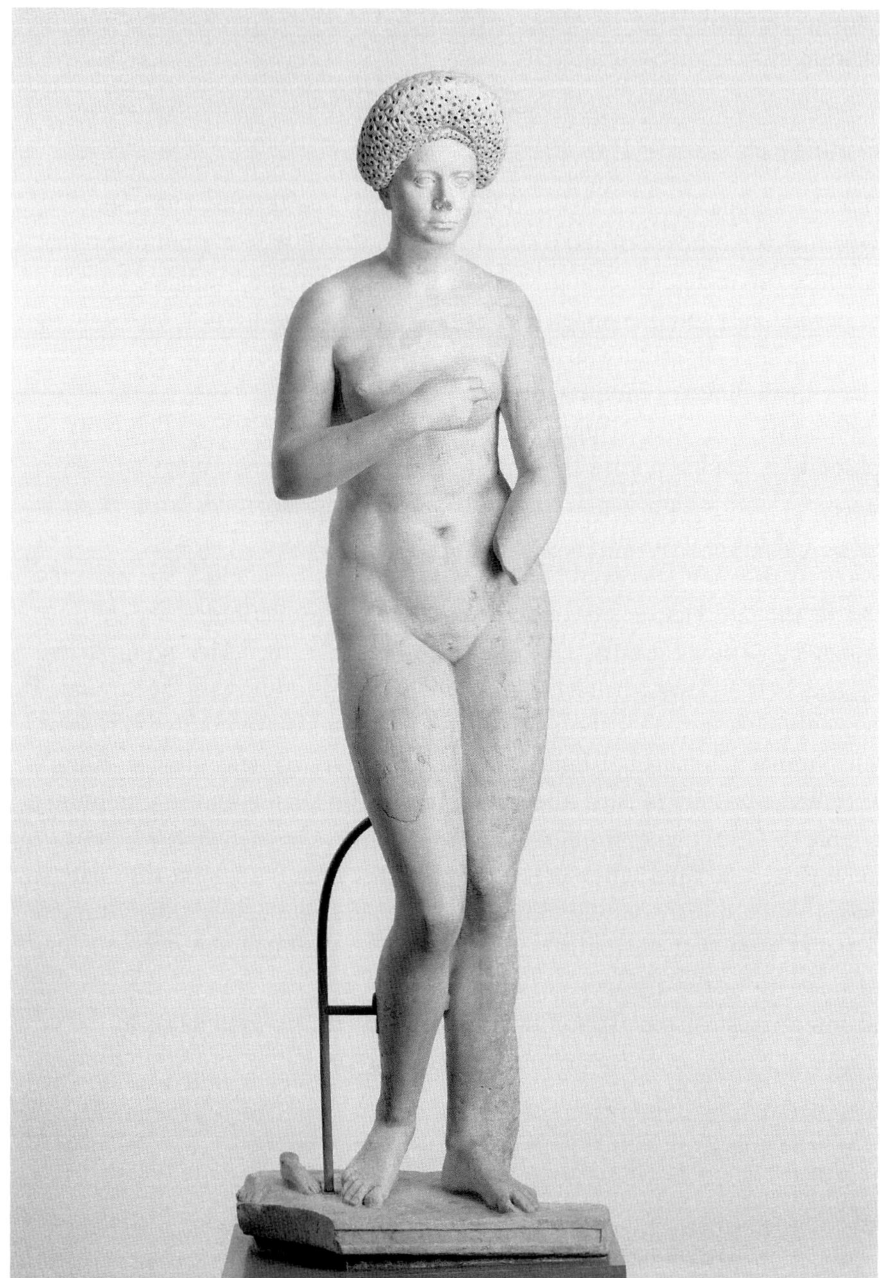

29. Roman woman as Aphrodite/Venus. Copenhagen, Ny Carlsberg Glyptotek.

her breasts with her arm. As many have observed, their "modest" gestures draw attention to that which they only partly conceal.[43]

[43] See, e.g., D'Ambra, "Nudity and Adornment," 104. We can see here rich possibilities for interpreting early Christian language of the flesh as a garment that Christ and all humans put on and take off.

30. Roman woman as Aphrodite/Venus. Museo Pio Clementine, Vatican Museums, Vatican State. Scala/Art Resource, NY.

These sculptures are theological as well as social statements; yet we scholars struggle to understand the choice to represent Roman matrons as naked Aphrodites. Goddesses or mythological figures might bare a breast or appear naked, but the naked body of a respectable Greek or Roman woman of the second century would be a less expected sight.[44] Although there are more than 320 known examples of portraits of men in heroic "costume" (that is, naked or semi-naked), only sixteen portraits of naked women survive, according to Hallett's count.[45] This may be due to the vagaries of archaeological finds and survival, but the difference is surprising. Of the sixteen remaining Roman female portraits, thirteen are quotations or interpretations of Aphrodite statues, and the majority of these interpret the Knidian Aphrodite.[46] These statistics do not include funerary portraits in relief that evoke the Knidia.

Literary sources from the Roman period help us a little in understanding the representation of Roman matrons as goddesses in funerary monuments.[47] From Statius we learn of the tomb of Priscilla, in which statues depict her as the goddesses or near-goddesses Ceres, Ariadne, Maia, and Venus; the last is defined as *non improba*, "not immodest," probably indicating that Priscilla was depicted nude or semi-nude, with the gesture of the hand over the *pubes* understood as an act of modesty (*Silvae* 5.1.222–235).[48] "The deities, unoffended, receive [your] beautiful visage" (*accipiunt vultus non indignata decoros/numina*),[49] writes Statius, referring to the mechanics of carving the deceased Priscilla's face onto the forms of goddesses. So too the "venerable marble breathes out" (5.1.230–231) and thus Statius's prose blurs the reality of the living breathing Priscilla, her dead unbreathing form, marble which can never breathe, and the power of the sculptor to simulate breath in stone. The tomb of Claudia Semne, wife of imperial freedman M. Ulpius Crotonensis, was discovered along the Via Appia and dates to the 130s. Like Statius's Priscilla she was multiply divine, depicted as Fortuna, Spes, and Venus.[50] In a famous relief depicting the tomb of the Haterii, Hateria Helpis seems to be depicted in a tiny aedicula as a naked Venus and in many other guises.[51] Elsewhere, as we shall see, Roman women were sometimes portrayed clothed or semi-nude alongside their husbands, in poses recalling the love between Aphrodite and Ares or Venus and Mars.

[44] In the Roman world, nakedness is often associated with Greek corrupting influences, with depravity, with degradation and even madness (Hallett, *The Roman Nude*, 61, 71–73, 83). For men, nakedness evoked all these things; for women, worse (see his chap. 4). In contrast, see Havelock, *The Aphrodite of Knidos*, 27–37.

[45] Hallett, *The Roman Nude*, 219. Hallett counts only confirmed portraits.

[46] See the catalog in appendix B of ibid., 331–32; see also D'Ambra, "Nudity and Adornment," 105. These naked statues (both male and female) are usually found only in Italy, and especially in Rome.

[47] See Hallett, *The Roman Nude*, 219–22.

[48] D'Ambra, "The Calculus of Venus," 222.

[49] The Latin is from Statius *Silvae* (LCL; trans. D. R. Shackleton Bailey; Cambridge, MA: Harvard University Press, 2003) 328. The poem denies the realities of death and its impact upon the human body (Statius *Silvae* 5.1.228–230).

[50] Henning Wrede, "Das mausoleum der Claudia Semne und die burgerliche plastik der kaiserzeit," *RömMitt* 78.2 (1971) 125–66; see also Hallett, *The Roman Nude*, 209–12.

[51] D'Ambra, "The Calculus of Venus," 222; Hallett, *The Roman Nude*, 219–21.

Yet even given this evidence of Roman matrons depicted as goddesses in funerary contexts, the juxtaposition of the sometimes weary head of a Roman matron with the lush body and form of any goddess, especially the naked Knidian Aphrodite, still raises questions. In general, scholars conclude that such portrait statues argue that a person is "worthy of comparison" with the god or goddess in whose form they are represented.[52] Those who depicted themselves as gods in their funerary monuments were seeking to collect for themselves the attributes of those gods, the "various virtues and attainments of the deceased": their fertility, modesty, beauty.[53] Especially in funerary contexts, where such statues could perhaps be seen by others moving around the tomb complex,[54] but were not publicly displayed, these women semi-privately "wore" the nudity of Venus, who was the mother of all Romans through Aeneas, as a costume, and were honored as "exemplary" mates.[55] "For Aphrodite/Venus beauty served as an erotic attraction; for the Roman matron, beauty reflected virtue and the display of the voluptuous female form, even if understood as a mythological conceit or a convention of art, had to be redefined as a sign of fertility," writes Eve D'Ambra, emphasizing the importance of conceiving and carrying a child to term for the continuance of the family name and property.[56] Venus the mother of the Romans is the model of matrons.

D'Ambra argues that the "frankly erotic" nature of many of these statues may be "tempered by Roman institutions, dynastic propaganda, marriage, medicine, and cult worship into socially acceptable desires," with the complicated coiffures of these women serving as a kind of "dress."[57] The hairpieces and careful adorning of second-century women allowed the Roman viewer to understand the body of Venus as an act of artifice, just like the portrait's hair;

[52] D'Ambra, "Nudity and Adornment," 101. Scholars have hypothesized that the *libertini* of the empire – former slaves, freed persons – found it important to represent themselves and their families in prestigious ways, and so imitated imperial portraiture and crafted themselves as gods. Wrede, *Consecratio in formam deorum*, 158–75; Diana E. E. Kleiner, "Second-Century Mythological Portraiture: Mars and Venus" *Latomus* 40 (1981) 512–44; Hallett, *The Roman Nude*, 202. See the methodological interventions of Lauren Petersen: *The Freedman in Roman Art and Art History* (Cambridge: Cambridge University Press, 2006) 1–13. While there is some evidence to associate certain portraits of Roman women in the guise of Venus with families of *libertini*, many others have no connected inscriptions or find sites to clarify their commissioners' identities. Perhaps this argument is fuelled by scholarly assumptions about freedmen as the ancient *nouveau riche*, as well as the vulgarity of being depicted as a god/dess in funerary monuments.

[53] Hallett, *The Roman Nude*, 221. See Wrede, *Consecratio in formam deorum*, 158–75 regarding portrait types and social context.

[54] See Lauren Petersen's analysis of the architecture of one mausoleum at the Isola Sacra: *The Freedman in Roman Art and Art History*, 184–226.

[55] Their depiction, Eve D'Ambra says, "*In formam deorum* suggests, at least, a significant emotional investment in conjugal relations and the pride taken in a faithful and exemplary mate" ("The Calculus of Venus," 222; see also 219–20); see also her "Nudity and Adornment."

[56] D'Ambra, "The Calculus of Venus," 221.

[57] D'Ambra, "Nudity and Adornment," 103.

these statues are "conceits for the cultivation of the female body as a work of art" as the "arts of Aphrodite become synonymous with the beauty of art and . . . the wonders of artifice."[58]

Yet do these explanations and socio-economic arguments, or even the idea of one's portrait body symbolizing divine virtues, really exhaust the philosophical and theological questions that such statuary evokes? Of course, there is no one meaning of the Knidia and there is no one meaning of her reproductions or reproductions of other Venuses; the Roman matron represented as Aphrodite may signal modesty and shame and, concurrently, the power of the goddess and the honor due her. Natalie Boymel Kampen wonders, "The figure of Venus may . . . keep some of its numinous force beneath the surface of the matron's portrait, may continue to signify the power of the goddess and notions of sensuality and plenitude even as the goddess Aphrodite is being trivialized in texts such as Lucian's."[59] Clement, we shall see, tries to trivialize her, but only because he understands the theological power of such images.

II. CLEMENT OF ALEXANDRIA

Although Clement (ca. 150–215 CE) was neither born in Alexandria nor remained there his entire life – he seems to have escaped in 202 or 203 during persecutions – he is associated with that "most important commercial city of the Mediterranean world," from which he wrote at the end of the second century.[60] "Eyes, you have met your match!" declares a character in *Leucippe and Clitophon* upon seeing Alexandria (5.1–2).[61] Alexandria is a key site for debates over ethnicity and the value of Greek *paideia*, and its visual stimuli are often mentioned in ancient sources.

Clement was probably in Alexandria during the reigns of Commodus and Septimius Severus, at a time when the city was famed not only for its double harbor, but also for its schools and its rich temples. Philo calls it a "megalopolis or many-citied Alexandria" (*In Flacc.* 163);[62] Aelius Aristides, in his *Roman*

58 Ibid., 111–12.

59 Natalie Boymel Kampen, "Epilogue: Gender and Desire," in Ann Olga Koloski-Ostrow and Claire L. Lyons, eds., *Naked Truths: Women, Sexuality, and Gender in Classical Art and Archaeology* (New York: Routledge, 1997) 270.

60 Alan K. Bowman, *Egypt after the Pharaohs: 332 BC–AD 642* (Berkeley: University of California Press, 1986) 218; Annewies van den Hoek, "How Alexandrian Was Clement of Alexandria? Reflections on Clement and his Alexandrian Background," *Heythrop Journal* 31 (1990) 179–94.

61 ET B. P. Reardon, ed., *Collected Ancient Greek Novels* (Berkeley: University of California Press, 1989) 233. The speaker comments on the gate of Helios, the long colonnaded streets, the massive population, and the procession for Zeus/Serapis.

62 The governor Flaccus proclaims that he was once τῆς μεγαλοπόλεως ἢ πολυπόλεως Ἀλεξανδρείας ἡγεμών (*In Flacc.* 163). I use the English translation of Pieter Willem van der Horst, *Philo's Flaccus: The First Pogrom: Introduction, Translation, and Commentary* (Leiden: E. J. Brill, 2003); for the Greek see L. Cohn and S. Reiter, *Philonis Alexandrini opera quae supersunt* (7 vols.; 1915; repr. Berlin: De Gruyter, 1962) 6.120–54. Ancient writers describe

Oration, calls it an ornament of empire flourishing under benignant Roman rule that treats Greek cities as if Rome were a foster-father (*Or.* 16.94–96).[63] The Roman prefect of the area was regularly and officially called "prefect of Alexandria and all Egypt,"[64] as if "all Egypt" were an afterthought to Alexandria.

Alexandria, the Mad, Hybrid, Spectacular City

Alexandria was also a site of fierce ethnic conflicts, where each group struggled for ethnic self-definition not only for its own sake, but also, and perhaps even more, for the tax benefits and cultural capital that could accrue if one were "Greek" or "Roman" and thus of the "right" ethnicity.[65] These struggles over ethnicity were forged in the crucible of shared space between Greeks, Romans, Egyptians, Jews, Christians, and Alexandrians, and of course any one person could inhabit more than one, and even more than two, of these identities.[66]

Philo embodies the complexity of ethnicity in Alexandria: He is a Jew, a writer of beautiful and sophisticated Greek philosophical prose, an emissary to Rome. His *Embassy to Gaius* and his *Flaccus*, often labeled as *apologiai*, likely date from the 40s CE.[67] In them he deploys polemical, ethnically charged language to describe how "a mixed and unruly mob of Alexandrians"[68] – the undertone is one of miscegenation – looks for a reason to attack Jews,

Alexandria's Pharos or lighthouse, its Serapeion, its Sebasteion (see Philo *Leg.* 151), and its Museum enlarged by Claudius and visited by Hadrian. See Bowman, *Egypt after the Pharaohs*, 223–33. Christians adopted the learned traditions of the city; a Christian catechetical school also seems to have flourished in Alexandria: Annewies van den Hoek, "The 'Catechetical' School of Early Christian Alexandria and its Philonic Heritage," *HTR* 90.1 (1997) 59–87; David Brakke, "Canon Formation and Social Conflict in Fourth-Century Egypt: Athanasius of Alexandria's Thirty-Ninth Festal Letter," *HTR* 87.4 (1994) 395–419.

63 Aelius Aristides mentions Smyrna and Alexandria as Alexander the Great's two prominent city foundations (*Or.* 21.19.4).

64 Bowman, *Egypt after the Pharaohs*, 205.

65 Greek identity, under Rome, extended only to the cities of Alexandria, Naukratis, Ptolemais, and later Antinoopolis, and a city could even lose the right to have a council and have to plead with the emperor to regain it, as Alexandria did with Augustus and again with Claudius (Bowman, *Egypt after the Pharaohs*, 209–15 esp. 211–12). On the radical difference Rome makes in the formulation of Philo's identity and ethnicity in Egypt in general, see Maren Niehoff, *Philo on Jewish Identity and Culture* (Tübingen: Mohr Siebeck, 2001) 7–9, 19–23, passim. I have benefited from conversations with and the papers of my students Cavan Concannon and Roberto Mata on Philo and ethnicity.

66 Niehoff, *Philo on Jewish Identity and Culture*. Denise Kimber Buell, "Ambiguous Legacy: A Feminist Commentary on Clement of Alexandria's Works," in Amy-Jill Levine, ed., *The Feminist Companion to Patristic Literature* (London: T & T Clark, 2008) 28–32. On areas of the city and their ethnic make up see Bowman, *Egypt after the Pharaohs*, 209.

67 van der Horst, *Philo's Flaccus*, 4–6.

68 ὁ Ἀλεξανδρέων μιγὰς καὶ πεφορημένος ὄχλος. Philo *Leg.* 18. I use the Greek edition of E. Mary Smallwood, *Philonis Alexandrini Legatio Ad Gaium* (Leiden: E. J. Brill, 1961) and have been helped by her translations.

and finds cause in Jewish refusal to offer *proskynēsis* or worship to the impious emperor Gaius (*Leg.* 16). Portraits of Gaius were forcibly hung in synagogues and a bronze statue of him with a quadriga (four-horse chariot) even placed in one synagogue (*Leg.* 18–20).[69] Philo points to the hypocrisy of Alexandrians who, in a city crowded with statuary, insist that images of the emperors must also be erected in synagogues. "Did they really want to honor the Emperor?" Philo questions. "Were temples scarce in the city? Have not the greatest and most important parts of the city been consecrated to gods, ready for the erection of any statues they wished?" (*In Flacc.* 51).[70] The emperor Gaius, says Philo, wants to be a god, and "he found no one, either among the Greeks or the barbarians, more suitable than the Alexandrians for the confirmation of his immoderate desire, which went beyond human nature" (*Leg.* 25). The Alexandrians are not Pharos-like, a beacon of light in the midst of a sea of native Egyptian ignorance. Philo instead conflates the Alexandrians with the ignorant indigenous Egyptians who worship anything, including animals, a calumny we find frequently used by Christian writers.[71] Still, the synagogues were confiscated, Flaccus issued a decree stigmatizing Jews as "strangers and immigrants" (*In Flacc.* 54), and Jews were herded into one section of town, into ghettos.

The trope of the Alexandrians as mob-like and seduced by spectacle is also found in Dio of Prusa's oration to the Alexandrians, probably written between 69–79 CE. He challenges the Alexandrians to realize that although their city is magnificent, they are not. When "countless Greeks and barbarians as well" return to their homes "at the ends of the earth" (ἐπὶ γῆς πέρατα), they will say:

> "Did we not see a city altogether amazing, and a spectacle greater than all human spectacles, with respect to the arrangement of sanctuaries and the multitude of citizens and the surplus of useful things? . . . But is it not a city that is maddened by song and horse races, and in these things they do nothing worthy of the city itself? For the people are moderate when they sacrifice and go about by themselves and do other things. But when they enter into the theater or the stadium, it is just as if there are drugs buried for them there; they know nothing of their former states

69 The statue itself in a synagogue is an offense, but Philo discusses a second offense as well. The quadriga was taken from elsewhere: it was a very old one from the gymnasium, in bad shape, but still, Philo questions: What about its original dedicator? (*Leg.* 20). See also Dio of Prusa's "Rhodian Oration" (*Or.* 31) on the danger of images being used in ways the donor would not have attended.

70 van der Horst, *Philo's Flaccus*, 63.

71 According to Philo, "Egyptian atheism" (τῆς Αἰγυπτιακῆς ἀθεότητος, *Leg.* 25) results in Egyptians' indiscriminate nomination of things as gods. Philo maps the different treatments accorded to different ethnicities (*Leg.* 79–80). The conditions of Roman rule do not serve to encourage possible alliances between subject groups.

> and they are not ashamed to say or to do any thing that should occur to them. . . . They are manifestly beside themselves and out of their minds – not only men, but also children and women." (*Or.* 32.41)[72]

The city shames itself globally. Dio offers a geographically far-flung list of nations that extends to Bactria, Scythia, and Persia that can witness to the Alexandrians' love of shameful spectacle (32.40, 32.43–44). While a *dēmos* should be gentle and democratic, open to listening and reform, the people instead are monstrous: They partake in a democracy "that is an altogether varied and fearsome wild beast, such as poets and artisans fabricate – Centaurs and Sphinxes and Chimaeras" (32.28). Dio argues that the Alexandrians are not only like a wild beast but also like "bad women . . . who sin most of all in the streets" (32.32).

The Alexandrian's attachment to spectacle makes them bad subjects and citizens, more inclined to dance than unity.[73] Dio states that God has given thoughtful *paidagogoi* to lead the Alexandrians as children (τοιγαροῦν ὡς παισὶν ὑμῖν παιδαγωγοὺς δέδωκε τοὺς φρονιμωτέρους τῆς πόλεως, 32.51). The Alexandrians need such pedagogues because in the midst of "the spectacle itself, as the things that take place are shameful and filled with every wantonness," they act "just as if, I think, they receive happiness through their ears; they call a wretched human savior and god. Do you know with how much laughter the gods jeer at you, when you, worshipping them, again offer the identical things and are constrained to honor divinity through the same terms? But the god is kind, I suppose, being god, and bears gently the stupidity of the masses" (32.50). The Alexandrians are apt to confuse those on stage who represent the gods with the gods themselves – we already saw in Philo that the Alexandrians flatter Gaius by treating him as god – and then their attempts at true worship of the gods are cheapened because they have to employ the same actions and terms.

Dio accuses the Alexandrians of being monstrous and effete, of seeing and hearing incorrectly, of confusing human and divine; they do not even walk their city correctly compared to the Rhodians, ancient Singaporians at heart, who do not run and who reprove those who walk incorrectly (32.52).[74]

[72] I was helped in my translations by Dio Chrysostom, *Discourses 31–36* (LCL; trans. J. W. Cohoon and H. Lamar Crosby; 1940; Cambridge, MA: Harvard University Press, 1995). The Greek edition is J. von Arnim, *Dionis Prusaensis quem vocant Chrysostomum quae exstant omnia* (1893–96; repr. 2 vols.; Berlin: Weidmann, 1962).

[73] Dio's double characterization of democracy and his use of terms of kingship and tyranny to describe democracy are fascinating but outside of the scope of this chapter; see *Or.* 32.27–29. See also his criticism of Alexandria's political history in *Or.* 32.69.

[74] Dio's criticism reminds us of de Certeau's idea of "walking the city" (see pp. 9–10, 58 above) but also of Clement's concerns with bodily control (regarding eating, talking, belching, laughing) in his *Paidagōgos*. "For Clement and others (Musonius, Plutarch, Dio), social order depends upon the negotiation of the rules through choices of actual behaviour when one

At every level, Dio seeks to shame and to reform the body, both the body politic of the city and the individual bodies of its inhabitants. He does so by a rhetoric of shame that uses pedagogical and theological terminology similar to that used by Philo or Clement, and that evokes the conversation about the confusion between human and divine in spectacle, which we have seen in Tatian and others.

Introducing Clement's Exhortation

According to Dio, the Alexandrians are seduced by spectacle and song; even their rhetors, sophists and physicians sing as they work; the dispensation of justice looks like a drunken gathering (*Or.* 32.68). He offers a myth of Alexandrian origins. They are the animals transformed by Orpheus's song, translated from Macedonia to Alexandria and thrill like animals at the sound of the lyre (32.63–66). Clement's *Exhortation*, too, begins with songs and a critique of those whom they mislead. It starts with a poetic and sonorous reference to Greek *mythos*, capped off by the dual form, no longer commonly in use at this time. The text begins:

> The Theban Amphion and the Methymnaion Arion
> both were musicians, both a myth.
> Ἀμφίων ὁ Θηβαῖος καὶ Ἀρίων ὁ Μηθυμναῖος
> ἄμφω μὲν ἤστην ᾠδικώ, μύθος δὲ ἄμφω. (*Prot.* I 1.1)

The Greek is rhythmic and musical. Assonance and alliteration move the lines along: The emphasis on the "amph" of Amphion meets emphasis on the "ar" of Arion; stress on the syllable "bai" of Thebaios matches the "nai" of Methymnaios. "Ampho" neatly begins and ends the second phrase.

Clement's sophisticated use of Atticized Greek and classical forms more generally is well known; we meet nothing like it in Justin, Tatian, Acts, or even Athenagoras.[75] His singing, rhythmic Greek matches his immediate topic of hymning and praise to God, and begins a text that is a Greek Christian supersession of the best of Greek culture. Both Amphion and Arion were famed, Clement writes, for the powerful effects of their music; the one lured a fish, the other built walls. Clement elaborates this theme of human lyric

is walking, sitting, speaking in the assembly, giving wealth, beating slaves, and so on. For moralists the public and the private spheres intersect; the modern argument, that someone's life is their own business, would have bewildered them." Simon Swain, "Polemon's *Physiognomy*," in Simon Swain, ed., *Seeing the Face, Seeing the Soul: Polemon's Physignomy* (sic) *from Classical Antiquity to Medieval Islam* (Oxford: Oxford University Press, 2007) 145.

[75] See the discussion of Clement's Greek and of Jakob Scham, *Der Optativgebrauch bei Klemens von Alexandrien* (1913) in John K. Brackett, "An Analysis of the Literary Structure and Forms in the Protrepticus and Paidagogus of Clement of Alexanderia" (Ph.D. dissertation, Emory University, 1986) 15–17.

power over objects and animals with the story of Eunomos and the Pythian grasshopper. Eunomos played beautifully for the funeral for the Python, the snake that Apollo conquered at Delphi. In the midst of this Greek festival assembly (πανήγυρις Ἑλληνική), the string of Eunomos's lyre broke. Among the crickets scraping away in the midday heat, one jumped onto the lyre to supply by his tune the sounds of the missing string. The usual moral of the story is that the grasshopper piously adds its strain to Eunomos's hymn. Clement rejects this; instead, the grasshopper leads Eunomos's tune away from "the dead serpent, the Pythikos," and "to the all-wise God" (I 1.2).

While Tatian within his first line clearly addresses the "Greeks," Clement only turns after the story of Eunomos to address an anonymous plural "you," and only once uses the term "Greeks" in the vocative, addressing the "Panhellenes" (II 34.1).[76] Rather than brutally confronting Alexandrians or Greeks, Clement instead brings together the poetics of song, so famously beloved in Alexandria (according to Dio) and the power of the image, so contentious in Alexandria (according to Philo). And at the very start, he offers a *different way of seeing* the story and its sculptural memorial at Delphi, a bronze depiction of Eunomos, the lyre, and the cricket. His *ekphrasis* of the event and the sculpture of Eunomos and the cricket offers a different hermeneutic for the story. The bug teaches the human about hymning the true god, rather than hopping up to sing for the daemonic Python.

The small gem of the tale of Eunomos and the cricket's song becomes the core for Clement's discussion of "a song that is a new one, a Levitical one," that offers "the eternal law of a new harmony" (I 2.4).[77] Thus, Clement puns, Eunomos – literally, "good law" – is surpassed. Moses is no false Orpheus or deceitful musician like the two singers whose names launch the *Exhortation*. These, according to Clement, "in the pretence of making music, destroy life; by some artful magic they are under the power of *daimones* to work for destruction; they ritually celebrate outrages; they make gods of sorrows; they were the first to lead people by the hand to idols, yes, stones and wood, that is to say statues and sketches. They opened up the stupidest of custom; they have really yoked together that good freedom of those who are citizens of heaven[78] and the lowest slavery by songs and spells" (I 3.1).

With slick sleight of rhetoric, Clement goes on to say that humans who believe statues and images to be gods are as stupid as stones and wood. But

[76] See Michael McGehee, "Why Tatian Never 'Apologized' to the Greeks," *JECS* 1 (1993) 143–58; Werner Jaeger, *Early Christianity and Greek Paideia* (Cambridge, MA: Belknap, 1961) 59.

[77] See Charles H. Cosgrove, "Clement of Alexandria and Early Christian Music," *JECS* 14.3 (2006) 255–82.

[78] In the phrase "citizens of heaven" Clement participates in a common conversation with Phil. 3:20 and offers a new ethnic-geographical map.

he then turns hopeful. He refers to the saying of John the Baptist (Matt 3:9 // Luke 3:8) that "God is able from these stones to raise children for Abraham." The "petrified hearts" of the Gentiles are raised to true piety through the Word (I 4.1–4). "See how mighty such a new song is!" Clement cries. "It has made humans from stones" (I 4.4). Stone becomes flesh, and flesh gains hope. Clement conjures for us images of stupid stone humans, stupid because they are deceived by stone and wood gods. But these stone-hard humans, looking so much like statuary, are then enlivened as the image of god. Clement alludes to the story of human creation from clay in Gen 2:7 – "The Lord perfectly fashioned a beautiful instrument, an in-breathed human after his own image" (I 5.4).[79] In an environment busy with statuary, Clement continues to use and reverse the language of sculpture in relation to the idea of human creation.

Clement argues that "our" ethnic origins predate those of other nations. (Phrygians, Arcadians, and Egyptians are mentioned.) "We were before the foundation of the world, we who were destined to be in him, have been begotten beforehand by God; we are the rational formations (τὰ λογικὰ πλάσματα) of God's Logos, through whom we have our origin,[80] because 'in the beginning was the Logos' (John 1:1)" (I 6.4). In this passage Clement reframes and expands the creation story of Genesis 1–2 in two ways. First, against other claims to ethnic primacy, and without defining his own use of the first person plural, he renders "us" to have existed before the creation of the world.[81] Second, he imagines that the formative act of human creation – the molding by hand of the human – was carried out by the Logos of God, just as God's sons carried out creation in Plato's *Timaeus*.

This creator-Logos became human.[82] Clement goes on to use Philippians 2's notion of how Christ became human to argue more generally for the

[79] Καλὸν ὁ κύριος ὄργανον ἔμπνουν τὸν ἄνθρωπον ἐξειργάσατο κατ' εἰκόνα τὴν ἑαυτοῦ. The Greek is rich with allusions: the term ἔμπνουν conjures the Genesis story of God's breath enlivening humans, but it also a term used to talk about the qualities of statuary and images so naturalistic that they seem to be breathing and alive. We also recall that for Aristotle, the slave is an *organon*. On Clement's anthropology and slippery use of the terms "image" and "likeness," see John Behr, *Asceticism and Anthropology in Irenaeus and Clement* (New York: Oxford University Press, 2000) 143–51.

[80] ἀρχαΐζω is difficult to translate. Lampe cites this passage and offers as definition A.1. "date from beginning of time or from eternity"; the term also refers to being archaic or copying the ancients according to both Lampe (A.3) and LSJ (A).

[81] On this passage and its language of ethnicity and worship, see Denise Kimber Buell, *Why This New Race? Ethnic Reasoning in Early Christianity* (New York: Columbia University Press, 1995) 73–74.

[82] For more on the topic of the creation story in Genesis 2 and how it is read by Clement, Philo, Tertullian, and others, see Laura Nasrallah, "The Earthen Human, the Breathing Statue: The Sculptor God, Greco-Roman Statuary, and Clement of Alexandria," in Konrad Schmid and Christoph Riedweg, eds., *Beyond Eden: The Biblical Story of Paradise [Genesis 2–3] and Its Reception History* (FAT II; Tübingen: Mohr Siebeck, 2008) 110–40.

possibility that humans can transcend their status and blur into gods. Clement writes, "The Lord himself will speak to you, 'who, though he was in the form of God, did not count equality with God a thing to be grasped, but emptied himself' (Phil 2:6–7a), the compassionate God who longs to save humanity. And the Logos itself already speaks to you manifestly, shaming unbelief. Yes, I say, the Logos of God became human, in fact in order that you too should learn by a human how it is ever possible that a human become a god" (I 8.4).[83] What we often call early Christian christology might better be described as anthropology. Early Christians are interested in Christ's revoking divine form and taking on human form (to be more literal to Philippians, a slave's form) in part because Christ is the first fruits of their own possible metamorphoses (cf. 1 Cor 15:12–58). Of course, as we have seen from Claudius as Zeus at Olympia or at Lanuvium to Roman matrons as the Knidian Aphrodite, Clement reacts in part to the theological messages available in the cityscapes of the Roman Empire, where physical reminders of human metamorphosis into the divine were common. In this environment he concludes that as God's Logos became human, so too humans can become gods.[84]

At the end of the first section of the *Exhortation*, Clement draws in the audience by asking it to engage in a rite of purification. "If you (sing.) desire *to see God truly*," he writes, "partake in cleansings fitting for divine majesty" (Σὺ δὲ εἰ ποθεῖς ἰδεῖν ὡς ἀληθῶς τὸν θεὸν, καθαρσίων μεταλάμβανε θεοπρεπῶν,

[83] αὐτός σοι λαλήσει ὁ κύριος, « ὃς ἐν μορφῇ θεοῦ ὑπάρχων οὐχ ἁρπαγμὸν ἡγήσατο τὸ εἶναι ἴσα θεῷ· ἐκένωσεν δὲ ἑαυτόν » ὁ φιλοικτίρμων θεός, σῶσαι τὸν ἄνθρωπον γλιχόμενος· καὶ αὐτὸς ἤδη σοὶ ἐναργῶς ὁ λόγος λαλεῖ, δυσωπῶν τὴν ἀπιστίαν, ναί φημι, ὁ λόγος ὁ τοῦ θεοῦ ἄνθρωπος γενόμενος, ἵνα δὴ καὶ σὺ παρὰ ἀνθρώπου μάθῃς, πῇ ποτε ἄρα ἄνθρωπος γένηται θεός. This idea and its connection to Phil 2:7 are not unique to the *Exhortation*: "That human person with whom the Logos is associated does not vary himself, or form himself. He has the form of the Logos, he is made like God; he is beautiful; he does not make himself up to be beautiful. He is truly beautiful, for God also is. That person becomes God, because God wills it. Indeed, Herakleitos says rightly, 'Humans are gods, and gods humans. For it is the same word.' The mystery is made clear: God is a human, and a human is god, and the mediator accomplishes the will of the father, for the mediator is the Word who is common to both, the son of God, the Savior of humans, and the servant of God, our Teacher. And since the flesh is a slave, just as Paul also witnessed, how can someone reasonably ornament a servant after the manner of a pimp? For the fleshly is the form of a slave, the apostle said concerning the Lord: 'Because he emptied himself, taking the form of a slave' (Phil 2:7a)" (*Paid.* 3.1.1.4–2.2). My translation; the Greek edition is Clément d'Alexandrie, *Le pedagogue livre III* (SC 158; trans. C. Mondésert and Chantal Matray; Paris: Cerf, 1970).

[84] On Clement and *theōsis*, see Norman Russell, *The Doctrine of Deification in the Greek Patristic Tradition* (Oxford: Oxford University Press, 2004) 121–40; see also Arkadi Choufrine, *Gnosis, Theophany, Theosis: Studies in Clement of Alexandria's Appropriation of His Background* (New York: Peter Lang, 2002) 159–212. Especially interesting is the discussion of image and likeness in Eric Osborn, *Clement of Alexandria* (Cambridge: Cambridge University Press, 2005) 233–53 on Clement's distinguishing between those who are in God's image (all humans) and those who are in God's image and likeness (those who are in Christ).

I 10.2; my emphasis). Later, Clement will practically carry objects over to us for our readerly inspection, dissolving the boundary of the written page, encouraging the audience to participate in religious rite and in judgment, in part through the act of viewing.[85] What constitutes piety will be visibly manifest. "I shall wheel [the so-called gods] out upon the stage of life for the spectators of truth" (II 12.1), writes Clement, in a spectacular city in every sense of the word, as we have seen, and in a world where the *scenae frontes* of theaters were complexly aediculated and covered with statuary and reliefs of gods and humans, and where of course gods were enacted on the stage itself.

Clement offers his readers amazing things to *see*: He claims even to offer a look at the mysteries (those things which the initiated should not say and the uninitiated should not know). He names objects that he should not have seen and he says out loud secret ritual words (II 12.2–22.6).[86] Outside of the context of the ritual, these sacred things are nonsensical and ridiculous: the words "I fasted, I drank the *kykeōn*, I took from the basket . . . " from the rites at Eleusis; the pyramidal cakes of the raving Dionysos, as well as pomegranates, fennel, ivy leaves, poppies; licentious behavior at the mystery rites. Clement heaps them on stage to be viewed as objects of misbegotten piety, even if emperors were initiates to the prestigious Eleusinian mysteries, as we recall from Herodes Atticus's induction of Marcus Aurelius himself.[87] Similar to Justin, Clement argues that the mysteries are actually constituted by "religious worship" (θρησκευομένη) that is the "the serpent's deceit" (II 22.3). "These are the mysteries of the atheists" (II 23.1): Clement turns back onto his inscribed audience the traditional accusation we have seen against Christians, that they are atheists.

The first book of the *Exhortation* lays out crucial themes for the rest of the text: the Logos as Song that helps to constitute the cosmos and that forms the human, the primordial antiquity of the people who follow this Logos, the folly of Greek myths and those who believe that stones and wood and bronze statues represent divinity, the possibility that stone-stupid humans can become images of God and indeed gods. As we move deeper into the *Exhortation*, Clement asks the reader who "desire[s] to see God truly" to open his eyes – Clement assumes a male subject – to the claims about gods that surround him in the cityscape and in the household.

85 Clement sometimes uses the second person, challenging the reader to understand and to turn away from misbegotten notions and practices. For charts of pronouns which he feels point to a better understanding of the structure of the *Exhortation*, see Brackett, "An Analysis," 49–67.

86 Clement introduces a discussion of Aphrodite with these words: "I will proclaim openly the things which have been hidden, because I am not ashamed to speak about things which you are not ashamed to worship" (II 14.1).

87 See p. 44.

III. "THEY SAY A GIRL LOVED AN IMAGE": THE *EXHORTATION* ON STATUES, PIETY, AND DESIRE

Scholars have long understood the *Exhortation* as invective against Greek culture, a kind of theological first step as Clement addresses a general audience.[88] What readers of Clement have not usually noticed is the extent to which the *Exhortation* fully engages the materiality of that culture and is concerned with contemporaneous interests in statuary and painting.[89] Throughout, Clement argues that images of the gods produce impiety because people become confused about the various registers of the cosmos. Because of such images, *daimones* are confused with true divinity; human lovers become models for images of the divine; dumb earth – mere matter – is associated with the eternal; idolatry is understood to be true worship; dead stone stands in for living flesh; immoral stories are confused with the true morality inspired by the one, true God.

Like Tatian, Clement wishes to demonstrate that there is something unseemly about images celebrated in or produced by Greek culture. At the beginning of his section on statuary, he offers himself as a kind of tour guide. He has just concluded an argument that temples and statues are established for the worship of *daimones*, and such temples are in fact tombs. He continues: "If... I, having carried over the statues themselves, should set them up for you to inspect, once you had approached them, you would find the custom is truly nonsense: You have been appealing to insensate things, 'works of human hands' (Ps. 115:4)" (IV 46.1). Clement continues the conceit of the moralizing tour guide and again seems to put his arm around the readers, leading them towards these images: "Therefore one must go the nearest as is possible to the statues (ἀγαλμάτων), as their related error is proved from their appearance. For indeed, the forms of the statues (τὰ εἴδη τῶν ἀγαλμάτων) quite clearly have been stamped by the bodily state of *daimones*" (IV 57.1).

Clement accuses the gods of having "shameful forms" (ἐπονειδίστων σχημάτων), emblematized by Dionysos's dress, Demeter's woe, Zeus and his swan, Aphrodite's nudity. "The fire signifies Herakles, and if someone should see a woman rendered nude, s/he thinks: 'The "golden" Aphrodite' (IV 57.2).[90] Clement implies that the attributes make the gods, with two

[88] Scholars have hypothesized that the *Exhortation* is the first of three stages in Clement's initiation of the individual into Christianity. See, e.g., Buell, "Ambiguous Legacy," 26; Brackett, "An Analysis," 4–5.

[89] See, however, Deborah Steiner, *Images in Mind: Statues in Archaic and Classical Greek Literature and Thought* (Princeton, NJ: Princeton University Press, 2001) 136–37; Simon Goldhill, "The Erotic Eye: Visual Stimulation and Cultural Conflict," in Simon Goldhill, ed., *Being Greek under Rome: Cultural Identity, the Second Sophistic and the Development of Empire* (Cambridge: Cambridge University Press, 2001) 172–80.

[90] "Figures that appear quite different to our demanding eyes could have been recognized as members of a type because of the recurrence of certain, vaguely defined features." Peter Stewart, *Statues in Roman Society: Representation and Response* (New York: Oxford University Press, 2003) 239.

results. First, a figure is legible as a god by means of form and attributes, even ridiculous and shameful ones. (We can remember the attributes of Jupiter that attach to Claudius; see Fig. 3.) Second, Clement implies, a viewer can interpret someone stripped of all attributes, including clothing, as Aphrodite, as we know from Roman elite women who represented themselves in her form. Clement moves us nearer to the images to convince the reader that such representations draw the viewer into an always deceitful interaction with the image.

The fourth book of the *Exhortation* focuses on images and statuary. Clement structures it through four main arguments against images. He begins by offering a history of the making of idols in order to argue that such objects (*xoana, bretē*) are not heaven-sent (IV 46.1–4).[91] Rather, "from the time that art (*technē*) flourished, error grew" (IV 46.4). This section also allows Clement to display art historical erudition of the day. Just as Pliny did in his *Natural History*, Clement urbanely discusses the evolution of representations of the gods from primitive forms to anthropomorphic sculpture and recites the histories of a range of famous sculptures. A very earthly etiology can be established for even the most ancient images of the gods. Since Clement can name their creators, he can pin the very human moment of the "divine" object's production, an argument that Athenagoras also made (*Leg.* 17.3–5). In addition, by entering into a long cultural conversation about these treasured objects, Clement is able to use ancient Greek writers of some prestige to support his arguments: "Apellas in the *Delphikoi* says that there were two Palladia [images of Pallas Athena], but that both have been created by humans" (*Prot.* IV 47.7), he happily reports.

Clement describes the biographies or the "social lives" of these images of gods in order to demonstrate their embarrassing histories or associations. He traces the famous kings who produced images and the provenance of famous images (Sarapis may have come to Alexandria from Pontus, for example). He even refers to Antinoos and finds the origins of this "new" divinity in lust (*epithumia*), since Antinoos was the beautiful beloved of an unnamed Roman emperor (IV 49.1) – Hadrian, of course. Clement offers this "social life of things" in order to prove that these images *are* things. They have histories. They are not divine or numinous but are the works of human hands, formed by known sculptors, commissioned by known kings, produced because of

[91] Clement briefly sketches a history of representation in his sentence, "When the *xoana* began to be represented in statues by humans, they reaped the name *bretē* ("wooden image of a god") from *brotōn* ("mortal, human")" (IV 46.3). He later explains that in Rome, for example, Ares was represented by a spear "since artisans had not yet started upon this specious evil craft [i.e., of representing gods in human form]" (IV 46.4). Clement puns: ἐπὶ τὴν εὐπρόσωπον ταύτην κακοτεχνίαν. Εὐπρόσωπος literally means "fair of face," but comes to signal hypocrisy ("fair in outward show," LSJ s.v. εὐπρόσωπος).

known pederasts; they are commodities traded from known city to known city. These images of gods, like Antinoos, are sometimes in reality images of the human dead, says Clement, and thus their temples are tombs. Confusion indeed.

Clement's second argument is that images of gods are insensate things, a topic familiar from Justin, Tatian, and Athenagoras. The images are worse than "worms and caterpillars . . . moles and the field-mouse" who at least have some sense perception (IV 51.3). In contrast stand the statues: "The *agalmata* are idle, impotent (do-nothings), insensate; they are bound and they are nailed on and they are fixed on, they are covered with pitch, filed, sawn, polished, carved" (τὰ δὲ ἀγάλματα ἀργά, ἄπρακτα, ἀναίσθητα, προσδεῖται καὶ προσκαθηλοῦται καὶ προσπήγνυται, χωνεύεται, ῥινᾶται, πρίεται, περιξέεται, γλύφεται, IV 51.5). In Greek, the sentence's assonance and alliteration, as well as the repeated force of the passive singular endings, make the argument rhythmic like the artisanal work described.

Clement uses Greek philosophers to bolster his point. Thus, for example, he cites "your own philosopher, Herakleitos of Ephesos, who mocks the senselessness (τὴν ἀναισθησίαν) of statues: 'And they pray to such statues, just as if someone were to chat with houses'" (IV 50.4). The statue's stupor makes them lower even than humans, who at least have sense perception. "The makers of cult images," Clement asserts, "dishonor the speechless earth" because they cause it to "stand outside of its proper nature." The "only true God is perceived by the intellect, not by sense perception" (IV 51.6). (Statues of) gods – Clement plays with the confusion between the statue and its referent – are shamefully powerless over their own care. They are melted and stolen, covered with guano and spider webs; they stand by insensate and helpless as their votive offerings are plundered (IV 52.2–6; see also IV 47.1). The passage echoes and may even borrow from Lucian, who laughingly depicts the powerlessness of the gods using similar stories of temple plunderers.[92]

Clement's third argument is against "those who craft images" (οἱ τῶν ἀγαλμάτων δημιουργοί). His main contention is they take their lovers as models for gods and goddesses (IV 53.1–6). Because of this, ancient kings such as Ptolemy IV and Alexander did not fear to proclaim themselves gods; even those of lower status did the same (IV 54.1–6). Moreover, lust produced the gods, since artisans used their lovers as models for their sculptures; flattery (*kolakeia*) too birthed gods as entire populations voted divine honors to humans. Gods are thus rightly called *eidōla* and *daimones* (IV 55.5) or *eidōla* and *skiai* (IV 56.1); *eidōla* of course can mean "idols" but also has overtones of the idea of shades. Thus Clement names the gods shades and shadows.

[92] See Lucian *Iupp. conf.* 8 for images of pirates stealing gods; *Iupp. trag.* 8 for images of mice inside statues of the gods. Minucius Felix *Oct.* 22 intensifies the image.

The fourth argument against the gods has to do with the stories and attributes associated with them (IV 57.1–63.5). Clement argues that images of the gods are intimately connected with deception and that their characteristic attributes – an eagle, a spear, nudity – should be understood as daimonic marks (IV 57.1). These images, moreover, deceive humans into falling in love with them; art or artifice (*technē*) implants an insane passion in the incautious viewer. Stories of the gods such as those found in Homer, enacted in the theater, and depicted in painted tableaux in homes offer theological justifications for out-of-control and immoral lifestyles. Clement argues that humans are living and moving statues and images of God, and, by implication, that the gods who are seen as statuary in the public square or the paintings at home are not. For Clement, God is the creator of all things, including the heavens, and this God rather than God's creation should be worshipped.

Clement on the Knidian Aphrodite

When Clement makes reference to the Knidian Aphrodite, he sees her as an example of his third argument against images. Those who make statues, says Clement, do so out of shameful impulses, crafting their own lovers into the form of the gods or leaving upon the body of the god some memorial of their lovers. "On the finger of the Olympian Zeus, Pheidias the Athenian inscribed, 'Pantarkes is beautiful,'" writes Clement, and, he sardonically explains, Pantarkes is not an epithet of Zeus, but is the name of Pheidias's beloved (IV 53.4).[93] He gives another example: "Praxiteles, then, . . . when he crafted an *agalma* of the Aphrodite of Knidos, made her nearly resemble the form of his beloved, Kratina, that the miserable people should have Praxiteles' beloved to worship." So also, according to Clement and as we have heard before, Praxiteles has a lover who is the model of his Knidian Aphrodite, and Phryne the Thespian *hetaira* is depicted as Aphrodite in the works of many painters at her time (IV 53.5–6).[94] Clement challenges the reader to decide "if you want to worship courtesans" (εἰ βούλει καὶ τὰς ἑταίρας προσκυνεῖν, IV 54.6).[95] Such images are the product of lustful desire, since tawdry artisans use their tawdry lovers as models for the bodies of gods. Statues also produce improper desire

[93] See Pausanias *Descr.* 5.11.2: Pheidias's statue of Zeus stands near reliefs of contests; among those reliefs, is one of Pantarkes, who is said to have been Pheidias's lover.

[94] On the idea that Praxiteles used Phryne as a model for the Knidia's body and Kratina as a model for her head, see Antonio Corso, *The Art of Praxiteles II: The Mature Years* (Rome: "L'Erma" di Bretschneider, 2007) 11 on Posidippus *Peri Knidou* frag. 147 and Clement's use of that tradition; p. 180 on Arnobius's use of it.

[95] On the idea that Christians and Jews can choose how to view Aphrodite, see also Seth Schwartz, "The Rabbi in Aphrodite's Bath: Palestinian Society and Jewish Identity in the High Roman Empire, in Goldhill, ed., *Being Greek under Rome*, 352–61.

as those who look on them are infected by the same lust that created them. (Of course, for Clement, sexual desire is not proper.)[96]

Tatian, in setting forth how images of gods and famed persons from the past celebrate the monstrous and lustful, makes only brief reference to the Knidian Aphrodite; Clement, in contrast, uses Aphrodite (including the Knidia) as a major figure in his argument. In the relatively short *Exhortation*, he refers to Aphrodite twenty-one times, compared with seven in the *Paidagōgos* and four in the *Stomata*. As in the texts we encountered in Chapter 6, so also in Clement we find that the production of statuary is bound up with desire and *eros*, and of course Aphrodite is the chief goddess of those. In a passage filled with supporting references and written in clipped clinical tones discontinuous with the lyricism of much of his writing, Clement criticizes such longing as it appears in ancient stories.

> Thus that Kypriot, Pygmalion, loved an ivory statue. It was the statue (ἄγαλμα) of Aphrodite and it was naked. The Kypriot is conquered by its form and he has sexual intercourse with the statue, and Philostephanos tells this story. Another Aphrodite in Knidos was stone and was beautiful; another man loved her and commingled with the stone. Poseidippos tells [this].... *Technē* has power to deceive such a man; it leads humans who are amorous into ruin. Now craftsmanship is efficacious, but such things should not deceive the rational person or those who have lived according to reason. (IV 57.4)

Clement begins by alluding to the famous tale of Pygmalion, the prime example of an image that blurs between object and person.[97] Ovid recounts the story of the sculptor Pygmalion, who was disgusted by women; they had denied the divinity of Venus and so she, angered, led them to public prostitution and "as all sense of shame left them, the blood hardened in their cheeks, and it required only a slight alteration to transform them into stony flints" (*Met.* 10.238–242).[98] In reaction to these live but stony, statue-like women, he sculpted a statue of a woman out of ivory and fell in love with it:

[96] See Clement *Paid.* 2.10 regarding modesty in sexual relations. Gaca, *The Making of Fornication*, chap. 9, esp. 251–53; see also Swain, "Polemon's *Physiognomy*," 136, which states that "the supposition underlying the whole of this work [Clement's *Paidagōgos*] is that one is being observed continually.... in the most intimate part of human life, in the bedroom, the wife is present to validate the husband's morality."

[97] The story of the artisan captivated by his own work has been depicted in art many times over. Regarding Ovid's Pygmalion and other examples of the blurring of humans and statuary in the Roman period, see Steiner, *Images in Mind*, chap. 4; Caroline Vout, *Power and Eroticism in Imperial Rome* (Cambridge: Cambridge University Press, 2007) 27–31. See a discussion of the Knidian Aphrodite in Spivey, *Understanding Greek Sculpture*, 186–87; for his full discussion of the Knidian Aphrodite, see 173–86.

[98] All translations are from Ovid, *The Metamorphoses of Ovid* (trans. Mary M. Innes; Baltimore, MD: Penguin Books, 1955) 252–53.

"Often he ran his hands over the work, feeling to see whether it was flesh or ivory, and would not yet admit that ivory was all it was. He kissed the statue, and imagined that it kissed him back, spoke to it and embraced it, and thought he felt his fingers sink into the limbs he touched, so that he was afraid lest a bruise appear where he had pressed the flesh. Sometimes he addressed it in flattering speeches, sometimes brought the kind of presents that girls enjoy" (10.254–259). He prays to have someone (something?) like the ivory woman, and Venus grants his prayer. Returning home from Venus's festival, he finds his sculpture with the ivory flesh pliant and the woman modest. One could say that the human is as quiet and coy as the thing – the statue – once was; the line between human and thing continues to be blurred. It is significant, of course, that Venus/Aphrodite, the goddess of love, enlivens the ivory statue and thus grants the sculptor the strange pleasure of marital and sexual relations with his own creation, and then a son who is another product of desire (10.280–297).

Clement uses the story of Pygmalion and a rapid reference to the Knidia in order to support his idea that statues are inextricably linked to error and, more specifically, that art is powerful to deceive. Ovid depicts Pygmalion's Venus as a purveyor of modest women, but Clement compares Aphrodite herself to a prostitute when he claims that "the initiates carry a coin in to the goddess, as lovers to a prostitute" (II 14.2).[99] A few lines after his reference to Pygmalion, Clement returns to the topic of Aphrodite, now in the form of the Knidia, to continue his argument about images, love, and deception.

> They say a girl loved an image and a beautiful boy the statue of the Knidia, but the eyes of the beholders were deceived by art. For no one would embrace a goddess, nor would someone have been buried together with a female corpse, nor would a sober-minded person have fallen in love with a *daimōn* and stone.
>
> Ἐρασθῆναι κόρην εἰκόνος λέγουσιν καὶ νέον καλὸν Κνιδίου ἀγάλματος, ἀλλ' ἦσαν τῶν θεατῶν αἱ ὄψεις ἠπατημέναι ὑπὸ τῆς τέχνης. Οὐδὲ γὰρ ἂν θεᾷ τις συνεπλάκη, οὐδ' ἂν νεκρᾷ τις συνετάφη, οὐδ' ἂν ἠράσθη δαίμονος καὶ λίθου ἄνθρωπος σωφρονῶν. (IV 57.4–5)

Clement introduces one of the only female viewers we have met, and so far the only desiring one,[100] and then reminds us of the beautiful youth who loved the Knidia, the unfortunate we met in Pseudo-Lucian's *Erotes*. Both the desirous girl and the desirous boy are condemned as deceived and lacking in

[99] For Clement's view of Aphrodite, see, e.g., *Prot.* II 14.1–2; II 33.7–9.

[100] Tatian mentions daughters at spectacle. Regarding female desire, we have an example perhaps in the Corinthian girl mentioned by Pliny and referenced in Athenagoras (p. 222). See Kampen, "Epilogue: Gender and Desire," 268 on imagining women as "desiring beings" and agents.

philosophical sobriety. It is folly to entangle oneself with a goddess (of stone) or to fall in love with a statue that is made of stone and houses a *daimōn*. These very acts, Clement says, are like being buried together with a corpse, a phrase that recalls a simile he offered at the beginning of the *Exhortation*: Those who worship statues are bound together with them to rot away, like the captives of barbarians were bound together with corpses (I 7.4–5).

Clement exposes the deceitful game of mimetic art, of which Praxiteles' Knidia is a prime example. Clement also admits that his audience does not really fall in love with the statues and paintings like the girl or the boy did; instead, Clement claims, they do something worse: "But *technē* deceives you by another witchcraft, leading you on to honor and worship the images and paintings, if not to fall in love with them" (IV 57.5). Clement is not concerned about the effects of male lust on statuary or real female bodies, but instead rails against the deceit and ruin these bodies effect on those (men) striving for self-control and *sōphrosunē*.[101] "Let art be praised, but let it not deceive a person into thinking that it is true" (IV 57.6), he goes on to say. Clement's concern is that *technē* beguiles and deceives the "mindless" (τοῖς ἀνοήτοις). To shame the reader who is entranced by images (and to delight the reader-in-the-know with his mocking humor), he offers examples from zoological experiments. Even monkeys know better, because they are not deceived by wax or clay toys or *korokosmioi* ("girls' toys"), while those he condemns worship stone, wood, gold, ivory, and paintings (IV 58.1–2).

Clement later reprises his argument about Praxiteles, images, and deception. He weaves in the concept of the human as God's image, by which of course he does not mean Praxiteles' courtesan in Aphrodite's image or Pheidias's Pantarkes in Zeus's image:

> For God is not at all unrighteous as the *daimones* are, but is the most righteous of all, and nothing is more similar (ὁμοιότερον) to him than the one among us who has become as righteous as possible: "Indeed, let every handcrafting artisan go his or her way!" . . . Stone-stupid artisans and worshippers of stones (ἠλίθιοι τῶν λίθων δημιουργοί τε καὶ προσκυνηταί)![102] Let your Pheidias and Polykleitos come; Praxiteles and Apelles too and as many as seek after the vulgar arts (ὅσοι τὰς βαναύσους μετέρχονται τέχνας), who are earthly workers of earth. For a certain prophecy says that when people believe in statues, then things in this world will be unfortunate. Therefore, again, (for I shall not cease my calling) let them come, these piddling artisans. None of them anyway has ever fashioned an in-breathed image, nor ever softened supple flesh from the earth. Who melted the marrow, and who fastened together bones? Who stretched out the nerves, and who grew forth the veins?

[101] See Harry Maier, "Clement of Alexandria and the Care of the Self," *JAAR* 62.3 (1994) 719–45; and Buell, "Ambiguous Legacy," 26–55.

[102] ἠλίθιοι (foolish, senseless) puns nicely with λίθων (stones); thus my free translation.

> Who poured blood into them and who stretched the skin around? How could any of them make eyes that see? Who implanted the soul? Who could give righteousness? Who promised immortality? Only the creator of all, the "best artisan father," has formed such an in-breathed statue as the human. But *your* Olympian Zeus, an image of an image, some great dissonance with the truth, is a mute work of Attic hands. (X 97.2–98.3)

The famed artisans of the classical and Hellenistic period are inadequate to the task of animating a real human, no matter if their statues can evoke belief and worship and even confusion over the life-likeness of the image. Clement lays heavily on the terminology of earth, of hands, of crafting in order to emphasize the work of creating statues – you can almost see the callused hands – and to recall the senselessness of those who are deluded into confusion about or even worship of life-like statues. At the same time, he employs the poetics of anatomical vocabulary to evoke the wonder of the living human and its creator.

We have already discussed how various images and stories of the Knidian Aphrodite (as well as other Aphrodites) circulated in the Roman world. Clement too offers an account of the social life of a thing, the Knidia. As the story goes, and certainly as Clement tells it, Praxiteles offers his lover as the form of a goddess or perhaps (to extend the adolescent humor of Alciphron's letters) may think that she has the body of a goddess; then the goddess again becomes human as she is the object of male sexual desire. She was also, as we know, a model for the memorialization of Roman matrons. If Clement were to have looked at the statues of Roman matrons in the form of the Aphrodite of Knidos, he would have concluded that the goddess is twice linked to the bodies of degraded and degrading human women. In Clement's eyes, Praxiteles' unphilosophical desire and the sexual availability of the woman who inspired the Knidian Aphrodite demand that the reader must consider if s/he wishes to bow the knee to a courtesan (IV 54.6). Whoever commissioned the face of a human woman to float on the form of Aphrodite memorialized that woman in a shameful, degraded way. Perhaps they would even be "buried together with a female corpse" (IV 57.4–5), to borrow Clement's description of the boy who loved the Knidian statue.

Stories of the Gods: The Pornographic Venus and Mars

Clement is especially concerned about images in statuary and paintings. Reversing the argument of Dio's *Olympian Oration*, which praised artisans and poets for how they depicted the gods,[103] Clement argues that artisans, stone masons, sculptors, painters, carpenters, and poets all deserve criticism,

[103] See pp. 230–33 for discussion of Dio's *Olympian Oration*.

the last because the shameful stories of the gods become the materials for drama. Clement mourns the spectacularization of false religion and mocks it: "You have made a stage of heaven and the divine has become for you action on the stage; and you have lampooned the holy by the masks of demons, making true religion (θεοσέβειαν) into satyr drama by your superstition" (IV 58.4). False religion mocks true religion. Homer, who has represented the love of Ares and Aphrodite in song, is especially enjoined. Clement starts out sarcastically:

> Sing to us, Homer, the beautiful saying:
> "Both beloved Ares and garlanded Aphrodite,
> How they first mingled in the house of Hephaistos
> Secretly: he gave her much and shamed the marriage and bed
> Of lord Hephaistos" (*Od.* 7.266–270).
> Cease the song, Homer. It is not beautiful; it teaches adultery.
> (IV 59.1–2)[104]

Such imagery, sung by Homer or manifest in paintings, can pervert in a variety of media. It makes its way indoors, into the household. The majority, Clement says, "throw aside shame and fear; their houses are painted with the unnatural lusts of *daimones*" (IV 60.1).[105]

Clement intentionally plays on the religious power of images in the household. There is no division between connoisseurship and piety, between looking and learning how to engage in lustful behavior: "Certainly, they have decorated their inner chambers with some painted tablets set high up like votive offerings, since they cleave to wantonness and consider licentiousness to be piety. And, lying upon the couch, still entangled together, they look towards that naked Aphrodite who was bound up in sexual intercourse" (IV 60.1–2).[106] These painted panels, Clement insinuates by his use of the verb *anakeimai*, are like votives hung up in the temples of the gods; he implies that such religion is perverted. The householders lie in their own embrace, looking up at Aphrodite and Ares similarly entwined and ensnared; he implies that the marriage is perverted. Perhaps the couple is caught tighter and tighter in some golden web like that forged by Aphrodite's husband-god Hephaistos, as Homer's story goes.[107]

[104] And so Plato is happy. The translation of the lines from Homer was made with reference to Clement's Greek and Richmond Lattimore's translation: *The Odyssey of Homer* (New York: Harper Perennial, 1965) 128.

[105] Clement's term ἐγγράφονται probably indicates that he is thinking of frescoes.

[106] Πινακίοις γοῦν τισὶ καταγράφοις μετεωρότερον ἀνακειμένοις προσεσχηκότες ἀσελγείᾳ τοὺς θαλάμους κεκοσμήκασι, τὴν ἀκολασίαν εὐσέβειαν νομίζοντες· κἀπὶ τοῦ σκίμποδος κατακείμενοι παρ᾽ αὐτὰς ἔτι τὰς περιπλοκὰς ἀφορῶσιν εἰς τὴν Ἀφροδίτην ἐκείνην τὴν γυμνήν, τὴν ἐπὶ τῇ συμπλοκῇ δεδεμένην.

[107] Homer *Od.* 8.267–70. Clement seems almost to be reading through this story and quoting from segments of it. See esp. Kleiner, "Second-Century Mythological Portraiture," 512–44; and now Rachel Kousser, "Mythological Portrait Groups in Antonine Rome: The Performance of Myth," *AJA* 111.4 (2007) 673–91.

Such objects are sacralized in the household as they are in public. You can hear the mounting outrage in Clement's rhetoric: "Yet you are not ashamed when you presently, in front of everyone, in public, look at the immortalized figures of utter licentiousness. When they are hung up as votive offerings you guard them even more,[108] as if they were doubtless the images of your gods. Your homes establish as sacred *stelai* of shamelessness – the figures of Philainis are inscribed as equal to the labors of Herakles" (IV 61.2).[109] We have already heard Tatian's mockery of Philainis, a woman who wrote a sex manual; Clement too introduces her here to highlight the scandalous sexual nature of such images. Clement understands sexual intercourse as something appropriate between married men and women only for the purposes of procreation; sex is something to be undertaken with philosophical sobriety and decency.[110] The audience he condemns in the *Exhortation* looks around during sex and enjoys it.[111] Clement briefly and censoriously depicts the inner chambers of the household and the endless loop of disgusting *mimēsis* within them: The gods embrace, the humans look; the gods look like humans, and the humans want to imitate the intertwined bodies of the gods.[112]

At Clement's time, the adulterous passion between Venus and Mars was sometimes used to depict or to memorialize the relationship between husband and wife. This was part of a larger trend at the time, which we have already been observing, to present "both aristocratic and freed men and women in mythological guise."[113] Marcus Aurelius and Faustina the Younger are thought from literary reference (Cassius Dio 71.31.1–2 [epitome]) to have been represented in statuary as Mars and Venus; even in the Augustan period there was in the Forum of Augustus a statuary group of Mars and Venus.[114] Thus the conceit

[108] I have imitated Mondésert's translation: "vous les gardez suspendues en ex-voto" (*Le protreptique*, 124).

[109] Ἤδη δὲ ἀναφανδὸν τῆς ἀκολασίας ὅλης τὰ σχήματα ἀνάγραπτα πανδημεὶ θεώμενοι οὐκ αἰσχύνεσθε, φυλάττετε δὲ ἔτι μᾶλλον ἀνακείμενα, ὥσπερ ἀμέλει τῶν θεῶν ὑμῶν τὰς εἰκόνας, στήλας ἀναισχυντίας καθιερώσαντες οἴκοι, ἐπ' ἴσης ἐγγραφόμενοι τὰ Φιλαινίδος σχήματα ὡς τὰ Ἡρακλέους ἀθλήματα.

[110] See Gaca, *The Making of Fornication*, chap. 9.

[111] On the erotic *pinax* in the bedroom of elites, see John Clarke, "Look Who's Laughing at Sex: Men and Women Viewers in the *Apodyterium* of the Suburban Baths at Pompeii," in Fredrick, ed., *The Roman Gaze*, 152; see also Goldhill, "The Erotic Eye," 174–75.

[112] For another angle of censure, see Clement *Strom.* 2.20.107: "Personally, I agree with Antisthenes when he says, 'I would shoot Aphrodite down if I could get hold of her; she has corrupted many of our best women.' He calls physical love a natural vice. The poor devils worsted by it call this disease a god. In these phrases he shows that it is the unlearned who suffer these defeats in ignorance of a pleasure which ought to be kept at a distance even if it is called a divinity, or rather even if it is actually a gift from God for the practical purpose of the production of children." ET Clement, *Stromateis* (trans. John Ferguson; Washington, D.C.: Catholic University of America Press, 1991) 228.

[113] Kleiner, *Roman Sculpture*, 280.

[114] A massive fragment of this group has likely been found; see Kousser, "Mythological Group Portraits," 681–82; Kleiner, "Second-Century Mythological Portraiture," 534.

of Mars and Venus was available visually even in moralistic, marriage-oriented Augustan times; it was available literarily (through Homer and retellings); it was available in performance, as Rachel Kousser argues, especially in the mime dramas so popular in the Antonine period.[115] Indeed, Clement's initial reference that the divine has become "action on the stage" (IV 58.4) hints at theatrical performance of the adultery of Venus and Mars. Recent information regarding the find sites of Venus and Mars portrait groups – that is, their location in the rare cases in which they were found *in situ* – indicates that such statuary may not only have been used in funerary settings, but also in private household contexts, evidence of elite Romans decorating their households and even understanding themselves in light of classically Greek imagery.[116] Kousser too pauses at the oddity – for us, at least; for Clement, the disgusting nature – of a married couple depicting themselves as the (adulterous) Mars and Venus. She puts such choices in a broader context: "In these, patrons, freed from the constraints of real-life decorum, could take on new roles in a fantasy world of romantic passion. Thus, Greek-inspired images served to express certain important aspects of Roman marriage more fully than could works of art of a more purely 'Roman' character."[117] Such images of the adulterous divine couple understood as a symbol of marital happiness evoke the famous narrative of their passionate union but also abstract from the well-known story to provide a pure moment of romantic union.[118]

Two examples demonstrate a presumably married couple represented or commemorated as Venus and Mars. These also bring together well-known sculpture types: the fourth-century Aphrodite of Capua type and the fifth-century Ares Borghese type. Thus, this style of portraiture not only blurs Roman elites with the gods; it also concatenates Romans with Greeks *and* brings side by side two different sculptures of Greek "origin" and intertwines

[115] Kousser, "Mythological Group Portraits," 687–89. On sexual mime popular with those of low status (in the Neronian period), see Clarke, "Look Who's Laughing at Sex," 155. From Lucian's "The Dance" we have the story of a dancer of Nero's time who "by himself danced the adultery of Aphrodite and Ares, Helios disclosing, and Hephaistos plotting and catching both in bonds like a net – both Aphrodite and Ares"; the story was so successful that the character who is skeptical of the function and power of dance shouts: "I hear, man, the things you're doing! I don't only see them, but you seem to speak with your very hands" (*Salt.* 63). Kousser ("Mythological Portrait Groups," 687) uses this passage to bolster her argument about the performance of myth contemporaneous to the production of Antonine period portraits of Venus and Mars.

[116] Kousser, "Mythological Portrait Groups," 678 regarding a find in a domestic context; see p. 674 regarding reading such sculptures in light of the "Second Sophistic"; and pp. 680–82 regarding Greek culture and Roman elite identity.

[117] Ibid., 685.

[118] On the trend in sarcophagus decoration from biographical narrative to the "symbolic and conceptual" by the middle and late Antonine period, see Natalie Boymel Kampen, "Biographical Narration and Roman Funerary Art," *AJA* 85.1 (1981) 47–58.

their bodies in stone. The first portrait group (Fig. 31), now in the Capitoline Museum, was found in the Isola Sacra (a necropolis approximately 30 km southwest of Rome).[119] Standing tall (1.88 m to the crest of the helmet),[120] the marble sculpture of Mars and Venus dates to ca. 145–150, based upon the portraits' similarity to Hadrian and Faustina the Younger in hairstyle and even facial characteristics.[121] The woman is depicted according to the Venus of Capua type, like the Venus who held the shield and wrote about victory on the Column of Trajan. She is fully clothed in a chiton with sleeves to the elbows, which is busy with tight vertical folds, and a mantle with looser folds is wrapped low on her hips. Her hair is caught up in a low bun, from which a thick wavy coil escapes to touch her shoulder; a diadem is high on her head. She grasps a naked and helmeted Mars, her right hand lightly touching his smooth chest at the point where his military cloak loops downward. Her left hand is extended behind him. Her body and her head are oriented towards her Mars; she is nearly in profile and gazes toward him, nose and diadem pointed his way. He holds a spear in his left hand, and a cuirass stands to his side. She is divinely his.

This Roman matron/Venus is fully clothed, but in another example, now at the Museo Nazionale delle Terme, the female figure is only partially draped (Fig. 32). This couple was found in an early Christian church in Ostia but was likely originally in a funerary context; it dates ca. 175–180 CE.[122] The unbearded man stands solidly, his body more reminiscent of the famous Doryphoros statue than the Capitoline Mars, whose upper chest was concealed by a cloak. The Ostian Mars has chiseled pectorals and abdominal muscles; his left hand would have held erect a spear, and his cloak lies draped over a cuirass to his left. His high warrior's helmet towers over both himself and his Venus; while his head is turned at three quarters toward her, it is her face and body which are more fully oriented toward him. Her right arm moves across her body, partially concealing high round breasts as she reaches to touch him; her

[119] For general information on the Isola Sacra see Petersen, *The Freedman in Roman Art and Art History*, 184–92.

[120] "The work is careful, hard, and poor"; the crest and top of the helmet are restorations: Henry Stuart Jones, *A Catalogue of the Ancient Sculptures Preserved in the Municipal Collections at Rome* (Oxford: Clarendon, 1912) 297–98 and pl. 73.

[121] Kousser, "Mythological Group Portraits," 676–78; or, Marcus Aurelius and Faustina the Younger, in Kleiner, "Second-Century Mythological Portraiture," 537–38; Wrede, *Consecratio in formam deorum*, 268–69 (no. 194); Hallett states that as male members of the imperial family began to be portrayed naked, male citizens followed suit, especially in their funerary monuments (Hallett, *The Roman Nude*, 199). On similar phenomenon, see Zanker, *Mask of Socrates*; but see also Smith's caution regarding the *Zeitgesicht* or "period face" of the citizen always following that of the imperial family, in R. R. R. Smith, "Cultural Choice and Political Identity in Honorific Portrait Statue in the Greek East in the Second Century A.D.," *JRS* 88 (1998) 59.

[122] Kousser, "Mythological Group Portraits," 677. For description and analysis see Kleiner, "Second-Century Mythological Portraiture," 539.

31. Roman man and woman as Mars and Venus. Originally found in the Isola Sacra. Musei Capitolino, Rome. Mai 1385.15959. Forschungsarchiv fur Antike Plastik, Köln.

hips are heavy and swathed in a thick mantle that twists at the top and falls in folds.[123]

The pervasiveness of such images of Mars and Venus in the Antonine period (on coinage, in statuary, and reliefs, among other media),[124] as well as the frank nature of the Venus's grasping adoration and the Mars's unphilosophical display, help us to understand more fully what is troubling Clement. These statue groups presenting husband and wife as Mars and Venus offer an interesting philosophical statement for the second century. They say something about idealized beauty, about valuing passion and desire, about couples orienting their bodies towards each other rather than standing facing forward, fully respectably clothed, with an image of a child, for instance, interposed between, as one finds in a contemporaneous funerary relief from Ostia.[125] Clement takes on an iconic image of his time, an image associated on coins and at least in literature with the imperial household, associated with Greek *paideia* and myth (Homer and his interpreters), associated with those wealthy enough to so commemorate themselves in sculpture. He offers his art-critical interpretation, exposing such images as disgusting and transgressive.

Clement presents himself as most concerned with the pedagogical or imitative potential of such images. They are, he insists, "models for your indulgence of pleasure; such are the theologies[126] of wantonness, such are the teachings of the gods who are engaged in *porneia* just as you are" (IV 61.1).[127] The solution to such images is a complete aesthetic transformation; that is, one's senses have to be retrained.

> We proclaim that not only the use, but also the sight and hearing of such things, should be forgotten. Ears have become prostitutes for you; the eyes have become fornicators, and – what is stranger – your gaze has committed adultery before you yourselves have had sexual intercourse. You violators of the human and those who by refutation have knocked down the divinity of the [human] form (τὸ ἔνθεον τοῦ πλάσματος ἐλέγχει ἀπαράξαντες), you are complete unbelievers in order that you may engage in passions. And you believe in the idols because you are eager to emulate their lack of self-control; you disbelieve God lest you should bear the burden of being modest (καὶ πιστεύετε μὲν τοῖς εἰδώλοις

[123] Regarding a similar Mars and Venus portrait group at the Louvre, see Kousser, "Mythological Group Portraits," 675–76; Kleiner, "Second-Century Mythological Portraiture," 538–39.

[124] For numismatic evidence see, e.g., Kousser, "Mythological Group Portraits," 675; Amyard, "Venus et les impératrices," 185–91.

[125] See Kleiner, "Second-Century Mythological Portraiture," 513–19, 541–43.

[126] More literally, "discourses on the divine." The verbal form means "discourse on the gods or cosmology" (LSJ s.v. θεολογέω); my translation "theologies" intends to help contemporary readers to understand that competing theologies are at stake in second-century "apologetic" debates.

[127] ταῦτα ὑμῶν τῆς ἡδυπαθείας τὰ ἀρχέτυπα, αὗται τῆς ὕβρεως αἱ θεολογίαι, αὗται τῶν συμπορνευόντων ὑμῖν θεῶν αἱ διδασκαλίαι.

32. Roman man and woman as Mars and Venus. Originally found in Ostia, now at the Museo Nazionale Romana (Terme di Diocleziano), Rome, Italy. Scala/Ministero per i Beni e le Attivita culturali/Art Resource, NY.

> ζηλοῦντες αὐτῶν τὴν ἀκρασίαν, ἀπιστεῖτε δὲ τῷ θεῷ σωφροσύνην μὴ φέροντες). . . . You have become spectators of virtue, but active champions of evil. (IV 61.3–4)[128]

[128] See also Goldhill, "The Erotic Eye," 174–75.

In a mix typical of Middle Platonic philosophy, Clement draws on the Stoic terminology for the good philosophical life with his references to a lack of self-control and to modesty or sobriety (*sōphrosunē*).[129] At the same time, his characterization of the senses as gateways for evil also corresponds with a larger cultural concern, often expressed by Platonists, over the epistemic reliability of sense perception in distinction to mental perception.[130] These images enter the eyes to teach an unphilosophical licentiousness and can even corrupt the divinity has indwelt the human form ever since Adam; Clement's use of *plasma* alludes to God's formation of the human according to Gen 2:7 and to his own description of humans as the *plasmata* of the Logos (I 6.4). The images do something to you, and then become a justification for licentious behavior: I saw the images (which themselves are mimetic of the gods), and I myself imitated them.

What viewer does Clement imagine? What reader does he inscribe? Clement discusses not only the viewer who is visually assaulted by the images embedded in and placed within the built environment of the city – that is, any person walking the cityscape. He addresses those in particular who have painted tablets within their homes and who own rings and statuettes; he constructs as his readers those men and women who would lie together, like Aphrodite and Ares in sexual embrace.[131] In the midst of his concern about *eros* and statuary, we see only two possible instances of female desire, the girl who lusts after a boy, and the female in her inner chamber who presumably enjoys the images of Aphrodite and Ares overhead. Both are condemned along with the rest of the *eros* evoked by images.

Clement briefly treats these women only to condemn their desire. It is not a surprise that Clement writes for the elite, cultured male.[132] But it is surprising to note how thoroughly Clement argues that images distract not only from the philosophical and theological differences between matter and the divine, but also from attempts at self-control, especially on the part of men. Anxious about such desire, Clement accuses his elite, philosophically inclined, cultured readers and viewers of seeking out precisely the sort of images that can lead them by the hand into wretched behaviors, ideally under the cloak of religiosity or culture. These images not only justify wrongdoing; looking at them can also knock down the divinity – *aparassō* has overtones of sweeping a statue off its pedestal or base – that was inbreathed at human creation.

[129] See, however, Gaca on the extent to which Pythagoreanism influenced Clement (*The Making of Fornication*, chap. 9).

[130] Goldhill, "The Erotic Eye," 175–84. See Tertullian *De virg. vel.* 2 on language of the seeing as sin, but see also Tertullian on reliability of sense perception, especially vision (*De an.* 18.38, discussed in Laura Nasrallah, *An Ecstasy of Folly: Prophecy and Authority in Early Christianity* [HTS 52; Cambridge, MA: Harvard University Press, 2003] 153–54).

[131] He does not address those at the time who eschewed sex altogether or who could not marry at all (being slaves) or who chose a lover of the same sex.

[132] See Maier, "Clement of Alexandria and the Care of the Self," 719–45.

CONCLUSIONS

In a landscape of having to repeat, filled with Roman interpretations and reworkings of the classical and Hellenistic sculptures of Pheidias, Praxiteles and the like, and in debate with this cultural context, Clement concludes his treatise by claiming visionary experience and speaking in the voice of Jesus who as eternal high priest prays for and encourages humans: "O former images, which all do not resemble [the model], I wish to restore you to the archetype, in order that you too may become similar to me. I shall anoint you with the ointment of faith, through which you cast off destruction, and I shall display the naked form of righteousness, through which you ascend to God" (XII 120.4–5).[133] Humans are the image of God, states the Logos, but they have lost their resemblance to the model. They need to be restored and anointed, as statues of divinities so often were in ancient ritual, and then they will rise to God in their naked form.

In response to the Logos's call, Clement exhorts humans not only to be images of God but also to be living, moving statuary: "Let us hasten, let us run, we God-beloved and God-imaged statues of the Logos!" (XII 121.1).[134] We perhaps imagine a great crowd of people, rising up to become living, breathing statues. He then continues: "Therefore it is time for us to say that only the God-fearing person is wealthy and [philosophically] self-controlled and well-born, and by this he is the image, together with the likeness, of God, and to say and to believe that he becomes, by Christ, 'just and holy with understanding,' and in such a way similar even also to God. Indeed, the prophet did not hide this gift when he said, 'I say that all are gods and sons of the highest' (Ps 82:6)" (XII 122.4–123.1).[135] We find blurring between human and divine in the images which are the focus of this chapter and book, but Clement proposes an even more radical blurring. He opens access to this *theōsis* or divinization, but how far? We are not surprised, but perhaps we are a bit disappointed, to find that Clement's concept of philosophical self-cultivation

[133] ὦ πάλαι [note: Mondésert has πᾶσαι] μὲν εἰκόνες, οὐ πᾶσαι δὲ ἐμφερεῖς, διορθώσασθαι ὑμᾶς πρὸς τὸ ἀρχέτυπον βούλομαι, ἵνα μοι καὶ ὅμοιοι γένησθε. Χρίσω ὑμᾶς τῷ πίστεως ἀλείμματι, δι᾽ οὗ τὴν φθορὰν ἀποβάλλετε, καὶ γυμνὸν δικαιοσύνης ἐπιδείξω τὸ σχῆμα, δι᾽ οὗ πρὸς τὸν θεὸν ἀναβαίνετε.

[134] Σπεύσωμεν, δράμωμεν, ὦ θεοφιλῆ καὶ θεοείκελα τοῦ λόγου [ἄνθρωποι] ἀγάλματα. See also *Strom.* 7.9.52.1–3, where the links between the Logos as *paidagōgos*, being made in the image of God, and spiritual progress are explicitly linked; this passage is well treated in Judith L. Kovacs, "Divine Pedagogy and the Gnostic Teacher according to Clement of Alexandria," *JECS* 9.1 (2001) 5–6.

[135] Ὥρα οὖν ἡμῖν μόνον θεοσεβῆ τὸν Χριστιανὸν εἰπεῖν πλούσιόν τε καὶ σώφρονα καὶ εὐγενῆ καὶ ταύτῃ εἰκόνα τοῦ θεοῦ μεθ᾽ ὁμοιώσεως, καὶ λέγειν καὶ πιστεύειν « δίκαιον καὶ ὅσιον μετὰ φρονήσεως » γενόμενον ὑπὸ Χριστοῦ Ἰησοῦ καὶ εἰς τοσοῦτον ὅμοιον ἤδη καὶ θεῷ. Οὐκ ἀποκρύπτεται γοῦν ὁ προφήτης τὴν χάριν λέγων, « ἐγὼ εἶπον ὅτι θεοί ἐστε καὶ υἱοὶ ὑψίστου πάντες ». The quotation from Ps 82:6 (LXX 81:6) contains "all." See Morton Smith, "The Image of God," *Bulletin of the John Rylands Library* 40 (1957–58) 477, 479 on rabbinic uses of this verse.

and progress of the self towards becoming the image of God is forged within and to some extent mirrors elite male philosophical practices and ideas of the time.[136] Clement holds out hope that "all are gods" and that only the god-fearer is truly wealthy and well-born. Yet such a message of wealth and divinity gained through self-mastery, Christian ritual, and control of one's in-breathed image was certainly harder for the slave (a body under another's control) or the woman to attain.[137] In the last quotation, Clement's terms for the person who is in the image of God draw from the model of the philosophically self-controlled person who is the "son" of the highest.[138]

In the first part of the chapter we found the sometimes vulnerable, sometimes powerful female or even goddess in the form of Aphrodite or Phryne. Stories about her origins and even her physical stance reveal her vulnerability. Some second-century types show an Aphrodite whose slightly rounded back defends her frontal nudity, her hand shields her genitalia and calls attention to her frozen pose of nakedness, as does the Capitoline Venus (see Figs. 26–27). It is not hard to imagine how ancient and modern viewers alike interpret these Aphrodites as startled and a little vulnerable. We are seeing what we should not see, and Aphrodite cannot prevent it. Indeed, by the Roman period, she cannot prevent the rapid proliferation of the images of her body, which multiply her literal exposure. We cannot know if the goddess of love evokes or disapproves the young man's actions as described by Pseudo-Lucian. The young man of the story might claim that it is he who suffered, that the goddess of love drove him to madness. But given the stain and the suicide, we can read this version of the famous story as a kind of rape. Athenagoras, Tatian, and Clement have all argued that material statues are powerless. Thus, the statuary goddess is helpless and vulnerable, subject to human care and abuse, at the same time as she is powerful and proliferating.

Today we find the idea of the human body as vulnerable commodity in accounts of slavery and sex trafficking.[139] This issue of human as commodity extends to conversations about reproductive technologies and the genetic manipulation of embryos.[140] Perhaps the most sinister manifestation of this issue is found in present-day organ "donation" and "medical tourism" in

[136] On the philosophical practices of the care of the soul more generally, see Maier, "Clement of Alexandria and the Care of the Self," esp. 720–25, 734.

[137] Ibid., 722 on how Clement's thinking finds its roots in speculation on the ideal male citizen from the classical period.

[138] Buell, "Ambiguous Legacy," 26–28, 54–55. On Clement and philosophical virtues, see Osborn, *Clement*, 236–51.

[139] E.g., E. Benjamin Skinner, *A Crime So Monstrous: Face-to-Face with Modern-Day Slavery* (New York: Free Press, 2008).

[140] Debora Spar, *The Baby Business: How Money, Science, and Politics Drive the Commerce of Conception* (Cambridge, MA: Harvard Business School Press, 2006); Susan Brooks Thistlethwaite, ed., *Adam, Eve, and the Genome: The Human Genome Project and Theology* (Minneapolis, MN: Fortress, 2003).

which the wealthy purchase the body parts of the poor, or rent women's wombs.[141] The question of who is human, who is a thing, who is a(n image of) god is significant in our own day. How are people differentially valued? Who is considered to be in the image of god, and who is treated as such?

It seems that Clement addresses this question for the second century by saying that all people, created by the Logos in God's image, are breathing statues. Yet Clement's own connoisseurship, his emphasis on the philosophical god-fearer who becomes the son of God, and his assumption elsewhere in his corpus that Christians are slaveholders[142] make us wonder whether Clement's vision of stone-hard humans transforming into moving statues in the image of God, and indeed into gods, extends to all bodies.

[141] See, e.g., Wacquant and Scheper-Hughes, eds., *Commodifying Bodies*.

[142] Throughout his corpus, Clement draws on slaves as a metaphor for what is licentious or problematic in behavior (e.g., *Paid.* 1.2 on drinking). In other places he seems to indicate that Christians will be slaveholders (e.g., *Paid.* 3.12 on not kissing wives in front of domestics [οἰκετοί], which he then immediately elides with a comment from Aristotle about slaves [δοῦλοι]).

EPILOGUE

Two texts by Lucian briefly encapsulate some of the key issues of this book. In Lucian's *Images* or *Representations*, the speaker Lykinos tells Polystratos the story of how he saw a woman and was practically turned to stone, "more motionless than statues" (*Imag.* 1).[1] The play between statues and people continues:

> "Have you ever travelled to Knidos, Polystratos?"
>
> "Yes, certainly!"
>
> "So then you saw their Aphrodite, no doubt?"
>
> "Yes, by Zeus, the most beautiful of Praxiteles' creations."
>
> "But have you also heard the story which the inhabitants tell about her, how someone fell in love with the statue, and, unnoticed, was left in the temple and had sexual intercourse with the statue, as much as that was possible?" (4)

Lykinos hints at the famous story of the Knidia's violation, and he and Polystratos display how they are connoisseurs of culture, tourists, or worshippers in Knidos.

1 The Greek title is *Eikones*; that of the volume that responds to it is *Hyper tōn eikonōn*. The edition for both is volume 4 of Lucian, *Works* (trans. A. M. Harmon; LCL; 10 vols.; repr. Cambridge, MA: Harvard University Press, 1999); the translations are mine.

After bantering sophisticatedly about other statuary, Lykinos and Polystratos return to the topic at hand: how to describe the woman Lykinos saw. He describes her as if a sculptor had formed her from the very best statues: ". . . he takes the head alone from the Knidia, for nothing else is needed, since the body is naked. Around the hair, and the forehead and the well-drawn brows, will be just as Praxiteles made them, and the softness of the eyes together with their brightness and graciousness – this too will be guarded according to Praxiteles' conception. The apple-cheeks and such front parts of the face by Alkamenes will be taken also from her in the Gardens, and besides the surfaces of the hands and the proportion of the wrists and the ease of the fingers in their fine tapering: also these things [will be] from the Lady in the Gardens" (6). Polystratos finally realizes who it is that Lykinos describes: "It is the emperor's consort!" (10).

As the dialogue proceeds, Polystratos's interest in the mistress's ethnicity becomes clear. "This precision of language and Ionic purity, and that she is able to engage in social discourse with chattering and much Attic loveliness is nothing to marvel at. For it is her hereditary and ancestral tongue (πάτριον γὰρ αὐτῇ καὶ προγονικόν), nor does she share in anything other than Athenian qualities, on account of the colony [that they planted in Ionia]. Nor again should I be amazed if she delights in poetry and converses much in it, she who is a countrywoman of Homer" (15). Her experience in statescraft is like that of Perikles' consort (17); she is even like Socrates' Diotima (18).

Lucian satirizes the many ways in which Greekness can be inherited and acquired. The Roman emperor's garrulous consort is Greek by heredity. She is literarily crafted as a composite of Greek literary references and language. She is a mix of pieces of classical and Hellenistic Greek statuary. The description of the woman in terms of multiple severed bits of famous ancient Greek sculpture is deliberately Frankensteinish. And, Lucian writes, she is painted not on a small canvas, as was the Athenian state, but on an enormous one, like "the present power of the Romans" (17). Lucian satirizes the cultural pretensions and political situation of the day. His characters flaunt their knowledge of Greek art, on the one hand, and joke that the Roman emperor has fallen for Greekness, on the other – and not just Greekness, but Greekness rendered huge by Rome.

In a follow-up dialogue, Lucian writes that the woman has heard about this literary portrait and demurely rejects it. Lykinos's friend reports: "She could not bear one thing, that you compared her to goddesses, to Hera and Aphrodite. 'Such things are beyond me,' she said, 'rather, beyond anyone of human nature. . . . Then, again, I am extremely pious [or superstitious, δεισιδαιμόνως] and timid regarding things concerning the gods'" (*Pro imag.* 7). Lykinos corrects her misunderstanding. He did not compare her to goddesses, he says, but only to their statuary. "But *I* – for she induced me to speak the truth – I did not say you were like goddesses, best of women, but like the creations of good artisans, what has been made from stone and bronze and ivory. It is not impious, it seems to me, to compare humans to things that have been made by humans – unless you have assumed that what Pheidias formed is Athena, or the heavenly Aphrodite is that which Praxiteles made in Knidos, not many years ago" (23). Lykinos has not confused the woman with goddesses, but the Roman emperor's Greek mistress has narcissistically missed the difference between the image and the thing itself, immodestly (while protesting too much) conflating herself with goddesses.

Lucian's stories about the emperor's mistress satirically investigate the blurring between human, divine, and statuary thing, the question of the relation between a representation and the thing itself, and the hyper-valuation of Greek *paideia* by the most powerful of elite Romans. The dialogues also show that Greek statuary and its re-presentations in the Roman era are not only aesthetic objects for connoisseurship, but are also theological documents in their production and use. Did Pheidias really form Athena, or Praxiteles Aphrodite? Has their work hobbled the theological imagination and caused impiety as humans cannot tell what is an image of a human, and what an image of a god?

The complex meeting of human and divine is explored in this wealthy, healthy, beautiful body of the Greek mistress of a Roman emperor. We have also seen such bodies in the Roman matrons who appear as the Aphrodite of Knidos, in the Roman men and women who pose as Venus and Mars, and in Claudius depicted with Jupiter's attributes or Commodus as Herakles. These idealized bodies did not conform perfectly to the range of bodies and faces at the time. Romans also exhibited the suffering, struggle, and subject status of some bodies. In Aphrodisias, in a sanctuary to the imperial cult, we saw Claudius subjugating the province of Britannia, figured, as is common, as a woman. She lies on her side, dragged upwards by Claudius's now-lost left hand, awaiting imminent violence from his right. Or, in Rome, we saw on Trajan's triumphal Column the fragmented bodies of the noble, conquered, barbarian enemy: Romans hold the Dacians' severed heads, while their women and children are led away as booty.

Many bodies, statuary and real, were abject[2] and objects in the Roman world. Not only were statuary bodies stolen, bought, and sold; so also were human bodies of prisoners of war and other slaves traded on the market, exposed naked on pedestals in public places, as if they were statuary on the market for connoisseurs. Aristotle had said centuries earlier that slaves are useful like animals and are objects or tools for human use. Yet even Aristotle had to admit that "although nature wishes to render different the bodies of

[2] See Lynda Nead, *The Female Nude: Art, Obscenity, and Sexuality* (New York: Routledge, 1992) 32 concerning Julia Kristeva's *Powers of Horror*.

the free and of slaves," and although those with inferior bodies should be enslaved, hypothetically, to those who are born with bodies "like the images of the gods," this is not how things really happen (*Pol.* 1254b). What is the divine potential of these enslaved bodies, who look like images of gods? Can they become the beautiful "living, moving statues" that Clement talks about? Are all created in the image of God?

Christians, among others, questioned the piety and purpose of individual humans and individual statues that confused the human and divine. They also turned to a larger stage as they responded to Roman-period representations of the broadest spaces of the world and the empire. On coins and reliefs in the ancient world, we sometimes see cupped in the hand of Zeus, Athena, or a Roman emperor a sphere – the world. Sometimes the emperor props one foot upon the globe; sometimes his image surmounts it, as in the depiction of Commodus as Herakles; sometimes the sphere is the size of a child's ball, balanced in the palm. These depictions, often on coins and statuary, offer two arguments: that the god or emperor both cared for and controlled the cosmos.

People in antiquity understood that the terrestrial sphere was round; they tried to map the cosmos, Earth, and their fragment of it, the *oikoumenē gē*, or "inhabited world." Geography was (and is) not only about the world's shape or about developing a mathematically precise understanding of space. Texts from the Roman period were concerned with mapping and articulating space in the face of and often for the sake of empire. Religious communities today still struggle with their place in the world and with the shape of the world, as new technologies and the flow of capital erase borders and bend space, bringing the distant near. Many Christians now also debate how to formulate ethical responses to globalization, on the one hand, and how to evaluate thoughtfully the centuries-long intersection of Christian mission with the goals of empires, on the other. This book has investigated the period before Christians had substantial material and political power that could significantly affect their place within the spaces of empire. Yet even at this time early Christians sought to articulate their places within these conceptions of the spaces of the world and the spaces of empire.

The five works closely examined in this book – Acts, Justin's *Apologies*, Tatian's *To the Greeks*, Athenagoras's *Embassy*, Clement's *Exhortation* – are evidence of how Christians in various ways articulate where Christianity belongs within the Roman Empire and in relation to Greek *paideia*. Tatian is most provocative, because he seems to offer a new map where what is usually considered marginal (Christianity, Assyria, the barbarian) is central. He asserts this while demonstrating that second-century cultural valuations are ridiculous. People can use Attic Greek and claim to be sophisticated, but in reality there is no pure Greek language; it is a hybrid from far-flung races. Romans can capture and display Greek statuary and images and claim to be connoisseurs of such culture, but if you take a closer look, you will see that this *paideia* is monstrous and effeminate. Far better the modesty of plain Christian women and the *paideia* of barbarian Christianity.

Tatian directed his treatise explicitly to the "Greeks." Clement's *Exhortation* focuses on the religious and cultural practices in which Greeks and Roman emperors take part. He mocks those who are seduced by Greek mystery cults (as were Hadrian, Marcus Aurelius, and Commodus); he mocks the statuary practices of the Roman Empire, where someone who has enough money or prestige can have a statue of him- or herself erected as a god, or where an emperor can have his lover's images set up for worship. In the midst of these practices of piety and these theological arguments in statuary, Clement asserts that all humans are "living, moving statues" in God's image. His argument is infused with the egalitarian possibilities of the creation story of Genesis, yet Clement does not fully realize that potential. It is the philosophically self-controlled (Christian) man who can most easily become a god.

Athenagoras, in contrast, directly addresses the emperors and calls on them to be who they say they are: pious and philosophical. He argues that their claims regarding their persons and their rule produce crises of *mimēsis*. What is the relation between a representation and the thing itself? Athenagoras lives in a world where Herakles represents both the emperor Commodus and a criminal forced to act out Herakles' labors and death – but not apotheosis – in the arena. Athenagoras does not reject Greek *paideia*, but uses philosophical debates over grammar and language to show the way in which signs have been usurped and how names and images of gods do not represent what they claim to represent.

Justin claims that he speaks to the imperial family and to the Roman Senate and people on behalf of himself and other oppressed races. His writings ask: What is one to make of imperial families that represent themselves as just, philosophical, and lovers of *paideia* when those same families persecute *paideia*-loving Christians "on the basis of the name alone"? As we saw, Athenagoras deals with this crisis through a sophisticated use of various grammatical and semiotic theories of his day. Justin, with more bombast, challenges the emperors to a divine trial and implies that they have already lost: They unwittingly hang their own trophies on the sign of the cross.

The Acts of the Apostles takes a different approach, presenting a Christian "Way" that moves toward the far reaches of the *oikoumenē* to bring all into the fold of the one God who is more than Panhellenic. While Tatian exited stage right into a barbarian land, Acts uses Paul's body as a metric to trace and bring together cities in a manner similar to the logic of Hadrian's Panhellenion, a Roman league of Greek cities. Acts offers scintillating narratives instead of expansive philosophical tracts, but like the other focal texts of my book, it presents "the Way" as something comprehensible to a Roman elite public that values Greek *paideia*. Paul's speech on the Areopagus occurs literally over and against the many statues and temples of the ancient Athenian agora. There he proclaims one true God who made all humans of one *ethnos*. The diversity of nations, with all their different notions of gods walking the earth (think of Lystra) or of philosophical-theological debate near the altar to the unknown god (think of Athens), can be won over to a Christianity that in the end remains fairly unscathed by the Roman Empire.

This book has perhaps emphasized too much the earliest Christian apologists' similarity with the surrounding culture. This is in response to the dominant trend in early Christian studies: Apologies have often been interpreted as marginal texts opposing Romans, Greeks, Jews, and other "heretical" Christians. Alternatively, they have been read as keys to the earliest Christian theological debates. In both cases, they are understood as largely separate from their world. Yet the Christian writers of the apologies should not be sequestered from the world of stone and other materials or from their fleshly contemporaneous writers. They were part of the frequent citations of high literature, discussion of prized images, and standard philosophical debates in the "landscape of having to repeat." Christians in the second century sought to assert their relationship to Greek culture and Roman power as surely as did the Fountain of Regilla and Herodes Atticus at Olympia, even if they did not have the funds to mount such a structure. They sought to enter as full participants in the spaces of the Roman Empire and to be tolerated as (some) others were and to be allowed to practice their piety.

Yet early Christians often demonstrated their sameness in order to deal with Christian difference – different rites, a different understanding of the Logos, a different idea of what images should be valued in the public square. The Christian sources we have treated would agree with Dio of Prusa regarding humans' quests for the divine. In the *Olympian Oration*, the famous Greek sculptor Pheidias defends the theology of his art: "For just as infant children artlessly have a terrible yearning and desire for father or mother when they have been torn away from them, and they stretch out their hands often while they are dreaming to those who are not present, thus also humans do to the gods, justly loving them on account of both their benefaction and kinship, eager to be with and to associate with them in every way" (*Or.* 12.61). Maximus of Tyre uses similar language of yearning for the gods and says that crafting images of the gods is an unphilosophical way to express this deep desire. Yet he will not judge: "Why then does it remain to me to examine and to lay down the law about images? Let them know the divine race; let them only know it. If the *technē* of Pheidias aroused the Greeks to the memory of God, if the honor rendered to animals roused the Egyptians, ... I am not upset at the diversity. Let them only know, let them only love, let them recollect!" (*Or.* 2.10).

Justin – or Tatian, Athenagoras, Clement, or the writer of Acts – would say that knowledge, love, and recollection of the divine are his goal too. He claims that an experience of diversity ended in his pursuit of Christianity. Justin talks of his testing of philosophical schools, his adherence to Plato's philosophy, and his recognition of Christianity as the highest philosophy, which came about by watching Christian martyrdom and realizing that these people must have attained to a great philosophy to face death so bravely. On the one hand, it is the traditions of Greek *paideia* – progress through philosophical schools, culminating in Plato – that led to Justin's embrace of Christian identity. On the other, it is his recognition of Christian courage in the face of unjust imperial power that leads him to Christianity. Christians engage the spaces of empire with a different vision, a vision that allows them everywhere to see the cross, whether in the masts of ships that sail the sea or the form of the trophies by which Romans declare their victories. Justin argued that all "who have lived by the aid of the Logos were Christians" (*1 Apol.* 46.3), from Socrates to Abraham and beyond. It is fitting to end with his expression of how his Christianness is simultaneously similar to and different from the valued *paideia* of his day: "I confess that I both pray for and with all my resources struggle to be found a Christian, not because Plato's teachings are different from Christ's, but because they are not similar in every way" (*2 Apol.* 13.2).

BIBLIOGRAPHY

A. ANCIENT SOURCES

Achilles Tatius. *Leucippe and Clitophon*, translated by John Winkler. In *Collected Ancient Greek Novels*, edited by Bryan P. Reardon. Berkeley: University of California, 1989.

———. *Leucippe and Clitophon*, edited by Ebbe Vilborg. Stockholm: Almqvist & Wiksell, 1955.

Aelius Aristides. *The Complete Works*, translated by Charles Behr. 2 vols. Leiden: E. J. Brill, 1981.

———. *The Roman Oration*, in James H. Oliver. *The Ruling Power: A Study of the Roman Empire in the Second Century after Christ through the Roman Oration of Aelius Aristides*. 1953. Repr. Philadelphia: The American Philosophical Society, 1980.

Aristotle. *Politics*, translated by H. Rackham. LCL. London: William Heinemann and New York: G. P. Putnam's Sons, 1932.

Artemidorus. *The Interpretation of Dreams*, translated by Robert J. White. Torrance, CA: Original Books, 1975.

Athenagoras. *Athenagorae Libellus pro Christianis, Oratio de resurrectione cadaverum*, edited by Eduard Schwartz. Leipzig: J. C. Hinrichs, 1891.

———. *Legatio and De resurrectione*, translated by William R. Schoedel. Oxford: Clarendon, 1972.

———. *Legatio pro Christianis*, edited by Miroslav Marcovich. Berlin: De Gruyter, 1990.

———. *Supplique au sujet des Chrétiens*, edited and translated by Gustave Bardy. SC. Paris: Éditions du Cerf, 1943.

Cassius Dio Cocceianus. *Dio Cassius Roman History*, translated by Ernest Cary and Herbert Baldwin Foster. LCL. 9 vols. Cambridge, MA: Harvard University Press, 1914–27.

Cicero. *De oratore, Books 1–2*, translated by E. W. Sutton and H. Rackham. LCL. Repr. Cambridge, MA: Harvard University Press, 2001.

———. *De Natura Deorum; Academica*, translated by H. Rackham. LCL. Repr. Cambridge, MA: Harvard University Press, 2000.

———. *Brutus; Orator*, translated by G. L. Hendrickson and H. M. Hubbell. LCL. Cambridge, MA: Harvard University Press, 1939.

———. *The Verrine Orations*, translated by L. H. G. Greenwood. LCL. New York: G. P. Putnam's Sons, 1927.

Cleanthes. *Cleanthes' Hymn to Zeus: Text, Translation, and Commentary*, translated by Johan C. Thom. Tübingen: Mohr Siebeck, 2005.

Clement of Alexandria. *Exhortation to the Greeks: The Rich Man's Salvation to the Newly Baptized*, translated by G. W. Butterworth. LCL. Repr. Cambridge, MA: Harvard University Press, 2003.

———. *Stromateis*, translated by John Ferguson. Washington, D.C.: Catholic University of America Press, 1991.

———. *Le pedagogue livre III*, edited and translated by Claude Mondésert and Chantal Matray. SC. Paris: Cerf, 1970.

———. *Le protreptique*, edited and translated by Claude Mondésert. SC. Paris: Cerf, 1949.

Dio of Prusa. *Dionis Prusaensis, auem vocant Chrysostomum, quae exstant omnia*, edited by J. von Arnim. 2 vols. Repr. Berlin: Weidmann, 1962.

———. *Discourses 12–30*, translated by J. W. Cohoon. LCL. Cambridge, MA: Harvard University Press, 1939.

Eusebius. *Die Kirchengeschichte*, edited by E. Schwartz and Th. Mommsen. GCS. 3 vols. Repr. Berlin: Akademie Verlag, 1999.

Geffcken, Johannes. *Zwei Griechische Apologeten*. Leipzig: B. G. Teubner, 1907.

Homer. *The Odyssey*, translated by Richmond Alexander Lattimore. New York: Harper & Row, 1967.

Horace. *Satires, Epistles and Ars Poetica*, translated by H. Rushton Fairclough. LCL. Cambridge, MA: Harvard University Press, 1966.

Justin. *Iustini Martyris Dialogus cum Tryphone*, edited by Miroslav Marcovich. Berlin: De Gruyter, 1997.

———. *St. Justin Martyr: The First and Second Apologies*, translated by Leslie W. Barnard. New York: Paulist Press, 1997.

———. *Iustini Martyris Apologiae pro Christianis*, edited by Miroslav Marcovich. Berlin: De Gruyter, 1994.

Juvenal. *Satires*. In *Juvenal and Persius*, translated by Susanna Morton Braund. LCL. Cambridge, MA: Harvard University Press, 2004.

Lucian. *De Dea Syria*, translated by J. L. Lightfoot. Oxford: Oxford University Press, 2003.

———. *Works*, translated by A. M. Harmon. LCL. 10 vols. Repr. Cambridge, MA: Harvard University Press, 1999.

The Martyrdom of Perpetua and Felicitas. In *The Acts of the Christian Martyrs*, edited by Herbert Musurillo. Oxford: Clarendon Press, 1972.

Maximus of Tyre. *The Philosophical Orations*, translated by Michael B. Trapp. Oxford: Oxford University Press, 1997.

———. *Dissertationes*, edited by Michael B. Trapp. Leipzig: Teubner, 1994.

Menander Rhetor, translated and edited by D. A. Russell and Nigel Guy Wilson. Oxford: Clarendon, 1981.

Minucius Felix. *M. Minuci Felicis Octavius*, edited by Bernhard Kytzler. Leipzig: Teubner, 1992.

The Mishnah, translated by Herbert Danby. London: Oxford, 1933.

Novum Testamentum Graece, edited by Eberhard Nestle, Erwin Nestle, Barbara Aland, and Kurt Aland. 26th ed. Stuttgart: Deutsche Bibelgesellschaft, 1987.

Otto, Johannes. *Corpus Apologetarum Christianorum Saeculi Secundi*. 9 vols. Wiesbaden: Sändig, 1851–1969.

Ovid. *The Metamorphoses*, translated by Mary M. Innes. Baltimore, MD: Penguin Books, 1955.

Pausanias. *Description of Greece*, translated by W. H. S. Jones and Henry Arderne Ormerod. LCL. 5 vols. Repr. Cambridge, MA: Harvard University Press, 2000.

———. *Pausaniae Graeciae Descriptio*, edited by Maria-Helena Rocha-Pereira. 3 vols. Leipzig: Teubner, 1903.

Philo. *Philo's Flaccus: The First Pogrom: Introduction, Translation, and Commentary*, edited and translated by Pieter Willem van der Horst. Leiden: E. J. Brill, 2003.

———. *On the Creation of the World*. In Philo, *Works*, vol. 1, translated by F. H. Colson and G. H. Whitaker. LCL. Cambridge, MA: Harvard University Press, 1971.

———. *Philonis Alexandrini opera quae supersunt*, edited by L. Cohn and S. Reiter. 1915. Repr. Berlin: De Gruyter, 1962.

———. *Philonis Alexandrini Legatio ad Gaium*, edited and translated by E. Mary Smallwood. Leiden: E. J. Brill, 1961.

Philostratus. *Philostratus, Imagines and Callistratus, Descriptions*, translated by Arthur Fairbanks. LCL. New York: Putnam, 1931.

Philostratus, Flavius. *Opera*, edited by C. L. Kayser. 1871. Repr. Hildesheim: Olms, 1964.

———. *The Life of Apollonius of Tyana*, translated by Christopher P. Jones. LCL. 2 vols. Cambridge, MA: Harvard University Press, 2005.

Plato. *Euthyphro, Apology, Crito, Phaedo, Phaedrus*, translated by Harold North Fowler. LCL. Repr. Cambridge, MA: Harvard University Press, 1995.

Pliny the Elder. *Natural History*, translated by H. Rackham et al. LCL. 10 vols. Repr. Cambridge, MA: Harvard University Press, 1967–2003.

Pliny the Younger. *Plinius, Epistulae. A Critical Edition*, edited by Edgar Selatie Stout. Bloomington: Indiana University Press, 1962.

Plutarch. *Plutarch's Moralia*, translated by Frank Cole Babbitt, Harold North Fowler, et al. 16 vols. Cambridge, MA: Harvard University Press, 1969.

Ptolemy. *Kriterion*. In *The Criterion of Truth*, translated and edited by Pamela Huby and Gordon Neal, 179–230. Liverpool: Liverpool University Press, 1989.

Res Gestae divi Augusti, in *Velleius Paterculus Compendium of Roman History; Res Gestae divi Augusti*, translated by Fredrick Shipley. LCL. New York: G. P. Putnam's Sons, 1924.

Sapientia Salomonis. In *Septuaginta*. vol. 12.1, edited by Joseph Ziegler. Göttingen: Vandenhoeck and Ruprecht, 1962.

———. *The Wisdom of Solomon: A New Translation with Introduction and Commentary*, by David Winston. The Anchor Bible. Garden City, NY: Doubleday, 1979.

Septuaginta, edited by Alfred Rahlfs. 2nd ed. Stuttgart: Deutsche Bibelgesellschaft, 1935.

Statius. *Silvae*, translated by D. R. Shackleton Bailey. LCL. Vol. 3. Cambridge, MA: Harvard University Press, 2003.

Strabo. *The Geography*, translated by Horace L. Jones and J. R. S. Sterrett. 8 vols. Cambridge, MA: Harvard University Press, 1960–70.

———. *Strabonis geographica*, edited by A. Meineke. 1877. 3 vols. Repr. Leipzig: Teubner, 1969.

The Tabula of Cebes, edited and translated by John T. Fitzgerald and L. Michael White. Chico, CA: Scholars Press, 1983.

Tatian. *Tatiani Oratio ad Graecos; Theophili Antiocheni ad Autolycum*, edited by Miroslav Marcovich. Berlin: De Gruyter, 1995.

———. *Tatiani Oratio ad Graecos*. Texte und Untersuchungen zur Geschichte der altchristlichen Literatur 4.1, edited by Eduard Schwartz. Leipzig: J. C. Hinrichs'sche Buchhandlung, 1888.

———. *Oratio ad Graecos and Fragments*, translated and edited by Molly Whittaker. Oxford: Clarendon, 1982.

Tertullian. *Apologetical Works, and Minucius Felix, Octavius*, translated by Rudolphus Arbesmann, Emily Joseph Daly, and Edwin A. Quain. The Fathers of the Church. Vol. 10. Washington D.C.: Catholic University of America Press, 1962.

Vitruvius Pollio. *De Architectura*, edited by F. Krohn. Leipzig: B. G. Teubner, 1912.

———. *Ten Books on Architecture*, translated by Ingrid D. Rowland. Cambridge: Cambridge University Press, 1999.

B. MODERN SOURCES

"'Apologetic,' 'Apology.'" In *Oxford English Dictionary*, edited by J. A. Simpson and E. S. C. Weiner, 553–54. 2nd ed. Oxford: Oxford University Press, 1989.

Abbasoğlu, Halûk. "The Founding of Perge and its Development in the Hellenistic and Roman Periods." In *Urbanism in Western Asia Minor: New Studies on Aphrodisias, Ephesos, Hierapolis, Pergamon, Perge, and Xanthos*, edited by David Parrish, 173–88. Portsmouth, RI: Journal of Roman Archaeology, 2001.

Adams, Colin and Ray Laurence. *Travel and Geography in the Roman Empire*. New York: Routledge, 2001.

Alcock, Susan E. *Archaeologies of the Greek Past: Landscape, Monuments, and Memories*. Cambridge: Cambridge University Press, 2002.

———. "The Reconfiguration of Memory in the Eastern Roman Empire." In *Empires: Perspectives from Archaeology and History*, edited by Susan Alcock et al., 323–50. Cambridge: Cambridge University Press, 2001.

———. *Graecia Capta: The Landscapes of Roman Greece*. Cambridge: Cambridge University Press, 1993.

——— et al., eds. *Pausanias: Travel and Memory in Roman Greece*. Oxford: Oxford University Press, 2001.

Alexander, Loveday. "Mapping Early Christianity." *Interpretation* 57, no. 2 (2003): 163–75.

———. "The Acts of the Apostles as an Apologetic Text." In *Apologetics in the Roman Empire: Pagans, Jews, and Christians*, edited by Mark Edwards et al., 15–44. Oxford: Oxford University Press, 1999.

———. "'In Journeyings often': Voyaging in the Acts of the Apostles and in Greek Romance." In *Luke's Literary Achievement: Collected Essays*, edited by C. M. Tuckett, 17–39. Sheffield: Sheffield Academic Press, 1995.

———. *The Preface to Luke's Gospel: Literary Convention and Social Context in Luke 1.1–4 and Acts 1.1*. Cambridge: Cambridge University Press, 1993.

Almagor, Eran. "Strabo's Barbarophonoi (14.2.28 C 661–3): A Note." *Scripta Classica Israelica* 19 (2000): 133–38.

Althusser, Louis. "Ideology and the Ideological State Apparatuses: Notes Towards an Investigation." In *Lenin and Philosophy and Other Essays*, translated by Ben Brewster, 106–26. New York: Monthly Review Press, 2001.

Ando, Clifford. *The Matter of the Gods: Religion and the Roman Empire*. Berkeley: University of California Press, 2008.

———. *Imperial Ideology and Provincial Loyalty in the Roman Empire*. Berkley: University of California Press, 2000.

———."Pagan Apologetics and Christian Intolerance in the Age of Themistius and Augustine." *JECS* 4, no. 2 (1996): 171–207.

Andresen, Carl. *Logos und Nomos: die Polemik des Kelsus wider das Christentum*. Berlin: De Gruyter, 1955.

Appadurai, Arjun. "Introduction: commodities and the politics of value." In *The Social Life of Things: Commodities in Cultural Perspective*, edited by Arjun Appadurai, 3–63. Repr. Cambridge: Cambridge University Press, 2003.

Arnold-Biucchi, Carmen. *Alexander's Coins and Alexander's Image*. Cambridge, MA: Harvard University Art Museums, 2006.

Asad, Talal. *Genealogies of Religion: Discipline and Reasons of Power in Christianity and Islam*. Baltimore, MD: John Hopkins University Press, 1993.

Athanassiadi, Polymnia and Michael Frede, eds. *Pagan Monotheism in Late Antiquity*. Oxford: Clarendon, 1999.

Attridge, Harold W. "The Philosophical Critique of Religion under the Early Empire." *ANRW* 2, no. 1 (1978): 45–78.

Austin, J. L. *How to Do Things with Words*, edited by J. O. Urmson and Marina Sbisà. 2nd ed. Cambridge, MA: Harvard University Press, 1975.

Aymard, J. "Vénus et les impératrices sous les derniers Antonins." *Mélanges d'archéologie et d'histoire* 51 (1934): 178–96.

Balch, David. "ΜΕΤΑΒΟΛΗ ΠΟΛΙΤΕΙΩΝ: Jesus as Founder of the Church in Luke–Acts: Form and Function." In *Contextualizing Acts: Lukan Narrative and Greco–Roman Discourse*, edited by Todd Penner and Caroline Vander Stichele, 139–88. Atlanta: SBL, 2003.

———. "Comparing Literary Patterns in Luke and Lucian." *The Perkins School of Theology Journal* 40, no. 2 (1987): 39–42.

Bann, Stephen. *The True Vine: On Visual Representation and the Western Tradition*. Cambridge: Cambridge University Press, 1989.

Barnard, Leslie W. *Athenagoras: A Study in Second Century Christian Apologetic*. Paris: Beauchesne, 1972.

———. "The Heresy of Tatian – Once again." *JEH* 19, no. 1 (1968): 1–10.

Barnes, Timothy D. "The Embassy of Athenagoras." *JTS* 86, no. 1 (1975): 111–14.

———. "Legislation against the Christians." *JRS* 58 (1968): 32–50.

Barth, Karl. *The Doctrine of the Word of God: Prolegomena to Church Dogmatics*. Edinburgh: T & T Clark, 1975.

Bartsch, Shadi. *The Mirror of the Self: Sexuality, Self-Knowledge, and the Gaze in the Early Roman Empire*. Chicago: University of Chicago Press, 2006.

———. *Actors in the Audience: Theatricality and Doublespeak from Nero to Hadrian*. Cambridge, MA: Harvard University Press, 1994.

Baur, F. C. *Paul: The Apostle of Jesus Christ*. 2 vols. in one. Peabody, MA: Hendrickson, 2003.

Baxter, Timothy M. S. *The Cratylus: Plato's Critique of Naming*. Leiden: E. J. Brill, 1992.

Beard, Mary. *The Roman Triumph*. Cambridge, MA: Belknap, 2007.

———. "The Triumph of the Absurd: Roman Street Theater." In *Rome the Cosmopolis*, edited by Catharine Edwards and Greg Woolf, 21–43. Cambridge: Cambridge University Press, 2003.

Béchard, Dean Philip. *Paul Outside the Walls: A Study of Luke's Socio-Geographical Universalism in Acts 14:8–20*. Rome: Editrice Pontificio Istituto Biblico, 2000.

Behr, John. *Asceticism and Anthropology in Irenaeus and Clement*. New York: Oxford University Press, 2000.

Benjamin, Anna. "The Altars of Hadrian in Athens and Hadrian's Panhellenic Program." *Hesp.* 32, no. 1 (1963): 57–86.

Benjamin, Walter. *Illuminations: Essays and Reflections*, edited by Hannah Arendt and translated by Harry Zohn. New York: Schocken, 1969.

Bergmann, Bettina. "Greek Masterpieces and Roman Recreative Fictions." *HSCP* 97 (1995): 79–120.

Bergmann, Marianne. *Die Strahlen der Herrscher: Theomorphes Herrscherbild und politische Symbolik im Hellenismus und in der römischen Kaiserzeit*. DAI. Mainz: von Zabern, 1998.

Bhabha, Homi. *The Location of Culture*. New York: Routledge, 1994.

Bignamini, Ilaria. "The 'Campo Iemini Venus' Rediscovered." *The Burlington Magazine* 136 (1994): 548–52.

Blank, David and Catherine Atherton. "The Stoic Contribution to Traditional Grammar." In *The Cambridge Companion to the Stoics*, edited by Brad Inwood, 310–27. Cambridge: Cambridge University Press, 2003.

Boatwright, Mary. *Hadrian and the Cities of the Roman Empire*. Princeton, NJ: Princeton University Press, 2000.

———. "Plancia Magna of Perge: Women's Roles and Statue in Roman Asia Minor." In *Women's History and Ancient History*, edited by Sarah Pomeroy, 249–71. Chapel Hill: University of North Carolina Press, 1991.

Bol, Renate. *Das Statuenprogramm des Herodes-Atticus-Nymphäums*. Olympische Forschungen XV. Berlin: De Gruyter, 1984.

Bonz, Marianne Palmer. *The Past as Legacy: Luke-Acts and Ancient Epic*. Minneapolis, MN: Fortress, 2000.

Botti, Guiseppe. "Atenagora quale fonte per la storia dell'arte." *Didaskaleion* 4 (1915): 395–417.

Bourdieu, Pierre. "The Forms of Capital." In *Handbook of Theory and Research for the Sociology of Education*, translated by Richard Nice and edited by John G. Richardson, 241–58. New York: Greenwood Press, 1986.

Boustan, Ra'anan. "The Spoils of the Jerusalem Temple at Rome and Constantinople: Jewish Counter-Geography in a Christianizing Empire." In *Antiquity in Antiquity: Jewish and Christian Pasts in the Greco-Roman World*, edited by Gregg Gardner and Kevin L. Osterloh, 327–72. Tübingen: Mohr Siebeck, 2008.

Bovon, François. "The Reception and Use of the Gospel of Luke in the Second Century." In *Reading Luke: Interpretation, Reflection, Formation*, edited by Craig Bartholomew et al., 379–400. Grand Rapids, MI: Zondervan, 2005.

———. "Israel, the Church and the Gentiles in the Twofold Work of Luke." In *New Testament Traditions and Apocryphal Narratives*, translated by Jane Haapiseva-Hunter, 81–104. Allison Park, PA: Pickwick, 1995.

Bowersock, Glenn. *Greek Sophists in the Roman Empire*. Oxford: Clarendon, 1969.

Bowman, Alan K. *Egypt after the Pharaohs: 332 B.C. – A.D. 642*. Berkeley: University of California Press, 1986.

Bowman, Alan, P. Garnsey, and D. Rathbone, eds. *The Cambridge Ancient History: The High Empire, A.D. 70–92*. 2nd ed. Cambridge: Cambridge University Press, 2000.

Boyarin, Daniel. *Border Lines: The Partition of Judaeo-Christianity*. Philadelphia: University of Pennsylvania Press, 2004.

———. "Justin Martyr Invents Judaism." *CH* 70, no. 3 (2001): 427–61.

———. *Dying for God: Martyrdom and the Making of Christianity and Judaism*. Stanford: Stanford University Press, 1999.

Brackett, John K. "An Analysis of the Literary Structure and Forms in the Protrepticus and Paidagogus of Clement of Alexandria." Ph.D. Dissertation, Emory University, 1986.

Brakke, David. *Demons and the Making of the Monk: Spiritual Combat in Early Christianity*. Cambridge, MA: Harvard University Press, 2006.

Branham, R. Bracht. "Authorizing Humor: Lucian's *Demonax* and Cynic Rhetoric." *Semeia* 64, no. 1 (1993): 33–48.

———. *Unruly Eloquence: Lucian and the Comedy of Traditions*. Cambridge, MA: Harvard University Press, 1989.

———. "Introducing a Sophist: Lucian's Prologues." *Transactions of the American Philological Association* 115 (1985): 237–43.

Brent, Allen. *The Imperial Cult and the Development of Church Order: Concepts and Images of Authority in Paganism and Early Christianity before the Age of Cyprian*. Leiden: E. J. Brill, 1999.

Brilliant, Richard. *Visual Narratives: Storytelling in Etruscan and Roman Art*. Ithaca, NY: Cornell University Press, 1984.

Brody, Lisa. *The Aphrodite of Aphrodisias*. Mainz: von Zabern, 2007.

Brooten, Bernadette J. *Love Between Women: Early Christian Responses to Female Homoeroticism*. Chicago: University of Chicago Press, 1996.

Buck, P. Lorraine. "Athenagoras's *Embassy*: A Literary Fiction." *HTR* 89, no. 3 (1996).

Buell, Denise Kimber. "Ambiguous Legacy: A Feminist Commentary on Clement of Alexandria's Works." In *The Feminist Companion to Patristic Literature*, edited by Amy-Jill Levine, 26–55. London: T & T Clark, 2008.

———. *Why This New Race? Ethnic Reasoning in Early Christianity*. New York: Columbia University Press, 2005.

———. "Race and Universalism in Early Christianity." *JECS* 10, no. 4 (2002): 429–68.

———. "Rethinking the Relevance of Race for Early Christian Self-Definition." *HTR* 94, no. 4 (2001): 449–76.

Burrows, Mark S. "Christianity in the Roman Forum: Tertullian and the Apologetic Use of History." *VC* 42, no. 3 (1998): 209–35.

Burrus, Virginia. "The Gospel of Luke and the Acts of the Apostles." In *A Postcolonial Commentary on the New Testament Writings*, edited by R. S. Sugirtharajah, 133–55. New York: T & T Clark, 2007.

Butler, Judith. *Excitable Speech: A Politics of the Performative*. New York: Routledge, 1997.

———. "Conscience Doth Make Subjects of Us All." *Yale French Studies* 88 (1995): 6–26.

Byron, Gay L. *Symbolic Blackness and Ethnic Difference in Early Christian Literature*. New York: Routledge, 2002.

Cadbury, Henry J. *The Book of Acts in History*. New York: Harper & Brothers, 1955.

———. *The Study and Literary Method of Luke*. HTS 6. Cambridge, MA: Harvard University Press, 1920.

Camp, John. *The Archaeology of Athens*. New Haven: Yale University Press, 2001.

Casson, Lionel. *The Periplus Maris Erythraei. Text with Introduction, Translation, and Commentary*. Princeton, NJ: Princeton University Press, 1989.

Castelli, Elizabeth. *Martyrdom and Memory: Early Christian Culture Making*. New York: Columbia University Press, 2004.

Chadwick, Henry. *The Early Church*. Baltimore, MD: Penguin, 1967.

Chin, Catherine M. *Grammar and Christianity in the Late Roman World*. Philadelphia: University of Pennsylvania Press, 2008.

———. "Origen and Christian Naming: Textual Exhaustion and the Boundaries of Gentility in Commentary on John 1." *JECS* 14, no. 4 (2006) 407–36.

Choufrine, Arkadi. *Gnosis, Theophany, Theosis: Studies in Clement of Alexandria's Appropriation of His Background*. New York: Peter Lang, 2002.

Clark, Kenneth. *The Nude: A Study of Ideal Art*. London: J. Murray, 1956.

Clarke, G. W. "The Date of the Oration of Tatian." *HTR* 60, no. 1 (Jan., 1967): 123–26.

Clarke, John R. *Art in the Lives of Ordinary Romans: Visual Representation and Non-Elite Viewers in Italy, 100 B.C.–A.D. 315*. Berkeley: University of California Press, 2003.

———. "Look Who's Laughing at Sex: Men and Women Viewers in the *Apodyterium* of the Suburban Baths of Pompeii." In *The Roman Gaze: Vision, Power, and the Body*, edited by David Fredrick, 149–81. Baltimore, MD: Johns Hopkins University Press, 2002.

Clarke, Katherine. *Between Geography and History: Hellenistic Constructions of the Roman World*. Oxford: Oxford University Press, 1999.

Clerc, Charly. *Les théories relatives au cultes des images chez les auteurs grecs du IIme siècle après J.-C.* Paris: Fontemoing, 1915.

Coarelli, Filippo. *The Column of Trajan*, translated by Cynthia Rockwell. Rome: Editore Colombo, 2000.

Cody, Lisa Forman. *Birthing the Nation: Sex, Science, and the Conception of Eighteenth-Century Britons.* Oxford: Oxford University Press, 2005.

Cohen, Shaye J. D. *The Beginnings of Jewishness: Boundaries, Varieties, Uncertainties.* Berkeley: University of California Press, 1999.

Coleman, Kathleen. "Fatal Charades: Roman Executions Staged as Mythological Enactments." *JRS* 80 (1990): 44–73.

Collins, John J. *Jewish Wisdom in the Hellenistic Age.* 1st ed. Louisville, KY: Westminster John Knox, 1997.

Conti, Cinzia. "The Restoration of Trajan's Column (1981–88)." In *The Column of Trajan*, edited by Filippo Coarelli and translated by Cynthia Rockwell, 245–49. Rome: Editore Colombo, 2000.

Conzelmann, Hans. *Acts of the Apostles: A Commentary.* Hermeneia. Philadelphia: Fortress, 1987.

———. *The Theology of St. Luke*, translated by Geoffrey Buswell. 1962. Repr. Philadelphia: Fortress, 1982.

Corso, Antonio. *The Art of Praxiteles II: The Mature Years.* Rome: "L'Erma" di Bretschneider, 2007.

Cosgrove, Charles H. "Clement of Alexandria and Early Christian Music." *JECS* 14, no. 3 (2006): 255–82.

D'Ambra, Eve. "Nudity and Adornment in Female Portrait Sculpture of the Second Century AD." In *I, Claudia II: Women in Roman Art and Society*, edited by Diana E. E. Kleiner and Susan B. Matheson, 101–14. Austin: University of Texas Press, 2000.

———. "The Calculus of Venus: Nude Portraits of Roman Matrons." In *Sexuality in Ancient Art: Near East, Egypt, Greece, and Italy, Cambridge Studies in New Art History and Criticism*, edited by Natalie Boymel Kampen and Bettina Ann Bergmann, 219–32. Cambridge: Cambridge University Press, 1996.

———. *Private Lives, Public Virtues: The Frieze of the Forum Transitorium in Rome.* Princeton, NJ: Princeton University Press, 1993.

Darwall-Smith, Robin. *Emperors and Architecture: A Study of Flavian Rome.* Bruxelles: Latomus, 1996.

Davies, Penelope J. E. "The Politics of Perpetuation: Trajan's Column and the Art of Commemoration." *AJA* 101, no. 1 (1997): 41–65.

Davis, Richard H. *Lives of Indian Images.* 1st paperback ed. Princeton, NJ: Princeton University Press, 1999.

de Certeau, Michel. *The Practice of Everyday Life*, translated by Steven Rendall. Berkeley: University of California Press, 1984.

Dench, Emma. *Romulus' Asylum: On Roman Identities from the Age of Alexander to the Age of Hadrian.* Oxford: Oxford University Press, 2005.

de Ste. Croix, G. E. M. *Christian Persecution, Martyrdom, and Orthodoxy*, edited by Michael Whitby and Joseph Streeter. Oxford: Oxford University Press, 2006.

Dibelius, Martin. *The Book of Acts: Form, Style, and Theology*, edited by K. C. Hanson. Minneapolis, MN: Fortress, 2004.

Dilke, O. A. W. *Greek and Roman Maps.* Baltimore, MD: John Hopkins University Press, 1998.

Dobrov, Gregory W. "The Sophist on His Craft: Art, Text, and Self-Construction in Lucian." *Helios* 29, no. 2 (2002): 173–92.

Dodds, E. R. *Pagan and Christian in an Age of Anxiety: Some Aspects of Religious Experience from Marcus Aurelius to Constantine.* Cambridge: Cambridge University Press, 1965.

Donohue, A. A. *Xoana and the Origins of Greek Sculpture.* Atlanta: Scholars Press, 1988.

Droge, Arthur J. "Apologetics, NT." In *The Anchor Bible Dictionary*, edited by David N. Freedman, 302–7. New York: Doubleday, 1990.

———. *Homer or Moses? Early Christian Interpretations of the History of Culture.* Tübingen: Mohr (Siebeck), 1989.

Dupont, Jacques. *The Sources of the Acts: The Present Position*, translated by K. Pond. London: Darton, Longman & Todd, 1964.

Eliav, Yaron Z. "Roman Statues, Rabbis, and Graeco-Roman Culture." In *Jewish Literatures and Cultures – Context and Intertext*, edited by Yaron Z. Eliav and Anita Norich, 99–115. *Jewish Literatures and Cultures: Context and Intertext*. Providence, RI: Brown Judaic Studies, 2008.

Elsner, Jaś. *Roman Eyes: Visuality and Subjectivity in Art and Text*. Princeton: Princeton University Press, 2007.

———. "Archaeologies and Agendas: Reflections on Late Ancient Jewish Art and Early Christian Art." *JRS* 93 (2003): 114–128.

———. "Describing Self in the Language of Other: Pseudo (?) Lucian at the Temple of Hierapolis." In *Being Greek under Rome: Cultural Identity, the Second Sophistic and the Development of Empire*, edited by Simon Goldhill, 123–53. Cambridge: Cambridge University Press, 2001.

———. *Imperial Rome and Christian Triumph: The Art of the Roman Empire A.D. 100–450*. Oxford: Oxford University Press, 1998.

———. *Art and the Roman Viewer: The Transformation of Art from the Pagan World to Christianity*. Cambridge: Cambridge University Press, 1997.

———. "Pausanias: A Greek Pilgrim in the Roman World." *Past and Present* 135 (May 1992, 1992): 3–29.

Elsner, Jaś and Joan-Pau Rubiés, eds. *Voyages and Visions: Towards a Cultural History of Travel*. London: Reaktion, 1999.

Elsner, Jaś and Ian Rutherford, eds. *Pilgrimage in Graeco-Roman and Early Christian Antiquity: Seeing the Gods*. Oxford: Oxford University Press, 2005.

Elze, Martin. *Tatian und seine Theologie*. Göttingen: Vandenhoeck and Ruprecht, 1960.

Esler, Philip. *Community and Gospel in Luke-Acts: The Social and Political Motivations of Lucan Theology*. Cambridge: Cambridge University Press, 1987.

Fanon, Frantz. *Black Skin, White Masks*, translated by Charles Lam Markmann. New York: Grove Press, 1967.

Felletti Maj, B. J. "'Afrodite Pudica': Saggio d'arte ellenistica." *Archeologia Classica* 3, no. 1 (1951): 33–65.

Ferguson, Everett. *Demonology of the Early Christian World*. New York: Edwin Mellen, 1980.

Fine, Steven. *Art and Judaism in the Greco-Roman World: Toward a New Jewish Archaeology*. Cambridge: Cambridge University Press, 2005.

Finney, Paul Corby. *The Invisible God: The Earliest Christians on Art*. Oxford: Oxford University Press, 1994.

Fittschen, Klaus and Paul Zanker. *Katalog der römischen Porträts in den Capitolinischen Museen und den anderen kommunalen Sammlungen der Stadt Rom*. Mainz: von Zabern, 1983.

Florescu, Florea Bobu. *Monumentul de la Adamklissi Tropaeum Traiani*. Bucharest: Editura Academiei Republicii Populare Romine, 1959.

Flower, Harriet I. *The Art of Forgetting: Disgrace and Oblivion in Roman Political Culture*. Chapel Hill: University of North Carolina, 2006.

Foakes-Jackson, F. J. and Kirsopp Lake, eds. *The Beginnings of Christianity: Acts of the Apostles*. London: MacMillan, 1920–33.

Foucault, Michel. *The Use of Pleasure*, vol. 2, *The History of Sexuality*, translated by Robert Hurley. New York: Vintage Books, 1990.

Frankfurter, David. "Introduction: Approaches to Coptic Pilgrimage." In *Pilgrimage and Holy Space in Late Antique Egypt*, edited by David Frankfurter. Leiden: E. J. Brill, 1998.

Fraser, P. M. "Hadrian and Cyrene." *JRS* 40, no. 1–2 (1950): 77–90.

Fredouille, Jean-Claude. "L'apologétique chrétienne antique: metamorphoses d'un genre polymorphe." *Revue des Études Augustiniennes* 41 (1995): 201–26.

———. "L'apologétique chrétienne antique: naissance d'un genre littéraire." *Revue des Études Augustiniennes* 38 (1992): 218–34.

Fredrick, David. "Introduction: Invisible Rome." In *The Roman Gaze: Vision, Power, and the Body*, edited by David Fredrick, 1–30. Baltimore, MD: Johns Hopkins University Press, 2002.

Freedberg, David. *The Power of Images: Studies in the History and Theory of Response*. Chicago: University of Chicago Press, 1989.

Frend, W. H. C. *The Rise of Christianity*. Philadelphia: Fortress, 1984.

———. *Martyrdom and Persecution in the Early Church: A Study of a Conflict from the Maccabees to Donatus*. Oxford: Blackwell, 1965.

Friesen, Steven. *Twice Neokoros: Ephesus, Asia, and the Cult of the Flavian Imperial Family*. Leiden: E. J. Brill, 1993.

Frilingos, Christopher A. *Spectacles of Empire: Monsters, Martyrs, and the Book of Revelation, Divinations*. Philadelphia: University of Pennsylvania Press, 2004.

Gaca, Kathy L. *The Making of Fornication: Eros, Ethics, and Political Reform in Greek Philosophy and Early Christianity*. Berkeley: University of California, 2003.

Gadza, Elaine, ed. *The Ancient Art of Emulation: Studies in Artistic Originality and Tradition from the Present to Classical Antiquity*. Ann Arbor: University of Michigan Press, 2002.

———. "Roman Sculpture and the Ethos of Admiration: Reconsidering Repetition." *HSCP* 97 (1995): 121–56.

Galinsky, Karl. "Herakles in Greek and Roman Mythology." In *Herakles: Passage of the Hero through 1000 Years of Classical Art*, edited by Jaimee Pugliese Uhlenbrock et al., 19–22. New Rochelle, NY: A. D. Caratzas and Annandale-on-Hudson, NY: Edith C. Blum Art Institute, Bard College, 1986.

Gamble, Harry. "Apologetics." In *The Encyclopedia of Early Christianity*, edited by Everett Ferguson, 81–87. New York: Garland, 1990.

Gates, Charles. *Ancient Cities: The Archaeology of Urban Life in the Ancient Near East and Egypt, Greece and Rome*. New York: Routledge, 2003.

Georgiadou, Aristoula and David H. J. Larmour. *Lucian's Science Fiction Novel True Histories: Interpretation and Commentary*. Leiden: E. J. Brill, 1998.

Gibbon, Edward. *History of the Decline and Fall of the Roman Empire*. 2 vols. Cincinnati: J. A. James, 1840.

Gilbert, Gary. "The List of Nations in Acts 2: Roman Propaganda and Lukan Response." *JBL* 121, no. 3 (2002): 497–529.

Glancy, Jennifer A. "Boasting of Beatings (2 Corinthians 11:23–5)." *JBL* 123, no. 1 (2004): 99–135.

Gleason, Maud W. "Greek Cities under Roman Rule." In *A Companion to the Roman Empire*, edited by David S. Potter, 228–49. Malden, MA: Blackwell, 2006.

———. *Making Men: Sophists and Self–Presentation in Ancient Rome*. Princeton, NJ: Princeton University Press, 1995.

Goldhill, Simon, ed. *Being Greek under Rome: Cultural Identity, the Second Sophistic, and the Development of Empire*. Cambridge: Cambridge University Press, 2001.

———. *Foucault's Virginity: Ancient Erotic Fiction and the History of Sexuality*. Cambridge: Cambridge University Press, 1995.

Goodenough, Erwin R. *Jewish Symbols in the Greco-Roman Period*. Bollingen Series, 37. New York: Pantheon Books, 1953.

———. *The Theology of Justin Martyr*. Jena: Verlag Frommansche Buchhandlung, 1923.

Gordon, Richard. "'The Real and the Imaginary': Production and Religion in the Graeco-Roman World." *Art History* 2 (1979): 5–34.

Gould, Peter and Rodney White. *Mental Maps*. 2nd ed. Boston: Allen and Unwin, 1986.

Graindor, Paul. *Athènes sous Hadrien*. Cairo: Imprimerie Nationale, Boulac, 1934.

Grant, R. M. "Five Apologists and Marcus Aurelius." *VC* 42, no. 1 (1988): 1–17.

———. *Greek Apologists of the Second Century*. Philadelphia: Westminster, 1988.

———. *Gods and the One God*. Philadelphia: Westminster, 1986.

———. "Sacrifices and Oaths as Required of Early Christians." In *Kyriakon: Festschrift Johannes Quasten*, edited by Patrick Granfield and Josef Jungmann, 1.12–17. 2 vols. Münster: Verlag Aschendorff, 1970.

———. "Athenagoras or Pseudo–Athenagoras." *HTR* 47, no. 2 (1954): 121–29.

———. "The Heresy of Tatian." *JTS* 5, no. 1 (1954): 62–68.

———. "The Date of Tatian's Oration." *HTR* 46, no. 2 (1953): 99–101.

Green, Miranda J. "God in Man's Image: Thoughts on the Genesis and Affiliations of some Romano-British Cult-Imagery." *Britannia* 29 (1998): 17–30.

Gregory, Andrew. *The Reception of Luke and Acts in the Period before Irenaeus*. WUNT 2.169. Tübingen: Mohr Siebeck, 2003.

Habicht, Christian. *Altertümer von Pergamon, III.3, Die Inscriften des Asklepieions*. DAI. Berlin: De Gruyter, 1969.

Haenchen, Ernst. *The Acts of the Apostles*. Philadelphia: Westminster, 1971.

Hall, Jonathan. *Hellenicity: Between Ethnicity and Culture*. Chicago: University of Chicago Press, 2002.

Hallett, Christopher. "Emulation *versus* Replication: Redefining Roman Copying." *JRA* 18 (2005): 419–35.

———. *The Roman Nude: Heroic Portrait Statuary 200 B.C.–A.D. 300*. Oxford: Oxford University Press, 2005.

Halliwell, Stephen. *The Aesthetics of Mimesis: Ancient Texts and Modern Problems*. Princeton, NJ: Princeton University Press, 2002.

Hannah, Robert. "The Emperor's Stars: The Conservatori Portrait of Commodus." *AJA* 90, no. 3 (1986): 337–42.

Harnack, Adolf von. *History of Dogma*, translated from the 3rd German edition by Neil Buchanan. 7 vols. in 4. Gloucester, MA: Peter Smith, 1976.

———. *Sokrates und die alte Kirche*. Berlin: G. Schade (O. Francke), 1900.

———. *Lehrbuch der Dogmengeschichte*. 3 vols. Freiburg and Leipzig: J. C. B. Mohr, 1894.

———. *Die Überlieferung der griechischen Apologeten des zweiten Jahrhunderts in der alten Kirche und im Mittelalter*. Texte und Untersuchungen zur Geschichte der altchristlichen Literatur 1.1–2. Leipzig: J. C. Hinrichs, 1882.

Harris, J. Rendel. *The Apology of Aristides on Behalf of the Christians: From a Syriac Manuscript Preserved on Mount Sinai*. 1891. Repr. Piscataway, NJ: Gorgias Press, 2004.

Hartog, François. *Memories of Odysseus*, translated by Janet Lloyd. Edinburgh: Edinburgh University Press, 2001.

Harvey, David. *Spaces of Hope*. Berkeley: University of California Press, 2000.

———. *Justice, Nature, and the Geography of Difference*. Cambridge, MA: Blackwell, 1996.

Hauken, Tor. *Petition and Response: An Epigraphic Study of Petitions to Roman Emperors 181–249*. Bergen: Norwegian Institute at Athens, 1998.

Havelock, Christine Mitchell. *The Aphrodite of Knidos and Her Successors: A Historical Review of the Female Nude in Greek Art*. Ann Arbor: University of Michigan Press, 1995.

Hawthorne, Gerald F. "Tatian and His Discourse to the Greeks." *HTR* 57, no. 3 (1964): 161–88.

Hayden, Dolores. *The Power of Place: Urban Landscapes as Public History*. Cambridge, MA: MIT Press, 1995.

Hekster, Olivier. "Propagating Power: Hercules as an Example for Second-Century Emperors." In *Herakles and Hercules: Exploring a Graeco-Roman Divinity*, edited by Louis Rawlings and Hugh Bowden, 205–21. Swansea, Wales: The Classical Press of Wales and Oakville, CT: The David Brown Book Co., 2005.

———. "Coins and Messages: Audience Targeting on Coins of Different Denominations." In *The Representation and Perception of Roman Imperial Power. Proceedings of the Third Workshop of the International Network Impact of Empire (Roman Empire, c. 200 B.C.–A.D. 476)*, edited by Lukas De Bois et al., 20–35. Amsterdam: Geiben, 2003.

———. *Commodus: An Emperor at the Crossroads*. Amsterdam: Gieben, 2002.

Hitzl, Konrad. *Die kaiserzeitliche Statuenausstattung des Metroon*. Olympische Forschungen Bd. 19. New York: De Gruyter, 1991.

Hodge, Caroline Johnson. *If Sons then Heirs: A Study of Kinship and Ethnicity in Paul's Letters*. Oxford: Oxford University Press, 2007.

Hoek, Annewies van den. "Apologetic and Protreptic Discourse in Clement of Alexandria." In *La littérature apologétique avant Nicée, Entretiens sur l'antiquité classique*, edited by A. Wlosok. Vandoeuvres-Genève: Fondation Hardt, 2005.

———. "The 'Catechetical' School of Early Christian Alexandria and its Philonic Heritage." *HTR* 90, no. 1 (1997): 59–87.

———. "How Alexandrian Was Clement of Alexandria? Reflections on Clement and his Alexandrian Background." *Heythrop Journal* 31 (1990): 179–94.

Hölscher, Tonio. *The Language of Images in Roman Art*, translated by Anthony Snodgrass and Annemarie Künzl-Snodgrass. Cambridge: Cambridge University Press, 2004.

Horner, Timothy J. *Listening to Trypho: Justin Martyr's Dialogue Reconsidered*. Leuven: Peeters, 2001.

Hunt, Emily J. *Christianity in the Second Century: The Case of Tatian*. New York: Routledge, 2003.

Hutton, William. *Describing Greece: Landscape and Literature in the Periegesis of Pausanias*. Cambridge: Cambridge University Press, 2005.

Hyldahl, Niels. *Philosophie und Christentum. Eine Interpretation der Einleitung zum Dialog Justins*. Copenhagen: Munksgaard, 1966.

Isaac, Benjamin. *The Invention of Racism in Classical Antiquity*. Princeton, NJ: Princeton University Press, 2004.

Jackson, Samuel Macauley and George William Gilmore, eds. *The New Schaff-Herzog Encyclopedia of Religious Knowledge*. London: Funk and Wagnalls Company, 1908–14.

Jacobs, Andrew. "Dialogical Differences: (De-) Judaizing Jesus' Circumcision." *JECS* 15 (2007): 291–335.

———. *Remains of the Jews: The Holy Land and Christian Empire in Late Antiquity*. Stanford, CA: Stanford University Press, 2004.

Jaeger, Werner. *Early Christianity and Greek Paideia*. Cambridge: Belknap, 1961.

Jensen, Robin Margaret. *Face to Face: Portraits of the Divine in Early Christianity*. Minneapolis, MN: Fortress, 2005.

Jones, A. H. M. *The Greek City from Alexander to Justinian*. Oxford: Oxford University Press, 1940.

Jones, Christopher P. *Kinship Diplomacy in the Ancient World*. Cambridge, MA: Harvard University Press, 1999.

———. "The Panhellenion." *Chiron* 26 (1996): 29–56.

———. *Culture and Society in Lucian*. Cambridge, MA: Harvard University Press, 1986.

Jones, Henry Stuart. *A Catalogue of the Ancient Sculptures Preserved in the Municipal Collections at Rome*. Oxford: Clarendon, 1912.

Kampen, Natalie Boymel. "Biographical Narration and Roman Funerary Art." *AJA* 85, no. 1 (1981): 47–58.

———. "Epilogue: Gender and Desire." In *Naked Truths: Women, Sexuality, and Gender in Classical Art and Archaeology*, edited by Ann Olga Koloski-Ostrow and Claire L. Lyons, 243–66. New York: Routledge, 1997.

———. "Gender Theory in Roman Art." In *I, Claudia: Women in Ancient Rome*, edited by Diana E. E. Kleiner and Susan B. Matheson, 14–25. Austin, TX: University of Texas Press and New Haven, CT: Yale University Art Gallery, 1996.

———. "Omphale and the Instability of Gender." In *Sexuality in Ancient Art: Near East, Egypt, Greece, and Italy*, edited by Natalie Boymel Kampen and Bettina Ann Bergmann, 233–46. Cambridge: Cambridge University Press, 1996.

———. "Looking at Gender: The Column of Trajan and Roman Historical Relief." In *Feminisms in the Academy*, edited by Donna Stanton and Abigail Stewart, 46–73. Ann Arbor: University of Michigan Press, 1995.

Kampmann, Ursula. "*Homonoia* Politics in Asia Minor: The Example of Pergamon." In *Pergamon: Citadel of the Gods*, edited by Helmut Koester, 373–94. Harrisburg, PA: Trinity Press International, 1998.

King, Karen. "Which Early Christianity?" In *The Oxford Handbook of Early Christian Studies*, edited by Susan Ashbrook Harvey and David G. Hunter, 66–84. Oxford: Oxford University Press, 2008.

———. *What is Gnosticism?* Cambridge, MA: Belknap, 2003.

Klauck, Hans-Josef. *Ancient Letters and the New Testament: A Guide to Content and Exegesis*. Waco, TX: Baylor University Press, 2006.

Kleiner, Diana E. E. *Roman Sculpture*. New Haven, CT: Yale University Press, 1992.

———. "Second-Century Mythological Portraiture: Mars and Venus." *Latomus* 40 (1981): 512–44.

Knox, John. *Marcion and the New Testament: An Essay in the Early History of the Canon*. Chicago: University of Chicago Press, 1942.

Koester, Helmut, ed. *Cities of Paul: Images and Interpretations from the Harvard New Testament Archaeology Project*. CD-Rom. Minneapolis, MN: Fortress, 2005.

Koester, Helmut and Holland Hendrix, eds. *Archaeological Resources for New Testament Studies*. Slides and Texts. 2 vols. Malden, MA: Trinity Press International, 1994.

Köhne, Eckart and Cornelia Ewigleben, eds., *Gladiators and Caesars: The Power of Spectacle in Ancient Rome*. Hamburg: Museum für Kunst und Gewerbe and London: British Museum Press, 2000.

Koltun-Fromm, Naomi. "Re-Imagining Tatian: The Damaging Effects of Polemical Rhetoric." *JECS* 16, no. 1 (2008): 1–30.

Konstan, David. "The Two Faces of Mimesis." *The Philosophical Quarterly* 54, no. 215 (2004): 301–8.

Kopytoff, Igor. "The Cultural Biography of Things: Commoditization as Process." In *The Social Life of Things: Commodities in Social Perspective*, edited by Arjun Appadurai, 64–91. 1986. Repr. Cambridge: Cambridge University Press, 2003.

Kousser, Rachel. "Mythological Group Portrait in Antonine Rome: The Performance of Myth." *AJA* 111, no. 4 (2007): 673–91.

———. "Conquest and Desire: Roman Victoria in Public and Provincial Sculpture Representations of War in Ancient Rome." In *Representations of War in Ancient Rome*, edited by Sheila Dillon and Katherine E. Welch, 218–43. Cambridge: Cambridge University Press, 2006.

———. "Creating the Past. The Vênus de Milo and the Hellenistic Reception of Classical Greece." *AJA* 109, no. 2 (2005): 227–50.

———. "Sensual Power: A Warrior Aphrodite in Greek and Roman Sculpture." Ph.D. Dissertation, New York University, 2001.

Kraemer, Ross S. "Jewish Tuna and Christian Fish: Identifying Religious Affiliation in Epigraphic Sources." *HTR* 84, no. 2 (1991): 141–62.

Kukula, R. C. *Tatians sogenannte Apologie*. Leipzig: Teubner, 1990.

———. *Alterbeweis und Künsterkatalog in Tatians Rede an die Griechen*. Vienna: Self-published, 1900.

Lampe, Peter. *From Paul to Valentinus: Christians at Rome in the First Two Centuries*. Minneapolis, MN: Fortress, 2003.

Lancaster, Lynne. "Building Trajan's Column." *AJA* 103, no. 3 (1999): 419–39.

Larsen, J. A. O. "Cyrene and the Panhellenion." *Classical Philology* 47, no. 1 (1952): 7–16.

Le Boulleuc, Alain. *La notion d'hérésie dans la littérature grecque (IIe-IIIe siècles)*. 2 vols. Paris: Études Augustiniennes, 1985.

Leander Touati, Anne-Marie. "Commodus Wearing the Lion Skin: A 'Modern' Portrait in Stockholm." *Opuscula Romana* 18, no. 7 (1990): 115–29.

Leeper, G. J. "The Nature of the Pentecostal Gift with Special Reference to Numbers 11 and Acts 2." *Asian Journal of Pentecostal Studies* 6, no. 1 (2003): 23–38.

Lefebvre, Henri. *The Production of Space*, translated by Donald Nicholson-Smith. Oxford: Blackwell, 1991.

Lepper, Frank and Sheppard Frere. *Trajan's Column: A New Edition of the Cichorius Plates*. Glouchester: Alan Sutton, 1988.

Levine, Lee I. *The Ancient Synagogue: The First Thousand Years*. 2nd ed. New Haven, CT: Yale University Press, 2005.

Leyerle, Blake. "Landscape as Cartography in Early Christian Pilgrimage Narratives." *JAAR* 64 (1996) 119–43.

Lieu, Judith. *Christian Identity in the Jewish and Graeco-Roman World*. Oxford: Oxford University Press, 2004.

———. *Neither Jew nor Greek? Constructing Early Christianity*. London: T & T Clark, 2002.

———. *Image and Reality: The Jews in the World of the Christians in the Second Century*. London: T & T Clark, 1996.

Liew, Tat-Siong Benny. "Tyranny, Boundary, and Might: Colonial Mimicry in Mark's Gospel." In *The Postcolonial Biblical Reader*, edited by R. S. Sugirtharajah, 206–23. Malden, MA: Blackwell Publishing, 2006.

Lightfoot, J. L. *Lucian On the Syrian Goddess* Oxford: Oxford University Press, 2005.

———. "Pilgrims and Ethnographers: In Search of the Syrian Goddess." In *Pilgrimage in Graeco-Roman and Early Christian Antiquity: Seeing the Gods*, edited by Jaś Elsner and Ian Rutherford, 333–52. Oxford: Oxford University Press, 2005.

Long, A. A. "Ptolemy on the Criterion: An Epistemology for the Practising Scientist." In *The Criterion of Truth: Essays Written in Honour of George Kerferd Together with a Text and Translation (with Annotations) of Ptolemy's on the Kriterion and Hegemonikon*, edited by Pamela M. Huby and Gordon C. Neal, 151–78. Liverpool: Liverpool University Press, 1989.

Long, A. A. and D. N. Sedley. *The Hellenistic Philosophers*. Cambridge: Cambridge University Press, 1987.

Loraux, Nicole. *The Experiences of Tiresias: The Feminine and the Greek Man*. Princeton, NJ: Princeton University Press, 1995.

———. "Herakles: The Super-Male and the Feminine." In *Before Sexuality: The Construction of Erotic Experience in the Ancient Greek World*, edited by David M. Halperin et al., 21–52. Princeton, NJ: Princeton University Press, 1990.

Love, Iris Cornelia. "A Preliminary Report on the Excavations at Knidos, 1972." *AJA* 77, no. 4 (1973): 413–24.

———. "A Preliminary Report on the Excavations at Knidos, 1970." *AJA* 76, no. 1 (1972): 61–76.

Lyman, Rebecca. "Hellenism and Heresy: 2002 NAPS Presidential Address." *JECS* 11, no. 2 (2003): 209–22.

———. "The Politics of Passing: Justin Martyr's Conversion as a Problem of 'Hellenization.'" In *Conversion in Late Antiquity and the Early Middle Ages: Seeing and Believing*, edited by Kenneth Mills and Anthony Grafton, 36–60. Rochester, NY: University of Rochester Press, 2003.

MacDonald, Margaret Y. *Early Christian Women and Pagan Opinion: The Power of the Hysterical Woman*. Cambridge: Cambridge University Press, 1996.

MacDonald, William L. *The Architecture of the Roman Empire*. 2 vols. New Haven, CT: Yale University Press, 1982–86.

MacDonald, William L. and John A. Pinto. *Hadrian's Villa and Its Legacy*. New Haven, CT: Yale University Press, 1995.

Maier, Harry. "Clement of Alexandria and the Care of the Self." *JAAR* 62, no. 3 (1994): 719–45.

Malherbe, Abraham J. *Ancient Epistolary Theorists*. Atlanta: Scholars Press, 1988.

———. "Athenagoras on the Pagan Poets and Philosophers." In *Kyriakon: Festscrift Johannes Quasten*, edited by Patrick Granfield and Josef A. Jungmann. Münster: Verlag Aschendorff, 1970.

———. "The Structure of Athenagoras, 'Supplicatio Pro Christianis.'" *VC* 23, no. 1 (1969): 1–20.

———. "The *Supplicatio Pro Christianis* of Athenagoras and Middle Platonism." Ph.D. Dissertation, Harvard University, 1963.

Martin, Dale. *Inventing Superstition: From the Hippocratics to the Christians*. Cambridge, MA: Harvard University Press, 2004.

Marvin, Miranda. *The Language of the Muses: The Dialogue between Roman and Greek Sculpture*. Los Angeles: J. Paul Getty Museum, 2008.

———. "Copying in Roman Sculpture: The Replica Series." In *Roman Art in Context: An Anthology*, edited by Eve D'Ambra, 161–88. Englewood Cliffs, NJ: Prentice Hall, 1993.

———. "Freestanding Sculptures from the Baths of Caracalla." *AJA* 87, no. 3 (1983): 355–84.

Matthews, Shelly. "Clemency as Cruelty: Forgiveness and Force in the Dying Prayers of Jesus and Stephen," *Bib. Int.* 17 (2009) 118–46.

———. "The Need for the Stoning of Stephen." In *Violence in the New Testament*, edited by Shelly Matthews and E. Leigh Gibson. New York: T & T Clark, 2005.

———. *Perfect Martyr: The Stoning of Stephen and the Making of Gentile Christianity in Acts*. Oxford: Oxford University Press, forthcoming.

McClintock, Anne. *Imperial Leather: Race, Gender, and Sexuality in the Colonial Conquest*. New York: Routledge, 1995.

McEwen, Indra Kagis. *Vitruvius: Writing the Body of Architecture*. Cambridge, MA: MIT Press, 2003.

McGehee, Michael. "Why Tatian Never 'Apologized' to the Greeks." *JECS* 1 (1993): 143–58.

Meeks, Wayne. *The First Urban Christians: The Social World of the Apostle Paul*. 2nd ed. New Haven, CT: Yale University Press, 2003.

Meneghini, Roberto. "Templum Divi Traiani." *BullCom* 97 (1996): 47–88.

Meneghini, Roberto and Riccardo Santangeli Valenzani. *I Fori Imperiali: gli scavi del comune di Roma* (1992–2007). Rome: Viviani, 2007.

Miles, Margaret M. *Art as Plunder: The Ancient Origins of Debate about Cultural Property*. Cambridge: Cambridge University Press, 2008.

Millar, Fergus. *The Emperor in the Roman World (31 B.C.–A.D. 337)*. Ithaca, NY: Cornell University Press, 1992.

Miller, Anna. "The Body of Christ as Demos: Democratic Discourse of the *Ekklesia* in 1 Corinthians." Ph.D. Dissertation, Committee on the Study of Religion, Harvard University, 2007.

Miller, J. Maxwell. "In the 'Image' and 'Likeness' of God." *JBL* 91, no. 3 (1972): 289–304.

Mills, Kenneth and Anthony Grafton, eds., *Conversion in Late Antiquity and the Middle Ages: Seeing and Believing*, Rochester, NY: University of Rochester, 2003.

Momigliano, Arnoldo. *Essays in Ancient and Modern Historiography*. Middletown, CT: Wesleyan University Press, 1977.

———. *Alien Wisdom: The Limits of Hellenization*. Cambridge: Cambridge University Press, 1975.

Mossman, Judith. "Heracles, Prometheus, and the Play of Genres in [Lucian]'s *Amores*." In *Severan Culture*, edited by Simon Swain et al., 146–59. Cambridge: Cambridge University Press, 2007.

Most, Glenn W. "Cornutus and Stoic Allegoresis: A Preliminary Report." *ANRW* II, no. 36 (1989): 2014–65.

Mount, Christopher. *Pauline Christianity: Luke–Acts and the Legacy of Paul*. Supp. Novum Testamentum 104. Leiden: E. J. Brill, 2002.

Moxnes, Halvor. *Putting Jesus in His Place: A Radical Vision of Household and Kingdom*. Louisville, KY: Westminster John Knox, 2003.

———. "'He Saw that the City was Full of Idols' (Acts 17:16): Visualizing the World of the First Christians." In *Mighty Minorities?: Minorities in Early Christianity, Positions and Strategies*, edited by Jacob Jervell et al., 107–31. Oslo: Scandinavian University Press, 1995.

Musurillo, Herbert. *The Acts of the Christian Martyrs*. Oxford: Clarendon, 1972.

Nandy, Ashis. *Time Warps: Silent and Evasive Pasts in Indian Politics and Religion*. New Brunswick, NJ: Rutgers University Press, 2002.

Nasrallah, Laura Salah. "The Knidian Aphrodite in the Roman Empire and Hiram Powers's *Greek Slave*: On Ethnicity, Gender, and Desire." In *Prejudice and Christian Beginnings: Investigating Race, Gender, and Ethnicity in Early Christian Studies*, edited by Laura Nasrallah and Elisabeth Schüssler Fiorenza, 51–78. Minneapolis, MN: Fortress, 2009.

———. "The Earthen Human, the Breathing Statue: The Sculptor God, Greco-Roman Statuary, and Clement of Alexandria." In *Beyond Eden: The Biblical Story of Paradise [Genesis 2–3] and Its Reception History*, edited by Konrad Schmid and Christoph Riedweg, 110–40. FAT II. Tübingen: Mohr Siebeck, 2008.

———. "The Rhetoric of Conversion and the Construction of Experience: The Case of Justin Martyr." In *Studia Patristica 18: Papers Presented at the Fourteenth International Conference on Patristics Studies Held in Oxford, 2003*, edited by E. J. Yarnold and M. F. Wiles, 467–74. Leuven: Peeters, 2006.

———. *An Ecstasy of Folly: Prophecy and Authority in Early Christianity*. HTS 52. Cambridge, MA: Harvard University Press, 2003.

Nast, Heidi J. and Steve Pile. "Introduction, MakingPlacesBodies." In *Places through the Body*, edited by Heidi J. Nast and Steve Pile, 1–14. New York: Routledge, 1998.

Nead, Lynda. *The Female Nude: Art, Obscenity, and Sexuality*. New York: Routledge, 1992.

Neumer-Pfau, Wiltrud. "Die nackte Liebesgöttin: Aphroditestatuen als Verkörperung des Weihlichkeitsideals in der griechisch-hellenistischen Welt." In *Approaches to Iconology*, edited by Hans G. Kippenberg, 205–34. Leiden: E. J. Brill, 1985.

———. *Studien zur Ikonographie und gesellschaftlichen Funktion hellenistischer Aphrodite-Statuen*. Bonn: R. Habelt, 1982.

Nicolet, Claude. *Space, Geography, and Politics in the Early Roman Empire*. Ann Arbor: University of Michigan Press, 1991.

Niehoff, Maren. *Philo on Jewish Identity and Culture*. Tübingen: Mohr Siebeck, 2001.

Nochlin, Linda. *Bathers, Bodies, Beauty: The Visceral Eye*. Cambridge, MA: Harvard University Press, 2006.

Nock, Arthur Darby. *Conversion: The Old and the New in Religion from Alexander the Great to Augustine of Hippo*. 1933. Repr. Baltimore, MD: John Hopkins University Press, 1998.

Noreña, Carlos. "The Communication of the Emperor's Virtues." *JRS* 91 (2001): 146–58.

Noy, David. "Rabbi Aqila Comes to Rome: A Jewish Pilgrimage in Reverse?" In *Pilgrimage in Graeco-Roman and Early Christian Antiquity: Seeing the Gods*, edited by Jaś Elsner and Ian Rutherford, 374–85. Oxford: Oxford University Press, 2005.

O'Neill, J. C. *The Theology of Acts in Its Historical Setting*. London: S.P.C.K., 1961.

OKell, Eleanor. "*Hercules Furens* and Nero: The Didactic Purpose of Senecan Tragedy." In *Herakles and Hercules: Exploring a Graeco-Roman Divinity*, edited by Louis Rawlings and Hugh Bowden, 185–204. Swansea, Wales: The Classical Press of Wales; Oakville, CT: The David Brown Book Co., 2005.

Oliver, James H. *The Ruling Power: A Study of the Roman Empire in the Second Century after Christ through the Roman Oration of Aelius Aristides*. 1953. Repr. Philadelphia: The American Philosophical Society, 1980.

———. "Hadrian's Reform of the Appeal Procedure in Greece." *Hesp.* 39, no. 4 (1970): 332–36.

———. *Marcus Aurelius: Aspects of Civic and Cultural Policy in the East*. Hesp. Supp. 13. Princeton, NJ: American School of Classical Studies at Athens, 1970.

———. "New Evidence on the Attic Panhellenion." *Hesp.* 20, no. 1 (1951): 31–33.

Osborn, Eric. *Clement of Alexandria*. Cambridge: Cambridge University Press, 2005.

———. *Justin Martyr*. Tübingen: Mohr (Siebeck), 1973.

Packer, James. *The Forum of Trajan in Rome: A Study of the Monuments in Brief*. Berkeley: University of California Press, 2001.

———. *The Forum of Trajan in Rome: A Study of the Monuments*. 2 vols. Berkeley: University of California Press, 1997.

———. "Report from Rome: The Imperial Fora, a Retrospective." *AJA* 101, no. 2 (1997): 307–30.

———. "Trajan's Forum Again: The Column and the Temple of Trajan in the Master Plan Attributed to Apollodorus (?)." *JRA* 7 (1994): 163–82.

Packer, James and John Burge. "TEMPLUM DIVI TRAIANI PARTHICI ET PLOTINAE: A Debate with R. Meneghini." *JRA* 16, no. 1 (2003): 109–36.

Pagels, Elaine. "Christian Apologists and the 'Fall of the Angels': An Attack on Roman Imperial Power?" *HTR* 78, no. 3/4 (1985): 301–27.

Pao, David. *Acts and the Isaianic New Exodus*. WUNT 2.130. Tübingen: Mohr Siebeck, 2000.

Parent, Rosa Cornford. "Mapping Identity in the Lucianic Corpus." Ph.D. Dissertation, Department of Classics, University of Southern California, 2000.

Pasquier, Alain. "Les Aphrodites de Praxitèle." In *Praxitèle,* edited by Jean-Luc Martinez and Alain Pasquier, 130–201. Paris: Musée du Louvre, 2007.

Passow, Franz. *Handwörterbuch der griechischen Sprache*. 1841–57. Repr. Darmstadt: Wissenschaftliche Buchgesellschaft, 1970.

Peachin, Michael. *Roman Imperial Titulature and Chronology, A.D. 235–284*. Amsterdam: Gieben, 1990.

Pearson, Lori. *Beyond Christianity: Ernst Troeltsch as Historian and Theorist of Christianity*. HTS 58. Cambridge, MA: Harvard University Press, 2008.

Penner, Todd. *In Praise of Christian Origins: Stephen and the Hellenists in Lukan Apologetic Historiography*. New York: T & T Clark, 2004.

Perkins, Judith. "Social Geography in the *Apocryphal Acts of the Apostles*." In *Space in the Ancient Novel*, edited by Michael Paschalis and

Stavros A. Frangoulidis, 118–31. Groningen: Barkhuis, 2002.

———. *The Suffering Self: Pain and Narrative Representation in the Early Christian Era*. New York: Routledge, 1995.

Perry, Ellen. *The Aesthetics of Emulation in the Visual Arts of Ancient Rome*. Cambridge: Cambridge University Press, 2005.

Pervo, Richard I. *Acts: A Commentary*. Hermeneia. Minneapolis: Fortress, 2008.

———. *Dating Acts: Between the Evangelists and the Apologists*. Santa Rosa, CA: Polebridge, 2006.

———. "Meet Right – and our Bounden Duty." *Forum* n.s. 4, no. 1 (2001): 57–60.

———. "My Happy Home: The Role of Jerusalem in Acts 1–7." *Forum* n.s. 3, no. 1 (2000): 31–55.

———. *Profit with Delight: The Literary Genre of the Acts of the Apostles*. Philadelphia: Fortress, 1987.

Petersen, Lauren. *The Freedman in Roman Art and Art History*. Cambridge: Cambridge University Press, 2006.

Petersen, William. "Tatian's Diatessaron." In *Ancient Christian Gospels: Their History and Development*, by Helmut Koester, 403–30. Valley Forge, PA: Trinity Press International, 1990.

Petsalis-Diomidis, Alexia. "The Body in Space: Visual Dynamics in Graeco-Roman Healing Pilgrimage." In *Pilgrimage in Graeco-Roman and Early Christian Antiquity: Seeing the Gods*, edited by Jaś Elsner and Ian Rutherford, 183–218. Oxford: Oxford University Press, 2005.

Porta, Giovanni. "La dedica e la data della *Πρεσβεία* di Atenagora." *Didaskaleion* 5, no. 1–2 (1916): 53–70.

Porter, James I. "Ideals and Ruins: Pausanias, Longinus, and the Second Sophistic." In *Pausanias: Travel and Memory in Roman Greece*, edited by Susan E. Alcock et al., 63–92. Oxford: Oxford University Press, 2001.

Porter, Stanley. "Excursus: The We Passages." In *The Book of Acts in Its First Century Setting*. Vol. 2, *The Book of Acts in Its Graeco-Roman Setting*, edited by David W. J. Gill and Conrad Gempf. 545–74. Grand Rapids, MI: Eerdmans, 1994.

Pouderon, Bernard. *D'Athènes à Alexandrie: études sur Athénagore et les origines de la philosophie chrétienne*. Québec: Presses de l'Université Laval and Louvain: Editions Peeters, 1997.

Pouderon, Bernard and Joseph Doré, eds. *Les apologistes chrétiens et la culture grecque*. Paris: Beauchesne, 1998.

Price, S. R. F. *Rituals and Power: Roman Imperial Cult in Asia Minor*. Cambridge: Cambridge University Press, 1984.

Puech, Aimé. *Recherches sur le Discours aux Grecs de Tatien suivies d'une traduction française du Discours*. Paris: F. Alcan, 1903.

Quasten, Johannes. *Patrology*. Vols. 1–3. Utrecht: Spectrum, 1964–66.

Rajak, Tessa. "Talking at Trypho: Christian Apologetic as Anti-Judaism in *Justin's Dialogue with Trypho the Jew*." In *Apologetics in the Roman Empire: Pagans, Jews, and Christians*, edited by Mark Edwards et al., 59–80. Oxford: Oxford University Press, 1999.

Raubitscheck, Antony E. "Hadrian as the Son of Zeus Eleutherios." *AJA* 49, no. 2 (1945): 128–33.

Reed, Annette Yoshiko. *Fallen Angels and the History of Judaism and Christianity: The Reception of Enochic Literature*. Cambridge: Cambridge University Press, 2005.

———. "The Trickery of the Fallen Angels and the Demonic Mimesis of the Divine: Aetiology, Demonology, and Polemics in the Writings of Justin Martyr." *JECS* 12, no. 2 (2004): 141–71.

Reynolds, Joyce. "Hadrian, Antoninus Pius and the Cyrenaican Cities." *JRS* 68 (1978): 111–21.

Ridgway, Brunilde Sismondo. *Roman Copies of Greek Sculpture: The Problem of the Originals*. Ann Arbor: University of Michigan Press, 1984.

Rist, John M. *Stoic Philosophy*. London: Cambridge University Press, 1969.

Rives, James. "Venus Genetrix outside Rome." *Phoenix* 48, no. 4 (1994): 294–306.

Rockwell, Peter. *The Art of Stoneworking: A Reference Guide*. Cambridge: Cambridge University Press, 1993.

Rohrbaugh, Richard L. "The Pre-Industrial City in Luke-Acts: Urban Social Relations." In *The Social World of Luke-Acts: Models for*

Interpretation, edited by Jerome Neyrey, 125–49. Peabody, MA: Hendrickson, 1991.

Romeo, Ilaria. "The Panhellenion and Ethnic Identity in Hadrianic Greece." *Classical Philology* 97, no. 1 (2002): 21–40.

Romm, James S. *The Edges of the Earth in Ancient Thought: Geography, Exploration, and Fiction.* Princeton, NJ: Princeton University Press, 1992.

Ronk, Martha Clare. *In a Landscape of Having to Repeat.* Richmond, CA: Omnidawn, 2004.

Rosenblum, Robert. *Transformations in Late Eighteenth Century Art.* Princeton, NJ: Princeton University Press, 1967.

Rowe, C. Kavin. "New Testament Iconography? Situating Paul in the Absence of Material Evidence." In *Picturing the New Testament: Studies in Ancient Visual Images*, edited by Annette Weissenrieder et al., 289–312. Tübingen: Mohr Siebeck, 2005.

Russell, Norman. *The Doctrine of Deification in the Greek Patristic Tradition.* Oxford: Oxford University Press, 2004.

Rutgers, Leonard Victor. *The Hidden Heritage of Diaspora Judaism.* 2nd ed. Leuven: Peeters, 1998.

———. *The Jews in Late Ancient Rome: Evidence of Cultural Interaction in the Roman Diaspora.* Leiden: E. J. Brill, 1995.

Rutherford, Ian. "Tourism and the Sacred: Pausanias and the Traditions of Greek Pilgrimage." In *Pausanias: Travel and Memory in Roman Greece*, edited by Susan E. Alcock et al., 40–53. Oxford: Oxford University Press, 2001.

Salomon, Nanette. "Making a World of Difference: Gender, Asymmetry, and the Greek Nude." In *Naked Truths: Women, Sexuality, and Gender in Classical Art and Archaeology*, edited by Ann Olga Koloski-Ostrow and Claire L. Lyons, 197–219. New York: Routledge, 1997.

Scheper-Hughes, Nancy and J. D. Wacquant. *Commodifying Bodies.* London: Thousand Oaks, 2002.

Schoedel, William R. "Apologetic Literature and Ambassadorial Activities." *HTR* 82, no. 1 (1989): 55–78.

———. "In Praise of the King: A Rhetorical Pattern in Athenagoras." In *Disciplina Nostra: Essays in Memory of Robert F. Evans*, edited by Donald F. Winslow, 69–90. Cambridge, MA: Philadelphia Patristic Foundation, 1979.

Schulze, Harald. "Vorbild Der Herrschenden. Herakles Und Die Politik." In *Herakles Herkules*, edited by Raimond Wünsche, 344–65. München: Staatliche Antikensammlungen und Glyptothek, 2003.

Schüssler Fiorenza, Elisabeth. *The Power of the Word: Scripture and the Rhetoric of Empire.* Minneapolis, MN: Fortress, 2007.

———. *Rhetoric and Ethic: The Politics of Biblical Studies.* Minneapolis, MN: Fortress, 1999.

———. *But She Said: Feminist Practices of Biblical Interpretation.* Boston: Beacon, 1992.

Schwartz, Seth. "The Rabbi in Aphrodite's Bath: Palestinian Society and Jewish Identity in the High Roman Empire." In *Being Greek under Rome: Cultural Identity, the Second Sophistic and the Development of Empire*, edited by Simon Goldhill, 335–61. Cambridge: Cambridge University Press, 2001.

Scott, James M. "Luke's Geographical Horizon." In *The Book of Acts in Its First Century Setting.* Vol. 2, *The Book of Acts in Its Graeco-Roman Setting*, edited by David W. J. Gill and Conrad Gempf, 483–544. Grand Rapids, MI: Eerdmans, 1994.

Seaman, Kristen. "Retrieving the Original Aphrodite of Knidos." *Rend.* 9, no. 15 (2004): 531–94.

Sinn, Ulrich. *Olympia: Cult, Sport, and Ancient Festival*, translated by Thomas Thornton. Princeton, NJ: Marcus Wiener, 2001.

Skarsaune, Oskar. *The Proof from Prophecy: A Study in Justin Martyr's Proof-Text Tradition: Text-Type, Provenance, Theological Profile.* Leiden: E. J. Brill, 1987.

———. "The Conversion of Justin Martyr." *Studia Theologica* 30 (1976): 53–73.

Skinner, E. Benjamin. *A Crime So Monstrous: Face-to-Face with Modern-Day Slavery.* New York: Free Press, 2008.

Sluiter, Ineke. *Ancient Grammar in Context: Contributions to the Study of Ancient Linguistic Thought.* Amsterdam: Proefschrift Vrije Universiteit, 1990.

Smith, Jonathan Z. *To Take Place: Toward a Theory in Ritual.* Chicago: University of Chicago Press, 1987.

Smith, Morton. "The Image of God," *Bulletin of the John Rylands Library* 40 (1957–58): 473–512.

Smith, R. R. R. "Nero and the Sun-God: Divine Accessories and Political Symbols in Roman Imperial Images [a review of M. Bergmann, *Die Strahlen Der Herrscher*]." *JRA* 13, no. 2 (2000): 532–42.

———. "Cultural Choice and Political Identity in Honorific Portrait Statues in the Greek East in the Second Century A.D." *JRS* 88 (1998): 56–93.

———. "*Simulacra Gentium*: The *Ethne* from the Sebasteion at Aphrodisias." *JRS* 78 (1988): 50–77.

———. "The Imperial Reliefs of the Sebasteion at Aphrodisias." *JRS* 77 (1987): 88–138.

———. "What a Difference a Difference Makes." In *"To See Ourselves as Others See Us": Christians, Jews, "Others" in Late Antiquity*, edited by Jacob Neusner and Ernest S. Frerichs, 3–48. Chico, CA: Scholars Press, 1985.

Snyder, Harlow Gregory. "'Above the Bath of Myrtinus': Justin Martyr's 'School' in the City of Rome." *HTR* 100, no. 3 (2007): 335–62.

Soja, Edward W. *Postmetropolis: Critical Studies of Cities and Regions*. Oxford: Blackwell, 2000.

Spar, Debora. *The Baby Business: How Money, Science, and Politics Drive the Commerce of Conception*. Cambridge, MA: Harvard Business School Press, 2006.

Spawforth, A. S. and Susan Walker. "The World of the Panhellenion. II. Three Dorian Cities." *JRS* 76 (1986): 88–105.

———. "The World of the Panhellenion. I. Athens and Eleusis." *JRS* 75 (1985): 88–104.

Spelman, Elizabeth V. *Inessential Woman: Problems of Exclusion in Feminist Thought*. Boston: Beacon Press, 1988.

Spencer, Diana. *The Roman Alexander: Reading a Cultural Myth*. Exeter: University of Exeter, 2002.

Spivey, Nigel Jonathan. *Understanding Greek Sculpture: Ancient Meanings, Modern Readings*. New York: Thames and Hudson, 1996.

Spyropoulos, Georg. *Drei Meisterwerke der griechischen Plastik aus der Villa des Herodes Atticus zu EVA/Loukou*. New York: Peter Lang, 2001.

Stanton, Graham. "'God-Fearers': Neglected Evidence in Justin Martyr's Dialogue with Trypho." In *Ancient History in a Modern University*. Vol. 2, *Early Christianity, Late Antiquity and Beyond*, edited by T. W. Hillard and E. A. Judge, 43–52. Grand Rapids, MI: Eerdmans, 1998.

———. "Other Early Christian Writings: 'Didache,' Ignatius, 'Barnabas,' Justin Martyr." In *Early Christian Thought in its Jewish Context*, edited by John Barclay and John Sweet, 174–90. Cambridge: Cambridge University Press, 1996.

———. "Justin Martyr's Dialogue with Trypho: Group Boundaries, 'Proselytes' and 'God-Fearers.'" In *Tolerance and Intolerance in Early Judaism and Christianity*, edited by Graham Stanton and Guy G. Stroumsa. 263–78. Cambridge: Cambridge University Press, 1983.

Steiner, Deborah. *Images in Mind: Statues in Archaic and Classical Greek Literature and Thought*. Princeton, NJ: Princeton University Press, 2001.

Sterling, Gregory. *Historiography and Self-Definition: Josephos, Luke-Acts, and Apologetic Historiography*. Leiden: E. J. Brill, 1992.

Stewart, Andrew F. *Art, Desire, and the Body in Ancient Greece*. Cambridge: Cambridge University Press, 1997.

———. "Baroque Classics: The Tragic Muse and the *Exemplum*." In *Classical Pasts: The Classical Traditions of Greece and Rome*, edited by James I. Porter, 127–70. Princeton: Princeton University Press, 2006.

Stewart, Peter. *Statues in Roman Society: Representation and Response*. Oxford: Oxford University Press, 2003.

Stowers, Stanley. *Letter Writing in Greco-Roman Antiquity*. Philadelphia: Westminster, 1986.

Stroumsa, Guy G. *Barbarian Philosophy: The Religious Revolution of Early Christianity*. WUNT 112. Tübingen: Mohr Siebeck, 1999.

Swain, Simon. "Polemon's Physiognomy." In *Seeing the Face, Seeing the Soul: Polemon's Physiognomy from Classical Antiquity to Medieval*

Islam, edited by Simon Swain et al., 125–202. Oxford: Oxford University Press, 2007.

———. "Dio's Life and Works." In *Dio Chrysostom: Politics, Letters, and Philosophy*, edited by Simon Swain, 1–12. Oxford: Oxford University Press, 2000.

———. *Hellenism and Empire: Language, Classicism, and Power in the Greek World A.D. 50–250.* Oxford: Clarendon, 1996.

Talbert, Richard J. A. and Kai Brodersen, eds. *Space in the Roman World: Its Perception and Presentation.* Münster: LIT Verlag, 2004.

Tannehill, Robert. "Paul Outside the Christian Ghetto: Stories of Intercultural Conflict and Cooperation in Acts." In *Text and Logos: The Humanistic Interpretation of the New Testament*, edited by Theodore W. Jennings. 247–63. Atlanta: Scholars Press, 1990.

Tanner, Jeremy. *The Invention of Art History in Ancient Greece: Religion, Society and Artistic Rationalization.* Cambridge: Cambridge University Press, 2006.

Thistlethwaite, Susan Brooks, ed., *Adam, Eve, and the Genome: The Human Genome Project and Theology.* Minneapolis, MN: Fortress, 2003.

Thompson, F. H. *The Archaeology of Greek and Roman Slavery.* London: Duckworth, 2003.

Tobin, Jennifer. *Herodes Attikos and the City of Athens: Patronage and Conflict under the Antonines.* Amsterdam: Gieben, 1997.

———. "Some New Thoughts on Herodes Atticus's Tomb, His Stadium of 143/44, and Philostratus *VS* 2.550." *AJA* (1993): 81–89.

Trakatellis, Demetrios. "Justin Martyr's Trypho." *HTR* 79 (1986): 289–97.

Trimble, Jennifer Ferol. "The Aesthetics of Sameness: A Contextual Analysis of the Large and Small Herculaneum Woman Statue Types in the Roman Empire." Ph.D. Dissertation, Department of Classical Art and Archaeology, University of Michigan, 1999.

Tyson, Joseph B. *Marcion and Luke-Acts: A Defining Struggle.* Columbia: University of South Carolina Press, 2006.

———."The Legacy of F. C. Baur and Recent Studies of Acts." *Forum* n.s. 4, no. 1 (2001): 125–44.

———. *Luke, Judaism, and the Scholars: Critical Approaches to Luke-Acts.* Columbia: University of South Carolina Press, 1993.

Van Dyke, Ruth and Susan E. Alcock. "Archaeologies of Memory: An Introduction." In *Archaeologies of Memory*, edited by Ruth Van Dyke and Susan E. Alcock, 1–14. Malden, MA: Blackwell, 2003.

Varner, Eric R. *Mutilation and Transformation:* Damnatio Memoriae *and Roman Imperial Portraiture.* Leiden: E. J. Brill, 2004.

Vermeule, Cornelius. "Herakles Crowning Himself: New Greek Statuary Types and Their Place in Hellenistic and Roman Art." *JHS* 77, no. 2 (1957): 283–99.

Vilborg, Ebbe. *Achilles Tatius: Leucippe and Clitophon.* Stockholm: Almqvist & Wiksell, 1955.

Volkmar, Gustav. "Die Zeit Justin's des Märtyrers, kritisch Untersucht." *Theol. Jahr.* 14 (1855): 234–83.

Vout, Caroline. *Power and Eroticism in Imperial Rome.* Cambridge: Cambridge University Press, 2007.

Waelkens, Marc. "From a Phrygian Quarry: The Provenance of the Statues of the Dacian Prisoners in Trajan's Forum at Rome." *AJA* 89, no. 4 (1985): 641–53.

Wagenaar, H. "Babel, Jerusalem, and Kumba: Missiological Reflections on Genesis 11:1–9 and Acts 2:1–13." *International Review of Mission* 92 (2003): 406–32.

Walker, Susan. "Roman Nymphaea in the Greek World." In *Roman Architecture in the Greek World*, edited by S. Macready and F. Thompson, 60–71. London: Society of Antiquaries, 2001.

Wallace-Hadrill, Andrew. *Rome's Cultural Revolution.* Cambridge: Cambridge University Press, 2008.

Watson, Gerard. "Discovering the Imagination: Platonists and Stoics on *Phantasia*." In *The Question of "Eclecticism": Studies in Later Greek Philosophy*, edited by John M. Dillon and A. A. Long, 208–33. Berkeley: University of California Press, 1988.

———. *Phantasia in Classical Thought.* Galway: Galway University Press, 1988.

Webster, Jane. "Creolizing the Roman Provinces." *AJA* 105, no. 2 (2001): 209–25.

Weinstock, Stefan. "The Geographical Catalogue in Acts II, 9–11." *JRA* 38, no. 1–2 (1948): 43–46.

Whitmarsh, Tim. "Varia Lucianea." *CR* 53, no. 1 (2003): 75–78.

———. "'Greece is the World': Exile and Identity in the Second Sophistic." In *Being Greek under Rome: Cultural Identity, the Second Sophistic and the Development of Empire*, edited by Simon Goldhill, 269–305. Cambridge: Cambridge University Press, 2001.

———. *Greek Literature and the Roman Empire: The Politics of Imitation*. Oxford: Oxford University Press, 2001.

Whittaker, Molly. "Tatian's Educational Background." In *Studia Patristica 13: Papers Presented to the Sixth International Conference on Patristic Studies Held in Oxford 1971, Part II: Classica et Hellenica, Theologica, Liturgica, Ascetica*, edited by Elizabeth Livingstone, 57–59. Berlin: Akademie Verlag, 1975.

Wills, Lawrence. "The Depiction of the Jews in Acts." *JBL* 110 (1991): 631–54.

Wilson, Elizabeth. *The Sphinx in the City: Urban Life, the Control of Disorder, and Women*. Berkeley: University of California, 1992.

Winckelmann, Johann Joachim. *History of the Art of Antiquity*, translated by Harry Francis Mallgrave. Los Angeles: Getty Research Institute, 2006.

Winden, J. C. M. van. *An Early Christian Philosopher: Justin Martyr's Dialogue with Trypho Chapters One to Nine. Introduction, Text and Commentary*. Leiden: E. J. Brill, 1971.

Wolfson, Harry Austryn. *The Philosophy of the Church Fathers*. 3rd ed. Cambridge, MA: Harvard University Press, 1970.

Wood, Susan E. *Imperial Women: A Study in Public Images, 40 B.C.–A.D. 68*. Leiden: E. J. Brill, 1999.

Woolf, Greg. *Becoming Roman: The Origins of Provincial Civilization in Gaul*. Cambridge: Cambridge University Press, 1998.

Wordelman, Amy. "Cultural Divides and Dual Realities: A Greco-Roman Context for Acts 14." In *Contextualizing Acts: Lukan Narrative and Greco-Roman Discourse*, edited by Todd Penner and Caroline Vander Stichele, 205–32. Atlanta: Society of Biblical Literature, 2003.

Wrede, Henning. *Consecratio in formam deorum: vergöttlichte Privatpersonen in der römischen Kaiserzeit*. Mainz: von Zabern, 1981.

———. "Das mausoleum der Claudia Semne und die burgerliche Plastik der Kaiserzeit." *RömMitt* 78, no. 2 (1971): 125–66.

Wünsche, Raimond. *Herakles Herkules*. München: Staatliche Antikensammlungen und Glyptothek, 2003.

Yong, Amos. "As the Spirit Gives Utterance: Pentecost, Intra-Christian Ecumenism, and the Wider Oikoumenē." *International Review of Mission* 92 (2003): 299–314.

Young, Robert. *Colonial Desire: Hybridity in Theory, Culture, and Race*. New York: Routledge, 1995.

Zanker, Paul. "The City as Symbol: Rome and the Creation of an Urban Image." In *Romanization and the City*, edited by Elizabeth Fentress, 25–41. Portsmouth, RI: JRA, 2000.

———. *The Mask of Socrates: The Image of the Intellectual in Antiquity*. Berkeley: University of California Press, 1995.

———. *The Power of Images in the Age of Augustus*. Ann Arbor: University of Michigan Press, 1988.

———. "Das Trajansforum in Rom." *AA* 4 (1970): 499–544.

INDEX LOCORUM

INDEX